THE CLINICIAN'S HANDBOOK

INTEGRATED DIAGNOSTICS, ASSESSMENT, AND INTERVENTION IN ADULT AND ADOLESCENT PSYCHOPATHOLOGY

FOURTH EDITION

ROBERT G. MEYER

University of Louisville

SARAH E. DEITSCH

University of Kentucky

ALLYN AND BACON
Boston   London   Toronto   Sydney   Tokyo   Singapore

Library of Congress Cataloging-in-Publication Data

Meyer, Robert G.
    The clinician's handbook : integrated diagnostics, assessment, and
intervention in adult and adolescent psychopathology / Robert G.
Meyer, Sarah E. Deitsch.—4th ed.
        p.   cm.
    Includes bibliographical references and indexes.
    ISBN 0-205-17181-8
    1. Mental illness—Diagnosis.   2. Psychodiagnostics.
3. Psychotherapy.   I. Deitsch, Sarah E.   II. Title.
    [DNLM: 1. Mental Disorders—diagnosis.   2. Mental Disorders—
therapy.   3. Psychological Tests.   WM 141 M613c   1995]
RC469.M457   1995
616.89—dc20
DNLM/DLC
for Library of Congress   95-4215
                                                                      CIP

Printed in the United States of America
10 9 8 7 6 5 4 3 2 1   00 99 98 97 96 95

RELATED TITLES OF INTEREST

DEDICATION

To our parents and grandparents, Bob and Ardelle, who gave so much.

CONTENTS

10. Impulse Control and Eating Disorders 239

11. CNSI, ADHD, and Retardation 259

12. Clinical Correlates of the MMPI-2 289

13. Clinical Correlates of 16 PF Test 339

14. Aggression, Rape, Child Abuse, and Suicide 359

15. Psychopharmacology 386

16. Malingering and the Factitious Disorders 412

PREFACE

As early as my graduate training and internship, I (the senior author) looked for a book that had not only integrated discussion of the common symptoms, personality styles, test patterns, and treatment recommendations but had also linked these with the various major psychodiagnostic categories that clinicians use every day. These data were available, but only as isolated pieces of information. Books such as Graham's (1973) *The MMPI: A Practical Guide* and Zimmerman and Woo-Sam's (1973) *Clinical Interpretation of the WAIS* took steps to incorporate the data, yet these books dealt with only a single test. Also, such texts, as well as others that followed that do deal with a number of tests, only occasionally linked general behavior patterns to particular test results. Furthermore, the test results are seldom related clearly to specific diagnostic classifications. Finally, there are no other books that linked all of these with the next step, treatment recommendations.

The Clinician's Handbook integrates these distinct, but necessarily related, considerations. This book links diagnostic issues and concepts with updated correlates for the most commonly used objective psychological test, the Minnesota Multiphasic Personality Inventory (MMPI-2), as well as complementary data from other tests, such as personality information from the Institute of Personality and Ability Testing's (IPAT) Cattell Sixteen Personality Factor Questionnaire (16 PF) Test (and, analogously, IPAT's High School Personality Questionnaire, the HSPQ, for adolescents and young adults age 12–18, because virtually the same factors are measured in each). Other psychological tests commonly used with adults and adolescents are discussed, primarily the Wechsler Adult Intelligence Scale-Revised (WAIS-R), the Millon Clinical Multiaxial Inventory (MCMI-II), the Rorschach Ink Blot Technique, and the Thematic Apperception Test (TAT) and drawing tests. This book then integrates common behavior features (and *Diagnostic and Statistical Manual of Mental Disorders* (DSM-IV) descriptors in most instances), test data, and the most valid treatment recommendations. This synthesis is based on the assumptions that (1) a multimodal treatment is almost always the optimal approach, (2) virtually all theories and schools are useful to some degree, and (3) that a major challenge in modern treatment is determining the best fit of client type with treatment type. The eclecticism inherent in the latter two assumptions dovetails with the multimodal approach to treatment recommendations. That is, it rarely appears that a single treatment approach is sufficient to treat clusters of disordered behaviors comprehensively, and the use of only one technique is seldom the best approach with any one client.

The Clinician's Handbook was designed first for practitioners, since they are likely to encounter the broadest variety of emotional disorders in their work. Even practitioners who do not regularly administer the tests previously noted should find this book useful, because test responses are tied to various functional aspects of each disorder and to treatment options that might be used. The practitioner can assess this information in several ways. Generally, it is most useful to begin with common initial diagnoses and to examine the book's behavioral descriptors, DSM-IV requirements, and various personality indices that are detailed for each. The relevant treatment recommendations can then be checked and incorporated into a report or overall treatment program.

Clinicians who prefer to look at MMPI-2 data before making a tentative diagnosis can use this book by going to Chapter 12 to locate the particular high score (or two-point code) that is obtained and then, if desired, use Table 12.1 (in Chapter 12). The table presents a list of probable diagnoses associated with virtually all of the two-point MMPI-2 codes. These probable diagnoses can then be checked as previously described.

Although originally designed for the practitioner—including clinical, counseling, health, educational, forensic, and industrial psychologists; psychiatrists; clinical social workers; psychiatric nurses; family and marital therapists; and pastoral counselors—*The Clinician's Handbook* is also useful as a text in graduate-level courses. The breakdown of the disorder patterns follows the same progression and schema as in DSM-IV and adds material about important allied topics, such as the criminal personality, acting-out potential, malingering, central nervous system dysfunction, and legal concepts (insanity, incompetency) as they relate to diagnostic categories. Thus, a full spectrum of adult and adolescent psychopathology can be studied. Numerous instructors have used this book as a primary text, which they supplemented with readings on research relevant to the various disorder patterns and with other textbooks. *The Clinician's Handbook* can also be used to supplement a standard text on abnormal psychology or in clinical courses and practicums as an adjunct to books on specific tests, test research, or test administration.

As noted in Chapter 1, this book incorporates most modern research available on the relationship of disorder patterns to diagnostic indicators and treatment options. Table 1.1 (in Chapter 1) lists many of the standard sources for the general and developing tradition of research studies noted throughout this book. Chapter 1 also details the long process by which this book evolved; the bedrock was the available research.

It is clear that this material, like any other body of information, will change with time. It is hoped that many of these changes will be spurred on by this book itself—that is, that researchers will refine, through more practical and precise studies, the clusters of diagnostic features, test results, and treatment options that are offered in the following pages. Reports of research and feedback from clinicians as they use these formulations would be most welcome. Please send any information to the senior author, Department of Psychology, University of Louisville, Belknap Campus, Louisville, KY 40292.

We are grateful to the American Psychiatric Association for its permission to convey generally the essence of the DSM-IV categories seen in this book. Readers who want a more detailed description of the behavioral and statistical correlates of these categories should consult the DSM-IV itself.

This book has been significantly aided by the contributions of the many teachers, colleagues, and students whom we have known over the years; each has in some way been helpful. A particular debt is owed by the senior author to professors Albert I. Rabin and Bertram Karon at Michigan State University, as well as to many other clinicians and colleagues, such as Norman Abeles, Curtis Barrett, Vytautas Bieliauskas, Mary Clarke, David Connell, Dan Cox, Herb Eber, Will Edgerton, Diane Follingstad, Ray Fowler, Carleton Gass, Alan Goldstein, Phil Johnson, William Kronenberger, Rhett Landis, Michael Nietzel, Paul Salmon, Steven R. Smith, Harvey A. Tilker, Wilfred Van Gorp, Martha Wetter, and Thomas Widiger, all of whom have been helpful and instructive throughout the years. I also wish to thank Professor James R. Rafferty, Wright State University, for his review and helpful comments on the revised manuscript for this fourth edition.

A special thanks is due our editor at Allyn and Bacon, Mylan Jaixen. A major acknowledgment and thank-you goes to Sandy Garcia, who contributed significantly with manuscript preparation and editorial assistance.

R.G.M.
S.E.D.

Robert G. Meyer, Ph.D., received his Ph.D. in psychology from Michigan State University in 1967. He was chief psychologist at the Psychiatric Clinic of the State Prison of Southern Michigan during 1968 and then was Assistant Professor in the Department of Psychiatry at the Medical School of the University of North Carolina at Chapel Hill. He came to the University of Louisville in 1969 as Clinic Director and Assistant Professor and is now a Full Professor in the Department of Psychology.

Dr. Meyer specializes in clinical and forensic psychology and in hypnosis. He is board certified in both clinical and forensic psychology by the American Board of Professional Psychology (ABPP), is a fellow in divisions 12 (Clinical) and 41 (Law and Psychology) of the American Psychological Society. He is a consultant to the Kentucky Corrections Cabinet and is a past-president of the Kentucky Psychological Association. He received the Grawemeyer Award for innovative curriculum development for his course in Law and Psychology. He is the author of *Law, Behavior and Mental Health* (with Dean Steven Smith of the Cleveland Marshall School of Law); *Law for the Psychotherapist* (with Rhett Landis); *Abnormal Psychology* (with Paul Solmon); *Case Studies in Abnormal Psychology* (with Yvonne Hardaway Osborne); *Case Studies in Developmental Psychology and Psychopathology; Preparation for Licensing and Board Certification Examinations in Psychology;* and *Practical Clinical Hypnosis* as well as several other books and over 50 scholarly articles. He is editor of the *Bulletin of the American Academy of Forensic Psychology.*

Sarah Deitsch has received her M.A. in psychology and has completed all coursework for a Ph.D. in clinical psychology at the University of Kentucky. She has carried out research on the MMPI-2 in conjunction with the MMPI-2 research group affiliated with the University of Kentucky, and is presently involved in research on the NEO-PI-R. She is Coordinator of the Harris Psychological Services Center in Lexington, KY. She has taught in the areas of psychological assessment, statistics, and other topics in clinical psychology.

CHAPTER 1

Overview and Introduction

This book provides overall diagnostic concepts and observations, links these with specific assessment and test data for diagnostic categories, and then integrates all of this with recommended intervention procedures. It would be unreasonable to expect that any one treatment approach or single pattern of test responses will be specifically relevant to only one diagnostic grouping and, conversely, that individual clients in any one diagnostic category will respond to only one type of treatment or show a single pattern on diagnostic tests. Hence, there is a multimodal assessment and treatment emphasis throughout this book.

All of this is anchored in the DSM-IV. Even though there are valid criticisms of the DSM, it's the official document of the American Psychiatric Association and is well respected by all varieties of mental health workers, both nationally and internationally. There were numerous changes from DSM-III-R to DSM-IV; indeed, the simple listing of changes took up twenty-eight pages in the 1994 edition. Concisely, some of the more important changes are: Only the Personality Disorders and Mental Retardation remain on Axis II; Rett's Disorder, Childhood Disintegrative Disorder, and Asperger's Disorder have been added as Childhood Disorders; there is no separate category of Attention Deficit Disorder, which is subsumed under ADHD; there is now a separate overall category of Eating Disorders; there are now two separate Bipolar Disorders, with Bipolar Disorder II referring to the traditional, severe form, where recurrent manic and depressive patterns are both observed; the phrase "outside the range of normal human experience" has been deleted as a criterion for PTSD, and the related category of Acute Stress Disorder has been added; the term Multiple Personality Disorder has been changed to Dissociative Identity Disorder; Passive-Aggressive Personality Disorder has been deleted as an Axis II Personality Disorder but has been retained in revised form as a "Criteria Set . . . for further study"; two new patterns in "other conditions that may be a focus of clinical attention" are "Religious or Spiritual Problem" and "Acculturation Problem."

There is an emphasis on integrating psychological test data with interview data because the combined information is a substantial improvement over interview data alone (Butcher, 1995; Kronenberg & Meyer, 1996). This is true even when the interview data are obtained in a controlled format, such as the Mental Status Examination, which traditionally includes assessment of the following: (1) identifying data—chief complaint and physical appearance; (2) personal and family history; (3) motor functions; (4) speech activity and patterns; (5) mood and affect; (6) alertness and attention; (7) content and organization of thoughts; (8) orientation and perception; (9) the general areas of memory—abstract thinking, judgment, and the client's fund of knowledge; and (10) the client's attitude toward the examination and toward his or her condition (Melton et al., 1987). Some of the questions that commonly appear in the Mental Status Examination are the following: What is this place? Who am I? What day is it? Who are you? Who is the president? Who was the president before he was? What does "Don't cry over spilled milk" mean?

Even though the Mental Status Examination interview is structured, the examination has the weakness of all data obtained from interviews: There are few or no statistical or normative standards for the obtained responses on which to base a communicable inference and an eventual diagnosis. Examiners are too often left to develop their own idiosyncratic notions of what a certain response means. While this procedure may be helpful in developing beginning inferences, first inferences are significantly strengthened (or called into question) when the more objective data of psychological testing are considered as well.

The senior author was confronted with the potential of idiosyncratic error in the first case conference examination of a patient that I ever witnessed. The senior clinician who was examining the client proceeded with the questions of the Mental Status Examination. The client did generally well on most questions, except that he did not remember what date it was, he had some trouble counting backward from 100 by 7s after he got to 86, and he gave a rather concrete interpretation to the "spilled milk" question. After the client left the room, the examining clinician suggested the diagnosis of schizophrenia, pointing out that the client's lack of awareness of what date it was suggested a global disorientation, the problem in counting backward from 100 by 7s suggested general confusion, and the difficulties with the proverb suggested concreteness.

By this time I was uncomfortable because I also had missed the date by a full seven days. In actuality, a simpler and better explanation for the client's behavior is available. A lack of knowledge of the exact date, even being off by a number of days, is common. In addition, people who have been in an institution for any period of time easily become confused about, if not indifferent to, the date. The problems with the other two pieces of data are explainable by the fact that this client was not very bright.

There are trends, probabilities, and even some hard data to link the categories typically used by clinicians to various patterns. This book presents these relationships to the extent they are known at this time. In that regard, it is hoped that this book will result in more research that relates patterns of responses on several tests (which is what most clinicians use in an individual case) to various syndromes. As in any other area of scientific knowledge, subsequent research may supplant little, much, or all of what is now known.

This book is based on research results that have been melded with reported consensual clinical experience. The extent of the research data and the clinical experience naturally varies, depending on the particular syndrome being discussed.

A single author or study that is the source of material leading to a diagnostic or therapeutic recommendation will be directly referenced. If the recommendation is the speculation of the author(s) alone, it will be so labeled. Where two or more different sources have provided information on which a recommendation is either directly based or inferred, this will be stated in ways such as "The evidence shows . . ." or "The classic profile for . . . ," or it will be put in a direct statement such as "Clients who are low on scale 8 are . . . ." The primary sources for the inferences for each of the four major tests used in this book—Minnesota Multiphasic Personality Inventory (MMPI-2), Cattell Sixteen Personality Factor (16 PF) Questionnaire, Wechsler Adult Intelligence Scale-Revised (WAIS-R), and Rorschach—are presented in Table 1.1.

The first section of this book (i.e., Chapters 1–11) proceeds in a standard sequence for each disorder, with a number of related syndromes grouped together under an appropriate chapter heading. In each chapter an overview of the material relevant to the specific diagnostic disorder being discussed is presented first. This is usually followed by a synopsis of what the *Diagnostic and Statistical Manual-IV* (DSM-IV) requires so that the clinician can apply this diagnosis to a client. In some cases, where there is little detail in the DSM-IV requirements, we incorporate this information into the first general subsection rather than having a specific DSM-IV subsection for that syndrome.

The next subsection presents the MMPI-2 code types and scale patterns one might expect with a client who exhibits this specific disorder. In most cases the disorder can manifest itself in a variety of ways, so the text attempts to detail the major possibilities. This same approach is used in the next subsection, the presentation of 16 PF correlates. Following the subsection on the 16 PF, corresponding information from other relevant test sources is presented, notably from the Wechsler Adult Intelligence Scale-Revised (WAIS-R) and the Rorschach.

For some of the syndromes, little information is available. If so, only a short subsection is included based on this limited information, and, combined with consensual speculation, it is presented under the heading of Diagnostic Considerations, a designation that supplants the categories usually used—for example, MMPI-2 and Other Test–Response Patterns.

The last subsection, usually entitled Treatment Options, succinctly presents a number of possible treatment methods appropriate for the particular disorder, since the clinician often faces this question. An important point is that we will not consistently mention psychotherapy, chemotherapy, or general schools of therapy as treatment options for the various syndromes. There is good reason to believe that psychotherapy is an appropriate treatment for

TABLE 1.1   Primary Sources for Four Test Inferences

MMPI-2

Ben-Porath and Butcher (1989)
Berry et al. (1991)
Butcher (1979, 1990, 1995)
Butcher and Graham (1988)
Carson (1969)
Colligan et al. (1983; 1994)
Dahlstrom and Dahlstrom (1980)
Dahlstrom and Welsh (1980)
Dahlstrom et al. (1972)
Dahlstrom et al. (1986)
Fowler (1981)
Gilberstadt and Duker (1965)
Graham (1987, 1993)
Graham et al. (1991a)
Greene (1980, 1991)
Gynther, Altman, and Slettin (1973)
Gynther, Altman, and Warbin (1973)
Kelly and King (1979a)
Lachar (1974)
Lewak et al. (1990)
Pope et al. (1993)
Webb et al. (1981)

RORSCHACH

Allison et al. (1988)
Aronow and Reznikoff (1976)
Beck and Beck (1978)
Beck and Molish (1952)
Cooper et al. (1988)
Exner (1974, 1978, 1988, 1993)
Gacono and Meloy (1994)
Gilbert (1978, 1980)
Goldfried et al. (1971)
Groth-Marmat (1990)
Klopfer and Davidson (1962)
Levitt (1980)
Maruish (1994)
Netter and Viglioni (1994)
Newmark (1985, 1989)
Ogdon (1977)
Phillips and Smith (1953)
Piotrowski (1979)
Rabin (1964, 1968, 1981)
Rapaport et al. (1968)
Rickers-Ovsiankina (1960)
Rorschach (1953)
Shafer (1948, 1954)
Siegel (1987)
Swiercinsky (1985)
Wagner and Wagner (1981)

WAIS-R

Allison et al. (1988)
Anastasi (1987)
Gilbert (1978, 1980)
Golden (1979)
Groth–Marmat (1990)
Guertin et al. (1962)
Holland and Watson (1980)
Klinger and Saunders (1975)
Kramer (1990)
Maruish (1994)
Matarazzo (1972)
Newmark (1985, 1989)
Rabin (1964, 1968)
Rapaport et al. (1968)
Shafer (1948)
Swiercinsky (1985)
Wechsler (1981)
Zimmerman and Woo-Sam (1973)

16 PF

Cattell, H.B. (1989)
Cattell, H.E.P. (1993)
Cattell, R. (1965, 1973, 1979, 1986)
Cattell, R. and Warburton (1967)
Cattell, R., et al. (1970)
Conn and Rieke (1994)
Eber (1975, 1987)
Golden (1979)
IPAT Staff (1963, 1972)
Karson (1959, 1960)
Karson and O'Dell (1976, 1989)
Krug (1978, 1980, 1981)
Krug and Johns (1986)
Lorr and Suziedelis (1985)
Reuter et al. (1985)
Russell and Karol (1994)

virtually every syndrome mentioned, either as the major component or as an adjunct to other techniques (Lipsey and Wilson, 1993; Zeig, 1987; Landman and Dawes, 1982; Smith and Glass, 1977). Hence, it would be redundant to mention it continually as an option. On those occasions when psychotherapy is specifically mandated, this fact will be noted. Similarly, the proponents of psychoanalysis and the other major therapy schools often assert that their techniques are valid for the majority of syndromes noted in this work. Where the literature indicates that a particular theoretical approach is especially efficient, it will be noted. Also, chemotherapy may be a useful adjunct in many of the diagnostic categories. It will be mentioned only where it is specifically warranted, with no implied assertion that it may be inappropriate in those groupings where it is not specifically listed.

The reader will also note that specific secondary or derived MMPI-2 or 16 PF scales for the diagnosis of a pattern or type of disorder are only mentioned when they specifically and clearly apply. Many secondary scales have been derived on the MMPI-2 for almost everything from depression to potential for happiness in marriage (Graham, 1987, 1993). In fact, there are secondary scales derived by researchers for almost every type of personality or affect pattern imaginable. The problem is that some of these scales are not routinely given in standard clinical assessments, and many of the others are not well validated and/or do not measure what the scale title suggests they do.

The clinical correlates of the MMPI-2 and the 16 PF scales are examined first in Chapters 12 and 13. Many researchers and clinicians have carried out similar work in this area, and much is owed to them. These chapters attempt to integrate and update previous efforts so that the reader has an up-to-date body of information along traditional lines—that is, the various behavior patterns associated with the scale patterns. For some readers much of this information will be new. For others it will at least offer a review and a handy section to refer to on occasion while using the rest of the book.

Chapter 14 examines issues in predicting various patterns of behavior that directly involve dangerous to self or others. Chapter 15 discusses psychopharmacology, and Chapter 16 examines malingering. The last two chapters deal with the forensic–legal arena. Chapter 17 discusses the issues of competency, criminal responsibility, and civil commitment; Chapter 18 deals with professional case preparation for the office or the courtroom.

■ The Rationale for Inclusion of Certain Tests

The reader might ask why the primary emphasis is on the MMPI-2, 16 PF, Millon Clinical Multiaxial Inventory (MCMI-III), WAIS-R, and Rorschach. The reason is obvious with the MMPI-2 and WAIS-R: They are the most commonly used and researched objective psychological tests (Butcher, 1995; Maruish, 1994; Nietzel et al., 1994; Graham, 1993; Allison et al., 1988). Virtually every clinician, regardless of theoretical orientation or type of training, has some familiarity with the MMPI-2 and WAIS-R. Such an extensive amount of normative data has been gathered on these tests and the MMPI-2 that they are by far the most useful standard objective tests among the clinician's diagnostic options.

Although certain clinicians question the validity of projective tests, there are data to support their usefulness in many situations, and the Rorschach has become one of the most commonly used and well known of these tests (Maruish, 1994; Nietzel et al., 1994). The Thematic Apperception Test (TAT) is also commonly used (Maruish, 1994; Bellak, 1993), and many of the observations on TAT in this book apply equally well to other, newer thematic tests. The MCMI-III was first included in the second edition of this book, and although there are a number of valid criticisms of this test (e.g., "overpathologizing," the scoring of too many scales from the number of items, questionable validity scales, etc.), it is still popular with many clinicians.

The Cattell 16 PF test is not as commonly used as the others. However, while the MMPI-2 is particularly good at assessing severe patterns and conditions of pathology and present adjustment, the 16 PF is a useful measure of personality patterns (Cattell, 1989), and there is increasing empirical support for using such measures (Goldberg, 1992). Thus, they dovetail nicely and provide the practitioner with an effective overview of the client. This is not to say that other tests, such as the Edwards Personal Preference Test, would not be useful as adjuncts to the MMPI-2 as well. However, the validity data on the 16 PF are certainly as impressive as the data on these other tests (Conn and Rieke, 1994; Russell and Karroll, 1994; Cattell, 1979). As Karson and O'Dell (1976) note, "It is important to remember that, in the search for significant variables in personality, the 16 PF has a decided edge over other tests, in that it is deeply embedded in a data-based multivariate personality theory" (p. 50).

The Cattell group has also formulated tests (using virtually the same scales) for persons in the lower age ranges. Thus, if practitioners use these tests with adults, they begin to develop some facility with a related set of children's tests, and vice versa. Also, it is felt that the motivational distortion scores derived for the 16 PF are more useful than those in other available tests, when they have them at all. Finally, from a personal standpoint, the senior author has worked with both the childhood and adult forms of the Cattell test since internship and has gathered a great deal more data regarding this test. Like numerous clinicians, I have continually used it in conjunction with the MMPI-2 and have found the combination to be especially effective.

The Information Evolution in This Book

Before proceeding to a discussion of DSM-IV, the senior author—sole author for the first three editions—would like to explain the procedure by which the information in this book was gathered and integrated. The following stages were followed to bring research information into coordination with consensual clinical experience.

1. For about fifteen years (up to the publication of the 1983 edition of this handbook), I continually used the most accepted diagnostic tests, especially the MMPI–2, 16 PF, and WAIS-R, in a wide-ranging diagnostic practice and kept written records that were cross-checked and compared to the research literature to develop correlations of test patterns with various syndromes and the syndromes with the most appropriate treatments. This was in keeping with the traditional admonition that too much dependence on memory quickly leads to error in clinical inference. These patterns also were used as a teaching tool in graduate courses in diagnostic testing and clinical psychopathology. Thus, the developing concepts were again continually checked against available clinical research literature and within the case itself.

2. A thorough formal review of the literature was instituted, and from this and the information collected in Step 1, a first draft was written that correlated the patterns on the 16 PF and MMPI-2 and appropriate treatments with the diagnostic categories in the initial DSM-III.

3. Graduate students in sequential clinical psychopathology courses were each assigned a subset of DSM-III categories. They were asked, independent of the information in the first draft, to find correlates of the DSM-III draft categories on the MMPI-2, 16 PF, WAIS-R, and Rorschach in the research and clinical literature. Another review of the most recent literature was coordinated with the corrections and suggestions gleaned from the production of these graduate students.

4. As soon as the final DSM-III was published, the work that emerged from Step 3 was coordinated with changes from the earlier versions to produce a polished draft.

5. The information derived up to that point was presented to a continuing-education seminar of twenty practicing clinical psychologists. These people responded via formal feedback procedures about the applicability and accuracy of the findings in this draft. There was substantial agreement between the views of these practicing clinicians and the draft that was produced at the end of Step 4, but corrections were noted, and some interesting suggestions were incorporated.

6. After integrating this information, the latest draft was presented to five of the most respected practicing clinical psychologists in the region, all of whom regularly used these tests in their practices. Each carried out a thorough review of the book, and again, although there was general agreement with the material as presented to them, they did offer much helpful commentary.

7. After this material was integrated and amplified in accordance with the publisher's reviewers, there was a last check with the relevant research literature, and the manuscript was again considered and put into a final state.

8. After the 1983 edition of this book was published, it was consistently used as the primary text in a graduate course on psychopathology and psychological testing. At various junctures, students were asked to critique and/ or update subsections of the book, including new diagnostic categories proposed for and then included in DSM-III-R. More diagnostic categories specific to adolescence were added. Taking cues and new points of view from the work of these students, the author carried out similar continuing updates and critiques himself, using all of this material to keep reworking the manuscript.

9. The MCMI-II was incorporated because of its increasing popularity with a number of clinicians. MCMI-III diagnostic correlates of the major syndromes are now included throughout the book. After being initially generated, they were critiqued and updated by several graduate students and local clinicians who had worked extensively with the MCMI; they were later thoroughly critiqued and reworked by Wilfred Van Gorp, Kenneth McNiel, and John Boles, all of whom not only have extensive clinical experience with the MCMI but also have carried out research on the instrument.

10. A chapter on professional practice (Chapter 18), relevant to the courtroom as well as the office, was developed.

11. For each chapter, at least two (and often more) experienced practicing clinicians, each of whom is recognized as having substantial expertise in the areas covered, contributed a thorough critique and update of that chapter to aid in finalization of the manuscript.

12. A final reworking of the manuscript incorporated the changes from DSM-III to DSM-III-R, as well as the publisher's reviews and a thorough check on the relevant literature.

13. After the publication of the 1989 edition, graduate student feedback and input was again incorporated; most chapters were submitted to experienced clinicians with specific expertise, and their input was also integrated.

14. Theodore Feldmann, M.D., Harvey A. Tilker, Ph.D., and Stephen G. Thein Jr., Ph.D., along with the authors of this book, authored Chapter 15 on psychopharmacology. Dr. Tilker also contributed numerous related additions to the overall text. With substantial help from Steven R. Smith, dean of the Cleveland–Marshall Law School at Cleveland State University, Appendix D on relevant legal cases was developed.

15. The material on the MMPI and MCMI was revised and updated so as to make recommendations in this book consistent with the respective revisions of these tests, MMPI-2 and MCMI-II. A final update based on the recent research and publisher's reviews produced the 1993 edition.

16. Sarah E. Deitsch joined in as junior author, and as with prior editions, critiques and contributions from colleagues for the various chapters were again incorporated into this fourth edition.

17. With the help of Laura Bolte, Appendix A, Bibliotherapy Suggestions, was developed.

18. Appendix B, which details two relaxation methods that can be directly applied in work with clients, was added.

19. The changes from DSM-III–R to DSM-IV were incorporated into the manuscript, and consequent related changes were made throughout the text.

20. A final update, based on publisher's reviews, colleague critiques, and new research, produced this edition.

Throughout this process, as much research information as possible was gathered and integrated and then complemented by consensual clinical experience.

In addition to the standard DSM-IV categories, this book examines several other topics of interest to practitioners: the issues of acting-out potential (for example, aggression and suicide potential); the criminal personality; rape; and the legal concepts and psychological correlates of insanity, involuntary civil commitment, and competency to stand trial. Malingering is included in the DSM-IV, but it receives relatively little notice there, as in most diagnostic texts. I consider it to be of considerable importance to the diagnostician, so it will be dealt with in some depth in Chapter 16.

Following the main text is Appendix A, which provides bibliotherapy recommendations for a wide variety of patterns and disorders. Appendix B is a client screening device, a set of paper-and-pencil test materials that I have revised and integrated over the past eighteen years. The reader can use the material as a classroom handout with the text without written permission, so long as it is not sold or reproduced for any other reason. You may want to insert a drawing test different from the Draw-A-Group Test, add some Bender-Gestalt–like figures (see the section on central nervous system impairment in Chapter 11), or otherwise modify it. The four proverbs included were selected because Johnson (1966) found these to be the most efficient in discriminating between cases of central nervous system impairment and schizophrenia. The validated short form of the Marlowe-Crowne Social Desirability Scale would also be a useful addition, in order to get a quick estimate of the client's response set (Zook and Sipps, 1985). Appendix C, Two Relaxation Methods, consists of a long- and a short-term technique for combatting stress and inducing relaxation. As noted earlier, Appendix D presents a listing of the major legal cases relevant to clinicians.

CHAPTER 2

Substance Use Disorders

■　**Overall Concepts**

Although we relish our combination of "Puritan" and "pioneer" traditions, the evidence is clear that we have an early tradition of substance abuse in the United States. In fact, a staggering amount of alcohol was consumed in early colonial times, abetted in part by the widespread belief (very possibly an accurate one) that drinking water was hazardous to one's health. Hard apple cider was the accepted substitute. Also, it's noteworthy that in the 1770s the city of New York had almost four hundred taverns, at a ratio of about one for every twelve adult males (compared to only twenty-two churches).

Unfortunately, modern society provides an increasing number of substances that are abused (Meyer, 1995; Beck et al., 1994, L'Abate et al., 1992), and this is reflected in the DSM-IV. The first matrix in the DSM-IV system refers to drugs that are commonly abused, such as marijuana (cannabis), cocaine, amphetamine, and heroin (opioids), and are given separate subcategories in the DSM-IV. Caffeine and nicotine use disorders are also included, the latter being especially important as a precursor to other forms of chronic substance abuse. Other categories in the DSM-IV are hallucinogens; inhalants; phencyclidines; sedatives, hypnotics, and anxiolytics; polysubstance use; and "other." Within this overall "substance" matrices or set of categories, the following "pattern" matrices are five diagnoses potentially available: dependence, abuse, intoxication, withdrawal, and "persisting." We say "potentially" because some pattern diagnoses are not available for some substances (e.g., the diagnosis of intoxication for caffeine; the diagnosis of withdrawal for caffeine, cannabis, hallucinogens, inhalants, and phencyclidine; etc.). This does not mean there are no such effects, just that there is no provision for a formal diagnosis per se.

Dependence and abuse are defined similarly across all these substances. Intoxication and withdrawal are defined by the specifics of each substance plus the fact that intoxication must be "reversible" and "maladaptive" and withdrawal involves a relationship to cessation of use and must be distressing or impairing in an important life arena.

A third matrix potentially fed into the diagnosis is the set of "phenomeno-logically similar" (to other DSM-IV diagnoses) disorders, that is, delirium, dementia, amnestic, psychotic, mood, anxiety, sex, and sleep disorder. Again, not all of these latter categories are available as sub-modifiers in the diagnosis of all substances; for example, dementia is only available to the overall sub-stance diagnoses of alcohol, inhalants, sedatives, and "other."

As noted, the two modifiers available throughout the substance matrix (i.e., a primary diagnostic term such as "alcohol"), are dependence and abuse, and they are defined similarly across substances.

Substance Dependence is a maladaptive pattern, signaled by impairment or distress, with three of the following seven occurring in a twelve-month period: (1) tolerance—need for greater amounts to achieve similar results, or dimin-ishing effect with use of the same amount; (2) withdrawal—individual symp-toms for each substance, or the use of the substance to relieve or avoid with-drawal symptoms; (3) unintended use of larger amounts or for longer than intended; (4) inability to control use, or persistent desire for the substance; (5) high time cost to obtain, use, or recover from the substance; (6) giving up of important life activities because of use; (7) continued use in the face of use–related psychological or physical problems. Diagnosis should specify if the Dependence diagnosis is "with" or "without physiological dependence," that is, "with" if either #1 (tolerance) or #2 (withdrawal) is present, or "without" if neither #1 or #2 is present.

A diagnosis of *Substance Abuse* presumes no prior diagnosis of Dependence. It does require impairment or distress from a maladaptive pattern, within a twelve-month period as evidenced by at least one of the following: (1) failure in a major life role obligation in some recurrent pattern; (2) hazardous status, for example, driving, in some recurrent pattern; (3) recurrent consequent legal problems; (4) persisting use despite use-related socio-interpersonal problems.

It would likely take several volumes to provide individual descriptions of each potentially applicable DSM-IV substance use disorder category. Hence, this chapter will concern itself with those diagnoses/substances that are both common and also challenging in their complexity of assessment and treatment, that is, alcohol, polysubstance use (often including cannabis), amphetamine (and phencyclidine), cocaine, opioids, and nicotine. Although not included in DSM-IV, prescription drug abuse will also be discussed. Alcohol is still the preeminent drug of abuse, as approximately 10–14% of Americans have prob-lems with alcohol, and well over 10 million are alcohol dependent. Approxi-mately 35% (higher by some other estimates) of people with an alcohol prob-lem have a comorbid mental disorder (McCreery & Walker, 1993). Note that there are many narrowly defined substance use categories in the DSM-IV, so many that it would be impossible to discuss each one here, especially since many of them are not often applied. We first take note of some general charac-teristics of substance use disorders.

In any evaluation one should be alert to "danger signs" signaling possible abuse—for example, disruption in job, marriage, or other significant relation-ships; deteriorating financial or physical health; frequent job changes; an arrest record; complaints of anxiety, depression, or insomnia; direct signs of addictive personality; and social patterns. Reports of significant others are useful here. For instance, young males who early showed a high tolerance to the effects of alcohol are much more likely to later become alcoholic, and having had an alcoholic father is a strong predictive factor for young males.

A critical component of the process of evaluation is to sort out the validity of the client's various self–reports. The following schemata may help in this process:

CONDITIONS CONDUCIVE TO INVALID SELF-REPORT	CONDITIONS CONDUCIVE TO VALID SELF-REPORT
1. Client shows positive blood alcohol/drug concentration, is experiencing withdrawal, and/or apparent substance-related distress	1. Client is alcohol/drug free and is not showing withdrawal symtoms or evident substance-related distress
2. Client referral generated primarily by objective coercion, e.g., DUI, threat of job loss	2. No objective coercion
3. Client referral generated primarily by interpersonal distress, e.g., threat of divorce	3. Interpersonal coercion not primary
4. Client doubts confidentiality of information he or she provides	4. Confidentiality is assured and apparently accepted
5. Client keeps interpersonal distance and/or contracts are brief	5. Adequate rapport has been established
6. Client is unaware that self-report data will be corroborated	6. Client understands self-report will be checked against other data
7. Vague, unstructured interview techniques are used	7. Structured interview techniques and psychological tests are employed
8. Client shows psychopathic and/or antisocial personality characteristics	8. Client is relatively low on psychopathic-antisocial dimension
9. Client shows inadequate compliance	9. Client shows adequate compliance
10. Adequate attendance and/or compliance is a condition of parole, continued relationship, or employment, etc.	10. Reasons for performance compliance are minimal or do not appear to be a primary motivation

☐ MMPI-2

Craig (1993) states that from a consensus of the literature, the 2-4/4-2, 4-8/8-4, and 4-9/9-4 profiles account for 40–50% of MMPI-2 profiles of substance abusers. Johnson et al. (1992) find the 2-4/4-2, 2-7/7-2, and 4-9/9-4 profiles to be especially common in substance abusers. Trethvithick and Hosch (1978) have noted that persons with substance use disorders in general are typically elevated on MMPI-2 scales 4, 8, 2, and 7, and others note that 9 is often high, too (Patalano, 1980). These elevations reflect the confusion, distress, and depression that are found in addition to the sociopathic traits of drug abusers. Scores on scale 9 will vary, depending on their need to affiliate with others and whether they are inclined toward the use of depressants or stimulants in response to their own typical physiological patterns. The rare spike-9 profile is indicative of drug abuse associated with antisocial patterns (King and Kelley, 1977).

An MMPI-2 content scale (forty-nine items) that is particularly useful in diagnosing substance abuse disorders, especially with alcohol, but also with heroin, heavy marijuana use, cocaine, polydrug use, etcetera, is the MacAndrew Alcoholism Scale (MAC) (MacAndrew, 1965; Craig, 1993). This scale is also useful with young adults in predicting later abuse patterns. When MMPI-2 was developed, four religious items were dropped and were replaced with four items that were found to differentiate alcoholics from nonalcoholics. The MAC is hard to fake unless one fakes the MMPI-2 in general, so it is usually accurate if the validity scales are within acceptable limits. According to Butcher (1990), a cutoff range (raw scores) at 26–28 strongly suggests past or present abuse and/or potential abuse; a score of 29–31 indicates an addiction problem of some sort is very likely; and with a score over 31, addiction is highly probable. Since minorities (especially blacks) and obese persons tend to score a bit higher on this scale, adjusting the cutoff 1–2 points higher is suggested for these clients; females tend to score slightly lower than males, so reducing the cutoff score by 2–3 points is recommended. From a more general perspective, persons scoring high on the MAC present themselves as self-confident; are risk-taking, assertive, exhibitionistic, extroverted; and show a history of concentration and persistence difficulties and acting-out problems such as in school.

The Addiction Prediction Scale (APS) and the Addiction Acknowledgement Scale (AAS) are also helpful. They are straightforward in their item content and are interpreted as their titles read, using 60 T as a reasonably effective discrimination point (Graham, 1993). Since the AAS has a more straightforward goal, the assessment of open acknowledgement of addiction behaviors, it so far has shown more validity and usefulness than the APS.

☐ 16 PF

In the typical testing situation, when disposition is at least one of the considerations, individuals with substance use disorders tend to score high on the H, I,

M, and Q_4 scales and low on F, which reflects their imagination and their disdain for typical societal standards, as well as their distress. They are likely to be moderately high on scale L, reflecting their concern about arrest and the eventual disposition of their situation. They tend to be moderately low on both scales G and Q_3, reflecting again their disdain for the standard mores. They are also lower on scales B, C, and E, and if their distress is relatively high, they are likely to show a lower score on scale F.

OTHER TEST-RESPONSE PATTERNS

Clinicians should of course look for physical signs of substance abuse (needle marks, abscesses over veins, constriction of pupils) and make sure that adequate physiological screening, such as urinalysis, has been carried out. Over a hundred structured interviews are available for substance abuse and its variations. Two of the most commonly used are the Addiction Severity Index (ASI) and the Michigan Alcoholism Screening Test (MAST) (Craig, 1993).

If the substance abuse has not been long-term, or if there is little in the way of allied psychopathology, WAIS-R scores are in the normal range and do not show marked subtest deviation (Hewett and Martin, 1980). In some instances, when clients are tested after having ingested low doses of cocaine or amphetamines, they do slightly better on certain tasks, such as digit symbol, that require speed and role learning (Washton, 1991). If individuals have been abusing drugs for some time, they do poorly on tests that reflect school achievement, such as information and arithmetic, although they still do reasonably well on vocabulary. If they have begun to develop confusion, which occurs in the polydrug abuse syndrome, they are likely to do poorly on the coding and the block design test. They do best in such subtests as similarities, picture completion, and comprehension.

Several factors on the MCMI-III have been noted (Choca et al., 1992; Bryer et al., 1990). Scores of 75 or higher on B or T have traditionally been thought to indicate the presence of some drug or alcohol abuse, while scores of 85 indicate a more severe abuse problem (although Bryer and his colleagues (1990) report a 50% false positive rate, and positive hit rates of 43% for alcoholics and 49% for drug abusers when using a score of 75 as a cutoff point). According to Craig (1993), general drug addicts peak on 6A, with secondary peaks on 6B and 8A and with lesser peaks on 5, 4, and C on the personality scales. On the clinical scales a primary peak on T and a secondary peak on 2B is expected. For alcoholics, peaks on 6A and 6B, with secondary peaks on 8A and C are expected on the clinical scales, with a peak on B and a secondary peak on T on the clinical scales. During periods of intoxication by drugs or alcohol, the severe symptom syndromes SS and PP may become elevated, and scale 3 and/or 5 is also high.

TREATMENT OPTIONS

A variety of treatment techniques has been used in substance use disorders (Beck et al., 1994; Roffman and Stephens, 1993; Prochaska et al., 1992; Barrett and Meyer, 1992). Common to most therapeutic situations involving substance abuse are (1) breaking through the often massive denial that there is a problem, (2) bolstering the often-wavering motivation, and (3) avoidance of manipulations and rationalizations.

Prochaska et al. (1992) provide a useful model for change behaviors. Though designed specifically to respond to substance abuse behaviors, it is helpful for responding to virtually all disorders. They conceptualize change as occurring in five stages:

1. *Precontemplation:* The person avoids any confrontation of true issues, and generally denies realistic consequences.

2. *Contemplation:* There is at least some acknowledgement of responsibility and problematic consequences and at least a minimal openness to the possibility of change, though effective change has not yet been instituted.

3. *Preparation:* This is the decision point. There is enough acknowledgement of problematic behaviors and consequences that the person can make the required cognitive shift to initiate change.

4. *Action:* There is a higher sense of self–liberation or willpower, generating sets of behaviors toward positive coping and away from situations that condition the undesired behavior.

5. *Maintenance:* Efforts are directed toward remotivation and developing skills and patterns that avoid relapse and promote a positive lifestyle.

Table 2.1, adapted from Prochaska et al. (1992), lists the major change processes. They are listed in the order in which they occur in the overall change process; that is, consciousness raising is more likely to occur in the precontemplation and contemplation stages, and self-disclosure and trust are more likely to be central to action and maintenance processes.

The achievement and maintenance of abstinence are critical to most treatment programs for substance abuse. Since comorbidity with other diagnoses (e.g., depression, psychopathy, physical disorder) is so common, the treatment program for any one individual will vary, depending upon the specific dual diagnosis. Ideally, the concurrent diagnosis is made only if the pattern persists for four weeks beyond obtained and maintained abstinence.

Initial brief therapy to teach deficient behavioral skills—self- and compliance monitoring, goal setting, avoidance of denial or displacement of responsibility, and recognition and avoidance of high risk situations—is often necessary. Over the long haul, relapse prevention includes stress reduction, improvement in interpersonal skills, the ability to "minesweep" the environment to rid it of conditioned stimuli for abuse, involvement of significant others, and the development of healthier physical and psychological lifestyles. Some version of the Twelve-Step Program is often included.

Aversive conditioning has been favored for working on the specific habits that form the matrix of substance abuse, as well as in helping develop an aversive response to the drug itself. It is also argued that relaxation training is

TABLE 2.1   Change Processes

PROCESS	DEFINITIONS: INTERVENTIONS
Consciousness-raising observations	Increasing information about self and problem: confrontations, interpretations, bibliotherapy
Dramatic relief	Experiencing and expressing feelings about one's problems solutions: psychodrama, grieving losses, role playing
Environmental reevaluation	Assessing how one's problem affects physical environment: empathy training, documentaries
Self-reevaluation	Assessing how one feels and thinks about oneself with respect to a problem: value clarification, imagery, corrective emotional experience
Choice and commitment	Choosing and commitment to act or belief in ability to change: decision-making therapy, New Year's resolutions, logotherapy techniques, commitment-enhancing techniques
Reinforcement management	Rewarding one's self or being rewarded by others for making changes: contingency contracts, overt and covert reinforcement, self-reward
Self-disclosure and trust	Being open and trusting about problems with someone who cares: therapeutic alliance, social support, self-help groups
Counterconditioning	Substituting alternatives for problem behaviors: relaxation, desensitization, assertion, positive self-statements
Stimulus control	Avoiding or countering stimuli that elicit problem behaviors: restructuring one's environment (e.g., removing alcohol or fattening foods), avoiding high-risk cues, fading techniques
Sociopolitical	Increasing alternatives for nonproblem behaviors available in society: advocating for rights of repressed, empowering, policy interventions

helpful for substance abusers, particularly those who use tranquilizers or depressant drugs. Where the disorder appears to be an escape response from fears and phobias, systematic desensitization is helpful. Analogously, assertive training may be included in the treatment package if social inadequacy is evident, as is often the case in substance dependence.

In the initial stages of the treatment, when the person is being detoxified in a controlled setting, a quasi-token economy may be helpful in getting the client to organize his or her behavior effectively. With regard to the cognitive behavioral treatments, many feel that covert sensitization is especially useful for the substance use disorders (Cautela and Wall, 1980). Within the psychoanalytic therapies it appears that the Adlerian approaches have the most to offer for this particular pattern, with their emphasis on personal responsibility for behavior. As the person progresses away from drug abuse, the cognitive and existential therapies take on a particularly important role (Beck et al., 1994). Certainly the critical issues in treatment success in any substance abuse pattern are the client's decision to change, the maintenance of that decision, and the ability to implement relapse prevention strategies over time. A "quit contract" that is written out and spells out specifics of that decision is recommended. Since the experience-seeking subfactor of the stimulation-seeking variable particularly characterizes the substance abuser (Zuckerman et al., 1980), the therapist needs to help the client channel this need into more legitimate and constructive pursuits. Family therapy also is usually necessary (Brown, 1991).

■ Alcohol Use Disorders

> *I was never a drunkard*
> *and I have not reformed.*
> Jack London
> *John Barleycorn* (1913)

☐ DSM-IV CONSIDERATIONS

The various DSM-IV subcategories discussed in the initial part of this chapter also applying to alcohol. Recall that the definitions of abuse (alcohol abuse, 305.00) and dependence (alcohol dependence, 303.90) are the same for all substances, as previously detailed. Alcohol intoxication (303.00) requires sufficient, recent ingestion, consequent and clinically significant maladaptive changes, with at least one of the following: slurred speech, lack of coordination, unsteady gait, mystagmus, impairment in attention or memory, or stupor or coma. Alcohol withdrawal (291.8) requires clinically significant distress or impairment upon cessation or reduction of use, with at least two of the following signs: autonomic hyperactivity (e.g., sweating, increased hand tremor, insomnia, nausea, or vomiting), transient hallucinations or illusions, psychomotor agitation, anxiety, or grand mal seizures. Diagnosis using those "phenomenologically similar disorders," the third matrix (e.g., alcohol delirium [291.0], alcohol sexual dysfunction [292.8], are defined by substance use resulting in that specific impairment.

☐ OTHER BEHAVIORAL CONSIDERATIONS

The psychological euphoria from alcohol is functionally a toxic response (Maltzman, 1994). Alcohol is not digested, but absorbed through the stomach and intestinal walls and metabolized in the liver by the process of oxidation.

In this process, alcohol fuses with oxygen, and the resulting pure grain alcohol, or ethanol, is converted by enzymes to acetaldehyde, which is further broken down to acetic acid (vinegar). The vinegar is then broken down by enzymes into water and carbon dioxide, which are passed out of the body. The liver can only break down approximately one ounce of 100-proof whiskey per hour, assuming the person is of average weight. Any excess that cannot be broken down directly affects the brain, causing intoxication. Interestingly, even when males and females are of equal weight, this process is still slower in females.

Pharmacologically, alcohol acts as a depressant that first inhibits the higher brain centers and only later depresses the lower brain centers (Maltzman, 1994; Meyer, 1995). The resultant decrease in control of overt behavior has led to the mistaken belief that alcohol is a stimulant. With continued alcohol intake, there is a loss of the more complex cognitive and perceptual abilities and eventually a loss in simple memory and motor coordination.

It is interesting that part of the strength of the effect depends on whether people are getting drunk or sobering up. Those who are sobering up perform better on short-term memory and perception tasks than those who have the same blood level of alcohol but who are getting high.

Long-term alcohol abuse is likely to result in central nervous system dysfunction, or organicity, especially in older alcoholics (see Chapter 11 for relevant diagnostic considerations). This dysfunction is not simply a result of B-vitamin deficiencies from the poor diet that often accompanies chronic alcoholism, but is at least in part caused by the effects of alcohol per se (Barrett and Meyer, 1992). The reader is referred to the important work of researchers (see review by Marlatt et al., 1988) who have indicated that the *belief* that one has ingested alcohol is often more critical than whether one has actually done so. These researchers show that both aggression and sexual behavior are highly dependent on the belief system of those individuals who use alcohol, and many times the alcohol is a learned excuse for acting-out behavior in these areas (Beck et al., 1994).

Fabian and Parsons (1983) addressed the question of whether cognitive deficits (decrements in problem solving, abstracting, and spatial-perceptual skills, but with intact verbal intelligence) found in detoxified alcoholics diminish over time. Results indicated that most, but not all, cognitive deficits continued to show up, but at reduced levels, at follow-up (1.8 years later), with the greatest and perhaps the earliest improvement occurring on complex abstracting tests. Continued deficits in the four-years-sober alcoholics were most notable on perceptual-motor tasks, such as WAIS-R Digit Symbol and the Trail-Making Test. Recovery of most functions for which recovery is possible occurs roughly within the first year of sobriety. Thus, differential recovery among cognitive abilities was noted over a four-year period: Some complex cognitive abilities appear to return to normal levels, while others (perceptual-motor speed, for example) remain lower than normal.

There are a number of structured interviews designed to assess alcoholism. Craig (1993) sees the Michigan Alcoholism Screening Test (MAST) as one of the best. It consists of twenty-five items, answered "yes" or "no," with a score of 5 or more indicating a likely problem. Other tests, such as the Alcohol Use Inventory (AUI) may be more helpful in developing individual treatment plans.

MMPI-2

As noted earlier, the MAC is especially useful here (MacAndrew, 1965; Craig, 1993). The MAC seems especially effective in picking up alcoholics or those predisposed to substance abuse because of traits of extroversion and/or sensation seeking. The scale is somewhat less effective in spotting the reactive and/or neurotic substance abuser.

Because chronic alcohol intoxication refers to one behavior pattern within an overall personality, and because that behavior can be generated by diverse trains of personality development, what one might expect on various tests is even less clear than with a number of the other disorders that will be discussed later. The 4-9/9-4 profile is especially common in alcoholics. Otto et al. (1988) found alcoholics to be high on all scales except L, K, 5, and 0. Holland and Watson (1980) reported elevations above the 65-T level on F, 2, 4, 7, and 8 in their sample of MMPIs from inpatient alcoholics. They compared this group to neurotic, schizophrenic, and brain-damaged groups and found that the only marked differences from the other groups in general were the alcoholics' low scores on L, K, and O. They assert that this is indicative of the introversion, somatization, and depression that are characteristic of this group. The 8-7 alcoholic is most likely to be psychotic and/or depressed (Conley, 1981).

The classic high 4-9 pattern that characterizes the psychopath is commonly found in outpatient alcoholics, although it is usually accompanied by a higher F score (Greene, 1991). When referring to the more acute alcoholic, experts like Conley (1981), Gynther et al. (1973a), and Lachar (1974) have noted that the 2-4/4-2 profile is particularly common. The 2-4/4-2 reflects the depression that a person in an acute state of alcoholic disorder is likely to experience (Barrett and Meyer, 1992). The 4-2 is more common than the 2-4, although the two scores are closer together here than in the 4-2 obtained with other drug disorders. This 4-2 pattern is particularly noted in those arrested for driving under the influence of alcohol.

Gynther and his colleagues (1973a) have also found that the 1-2/2-1 MMPI profile is common in alcoholics, particularly for males who show an episodic pattern with numerous physical complaints. This usually represents a person who has used alcohol for a significant period of time and who primarily manifests the abuse in episodic sprees. When 3 is also elevated and 7 is one of the next highest scores, a substantial and often severe neurotic component is involved (Conley, 1981). Profiles with an elevation on 4 and 7 frequently indicate persons who manifest a cycle of alcoholic indulgence, regret, and remorse and then repetition of the acting-out, while the 2-7/7-2 is noted where remorse is more chronic and has channeled into depression.

The 4-6/6-4 profile is commonly found in alcoholics who have a long history of alcoholic problems; as alcoholics age, however, scales 4 and 6 decline.

They are less inclined toward episodic drinking than those with the 1-2/2-1 profile, and they are likely to avoid treatment. The 6-4/4-6 alcoholics usually have very poor work histories and have had numerous marital problems, including the tendency to get married repetitively. When the 6 scale is higher, the individual is likely to be abusive, with the spouse probably the main target of this abuse. The 4-9/9-4 profile with a high F scale has already been noted; such persons tend to be long-term alcoholics.

There is also the 1-4/4-1 pattern, where the person is high on scale 9 and at least moderately low on the 0 scale. These individuals are the extroverted social alcoholics (or drug abusers in general) who do not have as severe underlying conflicts as those with other patterns.

☐   ## 16 PF

Some of the early research gathered by the people who developed the Cattell 16 PF test has delineated some characteristics on the 16 PF that are common to most alcoholics (IPAT Staff, 1963). They found the alcoholic to be high on the I, M, O, and Q_4 scales, as well as moderately high on the L and N scales. They reported the alcoholic to be low on the B, C, and F scales and at least moderately low on scales E and G.

Gross and Carpenter (1971) found somewhat similar results in a study of 266 alcoholics who showed elevation on O and Q_4, with slight elevation on B and M. They also found low scores on C, E, G, H, and Q_1, with a moderately low Q_3. They assert that these profiles characterize the alcoholic as having more imaginative capacity and intellectual ability than the normative group and indicate extroversion, passivity, emotional instability, anxiety, and interpersonal undependability.

Costello (1978) found two major subtypes of alcoholics reflected in the 16 PF. The first is characterized by high scores on L, N, O, and Q_4, with low scores on C, E, H, I, M, Q_2, and Q3. This group, which approximates the stereotype of the alcoholic, manifests anxiety, introversion, and ambivalent dependency. The second subtype shows high scores on G, N, and Q_3, with lower scores on B, C, F, Q_1, and Q_2. This group is more aggressive, more highly socialized, and has less immediate anxiety.

The scores on the O and Q_4 scales depend in large part on the degree of anxiety the alcoholic is experiencing at the time of the test. Some alcoholics no longer have immediately intense sources of anxiety and are involved with alcohol largely out of habit and personality factors. They are not likely to be as high on the O and Q_4 scales and are expected to be lower on the Q_3 scale.

☐   ## OTHER TEST-RESPONSE PATTERNS

In part, the response of the alcoholic to the WAIS-R is dependent on whether there has been a development of central nervous system impairment (CNSI) (Barrett and Meyer, 1992) (see Chapter 11). It has generally been assumed that alcoholics do well on tests that measure vocabulary (which may be the highest score), similarities, information, and comprehension but do less well on tests that tap visual motor coordination and on problems in impulsivity. They occasionally miss surprisingly easy items, reflecting a lack of attention and/or CNSI.

Holland and Watson (1980) administered the WAIS-R to alcoholic inpatients. Their subjects obtained average scores on similarities, comprehension, information, vocabulary, picture completion, and arithmetic. Scores were significantly lower on digit symbol, block design, object assembly, and picture arrangement, which suggests the decrements in visual motor coordination to which others have alluded.

Kish et al. (1980) tested four groups of alcoholics at 6, 15, 21, and 102 days of abstinence from alcohol, using the arithmetic, digit span, block design, similarities, and digit symbol WAIS-R subtests. At the time of the first evaluation (6 days) the alcoholics showed scores that were deficient on all the scales used. Scores improved, however, between 6 and 21 days on digit span, block design, and similarities. This pattern continued, indicating that, with reference to the degree of alcoholism they were studying in general, "recoveries in short–term memory and attention, visual, analytic and synthesizing ability, and abstracting ability" did occur, while the decrements in learning new material or handling arithmetic or digit-symbol tasks continued.

Highest elevation on scales B and T should occur on the MCMI-III (Choca et al., 1992). This may be accompanied by an elevated 2B and D, reflecting the depression often occurring in chronic alcoholics or in alcoholic withdrawal. Personality types most often associated with chronic alcohol intoxication are 2, 3, S, C, and P (Craig et al., 1985). Also, those who are schizoid should score high on scale 1. A score of at least 75 might be expected on one or more of these scales. The borderline passive-aggressive mixed-personality disorder is often seen in chronic alcoholic patients drying out (see Chapter 9). Depressed alcoholics tend to score higher on D, A, 2, 8, C, S, SS, and H than do nondepressed alcoholics.

On the Rorschach a high percentage of oral responses and anatomy responses have been reported. W responses and an increment of Dd responses have been reported by Rapaport et al. (1968) to be associated with addictive tendencies. Others (Gilbert, 1978, 1980) found a high number of anatomy responses, a low F+ percentage, a number of aquatic animal responses, and some color responses to be related to orality. Phillips and Smith (1953) found an absence and/or decrement of Popular responses in the record. Bug and/or beetle responses are alleged to denote the frustrated dependency commonly associated with alcoholism.

TREATMENT OPTIONS

Most alcoholics who have been chronically imbibing will need an initial period of detoxication (Meyer, 1995), especially in light of the mild confusion and memory and concentration problems commonly found as acute withdrawal symptoms in the one to three weeks following the cessation of drinking. In addition, a period of hospitalization or other controlled-living environment keeps them from giving in to strong immediate habits that would return them to drinking (Barrett and Meyer, 1992). Hospitalization was traditionally over-used—it is more profitable for the treater. Today it is more profitable for the insurance carrier to keep hospitalization to a minimum. While studies have found no significant difference between inpatient and outpatient treatment settings (McCreery & Walker, 1993), the diversity of patient characteristics makes hospitalization a necessity in some cases. It is common to administer 100 mg of thiamine parenterally, upon admission, and to follow this up with a daily 100-mg oral dose and a multivitamin with mineral and folate (1 mg).

Chemotherapy, especially with the benzodiazepenes, can be helpful in specific instances for weaning the person away from alcohol (Meyer, 1995), although it introduces the paradoxical problems of treating drug abuse with another drug, and secondarily, the implicit message in any chemotherapy that the client's efforts to change are not the critical factor. A combination of methadone and imipramine has been useful for alcoholics where depression is a strong feature.

The first critical steps in the treatment of alcoholics are simply getting them to admit they have a problem and then to become involved in any ongoing treatment program (Maltzman, 1994). Confrontation techniques are typically necessary here. When involved in consensual data gathering, it is good to write down critical agreements and pieces of data. Since alcoholics often have impaired and irritated nervous systems, written reference data is useful. Another helpful approach to this problem was demonstrated by Craigie and Ross (1980): They used videotape to model self-disclosing behaviors and treatment-seeking behaviors with one group of alcoholics who were in a detoxication unit. They compared their subsequent degree of involvement in treatment to those who had seen only general films about alcoholism and found that the modeling for self-disclosure and treatment seeking significantly improved the probability of staying in treatment.

Naltrexone is effective in helping to curb the need for alcohol. Drugs such as disulfuram (Antabuse), introduced in 1948 following the serendipitous discovery of its action by two researchers who became ill at a cocktail party, can also be helpful in controlling the immediate impulse to drink, although the effects of the Antabuse can be bypassed in short order (Ciraulo and Shader, 1991). Calcium carbimide (Temposil) is effective as an alternative to Antabuse in some cases. The implantation of time-release drugs similar in action to Antabuse is a future option, although there are potential legal liabilities if a client fatally overdoses by combining alcohol and the drug, which is possible (Slovenko, 1995). Aversion therapy is also helpful in giving the client additional control over impulses; aversion by electric shock can be supplemented by videotape replays of the person while he or she is drunk.

Many alcoholics, like other persons with impulse problems, are relatively unaware of their physiological reactions as they proceed in their abuse (Maltzman, 1994). Unlike depressives who don't trust "self," alcoholics overtrust their "alcoholic self." Yet analogous to obese individuals, alcoholics are less aware of how much more they drink than normal drinkers, a surprising finding in light of their substantial experience. Clients who are able to return to social drinking rather than to rely on total abstinence are usually better educated, have a shorter drinking history, and are more confident of their ability to avoid drinking that goes out of control (Marlatt et al., 1988). For all alcoholics there is a need for continued monitoring, cognitive-behavioral retraining, supportive therapy, and work with their social networks well beyond the point when they have stopped drinking (Barrett and Meyer, 1992).

Continued contact and long-term cognitive retraining are just two of the advantages of Alcoholics Anonymous (AA). A favorite AA saying is "Stinkin' thinkin' leads to drinkin'." In addition, AA forces alcoholics to publicly label themselves as in need of help and gives them a new social network composed of nondrinkers. Although AA's data supporting the claim of high rates of success are flawed methodologically, AA has clearly been helpful to persons who have trouble with impulse drinking, who need a new social network, and who are able to work within the somewhat rigid demands of the AA belief system (Marlatt et al., 1988).

Marital and family-help therapy are important for dealing with the disruption that has usually occurred in the alcoholic's family life and, most importantly, for helping the family offer positive support to the alcoholic while not subtly encouraging a return to drinking. This is especially helpful in confronting the "willpower" dilemma—that is, "If she loved me enough, she wouldn't drink so much." Such approaches may be extended beyond the nuclear family to friends and associates in order to keep them from reinforcing drinking (Marlatt et al., 1988). Social-skills training to improve communication skills and assertiveness training to help resist peer pressure may be useful here as well as in other patterns of substance abuse (McCreery & Walker, 1993).

Once alcoholism has developed, it appears that some nine to fifteen months are needed to adjust to an alcohol-free lifestyle. But many alcoholics can achieve a relapse-resistant lifestyle recovery program within two to three years. For many alcoholics the ability to have fun and enjoy life (and, as a result, to be more pleasant to have around) is a state-learned behavior (rather than a trait); that is, it has become associated with the use of alcohol. Total abstinence means the loss of conditioned cues for such behaviors. Without relearning the "skills" to have fun and enjoy life, some recovered alcoholics become tedious to be around, further fraying relationships with friends and significant others. Helping the recovered alcoholic to develop these lost skills is an area ignored by most therapists.

■ Prescription Drug Abuse

The DSM-IV differentiates a number of substance abuse patterns, yet never specifically discusses a pattern called "prescription drug abuse." I feel that this is an important pattern because it focuses on the common characteristics of clients rather than making a differentiation according to the specific drug that is abused, an approach that often cuts across personality patterns. Drug companies and physicians should openly acknowledge at least some degree of responsibility for the high level of prescription drug abuse in our society.

While the barbiturates were for many years the most commonly abused prescription drugs, amphetamines and minor tranquilizers are heavily abused in our present society (Ciraulo and Shader, 1991). Since this book will discuss some of the ancillary patterns common to amphetamine abuse, the focus will now be on prescription drug abuse involving minor tranquilizers. This latter abuse pattern typically emerges in individuals between the ages of 30 and 60, predominantly in middle-class and upper-class females. Female abusers are rather evenly divided between homemakers and those who work outside the home. They take prescribed tranquilizers initially for nervousness or insomnia, gradually increase the dosage, and commonly compound the problem with an increased use of alcohol. The likelihood of abuse is further compounded because more than 90% of the mood-altering drugs taken by women have been prescribed by physicians who have no special training in psychological disorders (Meyer and Salmon, 1988).

The common signs of prescription drug abuse are: (a) efforts toward making sure prescriptions are quickly filled; (b) efforts toward developing backup prescriptions and/or physician contacts; (c) resistance-avoidance toward any health care professional who begins to confront the pattern; (d) increased contacts with sympathetic health care workers; (e) depression and anxiety increase, especially if prescription-refills are delayed or renewals are threatened; (f) withdrawal from standard interests, friends, activities; and (g) increased use of alcohol to supplement the effects of the pills.

□ MMPI-2

It has already been noted that in substance abuse in general the clinician can expect elevations on MMPI–2 scales 2, 4, and 8 (Greene, 1991). This would generally hold for the typical prescription drug abuses as well, although I would accentuate the depression reflected in the 2 scale. The 8 scale (and to a lesser degree the 7 scale) is also likely to be substantially elevated, reflecting tension, a sense of being disturbed, and allied vague complaints. At the same time, I would expect the 4 scale to be less elevated than one would find in most drug abuse patterns. It will probably be above normal, particularly because these individuals are likely to use the more simplistic defense mechanisms of denial and projection and are also narcissistic in their personality orientation. These factors also predict moderately high scores on scales 1 and 3.

A low score on scale 5 is expected because these individuals usually identify with the female role, and lower scores on scale 5 are typical of the standard middle-class interest pattern for females. This would vary because of age and whether the woman had a paying job. Because these individuals often feel isolated, and many of them actually live alone, a moderately high score on scale 6 is not uncommon. The depression and the social isolation also suggest that scale 9 is likely to be lower than average.

☐   ## 16 PF

The 16 PF pattern should differ somewhat from the overall substance abuse pattern presented in the previous section. Similar to that pattern, a high I score likely reflects a tender-minded and somewhat dependent individual, and the Q_4 score, reflecting anxiety, may be somewhat higher than with the standard drug abuse pattern. I expect scale A to be only moderately high, at best, and in some individuals—possibly the homemaker who is bordering on agoraphobia because of her anxiety—I expect a low A.

The M score, unlike that obtained in many drug abuse patterns, should be no higher than average. In the case of the homemaker, particularly the middle-class one, it may tend toward the low end of the scale. Because anxiety is not being dealt with very well, there should be a high Q_3 score. I would expect at least a moderately high L scale, in coordination with a high scale 6 score on the MMPI-2. As in most psychological disorders, C should be low. Shyness and social isolation are likely to be reflected in a low H score and low F and E scores. Q_1 should be much lower than that of most drug abuse patterns. The B scale, measuring general intelligence, will depend on the social class and education of the individual, as well as on the degree of depression.

☐   ## OTHER TEST-RESPONSE PATTERNS

Prescription drug abuse is likely to occur in those personality types in which anxiety and depression are major components, and this would be reflected in the MCMI-III by high scores on 2B, 8A, C, and S. Those who score high on scale 7 may be more likely to turn to prescription drugs or alcohol than to illegal drugs because of the high level of conformity to social rules in these individuals. Because alcohol use is often combined with prescribed medications, elevation on B is probable.

☐   ## TREATMENT OPTIONS

Persons with a prescription drug abuse syndrome are oriented toward medical treatment and often have a middle-class value system, so hospitalization for detoxication fits well with their concept of what should occur. After the initial stage the clinician has to deal with the tension and depression that often underlie this pattern (Marlatt et al., 1988). The development of a relaxation response is important, particularly since it teaches clients that they can exert some control over their lives and thus do not need to be so dependent on external agents, such as drugs.

Many of these people have withdrawn socially, so assertiveness training and efforts to expand their social networks are most important. Along with this, the therapist can present the issue of taking drugs as a rational and/or existential choice (Beck et al., 1994), while emphasizing how the clients can determine many of the events that occur in their worlds and thus, the anxieties and responsibilities concomitant with these choices.

Because insomnia and obesity are common problems that lead to prescription drug abuse, as well as to drug abuse problems in general, it is important to help the person cope with them (Hauri, 1991). With either pattern, any form of relaxation training that emphasizes deep–muscle relaxation can help, although the habit-control procedures are more important. With regard to weight problems, the reader is referred to the treatment options in the section on amphetamine abuse later in this chapter.

■ Polysubstance Abuse

The term "polysubstance abuse" is also not included in DSM-IV, nor was it in prior editions. However, there is in DSM-IV the category Polysubstance Dependence (304.80), in which a person has used at least three different substances (not including caffeine or nicotine) for at least six months and no substance has predominated. The relative neglect of polysubstance abuse reflects an essential feature of our society: the belief that there is a particular remedy for virtually any physical or psychological disorder that occurs (L'Abate et al., 1992). The polysubstance abuser usually combines the expectancy that an external agent will take care of all problems with a high need for new experiences or sensation seeking (Petraitis et al., 1995; Zuckerman et al., 1980).

The use of a combination of drugs over a period of time is, of course, not new to human society, although in our present culture the pattern is magnified. The epidemic of this pattern is so recent that there are few significant data regarding how these individuals will eventually function in later life. These data are important to obtain, since polysubstance abusers appear to most clinicians to be more disturbed psychologically than those with other abuse patterns (Penk et al., 1980).

Polysubstance abusers could be described as psychotics without the loss of reality contact: They show deterioration of behavior in a wide variety of arenas—work, school performance, interpersonal relationships, and motivation—especially if they have been abusing drugs for a substantial length of time. Affect is generally flat, or, when emotion is manifest, it is quite labile. Like the alcoholic, there are many protestations of future positive change, and also like the alcoholic, the promises are seldom fulfilled. This does not appear to be a manipulative deception, as the person seems intellectually committed to changing, yet the motivation and behavior necessary to actuate that change cannot be generated.

Polysubstance abusers are likely to be late adolescents or young adults (Petraitis et al., 1995). They commonly begin ingesting some mood-altering substance in their early teens and quickly progress through the less potent substances to the point where they will use practically anything provided to them. There are some sex differences in the preferences for drugs: Males lean a bit more toward the use of alcohol, cocaine, opiates, marijuana, and hashish, and females are more prone to combine stimulants and/or tranquilizers, relaxants, sedatives, and tobacco.

☐   MMPI-2

As with alcoholics, scale 4 is consistently high in polysubstance abusers, as is 8, especially with late-adolescent polysubstance abusers (Archer, 1987). It is relatively lower in the subgroup of depressed polysubstance abusers, who tend to have high 2, 7, and 8 scales as well. The more psychopathic 6-8 and 8-9-4 patterns are less likely to show depression and more likely to act out in ways other than simply drug abuse. In those individuals who are high-sensation seekers, the F scale is consistently elevated above a T score of 70. Elevations on scales 1 and 3 are not consistently found with polysubstance abusers, although when these are at least moderately elevated, some feel it is a better prediction of successful participation in treatment programs. As a person continues in the polysubstance abuse pattern, apathy increases and scores on scale 9—and, to a lesser degree, on scales 6 and 4—will be lowered. The apathy and social problems that accompany this pattern predict a high O scale, especially if depression is still present and not diluted by the drug use.

Overall, polysubstance abusers have been found to have more MMPI-2 scores elevated over the 70-T level than do heroin abusers. The latter group on the average shows elevations above 70 T on 2, 4, and 8, whereas polysubstance abusers show them on F, 2, 4, 7, and 8 (Penk et al., 1980). As noted earlier, the MAC is useful here (MacAndrew, 1965).

☐   16 PF

Four factors consistently found in drug abusers are high F, low G, high H, and moderately high I. The high H measures their venturesomeness, more specifically their willingness to try nonapproved consciousness-altering drugs. The moderately high I, in conjunction with the other scores, reflects reliance and yet also the sensitivity and ambivalent dependency found in alcoholics. The low G measures the sociopathy to be expected here. The high F suggests extroversion and even a slightly manic quality; this primarily depends on when the individual is tested.

These persons' lack of a consistent value system, along with an imaginative although nonpersistent problem-solving approach, predicts a higher M score, and the orientation toward experimentation with drugs and disavowal of standard morality systems predicts a high Q_1 score. Similarly, emotional lability and a lack of discipline predict low scores on C and Q_3. In the early stages of the pattern, one could also expect relatively high scores on A, B, and Q_4, but with increased apathy and decreased ability to generate new behaviors, these scales should decrease. The lack of adequate social skills usually noted in this group (Washton, 1991) would suggest at least a moderately low N score and a moderately raised Q_2 score, although the latter is then more appropriately interpreted as group avoidance rather than as self-sufficiency.

☐   OTHER TEST-RESPONSE PATTERNS

A high score on the MCMI-III on T is indicated, and B if alcohol is involved. If psychotic symptomatology occurs, then SS, CC, and/or PP will become elevated. The lack of concern for social rules exhibited by the narcissist and the impulsivity and stimulation seeking of the aggressive and gregarious personalities predispose them toward polydrug abuse; elevations on scales 5 or 6A and sometimes 4 are likely.

☐   TREATMENT OPTIONS

In many instances there is an acute toxic drug reaction that must be dealt with first. For example, in an acute reaction to cocaine, the standard stabilization sequence may require the use of (1) oxygen to stabilize respiration, (2) Inderal for any cardiac arrhythmias, (3) a barbiturate to reduce central nervous stimulation, or (4) benzodiazepines to control convulsive reactions (Washton and Gold, 1987). This response must be short-term and very carefully monitored in order to avoid secondary abuse patterns.

Since the typical polysubstance abuser is an adolescent or young adult who is showing a deterioration of functions in a wide array of behaviors, a broad-spectrum treatment is necessary. The clinician should be aware of the probability that such clients, while in the detoxication phase, will attempt to obtain addicting drugs through manipulation of their peer group (Petraitis et al., 1995).

Group experiences that emphasize confrontive techniques are often necessary here, so rational-emotive (Lyons and Woods, 1991) or reality therapy (Glasser, 1980) can be an important adjunct to the treatment program. Polysubstance abusers easily verbalize promises and commitments, but they seldom tie commitments to future contingencies, and these therapies, of course, emphasize this linkage. Most importantly, clients should be forced to accept responsibility for the abuse behavior, as these persons often promote the idea that they were "seduced" into the drug culture. Aversive techniques can be helpful in dealing with specific habit patterns. Because family problems may have been a catalyst for the early drug abuse, these need to be worked out via family therapy.

■   ## Amphetamine Use Disorder

As previously noted, the DSM-IV lists a variety of substances for which abuse can be diagnosed, and numerous potential subdiagnoses. This book will comment on the most constant and challenging patterns—amphetamines, cocaine, opiates, and nicotine—because they are so important in today's society.

The first synthetic amphetamine, a methamphetamine, was compounded in 1919 by the Japanese scientist Ogata. Amphetamines were used to combat fatigue in World War II and are used today in treating hyperactive children.

They also have been too commonly prescribed as a diet aid in the past, although there are now increasing restrictions on physicians. Tolerance to amphetamines builds quickly, so abuse easily leads to increased intake and dependence. Continuation of an intake of amphetamines over a significant period of time leads to paranoid and other psychotic symptoms that may continue for some time after the drug is discontinued. Unfortunately, "ice," a smokable form of amphetamine, has now been synthesized. Its effect is analogous to "crack" and lasts longer. To the degree efforts to control cocaine are effective, the use of any analogous synthetic drug is likely to increase.

☐ ## DSM-IV

All of the DSM-IV diagnostic categories relevant to amphetamines include the concept "or related substances," as these are thrown together in the same diagnostic category. In addition to the standard categories of Abuse and Dependence, there is the category of Amphetamine Intoxication (305.70), which requires the toxic effects of recent usage and two consequent symptoms, such as tachycardia or bradycardia; elevated or lowered blood pressure; nausea; perspiration or chills; evidence of weight loss; psychomotor agitation or retardation; muscular weakness, respiratory depression, chest pain or cardiac arrhythmias; confusion, seizures, dystonia, or coma; or pupillary dilation and such maladaptive behavioral changes as psychomotor excitement, grandiosity, or hypervigilance.

A diagnosis of Amphetamine Withdrawal (292.00) requires dysphoric mood accompanied by at least two of the following, developing in a few hours to several days, with consequent distress or impairment: (1) fatigue; (2) vivid, unpleasant dreams; (3) hypersomnia or insomnia; (4) increased appetite; (5) psychomotor agitation or retardation.

"Delirium" is the term for the syndrome that used to be called "acute brain syndrome." It involves a clouding of consciousness and memory disruption, along with evidence of two of the following: speech difficulty, perceptual problems, sleep problems, or hypo- or hyperactivity. The duration of delirium is typically short, no more than a week. In the specific instance of amphetamines (Amphetamine Delirium, 292.81), delirium lasts only about five hours, starting about an hour after ingestion of the substance, and the DSM-IV requires evidence of onset within 24 hours of ingestion.

☐ ## MMPI-2

The elevation on scale 4 that is common to most drug abuse patterns is particularly evident in this syndrome. It is combined with an elevation on scale 9, reflecting the heightened activity and agitation associated with amphetamine use. There is also a significant elevation on scale 6, depending on the degree of abuse and whether paranoid ideation has begun. Elevations on scales 8 and 3 are also relatively common. Since amphetamine abuse is often a coping mechanism to deal with depression (Barnett and Gotlib, 1988), this will be manifest in a degree of suppression of scales 2 and 0.

☐   ## 16 PF

As in the other drug abuse patterns, low C and Q_3 scores are expected. The rejection of standard mores and the high activity level characteristic of amphetamine abuse are reflected in higher scores on E, F, M, and Q_1, and probably to a lesser degree on H. Prolonged abuse is likely to result in a higher L score, which reflects the development of a paranoid trend. Since these individuals, especially when they are still experiencing the effects of intoxication, are not likely to pay attention to a particular question for any length of time, scores on B should not be particularly high. A low score on G would be expected, as well as a moderately low score on H, the latter reflecting the autonomic over-reactivity generated by this particular drug.

☐   ## OTHER TEST-RESPONSE PATTERNS

In addition to elevated T, high scores on the MCMI-III on N are likely to occur as a result of physiological arousal and hyperactivity. Since these individuals often show acute paranoia, an elevation on P is possible. As psychomotor activity increases, scores on D will decrease. Long periods of amphetamine use may lead to psychotic symptoms that will elevate PP and SS. Personality elevations that are likely to occur include 4, 5, and 6A, and those with whom depression was initially a factor will show elevations on 2B, 8A, C, and S. The former elevations will be more likely after repeated amphetamine use, while the latter may be more probable in early states or preceding use.

☐   ## TREATMENT OPTIONS

Because amphetamine abuse or the abuse of other, similar stimulant drugs is often related to underlying anhedonia or depression, existential techniques to confront the apathy, as well as the cognitive behavior techniques described later for depression, are useful here. It is extremely important to teach persons that they can get involved with and control their worlds without the crutch of a stimulating drug (Beck et al., 1994).

Covert sensitization, a subcategory of the techniques known as covert conditioning, is useful for drug disorders (Cautela and Wall, 1980). This is an imagery procedure that asks the client to imagine a highly aversive contingency or event occurring immediately on the cessation (in imagination) of the behavior that one is attempting to eliminate (in this case, the specific components of the amphetamine abuse sequence). This is repeated over a number of sessions and is efficient to the degree that the client can develop adequate images that are experienced as vivid and real.

Since amphetamine abuse is often a logical extension of an abuse of other prescription or nonprescription pills for dieting, concomitant techniques to help with obesity are often useful to prevent the return to the use of amphetamines. Supportive group therapy, teaching of a relaxation response, hypnosis (in some cases), and especially behavioral and confrontive control therapies are useful here (Ellis, 1992). For example, it is important that the person never associate eating with other activities, such as reading or watching television; the eating has to come with independent cues. Teaching the person to be able to interrupt meals for brief periods of time is a useful exercise, as well as eating a salad or small bowl of soup before meals. Analogously, the person should be admonished to take smaller portions into the mouth, chew the food much longer, keep desirable foods out of the house as much as possible, purposely slow the pace of eating, and eat in only one spot in the house. A diary of eating behaviors should be kept so that awareness increases and therefore contingency contracting can be carried out.

■ Cocaine Abuse

Cocaine has become a favored drug in recent years (Washton, 1991). Its abuse by many sports and entertainment idols has received much media attention. Nevertheless, cocaine has been used for centuries. It is an alkaloid derivative of coca leaves, which were chewed by the Aztecs and are still used by at least four million Indians in South America. Such diverse people as Arthur Conan Doyle's character Sherlock Holmes, John Philip Sousa, and even Sigmund Freud have sung the praises of cocaine. A number of people became inadvertently habituated to cocaine in the United States during the late 1800s by drinking Coca-Cola. John Pemberton, an Atlanta druggist, combined cocaine with sugar and kolanut extract in a brass pot in his backyard to make the original Coca-Cola, which he advertised as a "brain medicine." When the Pure Food and Drug Law of 1906 outlawed the use of cocaine, caffeine was substituted in "the real thing."

Traditionally used cocaine is not pure (free-base) cocaine but cocaine hydrochloride, a salt that is approximately 85% cocaine by weight. "Crack," an alkalinized form of cocaine base, has a low melting point so it can be smoked; hence the effect, per unit of drug ingested, is quicker and more intense, leading to the potential for quicker and more severe addiction (Meyer, 1995). Short-term use of cocaine inhibits the reuptake of dopamine. This apparently leads to an increased concentration and transmission of dopamine, which apparently causes the euphoria. However, long-term cocaine use depletes the brain of dopamine, as well as norepinephrine and serotonin. When cocaine is mixed with alcohol, a new substance called cocaethylene forms in the liver, which amplifies the effects of cocaine and increases the risk of heart attack by almost twenty times.

☐ DIAGNOSTIC CONSIDERATIONS

The DSM-IV diagnostic considerations that apply to the diagnosis of Dependence (304.20) and Abuse (305.60) in all of the other substance use disorders apply here as well. The diagnoses of both Cocaine Intoxication (305.60) and Cocaine Withdrawal (292.00) have exactly similar symptom requirements as for Amphetamine Intoxication or Withdrawal (see prior section).

Spotts and Schontz (1984) have found that middle-class and upper-middle-class cocaine users, especially males, show an intense, narcissistic, competitive, and achievement-oriented personality, with a strong fear of intimacy and vulnerability in relationships, so diagnostic considerations for the narcissistic and obsessive-compulsive personality disorders (see Chapter 9) would also apply here. Johnson et al. (1992) find that the 2-4/4-2, 2-7/7-2, and 4-7/7-4 MMPI-2 profiles account for 65% of the profiles of cocaine abusers. A stairstep progression on scales 1, 2, 3, 4, 7, and 8 has been noted in a population of cocaine abusers, with scores in general being significantly elevated above normal and with an inverted V on the validity scales (F being the highest score). Since cocaine use will often facilitate paranoid ideation (Washton, 1991), scale 6 may be elevated.

OTHER TEST CONSIDERATIONS

MMPI-2 and 16 PF patterns are usually similar to the overall substance abuse pattern discussed at the beginning of this chapter. As in other patterns of substance abuse, a high T is very likely on the MCMI-III. To the extent that alcohol abuse is involved, B will be elevated. On the scales representing the persistent personality features (1–8), expect elevation on 4 and 5. Scale 4 reveals a sociable self-image and a preference for a fast-paced lifestyle. Also, the immature stimulus-seeking behaviors and manipulation of others to receive attention will be evident here. A high 5 shows the interpersonal exploitiveness that typifies a cocaine abuser. As the chronicity of drug use increases, so, too, do the elevations on scales C and N. High C scores reflect the endogenous mood or other depressive components that often underlie cocaine abuse, while high N scores reflect hypomanic characteristics that also may accompany abuse.

On the Rorschach, a heightened level of defensiveness will be manifested by a small number of total responses (R) and an increased number of W, F, and Popular responses. A disproportionately high L score is also predicted, indicating that the subject has refused to process the stimuli as requested. A high number of M and Y responses may indicate a situational crisis related to the abuse condition. Because FM answers are increased under altered states of consciousness (Exner, 1986), cocaine abusers should show a higher frequency of them.

TREATMENT OPTIONS

Any inpatient treatment plan should have the goals of detoxifying the person's biological system and directly and strongly confronting the destructive psychological patterns (Barrett and Meyer, 1992). Withdrawal effects can last from a few days to three months, and the extinction phase, which includes a high risk of relapse, can last from three to twelve months. Calcium channel blockers (e.g., nitrendipine) directly act to reverse the effects of cocaine toxicity. Agonists (i.e., drugs that substitute for the effects of the drugs), such as buprenorphine or even ibogaine (itself a hallucinogen), can be useful, as are drugs that soften withdrawal, such as desipramine. Catalytic antibodies, which split the cocaine molecule into two inactive ingredients, have shown potential in treatment and prevention.

Confrontation techniques, pioneered with heroin abusers by group treatment centers such as Synanon and Daytop Village, are used with cocaine addicts as well. The goal is to get the addict to assume control of his or her own decisions; to plan more adaptive behaviors to satisfy vocational, interpersonal, and sexual needs; and then to look at more characterological and existential issues. Similarly, many such addicts need intensive psychotherapy (especially those whose abuse pattern is trauma-generated) with a focus on the avoidance of dependency and unresolved spiritual and intimacy-betrayal and intimacy-avoidance crises. Such psychotherapy should take into account the often underlying depression and at the same time allow socially acceptable outlets for the commonly higher-than-average level of stimulation seeking. As some success is attained, involvement in group therapy modeled on AA principles can be effective (Washton, 1991). Cocaine Anonymous or Narcotics Anonymous is available in most areas. Yet, in the long run, the critical predictor appears to be the ability to learn, apply and maintain relapse strategies.

■ Opioid Use Disorder

Opioids are defined by their interaction with any of the opioid receptor groups (five have already been clearly identified). The mu receptor agonists receive the most attention since they are the site of action for morphine and heroin (Meyer, 1995). Agonists stimulate receptors; antagonists, such as naltrexone and naloxone, block the receptor's response to an agonist.

Even though the opium poppy has been used as a mind-altering substance for at least six million years, two events in particular spurred the increased abuse patterns noted recently. Early in the nineteenth century, morphine (ten times stronger than opium) was isolated from the opium poppy, and approximately fifty years later, Alexander Wood perfected a more effective drug-delivery system: the hypodermic needle. Morphine was soon included in many patent medicines, although it was supplanted in use near the end of the century when Wright discovered heroin, a semisynthetic opioid derived from morphine. Heroin (diacetylmorphine), a respiratory depressant, is more lipid soluble than morphine and efficiently and quickly crosses the blood–brain barrier; thus it is more addicting. Interestingly, heroin was at one time used to cure morphine addiction, just as another addicting drug, methadone, is now used to treat heroin addiction. However, since methadone has a greater percent of storage in plasma, peaks and declines in serum levels are more gradual, which lessens craving.

Heroin induces a warm, sensual euphoria, usually followed by sleepiness and lethargy. Tolerance develops rapidly, however, and six to twelve hours after an injection the individual is likely to experience withdrawal symptoms, the severity depending on the amount ingested and how long the person has been abusing. While these symptoms are seldom as severe as the mad ravings portrayed in the media, they usually cause symptoms similar to those of the flu, though with more severe distress.

Perhaps no one has expressed so clearly the reinforcement from heroin as French humanist and poet Jean Cocteau:

Everything we do in life, including love, is done in an express train traveling towards death. To smoke opium is to leave the train while in motion; it is to be interested in something other than life and death. (Jarvik, 1967, p. 52.)

☐   ## DSM-IV

The DSM-IV requires the same criteria for opioid abuse (305.50) and dependence (304.00) as it does for all the substances heretofore mentioned. The DSM-IV lists Opioid Intoxication (305.50), which is the effects of recent use toxic enough to produce clinically significant changes, accompanied by pupillary contraction (or pupillary dilation if the dose is so severe as to cause anoxia) and at least one of the following: drowsiness or coma, slurred speech, or impairment in attention or memory.

Prolonged or heavy use often results in Opioid Withdrawal (292.00), in which three of the following are experienced on cessation of use: dysphoric mood, nausea, muscle aches, lacrimation or rhinorrhea, pupillary dilation, piloerection or sweating, diarrhea, yawning, fever, or insomnia.

Unfortunately, in addition to the addiction and its natural sequelae, opioid dependence has other associated problems. Aging heroin addicts are very prone to develop alcohol addiction, and approximately 70% of heroin addicts easily earn another major psychiatric disorder diagnosis, for example, affective or anxiety disorder, and over 40% show clear evidence of a personality disorder (Craig, 1993). Also, the relapse rate after even long-term detoxification-treatment is extremely high.

☐   ## MMPI-2

Elevations on scales 2, 4, and 8, which are generally characteristic of the drug abuse patterns, are found in opiate abuse (Penk et al., 1980). Elevations on scales 3 and 6 are also likely, reflecting the egocentricity and problems with authority characteristic of this pattern, although it is true that the elevation on scale 6 may not be as high as it is for a person who is dependent on amphetamines. In certain opiate abusers there is a high scale 9, indicating a person who is easily bored and has a low frustration tolerance and is in that sense narcissistic. In another subgroup, the more relaxed or bohemian opiate abuser, a 4-5 code type is common. Scores on scales 2 and 9 will vary depending on whether the person is feeling euphoric or dysphoric. Because the person is not likely to be tested while in the midst of an episode, a rise on scale 2 is more likely. It is interesting that opiate abusers seldom show a profile as pathological as most of the other significant drug abusers do. The MAC may be useful here (MacAndrew, 1965), although it is usually more effective in pointing to existing or potential substance abusers who have higher levels of extroversion and/or sensation seeking (Allen et al., 1991), which is not always the case in opiate abusers.

16 PF

Opiate abusers are likely to be high on scales I and M. This reflects their paradoxical indulgence in fantasy while they maintain an apathetic view of events in their world, along with their avoidance of either stress or commitment whenever possible. They are also relatively high on O, although typically not as high as alcoholics. They are relatively high on scale A, which is different from a number of other drug abuse patterns; this reflects their lack of paranoid response toward the environment, at least in relation to the amount seen in the other drug abuse patterns. They tend to be slightly above average on L, although this will vary depending on the testing situation.

Opiate abusers tend to be average on scales H, Q_1, and Q_3 and lower on N, which again differentiates them from those with other drug abuse patterns. However, like all of these patterns, they are low on scales C and E. They are also low on B, reflecting their lower socioeconomic status and educational attainment, as well as the lack of initiative found in these persons.

OTHER TEST–RESPONSE PATTERNS

Keiser and Lowy (1980) present evidence that heroin addicts tend to be significantly higher on digit span scores than on other WAIS-R subtests. This fits with the evidence that a digit span score well above the mean of the client's other WAIS-R subtest scores is correlated with an interpersonal-detachment syndrome characterized by superficial and emotionally distant relationships.

TREATMENT OPTIONS

Because of the high risk of relapse, long-term therapy, methadone maintenance, and active involvement with a support group provide the best chance for success. Therapeutic communities (TCs), often peer-directed, which paradoxically but effectively give high levels of both support and confrontation, are often the best option, though TCs have occasionally been burdened by problems resulting from their resistance to any reliance on professionally trained staff. In any case, a method of providing a more therapeutic social network is critical in dealing with opioid addicts, as they easily return to their destructive peer-group setting (Petraitis et al., 1995).

Naloxone, a short-duration, intravenously administered antagonist, helps with overdose cases and also with the first stage of withdrawal. Naltrexone, a longer-acting antagonist with a 12-24 action, helps stabilize the post-withdrawal addict as long as clients continue taking it. Unfortunately, many stop taking it against therapeutic advice.

Methadone appears to be effective in many cases, although the clinician must be aware of possible secondary abuse of the drug used for treatment, particularly in addicts who are psychopathic. Methadone clients often request increasing dosages, so it's best if methadone blood levels are drawn before the morning dose (the "trough level"). Since, as an agonist, methadone does not cause the distinct euphoria of heroin, it can be taken orally and less often than heroin; also, its lower cost may allow the addict to move out of the criminal system. Similarity of client and therapist on ethnic and cultural dimensions facilitates success to a marked degree with these clients. Unfortunately, methadone maintenance clients have a high rate of relapse into cocaine abuse. Another narcotic, buprenorphine, which can substitute for methadone, carries a lower risk of relapse into cocaine abuse.

Tranquilizers and/or antidepressants can often be helpful in reducing psychological withdrawal or allied psychopathology. While clomidine has often been cited as effective, acetorphan has also been found to be effective (Hartmann et al., 1991).

Nicotine Dependence

In 1492, Luis de Torres and Rodrigo de Jerez, two of Columbus's crew, observed natives of Cuba drying and then smoking some plant leaves. De Jerez tried it himself, apparently becoming the first confirmed European smoker. When he tried it back in Spain, his countrymen were alarmed at the smoke coming out of his mouth, assumed him to be possessed by the devil, and imprisoned him via the Inquisition. Unfortunately, this did not prevent his legacy from being returned to North America.

Nicotine, the principal active component of tobacco leaves, acts as a stimulant on persons who use it rarely. It raises the heart rate and increases the blood pressure by simultaneously inducing greater cardiac activity and constricting peripheral arteries. It reduces the appetite, especially for carbohydrates, such as sugar and simple starches, a fact that must be considered if gaining weight upon stopping smoking is to be avoided. It is powerfully addicting and habituating—and it is also an effective pesticide.

Statistically, two-pack-a-day smokers can expect to live about six years fewer than their nonsmoking peers. Smokers in general are about 50% more likely than nonsmokers to require health care each year, and the smoke they disperse is harmful to those around them. Historically, efforts to deter people from smoking, such as warnings from the surgeon general's office, have had only limited effects, and those who do quit are extremely prone to relapse. In the seventeenth century, even Turkish sultan Murad IV's campaign of torturing and executing those addicted to tobacco was scarcely more effective, nor was a 1683 Chinese law that authorized beheading simply for possessing tobacco.

Seven major factors are usually considered to be crucial in initiating and maintaining tobacco addiction: (1) modeling and ease of access to tobacco, promoted by significant peers, authority figures, and media idols; (2) peer pressure, especially for early adolescents; (3) physiologic addiction; (4) genetic predisposition; (5) habit and ritual; (6) the paradoxical tranquilizing effect of nicotine on the chronic smoker (pharmacologically, it is a stimulant); and (7) the fulfillment of personality needs (such as oral eroticism) (Dalack et al., 1993; Scott et al., 1986).

It is difficult to set out clear diagnostic-test correlates for nicotine abuse or dependence given its legal acceptance by society, widespread patterns of accepted daily usage, society's traditional tolerance of smoking by adolescents, and society's failure to clearly discriminate use from abuse.

The DSM-IV does not even offer a diagnosis of nicotine abuse. Nicotine Dependence (305.10), first listed in the DSM-III, is defined by the same criteria as other substance dependencies. Nicotine Withdrawal (292.00) is defined as cessation or reduction of use, after at least several weeks of use, followed by at least four of the following within twenty-four hours: dysphoria or depressed mood, insomnia, irritability or anger, anxiety, difficulty concentrating, restlessness, decreased heart rate, or increased appetite or weight gain, with consequent life distress or impairment. A history of major depression is surprisingly common in the histories of heavy smokers, who are very prone to relapse.

TREATMENT OPTIONS

As a result of a severe flu attack at age 38, Dr. S. experienced an irregular heartbeat. His personal physician and colleague, Dr. F., told him that his habit of smoking cigars had caused it and advised him to stop smoking. When Dr. S. tried to do so, he became depressed and occasionally suffered an even worse pulse rate. After several attempts at stopping, he returned to smoking about twenty cigars a day and developed cancer of the jaw at age 67. Despite thirty-three operations and the removal of his entire jaw because of various cancerous and precancerous conditions, Dr. S continued to smoke. At age 73 he developed angina pectoris (chest pains from heart disease), which was relieved whenever he stopped smoking. Yet, although he continued to try to stop smoking, he could not. He died from cancer at age 83 after many years of severe suffering from operations, cancer, and heart disorder.

The fact that Dr. S. is Sigmund Freud offers strong testimony to the difficulty of changing this behavior. Numerous researchers have examined ways to help individuals control their smoking. Therapists have used scare tactics such as showing films of people dying of lung cancer, applied shocks to clients when they smoke, and had clients smoke as fast as possible in a closed space to induce nausea. Behavioral rehearsal of positive nonsmoking habits, psychotherapy, group therapy, hypnosis, and a mélange of other techniques have been tried.

Most of these efforts have had some limited success; none has shown complete success. In many cases, individuals are able to control their smoking significantly during the treatment phase, only to remit gradually afterward. The relapse rate is very high. Scott et al. (1986) found that a single relapse led to a resumption of smoking 50% of the time, and 100% of those who relapsed twice eventually resumed smoking. Quitting all at once has traditionally been considered the best strategy for most smokers, yet gradual weaning from the chemical addiction to the nicotine itself (e.g., by using nicotine gum) as well as other behavioral delay strategies (e.g., gradually but increasingly delaying smoking the first cigarette of the day), seems to help many. Continued success also requires that the significant persons around the smoker be supportive of a change to nonsmoking. Friends and family (particularly if they are also smokers) often give lip service to the smoker's pledge to quit, only to subvert—consciously or unconsciously—his or her efforts. As with many other substance abuse patterns, prevention is more efficient and effective than cure. The combined efforts of prevention and treatment caused the smoking rate in American adults to drop from 42.2% in 1966 to approximately 20% in 1995, and it continues to fall. It persists most strongly in lower socioeconomic classes.

Techniques that seem to help (best delivered in the context of a psychotherapy to control smoking and deal with related issues) are (Dalack et al., 1993; Bongar and Beutler, 1995):

- For most people, increasing delay strategies (behavioral and physical) up to the point of quitting all at once and/or the use of a planned "quit day"
- Use of nicotine gum to fade the addiction component
- Use of a short–term and/or "as needed" prescription for tranquilizers to mute anxiety and apprehension during the first couple of weeks to a month
- Use of hypnosis, autogenic training and/or relaxation training to develop long–term methods of coping with stress and situational anxiety and to enhance motivation
- Counseling to the client from the primary care physician on the need to quit smoking, and follow–up calls by physician and/or colleague-counselors
- Use of rapid smoking techniques to create aversion-extinction responses
- Attention to diet and exercise to enhance self-esteem and physiological health
- Direct treatment of any concomitant disorders such as depression anxiety
- Participation in a support group
- Work with significant others to facilitate their support of, and to negate any subversive behaviors toward, the client's attempt to change
- Behavioral skills training to cope with stress, to avoid high-risk situations, and to learn a psychologically healthier lifestyle

A successful "quit" typically proceeds in the following stages:

1. *Consideration of change:* The individual talks and thinks about the possibility of quitting and the personal ramifications.

2. *Crystallization:* A goal to actually quit is accepted. Cost-benefit analyses (e.g., health reasons), are explored. Lists should be prepared to concretize expectancies about annoyances, personal costs, traps for relapse.

3. *Concrete preparation:* The commitment to quit is finalized and a time to quit is picked, preferably a relatively stress-free period. Anti-stress mechanisms, such as hypnosis, yoga, prescription for benzodiazaprenes, and contracts with significant others are put in place.

4. *The "just do it" phase:* The move is made, with preparations put into action. New behaviors to fill "smoking time" are put in place; smokers are avoided. Some coping strategies are put in place to deal with the actual experience of the addiction, which continues for three to six months, and the change in metabolism that can lead to weight gain.

5. *Maintenance:* A more healthful lifestyle (physically, emotionally, and spiritually) must be put in place.

6. *Anti-Relapse:* The possibility of some relapse is expected (approximately 45% do so within one month), and coping for that is planned out ahead of time. Enhanced mechanisms to avoid relapse are put in place—for example, a public commitment to anti–smoking campaigns.

CHAPTER 3

The Schizophrenic and Paranoid Disorders

■ **Overall Concepts**

Many clinicians would argue that schizophrenia is the most serious of all mental disorders (Leff, 1994; Cromwell and Snyder, 1993). Although other disorders are more common or may involve more immediate distress, the pervasive effect of a schizophrenic disorder throughout all areas of an individual's functioning and the complexity of problems it presents in assessment and intervention support the assertion that it is the most serious mental disorder. Occurrence is approximately equal across sex, although there is frequently a milder course in women as well as a mean later onset of six years. Onset typically occurs between mid-teens to mid-twenties. About one out of every one hundred people will receive a diagnosis of schizophrenia in his or her lifetime (Michels and Marzuk, 1993). This is a percentage that is pretty stable across and within most cultures. This fits with the concept that genetic factors are critical in the development of most schizophrenics, just as there is evidence that brain dysfunction from other causes may be important in other schizophrenics. The schizophrenic who has been released after a first hospitalization unfortunately still has about a 50% chance of returning to the hospital within two years.

Negative symptoms (affective flattening, alogia, avolition/apathy, anhedonia/asociality, and attentional impairment) are directly correlated with a high rate of remission, slow onset, and higher probability of permanent disability. Positive symptoms (hallucinations, delusions, positive formal thought disorder, and bizarre behavior) predicted better response to medication and less permanent disability. Two negative symptoms, anhedonia and affective flattening, were the strongest independent predictors of negative outcome, and patients with the poorest long-term outcome tended to show an increase in negative symptoms during the early years of their illness. Early and progressive negative symptoms may signal a process leading to long-term disability (Knable et al., 1995).

There are a number of premorbid predictors of schizophrenia worth assessing in a client (Leff, 1994; Michels and Marzuk, 1993; Cromwell and Snyder, 1993; Potkin et al., 1993; Gottesman, 1991):

- A schizophrenic nuclear family member, a less potent variable being the presence of other schizophrenic blood relatives (There is approximately a fifteen-fold increased risk in developing schizophrenia when a nuclear family member is schizophrenic. There is evidence that for daughters, the earlier their mother became schizophrenic, the higher is the likelihood that they, too, will become schizophrenic.)

- A history of prenatal disruption, birth problems, viral or bacterial infections, or toxic situations during pregnancy, especially in the second trimester

- Low birth weight and/or low IQ relative to siblings

- Hyperactivity; cognitive slippage; any signs of central nervous system dysfunction, especially difficulties in attention tasks with distracting stimuli and/or eye tracking; convulsions; evidence of enlarged cerebral ventricles; significant reaction time problems; or an abnormally rapid recovery rate of the autonomic nervous system

- An early role as the "scapegoat" or odd member of the family

- Parenting marked by emotional and/or discipline inconsistencies, including double messages

- Rejection by peers in childhood or adolescence and perception by either teachers or peers as being significantly more irritable or unstable than other children

- Rejection of peers, especially if accompanied by odd thinking processes, ambivalent emotional responses, or a lack of response to standard pleasure sources

- An inability to develop a stable committed relationship, especially for men. For example, never–married men have 50 times higher odds of developing schizophrenia than men who married; for women it is 14 times higher for never–married over married

A common cause path (Meyer and Salmon, 1988) for the development of a long-term schizophrenic pattern is presented in Figure 3.1.

☐   DSM-IV

To apply the overall diagnosis of schizophrenia, the DSM-IV requires evidence of two of the following (Criteria A): (a) delusions, (b) hallucinations, (c) grossly disorganized or catatonic behavior, (d) disorganized speech or (e) negative symptoms, such as affective flattening, alogia, or avolition. But, if hallucinations involve "voices commenting" consistently or "voices conversing," or if delusions are bizarre, only one sign is required. These criteria must be present for at least one month, and some signs of the disorder must continue for at least six months with or without a prodromal or residual phase. Schizoaffective or Mood Disorder with Psychotic Features should be ruled out, as well as causation by a substance ingestion or general medical condition.

FIGURE 3.1   A Common Developmental Path in Schizophrenia

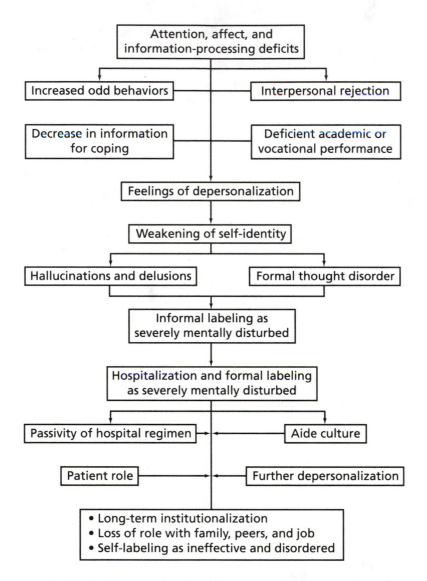

Typical delusions of schizophrenics include somatic delusions, delusions of being controlled, thought broadcasting, and grandiose delusions. This symptomatology must not be directly related to a substance use or depressive or manic disorder. Schizophrenic symptomatology must dominate the affective disorder, or else the affective disorder must be a relatively minor component. During the active phase of the disorder, there must be some significant impairment in areas of daily functioning, such as interpersonal relationships, school, or work.

☐ RELATED DIAGNOSTIC ISSUES

These are the common diagnostic dilemmas that may lead to the misdiagnosis of affective disorder as schizophrenia:

☐ Mistaking anhedonia and depressive depersonalization for schizophrenic emotional blunting

☐ The superimposition of a manic or depressive psychosis on the substrate of an introverted personality

☐ Affective psychosis in mentally retarded individuals

☐ Incomplete interepisodic recovery

☐ Rapid-cycling bipolar affective disorder

☐ The predominance of irritability, hositility, and cantankerousness

☐ Mistaking paranoid ideation for schizophrenia

☐ The equation of other "bizarre" ideation with schizophrenia

☐ Sleep deprivation and metabolic disturbances secondary to reduced caloric and fluid intake

☐ The superimposition of unsuspected alcohol and drug withdrawal states

☐ Difficulty in distinguishing formal thought disorder from flight of ideas

Pathological hallucinations or delusions may sometimes be difficult to separate from culturally sanctioned experiences that are not particularly pathological. These latter experiences are usually characterized by (1) socially appropriate, productive, and adequate coping behavior before and after the experience; (2) time limitations of a few hours to a few days; (3) a reasonable degree of family and/or subgroup support; (4) a resultant gain in social prestige or self-esteem; (5) culturally congruent experiences in the delusions or hallucinations; and (6) a relative absence of psychopathological indicators.

Auditory hallucinations, the most common in schizophrenia, are sometimes difficult to discriminate between true and faked hallucinations. They are more likely to be faked if (Rogers, 1988; Resnick, 1990):

1. They are vague or if the person reports it is hard to hear them or to understand them

2. They are reported as continuous rather than sporadic or intermittent

3. The hallucination is reported as not being associated with a delusion

4. Stilted language is reported as the content of the hallucination

5. The content specifically exonerates the individual from some blame or responsibility

6. The person reporting the voices can give no strategy to diminish the voices

7. The person says that he or she obeyed all commands in the hallucinations

Delusions that are most characteristic of paranoid schizophrenia (as well as paranoid disorders) also can be faked as part of an attempt to avoid responsibility. In general, the clues that lead one to believe that the reporting of a delusion may be faked are:

1. An abrupt onset or cessation

2. If the person is eager to call attention to the delusion or leads the discussion to this topic

3. If the person's conduct is not consistent with the delusion (and the person is not a "burned-out" schizophrenic who generates few or no behaviors anyway)

4. If there is reported bizarre content in the delusion without disordered thoughts or hallucinations

5. If the delusion (or hallucination) somehow specifically reduces the relevant responsibility or culpability

The preschizophrenic personality of individuals who later become schizophrenic can often be described as eccentric and isolated, mildly confused and disorganized, suspicious, and/or withdrawn. As a result, such individuals may require the additional diagnostic qualifier of such categories as schizotypal, borderline, introverted, or paranoid personality disorder (Widiger et al., 1991).

Several studies have pointed to the problems of making accurate subclassifications within the overall category of schizophrenia (Tamminga and Schulz, 1991). Most clinicians find such classification meaningful, however, because it clarifies communications and facilitates discussions of treatment and prognosis. Structured interviews, such as the Schedule of Affective Disorders and Schizophrenia (SADS), can be useful here, as well as in the overall diagnostic process. While relatives have a 5–10% increased risk of schizophrenia, depending on the diagnostic criteria used, well-defined subtypes do not tend to run in families. Regarding the overall diagnostic category of schizophrenia, a landmark study by the World Health Organization (1979) has demonstrated the reliability of this concept in a variety of sociocultural settings.

MMPI-2

As might be expected, most clinicians agree that scale 8 is typically elevated above 65 T in schizophrenics, since this directly reflects their tendency to escape reality through fantasy behavior and to process information inadequately. Most schizophrenics tend to score in the 70–85 range, particularly as they move toward chronicity. Extremely high scores are more likely to indicate severe patterns within other diagnostic categories or to reflect an attempt to fake-bad (Graham, 1993). They tend to be high on the Bizarre Mentation (BIZ) and Family Problems (FAM) content scales.

A variety of scale patterns have been noted (Moldin et al., 1987). Lachar (1974) points out that the 7-8/8-7 profile suggests possible chronic schizophrenia, whereas the 2-7-8 code type, or a similar combination, is more likely to be associated with an earlier stage of schizophrenia (Edell, 1987; Golden and Meehl, 1979). A pattern that appears especially predictive of schizophrenia is the F scale (in T scores) being in the range 65–85, scale 8 70–90, and scale 7 less than scale 8.

When a profile is obtained where scale 8 is high and scale 1 is around 85 T and at the same time 10 to 20 T greater than scales 2 and 3, this suggests a schizophrenic with somatic delusions. The unusual 3-8/8-3 profile, especially when 1 is also high, also indicates an individual with high somatic concerns but with a greater tendency to dissociate (Moldin et al., 1987). A primary elevation on scale 6 is not consistently obtained in schizophrenic profiles, although it is likely in paranoid schizophrenics and occurs occasionally in some catatonic schizophrenics.

The 8-4/4-8 profile can also indicate schizophrenia (Greene, 1991), particularly when hostility and anger are major components. If a 4-8 client shows an elevation on the BIZ and FAM content scales, it points to schizophrenia, whereas elevations on the Cynicism and Anger content scales should first suggest an aggressive personality disorder. When the clinician sees an 8-9/9-8 profile, it is commonly that of a schizophrenic who finds it extremely difficult to vocalize the issues at hand, who is consistently problematic to work with therapeutically, and who is often disruptive in functioning.

Schizophrenics are usually elevated on the F scale, and Gynther et al. (1973b) note that a very high F scale obtained in a psychiatric population is likely to indicate a confused individual rather than one who is faking-bad. Although it does occur in certain instances, a major elevation on scale 3 is not typical in schizophrenic profiles. A particularly high scale 5 in a woman who appears to fit within the traditional feminine role should alert the clinician to look for other indications of schizophrenia. In a somewhat similar vein, Holland and Watson (1980) find male schizophrenic VA-hospital inpatients to be high on F, L, 5, 6, and 8.

In this regard, Goldberg's formula for determining psychosis using T scores should be noted. The L score must be added to the scores for scales 6 and 8, and then the scores on scales 3 and 7 must be subtracted. Using a lower cutoff point of 45, one is allegedly correct 70% of the time in using the label schizophrenia, although this seems to be a sign of paranoid schizophrenia more than schizophrenia in general. Newmark's formula (T on Sc > 80, < 100; total Sc raw score is no more than 35% of K items; T score on F > 75, < 95; on Pt > Sc) was proven to be effective with the original MMPI, primarily with schizophrenics under 45 years of age (Newmark and Hutchins, 1980).

16 PF

On the 16 PF, schizophrenics tend to be high on I, M, O, and Q_4. This reflects their propensity to engage in fantasy as a way to control intrapsychic conflict and their tendency to withdraw and not deal in a practical fashion with the world. This pattern at the same time reflects the high level of anxiety and insecurity experienced by most of these individuals. This fits well with the concept that they are stimulation-avoidant, as opposed to the primary psychopath who is stimulation-seeking.

Schizophrenics also tend to be low on scale C (surprisingly often not as low as many of the other psychiatric disorder categories). They are consistently low on scales F and H, which reflects a stimulation-avoidant pattern as well as the depression that is likely to accompany such a high level of disturbed functioning. Numerous schizophrenic individuals may score in the average range, but in general they tend to be somewhat lower on G, Q_2, and Q_3. Corresponding with their significant inability to cope with the world, they also tend to be low on scale B. As schizophrenia becomes chronic, C, E, F, and H tend to be lower and I and M higher.

OTHER TEST-RESPONSE PATTERNS

Since lowered frontal lobe cortical activity and nonspecific structural brain abnormalities (especially bilateral ventriculomegaly with decreased brain volumes in certain regions such as the temporal lobes and the amygdalo-hippocampal area) are found in a number of schizophrenics, a variety of deficits on neuropsychological tests are common. On the WAIS-R, several patterns are commonly found (Feinberg and McIlvried, 1991; Newmark, 1985; Anastasi, 1987). First, subtest scatter is common, and the verbal-scaled score tends to be higher than the performance-scaled score. Within the subtests themselves there is a tendency to succeed on harder items and at the same time fail some of the easier items. Scores tend to be higher on block design and occasionally on information and vocabulary, while typically lower on arithmetic, picture arrangement, digit symbol, and comprehension. A low similarities score often includes several overinclusion responses, and a low score on comprehension is usually accompanied by evidence of irrelevant associations. A high similarities score is a good prognostic sign for schizophrenia. There are often peculiar arrangements in the picture arrangement test; in the picture completion test, frequent reference is made to items not intended to be together. In addition, process schizophrenics do less well than reactive schizophrenics on the picture completion test, relative to their other scores.

Ogdon (1977) reviewed a wide range of studies that used the Rorschach and noted several response patterns found to be associated with psychosis in general and schizophrenia in particular: (1) poor quality and a low number of human movement responses (those in which humans are perceived as involved in at least some minimal action), (2) animal movement responses in which the organization of the response is very poor, (3) an abnormally high or low number of pure-form responses (in which the client made the response based simply on the form of the blot, without reference to any other aspect), (4) responses dictated only by the color of the blot (that is, pure-C responses), (5) an abnormally low number of responses in which all aspects of the blot are integrated into the response (whole, or W, responses), (6) a lower-than-average number of Popular, or P, responses (responses perceived by most people), and/or

(7) perseverating by continually seeing the same or analogous responses throughout several blots in sequence.

Exner (1978, 1986) has noted several differences between schizophrenics and normals on the Rorschach. Schizophrenics obtain more F and M responses than do either borderlines or normal persons, although there may be a high percentage of F responses. Borderline individuals average 6.4 Popular responses, whereas schizophrenics average only 3.6. Not surprisingly, schizophrenics have almost twice as many unusual responses as borderline cases and certainly far more than normal individuals. Schizophrenics also give three times fewer S responses and two times fewer T determinates than normal individuals. More specifically, schizophrenics scored significantly lower than normals on R, D, DQt, Sum T, H, Xt%, Pop, and Afr and higher on Dd, (FQw) – (fQ-), Sum Y, L, Sum SP.SL (Mason et al., 1985).

Exner (1986) has developed a "Schizophrenic Index" that includes the following criteria:

1. $X+\% < 70$
2. Sum FQ– > Sum FQµ, or $X - \% > 20$
3. $M = 0$, or WSUMG > 11
4. (Sum DV + DR + INCOM + FABCOM + ALOG + CONTAM) > 4
5. (Sum DR + FABCOM + ALOG + CONTAM) > (Sum DV + INCOM), or M– > 1

Exner asserts that a cutoff score of 4 or 5 is indicative of schizophrenia, which would probably not always allow an acceptable number of false-positives or -negatives, but these signs are a useful general indicator of thought/perceptual distortion.

Others have noted that schizophrenics are more inclined than other groups to show a massing of pure-color responses, and they occasionally show very arbitrary FC responses (e.g., pink rats). Color-shock or pleasantly verbalized comments about color in the cards are considered to be favorable prognostic signs in schizophrenia (Phillips and Smith, 1953). Along with the deviant verbalizations—such as fabulized responses (two rabbits with a baseball bat), contaminations (the head of a beetle-tiger), and other incongruous combinations (a woman with a head of a horse)—schizophrenics tend to show overelaborate symbolism and absurd responses in the patterns and a number of mangled and distorted perceptions. Schizophrenics are more likely to show a perseveration of Dd responses, which reflects a high degree of overcontrol in their response patterns combined with underactivity in the actual perceptions. They also may show a massing of sex responses, particularly referring more often to the sexual act rather than to sexual organs. As in most of the tests, there is a tendency for the quality of responses to deteriorate toward the end of the test. Not only do schizophrenics show a higher percentage of F responses, but they also show higher levels of articulation of the object as they perceive it within the F response. In essence, their ego resources are being channeled into fantasy behavior.

The Thought Disorder scale (SS) on the MCMI-III is designed to reflect schizophrenic thinking, but it is not always effective because it is susceptible to faking-good (i.e., schizophrenics who tend to be nonreporters of symptoms do not show up on this scale) (Jackson et al., 1991). Schizophrenics do tend to be higher on 2A, S, 1, and 8B. During active phases of schizophrenia, disorientation, inappropriate affect, hallucinations, and delusions will be represented by SS scores above 84 on the MCMI-II. Elevations on CC and PP are likely to the extent that depression and paranoia are present. In general, elevations on 1, 2A+B, 3, and 8A have been found to be characteristic of inpatient samples, who are often schizophrenics (McCann and Suess, 1988).

On the Thematic Apperception Test (TAT), schizophrenics are prone to tell rambling, confused stories or to have a very restricted response record. They are more likely to make comments of self-reference or show personal reactions, such as disgust, in response to the cards. They make bizarre comments and show less ability to concentrate on their responses. From a thematic standpoint, schizophrenics are more likely than normals to show direct sexual and aggressive themes; themes of persecution and/or omnipotence; characters changing in confused, odd, or magical ways; ideas of reference (especially linking the present card to a prior card); juxtaposition of extremes (e.g., acts of murder and tenderness); disorientation as to person, place, and time; lack of clear body boundaries; gross deviation from the stimulus properties; and grossly destructive bizarre or sexual themes (Bellak, 1993; Karon, 1981).

Proverbs have also been used to distinguish schizophrenics from other groups. Johnson (1966) found that only those proverbs that are commonly understood ("It never rains, but it pours") are consistently useful in distinguishing schizophrenics from other groups, such as persons with organic brain damage (four such proverbs are included in the Meyer Information Battery listed in Appendix B). Schizophrenics are more likely to give peculiar, abstract responses to these proverbs. Figures on the Bender-Gestalt are likely to be boxed, to be drawn in a confused order, and to be drawn overly large (Rossini and Kaspar, 1987).

Persons with basic personality patterns encompassing traits of the schizoid, borderline, schizotypal, and avoidant personalities are more likely to use schizophrenic-like patterns as coping devices or to decompensate to a schizophrenic pattern. Elevations on scales 1, 2, C, and S may be present and representative of precipitating personality styles. Scales 4 and 7 should be somewhat depressed, as these patterns are not likely to develop schizophrenic disorders. Overall, the MCMI-II does not appear to be as effective as the MMPI-2 in assessing schizophrenia (Patrick, 1988).

Iacono (1991) notes several physiological markers for schizophrenia that could be integrated into a specialized evaluation, for example, dysfunctional smooth-pursuit eye tracking, differences in event-related brain potentials.

TREATMENT OPTIONS

There are several prognostic indicators that point to a positive chance of remission once schizophrenia does occur (Knable et al., 1995; Leff, 1994; Cromwell and Snyder, 1993; Potkin et al., 1993; Meyer and Salmon, 1988): (1) sexual-marital status: being married or at least having a history of stable, consistent sexual-social adjustment; (2) a family history of affective disorder rather than schizophrenic disorder; (3) presence of an affective pattern (either elation or depression) in the acute stage of the schizophrenic disorder; (4) abrupt onset of the disorder and onset later than early adulthood; (5) adequate premorbid school and/or vocational adjustment; (6) evidence of premorbid competence in interpersonal relationships and a higher socioeconomic status; (7) a short length of stay in the hospital with an absence of electroconvulsive therapy (ECT) treatment; (8) absence of evidence of cognitive dysfunction or deterioration; (9) nonparanoid subdiagnosis; (10) a family history of alcoholism; (11) psychomotor retardation; (12) lower levels of criticism, hostility, and emotional overinvolvement (Expressed Emotion—EE) upon hospital release; (13) evidence of clear precipitating factors at the onset of the disturbance; and (14) a low rate of occurrence of negative symptoms, that is, alogia, avolition/apathy, attentional impairment, and especially anhedonia and flat affect. The clinician should note the markedly increased risk for suicide in schizophrenics, at a rate ten times higher than normals, close to that of persons with severe depression.

More than almost any other disorder, schizophrenia warrants a multi-faceted treatment plan because of its complexity. Chemotherapy—traditionally with the phenothiazines, the butyrophenones, or the thioxanthenes—is useful as one component in the treatment of many schizophrenics, particularly for those who are hospital-prone clients of low competence (Wiesel, 1994) (see Chapter 17). The substituted benzamides (sulpiride, remoxipride, and raclopride) offer promise here (Michels and Marzuk, 1993). Clozapine, a dibenzodiazepane, has been helpful for some schizophrenics who do not respond well to other medications. However, 1–2% of persons taking clozapine are at risk to develop agranulocytosis, a life-threatening blood disorder, so consistent monitoring is required.

"Positive" symptoms—that is, those marked by their presence, such as hallucinations, delusions, and incoherent speech—respond more quickly to chemotherapy, while those "negative" symptoms noted earlier, as well as interpersonal deficits and disrupted quality of life, do not respond very well (Knable et al., 1995). Breier et al. (1994) did find clozapine superior to haloperidol, although the effect was by far most evident on positive symptoms. Since there can be major problems with a schizophrenic's ability to take medication after being released from the hospital, the long-acting agents, such as the phenothiazine Prolixin, can be useful, although they have a restricted range of effectiveness and there are problems with side effects.

As with all the antipsychotic chemotherapies, approximately 35% of the clients show muscular problems and feelings of lethargy alternating with restlessness. Up to 5% (up to 40% in the elderly) develop tardive dyskinesia, a typically irreversible syndrome (although it can be muted with other medications and even vitamin E) that involves grimacing, lip smacking, and involuntary neck and head movements. Also, particularly with the phenothiazines (the most commonly used drug), a significant number of deaths due to aspiration asphyxiation have been noted because the drug tends to suppress the gag reflex. In addition to these side effects, there is loss of creativity and spontaneity and a reinforcement of the patient role, because the client sees treatment as totally external to her- or himself. Although chemotherapy can be useful, antipsychotic drugs are prescribed too often and/or at too high a dosage (Rifkin et al., 1991).

Electroconvulsive therapy (ECT) has been used with schizophrenics since its discovery, but it has not shown any significant success. Psychosurgery, dialysis, and megavitamin therapies have been tried with increasing frequency in recent years, but as yet there is little significant evidence of their success with schizophrenia (Plotkin et al., 1993; Valenstein, 1986).

Inpatient hospitalization is often required, although many cases now hospitalized could be treated just as effectively with partial hospitalization. Either approach should provide structure, social-skills education, and social contact and support. Significant others and eventual aftercare staff should be involved as early as possible. Programs should attend to all seven domains of functioning, as defined by Lazarus (1971), that is, behavior, affect, sensation, imagery, cognition, interpersonal, and drug. Psychotherapy can be useful, especially when directed to such areas as problems associated with a chronic, debilitating disorder and the self-esteem and interpersonal problems inherent to the schizophrenic process.

Token economies have been used effectively in bringing the disrupted and institutionalized schizophrenic back to a semblance of normal functioning and the development of simple and basic behaviors. Milieu therapy, occasionally only a euphemism for sitting around the ward, is optimally a total treatment approach that adds the values of patient-governance and input to the concepts of group process and the "moral therapy" of the nineteenth century (Adler, 1988). Milieu therapy should also include an available combination of new and effective treatment techniques directed toward the overall improvement of schizophrenia. In this regard, occupational, activity, and art therapies can be useful adjuncts. Developing adequate vocational skills is important, and these skills should not be for obsolescent vocations, as is often the case in prison and mental hospital programs. Social-skills training is not only effective for the specific skills taught, but also generalizes to other situations outside the treatment environment. Cognitive retraining and other rehabilitation techniques used for head-injury patients can be helpful in dealing with the attention dysfunctions that are critical to the schizophrenic process. Family therapy, group therapy and social skills training are especially important as the person moves back into the home system (Leff, 1994).

Ellsworth et al. (1979) thoroughly examined the issues in milieu therapy and advised that the milieu is much more effective when there is a mixture of both chronic and acute patients. They noted a cluster of specific factors that facilitate the positive effects of milieu therapy, notably the availability of a separate television room, recent magazines and other reading materials, music at meals, stalls separating the toilets, and pleasant pictures on the walls.

Proactive efforts by an aftercare "case manager," that is, consistent contact, monitoring and support, sometimes referred to as "assertive community treatment" (ACT), can be very effective, though ACT is seldom applied. It works by helping the client stabilize during crises, apply already learned and new social and coping skills, and make more positive social and vocational contacts.

■ Undifferentiated Schizophrenia (295.90)

This category is marked by prominent schizophrenic symptoms and Criteria A is met; however, there are several symptoms from various subtypes, or for some reason the criteria for one of the other categories are not quite fulfilled. This category fits most clearly the previous comments, testing indicators, and treatment suggestions for the overall category of schizophrenia.

■ Disorganized Schizophrenia (295.10)

Disorganized Schizophrenia was termed Hebephrenia in earlier DSM classification systems. The DSM-IV diagnosis of disorganized schizophrenic denotes an individual meets the overall criteria of schizophrenia and who shows disorganized speech, disorganized behavior and flat or inappropriate affect (often in the form of random giggling), and does not meet the criteria for the Catatonic type.

Other elements commonly associated with disorganized schizophrenia include odd facial grimaces, extreme social withdrawal, and very peculiar mannerisms. Delusions and hallucinations do not show the structure or pattern common to other schizophrenic disorders. As would be expected from the preceding description, social functioning is severely disrupted.

Overall, disorganized schizophrenia is characterized by very poor premorbid adjustment, slow onset (usually starting in adolescence or early adulthood), neurological problems, and chronicity of adjustment. These individuals are likely to develop more chronic and apathetic patterns with time, and the likelihood of significant long-term remission is quite low.

☐   MMPI-2

Gynther et al. (1973a) note that the 8-9/9-8 profile is commonly associated with the behaviors typical of disorganized schizophrenia. This is particularly true if the affect is silly or inappropriate. When it is flat, scale 9 tends to be lower and scales 7 and 2 are likely to be higher. Disorganized schizophrenics are often so severely disturbed in functioning that they cannot adequately complete the MMPI-2, at least to the degree where it is suitable for scoring. The reader is referred to the section on malingering (Chapter 16), since some of that material relates to the patterns to be expected here.

☐   16 PF

The same problems in adequately scoring the MMPI-2 also hold true for the 16 PF. In those individuals who are able to perform the task adequately, their 16 PF profile is likely to fit the overall schizophrenic pattern mentioned earlier, with only a few minor changes: Scale C is likely to be lower in disorganized schizophrenics than in others, as are scales N and Q_3. They also tend to be higher on scale A and lower on scale L, which reflects their willingness to interact interpersonally as expressed through fantasy, but their inability to actuate this interaction in reality.

☐   OTHER TEST-RESPONSE PATTERNS

While the overall schizophrenic pattern is most likely to be reflected on the WAIS-R, this test emphasizes the very odd response patterns to an even greater degree. Proverbs are especially peculiar, and the disorganized schizophrenic is probably not able to provide even the distorted rationale that paranoid schizophrenics may volunteer if they feel comfortable enough with the tester (Feinberg and McIlvried, 1991). If the affect of the disorganized schizophrenic is silly or incongruous, there is usually an extreme scatter in the quality of responses, and this will affect the subtest patterns and the within-test scoring. They tend to do more poorly on block design, digit symbol, and object assembly than do other schizophrenic clients, reflecting the neurologic component.

On the Rorschach, form level is very low, and although there are occasional M responses, these are likely to be of poor quality and reflective of disrupted ideation.

On the MCMI-III, elevations above 84 on C and S are most common, with elevation of P and 1 likely. Because PP and SS are partly defined by hallucinations and delusions, they are not as likely to be very high in the disorganized schizophrenic, where these symptoms are not typically present, but moderate elevations (74–85) may occur. One personality pattern that is most likely to occur with the disorganized schizophrenic is the avoidant type; indeed, disorganization may be considered an extension of their characteristic protective maneuver in interfering with cognitive clarity (Millon, 1981). In this case, elevations above 74 may be expected on scale 2A.

☐   TREATMENT OPTIONS

The particularly low level of functioning of the disorganized schizophrenic warrants the use of most of the techniques discussed relative to schizophrenic disorders. Chemotherapy is commonly required (Wiesel, 1994), and token economies and milieu therapy are particularly useful (Adler, 1988). Until disorganized schizophrenics can develop the basic appropriate behaviors of even the most minimally normal individuals, many of the other therapy techniques—such as psychotherapy, group therapy, and occupational therapy—are virtually impossible. Since disorganized schizophrenics are likely to have a markedly poor premorbid adjustment, an emphasis on vocational training is important if they are to make any ultimate transition to normal living. Thus, rigorous training in basic social skills is necessary, first via the token economy and then later through a total-milieu approach. Genetic counseling is also encouraged (Gottesman, 1991).

In choosing a specific therapist for an extremely disturbed client, the clinician might recall the classic differentiation between A and B therapists, first studied by Whitehorn and Betz (Goldstein and Stein, 1976). They found that B therapists were significantly more successful with the extremely disturbed individual. These therapists are characterized as noncoercive problem solvers; they are able to persuade while at the same time communicate a sense of acceptance of and empathy with the schizophrenic's bizarre thoughts and fantasies.

Catatonic Schizophrenia (295.20)

Severe psychomotor disturbance is the essential feature of catatonic schizophrenia. The first of the two major traditional subdivisions found in the literature (not DSM–IV categories) is that of stuporous catatonia, in which movement is severely reduced and catatonic stupor, rigidity, or posturing is evident. Some may even show waxy flexibility, a condition in which the body is passively receptive to posture control. It is possible to manipulate such individuals physically just as one would move a store manikin, and they can remain in the manipulated position for extremely long periods of time.

The agitated catatonic, or excited type, is marked by uncontrollable verbal and motor behavior—apparently purposeless and not necessarily influenced by external stimuli. Individuals of this type can be quite dangerous and may break into frenzied violence in which they hurt or kill themselves or others. This is not an outgrowth of personal hostility, but rather a response to other persons as objects in their way. Before the use of psychomotor-control drugs, agitated catatonics would sometimes drive themselves to the point where they would die from severe exhaustion.

Two different courses are typically observed in catatonic schizophrenia. The chronic form of this disorder is primarily manifested in the stuporous types, and the progression in the disorder is slow and steady. The prognosis for remission is low, and the person may eventually develop into an undifferentiated schizophrenic.

In the periodic type an abrupt onset is usually followed by alternating periods of agitated and stuporous catatonia. Remission is more likely, yet there may be recurrences. These individuals are particularly dangerous at the point of the shift from stupor to agitation because hospital personnel have few cues as to when the shift will occur.

DSM-IV

In addition to meeting the standard criteria for schizophrenia, a diagnosis of catatonic schizophrenia requires that at some time during the active phase of the illness the symptom picture is dominated by a catatonic pattern that includes at least two of the following: (1) motoric immobility as shown by stupor or catalepsy (including waxy flexibility); (2) excessive motor behavior (apparently not purpose- or stimulus-related); (3) extreme negativism or mutism; (4) peculiar voluntary movements, that is, postures, grimaces, et cetera; or (5) echolalia or echopraxia. Interestingly, although the catatonic subtype was once considered to be one of the most common schizophrenic patterns, it is now relatively rare in Europe and North America.

MMPI-2

The 2-7-8 pattern, with 2 most likely to predominate, is often reflective of the catatonic who is confused and yet oriented toward stuporous catatonia. Agitated catatonics are more likely to show an 8-9 or 8-0 pattern (Moldin et al., 1987). If this agitation has been transferred intellectually into hostility, an elevation on scale 4 is more likely and scale 6 is usually elevated. The 0 scale is high, reflecting significant discomfort with and withdrawal from interpersonal relationships.

16 PF

This pattern is similar to the prototypical pattern for schizophrenia, although it will differ on certain scales depending on whether the person tends toward stupor or agitation. This will be reflected particularly in scales F, Q_4, and, to a degree, E and Q_3. Since this pattern may border on the hostility and social isolation of the paranoid, the L scale is likely to be affected more so than for other schizophrenics; to a degree, this is also evident in a higher Q_2 score.

OTHER TEST-RESPONSE PATTERNS

The schizophrenic profile would be expected on the MCMI-III, represented by elevations on SS along with the indicated patterns that seem to predispose toward schizophrenia (elevation on 1, 2A, C, and/or S). Additionally, CC would be more prominent in this type of schizophrenia than in others, representing the catatonic and agitated types of motor activity. Scores on this scale of 85 or higher would not be uncommon. The overactivity factor of the excited type would be represented by an elevated N.

TREATMENT OPTIONS

Agitated catatonic schizophrenics may force a coercive control of their behavior; chemotherapy, the "modern straitjacket," is often necessary to bring a semblance of order into their worlds (Wiesel, 1994). Intravenous amobarbital is often successful in breaking through the mutism seen in many catatonics. Token economies and milieu therapy are also useful for ameliorating the extremes of either agitated or stuporous catatonia (Adler, 1988). The possibility of an associated manic component in the agitated catatonic must not be overlooked, so a trial period of lithium therapy can be employed.

The stuporous catatonic is not unlike the severe depressive on several continuums, so the reader might consult some of the techniques useful for moving a person out of a depressive episode (Schuyler, 1991). Direct therapy, which can be seen as a psychoanalytic analogue to implosive therapy, can be useful primarily with regressed paranoid and catatonic schizophrenics (Karon, 1976). Through a prolonged verbal assault on his or her inner fantasies and fears, the client is goaded into at least a retaliatory response. Once this occurs, the therapist can move into more supportive and interactive roles.

Residual Schizophrenic Disorder (295.60)

This DSM-IV diagnosis is applied to the individual who has already been labeled schizophrenic under the previous criteria, but in whom the disorder has lessened to the point that there are no longer any prominent characteristic symptoms, but there are some negative symptoms or two or more attenuated characteristic symptoms from Criterion A.

This judgment can be difficult, especially in view of the potency of certain chemotherapeutic agents to mask or suppress a wide variety of behavioral responses. Nonetheless, the category is likely to be used often since it is potentially applicable to many individuals.

MMPI-2

Since the category is *residual* schizophrenia, it could be debated how much psychopathology is likely to be evident in the MMPI-2 profile. It is reasonable for the clinician to expect that in most cases the general profile of schizophrenia will be evident, but without the extremes of response. For example, a significant elevation on scale 8 would still be likely, but it should be less than in a person with active schizophrenia. Similarly, an elevation on scale F is reasonable, although on occasion this may be an individual who is trying to avoid remembering the schizophrenic episode and who becomes very defensive in that regard. As a result, scale K—and possibly L—would be high (Moldin et al., 1987). When this happens, the person is also likely to be defensive about any kind of intrapsychic exploration.

It is typical to expect a relatively low 9 score in most residual schizophrenics, particularly since many of them are still on medication to suppress behavior. Other changes will be dependent on the specific type of schizophrenia, as well as on the premorbid personality, which is likely to come to the fore as the schizophrenic symptoms are suppressed.

16 PF

Much the same suppression of extreme scales would be expected on the 16 PF. C, H, M, O, and Q_4 should still be on the negative side of the continuum, yet they will be somewhat muted from prior levels. Scale B should be somewhat higher and now more accurately reflective of the person's actual abilities. A higher score on Q_3 should reflect the fact that the individuals now have more control in their worlds. Other scores will be affected by the type of schizophrenia manifested, the premorbid personality, and the feelings of security about present adjustment.

OTHER TEST-RESPONSE PATTERNS

MCMI-III profiles of residual schizophrenic disorder may be similar to those of other schizophrenic disorders without such extreme elevations on the clinical-symptom scales CC, PP, and SS. The personality pattern elevations expected for schizophrenia—1, 2A, C, and/or S—should be more elevated relative to CC, PP, and SS, in contrast to the active phases in which clinical-symptom scales are more prominent relative to personality patterns.

TREATMENT OPTIONS

Since by definition the symptom picture of residual schizophrenia excludes pervasive and permanent psychotic symptoms, there should be a continuing cost-benefit analysis as to whether any values from chemotherapy are, or could be, offset by the physical and psychological risks. Certainly trial periods without medication, and/or lower dosages of medication such as haloperidol (Rifkin et al., 1991), should be more common for such persons than they are.

The residual symptoms are usually in the area of social and interpersonal behavior and, as such, require systems that provide adequate feedback to the schizophrenic about these behaviors. Expatient groups such as Recovery can be useful in helping previously hospitalized clients adjust, but there is the risk that mildly bizarre behaviors in the social and vocational world will be reinforced, or at least too easily tolerated, without feedback. Hence, it is important to move quickly into group-therapy situations in which the predominant ethic is normality and in which feedback without inappropriate behaviors is generated supportively and accurately. Similarly, the family can be trained to provide this feedback in a positive manner through family-therapy situations (Leff, 1994).

If attentional problems persist into the residual phase, which they often do, biofeedback of electroencephalographic (EEG) patterns can be employed to increase those patterns associated with attention, such as decreasing the percentage of alpha waves, the classic indicator of nonattention. Biofeedback of muscle patterns is potentially useful to decrease the motoric side effects of tardive dyskinesia, or even to lower the excitability level of the agitated catatonic, although the latter task would indeed be challenging.

Schizophreniform Disorder (295.40)

The major substantive differences between the schizophreniform disorder and the overall diagnosis of schizophrenia are duration and degree of dysfunction.

If the disorder lasts more than a month but less than six months but the symptoms are those of schizophrenia, or if the person is symptomatic but has been so for less than six months, or if social/occupational dysfunction is not marked, the term "schizophreniform disorder" is appropriate. The diagnosis of schizophrenia requires symptoms for six months or more. If the duration of disorder is less than a month, the appropriate diagnosis is usually brief reactive psychosis.

The major reason for the differential diagnosis is that the schizophreniform disorder shows several characteristics that differ from schizophrenia. There is usually a better prognosis in the schizophreniform disorder; the individual is far more likely to recover to the premorbid level of functioning (although the DSM-IV asks the clinician to note whether there are or are not "Good Prognostic Features").

DIAGNOSTIC CONSIDERATIONS

There is a high likelihood that the symptom picture is going to include much emotional upset and turmoil, reflecting the acute variable. This is opposed to chronic schizophrenic patterns, so scores on the MMPI-2, 16 PF, MCMI-III, and other tests are likely to be slightly accentuated. For example, on the MMPI-2 one is more likely to see a higher F scale than for chronic schizophrenics, but lower F, 7, 8, and 0 scales than for acute schizophrenics. This profile occurs in schizophrenia as well, although not so consistently. On the 16 PF, higher scores on scales O and Q_4 and lower scores on C and H are likely to be found more often than with schizophrenics.

TREATMENT OPTIONS

Since the schizophreniform disorder is essentially a schizophrenic adjustment that has not yet lasted for six months, the techniques appropriate for the treatment of schizophrenia are applicable here. This is particularly so for psychological techniques, as every effort should be made to help the client avoid the patient role and even worse, extended institutionalization.

Brief Psychotic Disorder (298.8)

The primary distinguishing features of this psychotic reaction are sudden onset and short duration, ranging from at least one day up to one month. It requires only one of the following symptoms: (1) delusions, (2) hallucinations, (3) disorganized speech, or (4) catatonic or grossly disorganized behavior (unless any of these are culturally sanctioned responses). There should also be a specification as to whether there are indications of marked stressors (thus bringing in the earlier DSM concept of Brief Reactive Psychosis), or if it is a Postpartum Onset response (i.e., within four weeks postpartum).

This disorder is often triggered rather suddenly by an event of extreme stress: the loss of a loved one, a traumatic war experience, or other such stress.

Unable to deal with the stress, the individual withdraws into a state of mental confusion, typically characterized by extreme emotional lability, bizarre behaviors, and perceptual distortions, including hallucinations and delusions. Individuals with histrionic, schizotypal, and borderline personality disorders, as well as adolescents and young adults manifesting emotional instability of various sorts, are especially prone to this reaction.

Unlike the schizophreniform disorder and the organic mental disorders that display comparable symptoms, the brief psychotic reaction is sudden in onset and of short duration. Unlike the factitious disorder, which in some respects may be considered a stress reaction, the person with a brief psychotic reaction appears to have little or no voluntary control over his or her symptoms.

OTHER TEST-RESPONSE PATTERNS

The test-response patterns are similar to the schizophrenic disorders, even more so to the exaggerated patterns of the schizophreniform disorder, particularly since acute emotional distress is apparent here. Those accentuations noted in the section on test responses in schizophreniform disorder are applicable here, with some minor exceptions. Those exceptions relate to the probability of lower ego strength and indications of a more permanent disorder than are found in the other patterns. Hence, scales 4 and 6 on the MMPI-2 would be even less likely to be elevated, and scale 0 is not as likely to be very different from normal in these individuals as in schizophrenia. Scale 2 is likely to be elevated, representing the present acute distress. On the 16 PF, the C and H scales are not as likely to be as low, as these are reflective of more disturbed ongoing personality functioning. Patterns similar to schizophrenic patterns would also be expected on the MCMI-III, along with greater elevations on A, N, and, to a lesser degree, D. Along with the expected accompanying personality disorders, elevation on 4 is possible since this type is related to the histrionic disorder.

TREATMENT OPTIONS

Since this diagnosis is warranted when the person has shown psychotic behavior only for two weeks or less, the techniques appropriate for the treatment of schizophrenia or severe affective disorder (see relevant sections) can be supplemented by the techniques of crisis intervention. Most importantly, every effort should be made to keep clients from withdrawing from their social or vocational worlds and adopting patient roles. If at all possible, the family should be involved in the treatment, both as a mode of cutting off pathological behaviors and as a means of providing emotional support (Leff, 1994).

In addition, the brief psychotic disorder is effectively treated with covert modeling. In this technique, clients are asked to imagine a whole set of new behaviors and imagine themselves performing these behaviors. With practice, and with contracting for gradually moving aspects of the imagery patterns into their existing worlds, a positive effect can be generated.

■ Psychotic Disorder Not Otherwise Specified (298.9)

This category is used to designate those individuals who for some reason do not fit into any of the previous categories. For example, atypical psychosis might refer to individuals with a monosymptomatic somatic delusional system or to someone with such a confusing clinical picture that a specific diagnosis would be wrong.

■ Psychotic Disorder Due to a General Medical Condition (293.8)

This new category in the DSM–IV requires prominent hallucinations or delusions, not exclusively occurring during Delirium or Dementia and not better accounted for by another mental disorder, and evidence that a general medical condition is etiologically related to the behavior.

■ Paranoid Schizophrenia (295.30)

This disorder is discussed here because it is a juxtaposition of concepts from both schizophrenia and the paranoid disorders, the focus of the next section. Paranoid schizophrenia shows the most fragmented thought processes of any of the paranoid disorders; for that reason, it is included under schizophrenia. At the same time, however, there is a delusional system that is the mark of a paranoid disorder. In order to warrant the DSM-IV diagnosis of Paranoid Schizophrenia, the person has to fulfill the criteria for schizophrenia and present a symptom picture dominated either by preoccupation with one or more delusions or with frequent auditory hallucinations. There should be no prominence of disorganized behavior or speech, inappropriate affect, or catatonic behavior.

Paranoid schizophrenia is a somewhat different disorder than other forms of schizophrenia. Paranoid schizophrenics show less anxiety (more of a counterphobic response to depressive ideation), relatively less judgment impairment, smaller deficits on most cognitive tests, and more concern with erecting boundaries in tasks and in their personal worlds than do other schizophrenics. There may even be differences in blood chemistry between these groups; however, these data have been contradictory to date. In addition, paranoid schizophrenia can be contrasted with other schizophrenic disorders on the dimensions listed in Table 3.1.

Although paranoid schizophrenics are typically more adequate socially than other schizophrenics, their reactions are consistently more stilted or intense than are normal responses. This is particularly so if anger and suspicion rather than grandiosity are the focus of the symptom picture. Reasonably appropriate affective responses often exist in paranoid schizophrenia, in contrast to the other schizophrenias.

TABLE 3.1   Contrasting Factors in Paranoid and Other Schizophrenic Disorders

PARANOID SCHIZOPHRENIA	OTHER SCHIZOPHRENIC DISORDERS
Depression not that common	More often show depression or other mood disorder
Develop later in life	Show first manifestations in adolescence or late adolescence
More common in males	Approximately equal incidence in males and females
Often show some reasonably normal-appearing outward behaviors	Appear more disoriented or withdrawn
Higher intellectual ability than other schizophrenics	Often of lower-than-average intelligence
Seldom occurs in many rural non-Western cultures	Approximately equal occurrence rate across cultures
Proportionately shorter hospital stays	Tend toward long periods of hospitalization
More often tend to be mesomorphic (the body of a powerful athlete)	Any body build

Another occasionally confusing differential diagnostic problem is between the temporary psychotic state induced by severe alcoholic abuse and that of paranoid schizophrenia. Table 3.2 offers some guidelines.

MMPI-2

When the profile is devoid of a T-score elevation over 70, the L score is greater than or equal to 7 (absolute values), and the person is not a minister, paranoid mentation with some delusions is likely and probability of acting-out is increased to the degree that scales 3 and 4 are high (Fjordback, 1985). The 8-4 pattern, with high scores on 2, 6, and 7, is characteristic of paranoid schizophrenia. The 8-6/6-8 and the 6-9/9-6 profiles are also typical for paranoid schizophrenics (Moldin et al., 1987); if the 6 is the predominant scale with 4 also raised, the person should be considered one of the more dangerous paranoid schizophrenics. If the 8 dominates in the profile, then prepsychotic schizoid traits are more likely.

A high F scale is typical, and an F – K (F minus K) ratio greater than 11 is not necessarily an indication of an invalid profile in a situation with high 4, 6, 8, and 9 scales. If the 7 scale is low, auditory hallucinations are particularly likely to occur. When the individual is more inclined toward grandiose rather than persecutory delusions, an 8-9/9-8 profile is more likely, with the 2 scale being lower than usual. The 1 and 3 scales are often relatively low in the proto-

TABLE 3.2 Differential Diagnosis Between Alcoholic Hallucinosis and Paranoid Schizophrenia

	ALCOHOLIC HALLUCINOSIS	PARANOID SCHIZOPHRENIA
Age of Onset	More often 30–60 years of age	Usually less than 35 years of age
Onset	Acute	Insidious
Family History	Usually no family history for schizophrenia	Typically a positive family history for schizophrenia
Distinguishing Characteristic Affect	Anxiety and depression	Flat or inappropriate
Thought Processes	Coherent thought processes	Loose associations, formal thought disorder
Intellectual Functioning	Slight impairment of cognitive functions	No compromised cognitive functioning
Length of Illness	Spontaneous improvement within days to weeks	Lifelong relapsing illness

Adapted in part from Surawicz, F. (1980). "Alcoholic Hallucinosis, a Missed Diagnosis. Differential Diagnosis and Management." *Can J Psychiatry, 25,* 57–63.

cols of paranoid schizophrenics, although Gilberstadt and Duker (1965) suggest that the 1-6/6-1 pattern with a 4 scale less than 70 T should be considered a cue to look for further evidence of paranoid schizophrenia. They tend to be moderate to high on the BIZ (Bizarre Mentation) content scale, higher to the degree that their adjustment is fragmented and deteriorating.

☐　　16 PF

The paranoid schizophrenic 16 PF profile is similar to the overall schizophrenic profile, with some significant differences. Paranoid schizophrenics, especially females, are more likely to be high on the L scale, reflecting the jealous paranoid component essential to the disorder. Paranoid schizophrenics are also more likely to be high on Q_3 because anxiety is more controlled by projecting conflict and feelings onto other agents. As a result, the O score is less, the C and E scales higher, and the Q_4 scale somewhat lower than is found in the usual schizophrenic protocol. Also, because paranoid schizophrenics on the average are more intelligent, scale B is higher.

☐　　OTHER TEST-RESPONSE PATTERNS

Elevations on 1 and P are expected on the MCMI-III, and to a lesser extent, 2A, 6A, and/or C. MCMI-II scores of 85 and higher occur on PP, whereas the relatively less psychotic thought processes and affects exhibited by this type produce relatively lower scores on CC and SS, placing them in the 75–84 range.

On the WAIS-R, paranoid schizophrenics are likely to be higher on the similarities and picture completion subtests, while relatively lower on the digit symbol and picture arrangement subtests. This reflects the unusual interpretations they tend to make, as well as their compulsive traits, which are usually more evident premorbidly. Because they exhibit less cognitive confusion, compared to disorganized schizophrenics, their overall scores are higher (Feinberg and McIlvried, 1991). On the comprehension subtest, paranoid schizophrenics are occasionally lower because they tend to make peculiar and overinclusive proverb interpretations. This trait is also found in the Benjamin Proverbs (Johnson, 1966).

This is one instance when the use of more exotic proverbs can be helpful. Paranoid schizophrenics, particularly if they are bright, often understand the popular interpretation of common proverbs and sayings and will state them, even though they may entertain other interpretations (Oltmanns and Maher, 1988). Exotic proverbs can bring out the delusional material more clearly.

On all tests, including the WAIS-R, paranoid schizophrenics show over-concern about the correctness of their responses and will often question the examiner as to what the correct response is. They tend to make deviant replies in response to numerous stimuli and are happy to argue about the meaning of any question presented to them (Heilbrun et al., 1985). On the Rorschach, paranoid schizophrenics are again very concerned about the meaning of the test, particularly since the ambiguous stimuli are not easily interpretable. They are more likely to look at the back of the card and to make excessive Dd responses. They show a fairly high F+ percentage, but not with the quality seen in the other paranoid disorders. If they are more oriented toward the persecutory dimension, a low number of responses is likely unless they can be made at least minimally comfortable in the testing situation.

If responsive, paranoid schizophrenics are likely to show a higher number of M responses and a lower number of C responses, particularly if there is a degree of integration in their adjustment. Responses are occasionally seen as "coming at" the person, and there are more "mask" responses than usual, as well as percepts of animals or humans being attacked or surrounded. There is an overemphasis on W responses, but often with poorer form than one would expect based on their intelligence level. Content often includes grandiose or cosmic concepts as well as responses that define boundaries, such as "edge" or "border" responses.

On the TAT, grandiose and pretentious stories are likely, with the person often being too negativistic to cooperate in pinning down details of the story. They are likely to use a story as a forum for making philosophical comments or moralizing about situations. Alternatively, if they feel threatened, they may refuse even to tell a story or will give very short and concrete descriptions of the pictures (Bellak, 1993). Gutters, fences, other indications of borders, castles, and similar concepts are found in the drawings of paranoids (Oster and Gould, 1987).

☐ TREATMENT OPTIONS

Neuroleptic drugs can be useful with the delusional component of severe paranoid disorders (Wiesel, 1994), and are typically more effective with persecutory delusions, as compared to somatic and erotomanic delusions. Pimazide has shown some success with somatic delusions. Although no single drug has been consistently effective, there is some evidence that chlorpromazine, haloperidol, and a trifluoperazine-amitriptyline combination may have some benefit when used as an adjunct to other treatment techniques in severe paranoid disturbance. Since "positive" schizophrenic symptoms are often central to an outpatient paranoid schizophrenic pattern, clozapine can be useful (Breier et al., 1994).

The significant level of disturbance and more bizarre quality of the paranoid schizophrenia, as contrasted to that of the other paranoid disorders, may warrant more intrusive methods. ECT has been used with some paranoid schizophrenics in an apparent attempt to disrupt the consistency of the belief system. However, ECT contains all the risks of any intrusive procedure, which are so important here because a fear of being intruded on in any number of dimensions is central to the paranoid disorders. In addition, there is the probability of short- and long-term memory loss, which could easily increase the sense of vulnerability so critical to many paranoids.

Chemotherapy can lessen the anxiety often found in the paranoid delusional system (Zigler and Glick, 1988). But again, there are the risks of apparent intrusiveness, plus increased delusions in response to any side effects, even those that have little long-term danger.

> *An envious heart makes a*
> *treacherous ear.*
>
> Zora Neal Hurston
> *Their eyes were watching* (1937)

■ The Paranoid (Delusional) Disorders

The paranoid disorders are psychotic conditions in which the symptom picture is dominated by persistent persecutory delusions or delusions of jealousy. This is not an official DSM-IV category, as the Delusional Disorder is lumped under "Other" psychotic disorders, Paranoid Personality Disorder under the Personality Disorders, and so forth. "Paranoia" was long used as a general term to denote bizarre behavior. In 1863 the term was refined by Kahlbaum to denote a persistent disorder marked by delusions. Although paranoids manifest social isolation secondary to their core suspiciousness, they show a relatively high marital rate, similar to affective disorders and as opposed to schizophrenics, possibly because peak age of first psychiatric admission is in their mid-forties. Actual onset apparently predates this period by a considerable amount, and hospitalization may never occur. Females suffer this psychotic disorder at a slightly higher rate than males.

The term "paranoia" means "knowledge" *(noia)* that is "alongside" *(para)*— to be beside oneself, or mad. While the DSM-IV emphasizes the "delusional" rather than "paranoid" terminology, we will use the traditional and still more generally accepted "paranoid" terminology. There are usually no significant hallucinations in the paranoid disorders, and the symptoms are not primarily attributable to a schizophrenic, affective, or organic mental disorder or to any combination of the three. Unlike paranoid schizophrenia, there is not much fragmentation of thoughts or bizarreness in the delusions. Typically, there is only one delusional theme. Also, there is seldom as severe an impairment in daily functioning as there is in paranoid schizophrenia (i.e., the latter show more characteristics of an "autistic retreat" from life). Paranoid schizophrenics typically have more than one delusional system, but it is not uncommon in the paranoid disorder that there is only a single focus in the delusions (Oltmanns and Maher, 1988).

The paranoid disorders can be oriented on a continuum based on the degree of integration in the delusions, with paranoid schizophrenia being the most fragmented and delusional (paranoid) disorder the least. The paranoid personality disorder can be seen as an extension of this continuum in that there is no true delusional system at all (Turkat, 1990).

The paranoid disorders seldom show marked disruption in occupational functioning or intellectual activities, but they do show disruption in marital and interpersonal functioning. These are relatively rare disorders, and since these individuals are usually coerced into treatment, they are not always cooperative in a diagnostic situation. For that reason, the reader should consult the section on malingering (Chapter 16). Because anger is often a factor in the personality makeup and occasionally is so extreme that there is danger to others, the reader should consult the section of this book on aggression potential (Chapter 14).

☐   ## MMPI-2

While one would expect scale 6 to be elevated in this disorder, this is not always the case. Paranoids with good defenses may not want to reveal their delusions and as a result may score rather low on scale 6, in some instances being inordinately low, even relative to normal scores (Heilbrun et al., 1985). It must also be remembered when making a diagnostic judgment that blacks tend to score higher on scale 6 throughout the range of normal and paranoid patterns (Dahlstrom et al., 1986). Overall, paranoids are likely to skip a number of the questions and often express irritation at being forced to make true-false decisions.

Unlike persons with other psychiatric disorders, paranoids will show a high K score and a relatively low F score and, consistent with that, a lower score on scale 4 than would be expected. The more disturbed the individual is (the more toward the paranoid schizophrenic end of the continuum), the more likely the "paranoid trough" will occur, that is, high scores on scales 6 and 8 and a relatively lower score on scale 7. Since denial and projection are common features of the paranoid disorders, reasonably high scores on scale 3 can be expected. As noted in paranoid schizophrenia, with a profile of T well below 70 and L (in absolute numbers) greater than or equal to 7, paranoid mentation is probable, and elevations on 3 and 4 increase the probability of acting-out (Fjordback, 1985). They tend to be high on the Overcontrolled Hostility (OH) supplementary scale and the Cynicism (CYN) content scale and, to the degree they approach psychosis, on the BIZ content scale.

☐ ## 16 PF

It was originally thought that paranoids would score high on the L scale, but this is not always so, which again reflects the situation where the client is guarded in revealing the content of his or her concerns. Hence, the diagnostician should score for faking-bad (Winder et al., 1975; Krug, 1980) in order to check for the extremity of this response pattern. On the paranoia end of the continuum, as opposed to the paranoid schizophrenic end, scores on B, N, and Q_3 are likely to be higher, while I is lower.

☐ ## TREATMENT OPTIONS

The concerns of the paranoid about intrusiveness make this set of disorders most difficult to treat, and the possibility of an underlying depression has to be kept in mind (Zigler and Glick, 1988). The therapist can crash through the defenses via techniques such as direct analysis, chemotherapy, or even psychosurgery. The consequently disrupted psychological functions then have to reintegrate—not always an easy task. In addition, the iatrogenic effect of coercively intruding on an individual who already has a low threshold for perceiving intrusiveness presents substantial difficulties in the later development of trust.

To the degree the paranoid individual is more integrated in functioning, intrusive techniques can be avoided and the therapist can focus on developing trust. In that way, paranoids may now gain recourse to another individual, a pattern usually absent. Once some trust is gained, efforts can be made to help the client learn self-monitoring and self-evaluation skills, and then move toward developing adequate social skills. Therapists must attempt to maintain their integrity and honesty while empathizing with the paranoid's delusional beliefs. The critical feat is to gain the trust of an individual who is pervasively untrusting and, at the same time, accept but not participate in the paranoid's delusional system. (Also see the section on treatment for the paranoid personality disorder in Chapter 9.)

■ Delusional Disorder (297.1)

Delusional Disorder (DD) is rarely observed in clinical practice for several reasons. First, DD apparently does not exist as commonly as many other disorders. Second, the higher level of personality integration allows DDs to avoid seeing a clinician, even when their lives are being disrupted. Since they are inclined to isolate themselves under stress, it is very hard to even coerce them into treatment.

A DSM-IV diagnosis of Delusional Disorder requires that (1) there is evidence of nonbizarre delusions (which, at least at first blush, seems to be an oxymoron), (2) for at least a month the individual has never met Criteria A for Schizophrenia, (3) functioning is not impaired markedly, (4) behavior is not obviously odd or bizarre, (5) generation by effects of a substance is ruled out, and (6) mood episodes are brief relative to delusion duration. In the DSM-IV the following are subtypes of the Delusional Disorder: Erotomanic, Grandiose, Jealous, Persecutory, Somatic (and Mixed or Unspecific).

The two classical variations of paranoia are conjugal paranoia and erotomania. Conjugal paranoia is marked by delusions of jealousy that involve the spouse. This condition, sometimes termed the *Othello syndrome*, progresses from minor criticism of the marital partner through suspiciousness to full-blown delusions involving thoughts of the spouse's infidelity. Psychotic jealousy may lead to acts of violence against the spouse or lover, who is the subject of the delusional system. Conjugal paranoia should be distinguished from pathologic jealousy, which occurs simply as an accompanying symptom in many disorders, including organic mental disorders, alcoholism, schizophrenia, and the affective disorders.

Erotomania, also referred to as Clerambault's syndrome, has been more often reported in women, although more recent reports seem more equally distributed. The patient develops an intense delusional belief that a man, usually older and of higher social standing, is in love with her. One pattern, considered a subset of paranoia, is characterized by the sudden onset of a delusional belief that focuses on one object and becomes fixed and chronic. The second type, a subset of schizophrenia, is characterized by an erotic delusion superimposed on other symptoms of schizophrenia. A third type is characterized by recurrent and short-lived delusions in the absence of other symptoms of schizophrenia.

☐   MMPI-2

There are fewer data in the literature on the MMPI-2 responses of DDs than there are for most other psychopathology groupings. On occasion a DD will show a spike on scale 6, with most of the other scales relatively low. This is not common, however, as the defenses usually do not allow that kind of disclosure. A moderate elevation on scale 6 along with an elevation on scale 4 is more common, reflecting the paranoid delusions and the hostility and social alienation that typically accompany them. At the same time, this suspiciousness and anger can result in a complaining attitude if the client has been forced into a diagnostic situation, and hence a higher K scale relative to other psychopathology groups, with a concomitant lower F scale, can be expected. In addition, scale 9 is usually moderately elevated.

□ ## 16 PF

Delusional individuals may skip many items, and the clinician should check for this if someone else is doing the scoring. Scale L may be elevated, although DDs are often well enough defended so that this is not the case. Q_3 is likely to be particularly high, and scales N and Q_1 are likely to be low. These scores reflect the guardedness and the integration around the delusional system that mark DDs. They are likely to be lower on scale A than their behavior would suggest, which reflects the inner guardedness not always directly manifest in their initial interpersonal contacts.

DDs are likely to be relatively low on Q_4, indicating the denial of anxiety, and low on Q_1, again indicating a conservative and guarded approach toward the world. Scores are relatively high on B because DD is a coping mechanism more common in brighter individuals. The chronic and unshakable aspects of the delusions are reflected in higher scores on scales G and E. Scale G points to the persistently moralistic nature of DDs' belief systems, and scale E points to the need for dominance that is embedded in DDs' coping strategies. DDs are likely to be relatively low on M, as reflective inner fantasy is antithetical to the use of projection and denial (Heilbrun et al., 1985).

□ ## OTHER TEST-RESPONSE PATTERNS

On the WAIS-R, DDs are likely to attain high arithmetic and picture completion scores, reflecting their hyperalertness toward the environment. They also do well on similarities and comprehension, in large part because they take a meticulous approach to these tests and are thus likely to gain 2-point answers. Their propensity toward abstraction also helps them in the similarities tests.

During the tests they are likely to be argumentative, critical, and condescending about both the purpose of the test and the actual questions used. They may even object to the examiner's writing down responses or ask to examine what has been written. On the Rorschach they are likely to attain a very high F and F+ percentage, reflecting their constriction, as well as many Dd and space responses. Unless they feel comfortable, they are likely to reject cards that the clinician is reasonably sure they could handle intellectually, and, in general, the record provided is sparse. Although they characteristically have few M and color responses, the more grandiose DDs do show M responses. Phillips and Smith (1953) suggest that any "eye" or "ear" responses, as well as any looking at the back of the cards, are indicative of a paranoid orientation. There is a concern for the symmetry in the cards, and, as in other tests, there is criticism of the test itself, particularly if the ambiguity of the Rorschach stimuli becomes threatening.

Most common on the MCMI-III is the elevated P score—at least 75 and very possibly greater than 85—because this personality type is likely to develop acute paranoid disorders; PP may be raised, depending on the extent to which the paranoid defenses allow disclosure (Choca et al., 1992). Except for the occurrence of delusions, paranoids are generally cognitively intact, so scores less than 75 on SS should occur. Elevations on scale 6A commonly occur, indicating an aggressive component of paranoia and possible acting-out. Elevations on 5 are rather common, as paranoid features are present in the narcissist; variable scores on 7 occur, depending on the degree of obsessive-compulsive features. Patrick (1988) found the MCMI to be more effective than the MMPI in assessing paranoid disorders.

☐   TREATMENT OPTIONS

DDs will typically undergo treatment only when coerced by possible legal sanctions or the threat of the loss of a relationship. They are inclined to be condescending and only make a pretense of interest, at least at first.

Since DD is marked by a well-integrated system of personality functioning, albeit based on bizarre premises (Oltmanns and Maher, 1988), intrusive techniques are likely to backfire and further alienate the client from the treatment process. It is hoped that consistent contact in psychotherapy will lead to a development of some minimal trust in the relationship. This trust gives DDs a much needed feedback resource, a person with whom they might test out the adequacy of their delusional system.

The therapist must accept and empathize with the DD and yet not lose integrity as a therapist by participating in the delusional system. For example, the therapist may note correlates between his or her own life and the client's, which gives the client a potential new frame of reference as well as a new model for coping with vulnerability and fear. Humor, notably absent in many DDs, can be modeled, as can other cognitive coping systems.

As DDs move away from their delusional systems, a variety of cognitive retraining procedures can be brought into play. The clinician might also consider group therapy; however, the transition from individual to group therapy is particularly tricky for DDs. If it can be accomplished, an even greater potential for consensual feedback, so lacking for most DDs, is then available.

■   Shared Psychotic Disorder (297.3)

The Shared Psychotic Disorder has traditionally been termed *folie à deux* ("the madness of two"), and traditionally recognized both the person who was originally paranoid in some form and the receiver who passively incorporates the paranoid beliefs into his or her own system. The DSM-IV recognizes this diagnosis as only appropriate for the receiver, who typically is in an intimate relationship with the dominant individual and has a history of being psychologically dependent on the controlling person. The DSM-IV also requires that the delusion be similar to that of the sender. Since the disturbed ideation of the receiver is likely to dissipate if the relationship is broken (Oltmanns and Maher, 1988), the paranoid elements are not the dominant focus of the personality. The need for affiliative dependency is a primary factor, usually in conjunction with passive-aggressive hostility that is expressed through the channel of the shared psychotic belief system.

☐ ## MMPI-2

The receiver is typically very defensive about the delusional beliefs and in one sense wishes to manifest them to gain the approval of the dominant other. Thus, a raised score on scale 6 is likely. Several questions on L tap a willingness to trust others, so the receiver's dependency keeps the L scale from being extremely high.

Interestingly, depression is common here, as are psychopathic components; hence, scales 2 and 4 are likely to be raised. Males who are receivers are higher on scale 5 than other paranoids, whereas females are lower on scale 5. Scale 7 is also likely to be moderately raised, as is scale 8.

☐ ## 16 PF

Since these individuals are fairly open about their delusional beliefs, they score high on L, and the submissiveness is reflected in lower scale E and H scores. They are also, for the same reason, relatively higher on I and N. They are not likely to show as high a Q_3 score as other paranoid individuals, as their personality integration derives from the other person rather than from their own personality. They are also not likely to be as bright as other paranoids; hence, B should be lower.

☐ ## OTHER TEST-RESPONSE PATTERNS

On the MCMI-III the features of the paranoid profile are present. While elevated 5 and 6A are likely in the dominating member of the pair, elevations on 3 and 4 would be the most prominent patterns in the dependent member of the pair.

☐ ## TREATMENT OPTIONS

The sender, the dominant individual in the shared psychotic disorder, often manifests classic paranoia and is thus now diagnosed as having a delusional (paranoid) disorder; the reader is referred to the previous section for the modes of treating this pattern. The first issue for the shared psychotic system is to separate the parties, either by hospitalization or some other means. At this point the paranoid elements of the receiver are likely to dissipate since they are heavily based on the dependent relationship with the dominant personality. Cognitive retraining procedures and assertive therapy for the dependency are especially appropriate. A group-therapy experience can give the person the much needed personality support and at the same time provide access for modeling new and more appropriate belief systems.

CHAPTER 4

Mood (Affective) Disorders

■ **Overall Concepts**

The mood disorders have always been a common problem, but appear especially so in modern society (Cohen, 1994; Riedlinger and Riedlinger, 1994; Keller and Baker, 1992). In DSM-IV the focus is on two major subcategories: bipolar disorders and depressive disorders. It is important to note that DSM-IV provides for a diagnosis of mania without some evidence of depression, in contrast to DSM-III-R, wherein it was assumed that such a pattern occurs very rarely, if at all. The DSM-IV offers a somewhat mind-numbing array of options for subcategorizations for Major Depressive Disorder and Bipolar Disorder (Types I and II). Also available is the diagnosis of Cyclothymic Disorder (301.13), Dysthymic Disorder (300.4), Medical Disorder Due to a Medical Condition (293.83), and Substance-Induced Mood Disorder (code specified by the substance). Most mood disorders can be specified by "Cross-Sectional Symptom Features," that is, "Melancholic," "With Atypical Features," or "With Catatonic Features," as well as with such "Course Specifiers" as "With Seasonal Pattern" and "With Postpartum Onset."

□ TREATMENT OPTIONS

Treatment of the mood disorders depends on which affect is predominately manifested, mania or depression. When it is mania, the primary treatment of choice has been lithium therapy (Nathan et al., 1995; Goodwin and Jamison, 1990). If this is not successful, others have used some of the antipsychotic medications, which can at least suppress the behavior. ECT has also been used, but this is only reasonable as a last resort. When the quality of the manic episode shifts toward irritability and suspiciousness, appropriate techniques for the paranoid disorders can be considered (see Chapter 3).

A wide variety of treatments have been useful for depression, yet depression still remains a pervasive problem for our society. Classic treatment wisdom advises the use of chemotherapy and/or ECT. The problems with chemotherapy are the significant side effects, the further disruption of any sense the depressives might have that they can control their destinies, the fact that they do not work in all cases (although they do in the majority of them), the delay in action of often up to two weeks, and the fact that drugs only work to improve the activity spectrum and not the interpersonal dimension (Chorney et al., 1995).

ECT has been recommended where immediate disruption of the depression response is required, especially when suicide is a possibility. ECT is appropriate for the severe psychotic depressions (especially with melancholic features); however, the treater must consider the cost-benefit issues of short- and long-term organic dysfunction as a result of the ECT and the possible exaggeration of learned helplessness through the use of such a coercive treatment (many theories of depression emphasize learned helplessness as a generic factor).

Every effort should be made to minimize consequent cognitive deficits: unilateral electrode placement, use of more widely spaced treatments with only one seizure per session, lower electrical dosages, brief-pulse rather than sine-wave stimuli forms, lower pre-treatment barbiturate dosages, and avoidance of concomitant psychotropics (Michels and Marzuk, 1993). Although a number of studies report no detrimental long-term effects from ECT, many such studies contain methodological flaws. Depending on various factors, the use over time of ECT can result in impaired judgment and insight, shallow emotional reactions, confusion, and global disruption of intellectual functioning, apparently resulting from electrical insult to the brain.

Existential therapies are useful where the central quality of the depression is apathy rather than psychomotor retardation. Also, the cognitive behavior therapies have been specifically helpful throughout the range of depressive disorders. Burrows (1992) recommends this follow-up treatment, after remission, if there has been either more than one severe episode or several minor episodes: use of a tricyclic antidepressant or lithium, at least a single dose at night; at least two contact visits a month; and a review of medication after a two year euthymic period. The reader is referred to the individual sections in this syndrome grouping for further elaboration.

Manic Episode

Mania has been described since ancient times (Cohen, 1994). Hippocrates accurately noted many of the symptoms but attributed manic behavior to an excess of yellow bile. While depression is a common affective disorder, mania is not; it accounts for only about 4% of psychiatric hospital admissions. Its incidence, however, appears to be increasing in the United States. A possible explanation for this increase is that there is now a reasonably effective and straightforward cure for mania, while in the past it was considered very difficult to treat (Goodwin and Jamison, 1990), so clinicians may be more amenable to putting borderline cases into a category that now has a better prognosis.

While clear manic episodes are more often evident in adulthood, adolescent manics are very prone to relapse and reoccurrence, especially upon lithium discontinuance.

Throughout the literature, three classic-cardinal features of the manic phase have been described: (1) hyperactive motor behavior, (2) labile euphoria and/or irritability, and (3) flight of ideas.

Four important behavioral variables are useful in making a differential diagnosis between severe manic episodes, schizoaffective disorder, and a more emotionally labile form of schizophrenia. First, while all three categories are distractible, schizoaffectives and schizophrenics are primarily distracted by internal thoughts and ruminations, whereas manics are distracted by the external stimuli that often go unnoticed by others. Second, schizoaffectives and schizophrenics during an active phase tend to avoid any true relationships with others, whereas the manic is usually profoundly open to contact with other people (Mester, 1986). Third, another useful distinction between mania and schizophrenia involves language organization. Although both manics and schizophrenics may exhibit thought disorder, the incoherence in manic speech is due to shifts from one coherent discourse structure to another, while the ability of schizophrenics to construct any discourse structure is different (Feinberg and McIlvried, 1991). Fourth, while the thought problems of schizophrenics are marked by disorganization, confusion, and peculiar words or phrases, the thought problems of manics are marked by odd combinations denoted by playfulness, flippancy, and humor (Solovay et al., 1987). Additionally, supersensitivity to light (noted, for example, by a marked reduction in plasma melatonin levels upon exposure to light at night) has been found to be a marker for manic reactions (Lewy, 1993). Disturbance in the epinephrine-norepinephrine balance is common, pointing to a disruption in the adrenal medulla as a likely marker (Swann et al., 1991). Persons with right frontal or diencephalic strokes or hyperthyroidism often show mania.

Positron-emission tomography (PET) is a radiological technique that determines patterns of glucose metabolism in the brain. These patterns can be abnormal for both manics and schizophrenics and yet still differ from each other. Schizophrenics, especially schizophrenics of low competence, show decreased glucose metabolism in the frontal cortex; manics in the midst of an attack show increased glucose activity in the right temporal region. There are some drawbacks to this diagnostic technique. First, there is little evidence that PET can make that differentiation with any consistency when the behavior patterns are somewhat similar. PET is also expensive and requires the introduction of a catheter into a blood vessel, a small but clear risk. In addition, a radioactive substance is introduced into the brain, and the long-term risks of such a procedure are not yet known.

☐ DSM-IV

To earn the DSM-IV appellation (i.e., not a diagnosis itself, but required for other diagnoses) of Manic Episode, it is required that the behavior (persistently or abnormally elevated expansive or irritable mood) generates hospitalization or at least last for a week, the behavior generates some impairment, it is not due to a substance, and there are at least three (or four if the mood is irritable) of the following: (1) inflated self-esteem or grandiosity; (2) lessened need for sleep; (3) increased talkativeness or feeling of pressure to be so; (4) flight of ideas or reports that thoughts are racing; (5) distractibility; (6) increased goal-directed activity, or psychomotor agitation; (7) excessive involvement in potentially costly activities, that is, from a personal cost-benefit perspective, as in sexual or financial risk-taking. The diagnosis is complicated by the alternately available appellation of Hypomanic Episode, which has exactly the same requirements, except for the duration issue; in hypomanic episode the duration is "throughout at least four days." There are then eight different Bipolar Disorder diagnoses, depending upon number and sequencing of types of episode (depressed, manic, hypomanic). Rapid cycling is a valid course modifier for bipolar disorder; the rapid-cycling group contains more women and more persons from higher social classes, yet does not appear strongly related to family history (Bauer et al., 1994). It does predict a poorer prognosis.

MMPI-2

It is often difficult to get a true manic who is in the throes of an active episode to produce an adequate MMPI-2. But if you do, a high 9 scale and elevated scores on 6 and 8 and usually 4 are predominant (Graham, 1993). A very low 2 scale may indicate the manic component of a cyclothymic process. Winters et al. (1981) found the 9-6 code discriminated manics from schizophrenics effectively. Scales 3 and 0 are usually elevated in manics, and scale 2 is low, except in the depressive phase of bipolar disorders (Silver et al., 1981). The 6 scale is particularly related to the irritability factor. Individuals who are not irritable but are primarily euphoric usually do not score high on the 6 scale or even on the 4 scale. Very irritable manics will occasionally have their highest elevations on scales 3 and 4, with lesser elevations on scales 6, 8, and 9. To the degree that there is an attempt to control tension and anxiety, scale 7 is higher. Severity is related to the F scale: The higher it is, the more likely the individual will manifest a psychotic level of disorder. In moderate-level manics the F scale may be lower with the K scale raised, reflecting a denial of psychopathology.

16 PF

Manics score high on scales F and H and low on N. This results from their high activity levels, combined with a lack of insight about the reactions they engender in others. They also tend to be high on scales A and E.

To the degree they are euphoric, manics are a bit higher on A relative to E and lower on L, whereas they tend to be opposite to the degree they are irritable. Their high level of tense and driven behavior is reflected in a low Q_3 scale, with a tendency to be moderately low on C and Q_2, while moderately high on O.

☐   OTHER TEST-RESPONSE PATTERNS

The frenetic behavior patterns that mark the manic (Goodwin and Jamison, 1990) should result in higher WAIS-R scores when speed per se is an issue, such as in digit symbol. However, the lack of allowance for feedback through checking of one's own performance results in lower scores on block design, picture arrangement, and object assembly. They may often come quite close to the required response, but in their impatience they offer an incomplete solution as the finished solution. If their manic behavior includes continuous talking, they may do well on subtests such as comprehension, vocabulary, and similarities, in which persistence can result in extra points. However, at the same time, if the mania takes the form of impatience, they would likely score low on these tests. Throughout both the WAIS-R and the Rorschach, they are likely to manifest a desire to move on to a new item or task.

This frenetic behavior should result in a number of poor W responses on the Rorschach, with simultaneous notice of details that others often ignore. Response latencies are typically very short, and there are usually a number of M responses (Wagner and Wagner, 1981). Shafer (1954) asserts that a high number of confabulation responses and/or shading responses, in combination with a high percentage of C, CF, Dd, S, and W responses, are indicative of mania, a result generally confirmed by Wagner and Heise (1981).

The emotional lability and ambivalence indicated by high scores on S and C on the MCMI-III suggest the predisposition of these persons toward development of manic episodes (Choca et al., 1992). During the period of mania an N of 85 or higher should occur. Impulsive behavior during these periods may cause increase in the likelihood of drug abuse, evidenced by a T score of 74–85. The flight of ideas and sometimes confused state of the manic may produce some elevation on SS, but when it is 75 or higher, a diagnosis of schizoaffective disorder may be warranted.

☐   TREATMENT OPTIONS

The single most recommended treatment for mania is lithium therapy; it appears to reverse the manic factor in approximately 75% of the cases treated, to an average symptom ratio of about 50%. Two to three weeks are required for maximum efficacy. However, research demonstrates that combining psychotherapy with lithium therapy is superior to the use of lithium alone (Mester, 1986). In about one-third of those cases refractory to lithium therapy, divalproex sodium is effective, again to about an average symptom recovery ratio of 50%. Also, benzodiazepenes can help restore the disrupted sleep so common to manics.

Lithium salts were originally used, but lithium carbonate is now used because it is less toxic, is chemically convenient, and contains a high percentage of lithium relative to weight. Since lithium is rapidly absorbed by the kidneys, it has to be taken in divided doses to prevent any cyclical physiological response from overwhelming the client. As a result of the need for consistently administered divided doses, education of the patient is critical. Doses must be taken on a schedule, so when a patient indicates a lack of intelligence and/or discipline, mechanisms for controlled administration of the drug are necessary.

As noted, divalproex sodium can be useful in refractory cases. Other drugs are sometimes used if lithium is ineffective, such as imipramine if there is a substantial depressive feature. Carbamazepine is a good second-line treatment, and valproic acid and clonazepam should receive third-order consideration if other drugs are ineffective. Neuroleptics may stimulate a depressive episode or lengthen the next depressive episode. Valproic acid is most useful with dysphoric mania. Tranylcypromine has also been of value.

Since manics may have elaborated some negative behavioral habits in addition to the apparent physiological disorder, behavioral training is advised in addition to the lithium. It is helpful to teach the client to consider plans thoroughly before beginning to actuate them, to follow through with them once the decision is made, and to stay with interpersonal commitments (Goodwin and Jamison, 1990).

Major Depressive Episode

As with the manic disorders, depressive disorders are divided between major depression and dysthymia (or depressive neurosis), based again on chronicity and severity (Keller and Baker, 1992). Peak occurrence is in the 20–45 age range; episodes in older people are likely to include more severe symptoms and a more precipitous onset. Predisposing factors include a family history of depression, a depressive episode in childhood (e.g., there is a 75% chance of recurrence in later life if a child has a first episode during the period of age 8–13), alcohol abuse, high negative stress, recent losses, chronic low self-esteem, and any history of chronic illness. Co-morbid anxiety or panic disorder predicts a more negative prognosis, as does melancholia (a syndrome including such symptoms as early morning awakening; more severe dysphoria in the morning; psychomotor agitation or retardation; loss of ability to experience pleasure; and, occasionally, anorexia) (Michels and Marzuk, 1993). Melancholic features are associated with a family history of depression, but also with a better response to ECT and tricyclic antidepressants. One in seven with a major depression will make a suicide attempt, and one in three will develop some form of substance dependency (Tollefson, 1993).

It's sobering to realize that in nations as separate as the United States, Taiwan, Lebanon, and New Zealand, there is evidence that each successive recent generation is growing more susceptible to depression. Of those Americans born before 1905, only 1% had experienced a major depression by age 75; of those born after 1955, 6% had suffered a significant depression by age 30. Certainly better recognition is a factor, but so is the stress of modern life. It is estimated in DSM-IV that approximately 3% of males and 6% of females have had a depressive episode sufficiently severe to require hospitalization. However, it's also clear this "gender gap" is narrowing, especially for those under the age of 40. An important aspect of the explanation for the greater incidence of depression in females is the accentuation of behavior prescribed by traditional sex-role expectations. Also, abuse early in life, other patterns of victimization, unhappy marriages, and infertility or a large number of children (especially when the latter is combined with low economic resources) are factors that predispose women to depression (Tollefson, 1993). Several other factors predict depression in women: economic deprivation, low self-esteem, a preoccupation with failure, a sense of helplessness, a pessimistic attitude toward the world, and narcissistic vulnerability.

☐   DSM-IV

If there is a single major depressive episode, the formal DSM-IV diagnosis is Major Depression, Single Episode (296.2x), whereas the occurrence of more than one is diagnosed Major Depression, Recurrent (296.3x). Both require an absence of any manic episodes.

The diagnosis of major depressive episode requires evidence of either (1) depressed mood or (2) a marked loss of interest or pleasure in most of one's usual activities for at least two weeks most of the day, nearly every day. This reaction cannot be the result of a schizophrenic or organic disorder or simple bereavement such as follows the loss of a loved one. At least five of the following (including one or both of the prior symptoms) consistently present depressive symptoms are required for the diagnosis: (1) agitated or retarded psychomotor ability, (2) significant weight loss or weight gain or loss of appetite, (3) consistent insomnia or hypersomnia, (4) fatigue or loss of energy, (5) guilt or sense of worthlessness, (6) slowed or disrupted thinking or indecisiveness nearly every day, or (7) suicide or death ideation.

A major depressive episode is delineated on the fifth digit by most of the same qualifiers as used for a manic episode—for example, "in partial remission" is between "in full remission" and "mild," but "moderate," "severe with psychotic features" and "with psychotic features" are also available. The last qualifier can also be sublabeled as to mood-congruent or mood-incongruent psychotic features. Again, severity per se is not enough to warrant a psychotic diagnosis.

☐   MMPI-2

Scale 2 is, of course, consistently elevated in chronic depressive disorders (Nelson and Cicchetti, 1991), as is the DEP (depression) content scale. In women the ANX content scale is often elevated. The 2-7/7-2 combination is commonly noted across the depressive spectrum. A concomitant high scale 4 suggests possible passive-aggressive accompaniments to the depression (Anderson and Bauer, 1985), and it has been noted by several observers that a high scale 4 in depressives correlates best with both hostility and depressive thoughts rather than with psychomotor retardation. The 3-2 and the 2-8 profiles are also indicative of possible depression (Lachar, 1974; Silver et al., 1981). As the 8 score rises, the latter profile is more likely to be schizoaffective, and such persons are likely to be agitated and have a specific suicide plan. Johnson et al. (1980) found the 2-8-7 combination to be characteristic of severe depression. Overall, Winters et al. (1981) found codes 2-7-8, 2-8, and 4-8-2 to discriminate a group of depressives from schizophrenics effectively.

In all of these situations, as scores rise on both F and 8 and scores on scale 9 become lower, the depression is proportionately more severe, there is retarded motor behavior, and the depression is prone to move into the psychotic range. Scale 9 is also an indication of avoidance patterns and correlates with the depression. In some cases a high 9 signals a frenetic counterphobic response to depression, and the 1-9 code is often a masked depression. The clinician occasionally sees a 2-0 profile, which suggests a chronic depression. Also, the profile of a high 1 and relatively low 2 scale, along with verbalizations of depression, suggests a situationally generated depression, possibly even an extended bereavement. The subtle items of scale 2 have consistently proved to be a better predictor of depression than the obvious items (Nelson and Cicchetti, 1991).

16 PF

In the marked and moderate range of the depressive episode, individuals are likely to score relatively high on scales I, L, M, O, and Q_4, particularly where there is still a degree of agitation in the depressive response. They also score high on Q_2. As the disorder moves toward a psychotic dimension, scores are higher on L, M, and O and lower on C, H, and Q_3. They revert to average on Q_2 and are now lower on A. Because of their apathy toward the environment, they also score low on B.

OTHER TEST-RESPONSE PATTERNS

There are several good rating scales—such as the Beck, Zung, and Hamilton scales—designed specifically to assess depression, each with its own strengths and weaknesses (Lambert et al., 1986), and a number of these are already in revised form. A structured interview, such as the Schedule of Affective Disorders and Schizophrenia (SADS) can be especially useful here.

On the WAIS-R the classic sign of depression has been an overall performance-scale score significantly less than the verbal-scale score, as well as generally brief responses (Swiercinsky, 1985). Depressed clients are likely to fail on WAIS-R items that they should typically be able to answer, simply because they give up on them, and they usually do poorer on the timed components of any test, including the WAIS-R. Within the performance-scale scores, picture completion is usually the highest. Within the verbal-scale scores, digit span is expected to be the lowest (Keiser and Lowy, 1980), with arithmetic also being very low, and vocabulary rather high. "I don't know" responses and general lack of persistence are common.

Depressive inpatients, in common with other inpatients, are likely to score high on MCMI-III scales 1, 2B, 3, and 8A (McCann and Suess, 1988). Both CC and D of 85 or higher should occur on the MCMI-III in most major depressive episodes, especially where there are psychotic features. The uncomfortable depressed state may be represented by some elevation on A. The intense moods and dysregulated activation of the borderline will predispose him or her to react with a depressive episode. The emptiness and dysphoria experienced by the avoidant can often escalate to a major depressive episode. Therefore, elevations between 74 and 85 are likely on scales C and 2. Overall, the MCMI-III does not appear to be as effective in assessing depression as does the MMPI-2 (Patrick, 1988).

On the Rorschach, long reaction times to the cards and the rejection of several cards are probable. Furthermore, the number of responses is usually less than twenty. The individual is often highly self-critical while responding to the Rorschach. A low percentage of good W or original responses and high F percent and a high percentage of Popular responses are common (Swiercinsky, 1985). FY or MY responses are seen as indicative of depression (Phillips and Smith, 1953), and something like a YF response would in particular suggest depression. There are typically few C and CF responses, a low number of M responses, and a low number of W or Wt responses (Wagner and Heise, 1981). Dysphoric content is common, and cloud and vista responses occasionally occur. Within the Exner system, Mason et al. (1985) found that depressives scored significantly lower than normals on Rorschach scoring criteria M, Xt%, Pop and significantly higher on DQv, Col-Shd, Sum V, Sum SP.SC. They also scored lower than normals but higher than schizophrenics on (FQw) – (fQ-), Xt%, Pop.

Analogous to the schizophrenic index, Exner (1986) has a "Depression Index." Again, it is best to avoid using a hard and fast cutoff point, but simply to use the following as helpful general indicators of depression:

Sum FV + VF + V > 0

Color Sh Blend > 0

$(3r + (2))/R < .30$

Sum FC^1 + C^{1}F + C^1 > 2

Sum MOR > 3

Figures on the Bender-Gestalt are likely to be boxed, to show a confused order, and to be drawn overly large (Rossini and Kaspar, 1987). Stories on the TAT are short and stereotyped and are often only descriptions of the cards rather than an actual story. It is difficult to carry on an inquiry in either the TAT or the Rorschach since the person may give only monosyllabic portrayals of each card. Themes of guilt, lack of success, and expiation through suffering are common. Bellak (1993) points out that cards 12BG, 14, 3BM, and 3BF may bring out the depressed feelings of a subject. Card 9GF can also bring out depressed feelings, even suicidal tendencies, as when a story involves circumstances in which the girl in the picture is made into someone who panics and runs into the sea.

☐   TREATMENT OPTIONS

Since the major depressive episode often involves a severe level of depression, possibly including psychotic components, more intrusive techniques are likely to be used (Charney et al., 1995; Burrows, 1992), at least initially. However, the techniques discussed in the next subsection (Dysthymia) are needed as well for any long-term remediation.

ECT has often been used for severe depression; it is probably one of the few syndromes for which there is good evidence of ECT's effectiveness (Valenstein, 1986). Similarly, psychosurgery has been used in which a lesion is placed in areas that control emotional response, such as the limbic system. However, any effectiveness must be balanced against the high psychological and physical costs of these techniques.

Clients usually receive six to twelve ECT treatments administered every other day. The sine-wave, or brief-pulse electric stimulus, typically ranges from a minimum of ten 2-watt seconds to several 90-watt seconds. Briefer pulse stimulus is correlated with less cognitive deficit, and the lowest stimulus for an adequate seizure response should be used. ECT is strongly contraindicated if the patient (1) shows any increased intracranial pressure; (2) shows cerebral pathology; (3) shows impaired cardiac function, especially if from an aneurysm or recent myocardial infarction; or (4) is pregnant.

Since ancient times, humans have used drugs to alleviate depression, notably alcohol and other self-medications. New medications are constantly being developed (see Chapter 15), but the two traditional major subcategories of antidepressants used in recent times are the tricyclics and the monoamine oxidase (MAO) inhibitors (see Chapter 15). Both drug classes require substantial trial-and-error adjustment on dosages (titration), and both require from several days to several weeks before any positive effects occur. Because the MAO inhibitors have more significant side effects, the tricyclics have been favored in recent years (Tollefson, 1993). The MOA inhibitors (which reduce the catabolism of neurotransmitters) are most useful with depression associated with panic, and with atypical depressions (especially if marked by mood reactivity and interpersonal avoidance). Phenelzine appears especially helpful with atypical depressives. The tricyclics (which block the uptake of neurotransmitters at the synapse) are most effective with severe depressions that have a significant endogenous component, but the rate of effectiveness is seldom better than 70%. Also, tricyclics offer a greater risk of suicide by overdose than most other antidepressants. When the tricyclics are administered to someone who actually has a bipolar disorder in a depressive phase, there is a very real danger of stimulating a manic episode. Where weight loss is also clinically desired and agitation and destructive ruminations are not prominent, fluoxetine or bupropion can be useful. Paroxetine and sertraline can be useful, especially if there is an absence of melancholic symptoms. Some depressives have responded well to high doses (3,000 mg) at bedtime of L-tryptophan, a naturally occurring amino acid. A dose of nicotinic acid needs to be taken at the same time to keep the liver from destroying all of the L-tryptophan. Also, in a study in which imipramine and lithium were used, Prien and Klupfer (1986) found that drug therapy should be maintained for at least sixteen to twenty weeks following a cessation of significant depressive symptoms. Additionally, even mild symptoms during the period indicated that the depression had not run its course and that continued drug therapy was essential to contribute to the absence of relapse in the treatment group.

There is some evidence that a certain small subgroup of major depressives may have a disturbance in rapid eye movement (REM) sleep patterns. This specific pattern is marked by an abnormal temporal distribution of REM sleep. This inadequate capacity to sustain REM sleep tends to worsen with age in all individuals and may explain why sleep problems are much more common as persons age. Vogel and his colleagues (1980) treated this subgroup of depressives by depriving them of REM sleep for short periods of time and found that this significantly decreased their depression. It is interesting that depressed patients who were responsive to this technique were unresponsive to the tricyclic antidepressives, though in a comparison among studies, REM sleep deprivation and drug treatments were equally effective. However, it takes about three weeks for the REM sleep deprivation technique to bring about improvement. When specific brain dysfunction has caused depression, the disease is more likely to be found in the left frontal region.

Any of the intrusive techniques have a number of risks, which, of course, can be balanced by gains in controlling the depression and in preventing any suicide behaviors. Yet it is most important that they be implemented in an overall treatment that includes a variety of techniques designed to control the depression psychologically and to upgrade the skills needed to prevent future depression (Chiles and Strosahl, 1995).

Table 4.1, adapted from Tollefson (1993), provides a guideline to consensus drug treatments for depression, depending upon symptom pattern.

TABLE 4.1   Consensus Drug Treatments for Depression

TARGET SYMPTOMS	AGENT(S)
Agitation	BDZ + AD/buspirone + AD
Psychotic	NL + AD/amoxapine/ECT
Obsessive	Fluozetine/clomipramine
Retarded	Bupropion
Bipolar (rapid cycler)	Carbamazepine/valproate/verapamil
"Atypical"	Phenelzine/imipramine/fluoxetine
Insomnia	BDZ + AD; trazodone + other AD
Bipolar (depressed)	Lithium + AD/carbamazepine
Obesity	Bupropion/fluoxetine
Peptic ulcer	Doxepin/imipramine

AD, antidepressant; NL, neuroleptic; ECT, electroconvulsive therapy; BDZ, benzodiazepine.

■ Dysthymic Disorder (300.4)

Many of the symptoms characteristic of the depressive episode are noted here. However, they are not as severe or as common, but they are of longer duration. Evidence of depressed mood for most of the day, more days than not, for a duration of two years is required for the DSM-IV diagnosis (except for children and adolescents, where the requirement is one year and where irritability can substitute for depression), and periods of dysphoria cannot be separated by periods of normal mood of more than two months. There can be no evidence of an unequivocally diagnosable manic or hypomanic episode. Dysphoria and apathy are commonly noted, and severe impairment in social or vocational or some other life area is present. If there is a history of apparent major depressions, the prognosis is much more negative. Along with the characteristics just noted, the DSM-IV requires that at least two symptoms accompanying the depressive symptoms occur: (1) low self-esteem, (2) fatigue, (3) problems in concentration or decision making, (4) poor appetite or overeating, (5) insomnia or hypersomnia, or (6) feelings of hopelessness. If onset is prior to age 21, it is specified as Early Onset; if over age 21, Late Onset.

☐   ## MMPI-2

Since this personality profile does not show the anxiety, agitation, and possible psychotic components of major depression, a lower overall profile is expected. For example, scale 9 is not as likely to be low nor is scale 0 likely to be as high as in the depressive episode. Yet, scales F, 2, and 7 are high. If scale 4 is raised, there is reason to look for a passive-aggressive use of the depression (Anderson and Bauer, 1985). If somatization is a major factor, scale 1 should be high. The DEP content scale is usually high.

☐   ## 16 PF

Similarly, the 16 PF profile is not as extreme for dysthymia as in the depressive episode, yet the general outline is the same and is similar to the pattern for the more neurotic aspects of the depressive episode. With that stipulation, scale C is not as likely to be low, nor is Q_4 likely to be quite as high.

☐   ## OTHER TEST-RESPONSE PATTERNS

In contrast to the profile of the major depressive episode, the highest elevation on the MCMI-III is likely to occur on 2B and D, with the more severe symptomatology of CC less prominent. To the degree anxiety is present, there is an elevated A. Borderline and negativistic personalities can be susceptible to developing this disorder, so elevations on scales 8A and C are indicated. Very low scores on 7 are expected, because the restrained affectivity and conscientious self-image of the conforming personality are not compatible with the depressive affective features of the dysthymic disorder.

As noted earlier, several short scales (approximately twenty questions) have been specifically designed to measure depression and can be helpful in screening procedures and measuring outcome (Lambert et al., 1986). Three of the most commonly used have been the Zung Self-Rating Depression Scale, the Hamilton Rating Scales, and the Beck Depression Inventory. All three have been found to have adequate validity, although Lambert's data seem to favor the Zung. Others have commented, however, that the Zung Scale is too age-specific for certain groups, since normals under 19 years of age or over 65 unfortunately tend to score in the depressive range.

Performance on other tests will be similar to that of the depressive episode; though again, the clinician should temper the interpretation of these patterns with the awareness that this is less severe than major depression, with the symptoms more integrated into the ongoing personality.

TREATMENT OPTIONS

Monitoring is a worthwhile first step in any treatment of depression (Cohen, 1994). Simple self-monitoring of both mood and activity produces decreases in depressed mood, as well as some increase in self-reported participation in chosen activities. To aid in self-monitoring, it is useful to teach them to keep a daily log of their automatic thoughts, especially those that are dysfunctional—"I can never succeed to the point that (Mommy, Daddy, . . . I) will love me," "If I'm alone, I'll be unhappy," "If I become unhappy, I won't be able to stop it," and so on. The most straightforward method for uncovering automatic thoughts is to ask clients what thoughts went through their minds in response to particular events. Modeling the assessment of some of your own automatic thoughts can also be useful. Such thoughts can then be analyzed "scientifically" and/or confronted, for example, via rational-emotive techniques (Lyons and Woods, 1991).

With regard to their future outlook, depressives should understand that occasional upsurges of anxiety and depression will occur throughout their lives and that these should not be construed as indications of a return to pathology. This is an important admonition for all groups with psychopathology. In many cases, as these persons move toward a cure, they develop hope that they will never encounter any experiences similar to their past disorder. Hence, when these experiences naturally emerge, even in a minor form, there is a tendency to drop their coping patterns. Adopting a cognitive set to counteract this phenomenon is most important.

Chemotherapy is often used with dysthymia, but it is not as appropriate as it is for the more severe depressive episode (Burrows, 1992). Since learned helplessness is often a factor in dysthymia, chemotherapy, ECT, or similar treatments can easily exacerbate this component by pointing out in a direct way that patients cannot play a major role in redirecting their life situation (Cohen, 1994). Therefore, a package derived from the following psychological treatment methods is recommended.

Keeping in mind that the term *depression* derives from the Greek *Barunomenon,* meaning "weighted down" or "being burdened," the clinician can employ contingency management techniques, which can aid the client especially in developing a new self-percept less confounded by helplessness and apathy. It is initially advisable for the therapist to avoid reinforcing any of the client's depressive verbalizations. The clinician can use audiotapes of the sessions to indicate to a client how thoroughly he or she is inclined toward these verbalizations. This approach can be augmented by a contractual agreement with the client to avoid such verbalizations and instead to increase the number of positive verbalizations (Meichenbaum, 1985). Such behaviors can be consolidated by using the Premack Principle and, in addition, by training the client's family and friends to reinforce positive behaviors and verbalizations. Interpersonal-based therapies are especially important in rehabilitating the severely depressed, especially where there are issues of (1) long-term family conflicts, (2) loss issues, (3) developmental transition conflicts, or (4) social-skills disruptions or deficits.

Imagery techniques are also helpful. For example, Lazarus (1971) recommends a variation of systematic desensitization that he terms "time projection with routine reinforcement." Clients are first hypnotized, deep relaxation is induced, and then they are asked to imagine that they are in the future and are engaged in what had been previously pleasant activities. Clients are then asked to return to the present while still maintaining these positive feelings and images from the future. By continually shifting back and forth, this time-projection strategy aids depressed persons to develop more consistent present images of pleasurable activities; Lazarus indicates that this then generalizes into behavior.

Probably the most important psychological treatment methods of depression are the cognitive-behavioral techniques, derived originally from Beck (1976). Through discussion and consciousness-raising techniques, clients are taught to view their thoughts more objectively (to distance themselves from these maladaptive thoughts). Such common depressive thoughts as "I am totally worthless" are suggested as hypotheses rather than facts, a phenomenon rather than a reality. In addition, clients are taught to "decenter." Through feedback, possibly in a group, depressives learn that they are not the focal point of all events, such as a disparaging glance on the street. Implicit in all this is the need for clients to learn to validate any self-made conclusions more objectively, a behavior notably absent in depressives. The belief systems that a person lives by are then examined, since impossible standards are commonly promoted within the self-system.

Another useful cognitive-behavioral treatment for dysthymia is covert negative reinforcement, because depressed individuals often find it difficult to envision positive behaviors at all and therefore are not particularly responsive to covert positive reinforcement techniques. In covert negative reinforcement with depression, a highly aversive image is developed and is then terminated by the imagination of the performance of the desired behaviors. It is critical that the switchover of images take place as quickly as possible.

Finally, a number of lifestyle modification techniques can be used. Assertiveness training is appropriate (Wickramesekera, 1988), so that the person does not introject anger and frustration. Inducing the individual to take more frequent and more strenuous exercise helps in many cases, and, if the depression has a seasonal component, sessions of bright, incandescent light can be helpful (see the upcoming section in this chapter on SAD) (Lewy, 1993; Oren et al., 1991). Within the context of group therapy the person can contract for a series of graded tasks, all of which are increasingly pleasurable and thus likely to change the overall negative set the individual carries. Such experiences are especially therapeutic to the degree that they also increase the client's sense of mastery over events in the world.

■ Bipolar Disorder

DSM-IV introduces major changes in the diagnosis of Bipolar Disorder. Bipolar I Disorder is characterized by an occurrence of one or more Manic or Mixed episodes; Bipolar II Disorder (296.89) by the occurrence of one or more episodes that constitute a Major Depression, along with at least one episode that constitutes a Hypomanic Episode. Bipolar I Disorder is subdivided into six separate, specific DSM-IV diagnoses. Single Manic Episode (296.0x), Most Recent Episode Hypomanic (296.4x), Most Recent Episode Manic (296.4x), Most Recent Episode Mixed (296.6x), Most Recent Episode Depressed (296.5x), and Most Recent Episode Unspecified (296.7). Different specifications are available for each subdiagnosis of Bipolar I, as well as for Bipolar II. For example, for Bipolar II (the classic, severe form of "manic-depressive disorder") the most recent episode is specified, that is, Hypomanic or Depressed; if the most recent episode was a Major Depression, it is specified by Severity/Psychotic/Remission Specifiers and/or as "Chronic," "With Melancholic Features," "With Atypical Features," "With Postpartum Onset," and also with Longitudinal Course Specifiers, or as "With Seasonal Pattern," or "With Rapid Cycling."

Cycles tend to become more frequent with time in most bipolars, theoretically from behavioral sensitization and electrophysiological kindling from repeated brain stimulation; thus the value of anticonvulsants for some depressives (Michels and Marzuk, 1993). Persons who show "rapid cycling" are difficult to treat, as they respond poorly to treatment and present a higher suicide risk and more negative prognosis (Chiles and Strosahl, 1995). It often develops later in the disorder pattern. Unlike standard bipolars, rapid cyclers are more likely to have a depressive episode as a first manifestation. It is more common in women and may be associated with hormonal disruptions (especially in women), hyperthyroidism, or neurological trauma (Nathan et al., 1995).

The MMPI-2, 16 PF, and other test data patterns are generally similar to what is expected in single episodes. The reader is referred to the appropriate sections for the behavior pattern manifest at the time. Clients with bipolar affective disorder show larger average cortical-evoked potentials than do normals, who in turn are higher than schizophrenics, with this particularly so at high stimulus intensities. It has also been found that the shift from mania to depression is physiologically marked by increases in blood levels of phosphorous and calcium, as well as differences in the epinephrine-norepinephrine balance (Swann et al., 1991). A similar phenomenon has been observed when certain withdrawn depressives move toward more agitated behavior.

☐ ## TREATMENT OPTIONS

The treatment of the bipolar is directed in large measure toward the dominant affective mode at the time. Lithium therapy is used to alleviate severe mania and has occasionally been effective with the depressive component as well, though the standard chemotherapy for the depressive component is that noted in the previous section on the depressive episode. It should again be noted that administration of the tricyclic antidepressants to an individual with bipolar disorder can induce a manic episode, or even rapid cycling. As the person moves toward a better level of functioning, the psychological treatment techniques noted in the sections on manic episode and dysthymic disorder become the primary mode.

■ # Cyclothymia (301.13)

Cyclothymia is the DSM-IV term for the traditional term "cyclothymic personality." As with dysthymia, this diagnosis requires a disorder duration of two years (but not symptom-free for more than two months), and one year for children and adolescents, as well as alternating numerous hypomanic episodes and depressions that were not major depressions or clearly diagnosable manic episodes. The reader is referred to previous sections for those diagnoses as well as the concomitant patterns expected on the MMPI-2, 16 PF, MCMI-III, and other tests. This disorder has traditionally been thought to be very rare, but recent evidence suggests that it is at least moderately common, that is, 0.4% to 1% in the general population, with a 15–50% risk of such individuals later developing some form of bipolar disorder.

☐ ## TREATMENT OPTIONS

In most instances the manic phase of cyclothymia is not severe enough to warrant significant intervention. Rather, it is more like a relief stage and, at worst, requires the psychological techniques noted in treatment of the manic episode. The depressive components are appropriately treated by the techniques detailed in the section on dysthymia. The clinician should watch for the possible emergence of a classic bipolar disorder, and if the client shows any increasing pathology, lithium might be considered. Some clinicians have found the use of a diary helpful with cyclothymia. When a client keeps a diary, he or she becomes more attuned to the factors that are likely to set off the pattern.

■   ## Seasonal Affective Disorder

Seasonal Affective Disorder (SAD) is not formally included in DSM-IV as a separate disorder, but is included as a "longitudinal course specifier" that can be applied to either a diagnosis of Bipolar Disorder or Major Depressive Disorder (recurrent). However, many who work with SAD sufferers see it as a pattern that is qualitatively different than the standard mood disorders. While it may take several forms, by far the most common SAD pattern is winter depression (Oren et al., 1994), and that is what SAD will refer to herein. SAD is typically unipolar, depressed, and primarily marked by decreased energy with vegetative changes in appetite and sleep, with related (probably consequentially) negativism and lowered self–esteem. Woman are affected three to five times as often as men, and a degree of Premenstrual Dysphoric Disorder (see upcoming section) may be a comorbid symptom. Estimates are that as high as 5% of the population suffer SAD. Though referred to as "holiday blues," it is clear that SAD occurs in people in the Southern Hemisphere, where Christmas is a summer holiday. SAD does occur in children, but severity usually reaches clinical significance when SAD sufferers are in their twenties or thirties. A move to a higher latitude may set off SAD in vulnerable individuals (Lewy, 1993).

□   ## TREATMENT OPTIONS

The treatment of choice for the most common form of SAD, winter depression, is exposure to light (Oren et al., 1991, 1994). This apparently acts by affecting melatonin production and the circadian rhythm. Of course, anyone embarking on light treatment should be cleared by their ophthalmologist if there is any history or indication of eye disease.

Delivery of light can be adjusted on four parameters: intensity, wavelength, duration, and timing (Lewy, 1993). Intensity has to be bright enough to suppress nighttime melatonin production; 2500 lux is suggested. Since intensity increases as an inverse function of the square of the distance from the source of light, then the closer to the light source, the greater the effect. The light source should be positioned at a 45-degree angle to the line of sight. The client should not stare at the light, but should quickly scan the eyes across the light source two or three times a minute.

The peak wavelength is the blue-green range, around 509 nm, where rods and rhodopsin are most sensitive. The amount of infrared and ultraviolet radiation should be minimized as much as feasible. A plexiglass diffuser is recommended.

Duration is effective as a linear variable; that is, thirty minutes at 10,000 lux is equal to two hours at 2500 lux. Also, given the distance law noted above, by halving the distance from a 2500-lux light source, a 10,000-lux intensity is produced. Exposure to intensity over 10,000 lux is not recommended. A standard dosage is 2500 lux for about two hours, once a day at first, then tapered to once every other day if improvement is maintained.

Traditionally, timing of treatment was not held to be important. However, more recent findings suggest that the majority of SADs are "phase-delays" (referring to circadian rhythm delays), indicated by characteristic morning hypersomnia and clear vulnerability to shortened photoperiod exposure (Oren et al., 1994). For the phase-delays, whose circadian rhythms are cued by dawn rather than dusk, light therapy should be administered as soon as feasible upon awakening. For "phase advance" types, cued by dusk, whose sleep disruption is usually more toward morning, light therapy should be administered at night, preferably between 7 and 9 p.m. To help orient the circadian rhythms, phase-delays should avoid bright light exposure at night (e.g., in bright malls); phase-advances should minimize it in early morning (Lewy, 1993). Persons with characteristic early morning awakening and early evening fatigue ("advanced sleep-phase syndrome,") should receive light therapy before bedtime. Occasionally people will shift from one pattern to another, requiring a timing change for the light therapy.

In addition to the above, counseling toward good sleep habits (see Chapter 7) is recommended, and the amount of sleep time should be held relatively constant.

There is some indication that the oral administration of melatonin, a hormone produced by the pineal gland and available without a prescription, can produce results similar to light therapy. Melatonin production has a strong diurnal rhythm. It is released primarily and in most cases only at night, as its production shuts down when daylight reaches the eyes and is perceived by the brain, thus it is seasonally patterned. Manipulation of serotonin levels can also help SAD sufferers as the suprachiasmatic nuclei, thought to be a critical component in our "body clock," are abundantly endowed with nerve cells rich in serotonin.

Atypical Mood Disorders

The DSM-IV has provided a category labeled Bipolar Disorder NOS (296.70) and Mood Disorders NOS (296.90). These are simply residual categories in which there is clear evidence of a general pattern, though it does not exactly fit the specific diagnostic requirements of any mood disorder or the adjustment disorder with depressed mood. However, the latter category does include provision for diagnosis of "Premenstrual Dysphoric Disorder." Atypical depressions, marked primarily by mood reactivity (the capacity to respond appropriately to positive environmental stimuli) but also by fear of interpersonal rejection, hypersomnia, hyperphagia (marked by excessive eating or appetite), and/or feelings of heaviness/paralysis, are now recognized as relatively common, with age of onset often before age 20. The psychological treatments recommended for dysthymia are indicated here, and the MAOs, especially phenelzine, are often the drug treatments of first choice.

■ Schizoaffective Disorder (295.70)

This disorder was traditionally (i.e., in DSM-II) included as a subgroup under schizophrenia. It was then listed as a separate disorder in DSM-III-R, probably because of the evidence that it has several characteristics different from those disorders that were kept under the "schizophrenic" rubric. It is now again included in DSM-IV under Schizophrenia and Other Psychotic Disorders. Schizoaffective disorder is more likely than most schizophrenias to have an acute onset, and it has a generally better prognosis for avoidance of long hospitalization and for recovery to a premorbid level of functioning. In addition, it has been noticed that blood relatives of persons with the schizoaffective disorder do not have a markedly higher proportion of the same disorder than do normals, a finding different from that of schizophrenia.

☐   DSM-IV

The essential feature of this disorder is a combination of schizophrenic and affective symptoms. The DSM-IV requires an unspecified but uninterrupted period of time during which a substantial portion of the symptomatology is a mood episode (a major depressive episode marked by depressed mood, or a manic episode), concurrent with the "characteristic" Criterion A symptoms of Schizophrenia (delusions, hallucinations, disorganized speech, grossly disorganized or catatonic behavior, or "negative" symptoms); there must be a two-week period during which there are delusions or hallucinations without prominent mood symptoms, and symptoms that fulfill the criteria for a mood episode are present for a substantial portion of the total time of active or residual disorder. It is subtyped as "Bipolar" or "Depressive." This is functionally a residual category, as the clinician has usually ruled out the major depressive disorders, schizophrenia, and the schizophreniform disorder.

☐   MMPI-2

Because of the confluence of two pathological trends, the profiles in schizoaffective disorders are likely to appear quite disturbed. Johnson et al. (1980) find that a spike 8, with high scores on scales 2 and 7, is characteristic of the schizoaffective disorder, particularly when depression predominates. Another common pattern for the depressed schizoaffective is the 8-2 profile (Kelley and King, 1979c). It is probable that these individuals have considered suicide and even have a specific suicide plan. The possibility of acting out this plan is often related to the 9 scale. As the score moves up, it indicates an increase in the amount of available energy and makes actualization of the plan more likely.

If the affective component is more in the manic direction, a common profile is an 8-9/9-8, with a higher score on scale 4 as compared to the depressed schizoaffective. In both types, scale 7 is elevated, as is the F scale (although both are more elevated in the depressed type).

□ 16 PF

The 16 PF resembles the overall schizophrenic profile, but with the following qualifications. In the manic type of schizoaffective disorder, a higher A, F, and H and a lower N and Q_4 are more probable than in schizophrenia or schizoaffective, depressed type. Conversely, depressed schizoaffectives are inclined to show the reverse profile, having a fairly low F score, as well as lower scores on A, B (reflecting less attention to the task), E, H, and M. They also manifest a lower C and a higher O score, indicating more blatant distress and emotional upset.

On the other tests the typical patterns obtained by schizophrenics are likely, with the added content and style factors specific to either the manic or depressed syndrome.

□ OTHER TEST-RESPONSE PATTERNS

The characteristics of the schizophrenic and affective disorders will appear in varying combinations on the MCMI-III as well. Typically, one would expect the profile of the affective disorder that is present along with elevation above 74 on S and a higher elevation on SS. Avoidant characteristics often occur, so there may be a moderately high score on 2A.

□ TREATMENT OPTIONS

As with the bipolar disorder, the treatment in large part depends on the affective flavor of the disorder. Since it is usually depression (which has a more negative prognosis), the reader is referred to the sections on the depressive episode and the dysthymic disorder. In those rarer cases that have a manic component (where lithium combined with a neuroleptic is the treatment of choice), the reader is referred to the section on the manic episode. The section on the schizophrenic disorders is also relevant here.

Premenstrual Dysphoric Disorder

The concept of a specific syndrome related to negative mood changes premenstrually was first introduced by Frank in 1931 (Dawood, 1985). Since then, many studies have been conducted on premenstrual syndrome, but there is still much that is not known about the disorder (Aganoff and Boyle, 1994; Corney and Stanton, 1991). What is evident is that the pattern of menstrual cramps, water retention, emotional disruptions and decreased activity related to the onset of menstruation is found equally in such diverse cultures as the United States, Italy, and Bahrain. As with many syndromes, failure to agree on a definition has led various investigators to utilize different criteria, creating inconsistencies among research findings.

Traditionally termed "premenstrual syndrome," the DSM-III-R used the term "late luteal phase dysphoric disorder," but DSM-IV uses the more recognizable term of Premenstrual Dysphoric Disorder (PDD). However, this category is not an official DSM-IV diagnosis; it is included in the DSM-IV as a "criteria set" or optional diagnosis, but it may also be included as a Depressive Disorder NOS.

The DSM-IV diagnostic requirements are that at least five of the following occurred in most menstrual cycles during the past year: (1) markedly depressed mood, feelings of hopelessness, or self-deprecating thoughts; (2) marked anxiety or tension-agitation; (3) marked affective lability; (4) persistent and marked anger, irritability or interpersonal conflict; (5) lessened interest in usual activities; (6) subjective experience of difficulty concentrating; (7) lethargy or marked loss of energy; (8) appetite change or cravings or overeating; (9) insomnia or hypersomnia; (10) subjective experience of being overwhelmed or out of control; (11) other "traditional" physical symptoms, for example, bloating, breast tenderness. At least one symptom must be 1, 2, 3, or 4.

Just as importantly, these symptoms must occur during the last week of the luteal phase and be remitted within a few days after onset of the follicular phase (in nonmenstruating females, determination of these phases may require measurement of circulating reproductive hormones). Although up to 80% of women occasionally experience some symptoms of PDD, the authors of this DSM-IV category expect only about 3–5% of women to clearly fit the PDD diagnosis.

Some PDD women have been found to have personality characteristics of instability, suspicion, guilt-proneness, apprehension, tension, and self-conflict. Women with PDD commonly show problems in coping successfully with environmental stress or the added stress from internal changes. On the average, PDD sufferers were found to have significantly lower self-esteem; more negative attitudes about their bodies, their genitals, sexual intercourse, and menstruation; and the feeling of less control over the events of their lives (Corney and Stanton, 1991; Dawood, 1985). One of the more thorough reassessments of the literature suggests that the incidence of PDD is about 2–5% (Dawood, 1985), reflecting the extent to which women are seriously debilitated by the disorder. It is most common in the 30–45 year age range.

In the past, clinicians used questionnaires that focused on premenstrual symptoms to diagnose patients with PDD. However, these questionnaires are often unreliable because they depend on retrospective reporting of symptoms. Patients tend to remember the symptoms that occur near menstruation but ignore those symptoms during the intermenstruum.

The specific cause of PDD is still unknown, although numerous hypotheses have been generated, with the most popular explanations focusing on hormonal disruption. But it appears that PDD is a complex disorder comprising of several overlapping syndromes (Aganoff and Boyle, 1994; Dawood, 1985). It is likely that there is more than one specific cause in any individual case.

☐ MMPI-2

Stout and Steege (1985) administered the Minnesota Multiphasic Personality Inventory to women suffering from PDD during their non-premenstrual phase and found that almost all of them had normal profiles. The most common feature of the profiles was a low scale 5, which reflects a strong endorsement of the traditional feminine role. This is in striking contrast to the overall characteristics of that sample. Most of the women had completed college and were working outside the home. This may suggest that this group of women is particularly stressed by role conflicts related to career goals and stereotypical female values. Along with a low scale 5, a good percentage of the women had two-point codes of either 3-4 or 3-6, reflecting strong tendencies to overcontrol or repress angry feelings. Surprisingly enough, in light of all the physical symptoms experienced during the premenstrual phase, only 3 percent of the profiles met the criteria for conversion V on scales 1, 2, and 3.

As women move into their premenstrual phase and their PDD symptoms become extreme, one would expect a rise in scales 1, 2, and 3, reflecting the physical changes and symptoms: edema, weight gain, breast tenderness, headache, and depression. Scales 7 and 8 would also likely increase mildly as symptoms of anxiety, irritability, depression, and dissatisfaction increase. Scores on scale 9 should be in the moderately low range, reflecting the lethargy experienced by some women.

☐ MCMI-III

Women with PDD may show basic personality patterns of a high scale 8A & B with a possible increase on scale 3. This would reflect emotional lability, hypersensitivity to criticism, and a lower frustration tolerance. PDD women should show an average response level to the pathologic personality disorders scales C, P, and S.

On the clinical symptom scales, scale A would tend to be a bit high, reflecting feelings of restlessness, tension, and physical discomfort. Scale H would be elevated to the extent that the woman is affected by physical symptoms. Scales N and CC are likely to be mildly elevated. This may seem contradictory, but it reflects the extent to which the client experiences unstable moods, distractability, impulsiveness, and irritability, as well as depressed mood and lack of hope for the future.

☐ 16 PF

For the woman with PDD, the 16 PF profile would generally resemble a normal profile, but it might destabilize somewhat as the woman approached the premenstrual days of her cycle.

Q_4 and I are likely to be high, reflecting the frustrations and overall sensitivity and stress. A low score on C, combined with a high Q_1 and low Q_3, may indicate the extent to which the woman is suppressing anger. Scale F is likely to be lower, as well as scale H, consistent with her tendency to focus on the inner aspects of the self, more often with negative perceptions and a feeling that she is being threatened.

OTHER TEST-RESPONSE PATTERNS

If PDD women took the Rorschach during the premenstrual cycle, one would expect a higher CF + C response, emphasized by several pure C responses. There would be an elevation of An + Xy responses, a high F+%, and possibly the presence of a V response. D scores would be around the –1 or –2 range (Exner, 1986). A person with this type of profile is one who is fairly intelligent but who is unable to respond cognitively as well as usual because the affective experience is so intense.

On the TAT, women with PDD are likely to tell stories with themes of an overall depressed mood and self-deprecation, without reference to the future. They may show affective lability, overreacting affectively to the stimulus picture. The overreacting may take the form of explanations, criticisms, affectively charged descriptions, arbitrary shaping of the story, and emotional eruptions, even to the point of crying. They may also show blocking on a picture as a result of the interference of affects or of being able to describe only the mood or affective tone of the picture. There may be plots emphasizing sudden physical accidents and emotional trauma, such as the loss of husband, mother, sweetheart, job, or house by fire.

TREATMENT OPTIONS

There are almost as many treatments as there are proposed etiologies for PDD. Since the 1950s, progesterone has been used extensively on the basis that premenstrual syndrome patients have either progesterone insufficiency or a high estrogen-to-progesterone level premenstrually. Although results of well-controlled double-blind studies show that progesterone and drugs like spironolactone are seldom more effective than a placebo, all were better than no therapy at all (Dawood, 1985). Indeed, reports of improvement of up to 40% of sample are found with placebo and/or longitudinal monitoring. Other common treatments include diuretics, oral contraceptives, and vitamins A and E, with varying although not marked success.

PDD has biological, behavioral, and psychological components, and in that vein, a multidimensional biopsychosocial approach can be effective. The first step is to record daily symptoms of mood and physical well-being in order to chart out a monthly pattern. Next, the client is asked to regulate the intake of certain foods and beverages. Reduction in caffeine and nicotine can help reduce premenstrual anxiety and irritability. Women with PDD should avoid alcohol because it can facilitate depression and feelings of hopelessness. They can cut down on their salt intake to help reduce the physical symptoms of edema, weight gain, and breast tenderness, but they should not cut down their water intake (continuing to drink at least six glasses of water a day). Naturally diuretic foods, such as cucumbers, asparagus, and watermelon, can help here. Also, women with PDD should be encouraged to eat small, frequent meals, rich in protein and complex carbohydrates, in order to decrease symptoms of anxiety, irritability, and lethargy. This helps to keep blood glucose levels stable (so they should also lower the intake of refined sugar), which in turn stabilizes estrogen-linked increases in insulin production.

Another step is to engage in a daily aerobic (but not overly vigorous) exercise program (Aganoff and Boyle, 1994). Exercise cuts down the amount of body fat, which in turn reduces the amount of estrogen the body produces. It has consistently been found that women who are physically active tend to suffer less from PDD (Aganoff and Boyle, 1994; Corney and Stanton, 1991). Also, as with SAD, light therapy is effective with many PDDs. Efforts should be made to decrease stress, especially premenstrually, because stress exacerbates the symptoms of PDD. A stress-reduction program may include yoga, meditation, or relaxation exercises.

Finally, if these measures fail to alleviate the symptoms of PDD, medications may need to be prescribed, often amplified by standard treatments for depression and/or anxiety. The choice of medication should be determined by the prominent symptoms. In this regard, clinicians group PDD clients into four categories, characterized by different clusters of symptoms and thus by different therapies.

First, there are women whose main symptoms are anxiety, irritability, and mood swings. They respond best to the diuretic effects of metolazone and to magnesium and B6 supplements and sometimes progesterone suppositories. Other women with PDD experience depression, irritability, insomnia, and mental confusion and are best treated with a triamterene and benthiazide combination, or with progesterone suppositories and, in some cases, an antidepressant. A third category includes women who primarily report bloating, swelling, weight gain, headaches, and breast soreness. They may be helped by the drugs bromocriptine or spironolactone or by supplements of B6 and vitamin E. The fourth group of women is characterized by increased appetite and cravings for sweets. They respond well to the hypoglycemic diet and a B-complex supplement.

If all else fails, severe, persistent symptomatology may be relieved by surgical hysterectomy and bilateral oophorectomy, with estrogen replacement.

CHAPTER 5

Anxiety Disorders

■ Overall Concepts

This grouping of disorders is primarily a subgroup of the disorders traditionally termed "neurosis." However, the anxiety disorders in DSM-IV do not encompass such traditionally included categories as conversion reactions or dissociative reactions, which are now dealt with in separate sections. Many clients show symptoms from various diagnostic categories, so a single DSM–IV diagnosis may not communicate the complexity of their disorders. Several significant changes occur in the Anxiety Disorders category of DSM–IV. There is no attempt at subcategorization, as in DSM-III-R. The diagnostic requirements for Post-Traumatic Stress Disorder are changed considerably, and the category of Acute Stress Disorder is added.

☐ MMPI-2

The classic general signs for neurosis on the MMPI-2 are elevations on scales 1, 2, 3, and 7. In fact, scales 1, 2, and 3 are often referred to as the "neurotic triad." The neurotic disorders, of which the anxiety disorders are a traditional subclassification, have an MMPI-2 that slopes from left to right; the psychoses are expected to slope from right to left; and the character disorders tend to peak more in the middle (Ben-Porath, 1994), with emphasis on the word *tend*.

The F scale is high in the neurotic profile. If it is very high, and scales K and L are 50 T or less, the clinician should look for (1) a blatant cry for help that could point to a variety of disorders, (2) faking-bad, or (3) in a hospitalized psychiatric population, the diagnosis of confused psychotic (Gynther et al., 1973b). As a result of the relative openness about anxiety, anxiety disorder profiles show some elevation on most of the scales, with the exception of 5, 6, and 9. They are typically high on the A and ANX (anxiety) scales, and, to the degree the fear is specific, on the FRS (Fears) scale.

☐ ## 16 PF

The general profile for the anxiety disorders has higher scores on I, L, M, O, and Q_4, with a moderately high score on Q_2. In addition, one would expect scores to be lower on C, E, F, G, H, and Q_3.

Karson and O'Dell (1976) list the individual scales in their order of importance in contributing to the second-order anxiety scale derived from the 16 PF as Q_4, O, C, L, and Q_3. If very high, Q4 can additionally be interpreted as a cry for help, as it shows an r of .75 with scale 7 of the MMPI-2. Q_3 is an index of emotional lability, that is, a reflection of the ability to bind up anxiety. Scales I and M pick up an ongoing vulnerability or sensitivity to stress.

Individuals with anxiety disorders, especially males (Krug, 1980), are relatively higher on scale M than are those who suffer psychosomatic disorders. It is hypothesized that in neurotics with anxiety, the greater inclination to fantasy makes them more prone to anxiety reactions, whereas psychosomatics have a more practical and concrete cognitive process, so they are more likely to use denial (Silverman, 1976) and less prone to use fantasy behavior to cope with distress.

☐ ## OTHER TEST-RESPONSE PATTERNS

On the MCMI-III, the single most prominent indicator, in most cases, of the presence of an anxiety disorder is the highest elevation on A (Choca et al., 1992). Because features of somatic disorders and depression are often involved, scales D and H frequently lie in the 75+ range. Personality types indicated by elevated scales on 2A&B, 8A, 8B, C, and S are subject to anxiety experiences that may develop into anxiety disorders. Scale 7 is negatively correlated with the overt experience of anxiety. To the extent to which alcohol is used to cope with chronic anxiety, high scores on B occur.

Impaired concentration from high anxiety would likely result in lower scores on arithmetic and digit span on the WAIS-R. In addition, as a result of anxiety and its accompanying inefficiency, lowered performance scores in general could be expected. In particular, awkwardness and a lack of orderly checking could lead to unexpected mistakes on object assembly and block design. This anxiety may also result in surprising errors in the early part of the information subscale.

A classic sign on the Rorschach of high anxiety and the inability to cope with it is extreme (both ways) reaction time to the cards. Color shock, or the inability to integrate and respond appropriately to the color cards, is also commonly noted as a sign of anxiety or neurosis (Exner, 1986). The novelist Joseph Heller (1974, p. 435) described the phenomenon of color shock well:

Some look like Van Dykes, and these I'm tempted to tug. Others have sideburns and shock me a moment like card number eight on the Rorschach test again. I was struck speechless when that damned color shock card appeared. I was stupefied.

Poorly integrated W responses, a form level below the acceptable range of 65–80%, and vague responses—such as clouds, smoke, maps—are also a common result of high anxiety. Shafer (1954) states that several C or P responses, a moderately low F percentage, and oral-threat-content responses (such as wolves) are indicative of potential for anxiety moving into panic. Shading, tiny figures, and fine and/or broken lines are traditionally thought to connote anxiety in figure drawings (Oster and Gould, 1987).

TREATMENT OPTIONS

A wide variety of techniques are used in the treatment of the anxiety disorders (Taylor, 1995; Bedrosian and Bozicas, 1994; Wolfe and Maser, 1994; Hecker and Thorpe, 1992; Hoehn-Saric and McLeod, 1988). Besides the standard reasons, treatment is critical to reduce the heretofore unrealized high rate of suicide, which is almost as high in anxiety-disorder clients as in those with depression (Allgulander and Lavonri, 1991). A combination of anxiety management, cognitive retraining, and social-skills training is often indicated. Related possible options include relaxation training, systematic desensitization, implosive therapy techniques, chemotherapy, and covert conditioning techniques. They aid in the avoidance of anxiety-generating situations and facilitate the ultimately critical variable in the treatment of the anxiety disorders: helping clients to confront the sources of their fears (Lyons and Woods, 1991). To the degree that the client is highly labile and physiologically reactive, the anxiety-lessening techniques, such as relaxation training, are useful; if that is not as strong a factor, an emphasis on skills training may be more productive (Cattell, 1986). Stress-inoculation training and/or cognitive reframing are also effective and have been proved to be superior to chemotherapy, if you consider the issue of side effects (Hecker and Thorpe, 1992). Whenever feasible and potentially useful, a spouse or significant other can be a helpful therapist assistant (Bedrosian and Bozicas, 1994) for such techniques as monitoring, re-education, cognitive reframing, and in vivo exposure. When these techniques are used efficiently, compliance and effectiveness are markedly enhanced.

The following is a list of cognitive distortions that are particularly common in anxious clients and tend to amplify their anxiety:

1. Catastrophizing. Anxious clients tend to dwell on the most extreme negative consequences conceivable, assuming that a situation in which there is any possibility of harm constitutes a highly probable danger. Agoraphobics expect disaster as the consequence of their own internal experience of anxiety or panic attacks.

2. Personalization. Anxious individuals often react as though external events are personally relevant and are indications of a potential danger to him or her.

3. Magnification and minimization. When anxious, individuals tend to focus on signs of danger or potential threat to the exclusion of other aspects of

the situation. Thus the anxious client tends to emphasize any aspects of a situation that might be seen as dangerous and minimize or ignore the non-threatening or rescue factors in a situation.

4. Selective abstraction. The anxious person often focuses on the threatening elements of a situation and ignores the context.

5. Arbitrary inference. The anxious client frequently jumps to dire conclusions on the basis of little or no data. A client may assume that any unusual feeling in the body must be a heart attack or that any turbulence means the airplane will crash.

6. Overgeneralization. The client may view a time-limited situation as lasting forever (for example, a panic attack will never end), may assume that because a particular problem has occurred previously it is bound to reoccur frequently or may assume that if he or she had any difficulty in a particular situation that shows that the situation is dangerous.

■ ## Panic Disorder

The panic disorder, suffered by about 1.5–3.5% of adults, is primarily denoted by recurrent anxiety attacks and nervousness that the individual recognizes as panic. The person typically experiences anticipatory anxiety, an initial period of often intense apprehension, and the thrust of anxiety accompanied by autonomic symptoms and discharge. Occasionally these attacks may last for hours, although attacks are typically for a period of about fifteen minutes during which the person literally experiences terror (Hoehn-Saric and McLeod, 1988). They present a high suicide risk (Chiles and Strosahl, 1995). About one-third to one-half of such individuals develop agoraphobic patterns. The disorder seldom first emerges after age 45 or before age 14, and modal ages of onset are late adolescence or the mid–thirties. Genetic factors play a part, possibly coded on chromosome 16, position Q22.

The disorder is recurrent and episodic; in at least 50% of these cases the course is chronic (Keller and Baker, 1992). Also, in approximately 50% of cases, the onset is gradual, almost with subpanic attacks, rather than being marked by an initial full-blown panic attack. The panic attacks are clearly separate incidents, and the anxiety experience is not a response to a phobic stimulus or to any event that is very dangerous in reality. Also, unlike the avoidance patterns noted in the phobias, panic disorder focuses more on the experience of terror and the temporary physiological discharge symptoms, such as cold sweats or hyperventilation. The terror experiences are not unlike severe free-floating anxiety, an experience of anxiety with the inability to specify any source or reason for the anxiety, combined with discomfort anxiety, the fear of being overwhelmed by the experience of anxiety (Walker et al., 1991). Depression, hypochondriasis, and somatization are common comorbid disorders. This is not surprising since panic disorder most resembles depression at the neurotransmitter level. Noradrenergic dysregulation is involved, and accumulating evidence suggests the locus coeruleus and pontine nucleus as the anatomical substrate of panic disorder (Michels and Marzuk, 1993).

☐   ## DSM-IV

The DSM-IV offers the specific diagnoses of Panic Disorder With Agoraphobia (300.21) or Without Agoraphobia (300.01). To diagnose either type of panic disorder the DSM-IV requires (1) recurrent unexpected panic attacks and (2) at least one of these attacks being followed by at least a month of one or more of (a) persistent anticipatory concern about attacks, (b) worry about implications or consequences of having an attack, or (c) a resultant significant change in behavior.

In order to diagnose a panic "attack," the DSM-IV requires the fear-discomfort and presence of at least four of the following symptoms during most of the attacks: (1) palpitations, pounding heart, or accelerated heart rate; (2) chest discomfort; (3) choking sensations; (4) feeling faint or dizzy; (5) feelings of unreality or depersonalization; (6) paresthesia (numbness or tingling); (7) hot or cold flashes; (8) sweating; (9) shaking or trembling; (10) nausea or abdominal distress; (11) fear of dying; or (12) fear of going crazy or losing control.

To complete the diagnosis of Panic Disorder Without Agoraphobia, one has to establish an absence of agoraphobia and evidence the panic attacks are not substance-generated or better accounted for via another diagnosis, for example, PTSD (a reaction to a severe stressor), Obsessive Compulsive Disorder, or Social Phobia.

To cope with these panic attacks, some individuals respond to the anticipatory fear of helplessness by becoming increasingly reluctant to leave the comfort and familiarity of home. If this pattern crystalizes, the diagnosis will likely change to agoraphobia with a panic attack. To complete the diagnosis of Panic Disorder with Agoraphobia, one has to again establish that the panic attacks are not accounted for by another diagnosis and establish the presence of agoraphobia (which is abstractly rather than operationally defined in DSM-IV—see following discussion of Agoraphobia). With this disorder it is important to rule out physical disorders such as hypoglycemia and hyperthyroidism.

☐   ## MMPI-2

A common MMPI-2 pattern for the anxiety neurosis—particularly where the emphasis is on anxiety, such as in the panic disorder and the generalized anxiety disorder—is a 2-8 code, with high scores on 7, 3, 1, and 4, in that order (Johnson et al., 1980). As such individuals move toward chronicity, they show profiles similar to agoraphobics (see the preceding section). One fairly rare MMPI–2 profile, the 3-9/9-3 pattern, has been characterized as typical of free-floating anxiety. As such, it would predict this disorder, as well as generalized anxiety disorder.

The 1-3-7 profile has been characterized as showing high anxiety, passive dependency, and proneness to develop psychophysiological disturbance. Hence, it is possible for this profile to show up in a panic disorder. Scale 7 is likely to be consistently elevated in this profile, as well as scales 1 and 3, whether or not there is a primary elevation on other scales. In some individuals an accompanying high scale 2 reflects a feeling of loss of control and a sense of hopelessness. As these feelings increase, 2-3/3-2 or 1-3/3-1 profiles are likely. They tend to be high on the A and ANX anxiety scales.

16 PF

The 16 PF profile of the panic disorder is similar to the standard profile for the anxiety disorders: high scores on I, L, M, O, and Q_4; a moderately high Q_2; and low scores on C, E, F, G, H, and Q_3. Since the Q_4 score is the quintessential measure of anxiety, it should be particularly elevated here, and in that regard Q_4 shows a consistently high correlation with scale 7 on the MMPI-2. Other differences from the standard anxiety disorder profile are that scale L is not quite as high, Q_2 may be moderately low rather than moderately high, and scale G is not as low.

OTHER TEST-RESPONSE PATTERNS

High scores on A and D are expected on the MCMI-III. The autonomic arousal that occurs may produce substantial elevation on H. If these individuals become increasingly withdrawn and begin to confine themselves to avoid the possibility of panic, they may become more dependent, producing increasing elevation on 3.

TREATMENT OPTIONS

Understand that panic attack clients are especially prone to suicide attempts (Chiles and Strosahl, 1995), so consider the issues discussed in Chapter 14 on suicide potential. Since the hallmark of the panic disorder is episodic anxiety reaction accompanied by a high level of psychological tension, the development of a sense of mastery over anxiety and a controlled relaxation response is one priority (Wolfe and Maser, 1994; Keller and Baker, 1992). Progressive relaxation, autogenic training, or any other form of systematized relaxation training is helpful. Also, inhalation therapy using carbon dioxide can be effective in some cases (Wolpe, 1987). They need to be guided into mastery of techniques of anxiety interception, that is, anything that blocks their tendency to "catastrophize." This could entail learning to focus on specific details as distractors; resorting to overlearned, comforting rituals; learning to "dissect" the anxiety by focusing on an abstract rendering of the experience in some dimension (physiological or psychological or both), et cetera. These approaches can be amplified by encouraging clients to take up ancillary interests, such as meditation or yoga. They need accurate information about their nervous system, emphasizing the nonpathological nature of the "misfiring" of their nervous system, as well as confrontation of their catastrophic thinking, such as "If I panic . . . (I'll die) (they'll think I am a fool) (the pain will never end)." Interoceptive exposure (repetitive exposure to internal somatic cues) acts to mute conditioned fear responses. The therapist guides clients into inducing specific symptoms, for example, by watching horror movie clips, consuming caffeine, spinning in a chair, or breathing through a straw. This helps to desensitize the behavioral aspects of panic. Breathing training to counteract feared hyperventilation is also employed.

In the initial treatment stage it may be helpful to give clients a small prescription of tranquilizing medication to be used as needed. This helps avoid problematic side effects, only moderately intrudes on their sense of being able to handle the problem alone, and gives them a sense that control is immediate and available (Foa and Kozak, 1986). If more long-term medication is needed, alprazolam, imipramine and desipramine have been effective here, as have phenelzine, fluoxetine, the other tricyclics, and a tetracyclic (mianserin) not yet available in the United States. Unfortunately, there is a high (30–90%) rate of relapse within six to twelve months after discontinuance of these medications (Michels and Marzuk, 1993).

Treatment can be amplified by having clients work on the relaxation training in a group setting. Not only does this give them the awareness that others share this problem, but it also easily sets up a discussion of problems in a quasi–group-therapy setting. Later they are more amenable to entering actual group therapy and thus may come into closer touch with the sources of their anxieties. As they do so, techniques more appropriate for the phobias, discussed in subsequent subsections, can be brought into play so that they can confront and stay with the feared stimuli, a critical variable in obtaining a significant cure (Wickramasekera, 1988).

Agoraphobia

Agoraphobia can be first thought of as a more complex phobia. The essential marker is a severe fear of being left alone in unfamiliar circumstances or of being "stranded" in the midst of people with no help available. The ultimate fear of agoraphobics seems to be that they will be left alone, with the possibility that fear or panic will occur and overwhelm them (Wolfe and Maser, 1994). Such individuals have a very low threshold for discomfort anxiety.

Agoraphobia was not even listed in DSM-I and II. It could be hypothesized that the rapid rise in the occurrence of this disorder reflects the increasing interpersonal alienation and heightened requirements for competence in vocational and social functioning that mark our society. In addition, such factors as the rising divorce rate and alleged breakdown of the family unit, along with our increased urbanization and the high level of social and geographic mobility, make it easier than ever to experience being alone in facing change and stress.

Such pressures often first coalesce in adolescence, although they may have been preceded by attacks of separation anxiety and occurrences of school phobia in childhood (Hoehn-Saric and McLeod, 1988). Social or vocational role changes make one particularly vulnerable to this disorder. Hence, women in a traditional housewife role who are going through menopause at the same time their children are leaving home are likely to be vulnerable to this pattern. Agoraphobics are prone to become housebound and attempt to break up their anxiety by manipulating significant others. Since these defenses are seldom effective, such individuals may with time become bothersome to those around them, and consequent depression will then complicate the agoraphobia. Alcohol and other drugs may be used to dilute the anxiety, leading to an overlay pattern of addiction. Approximately 5% of the population has at some time suffered from agoraphobia; the disorder is common in both psychiatric and cardiac practices.

DSM-IV

The two specific DSM-IV diagnoses are Agoraphobia without History of Panic Attack (300.22) (see preceding discussion) and Panic Disorder with Agoraphobia (300.21). Agoraphobia is specifically defined as the avoidance (or endurance with distress) of any situation, particularly being alone, where people fear they would be embarrassed and/or could not be helped or get in touch with help in the event of a panic attack or having panic–like symptoms. These fears pervade their worlds, and, as a result, they avoid being alone in open spaces or avoid public places where help is possibly not available if there is an emergency. As a result, their normal behavior patterns and experiences are severely disrupted. Some believe this diagnosis has been overused—agoraphobia without accompanying panic is rare and may be better accounted for by other diagnoses, such as Specific Phobia, OCD, or PTSD.

MMPI-2

Agoraphobics, whether or not they experience panic attacks, should score relatively close to the modal pattern for anxiety disorders presented in the previous subsection, with high scores on the A and ANX (anxiety) scales, and usually on the LSE (low self-esteem) scale. Even when the diagnosis "with panic attacks" is warranted, it is not likely that the person would be experiencing the panic at the time of testing. It would, however, suggest that the individual is not adept at binding up anxiety, so there will be some scores on the MMPI-2 and 16 PF that will differ. The 2-7/7-2 profile with scales 1 and 3 close to average is a likely one here, reflecting the high level of anxiety, the rather vague targets for the anxiety, and the absence in most cases of accompanying extensive somatic concerns or conversion reactions. Scales 4 and 9 would also be expected to be relatively low, and scale 8 would depend partially on how well the anxiety is integrated. The O scale is likely to be raised, even above the other neurotic disorders. The uncommon 7-0/0-7 profile, which reflects anxiety and inadequacy, might well suggest an agoraphobic orientation.

☐   ## 16 PF

Mlatt and Vale (1986) found that female agoraphobics who have families score significantly higher on the relaxed-tense dimension (Q_4) on the 16 PF, while male agoraphobics who are married with children score significantly higher on the dimension of tension (Q_4), warmth (A), and suspiciousness (L) and significantly lower on emotional instability (C). Generally, scales such as O and Q_4 will be high and somewhat dependent on whether or not there are panic attacks, with the latter suggesting higher scores. Slightly higher scores on scales I and L might also occur, reflecting the isolation of the individual who has developed agoraphobia. Similarly, scale A would probably be low in this disorder, but it is not commonly as low in the anxiety disorders.

☐   ## OTHER TEST-RESPONSE PATTERNS

The typical indicators of anxiety on the MCMI-III—great elevation on A and possibly on H and D—are expected here. With respect to precipitating personality styles, however, dependent types (scale 3) are more vulnerable to agoraphobic attacks.

☐   ## TREATMENT OPTIONS

Chambless (1985) points out that agoraphobia is particularly difficult to treat, with only about 20% of cases receiving significant, lasting relief. Chambless states that the agoraphobic very much needs to feel accepted, and the initial fostering of dependency is encouraged here more than with most other types of clients. As clients are eventually weaned from dependency, assertiveness training is useful to help them deal with their personality dependency and general lack of self-sufficient behaviors. The repressed feelings, often directed toward significant others, can be elicited by having the client write a diary with a focus on those feelings, and then catharsis techniques can be more systematically employed. Cognitive restructuring of the negative thoughts is also crucial to success (Hecker and Thorpe, 1992).

The tricyclic antidepressants, especially imipramine, which appear to block the reuptake of serotonin and norepinephrine by the presynaptic neurons and thus increase their concentration at the synaptic cleft, can help eliminate the panic aspects of agoraphobia with panic attacks, but they seldom do much for the agoraphobia (Hecker and Thorpe, 1992). Down-regulators of 5-HTZ receptors, such as busiprone, have proved helpful here, as has alprazolam.

The panic experience so common in agoraphobia can sometimes be effectively dealt with by implosive therapy, or flooding. Implosive therapy can be presented either in imagination or in vivo, depending on the particular case, and it is more successful if the implosion is carried out when anxiety is not muted by tranquilizing drugs. The stimuli can be presented either live or via audiotape, although therapist presence facilitates the effects in the latter condition. The client's ability to develop vivid imagery is a positive factor (Walker et al., 1991).

Even clients who are able to approach and handle the feared object after implosive therapy may still retain a basic fear sensation. This feeling typically dissipates with time; initially it can be disconcerting to the client and even to the therapist. An in vivo desensitization involving successively difficult practice tasks can be helpful here (Wolfe and Maser, 1994). As the fears of the agoraphobic become more specific, usually as the panic recedes, techniques such as relaxation training, systematic desensitization (SDT), and other behavioral control methods offer the highest chance of a successful intervention (Foa and Kozak, 1986). In certain situations the use of a neighborhood self-help group can reduce agoraphobia, and the training of the spouse to be a "coach" and supportive companion is also effective.

■ Generalized Anxiety Disorder (300.02)

Although the next consecutive listing in the DSM-IV is the Obsessive Compulsive Disorder (300.30), the Generalized Anxiety Disorder (300.02) will be discussed first because it is functionally a chronic and less cyclical version of the panic disorder. Again, as in the panic disorder, there is autonomic disturbance, although here this is evident in more chronic manifestations. Some free-floating anxiety may be present in the generalized anxiety disorder, but the essential feature is chronic autonomic hyperactivity (Rapee, 1991). Thus, it is similar to the general physiological-stress syndrome originally described by Hans Selye (1956), and its diagnostic predecessor is "anxiety neurosis," introduced by Freud.

Because it is a chronic disorder, persons have more apprehensive rumination and muscular tension than would be expected in a panic disorder. Clients with this disorder view many situations as insurmountable threats and see themselves as lacking adequate resources to cope with them. Emerging patterns of hypervigilance and self-checking may crystallize into the variety of patterns that are subsumed under the diagnosis of obsessive-compulsive disorder, which will be described next.

☐ DSM-IV

The DSM-IV requires evidence of excessive anxiety and worry as manifested in at least three symptoms out of a possible six: (1) irritability, (2) muscle tension, (3) becoming fatigued easily, (4) problems in concentration, (5) sleep disturbance, or (6) restlessness or feeling on edge or agitated. Only one symptom is required to make the diagnosis in children. The DSM-IV also requires that some symptoms of this anxiety occur more days than not during a six-month period, that the person finds it difficult to control the worry, there is some significant life area impairment, it is not caused by an organic factor and is not a part of a mood or psychotic disorder, and it is not confined to the features of another Axis I Disorder, such as PTSD, OCD, or Hypochondriosis.

☐   ### MMPI-2

The profile of this disorder parallels the general profile for the anxiety disorders. Similarly to the panic disorder, the profile will show high 2, 3, and 7 scores. The chronic autonomic hyperactivity is reflected in a relatively high 9 score, and if the person is beginning to fear loss of control about these behaviors, a rise on scale 8 is likely. A high F scale is also expected.

☐   ### 16 PF

As with the MMPI-2, the profile should resemble the modal anxiety disorder profile, with the extremes accentuated, as in the panic disorder. O and Q_4 should be very high, and H should be low.

☐   ### OTHER TEST-RESPONSE PATTERNS

The impairment and tension resulting from high anxiety should lower the digit span and arithmetic scores within the WAIS-R verbal scale scores. In general, the performance scores should be lower than the verbal scores, particularly object assembly. The rest of the notations in this section about overall anxiety disorders are also applicable.

High scores on A are expected on the MCMI-III, along with H, representing the considerable physiological symptoms that occur. For the most part, the scores here should be similar to those of anxiety disorders. Elevation on scale 2A indicates the individual's feared cognitive failure, low self-esteem, and helplessness. Scale 8A would also be high, stemming from the impatience and irritability usually present in the anxious individual. Among the pathologic personality scales, an elevated S may occur if the individual is withdrawing from other people and social situations because of not being able to handle the ensuing pressure. The interrupted sleep patterns, moodiness, and anxious worry typified by the borderline predisposes to this disorder. Combinations of elevations on A, D, and H may be expected, depending on the individual pattern of disturbance.

☐   ### TREATMENT OPTIONS

The focus in the generalized anxiety disorder is on chronic states of autonomic arousal, which to some degree is genetically based, accompanied by apprehension (Taylor, 1995; Rapee, 1991). An overall program including anxiety management and cognitive behavior modification is the treatment of choice. For example, a common central cognitive error is "probability overestimation," for example, worrying that one cannot perform a task or role adequately in spite of consistent prior data to the contrary. Relaxation and biofeedback are often central to anxiety management. The clinician is advised to use a variety of biofeedback modalities sequentially, such as electromyography (EMG), EEG, or the various measures of skin change (Schwartz, 1987). Frontal EMG training has been the most effective modality with this disorder. Concomitantly, teaching the client a controlled relaxation response is helpful (see prior section on panic disorder). Some form of meditation training may be useful, as is inhalation therapy using carbon dioxide (Wolpe, 1987).

It may be necessary to administer tranquilizing medication as needed in the initial stages, then to move quickly toward treatments that emphasize the client's increasing ability to control the response. As a client begins to gain more control over the anxiety, a treatment technique such as client-centered therapy, as originally advocated by Carl Rogers (1951), may become the primary treatment mode. The focus on empathy and warmth, combined with the initial low demand for specific discussion material, proves helpful here. When longer-term pharmacological treatment is necessary, the benzodiazepenes and buspirone are worth considering first.

If the person is under 18 and is manifesting significant anxiety, the appropriate diagnosis could be either Generalized Anxiety Disorder (which in DSM-IV now encompasses the traditional, separate diagnosis of Overanxious Disorder), or it could be Separation Anxiety Disorder (309.21). These two patterns are typically seen in childhood or early adolescence rather than in late adolescence. They predict later disorders, such as agoraphobia, the phobic disorders in general, the generalized anxiety disorder, or other similar patterns.

Separation Anxiety Disorder (309.21)

It has long been recognized that the correlation of separation anxiety and school phobia is high and in some cases may precipitate referral for treatment (Bloom-Feshbach and Bloom-Feshbach, 1987). While refusal or reluctance to go to school often accompanies separation anxiety, the term "school phobia" to describe these children is frequently misapplied. Whereas simple phobias refer to anxiety responses associated with specific stimuli, such as school, and typically involve otherwise stable personalities, disorders such as separation anxiety and agoraphobia generally suggest more deep-seated personality disorders and are characterized by an overlay of symptoms that may include generalized anxiety, depression, and somatic complaints. For the child experiencing separation anxiety, it is usually not the stimulus of school from which she or he retreats that is of clinical significance, but the attachment to parents or others that is sought (Bedrosian and Bozicas, 1994). Thus, "school phobia" is a misnomer when applied to children experiencing separation anxiety associated with refusal or reluctance to attend school; the term "school refusal" is generally more appropriate. Separation anxiety disorder commonly develops after a loss (the death of a relative or pet), after a change in the child's environment, or after a change in school or neighborhood.

A DSM-IV diagnosis of Separation Anxiety Disorder requires evidence of disturbance for four weeks, socio-interpersonal impairment, onset before age 18, and developmentally inappropriate and significant anxiety regarding separation from attachment figures, as evidenced by consistent, persistent indications of at least three of the following symptoms: (1) persistent worries that major attachment figure, such as a parent, will be harmed or will not return; (2) worries about events that could generate separation from attachment figures, such as being lost or kidnapped; (3) resultant persistent school phobia; (4) related reluctance or refusal to sleep; (5) nightmares about separation; (6) related, repeated physical symptomatology at points of potential separation; (7) recurrent, excessive distress when separated from home or attachment figures; or (8) reluctance to stay alone or at home without the major attachment figure.

School refusal is often hard to sort out from a normal response (Bloom-Feshbach and Bloom-Feshbach, 1987). Most school children's worst fear on entering kindergarten or the first grade is leaving their home and their mother. The first symptoms may include waking up in the morning with somatic complaints such as headache, stomach pain, vague "aches," or nausea, but no fever. After recurrences of these alleged illnesses, most parents become concerned. As school refusal worsens, actual symptoms may occur, including sleep disorders, disrupted peer relationships, low school achievement, and distinct school avoidance. Poor attendance in school naturally disrupts peer relationships and school achievement. A fear of being teased by other children and disapproval from the teacher for the child's ongoing absenteeism can cause the child to further refuse school. Such fears may also be expressed in nightmares and fantasies, resulting in requests for someone to sleep with him or her at night. School refusal is often preceded by episodes of separation anxiety.

TREATMENT OPTIONS

Cases of school refusal and separation anxiety provide an opportunity for treatment from a variety of theoretical perspectives, largely due to the range of clinical symptoms that arise and the nature of etiological factors (Duncan et al., 1995). From a behavioral perspective, treatments involving contingency-management programs and systematic desensitization have been found to be successful in reducing symptoms of anxiety and improving school attendance (Dangel and Polster, 1986). In SDT, the emphasis is placed on developing a relaxation response in association with a feared stimulus—school, separation from mother, riding a school bus—in an attempt to reduce and eventually eliminate fear responses, while at the same time assessing the system of overt and covert reinforcements that is maintaining the target behaviors. In a contingency-management program, reinforcers are used to reward school-approach behaviors rather than school-avoidance behaviors, and school refusal results in such punishments as time-out, loss of privileges, or extra household chores.

From a psychodynamic or developmental perspective, symptoms of separation anxiety may be seen as mechanisms of defense that function to reduce the anxiety generated from intrapsychic conflict (Bloom-Feshbach and Bloom-Feshbach, 1987). Unconscious conflicts are worked through using the therapeutic relationship as a mechanism of change, perhaps involving such techniques as psychodynamic play therapy, fantasy storytelling, and art therapy to express unconscious material indirectly.

In many cases the parent is subtly (or not so subtly) reinforcing the child's separation anxiety. It is always worthwhile to interview the parent for current stresses or concerns and to see if the parent is overreliant on the child. Using a family systems model, the structure of family relationships might be emphasized, with a goal of treatment being to restructure family boundaries and communication patterns. Attempts are made to strengthen the boundary between parent and child and to more clearly establish family roles.

■ Social Phobia (Social Anxiety Disorder) (300.23)

Social phobics are marked by anxiety about possible scrutiny of their behaviors by others, usually accompanied by clear anticipatory anxiety of panic and/or acting in a manner that will be considered shameful by others (Walker et al., 1991). As a result of the anticipatory anxiety, social phobics make strenuous efforts to avoid such situations. Social phobias are centered on such behaviors as eating or riding in public, using public lavatories, or blushing. The most common social phobia, however, is one in which the person is acutely fearful of public speaking. This often leads to a classic vicious cycle (Hecker and Thorpe, 1992). First, such persons experience anxiety about a public performance. If they then attempt to proceed in spite of the anxiety, the upset often detracts from the adequacy of the performance, possibly even causing them to twitch or shake visibly. Their prophecy that they will perform poorly and be embarrassed is then fulfilled, and future anticipatory anxiety is facilitated.

This disorder in severe form is relatively rare; it usually begins to evolve in late childhood or early adolescence, although spontaneous eruptions in adult life are not that uncommon (Hoehn-Saric and McLeod, 1988). The disorder is rarely incapacitating, but it may stunt an individual's professional and economic advancement, particularly if the person's position requires making public presentations. Social withdrawal is not characteristic of this pattern, and if this is present substantially, the diagnosis is not appropriate.

☐ DSM-IV

Social phobics show consistent avoidance of specific social situations in which they could be exposed to unfamiliar people and/or be scrutinized and as a result possibly be embarrassed or humiliated. Exposure to the feared situation generates immediate distress, which is impairing and may even become a situation-bound panic attack. There is insight that the fear is excessive or unreasonable, and feared situations are avoided or are endured with distress. Children can be diagnosed with this disorder without the recognition that the fear is inappropriate.

☐ MMPI-2

Since these individuals are not markedly disturbed in any area other than their social phobia, their MMPI-2 profiles are relatively normal. The F scale is at least mildly elevated, which reflects their concern about obtaining help. They are higher on the O scale, reflecting their problems in social functioning, although this elevation is not consistently high. They are a bit lower on the 9 scale, indicating their lowered interest in interacting with the environment, and scales 3 and 2 may be somewhat elevated.

☐   ## 16 PF

Again, there is an absence of the more extreme scores that are found in the anxiety disorders, even including the obsessive-compulsive personality. Yet, scores on scales E and H are usually low, and scores on I and Q_4 are reasonably high. Scores on scales C and L should be more toward the average than they are in the more blatantly disturbed anxiety neurotics.

☐   ## OTHER TEST-RESPONSE PATTERNS

In social phobia the related symptoms indicated by elevation on D and H are less likely to occur on the MCMI-III than in other anxiety disorders. The elevation of A may vacillate depending on the imminence of a situation in which they may be scrutinized. Social phobias are deeply ingrained in the style of the avoidant so that some elevation on 2A is probable; however, an extremely withdrawn avoidant would not receive a diagnosis of social phobia.

☐   ## TREATMENT OPTIONS

The standard anxiety-management treatments for phobias, for example, systematic desensitization, are helpful with the social phobic, especially when combined with cognitive re-education and restructuring and guided imagery (Hecker and Thorpe, 1992). Analogously, the clinician can train clients to overcome their fear in a graded-task approach, wherein they gradually develop their public presentation and social skills in front of increasingly larger groups, using video feedback as well. Role playing along with self-directed in vivo homework tasks can help to develop specific skills, such as rescuing a mistake made in front of an audience (a technique refined and made famous by Johnny Carson) that can give such clients a sense of control that allows them to go on if the anticipated and feared mistake does occur.

Social phobics who fear giving a public presentation can have anxiety reduced by being counseled on the following techniques: (1) The client should write out the speech in his or her own words, which facilitates comfort and learning; yet (2) avoid reading from a text—use index cards to order key points or phrases; (3) break tension before you give the speech—take a deep breath, drink some water, shake your hands or limbs, tell a joke to a supportive friend; (4) maintain eye contact with the audience—pick persons who seem sympathetic and who are at diverse spots in the audience and scan among them; (5) avoid using humor unless you are very comfortable with it; (6) monitor your body language to set up a more positive feedback cycle—for example, keep hands out of pockets, don't grip the lectern; (7) make sure that you feel comfortable that you will get across the message you wish—prepare a description of what will be presented, and repeat the message.

Beta blockers and certain MAO inhibitors (especially phenelzine) can be helpful (Taylor, 1995). More generalized social phobics, that is, those who are apprehensive in the face of numerous social situations, appear to be most helped by phenelzine. Those whose social phobia is more discrete, such as a fear of public speaking, do better with a beta blocker like atenol. Similarly, propranolol, as well as the standard minor tranquilizers, can at times be helpful with the anxious mood that often accompanies the social and simple phobias, although these drugs "allow a cure" rather than cure the phobia. Drugs like propranolol, however, are contraindicated when there is indication of a tendency toward asthma or congestive heart failure.

■ Specific Phobia (300.29)

Phobias in general are patterns in which chronic avoidance behavior is combined with an irrational fear of a particular object or situation. Many people experience phobias of one sort or another; for example, many people avoid extreme heights or strongly fear touching snakes. Because these types of fears can easily be controlled by environmental avoidance patterns, they are not usually disabling. A classic phobia is disproportionate, disturbing, and disabling and is marked by responses to a discrete stimulus. People with phobias may assert that their avoidance is reasonable because of the overpowering anxiety they feel, but they do not usually claim that this is rationally justified.

While phobias can develop at any age, the mean age of onset of all phobias is 11–17 years, with the modal onset occurring in early childhood. The overall prevalence rate is approximately 6%. Severe phobias are especially likely to occur in families where there was a severely traumatic precipitating event at a time of psychological vulnerability and where the family is marked by a general naiveté and/or avoidance of emotional issues. A potent, early influence, almost certainly of genetic origin, is a contributing factor; there is consistent support from twin studies as well as evidence that infants who show strong right frontal activity in their first two years in response to unfamiliar faces and other stimuli are more likely to be fearful, inhibited, and shy later in life. Simple phobias (usually concerned with the nature of the fear response) are less severe than social phobias (concerned with the negative evaluations of others), which are in turn less severe than agoraphobia (concerned with issues of personal control and raw vulnerability).

The specific phobias are those that most people commonly associate with the term: fear of bugs, snakes, or any other discrete objects or situations not included in social phobia or agoraphobia. The specific phobias are usually relatively chronic disorders, typically arising in childhood, and tend to occur more frequently among (or are more commonly reported by) women (Kleinknecht, 1991). A common traditional typology of phobia lists (1) animal-insect, (2) blood-injury, (3) choking-vomiting-fainting, and (4) situational. The DSM-IV allows the following specification of types: (1) animal; (2) natural environmental, for example, heights, water; (3) blood, injection, injury; (4) situational, for example, planes, closed spaces; and (5) other.

DSM-IV

The DSM-IV criteria for Specific Phobia requires that the person shows avoidance behavior (or distress when enduring exposure) that is distressing to the individual and interferes with some important area of functioning. The stimulus cues a marked and persistent fear that is excessive or unreasonable. Also, exposure to the feared stimulus generates an immediate anxiety response. This behavior must be in response to an irrationally feared situation or object. If there is an element of active danger in this situation or object, such as in fear of heights, the reaction must be disproportionate. It is also required that they recognize the irrational aspect of their anxiety, except when the diagnosis is applied to children.

Fear of dirt or contaminated objects may at first appear to be a simple phobia. However, such a fear is more often a sign of the complex anxieties and conflicts that suggest an obsessive-compulsive disorder.

MMPI-2

Specific phobics are more logical and rational in their thought processes, as well as less emotionally labile, than are people with more complex phobias, such as agoraphobia. As a result, their MMPI-2 profiles usually are not particularly remarkable. They do tend to be high on the FRS (fears) and PHO (phobias) content scale, especially if they are multiphobic. Both F and K may be at least mildly elevated, the F elevation reflecting the expression of concern and the K simultaneously reflecting an attempt to keep the disturbance compartmentalized as to type of phobia. Minor elevations on scales 2, 3, and 7 can be expected, reflecting the mild to moderate anxiety combined with the symptomatic depression that can be expected by the time they seek help. This also reflects the tendency toward denial and a lack of insight that is occasionally characteristic of such persons. If their controls appear to be breaking down and they are becoming concerned that panic will set in as a result of an expansion of the phobia, an elevation of scale 8 occurs, and possibly on scale 6, too.

OTHER TEST-RESPONSE PATTERNS

On the MCMI-III, the degree of elevation on A, D, and H may depend on the depth of the confrontation with the feared stimulus. Those whose prominent personality features are represented by scales 2A, 8A, C, or S may be more likely to develop phobias in that they may connect their anxieties to many aspects of life, increasing the chance that a formerly innocuous situation will become phobic.

16 PF

As with the MMPI-2, it would be extremely difficult to differentiate a specific phobic based on the 16 PF profile, since such phobics are so common and so close to normal functioning. However, following the theory that the individual has attempted to provide a focus for vague anxieties with the phobia, one would hypothesize at least some elevation on the Q_3. Yet the fact that it has not been entirely successful should lead to a mild elevation on O and Q_4. The H scale has been hypothesized as a measure of autonomic overreactivity, or what might be more broadly termed "emotional lability," and, as a result, a lower score on H would be expected.

TREATMENT OPTIONS

The classic treatment for specific phobia is systematic desensitization, and it is effective throughout the range of phobias usually seen by clinicians (Kleinknecht, 1991). The clinician can actuate this approach either in imagination or in vivo, though in vivo appears to be more effective.

The therapist can vary the desensitization procedure by including a modeling phase. In this approach the therapist first models the desirable behavioral pattern and then physically guides the person through the performance of the desired behavior (e.g., actually helping the person pick up the feared object). This can be combined with verbal support as one goes through the procedure and with covert conditioning techniques. Such treatment should be followed by opportunities to be exposed to the feared situation, along with "emotional education" and help in rehabilitating deficient social skills (Taylor, 1995).

For those clients who are not responsive to SDT, implosive therapy, or other cognitive-behavioral interventions, the controversial technique of aversion relief, pioneered by L. Solyom, can be effective. Specific phobics who have obsessive or hysteric trends benefit more from this procedure. An application of aversion relief would be to ask the client to tape record organized narratives of past and potential phobic experiences in the first person, present tense. The tape is then played back to the client through earphones, and lapses of silence, approximately twenty seconds in duration, interrupt the narrative at the appropriate juncture and are followed by electric shock. The tape then resumes immediately after the cessation of the electric shock (see Solyom, in Goldstein and Stein, 1976).

Beta blockers and phenelzine (an MAO inhibitor) can be helpful with refractory cases. As noted in the prior section on social phobia, propranolol can reduce some of the accompanying anxious mood, though it does not cure the phobia. Propranolol is contraindicated where there is any evidence of asthma or congestive heart failure.

Obsessive-Compulsive Disorder (300.30)

Although the obsessive-compulsive disorder (OCD) is listed as one of the anxiety disorders in the DSM-IV, the direct experience of the anxiety is not as evident as in the other anxiety disorders (van Oppen et al., 1995; Steketee, 1993). OCD patterns are seen by the person performing them as irrational and ego-alien, yet there are usually no panic experiences or sudden upsurges of anxiety on encountering the anxiety-arousing stimuli or mental images. At least initially, the person attempts to resist the obsession or compulsion (Pato et al., 1991).

OCD is an excellent transition category to the somatoform disorders. These latter disorders were traditionally included in the term *neurosis*, but anxiety is often not apparent in them, just as it is also not so obvious in OCD. The ego-alien quality is what discriminates the OCD from the obsessive-compulsive personality disorder (Kozak et al., 1988). In the personality disorder the compulsions are ego-syntonic (that is, they are not viewed by the person as in conflict with the essential qualities of the personality).

About 50% of OCDs show some symptoms by age 15, and by the age of 25, more than half of the treated obsessive-compulsives have already shown a clear set of symptoms. The lifetime prevalence rate of OCD is approximately 2.5%. About 25% are clear obsessionals. OCD occurs proportionately more often in middle- and upper-class individuals. This should not be surprising, especially in a society that so highly values achievement, since those with compulsive patterns are often quite efficient and productive (Steketee, 1993). OCDs are brighter on the average than individuals with the other anxiety disorders—obsessions are intellectual coping strategies for anxiety (van Oppen et al., 1995).

As Freud emphasized in his comment (1906–1908) that "sufferers from this disorder are able to keep their suffering a private matter," OCD is often hidden. As a result, it has traditionally been thought to be relatively rare, but more recent estimates suggest OCD occurs at about a 2.5% lifetime prevalence rate in the general population. Many who might be willing to report phobic anxiety would be more distressed to disclose that they think and act in ways they cannot control (Kozak et al., 1988).

The most common symptom clusters are (1) washers, (2) sinners/doubters, (3) checkers, (4) counters/organizers, and (5) hoarders. The most common obsessions seen by clinicians are repetitive thoughts of contamination or of violence, scrupulosity and/or doubts about religion and one's duties, and self-doubts. The most common compulsions include checking behaviors, repetitive acts, and handwashing. OCD does not include compulsions to perform behaviors that are inherently pleasurable, such as alcohol indulgence or overeating. A person may not be able to control these latter behavior patterns, but they are not ego-alien. While they do not want the detrimental effects of their behavior (i.e., alcoholism or obesity), they do not experience inherent discomfort about eating or drinking behaviors.

DSM-IV

The DSM-IV requires evidence of either obsessions (recurrent and persistent thoughts, images or impulses are experienced at some point as inappropriate and intrusive; they absorb at least one hour a day; cause distress; they are not just an excessive response to real-life issues; there are attempts to resist; and the thoughts are recognized as one's own), or compulsions (repetitive behaviors that are somehow a product of an obsessional pattern, accompanied by behaviors designed to change the situation and that these behaviors are not realistic for such an endeavor). The obsessions or compulsions must then be recognized as excessive or unreasonable, and the pattern is not explained within another Axis I disorder or substance abuse. In addition, the person must be distressed or impaired in everyday life and recognize the irrationality of the behaviors (although the DSM–IV allows the specification of a "Poor Insight Type" if there is little insight in the current episode). OCD is often chronic and accompanied by some disruption in personal functioning. The prognosis is guarded, since close to 50% will persist in some of their symptomatology, even with treatment. A common co–morbid pattern is depression, and common associated personality disorder patterns are avoidant, dependent, and histrionic.

There is also some overlap with Tourette's syndrome. However, the pattern is more focused in Tourette's syndrome and is marked by signs of restlessness such as head jerking, eye blinking, nail biting, humming, foot banging, pencil tapping, repetition of phrases (e.g., obscenities or TV commercials), grunting, throat clearing, and a short attention span. OCD traits such as inordinate, compulsive touching or the need to straighten things up are often noted. Since eye rubbing is common, Tourette sufferers often have circles under their eyes.

MMPI-2

The two common profile combinations related to the obsessive-compulsive disorder are the 7-8/8-7 and 2-7/7-2 (Lachar, 1974). The 7-8/8-7 commonly includes an intense preoccupation with inner mental processes. Inspection of relative scores on the Harris-Lingoes subscales is often very useful with these clients, both as a diagnostic tool and as fodder for the therapy hour. If a person obtains an 8-7 profile, the clinician is more likely to encounter a combination of deteriorating personality function and depression, whereas a 7-8 profile indicates some continuing struggle and in that sense is more benign. In the 2-7/7-2 profile, depression about one's functioning is a major component, and the person may have begun to show signs of social withdrawal.

It has been noted that the 2-7-8 high-point combination is a common profile in patients but rare in normals. It reflects people who are self-analytic and inclined toward catastrophic expectations and a sense of hopelessness. They require goal-directed therapy combined with emphasis on reinforcement for any achievements, with a concomitant deemphasis of their tendency toward introspection and extensive self-analysis.

The spike 7 profile is rare but suggests an obsessive-compulsive diagnosis. Such individuals show a high number of phobias and obsessions, which should be reflected on those content scales, and are close to breaking down and deteriorating into a psychotic condition. It should be noted that the scores on the 7 scale predict obsessiveness more than the compulsive aspects of the disorder. If health concerns are a central focus, they should score high on the HEA content scale.

☐ 16 PF

The modal 16 PF profile obtained by persons with an obsessive-compulsive disorder (IPAT Staff, 1963) shows high scores on I, O, and Q_4 and moderately high scores on L and M. They obtain a moderately low score on C and low scores on E, F, H, and Q_3. A comparison with the modal profile for the anxiety disorder shows that obsessive-compulsives are only moderately low on C and only moderately high on L and M, whereas persons with the anxiety disorders are high on C, L, and M. Also, persons with anxiety disorders show a low score on G and a moderately high score on Q_2, whereas obsessive-compulsives perform in the average range on these variables. This is surprising; I would expect the obsessive-compulsive to score high on Q_2, relative to anxiety neurotics. Also, we would expect obsessive-compulsives to score high on scale B because they tend to be brighter than most individuals with a diagnosis of psychopathology. Clinicians should be aware of the possibility that the IPAT sample did not tap these variables. It also is probable that obsessive-compulsives—particularly if they are still gaining a sense of control from the patterns and thus are not yet deteriorating—should score higher on Q_3 than those with most other disorders, with the possible exception of the paranoid disorders. Furthermore, one should consider the possibility that the G score will be higher than average in obsessive-compulsives.

☐ OTHER TEST-RESPONSE PATTERNS

On the MCMI-III, extreme elevations of D and H are more prominent than on A. Indeed, overt expression of anxiety may not be present at all. Yet, obsessive-compulsives are very likely to express dismay regarding the ego-alien quality of their disorder and to express their anxiety through somatic channels. Unlike the personality profiles typically associated with anxiety, elevations on C, S, 2A, and 8A are not as likely to be present in the obsessive-compulsive disorder. Rather, the controlled, conforming type is more likely to react to anxiety in an obsessive-compulsive way, very likely indicated by an elevated 7.

On the WAIS-R there is an overall higher IQ than in other disorders, reflecting the obsessive-compulsive's average to above-average intelligence (Kozak et al., 1988). Those who are primarily obsessive score higher on the overall IQ score and also have a higher verbal than performance IQ score. Self-deprecation and questioning of their performance, along with rather detailed verbalizations, are common. A meticulous approach to the block design and object assembly subtests is probable, occasionally leading to a loss of speed-bonus points but seldom resulting in inaccurate responses. Obsessive-compulsives usually do very well on vocabulary, similarities, and comprehension because of their meticulousness. At the same time, however, their inability to change "set" can sometimes penalize them on similarities. They also do well on both arithmetic and digit span (Rapaport et al., 1968). The intellectualization characteristic of the obsessive-compulsive disorder can result in a decrease in picture arrangement performance. A rather precise approach can again be expected on the Bender-Gestalt figures. The figures may be placed in a linear path, and a counting of the dots in appropriate cards is common.

On the Rorschach, expressions of doubt are expected, along with pedantic and esoteric verbalizations. Additionally, one expects a high number of responses overall, a high number of W and/or Dd, a high F+ percentage, edge details, and the likelihood of space responses. There are generally few color responses, and if color responses of poor form occur, they are thought to indicate decompensation (Shafer, 1954).

Obsessive-compulsives like to criticize the blots as well as their own responses and may express concern about the symmetry of the cards. Some surprising combinations or imagined responses (e.g., "two earthworms coming out of a rabbit's eyes" on card X) may occur. Similarly, pedantic wording, ambivalence over themes and an emphasis on details rather than story content are common on the TAT, especially if the individual is oriented toward paranoia as well. Idealistic stories and esoteric, although nonemotional, fantasies may occur.

Several questionnaires and inventories have been specifically devised to further elucidate the obsessive-compulsive patterns, for example, the Leyton Obsessional Inventory and the Maudsley Obsessional-Compulsive Inventory (Wetzler, 1989).

TREATMENT OPTIONS

Most experts recommend a combination of treatments for OCD (Taylor, 1995; Steketee, 1993; Kozak et al., 1988). A clear and consistent program of response prevention (e.g., taking all soap and towels away from a handwasher) combined with constant exposure to the eliciting stimuli to promote extinction provided in the context of a firmly and consistently demanding, yet supportive, therapy relationship is the core of an effective treatment program for the compulsive aspects of the disorder.

A dramatic example of this regimen is provided by Lazarus (1987):

We had him under 24-hour surveillance. He was not to do the circles. We even put mittens on his hands. Second, in terms of the germ phobia and the flooding, we got him to handle all of the dirty laundry in the hospital and he was not allowed to wash his hands for a week. He had to eat his food everyday without even washing his hands once. I was terrified that, with my luck, he would come down with the flu or a cold, and that would be the end of the therapy. Luck does play a great part. However, he was fine and of course he was flooded with anxiety. As for the obesity, we got everybody who was fat to sit on him, to roll him, to touch him; this was the flooding technique. Some people said to me, I hope you get a good EKG before you start these things. But the point is that sometimes these heroic methods are essential or else you are not going to get anywhere with these kinds of encrusted problems. However, if this is all you do, if breaking the web of obsessive compulsive rituals is all you do, my prediction is that relapse will be pretty rapid. But having broken through with response prevention and participant modeling and flooding, in my approach you proceed to work on the other residual problems; sensation, imagery, cognition, and personal and biological malfunctions have to be looked at as well. That is the multimodal concept. (p. 262)

As is evident, level of motivation is a critical predictor of success in such a program, so a degree of both courage and confidence is necessary (Steketee, 1993). Poor prognosis is correlated with associated major depressions, absence of rituals, and associated personality disorder diagnoses that enhance noncompliance.

The anxiety discomfort component can be handled by SDT techniques and in vivo exposure supplemented by self-instructional training and cognitive reframing (Hecker and Thorpe, 1992). This approach is effective to the degree that the individual becomes more adequate in focusing on the sources of anxiety. It is also very helpful to first reduce any depressive components before administering any full-blown treatment directed at the obsessive aspects. Thought-stopping or paradoxical-intention techniques can also work to eliminate the ritualistic behaviors and to counter the specific automatic thoughts that are unique to that individual client. Although thought stopping is especially efficient in dealing with the obsessive component, paradoxical intention (discussed in the subsection on the compulsive personality disorder) is most efficient in controlling the compulsive aspects (Seltzer, 1986). As progress occurs on these fronts, standard group therapy and/or psychotherapy can be used, as these help obsessive-compulsives get in touch with their high level of repression and suppression and at the same time help them become willing to self-disclose more easily. Of the possible adjunct chemotherapies, chlorimipramine has traditionally been viewed as the most effective.

The standard thought-stopping procedure for the obsessions asks clients to let the obsessions flow as in free association. Clients are then told that on a cue (e.g., a raised hand by the therapist), they should shout "stop!" Generalization is introduced by having clients practice this at home and to vary randomly the amount of time before vocalizing.

Thought stopping can be amplified by having clients visualize a pleasant scene immediately after saying "stop," thus furthering the relaxation and the control of the interruption sequence. In addition, moderately painful although harmless shocks can be administered by the therapist as the word *"stop"* is uttered; this significantly reinforces the effect. The clinician can add biofeedback training to increase the percentage of alpha brain rhythms, since they are antagonistic to problem solving or ruminative thought sequences (Schwartz, 1987). However, remember that obsessives are so perfectionistic, particularly early in therapy, that they fight the process, which hinders progress and results in their viewing themselves as failing.

In those cases that do not show some reasonably immediate response to psychological techniques, especially where depression is interfering with motivation, a regimen of chemotherapy, traditionally imipramine, has been found to facilitate progress. In recent years, clomipramine has been found to be effective, as well as fenfluramine, fluoxetine (ironically, often at a higher dose, 60–80 mg, than with depressives) and fluvoxamine. In contrast to the affective and anxiety disorders, the serotonin-selective uptake inhibitors are specifically appropriate for OCD. However, even effective agents often require four to ten weeks before any significant effect is noted; the effect is usually partial, they are more effective with compulsions than obsessions, and there is a high risk of rapid relapse after drug discontinuance. Psychosurgery has had some traditional acceptance as a treatment for severe obsessive-compulsive patterns, but other than an approximately 25% rate of moderate success in severe cases using stereotactic cingulotomy, sometimes in combination with subcaudate tractotomy, this has not received any consistent research support. Ironic anecdotal support comes from the report about a young Canadian (*The New York Times*, 2/25/88) whose severe phobia of germs and obsession with washing his hands disappeared after a .22-caliber slug lodged in his frontal lobe during an unsuccessful suicide attempt. The left frontal lobe is the usual target for psychosurgery for obsessive-compulsive patterns.

Post-Traumatic Stress Disorder (309.81) and Adjustment Disorder

The essence of the post-traumatic stress disorder (PTSD) is a delayed distress response pattern to an atypical and significantly traumatic event, an event such that most people would have very negative and disturbed responses. Such clients generally reexperience the stressor in intrusive thoughts and dreams, and depression and anxiety are common. Delayed disturbances in combat veterans—as from the Vietnam conflict, which was a spur to the modern conceptualization of this disorder—are often appropriately diagnosed here (Pitman and Orr, 1993; Kroll, 1993; Watson, 1990).

If the stressor is more within the normal range, with little in the way of a vivid reexperience of the trauma, but is not just bereavement; is excessive and impairing; and the symptoms don't persist six months beyond the stressor, the appropriate diagnosis is the traditional one of Adjustment Disorder. This latter diagnosis is appropriately qualified by the following terms:

With Depressed Mood (309.0)
With Anxiety (309.24)
With Mixed Disturbance of Emotions and Conduct (309.4)
With Mixed Anxiety and Depressed Mood (309.28)
With Disturbance of Conduct (309.3)
Unspecified (309.9)

Pitman and Orr (1993) point to literature that indicates an incidence rate of from 1% to 9% in the general population, from 34% to 78% in rape victims, from 3% to 37% in assault victims, and from 15% to 31% in Vietnam vets. They suggest an "r" of .65 for reliability of diagnosis under ideal conditions by trained observers.

☐   ## DSM-IV

The requirements for a DSM-IV diagnosis of PTSD are quite complex, possibly reflecting the combination of high controversy, use in the legal arena, and potential common usage of the diagnosis. The DSM-IV requires: (1) exposure to a traumatic event in which there is actual or threatened serious trauma or threat to self or others *and* there is intense fear, helplessness, or horror (or at least disorganized or agitated behavior in children); (2) the event is persistently re-experienced as evidenced by at least one of [a] recurring and intrusive distressing recollections, [b] recurrent distressing dreams, [c] acting or feeling as if the event is recurring, or [d] intense psychological distress at cues (internal or external) that symbolize or resemble the event, [e] physiological reactions; (3) persistent avoidance of stimuli associated with the event and a numbing of responsiveness as evidenced by three of these: [a] efforts to avoid related feelings or thoughts, [b] efforts to avoid related activities, places, or people, [c] inability to recall an important event component, [d] reduced participation in significant activities, [e] feelings of detachment or estrangement from others, [f] restricted affect range, [g] sense of a foreshortened psychological or physical future; (4) two persistent, subsequent-to-trauma symptoms of arousal, from [a] difficulty falling or staying asleep, [b] irritability or anger outbursts, [c] difficulty concentrating, [d] hypervigilance, [e] exaggerated startle responses. These must significantly impair the individual in some dimension and last for at least one month. The PTSD is specified as "Acute" if symptom duration is less than three months, "Chronic" if more, and is also specified as "With Delayed Onset" if onset is more than six months after the stressor.

Evidence of associated major depression episode(s), substance abuse, significant delay before seeking treatment, secondary gain, and detachment or denial patterns suggest a negative prognosis.

☐   ## DIAGNOSTIC CONSIDERATIONS

A critical predictor of a later PTSD is evidence of dissociation at the time of trauma, which may appear to onlookers to be a calm and collected response. Evidence of dissociation is in such patterns as blanking out, reporting or appearing to be "in a daze," reporting feeling as if time slowed down or watching oneself in slow motion, or any reports of feelings of unreality or depersonalization (see also Chapter 7). So, those who are at the greatest risk are at either end of the observable spectrum, that is, those who show rather immediate evidence of panic–high anxiety, and those who show little or none (which may be a process of dissociation from underlying feelings of panic). This suggests that "on-scene" evaluations have to be more in-depth and sophisticated than they have been at times.

In this same vein, PTSD can closely resemble the patterns seen in individuals with a panic disorder. A major difference is that the person with a post-traumatic stress disorder or adjustment disorder may show fewer acute signs of disruption in overall personality functioning (Hammarberg, 1992).

Interestingly, F scores were significantly lower among persons suffering from PTSD than among those who were *faking* suffering from PTSD. Yet, the F-2-8 code type appears to be the most common code type in those actively suffering from PTSD (Litz et al., 1991). The 7-2 code type is also particularly likely, as it incorporates the emotional distancing and the distress that are characteristic of this disorder. Graham (1987) suggests that a 1-9/9-1 code is indicative of this disorder. Burke and Mayer (1985) found that PTSD patients in a VA hospital showed an 8-2-7 profile, as opposed to an 8-2-6 profile shown by random psychiatric VA patients, with the PTSD patients being noticeably lower in F, 6, 9, and the Goldberg Index. They tend to be high on the PK and PS supplementary MMPI-2 scales.

On the 16 PF, scales C, G, and Q_3 should not be as low as in the panic disorder. Scores on O and Q_4 are especially likely to be high. Clues to methods of crying come especially from selected TAT plates, for example, cards 4, 6BM, 7BM, and 8GF (Swiercinsky, 1985). Otherwise, the diagnostic comments on panic disorders, the generalized anxiety disorder, and the anxiety disorders generally apply. In addition to the indicators of the panic disorder, 2, 6, and 8 may become more elevated on the MCMI-III as the disorder becomes more chronic, reflecting the lessened affect and the detachment that occur. Also, they should be high on R, a scale introduced in the third edition.

A number of specific scales have been designed to measure PTSD. Some of these are embedded in MMPI-2. Most use face-valid responses, and the reader is referred to Watson (1990) for an extended discussion of these scales and their usefulness. The Penn Inventory appears to be especially useful (Hammarberg, 1992).

Pitman and Orr (1993) propose an interesting assessment approach for PTSD. They use an interview to generate a thirty-second script they term "script driven imagery of personal events," that is, those events that are related to the individual client's PTSD. This script is delivered in an almost hypnotic-like patter while reactions are measured physiologically, for example, by heart rate, skin conductance, EMG.

TREATMENT OPTIONS

Based on a comparison of psychodynamic, behavioral, and biochemical treatments for PTSD, it appears that direct therapeutic exposure to the trauma (e.g., via systematic desensitization or flooding or even focused group discussion) and cognitive reframing have emerged as the most important factors in treatment (Taylor, 1995; Kroll, 1993). A working-through process in which the client's world-beliefs or overall cognitive schemata are modified in accord with the traumatic memory is often necessary for a successful treatment.

In treating post-traumatic stress disorders and adjustment disorders, the clinician is advised to keep in mind the principles of crisis intervention—immediacy, proximity, and expectancy—that were developed in World War II to decrease the consequent problems of the severe distress of combat. Immediacy emphasizes early awareness and detection by others close to the person, treatment as quickly as possible, and returning clients to their typical life situations as quickly as possible. Proximity emphasizes the need to treat clients in their own worlds—not distancing them from their upset by hospitalization. Lastly, the clinician must communicate a clear expectancy that although fear and anxiety are normal processes here, they do not excuse clients from functioning adequately; the sick role is not reinforced, and there is an emphasis on experiences that demonstrate that they are regaining control of their worlds.

These principles can be specifically amplified by the treatment techniques used for the panic disorder and the generalized anxiety disorder (the reader is referred to those sections), as well as those used for the borderline personality disorder (Kroll, 1993). As the fears begin to focus more on specific concerns, SDT or implosive therapy is appropriate. Antidepressants are often needed in more chronic and/or severe cases. Mild tranquilizers to be used as needed can also be a helpful adjunct treatment. Group therapy and sessions with family and/or friends that help clients implement new behaviors in their immediate worlds are often critical to a return to adequate functioning.

■ Acute Stress Disorder (308.3)

This diagnostic category is a new addition to DSM-IV; it is designed to complement and allow more specification of the PTSD diagnosis. The DSM-IV diagnostic requirements for this diagnosis are: (1) the exact same "1" requirement as for PTSD—see prior section on PTSD; (2) during or right after the distressing event, three of the following occur: [a] a sense of emotional numbing or detachment, [b] reduced awareness of surrounds, [c] derealization, [d] depersonalization, or [e] dissociative amnesia; (3) persistent reexperiencing of the event in at least one mode, for example, flashbacks, dreams, thoughts, et cetera, or distress upon exposure, (4) related stimulus avoidance, (5) marked anxiety or arousal, (6) distress or life-area impairment, (7) symptoms lasting at least two weeks, no more than four weeks, and within four weeks of the event; (8) not due to a substance response, a medical condition, or exacerbation of a preexisting Axis I or II disorder.

Diagnostic indicators are similar to those found in PTSD, and to the anxiety disorders in general (see prior sections in this chapter).

□ TREATMENT OPTIONS

Everyone encounters significant stressors at various points in their life. The most common ones (death of a loved one, divorce, loss of a relationship, loss of a job) inherently involve dealing with the loss as part of the coping strategy. The treatment options noted for PTSD, and for the anxiety disorders in general, are also relevant here. In addition, clients can be guided into both a short- and long-term strategy for such coping. The following list of such strategies can be presented to the client as a basis for work in psychotherapy and in homework.

SHORT-TERM TRAUMA-LOSS RECOVERY STRATEGIES

1. Withdraw from stress; seek and accept support.
2. Accept that you hurt.
3. Allow yourself to mourn.
4. Get any professional help you need, being careful not to stop dealing with the more important issues once the initial hurt lessens.
5. Delay any decisions and commitments.
6. Acknowledge objectively any other's share of the responsibility.
7. Direct your focus away from those perceived as responsible, and, when able, forgive them, and, for the most part, forget.
8. Acknowledge and respond to your responsibility in the loss.
9. Forgive yourself; participate in rituals of forgiveness.
10. Learn your vulnerability points; e.g., Sundays are weak days; i.e., the effects of the loss are more evident to us.
11. Know and live with your relationship limits.
12. Avoid previously ineffective relationships.
13. Avoid your addictions, including addictive relationships.
14. Accept the finality in your loss.
15. Affirm your survival; appreciate (in theory and in practice) those who helped.

LONG-TERM TRAUMA-LOSS RECOVERY

1. Return to your routines.
2. Eat well, sleep well, exercise well.
3. Return to your friends; expand your networks (although avoiding "rebound" or "co-dependent" relationships).
4. Heal with your family.
5. Organize and preserve selective mementoes; keep a diary or log.
6. Work directly on probable issues of resentment, hostility, anger, and dependency.
7. Become easy and accepting toward yourself, positive and forgiving toward others.
8. Become someone who can truly be with others, that is, become a "carer," maybe even a lover, but not a hurter.
9. Find places of belongingness, both persons (and animals) and places.
10. Reawaken your spiritual life.

■   ## Anxiety Disorder NOS (300.00)

This category is a catch-all applied to apparent anxiety disorders that do not exactly fit the previous categories. For example, where all the criteria for the generalized anxiety disorder are met, but the anxious mood has not lasted for up to six months, an anxiety disorder NOS diagnosis would be appropriate. Any other such mixtures of symptomatology where anxiety and its control are still the primary features can be placed in this category.

CHAPTER 6

Somatoform and Pain Disorders

■ ## Overall Concepts

Persons with somatoform disorders, like those with the factitious disorder, manifest complaints and symptoms of apparent physical illness that cannot be fully explained by a known medical condition or that are in excess of what would be expected from physical findings or cultural expectations. However, the symptoms of the somatoform disorders are not under voluntary control, as are those of the factitious disorders (Bell, 1994; Spivak et al., 1994). While factitious disorders are more common in men, somatoform disorders occur more frequently in women.

The diagnosis of somatoform disorder is made when there is good reason to believe that the person has little or no control over the production of symptoms. Note that (1) 50–70% of clients with a mental disorder first present themselves with a physical symptom, (2) about half of the 10% of patients who utilize half of the hospital inpatient days show psychological disorder, and (3) any co-morbid psychological disorder increases the hospital stay of true medical patients, even when controlling for severity of medical disorder (Katon, 1993).

□ ## SUBCATEGORIES OF SOMATOFORM DISORDERS

There are six major subcategories of the somatoform disorders: somatization disorder, undifferentiated somatoform disorder, conversion disorder, pain disorder, body dysmorphic disorder, and hypochondriasis. There is also a catch-all category, somatoform disorder NOS, in which individuals are placed if they fit the general criteria for somatoform disorder but not the specific criteria of the other categories.

The somatization disorder is chronic with multiple, vaguely presented symptoms and complaints. The conversion disorder usually focuses on one or two specific symptoms suggestive of a physical disorder, which on closer examination reflect primarily a psychological issue. Pain disorder is quite similar to a conversion disorder that refers specifically to psychologically induced pain states. Hypochondriasis is the consistent overresponse to and concern about normal and/or insignificant bodily changes, in spite of expert reassurance that there is no reason for concern. Body dysmorphic disorder (dysmorphophobia) refers to rumination and preoccupation with some imagined defect in physical appearance; in one sense, it is a variation of hypochondriasis.

TREATMENT OPTIONS

Several overall principles are useful in the treatment of the somatoform disorders (Katon, 1993):

1. Accept the clients as truly suffering—first, to mute the hostility that has accumulated over many years of dealing with disbelieving physicians; second, to set up and maintain an effective treatment relationship.

2. Set up regularly scheduled visits, based on the clients' apparent pattern of visits to treaters over the past several months. This obviates the clients' need for a physical symptom as an "admission ticket" to a treater.

3. Arrange for a straightforward and thorough physical exam. But coordinate so that exams are not repeated and secondary consultations or extensive lab testing is avoided. If consults are used, help to select conservative physicians who will only use needed tests, and who won't elicit further anxiety and ruminations by comments about low-probability disease possibilities based on statistical artifacts generated by multiple testing.

4. Avoid referrals for antianxiety or sleeping medications as this allows avoidance of psychological issues, as well as spurring abuse.

5. Consider the use of antidepressants for any significant depressive or panic episodes.

6. Make sure that any pain medication is controlled by the treaters, not the clients, nor by the clients' varying levels of pain. Use "time-contingent" rather than "as needed" medications.

7. Realize that exposure to some form of physical or sexual abuse, in the recent or distant past, is common in such clients, as is exposure to an environment where emotion was expressed through physical symptoms.

8. Start with concrete intervention techniques that can be construed as directed at physical problems, for example, biofeedback, relaxation training; move into supportive discussions, and then into more in-depth cognitive and emotive therapies. Such clients respond well to any "laying on of hands" but do so with consideration of relevant professional and ethical issues.

9. Help them set realistic treatment goals. Total "cure" is not always a realistic goal, so help them to learn coping and management techniques for whatever symptoms remain. Focus on what they do now, and can do in the future, rather than on "pain talk" (though you may occasionally allow a brief "organ recital").

10. Get them moving, psychologically and physically. This is the primary means to effect any change. They have to learn to push their limits, to walk an extra half mile, to clean another room, to sit up to watch TV rather than lie down. Have them learn that "resting" and inactivity are negative for them.

11. Try to involve the clients' families to build their understanding and acceptance of how they can respond to crises in terms of verbalized psychological needs rather than addressing physical symptoms. Help them to get the patient moving, to stop "pain" or "disease talk," and to not facilitate "rest" and withdrawal.

Even though conscious deception is not a factor with somatoform disorders, reality therapy (Glasser, 1980) can be appropriate, particularly to the degree the person becomes aware of the unreality of the physical symptoms. The therapist can also facilitate that awareness through such methods as consciousness raising, hypnosis, amytal interviews, or other methods of getting in touch with the repressed facets of the personality. In this regard, biofeedback may not only be useful in modifying some of the symptomatology; it may give the person some insight that the disorder is not primarily physiological (Schwartz, 1987).

Through supportive therapy, one may be able to counteract the commonly noted trait of "negative affectivity," marked by high indices of hostility, anxiety, and depression. This factor leads to resistance to treatment as well as chronically heightened autonomic response thresholds.

Rehabilitative medical-physical therapies can also be useful here because they (1) can deal with some of the secondary though actual physical problems that are common, (2) reassure such clients that their condition is not being dealt with lightly, and (3) allow them a "face-saving" way of dropping the somatoform system.

Somatization Disorder (300.81) and Undifferentiated Somatoform Disorder (300.81)

Somatization disorder was originally called "Briquet's syndrome" and was also included under the term *hysteria*. The chronic although cyclic multiple somatic complaints that mark this subcategory of the somatoform disorders are not primarily due to any physical illness. They may be mixed with other symptoms derived from an actual disease, so arriving at this diagnosis is initially difficult. It is not uncommon for this disorder to be an exaggeration of symptoms associated with a previously cured physical disease (Katon, 1993).

Somatization disorder is a relatively stable disorder, but is often co-morbid with major depression, panic disorder, mania, and/or phobias. It is more common in women, and the most common medical problems in somatization disorder are irritable bowel disorder and ovarian cysts (Bell, 1994). Bell further asserts that in a number of cases limbic kindling and/or other neurobiological sensitizing mechanisms in part account for the diffuse pattern of pain and disorder.

The diagnosis of somatization disorder is often difficult because a self-report of symptoms combined with apparent prior history is convincing to most physicians. Family physicians or general practitioners are more often than not the target of these complaints and are not inclined to see the somatization disorder as real. Physicians often believe such people (and hypochondriacs as well) are only malingering or that, at the very least, there is a degree of faking involved. Hence, they are inclined to put them in the too commonly used category of "crank" and attempt in various ways to avoid spending any time with them.

Since it is the supportive atmosphere of the physician's manner and/or the hospital structure that is at least one of the needs of persons with a somatization disorder (and to a degree the conversion disorders), such evident rejections begin to lay bare the underlying inadequacy of these persons to cope effectively with their worlds (Kellner, 1986). Depression often becomes an emergent and eventually paramount symptom, and the person may develop methods (e.g., alcohol) to deal with the depression. Alternately, the person with a somatization disorder may develop a new symptom picture and generate new systems of hospitals and physicians to work through. Restrictions of time and money, however, often bring the person full circle.

Symptoms are often presented in a vague but exaggerated fashion. Incidentally, this dramatic component was the linkage between the traditional diagnostic terms "hysterical neurosis" and "hysterical personality." Fortunately, the DSM-IV terminology does away with some of the confusion inherent in these labels. Hysterical personalities are now referred to as having a histrionic personality disorder. Hysteria is typically subsumed under one of the somatoform disorders, usually as a conversion disorder that is still referred to by some as the hysterical neurosis, conversion type.

One disorder occasionally misinterpreted as a somatization disorder, hypochondriasis, a conversion disorder, or even depression is myasthenia gravis, an immune-mediated polyclonal antibody disorder of receptors in the postsynaptic membrane. Referral to a neurologist for further consideration is particularly advisable when the client shows the following symptoms: (1) significant somatic weakness, occasionally resulting in collapse after use of any particular muscle group, (2) visual disturbances, including the dropping of one or both eyelids (more likely to occur in the evening), and (3) difficulty in speaking and swallowing.

☐ DSM-IV

The DSM-IV requires evidence of history of physical complaints, occurring over several years, resulting in seeking treatment or a significant life impairment, with evidence that the physical symptoms began before the age of 30. The clients must also show, at some time in the course of disorder, four pain symptoms, two gastrointestinal symptoms, one sexual symptom, and one pseudoneurological symptom, and either (1) these symptoms cannot be directly explained by a medical condition or substance, or (2) if there is a relevant medical condition, the response is excessive, and it is not a Factitious Disorder. The Somatization Disorder is thought to be diagnosed rarely in males, but approximately 1% of females are alleged to have this disorder at some point in their lives.

The Undifferentiated Somatoform Disorder requires only one physical complaint, again not directly explainable by a substance or a general medical condition, or being an excessive response if there is a medical condition; causes a life impairment; lasts at least six months; and is not better accounted for by other mental disorder diagnoses.

Systems of health care based on the group practice model make restriction and detection of this disorder easier, since this model facilitates higher levels of interspecialist communication. Also, these practices are more likely to include psychological services and be more sophisticated in implementation than an individual physician. Inclusion of psychological services actually reduces the cost of health care in most physical disorders, mainly by a reduction of repeated visits and unnecessary surgery.

MMPI-2

Scales 1, 2, and 3, and to a lesser degree, 7 are elevated in most of the somatization patterns (Dahlstrom et al., 1986), and they are typically close to the HEA (health concerns) content scale. Combinations of 1, 2, and 8 accompany the more bizarre somatic complaints. As has been noted, some depression naturally accompanies this syndrome and is reflected in the moderate elevation on scale 2. If scale 2 is high, it is possible that the person is beginning to feel that he or she is losing control. Scale 1 is elevated in most of these profiles, and the 1-2/2-1 profile is best thought of as somatization disorder with underlying depression. In this instance, one might also consider alcohol abuse as a compounding variable.

Elevations on scale 7 point to the degree of passivity and complaining that can be expected (Greene, 1991). The 1-7/7-1 client expresses chronic tension-related complaints and demands physical care and responsiveness from physicians but is resistant to following orders and is difficult to change. A 3-8/8-3 profile has also been associated with this disorder, although the chronic worry, dependency, and schizoid tendencies of these individuals should warrant consideration of a psychotic diagnosis.

The 1-4/4-1 profile reflects a high level of physical complaints, as well as excessive narcissism and egocentricity. If 6 is elevated, anger or rage in the face of rejection by the physician is to be expected. The 3-6/6-3 profile is similar—there is anger as well as rigidity and lack of cooperation. This anger is more often directed toward family members; clients are not quite as manipulative toward physicians.

When actual physical disorder is an accumulation of chronic psychological stress and accompanied by an equally high level of psychological repression (Bell, 1994), the 3-7/7-3 profile is common. A circumscribed physical disorder to which the person has responded with a reactive depression is more likely to produce a spike scale 2 profile.

The 3-9/9-3 profile is on the border between actual physical disorder and somatization disorder. A common complaint is acute upset accompanied by chest pain and anxiety. These individuals in particular respond well to superficial assurance and to continuing therapist contact.

A small subgroup of clients with a somatization disorder show virtually psychotic profiles. They are remarkably elevated on scale 4, sometimes above the 100-T level, and are also high on scales 6, 8, 2, 3, and 1, in that order. In fact, all scales except 0 and 5 may be well above the 70-T level (Propkop et al., 1980).

☐   ## 16 PF

Characteristics of the 16 PF commonly noted throughout all somatoform disorders, but particularly in the somatization disorder, are at least moderately high scores on I, N, and Q_4, moderately low scores on H and Q_1, and often lower on B. Karson (1959) suggests that individuals who are lower on A and M are also inclined toward this disorder. The B and M scores reflect the client's degree of sophistication and in that sense correlate with different somatization patterns. The less sophisticated symbolic conversion patterns, which were seen more commonly in Freud's era, are more typical of naive and less educated individuals.

Men who have high E and I scores have conflicts between the need to be sensitive in interpersonal relationships and yet to dominate relationships. Ambivalence about assertion and aggression is common and may surface in a somatization pattern. It has been hypothesized that women will encounter the same conflict as they move away from traditional female roles.

Clinicians have noted that persons with a somatization disorder also tend to be more average on C and Q_4 than do those with the anxiety disorders. They vary markedly on scales I and Q_3, depending on the degree of depression. Although a pattern with a combination of a low E and a high Q_1 score is relatively rare, it indicates a predisposition to the somatization disorders.

☐   ## OTHER TEST-RESPONSE PATTERNS

Performance scale scores on the WAIS-R are usually higher than verbal scale scores. In particular, the performance subtests that depend on motor coordination and speed are relatively high, with an occasionally surprising exception in object assembly. Within the verbal scale scores, lower information and digit span scores are expected, relative to higher comprehension scores. In those females where the somatization disorder incorporates histrionic components, the arithmetic score is low.

The typically salient feature of the MCMI-III profile is elevation of 85 or higher on H. Somatically channeled anxieties are often the source of somatization disorders, and this is indicated by considerable elevation on A. Both 4 and 7 are often also high (Choca et al., 1992). Somatization also occurs as a result of motoric dysfunction present in psychotic depression, so an elevation of 75 or higher on CC may occur. Personality types most prone to developing somatization disorders are the avoidant, the negativistic, the schizoid, and the cycloid, so elevations of 75 or higher may be predictive of the development of this disorder as a coping mechanism or during periods of stress.

Persons with a somatization disorder typically do not provide a high number of responses on the Rorschach and occasionally "fail" to give a response, and the percentage of W or complex M responses is usually low. They are more likely to give simple, Popular responses, using only the easily discerned details. A high number of M responses is rare, and when they are provided, they often have a more static quality than do normal M responses. Responses involving color as a determinant are uncommon. Responses focusing on bony-anatomy content and occasionally pure C responses, such as "blood," do occur (Wagner and Wagner, 1981).

TREATMENT OPTIONS

The comments in the section on somatoform disorders are also applicable to the somatization disorders. The symptomatology here is more similar to actual physiological disorder than it is in several of the other somatoform disorders (Bell, 1994). Hence, biofeedback can be useful in turning around some of the surface physiological symptomatology and at the same time can give clients concrete feedback that may, along with supportive therapy, convince them to look at psychological vulnerability as the source of their disorders. Most persons with this disorder are defensive about it, and, as a result, the comments about the paranoid disorders are applicable. At some point a shift into an existential orientation may be necessary to confront clients fully with their escape mechanisms.

Conversion Disorder (300.11)

The conversion disorder is similar in many respects to the somatization disorder. The difference is that in the conversion disorder there is a specific symptom or a related set of symptoms affecting a voluntary motor or sensory function indicating a medical condition, often used for the attainment of some secondary gain or to express a psychological conflict. Gait disturbances, pseudo-epilepsy, tremor, and paralysis make up the great majority of conversion symptoms. Although conversion disorder is often functionally a diagnosis of exclusion, up to 50% of conversion disorder clients have an associated neurological disorder (Katon, 1993).

Conversion symptoms are not under voluntary control. With some of the psychosexual dysfunctions (discussed in Chapter 8) it may be difficult to decide whether the problem directly expresses a psychological issue and is thus technically a conversion disorder or whether it is a physiological response to anxiety. In actuality, it may be a mixture of both. For this reason, as well as for convenience, these cases are included among the psychosexual disorders.

A conversion disorder is still occasionally referred to in the literature as a "hysterical neurosis, conversion type," and an individual with one is said to manifest *la belle indifférence,* an attitude in which there is little concern about the apparent serious implications of the disorder. Persons with a conversion disorder appear to be aware at some level that their complaints do not predict the further dire consequences that others might infer from them. Although often relatively indifferent to their presenting symptoms, emotional lability in response to other stimuli is commonly noted (Kellner, 1986).

The attitude of *la belle indifférence* is not found in all conversion disorders; some people develop their symptoms under extreme stress and manifest that stress quite directly. Even in these individuals, however, anxiety seems to dissipate over the duration of the disorder in favor of a focus on physical symptoms.

A dependent or histrionic personality predisposes individuals to the development of conversion symptoms. Another important predisposing factor is a history of actual physical disorder during which excessive caretaking behaviors or other secondary gains occurred.

DSM-IV

The DSM-IV requires at least one symptom or deficit affecting voluntary motor or sensory function indicating a general medical or neurological condition; psychological factors are associated with and affect the condition; it is not explained by a general medical condition, a substance, or a culturally sanctioned variable; there is a life impairment; and the symptom is not limited to pain or sexual dysfunction and is not better accounted for by another mental disorder. The possible specifications are "With Motor Symptom or Deficit," "With Sensory Symptom or Deficit," "With Seizures or Convulsions," or "With Mixed Presentation."

MMPI-2

Most of the comments made about diagnostic observations on somatization disorders are relevant here. It has been traditional to expect that in most cases of conversion disorder there is a classic conversion V, wherein scales 1 and 3 are both high and 2 is relatively low. Note that conversion Vs do show up in a number of people with actual physical disorder, so it should not be used as any per se diagnostic indicator. When actual physical disorder is not supported, the conversion V is especially indicative of a conversion reaction in which the individual takes a naive and Pollyannaish attitude and manifests *la belle indifférence.* However, Johnson et al. (1980) found that the 2-1-7 pattern, with a high score on 3, is more common in this disorder. If scale 3 is very high, scale 4 is low, and scale 1 is around 60–70 T, histrionic characteristics are emphasized. In persons where *la belle indifférence* is lacking, a higher scale 4 is likely.

Another profile occasionally seen in conversion disorders is the 3-9/9-3. These people experience conversion reactions in acute form, accompanied by at least moderately high anxiety levels. Over time, they are likely to show more histrionic characteristics, and the 9 scale should be somewhat lower.

16 PF

The observations on the 16 PF relevant to somatization disorders are applicable here as well. However, if there is *la belle indifférence*, N and Q_3 are higher and there is a relatively lower score on L. A high F score is also probable. Since these individuals are usually not as sophisticated as others in the overall group of somatoform disorders, a lower B scale is noted. Also, the concrete quality of their thinking predicts a lower M score.

OTHER TEST-RESPONSE PATTERNS

Although the overall group of conversion disorders is similar to the somatization disorders, those with *la belle indifférence* in particular show higher scores on digit symbol and digit span, relative to the other scales, on the WAIS-R. In addition, they seldom show bright-normal or superior intelligence and do poorly on tests that measure more subtle intellectual discriminations, such as comprehension, similarities, and picture arrangement. Emotional distancing from the Rorschach cards (through such comments as "they are weird" or "they are ugly") is common. They are prone to deny depressive or aggressive feelings in the content of the Rorschach and the TAT.

Because physical symptoms in conversion disorder are usually specific, elevated H is not highly likely on the MCMI-IIII. The submissive personality (scale 3) and the gregarious personality (scale 4) are most likely to develop conversion disorders as a way to achieve secondary gain. The submissive personality is especially likely to exhibit *la belle indifférence*. High scores indicating the presence of these personality patterns may be predictive of the development of conversion disorders. Those whose ambivalence and psychological conflicts produce elevated scores on scale 8A may be predisposed toward developing this disorder.

TREATMENT OPTIONS

Since the time of Freud, hypnosis as a means of directly suggesting a cure or as a means of exploring unconscious conflicts has been effective in the treatment of conversion disorders (Meyer, 1992b). Also, it is worthwhile to include several placebo and/or physical techniques with a client with conversion disorder, particularly one who focuses on the dramatic. Physical therapies in conjunction with psychotherapy are the standard intervention mode.

Hendrix et al. (1978) successfully used behavioral techniques to cure the conversion disorder symptom of a clenched fist. In general, aversion relief and variations of the time-out technique (removing the person from the situation and not responding to his or her disturbed behaviors) can be useful here. In the cognitive behavioral technique of covert extension the conversion disorder client would be asked to imagine the general conversion pattern while at the same time imagining that the reinforcing events that usually occur with this behavior in the real world do not occur in imagination. The effectiveness of the technique depends on already having attained some awareness as to the source of the conversion disorder. Thus, it is best used as a subsequent procedure to such techniques as hypnosis, psychotherapy, or free association, which are used to first explore these unconscious ties.

Pain Disorder

Pain disorder is diagnosed when psychological factors play an important role. As with the other disorders, a history of physical disorder involving the actual symptom is common (Katon, 1993). The emergence of a pain disorder, often referred to as chronic pain syndrome, is facilitated by developmental-stage transitions and by specific stressful events. Pain disorder also differs from the conversion disorders in that the commonly associated histrionic features of sexual ambivalence, *la belle indifférence,* and dependency are not usually observed.

As with the conversion disorders, pain disorder may reflect a psychological conflict and/or exert a controlling influence on the person's interactions with other people, resulting in some secondary gain and/or allowance for avoidance.

DSM-IV

The DSM-IV requires evidence of pain that is significant enough to warrant clinical attention and is the predominant referral focus; impairs a significant life area; has psychological factors that are important in all phases of its evolution; and is not better accounted for by diagnoses of malingering, Factitious Disorder, Dyspareunia, or a Mood, Anxiety, or Psychotic Disorder. When psychological factors are predominant in all phases of the evolution of the pain, the diagnosis is Pain Disorder Associated With Psychological Factors (307.80); if both psychological and a general medical condition play a role in that pain evolution, the diagnosis is Pain Disorder Associated With Psychological Factors and a General Medical Condition (307.89). When psychological factors are not deemed important in a pain disorder, the diagnosis is based on the pain site.

From an overall diagnostic perspective, the diagnostician should consider (1) the client's specific pain history (including treatment) and including historical issues such as family role models; (2) initiating and maintenance stressors; (3) the meaning of and value to the client of the pain; (4) issues of secondary gain, compensation and litigation issues, and other pain-maintenance variables; (5) overall physical, psychosocial and intellectual functioning; and (6) possible co-morbid pathologies, especially substance abuse and depression.

■ Chronic Pain Syndrome

The common characteristics of Chronic Pain Syndrome (a variation of the DSM-IV diagnoses) are (1) consistently manifested periods of intractable pain; (2) a restriction and/or disruption of daily activities; (3) alterations in related behaviors and mood, for example, depression; (4) no clear evidence of any relationship to organic disorder; (5) a history of multiple nonproductive assessments and interventions; and (6) excessive use of medications. The pain seldom follows known anatomic or neurological patterns. In the more sophisticated patient it may mimic well-known diseases, such as angina or arthritis. There are indications that people with certain lifestyles or family backgrounds are more likely to use pain as a manipulator:

People who have a history of extensive medical treatment and multiple surgical procedures

People with a history of hypochondriasis or of factitious disorders

People who have a history of taking significant dosages of pain medicine

People who are highly suggestible

People who had stressful childhoods and/or are from large families

People who began working full–time and/or had children at an early age

People who complain of too little pain for their injuries as well as those who complain too much

Consensus estimates are that over half of those people presenting chronic pain syndrome have back pain, often lower back pain. Benedikt and Kolb (1986) found in a study of those presenting themselves at a chronic pain center of a VA hospital that a large subgroup had undiagnosed post-traumatic stress disorder. They postulated that since the pain was usually focused in areas of injury related to the disorder, such as shrapnel wounds, the reexperiencing of the events had precipitated in this form. Many in this subgroup had been previously treated for the chronic pain with medications, surgery, or electric stimulation; it seems the psychological nature of their pain had been unrealized. The finding that chronic pain may be associated with post-traumatic stress syndrome should alert the clinician to alternative treatment strategies. Underlying depression is also a common accompaniment.

☐ MMPI-2

Although some forms of pain disorder can be considered as conversion disorders, the classic conversion V is not always found (Butcher and Williams, 1992). Because depression is evident in many cases, the 2 scale and the DEP (depression) content scale may be elevated, and the HEA (health concerns) content scales are usually elevated. Elevations (in order of degree) in the 1-2-3 scales are common (Love and Peck, 1987). Interestingly enough, clients with a single pain complaint tend to score higher on these scales than do clients with multiple pain complaints. Clients who are using their illness to obtain compensation are more likely to score higher on scale 4 and, to a lesser degree, on scale 9, and other cues for malingering should be considered.

As symptoms become more chronic and patients are more often rejected by diagnosticians and treaters, a rise in scale 7 is probable. When pain is focused in the extremities or is manifested in headaches or back problems (a pattern in which repression and denial are common), a 1-3/3-1 profile is likely.

One group of patients with multiple pain complaints shows high scores on 1, 3, 7, and 8, in that order. This group is characterized by somatic preoccupation, obsessive thinking, isolation, and denial of psychological problems. Another subgroup is denoted by high scores on scale K and scale 1 and a low score on scale 6. This group is particularly inclined to deny their psychological difficulties, almost naively, and is interpersonally insensitive (Propkop et al., 1980).

Clients with actual chronic pain do not often show much elevation immediately after the injury. However, if they are tested several months after it occurs, elevations on scales 1 and 3 are more likely. Also, an elevated conversion V along with an elevated scale 4 predicts poor recovery from pain or from surgery in general (Love and Peck, 1987).

Patients with chronic pain are also likely to become increasingly depressed, so elevations on the 2 and DEP scales are even more common (Butcher and Williams, 1992). Many patients with chronic pain become addicted to toxic levels of pain-killing drugs and as a result begin to show cognitive slippage and other indications of brain damage. A 2-9, with an 8 that is high and greater than 7, or other markers of disinhibition, such as a high 4, accompanied by indications of distress are potential indicators of this addiction and toxicity.

Certain patients with chronic pain appear to reflect a one-trial learning process associated with the originating trauma. As a result, they indicate phobiclike behavior on the MMPI-2. They are often suggestible and thus manifest high K and L scores, with a high scale 3 and a relatively high scale 1, often accompanied by a 7 scale that is elevated at least 10 points over scale 8.

16 PF

The comments regarding conversion disorders are appropriate here, except those that focus on the symptom of *la belle indifférence*, since this is not typical for most pain disorders.

OTHER DIAGNOSTIC CONSIDERATIONS

Extreme elevation on H on the MCMI-III is not likely here, although some specific patterns of pain may be indicated by elevations between 75 and 85. Some elevation on A and D is also likely. Those with elevations of 75 or higher on 2A may utilize psychogenic pain as a way to avoid interpersonal interactions, while the psychological conflict and ambivalence of the 8 and C patterns predispose them to the development of psychogenic pain. The personality patterns indicated by elevated scores on 2B and 8A are more likely to be present here, in contrast to conversion disorder, where the most likely patterns are indicated by elevations on 3 and 4.

Beyond the standard means (psychological tests, hypnosis, "truth serums") for differentiating a conversion disorder from an organic condition, there are other methods specifically helpful in discriminating psychogenic from organic pain (or from malingering; see Chapter 16). Cortical evoked potentials have shown promise as a diagnostic instrument in this area, as well as in many other diagnostic situations. Also, certain EEG patterns appear more consistently in organic than in psychogenic pain, and assessment of blood plasma cortisol can be a helpful discriminator. Unfortunately, most people with somatoform disorders, particularly conversion disorders or pain disorders, are seldom seen by a psychologist or psychiatrist, and such specific and more sophisticated assessments are never made.

TREATMENT OPTIONS

Employ the principles enumerated in the first "treatment options" section, at the beginning of this chapter, as they are very appropriate here. Most clients do better if they have some kind of scenario that helps to explain their disorder, in this case pain, to them (Omer, 1994). Gate-control theory is a good choice as it has a face-valid quality for most clients. The various treatment options commonly used (increasing activity and life meaning, changing negative "self-talk," emotional stabilization and physical relaxation, behavioral control of pain behaviors, medications, nerve blocks, etc.) can then be offered as ways of closing various gates. However, the major thrust of any pain-management approach is to help patients through social-skills training, assertiveness training, vocational rehabilitation, and the like to a more independent, active lifestyle, rather than to focus on pain reduction per se (Love and Peck, 1987). They must come to understand that they "use it or lose the use of it" and find something more meaningful in life than their pain. The overall goals of any pain-management program usually include (1) identifying and modifying behavioral and social pain reinforcers; (2) increasing more positive lifestyle behaviors, for example, increased exercise, better diet, stopping smoking; (3) decreasing pain communications, and associations with pain-communication reinforcers; (4) decreasing the use of pain as an allowance for avoidance behaviors; (5) weaning from the use of analgesic, "rest," sleep, and psychotropic medications; and (6) increasing the ability to communicate directly about emotions and feelings, to decrease the channeling of general life experience into pain experience and communications.

Poly-prescription drug abuse must be considered, as many such clients "doctor-shop" in order to find physicians who will tell them there may be an organic cause (which they believe extended, expensive, testing may detect) and will prescribe medications the client desires. A "pain cocktail" detoxification approach may be necessary. Dosages of abused opiates are converted into equivalent dosages of methadone, and sedative dosages into doses of phenobarbital, with acetaminophen and hydroxyzine added to enhance efficacy. The methadone is then decreased by 10–20% daily and the phenobarbital by 5–10%.

When there is clearly genuine, intractable long-term pain (for example, with certain cancers, reflex sympathetic dystrophy, etc.), daily, stable long-term doses of narcotics are an increasingly accepted option. Unlike street addicts, such clients show a low rate of addiction, get relief rather than a high, and show a low level of side effects.

A history of or present manifestation of depression is common in pain disorder clients, so treatment directed at this factor is often indicated. Also, since pain disorder is in some cases reasonably considered a specific form of the conversion disorder, the comments in that section are appropriate.

Cheek (1965) pioneered the use of hypnosis to find the subconscious causes in certain cases of chronic psychogenic pain. While his clients are under hypnosis, Cheek asks them to gradually release this symptom, often having them point to a date on the calendar designating when they might be willing to give up the symptom. He then makes an appointment for that day and gradually ties the insights under hypnosis into conscious awareness. Other hypnotic techniques are also helpful here (Meyer, 1992b).

With chronic pain the musculature has often conformed over time to a bodily posture that continues the pain and may even become the only true physiological pain source. This is one reason why expert clinicians in this area don't allow more than two days bedrest and quickly push such clients into increased activity, physical therapy, and the like. Biofeedback to release this tense muscle posture can be helpful. Other clinicians would argue that techniques derived from chiropractic, such as Rolfing, are useful here as well. Techniques such as biofeedback and relaxation training can be used to "bridge" cognitive and emotive techniques that are often needed for any significant long-term cure.

Secondary gain can be very important in the pain or conversion disorders, especially when these occur in adolescents and young adults. Therefore, the clinician should look at family and marital situations for possible reinforcement patterns, as well as for possible sites for intervention.

■   Hypochondriasis (300.70)

The term "hypochondriasis" was first used by the Greeks and referred to ailments of the region of the body below the ribs and xiphoid cartilage; they believed mental status changes were associated with changes in the organs of the hypochondria (Katon, 1993). The modern concept is that hypochondriacs unreasonably interpret normal or relatively unimportant bodily and physical changes as indicative of serious physical disorder. They are constantly alert to an upsurge of new symptomatology, and since the body is constantly in physiological flux, they are bound to find signs that they can interpret as suggestive of disorder. In many hypochondriacs their distorted coping strategy is an attempt to avoid a feeling of loss of control (Barsky et al., 1994) and, in that sense, parallels the panic disorder.

In one sense, hypochondriacs do not fear being sick; they are certain they already are. Hypochondriasis is a relatively common pattern from adolescence to old age. It is traditionally viewed as most frequently occurring in the age range 30–40 for men and 40–50 for women (Meister, 1980). Meister also believes there are many "closet hypochondriacs," those who do not constantly go to physicians, yet are heavily involved in health fads, checking of body behaviors, and discussion of their concerns with close friends (who may relish this quasi-therapist role). These closet hypochondriacs would not earn a formal DSM-IV diagnosis because they do not fit some of the specific requirements, such as seeking out medical reassurance and going through physical examinations. Nonetheless, they manifest the disorder.

A number of common factors have been observed in the development of hypochondriasis (Barsky et al., 1994; Katon, 1993; Kellner, 1986; Meister, 1980):

□ Most hypochondriacs have a background marked by substantial experience in an atmosphere of illness. This could include identification with a significant other who was hypochondriacal or early exposure to a family member who was an invalid.

□ Hypochondriacs often have had a strong dependency relationship with a family member who could express love and affection in a normal or intense fashion during periods when the hypochondriac had been ill, yet was distant or nonexpressive at other times.

□ Hypochondriacs often channel their psychological conflicts and their needs for existential reassurance into this pattern. As a result, the hypochondriac pattern of behavior may mask a mid-life crisis or some other challenge that is not being met effectively.

□ A certain subgroup of hypochondriacs is postulated as having a predispositional sensitivity to pain and body sensations. This could be stimulated by prior physical disorder in systems in which the hypochondriacal pattern is now manifest.

All of these factors are facilitated by reinforcement of the hypochondriasis in the client's world, and avoidance of tasks or demands because of being sick is often noted here.

DSM-IV

There is not so great a focus on actual physical symptoms in hypochondriasis as in the somatization disorder. Rather, such people are preoccupied with having a significant physical disorder—although not at a delusional level and not just in the midst of a panic attack—in spite of expert evaluation and assurance that there is little danger. The duration of disorder is at least six months, and some important area of life functioning is disrupted. Persons with a cardiac neurosis or cancer phobia may be placed in this category. If the person does not for the most part recognize the concern as inappropriate, the specification "With Poor Insight" is added.

DIAGNOSTIC CONSIDERATIONS

Hypochondriacs often function similarly to individuals with the somatization disorder, except that hypochondriasis is more focused and intellectualized. As a result, the MMPI-2 profile will be somewhat tempered, being lower on scales 7 and 8 in particular. Scale 1 is at least moderately elevated, and a common code type here is the 3-1/1-3 profile, as is the 1-2/2-1 when there is evident distress. Since there is at least a moderate amount of defensiveness associated with this disorder, scales K, 6, and 7 are usually moderately high. If the person is relatively naive in response to personal conflicts, the L scale is also somewhat elevated. Hypochondriacs who are inclined to discuss their problems with others should score lower on scale 0, indicating the extroverted aspect of their pattern.

As with the MMPI-2, the 16 PF is tempered from the profile usually noted with the somatization disorder. Specifically, C is usually not as low nor is Q_4 as high. However, E, I, and Q_3 are usually higher, reflecting the even more controlled psychological world of hypochondriacs in comparison to that of persons with a somatization disorder.

Preoccupation with matters of health will serve to moderately elevate H on the MCMI-III, so that scores of 75 or higher might be expected. A and D scores of 75 or higher are likely because hypochondriacal symptoms often occur in response to underlying anxiety and/or depression relevant to external situations. Those personality patterns that are likely to develop hypochondriacal disorders are those presenting a great deal of anxiety and compulsive behavior. Prominent patterns indicated by elevated 7, 8A, R and C scores are particularly likely.

Due to the mild obsessive component usually found in this disorder (Kozak et al., 1988), hypochondriacs overelaborate their responses on the WAIS-R and thus tend to do better on comprehension, similarities, and vocabulary. These are people who cope with words; as a result, the verbal scale is often higher than the performance scale. Blatt et al. (1970) found that a low score on object assembly was predictive of high bodily concern, including hypochondriacal patterns.

This same mild obsessive factor should result in longer latencies to the Rorschach cards, as well as a number of the other response patterns manifest in the obsessive-compulsive disorder. Anatomic responses to the cards are expected, and there is some indication that this anatomy content increases as they proceed through the cards. CF is usually greater than FC, and there is a relatively low production of M responses.

TREATMENT OPTIONS

Direct reassurance on medical symptoms is usually not a curative factor, although it is important that there be a thorough physical exam that allows reassurance so that the therapy can focus on consideration of psychological concerns. Acquiescing to pressure for repeated or secondary exams and tests easily leads the client to believe that his or her treaters are actually unsure about what's going on. It is important to follow the recommended therapeutic concepts noted in the first section of this chapter. The development of trust is especially critical in this disorder. In that regard, the reader is referred to the discussion of trust development in the section on the paranoid disorders (Chapter 9).

Another approach can be helpful with specific hypochondriacs: Therapists can suddenly state that they feel a hypochondriac client is "dead right" about his or her concerns. The shock from this unexpected agreement, with the apparent verification of their dreaded suspicions, can often elicit the underlying psychological concerns. This technique must be carried out with care, as it can backfire and solidify the hypochondriacal concerns.

Family therapy is also helpful with certain hypochondriacs (Barsky et al., 1994). Many of them have evolved a response system in which significant others consistently reinforce their pattern; with the supervision of the therapist, this pattern can be broken. Family members can be taught to give the person psychological reassurance and caring responses, while at the same time ignoring or otherwise avoiding the reinforcement of the concerns about physical disorder.

Such a technique takes into account the importance of underlying existential issues in the treatment of subcategories of hypochondriasis, such as cancer phobia and cardiac neurosis. Several clients appear to use specific concerns in these areas as a distraction from more anxiety-arousing issues, such as a basic realization of mortality or facing the potential to fail. Existential confrontation, in a context of supportive psychotherapy, allows the hypochondriacal concerns to cease so that clients can confront these deeper problems. Similarly, many of the techniques specific to the obsessive-compulsive disorder are applicable here.

Physicians who take the overall disorder as a serious problem and who do not write these patients off as "crocks" can go a long way toward breaking the hypochondriacal pattern. Once such patients begin to trust the physician, they can open up more about their total problems and then, under the umbrella of trust, possibly accept referral for psychological treatment (Katon, 1993).

■ Body Dysmorphic Disorder (300.7)

Body dysmorphic disorder (BDD) has been traditionally referred to as "dysmorphophobia." BDD is defined in DSM-IV as a preoccupation with some imagined imperfection in physical appearance or an exaggerated reaction to some minor defect that impairs an important life area and is not better accounted for by another mental disorder, for example, occurring during transsexualism or anorexia nervosa.

Victims may, if pressed, admit to the possibility that their concerns are excessive, but they persist in their concerns and in behaviors related to them (Kellner, 1986). For example, they may make repeated visits to plastic surgeons or dermatologists in order to have their concerns confirmed and to get some relief from the imagined defects. Unfortunately, there are a number of cases of such individuals undergoing extensive plastic surgery at the hands of careless or unscrupulous surgeons.

As is probably evident, BDD can be considered as a variation of hypochondriasis. Hence, the comments on diagnostic indicators and therapeutic considerations for hypochondriasis apply to BDD as well, although there is usually a greater degree of narcissism and a general concern with controlling interpersonal relationships in BDD. Thus, on the MMPI-2, BDDs tend to be higher on scales 4 and 0 and lower on scales 1 and 3 than classic hypochondriacs. Also, the BDDs tend to score higher on A on the 16 PF and generally show more of the indicators of narcissism on the MCMI-III.

■ Somatoform Disorder NOS (300.81)

This catch-all category includes a pattern that generally fits the requirements for somatoform disorder but does not fit the specifics of the individual patterns just covered. Also, see the discussion of the Undifferentiated Somatoform Disorder (300.81) earlier in this chapter. In actual practice, many individuals do not fit a specific somatoform disorder—not fulfilling the requirement of evidence in four or five symptom groups—and hence are included in one of these two categories. In general, the "Undifferentiated" label is used when the pattern persists for more than six months; "Somatoform Disorder NOS" if the duration is less than six months.

CHAPTER 7

Dissociative and Sleep Disorders

■ Overall Concepts

The dissociative disorders, traditionally referred to as the "hysterical neuroses, dissociative type," are characterized by a sudden disruption or alteration of the normally integrated functions of consciousness, memory, identity, or perception of the environment. This disturbance is usually temporary, although it may wax and wane, particularly in amnesia and fugue.

The various subcategories are dissociative amnesia, usually an acute disturbance of memory function; dissociative fugue, a sudden disruption of one's sense of identity, usually accompanied by travel away from home; dissociative identity disorder (formerly the multiple personality disorder), the domination of the person's consciousness by two or more separate personalities; and depersonalization disorder, a disturbance in the experience of the self in which the sense of reality is temporarily distorted. There is also a category referred to as dissociative disorder (NOS) (300.15), a residual category.

☐ DIAGNOSTIC CONSIDERATIONS

With the exception of the depersonalization disorder, the dissociative disorders are not especially common (Dunn, 1992), although there is much controversy regarding incidence rates (Kluft and Fine, 1993). In any case, there is not much significant literature on discrimination of these states by psychological tests (Maruish, 1994). This is not as unfortunate as it might seem. In the dissociative disorders the symptoms are usually reasonably clear indicators of the particular subcategory, even though other disorders have to be screened out. For example, many of these disorders have to be initially differentiated from schizophrenia. However, people with a dissociative disorder do not show the confusion and deteriorated functioning in most personality areas that are indicative of schizophrenia. A history of sexual or physical abuse (with derealization as a common later sequelae of sexual abuse) occurs more often than not in the dissociative's history (Finkelhor and Dziuba-Leatherman, 1994).

These disorders may also need to be distinguished from those in which the behavior mimics an organic condition, such as a head trauma, tumor, or epilepsy (Iacono, 1991; Gass and Russell, 1991). Indeed, when the clinician is confronted with the symptomatology noted here, a medical consultation is usually warranted.

■ Dissociative Amnesia (300.12)

This is a category where the commonly understood use of the term "amnesia" almost directly reflects the diagnostic implications. Dissociative amnesia is a temporary loss of ability to recall personal information. It can be information about a specific topic or memories of the immediate or distant past. Although media portrayals lead people to believe that the memory for *all* past events is lost in amnesia, this is rare. Recovery of memory is usually rapid, whereas the recovery is gradual in organic conditions, if it takes place at all. The alcohol amnestic disorder differs from dissociative amnesia. In the former the person is able to recall information for only a few minutes after it is obtained, since the ability to transfer information from short-term to long-term memory has been lost. This condition is also observed in some individuals who have had significant ECT treatments. Those with a history of traumatic sexual abuse are predisposed to dissociative amnesia. Since malingering needs to be considered (Slovenko, 1995) (approximately one-third of accused murderers plea some degree of amnesia), the reader is referred to Chapter 16.

□   DSM-IV

The DSM-IV requires evidence of sudden memory failure for important personal information that is too significant to be explained by ordinary forgetfulness; impairs a significant life area; and is not explained by alcohol-related "blackouts," by other organic conditions, or by such disorders as catatonia and stupor or multiple personality. It also needs to be discriminated from malingering, but such discrimination is often quite difficult (Wiggins and Brandt, 1988). The findings of faking scales on psychological tests are helpful here, as are interviews with the use of amytal or hypnosis.

This disorder is often observed in young adults and adolescents who are undergoing significant stress and in young persons first experiencing the distress of wartime. A subjectively intolerable life experience, such as an unexpected loss, is a common catalyst for amnesia, as well as for the related category dissociative fugue, which will be discussed next. Dissociative amnesia is also a common referral pattern following a public emergency. Since depression is a common factor in all of the above, consideration must be given to potential suicidal behaviors.

There are four common (non–DSM-IV) subgroupings of amnesia. The first and most common type, localized, refers to the loss of memory for events during a circumscribed period of time (following a severe stressor, such as an accident). Selective amnesia is a loss of memory for only certain types of events during the circumscribed period of time. Generalized amnesia, a failure to recall all events in one's life, and continuous amnesia, a loss of memory from one time to another, are both rare.

MMPI-2

A high 3-4/4-3 pattern on the MMPI-2, particularly the 3-4 profile, means fertile ground for the development of dissociative experiences. This pattern is marked by immaturity and significant difficulty in coping directly and maturely with disturbances in one's psychological world. It implies the use of denial, either psychologically (as in amnesia) or physically and psychologically (as in the fugue state). While scale 4 usually means sociopathy, it is also a measure of lack of social poise, naiveté, and immaturity and so may be high here.

Scale 1 is occasionally raised in this profile, as is scale 8, depending on whether the person is gravitating toward somatic concerns as an expression of disorder or into a general loss of integrated decision making. The F scale is low compared to other groups of pathology. If anger and hostility are being denied and avoided, an elevation on scales K and L is likely. The naiveté of the amnestic is especially reflected in a higher L score than would usually be obtained in an individual of similar social and intellectual levels.

16 PF

A modal profile for this type of disorder has not been determined. However, most clinicians agree that low scores on H, C, and N are to be expected. Suppressed anxiety should result in at least a moderate elevation on Q_4, and although Q_3 may be initially high, any increasing loss of integration of self-concept should lower Q_3. Higher scores on O and I reflect oversensitivity and apprehension. Also, E is usually high. The suggestibility and sense of inadequacy often found in such individuals also reflect the contrast between their rigid problem-solving skills and their desire to place trust in an authority figure.

TREATMENT OPTIONS

Hypnotic techniques to gain access to subconscious material have been a traditional treatment for amnesia, and they are generally effective (Meyer, 1992b). Psychotherapy, with an emphasis on interpretation of possible conflicts before adequate realization of them, is also useful, particularly if a supportive atmosphere both in and out of the therapy hour can be generated (Storr, 1990). This gives clients the sense of safety and potential for reintegration that they so desperately seek. Since this disorder is so often a response to a significant stressor, the techniques discussed in the treatment of the post-traumatic stress disorder are also applicable here.

■ Dissociative Fugue (300.13)

Dissociative fugue is a specific form of amnesia in which people are unable to recall some essentials of their personal identity and, in addition, they are likely to wander away from their home environment and assume an entirely new identity. Although they are seldom able to recall the behaviors that they carried out while in the fugue state, the recovery is usually complete.

The syndrome often occurs as a reaction to a severe psychosocial stressor, such as the unexpected breakup of a marriage or loss of a job without warning (Kluft and Fine, 1993). It is facilitated by previous heavy alcohol or drug use, which points to the dissociative quality inherent in states of consciousness engendered by drug abuse. An episode of depression or hypomania often precedes the emergence of a fugue state.

Somnambulism, traditionally considered a dissociative reaction, is now listed in DSM-IV as sleepwalking disorder (307.46). This is reasonable since it is usually not associated with any significant pathology. When it is clearly not associated with organic disorder (especially with temporal lobe epilepsy), as is true in most cases, it is best considered a simple learned behavior that was not suppressed in the early stages of development (Hauri, 1991).

☐ DSM-IV

To diagnose dissociative fugue, the DSM-IV requires evidence that the individual became confused about his or her identity or assumed at least some elements of a wholly or partially new identity, suddenly and unexpectedly left the normal home or workplace, and could not recall the past. This is not due to organic conditions or multiple personality, and impairs a significant life area.

This relatively rare disorder is somewhat similar to the multiple personality, in that the new identity is often in sharp contrast to the previous one. As previously noted, the pattern usually occurs in response to a significant loss of some sort and is catalyzed in some individuals by the shock of a natural disaster or a war.

☐ TESTING CONSIDERATIONS

These individuals are seldom tested while they are in the midst of the fugue state. As they are brought back into their natural environment, the recovery of memory begins to occur. When they are tested, they show patterns similar to dissociative amnesia.

☐ TREATMENT OPTIONS

Since dissociative fugue is analogous to dissociative amnesia, the techniques described for the treatment of the post-traumatic stress disorder are also applicable; a subjectively disturbing stressor is almost always a critical catalyst here. Hypnosis and sodium amytal interviews may aid in the recovery of missing memories. But care has to be taken because what appears to be a reintegration of true memories may in actuality be virtually new memories. As a followup, it would be useful to deal with the subjective reasons for the severity of this trauma through humanistic and existential techniques, for example, through gestalt therapy, since its emphasis is on reintegration of the person's wholeness.

Dissociative Identity Disorder (formerly Multiple Personality) (300.14)

Multiple personality, now termed Dissociative Identity Disorder (DID) in DSM-IV, receives much attention in the media, in part because it has traditionally been confused with schizophrenia. From this attention, it could be concluded that DID is a common disorder. However, Winer noted in 1978 that there have been only about two hundred reasonably well-documented cases at that time. Although no doubt an underestimate even then, this skepticism can be a good antidote to those mental health professionals who are far too quick to conclude a client is a "multiple" (Weissberg, 1993; Dunn, 1992).

A common presenting symptom is depression, usually through symptoms like labile mood, suicidal thoughts and sleep disorder. There is often a related diagnosis of personality disorder and/or somatization disorder (Dinwiddie et al., 1993). DIDs often come into treatment because they note some peculiarities in their worlds: forgetting of certain interactions with people, general confusion, and loss of memories. From either course a different personality is then acknowledged or even discovered through psychotherapy, which is often supplemented by hypnosis. In some cases, personalities continue to be produced, first by the indirect suggestion of the therapist's interest and reinforcement, then by the reinforcement of the therapist's reinvigorated concern for the person's problems. Though indications of dissociation are often noted even in early childhood, the mean age of diagnosis is approximately 28.

Amnesia is a sign of a possible future DID, and it is critical to reliable diagnosis (Dunn, 1992). A history of physical or sexual abuse (especially incest) is a common precursor; stress is an important precipitating factor, as are developmental or social transition points (Kluft and Fine, 1993). New personalities are usually a crystallization into a personality of opposite facets from the original one.

DSM-IV

According to DSM-IV, the DID is a person who is recurrently dominated by at least two separate and distinct personalities that determine separate thinking and behavior patterns, and at least two of these personalities alternately take control of the person's behavior. In this process the inability to recall personal information cannot be explained by a substance, a general medical condition, or ordinary forgetfulness, and, in children, cannot be attributed to fantasy play.

☐   TESTING CONSIDERATIONS

From an overall perspective, assessment should be validated by (1) an initial checklist approach to the critical and related symptoms in DID; (2) discussion with family, friends, and other potential information sources; (3) formal interviews and testing; (4) differential diagnosis from other possible diagnoses; and (5) followup to assess stability of the symptoms.

Because the personalities of a DID will vary markedly (Weissberg, 1993), depending on what facets of that individual they are expressing, no particular patterns can be expected. A high L scale is occasionally noted, and the 3-8/8-3 pattern is common. Fowler (1981) suggests that a 1-3/3-1 code type is also probable here. Histrionic and dependent personality components are often found in the separate personalities, and there is a greater likelihood of an acting-out of aggressive and sexual impulses. However, the overall personality is often marked by obsessive and introverted components, rather than blatant histrionic or labile patterns. The confusion and peculiarities initially presented by the DID may be present as an elevated S, R or SS on the MCMI-III. However, because of the nature of the disorder, no single prediction can be made; profiles should vary as personalities do.

Specific scales can be helpful. The Dissociative Experiences Scale (DES) is a 28-item self-report technique that has proven validity, and the Dissociative Disorders Interview Schedule (DDIS) is a 131-item structured interview that also has some proven validity (Dinwiddie et al., 1993).

Osgood et al. (1976) demonstrated an early and ingenious application of the semantic differential to the assessment of the contrasting features of a DID. Clinicians who happen to see this rare disorder could apply this method to monitor changes in the individual as he or she goes through various personalities and then begins to integrate again into a single personality. Also, in a few cases, EEG indicators of amplitude (attention) and latency have discriminated various personalities over time. Chapter 16 is useful here since some people are inclined to feign this disorder for the sake of media attention.

☐   TREATMENT OPTIONS

The initial thrust in therapy should be toward developing a therapy relationship the client can regard with trust and a sense of security (Kluft and Fine, 1993). The treatment contract needs to be clearly spelled out and put in writing for future reference. Audio or video taping of sessions is also useful for corroboration, and confrontation if necessary, and later to help in integration of the dissociated subpersonalities or "alters." Medication and heterogeneous group therapy should be avoided. An "internal group therapy" may be employed with the various alters, but this is a difficult technique that should not be attempted without specific and substantial supervision.

The classic treatment for the DID has been hypnosis, which is used to get in touch with the alters (Meyer, 1992b). In the few cases that have been available to clinicians for study this has generally been reasonably successful, but the cost in time has been high. Also, it is arguable that since hypnosis itself may involve a dissociative experience, it may iatrogenically increase the tendency to produce more personalities, particularly in the short run.

One could also argue that transactional analysis could further the dissociative process, since it so clearly emphasizes separate ego states. However, it could be useful in getting the DID in touch with the message that all of us play different roles and when these roles become crystallized, the potential for dissociative experience is heightened. This would at least place this experience closer to a normal experience and thus foster reintegration. Psychoanalysis has been used effectively with the DID (Osgood et al., 1976), although the therapist may have to deal with the unique problem of multiple transferences.

■ Depersonalization Disorder (300.6)

As noted earlier, the depersonalization disorder is dissimilar to other dissociative reactions, since consciousness is never truly segmented and significant memory loss is not a factor. Because there is no better place for depersonalization disorder in the DSM-IV and because it includes dissociation from the usual sense of reality, it is listed here.

In the depersonalization disorder, individuals experience a sense of separation from normal consciousness and may report feeling as if they are a separate observer of the self. The typical reality of the usual world seems altered. This is an experience that many people have on occasion—the issue is whether it is a consistent pattern. (It is interesting to note that if one follows certain modern gurus, the ability to constantly perceive one's functioning as a separate observer is the mark of progress toward enlightenment.)

Since depersonalization is experienced by many people at times, the definition of disorder is appropriate on the basis of either frequency or a feeling of lack of control. Many people are not really bothered by such experiences, whereas others feel as if they are going crazy. In the latter situation the sense of depersonalization can be conditioned to anticipatory anxiety, leading to a vicious cycle: reinforcing the belief that they might indeed be going crazy.

Because this disorder focuses on an experience of a changing identity, it is not surprising that it occurs most frequently during adolescence. There is little impairment from the experience itself, but when it is accentuated by a conditioned anxiety response, it becomes troublesome. In that sense it is similar to the conditioned anxiety response that many argue is the cause of the flashbacks during certain drug experiences. Abuse of alcohol or drugs facilitates the development of this disorder.

□   DSM-IV

Referred to historically as the "depersonalization neurosis," the present DSM-IV category requires indication of persistent or recurrent episodes of depersonalization potent enough to cause significant distress or impairment in an important life area, although reality testing remains intact—that is, an experience of either being outside of and/or detached from one's body, or feeling as if one were an automaton or in a dream. The possibilities of minor organic dysfunction, anxiety disorders, or even a developing schizophrenic or depressive episode must be ruled out. For example, people with anxiety disorders, especially if there is a panic component, will sometimes report depersonalization-type experiences. These are primarily offshoots of their constant self–monitoring rather than a true depersonalization.

MMPI-2

This disorder was included in the DSM-II as the depersonalization neurosis, and the modal profile reflects this conceptualization. Elevations on scales 3, 7, and F are likely, as these tap both the anxiety and hysteric components. The anxiety and identity confusion also lead to an elevated 8 scale, and since identity is threatened, changes in scale 5 away from stereotypical sexual-role scores are expected. Since these individuals are usually young, active in their response to their distress, but inclined to denial accompanied by somatic concerns, elevations on scales 1 and 9 may also occur. The various possible scale 4 elevations reflect the degrees of hostility and anger and the lack of social sophistication, which vary within individuals with this disorder. In rare cases a spike-0 profile may be noted early in its development (Kelley and King, 1979a).

16 PF

Instability and loss of a sense of reality are reflected in moderately low C and Q_3 scores. O and M are likely to be high, while the low score on N reflects naïveté and a relative lack of sophistication. Individuals who manifest a depersonalization disorder are usually of higher intelligence, so scale B should be average or above.

TREATMENT OPTIONS

In some respects the depersonalization disorder is as much an identity development disorder as it is a dissociative experience, so any techniques useful for getting in touch with the less integrated aspects of the personality might be useful here. This could range from Rogers's (1951) client-centered therapy through Gestalt therapy, supplemented by an emphasis on the problems of self-labeling, as detailed by Meichenbaum (1985). In this approach, clients are trained to label experiences viewed as alien as actually an integral part of their personality, to be confronted honestly.

Psychodrama could also be useful here. In this vein, Yablonsky (1976, p. 4) states, "In psychodrama a person is encountering his conflicts and psychic pain in a setting that will more closely approximate his real life situation than in most other therapeutic approaches. A young man in conflict with a parent talks directly to a person as an auxiliary ego playing his parent. His fantasy (or reality) of his hostility or love can be acted out on the spot." The acting-out of such fantasies about one's own reality, or the experiencing of that reality, can ultimately lead to a positive, integrative experience.

■ Sleep Disorders

The humorist and movie star W. C. Fields once quipped that "the best way to get a good night's sleep is to go to bed." Unfortunately, it is not that simple for many people. In fact, sleep disorder plagues everyone at one time or another. While estimates range widely, it is reasonable to assume that up to 15% of all adults will suffer a period of chronic insomnia at some point in their lives (Harsh and Ogilvie, 1995; Hauri, 1991; Montplaisir and Godbout, 1991).

There is a wide variety of sleep disorders, even though such disorders were not clearly recognized in the DSM until DSM-III-R. In the DSM-IV the sleep disorders are divided into (1) Sleep Disorders Related to Another Mental Disorder, for example, a mood or anxiety disorder; (2) Sleep Disorder Due to a General Medical Condition; (3) Substance-Induced Sleep Disorder; and the focus of this chapter, Primary Sleep Disorder. The Primary Sleep Disorders are subdivided into the Dysomnias (abnormalities in the sleep cycle, i.e., its amount, quality or timing) and the Parasomnias (sleep-related abnormal events, e.g., nightmares).

The Dysomnias include (1) Primary Insomnia (307.42) (at least a month of difficulty initiating or maintaining sleep, with life impairment, and not better explained by other sleep disorders or other disorders); (2) Primary Hypersomnia (307.44) (at least a month of excessive sleepiness, less if recurrent, and life impairment, etc.); (3) Narcolepsy (347) (at least three months of daily and irresistible attacks of refreshing sleep that include at least either catalepsy or recurrent intrusions of REM sleep into the sleep–wakefulness transition); (4) Breathing-Related Sleep Disorder (780.59) (evidence of a sleep-disrupting breathing condition); (5) Circadian Rhythm Sleep Disorder (307.45) (impairing and persistent or recurring excessive sleepiness or insomnia due to a mismatch of the sleep–wake cycle to the individual's circadian rhythm and/or environment requirements, and this can be further specified as "Delayed Sleep Phase Type," "Jet Lag Type," "Shift Work Type," or "Unspecified Type"; and (6) Dysomnia NOS (307.47).

The Parasomnias are Nightmare Disorder (307.47) (impairing and repeated sleep awakenings, with recall of extended and very frightening dreams, with rapid reorientation upon awakening); Sleep Terror Disorder (307.46) (impairing sleep awakenings, usually with a panicky scream, intense fear with related autonomic signs, relative unresponsiveness to comforting, with little recall of the dream); Sleepwalking Disorder (307.46) (impairing repeated sleepwalking episodes, with unresponsivity in the episode, relatively quick reorientation, and amnesia for the episode); and Parasomnia NOS (307.47).

☐ DIAGNOSTIC CONSIDERATIONS

The first diagnostic recommendation is that any apparently serious sleep disorder should be evaluated at a sleep disorder center; a thorough evaluation should include some observation and physiological monitoring, ideally of at least a couple of nights of sleep.

As regards standard psychological tests, Keles (1983) found that chronic insomniacs show a significant level of pathology on the MMPI-2. The highest three-scale code was 2-7-3. Fifty-six percent of the insomniacs tended to have a pathologic elevation on scale 2, while 42% had a pathologic elevation on scale 7 and 38% a pathologic elevation on scale 3. The 2-7-3 code reflects the chronic anxiety, difficulty expressing feelings, denial, and feelings of depression common to the insomniac. Interestingly, Keles found that 30% of his subjects had pathologic elevation on scale 8, which reflects self-image problems and difficulty integrating emotions. Scale 1 was significantly elevated in 20% of his subjects. Keles also found significant differences between age groups in their MMPI-2 scores. The most common three-scale code in those younger than 30 was 2-7-8; in ages 30–49, 2-7-3 was the most common.

On the 16 PF, it is hypothesized that insomniacs would have high scores on scales I, L, O, and Q_4, while scores on scales E, F, and H would be low and C relatively low. A high Q_4 would tap the high anxiety level that is common to most insomniacs. A high score on O would reflect the insecure and oversensitive nature of the insomniac. Introspection, rumination, and inability to deal with conflict would be reflected by a high scale I and at least a mildly elevated M.

On the ten basic personality pattern scales of the MCMI-III, an elevated scale 2B and moderately elevated 8A may be expected. A high scale 2A (avoidant) would tap two common personality characteristics of the insomniacs: mild cognitive intrusions and perceptual hyperactivity. Since many insomniacs have problems expressing their emotions, this may be reflected on scale 1. On the pathologic personality disorders (scales C, P, and S), little elevations are expected.

☐ TREATMENT OPTIONS

Many insomniacs have significant anxiety, depression, and/or obsessive-compulsive features that contribute to the insomnia, as well as to other aspects of functioning. If these exist, the reader is referred to those chapters for relevant treatment recommendations (Harsh and Ogilvie, 1995).

Chemotherapy is commonly used for insomnia, sometimes with a very specific focus—for example, oxycodone for restless-leg syndrome. Benzodiazepines, especially those with a short (diazepam) or intermediate (triazolam or temazepam) absorption rate, are the preferred hypnotic-sleeping drug for most clients. Antihistamines can be useful in the short run, but tolerance develops quickly. Numerous other agents are available for specific client needs (e.g., sedative antidepressants, barbiturates, chloral hydrate, etc.), but most have some problematic side effects if used for any length of time, and many quickly produce physical dependence. Indeed, any chemotherapy directed toward the sleep disorder as a whole must be administered with caution (Montplaisir and Godbout, 1991): It can be especially useful in breaking the insomnia cycle (e.g., if prescribed for no more than a week), but if prescribed for any length of time loses its effectiveness, brings on the risk of drug dependence and/or addiction, and can generate a rebound effect of even greater insomnia. Blood levels of melatonin, a natural hormone produced in the pineal gland, have been related to sleep-pattern disruptions. Melatonin at a dosage of 2–3 mg administered one to two hours before bedtime appears to restore disrupted sleep–wake cycle insomnia in as little as a week and to be especially useful for the elderly.

Various behavioral techniques have been found to be effective (Harsh and Ogilvie, 1995; Hauri, 1991; Montplaisir and Godbout, 1991), but the most efficient techniques are probably cognitive therapy, relaxation training and biofeedback where the emphasis is on muscle-tension release. Ancillary techniques include (1) initiating a regular program of vigorous exercise, although it is best to avoid vigorous exercise late in the evening—ideally, do aerobic exercise three to five hours before bed; (2) avoiding large or late meals or, conversely, going to bed very hungry—a high carbohydrate snack is helpful; (3) avoiding napping, especially long or late naps during the day—keep any naps to forty-five minutes or less; (4) go to bed only when sleepy, and limit allotted time in bed to estimated need, usually no more than seven hours—this creates an actual, controlled sleep debt and helps to break the cycle of rumination in bed; (5) cutting down on caffeine or heavy smoking or alcohol use, especially later in the evening; (6) ceasing to fret over inconsistencies in the sleep pattern—give yourself some "quiet time" before going to bed, ideally one to two hours, and tell yourself as you prepare for bed that you will sleep well; (7) keeping the bedroom as quiet, dark, and comfortable as possible—most find a temperature of 65 degrees to be optimal—and possibly using a "white noise" generator or audio tapes to introduce masking or restful sound; and (8) relearning a more appropriate bedtime routine by (a) going to bed only when feeling tired, (b) awakening at the same time each morning, (c) avoiding all nonsleep-related activities (within reason) in the bedroom, and (d) leaving the bed in twenty to thirty minutes if sleep has not occurred, to do something like read a book, and not returning until again feeling drowsy. As the philosopher Friedrich Nietzsche said in *Thus Spake Zarathustra*, "It is no small art to sleep: To achieve it one must stay awake."

Sleepwalkers often present management-control issues, and any therapist who works with such problems is advised to present the client with the following recommendations, as adapted from Gilmore (1991):

1. Use no drugs, alcohol, or caffeine, and use no psychotropic medications unless prescribed by a physician who is aware of the potential of such medications to exacerbate sleepwalking. Avoid any over-the-counter cold remedies or diet pills that contain stimulants.

2. Remove and/or dismantle any lethal weapons from access by the sleep-walker.

3. Take special precautions, such as placing locks on doors and windows, tying one's ankle to the bedpost, and placing a "kiddie fence" by the bedroom door.

4. Sleep on the ground floor.

5. Get treatment for depression and/or other concurrent emotional problems.

6. Learn stress-management skills and obtain skills and reassurance to lower anxiety, and consider marital counseling for related stress.

7. Maintain a regular sleep–wake cycle and get adequate sleep at regular intervals.

8. Get a complete assessment by an expert in sleep disorders who can monitor physiological measurements.

CHAPTER 8

The Sexual Disorders

■ Overall Concepts

This overall category in the DSM-IV is used for those disorders in which a psychological variable is a significant factor in a sexual disturbance or disorder. If the disorder is caused by a physical factor, such as impotence from arteriosclerosis, it would be coded as an organic mental disorder.

In DSM-IV there are three divisions: the paraphilias (the DSM-IV term for the traditional "sexual deviations"), the gender identity disorders, and the sexual dysfunctions. There is also a residual category: sexual disorder NOS. Although the DSM-IV does not directly provide for a diagnosis of sexual compulsion, it is a factor in many of the following diagnoses, and there is evidence that it may even be a recognizable pattern occasionally found apart from these other diagnoses (Schmidt, 1995; Masters et al., 1991, 1994).

■ Paraphilias

"Paraphilia" is the DSM-IV term for "sexual deviations," and both terms will be used interchangeably. The deviation *(para)* is in that to which the individual is attracted *(philia)*. In the DSM-IV, all diagnoses of Paraphilia first require fulfillment of (1) Criteria A—recurrent, intense, sexually arousing fantasies, sexual urges, or behaviors [with the specificity required by the particular disorder], over at least a six-month period *and* (2) Criteria B—these fantasies, urges, or behaviors cause clinically significant distress or impairment in an important area of one's life. As with most of the DSM-IV categories, the paraphilias are classified as (1) mild—few, if any, symptoms in excess of what is minimally required, (2) moderate—between mild and severe, and (3) severe—many symptoms in excess of the minimum, or several particularly severe symptoms.

The specific paraphilia categories included in DSM-IV are (1) Fetishism, (2) Transvestic Fetishism, (3) Pedophilia, (4) Exhibitionism, (5) Voyeurism,

(6) Frotteurism, (7) Sexual Masochism, and (8) Sexual Sadism. There is also a residual category, Paraphilia NOS (302.9), that could be used often when making a diagnosis, since the confabulation of potential sexual deviations is restricted only by the limits of the imagination (Janus and Janus, 1994). The specific variations included in the DSM-IV are those that have traditionally been labeled as deviant and/or that have involved a legal issue. Thus, "variation" is an even more appropriate term than "deviance," since "variation" more clearly implies this wide range of potential behaviors and the fact that many of these patterns may in certain circumstances be acceptable and adaptive and that the "deviance" of the disorder is often only in the eye of the beholder.

The essential disorder is in the lack of capacity for mature and participating affectionate sexual behavior with adult partners. Traditionally these disorders have been far more common in males, but this discrepancy has decreased slightly in recent years (Masters et al., 1994). Note that occasionally engaging in such fantasy or behavior does not usually qualify one as a paraphiliac. Exclusivity, persistency (even compulsivity), and pervasiveness are the hallmarks of the disorder. It is typically a driven, focused pattern, often seen initially in fantasy or behavior in mid-adolescence (Hollin and Howells, 1991).

Research does not support sex hormone or neurotransmitter abnormalities as the primary or major cause in the paraphilias (Masters et al., 1991, 1994). As Lo Piccolo (1993) asserts:

paraphilias are complex, multiply determined conditions, and . . . any single-element theory of etiology is oversimplified and incorrect. Rather, we should realize that paraphilias clearly involve a host of factors, including arousal conditioned to inappropriate objects, lack of internalized moral values, inability to weigh long-term negative consequences against short–term sexual pleasure, distorted thinking about sexuality, lack of access to gratifying normal sexual outlets, lack of empathy for victim distress, disinhibition by alcohol or drugs, and, possibly, temporal lobe pathology. In individual cases, various combinations of these factors may be more or less important. (p. 340)

DIAGNOSTIC CONSIDERATIONS

In general, the paraphilias, unless they are confounded by the presence of other psychopathology, do not present modal abnormal patterns on either the MMPI–2 or the 16 PF, although convicted sex offenders tend to obtain 4-5/5-4 or 4-8/8-4 profiles (Erickson et al., 1987). Because they are obtained in a clinical setting, some pathology is suggested, or else society, through a legal or social agent (e.g., a marital therapist) is concerned about the pattern. Certain scales may then be markedly elevated.

Useful measures specifically designed for this area include the Clark Institute Sexual Questionnaire, Abel-Becker's Sexual Interest Cardsort, Mosher Sexual Guilt Questionnaire, the Derogatis Sexual Function Inventory, and Abel-Becker's Cognition Scale.

Measuring sexual responses to suggested imagery or to actual pictures of various stimuli is helpful in specifying the focus of the sexually deviant fantasies that are a key to behavior. In a cooperative subject, direct measures of penile tumescence (usually via changes in a rubber tube encircling the penis, as in a pneumograph) are the most precise, although, in some cases, thermography has distinct advantages of ease of access and less embarrassment.

TREATMENT OPTIONS

Since the paraphilias range from disorders that involve passivity (sexual masochism) to those that involve coercive aggression and legal sanctions (pedophilia), treatments will differ as well (Woody, 1992). Indeed, a clinician working in this area is constantly challenged by the creative diversity found in sexual preferences. For example, antisex crusader John Harvey Kellogg in part originated Kellogg's breakfast cereals to calm sexual lust and promote a generally healthy lifestyle in the general population. Yet, Kellogg avoided sex with his wife and obtained gratification from enemas—a pattern known as klismaphilia.

In general, all of the paraphilias are difficult to treat—success is often negligible and/or short-term, and relapse is common. Castration is a time-honored method, although even it is not as effective as its admirers believe. Medroxyprogesterone acetate (Depa–Provera) is effective as a short-term chemocastrator. Neuroleptics such as thioridazine (Mellaril) produce a moderate reduction in arousal in at least 50% of clients, and Prozac has received some support as effective here. Neurosurgical castration via temporal lobe ablation has been used in eastern Europe.

Most individuals with a paraphilia are best treated within a formal treatment program, usually referred to as a Sex Offender Program. It is helpful if the program can be delivered in the context of a psychotherapy or counseling relationship wherein a degree of trust has been generated. Yet, understand that such clients, within a continuum of conscious deception to unwitting self-deception, are likely to overstate gains, resist treatment, and prematurely terminate. Be especially suspicious of statements that the client has spontaneously or quickly lost interest in deviant activities and/or has easily (or ever) become primarily interested in consensual sex with adult females. It almost never happens that way.

The following are potential components of a typical sex offender treatment program (Lo Piccolo, 1993; Woody, 1992):

1. *Assessment of the offender.* This includes nature of specific offense, victim characteristics, antecedents of the offender's crime, previous offenses, level of psychopathology, developmental history, educational history, social history, sexual history-knowledge-experience, religious beliefs, occupational history, level of anger, level of ability to empathize, awareness of emotions, cognitive distortions about men-women-children, and sexual arousal. Techniques to assess and evaluate the offender include clinical interviews, self-reporting, psychological tests, questionnaires, rating scales, and physiological measures.

2. *Any necessary acute measures,* e.g., short–term chemocastration. Other medications, e.g., antidepressants, may be necessary in some cases. Also, mandate any life situation changes that reduce the opportunity to engage in the deviant behavior, e.g., a temporary change of residence.

3. *Group and individual therapy.* This is necessary to clarify the individual's range of deviancy, level of disorder, level of commitment to change, and ability to tolerate confrontation. It provides a context for retraining more prosocial sexual patterns. This is an appropriate place to deal with cognitive distortions, such as "Women may act like they don't, but I can tell they secretly like it when I . . . ."

4. *An adequate system of phallometric measurement,* e.g., penile plethysmography. Self-report of offenders is faulty due to their tendencies to minimize involvement and their wishes to conceal information, and some suffer from disorders that affect their thought process to such an extent that self-reported information is invalid. Plethysmography is defined as the use of an instrument for determining and registering variations in the size of an organ or limb. Typically, an electronic device, called a penile transducer, is attached to the penis by the client. It detects changes in the size of the penis when sexual stimuli of both deviant and nondeviant content are presented (Fedora et al., 1992). The associated degrees of erection provide an indication of his sexual interests, preferences, and inhibitions. However, it is subject to inaccuracy due to malingering by conscious control, unconscious components, stress, etc. Therapists are trained to utilize the plethysmograph to condition the offender to appropriate sexual stimuli as well as to counter-condition him to inappropriate stimuli.

5. *Covert sensitization* is an imagery-based counter-conditioning procedure in which a client is instructed to imagine the relevant deviant sexual act or stimulus followed by the imagining of some negative reaction, usually either severe anxiety, terror, or nausea. Assisted covert sensitization employs a strongly noxious odor to aid in the development of a nausea response.

6. *Aversive conditioning* is when inappropriate sexual stimuli are presented to a client via slides, audio tapes, or video tapes, followed by the presentation of the noxious stimuli, such as the inhalation of valeric acid or ammonia.

7. *Masturbatory satiation therapy* involves having the offender masturbate to an appropriate sexual fantasy while verbalizing it aloud. Following this, the offender is required to continue to masturbate for a period ranging from forty-five minutes to two hours (or try, in some cases) while verbalizing deviant sexual fantasies. This should all be tape recorded to check progress, possibility of malingering, etc.

8. *Aversive behavioral rehearsal* attempts to decrease sexually deviant behaviors and arousal by making the behavior publicly observable. The offender describes in detail the types of offense committed and then by use of mannequins, clothing, apparatus, etc., reenacts the offense. The tape is narrated by the offender while discussing his plans, actions, feelings, and thoughts. Having victims, friends, and/or family members as an audience heightens the aversive effect.

9. *Education programs* that focus on sexual education, social-skills training, assertiveness training, and cognitive re-education are typically necessary.

10. *Enrollment in a support group* such as Sexaholics Anonymous or Sex and Love Addicts Anonymous.

11. In many cases it is critical to develop an *ancillary surveillance and report group,* specific to the individual client. This may involve family, friends, neighbors, etc. who are made aware of the situation on a need-to-know basis and who agree to report inappropriate or suspicious behaviors.

12. *Relapse prevention* emphasizes that sex offenses are not totally impulsive criminal acts, but have varying levels of control and planning. Offense precursors, a common sequence of risk factors that cumulate in sexual violence, set off chain-like processes. Offense precursors are emotion, fantasy, cognitive distortion, plan, and act. The two models of relapse are the internal, self-management dimension and the external, supervisory dimension. The first model increases the client's awareness and range of choices concerning his behavior, in developing specific coping skills and self-control capacities, and in creating a general sense of mastery over life. The second model imposes external controls involving the parole officer, the therapist, the parole board, and the ancillary surveillance and report group. Much attention should be paid to developing avoidance and escape strategies from risk situations, learning how to deal with frustrations in developing or existent appropriate sexual relationships and how to deal with boredom and involuntary thoughts, etc.

The offender typically has to admit guilt before he can be accepted into sex offender programming. He has to participate in the assessment process by taking tests, by relating his life's history, and by cooperating fully. Most programs require the offender to sign a contract outlining his responsibilities and the results that can occur if he does not meet these responsibilities. The goals and responsibilities agreed to are developed by the treatment team. Appropriate goals of treatment include, but are not limited to, the following:

- To actively participate in and follow all treatment requirements
- To learn to control his deviant arousal pattern
- To place obstacles in the path of converting nonsexual problems into sexual behavior
- To learn to solve nonsexual problems in nonsexual ways
- To take responsibility for his behavior without minimizing, externalizing, or projecting blame onto others
- To make some form of restitution to the victim

Fetishism (302.81)

The DSM-IV defines fetishism as a condition wherein nonliving objects (not including clothing used in cross-dressing or objects directly designed for sexual facilitation, e.g., vibrators) are specifically used to fulfill Criterion A and B for the paraphilias. The traditional use of this term included an attraction to isolated though still-attached body parts, but this does not fit with the DSM-IV definition. If the fetish is simply articles of clothing used in cross-dressing, the diagnosis could be transvestic fetishism.

Sexual stimulation from fetishes is typically obtained by tasting, fondling, kissing, or smelling the objects. Bras, panties, and shoes are the most common objects. The objects may be used while masturbating alone or, in some cases, as a necessary preliminary to intercourse. A degree of fetishism is associated with any sexual experience. Normal foreplay includes attention to sexually arousing objects or parts of the body, with consequent sexual arousal and progression toward coitus. In fetishism, however, the fetish takes primacy as a necessary means for developing arousal and allows avoidance of intimacy (Levin and Stava, 1987).

A confounding variable in fetishism, as well as in a number of other paraphilias, is the potential legal issue (Slovenko, 1995). Acts of breaking and entering are occasionally committed by the fetishist who is seeking a supply of women's used bras or panties. New articles of clothing are seldom arousing, in part because they are not identified with any individual person and also because they do not have the odors that are often arousing to the fetishist. In many cases the illegal behavior itself increases the excitation and consequently increases the sexual arousal.

Although fetishism tends to crystallize as a behavior pattern in adolescence, it often has precursors in childhood. It is chronic, and most fetishists are men.

MMPI-2

Fetishists seldom show a markedly elevated MMPI-2 profile. If the fetishism reflects some insecurity with the male sex role or some disguised homoerotic trends, an elevation on scale 5 is expected (Graham, 1987). In fetishists who indulge alone, a fear of the opposite sex may exist, which would elevate scales 4 and 7 to a degree. When the fetishism is embedded in heterosexual relationships, such elevations are less probable. When there is a legal problem involving fetishism, the reader should consult the section on malingering.

16 PF

The fetishist who indulges while alone is more likely to be low on factor A. Those who accept their fetishistic behavior should have a reasonably high Q_1, whereas if they do not accept it, Q_1 may be at an average level or even lower. These clients are also likely to be relatively low on scale G and moderately high on M. If distressed by their pattern, high scores on O and Q_4 are likely. If they are being legally or socially coerced because of their behavior, such defensive patterns as malingering may be expected, with a higher score on L.

TREATMENT OPTIONS

The aversive conditioning therapies are especially appropriate with fetishism, since specific behavior patterns are the central focus. Mild electric shock, inhalation of valeric acid, and nausea-inducing drugs have been successfully used in aversive conditioning procedures in which the object of the fetish, or fantasy of it, is paired with the aversive stimulus. In theory at least, mild electric shock is preferable to such nausea-producing drugs as apomorphine because the contiguity between the avoidance stimulus and the deviant response is more easily controlled when shock is used. The aversion therapy procedures of both fear conditioning and aversion relief have also been used. Once the person has decreased the arousal value contingent on the fetishistic object, training in more normal sexual patterns is possible (Lo Piccolo, 1993).

Transvestic Fetishism (302.30)

Transvestism, or transvestic fetishism (TF) in the DSM-IV, is the fulfillment of Criterion A and B of the paraphilias, with the specific focus on cross-dressing. In most transvestites the cross-dressing behavior was initiated in childhood and, in some, was significantly reinforced by parents, sometimes by "petticoat punishment," the humiliation of a boy by dressing him in girl's clothes. It typically becomes paired with masturbation and eventuates in the classic transvestite pattern.

Transvestic fetishism is considered to be a rare disorder; an even smaller subgroup eventually goes from TF to transsexualism, where the diagnosis of transsexualism takes precedence (Schmidt, 1995). TF is obviously related to fetishism. Just as in fetishism, an inanimate object is the stimulating variable, and there is often little or no dependence on human relationships for sexual gratification. When the transvestite has a partner, there may be masochistic fantasies that progress into behavior (Hollin and Howells, 1991). This then adds a secondary diagnosis of sexual masochism.

DIAGNOSTIC CONSIDERATIONS

Transvestites do not show particularly pathologic MMPI-2 or 16 PF profiles. A high GF scale score for male transvestites is highly likely, as is a high GM scale score for female transvestites (Gentry and Meyer, 1991). The clinician can expect a high scale 5 whether this is a male or female transvestite (although DSM-IV limits this disorder to males dressing as females). There is also a moderate rise in scale 3, which indicates some histrionic components, and possibly mild elevations in scales 4 and 6, reflecting concern about being discovered in a secret lifestyle and hostility toward standard social mores.

On the 16 PF, moderately elevated L and Q_1 scales and moderately low scores on G and Q_3 occur. A higher score on N is also probable, and if anxiety is a reason for this clinical situation, elevation on Q_4, and possibly on O, could be expected.

Anxiety and depression may occur if cross-dressing is inhibited, producing significant elevations on A and/or D on the MCMI-III. As in other psychosexual disorders, 1 and/or 2A may occur as the most prevalent personality syndrome. C is also likely to be high. Additionally, the indifference to social expectations may be reflected by elevation on 5.

TREATMENT OPTIONS

Since TF is easily considered a subcategory of fetishism, the procedures noted in that section are equally applicable here. In addition to using aversive procedures, the therapist could use thought stopping to control the initial impulse to cross-dress. TF may have certain compulsive features, so the reader is referred to the section on the obsessive-compulsive disorder. Both the aversion therapy and the thought stopping can be amplified by the use of a portable, self-administered shock unit. The person can wear this unit discreetly under clothing, and when the impulse arises, a shock can be administered in conjunction with the aversion or thought-stopping procedure.

Covert sensitization (Cautela and Wall, 1980) is particularly helpful in the habit disorders and can easily be dovetailed with the aversive conditioning procedures in the therapist's office. In the covert sensitization procedure, some highly aversive contingency is imagined immediately on the occurrence of the fantasy of the undesired behavior. In this case it is the transvestite pattern. As a result, the undesired impulse toward TF is weakened.

Pedophilia (302.2)

Pedophilia literally—and ironically—means "love of children," and a pedophiliac is one who consistently seeks out sexual experiences with children. To qualify for a DSM-IV diagnosis, one must meet Criteria A (involving sexual activity with a prepubescent child, "generally" younger than 14 years of age) and Criteria B (for paraphilias), and the perpetrator is at least 16 years of age and is at least five years older than the child. The diagnosis should specify if (a) "Sexually Attracted to Males," . . . "Females," or . . . "Both," (b) if "Limited to Incest," and (c) if "Exclusive Type," that is, only children, or "Nonexclusive Type."

Pedophilia is extremely rare in females, and although it is not a particularly common behavior in *any* demographic group (Seidman and Rieder, 1994), it has traditionally been viewed as a disorder of middle-aged males—"dirty old men." Research (Abel et al., 1986; Levin and Stava, 1987; Finkelhor and Dziuba-Leatherman, 1994) has shown, however, that while the offender is almost always male, the molestation typically started by age 15. Most early victims are known to the pedophile. Boys are more likely to be victims than girls; girls are more likely to be victims of "hands-off" crimes like exhibitionism. Most pedophiles over time commit a wide range of crimes, including exhibitionism, voyeurism, and rape; and pedophiles who molest boys do it a great deal (an average of over two hundred incidents), whereas female-oriented pedophiles average approximately twenty-five incidents and rapists of adults five to ten incidents. Not surprisingly, few sex offenders will admit to such numbers unless given complete anonymity.

There are significant differences between those pedophiliac men who are exclusively inclined toward sexual experiences with male children and those who primarily seek out females. Heterosexual pedophiles are more likely to be married and prefer a younger target—females age 8 to 10—as opposed to the homosexual pedophile's preference for boys age 12 to 14. Homosexual pedophiles show a poor prognosis for change, are less likely to know their victim, and are more interested in proceeding to orgasm rather than focusing on the touching and looking behavior often preferred by heterosexual pedophiles. Many heterosexual male pedophiles have problems with potency and are likely to prefer ejaculation achieved through voyeuristic-exhibitionistic masturbation. When they do attempt intercourse with a child, they are more likely to generate trauma and pain and in that way raise their chances of being reported and eventually apprehended.

Pedophiles, whether homosexual or heterosexual, often feel inadequate about their sexuality, and the contact and/or comparison with the sexually immature target may alleviate this anxiety and allow a nonthreatening release for sexual tension.

Alcohol abuse is a common catalyst for this behavior, as are marital problems among married pedophiles. Another catalyst (which does not detract in any way from the pedophile's responsibility for the act) is victim behavior. Finkelhor (1985) points to interesting data showing that an unusually high percentage of sexually victimized children had lived without their mothers for a significant length of time prior to the age of 16. It is possible that they may have missed a subtle training in behaviors conducive to fending off this type of sexual coercion. Evidence shows that when the pedophile is mentally retarded or schizophrenic, the victim sometimes initiated the contact (Friedrich, 1991).

A subcategory of pedophilia is incest. While incest occurs in any potential family structure relationship, father–daughter incest is by far the most common target of societal concern. Three psychological subpatterns occur in this specific form of incest (Finkelhor, 1985; Smith and Meyer, 1987). The first pattern is the inadequate and psychosexually immature father who is functionally a pedophile and who often has sexual contact with his daughters, sons, and other children. Such individuals show a combination of pedophiliac and psychopathic diagnostic indications. The second is a true "primary psychopath." This person relates to virtually all people as objects, is promiscuous in all directions, and shows little remorse over any behavior patterns.

Family-generated incest is the third pattern, and it is usually marked by a passive and inadequate father and an emotionally disturbed mother. These are often symbiotic personalities, who use the incestuous relationship to satisfy emotional and sexual needs. Sexual estrangement from the spouse is often the catalyst. Persons engaging in this type of incest show characteristics of the pedophile plus aspects of the passive-aggressive and dependent personality disorders.

MMPI-2

As might be expected from society's repugnance for this type of behavior, pedophiles are far more defensive than persons with most other paraphilias. As a result, elevated K and L scales are common, and elevations on 4 and 8 are most common in the clinical scales (Hall et al., 1986). Denial, along with an avoidance of intrapsychic concern, is reflected in an elevated 3 scale.

Erickson et al. (1987) found that offenders against children were more likely to obtain 4-2/2-4 profiles, whereas offenders against adult women tended to obtain 4-9/9-4 profiles. While the most common MMPI-2 profile in child molesters is a 2-4/4-2, the particularly inadequate pedophile who has significant difficulties in dealing interpersonally with the opposite sex often presents a 1-8/8-1 profile. Likewise, incestuous pedophiles score higher on 0 than nonincestuous pedophiles, who in turn are higher than normals (Levin and Stava, 1987). Those who show a consistent immaturity throughout many of their behavior patterns and who have problems in controlling impulse behavior may show a 3-8/8-3 code. Where the pedophiliac behavior is a classic counterphobic mechanism to deny feelings of inadequacy about masculinity, the 4-8/8-4, with a surprisingly low scale 5 score (considering the person's general behavior patterns), is obtained. Where the person is more aware of the disturbance in sexual identity, an elevation on scale 5 is seen.

16 PF

On the 16 PF the emotional disturbance, impulsivity, and deviant mores are reflected in low scores on A, C, G, and Q_3. Anxiety and insecurity, possibly induced by the potential for being apprehended, elevate scores on O and Q_4. The deviant fantasy and the isolation from society because of the repulsiveness of the acts result in high scores on L and M. Homosexual pedophiles are moderately high on E and H and moderately low on I; the reverse is true for heterosexual pedophiles. Scores on scale B vary markedly, although they are usually moderately low.

OTHER TEST-RESPONSE PATTERNS

In human-figure drawings, Johnson and Johnson (1986) found pedophiles, when compared to normals, to show poorer overall quality in the drawings, poorer gender differentiation, the female figure often larger than the male figure, and a number of male figures with blank or missing eyes.

Except for possible elevation on B and 3, the clinical-symptom syndromes do not usually show much disturbance on the MCMI-III. The interpersonal indifference and behavioral apathy indicated by elevated 1 are less likely here than elevated scores on 2A, 5, and 6A. Although high scores on 2A indicate a detached style, pedophiles may seek less threatening children as a source of sexual satisfaction to deal with their interpersonal inadequacy. A and D are likely to be high if the behavior is ego-dystonic, and 6 may be high if the person has become embroiled in legal troubles.

TREATMENT OPTIONS

Because of the disgust with which most people respond to this disorder, it is not surprising that the typical treatment approaches are somewhat coercive. Pedophiles rarely bring themselves into treatment and are typically coerced by sociolegal pressure (Finkelhor and Dziuba-Leatherman, 1994). Castration is still a favored response in some cultures, and, in our society, chemocastration is still considered to be a reasonable option. Antiandrogens such as cyproterone acetate (in Europe) or medroxyprogesterone acetate (in the United States) suppress the sexual libidos of male pedophiles; these drugs also have been used with rapists and exhibitionists (Abel et al., 1986). They function by reducing serum testosterone to levels at which sexual arousal is diminished or absent, and they have moderate success when combined with psychotherapy. The aversion therapies have also been used, with moderate success.

Covert sensitization can be helpful. Aversive mental images are immediately associated with images and impulses for initiating and continuing pedophiliac behaviors. Forgione (1976) presented an interesting variation on this approach. He filmed pedophiles while they reenacted their pedophiliac behaviors in response to a childlike manikin; simply watching the playback proved aversive and reduced the pedophiliac behavior. The clinician could vary this procedure by making slides from the tape and pairing electric shock with them to further the aversive response.

Work to correct such cognitive distortions as (1) "My sexual contact with children is not really bad for them, and may even be good for them," (2) "children are able to reason, so if they consent to it, it is really not molesting," and (3) "if they don't resist (or strongly resist), they actually want the sexual contact." Since inadequacy in social interactions is a major factor in most pedophiles, assertiveness training, particularly directed toward adults of the opposite sex, is helpful here. It can be complemented by general social retraining toward an ability to attain mature heterosexual partners (Finkelhor and Dziuba-Leatherman, 1994).

In one of the better studies on recidivism from treatment, in this case a maximum security psychiatric institution, Rice et al. (1992) found that the recidivism of 136 such extrafamilial child molesters who had received phallometric assessment and treatment from 1972 to 1983 was determined over an average 6.3-year followup. Fifty had participated in behavioral treatment to alter inappropriate sexual age preferences. Thirty-one percent of the subjects were convicted of a new sex offense, 43% committed a violent or sexual offense, and 58% were arrested for some offense or returned to the institution for a parole violation. Those convicted of a new sex offense had previously committed more sex offenses, had been admitted to correctional institutions more frequently, were more likely to have been diagnosed as personality disordered, were more likely to have never married, and had shown more inappropriate sexual preferences in initial phallometric assessment than those who had not returned to the penal system. Unfortunately, behavioral treatment did not significantly affect recidivism.

■ Exhibitionism (302.4)

The term "exhibitionism" was first introduced into psychopathology by Lasegue in 1877, although the act itself was described as early as 4 B.C. (Cox, 1980). Exhibitionism is the act of exposing one's genitals to a stranger in order to obtain sexual arousal. Certain rare individuals do expose themselves without ever having been aroused, but they usually turn out to be psychotic, senile, or at least moderately mentally retarded.

The DSM-IV requires the fulfillment of Criterion A and B for paraphilias, involving the exposure of one's genitals to an unsuspecting stranger. The DSMs traditionally argued that the condition was found only in males, but this proviso was dropped in DSM-III-R. There are few reports to police of females who exhibit themselves, but to assert that the behavior *never* occurs in females is unsubstantiated (Masters et al., 1991). Although it is treatable, exhibitionism, along with voyeurism, has had the highest recidivism rate of all the sexual disorders (Cox, 1980; Marshall et al., 1991).

☐ DIAGNOSTIC CONSIDERATIONS

From the legal perspective, exhibitionism is probably the most commonly reported paraphilia, but the cost to victims and society is lower than that of some of the other disorders, such as pedophilia (Slovenko, 1995). It is estimated to account for about one-third of all sexual offenses reported to authorities, and only a small percentage of exposure acts are ever reported to the police (Abel et al., 1986; Hendrix and Meyer, 1976). Indications are that there is a bimodal distribution of the mean age of onset of first exposure, with peaks in the age ranges 11–15 and 21–25. The mean age of first arrest is approximately 25. Exhibitionists seldom gravitate toward more serious sexual offenses (Cox, 1980).

The high overall recidivism rate is partially explained by a markedly increasing recidivism rate for those who are convicted more than once. Even though there is a conviction rate of only 10% for first offenders, the rate is almost 60% for those with more than one previous sexual offense and 70% for those with previous sexual and nonsexual offenses. If intervention can keep the exhibitionist from exposing himself for at least eighteen months after treatment, there is a low likelihood of future exposures (Cox, 1980).

There is a high incidence of disrupted father–son relationships in the background of exhibitionists—indeed, this is true to a degree for most of the paraphilias (Levin and Stava, 1987). Exhibitionists show poor interpersonal relationships during adolescence, and masturbation is always of unusual importance to them as a sexual outlet, even when other partners are available.

Of the personality types that eventuate in exhibitionism (Smith and Meyer, 1987), the "characterological type," a small group, is the only one that shows any significant danger to the victim. They have profiles similar to rapists, with the same elements of anger and hostility. The shock response of the victim is a major reinforcement, and there is little guilt or remorse.

A second subtype is the "unaware group," where the act is an outgrowth of extreme alcohol intoxication, organic brain disorder, or severe mental retardation. A third type is the "inadequate group." These individuals are similar to those with the avoidant personality disorder, although they have a few more obsessional features and more anger. The reader is referred to the section on the avoidant personality disorder, with the notation that scales 4 and 6 on the MMPI-2 and the correlated scales on the 16 PF should be a bit more elevated here.

The fourth group, the "impulsive-compulsive type," is obsessional, tense, anxious, and both sexually compelled and confused. Their behavior is an impulsive response to intrapsychic conflict and distress. It is this last group, the largest group of exhibitionists, that we will focus on in the following discussion of diagnostic parameters.

MMPI-2

A summary of MMPI-2 data collected on exhibitionists shows them to be moderately nonconforming individuals who have a history of mild violations of social norms, but with no extensive allied psychopathology (Cox, 1980). Throughout most studies the standard elevations are on scales 4, 5, and 8, but these are often below 70 T. The elevations on scales 4 and 8 reflect the mild antisocial nature of the behavior, the lack of impulse control, and a degree of hostility toward the general environment. The elevation on 5 reflects sexual confusion, but there are "macho" exhibitionists who are low on 5. Exhibitionists are usually very low on scale 0 and moderately low on scales 1 and 9. To the degree scale 8 is elevated in relation to other scales, these persons are likely to be self-defeating and their exposure patterns more likely to be discovered. For example, the senior author is aware of numerous exhibitionists who have admitted exhibiting themselves over five hundred times without ever being apprehended. Similar cases have shown a low 8 scale, with a high 4 scale and moderately high 5 and K scales. Exhibitionists are generally lower than rapists on 4, 8, 6, 3, 2, and F, in order of magnitude (Levin and Stava, 1987).

16 PF

Exhibitionists score moderately high on O and Q_4; however, their scales may revert to average if they are not under some kind of legal scrutiny. Similar to obsessives, they are only moderately low on C and moderately high on L and

M. To the degree they have been self-defeating in their exposure patterns, they are likely to show a low score on N and Q_3 and a high score on H. Other scales are usually not remarkable.

TREATMENT OPTIONS

Exhibitionism, like pedophilia, has a high rate of recidivism (Schmidt, 1995). For that reason, some therapists eventually resort to chemocastration through the use of such antiandrogen drugs as medroxyprogesterone acetate. However, the major treatment for exhibitionism is some form of aversion therapy, and cognitive therapy and relationship-skills training appear to be necessary to produce any long–term change (Marshall et al., 1991). Some retraining in social skills and orgasmic reconditioning are also usually necessary. Covert sensitization can be used, amplified by adding noxious odors and shocks at the time the exhibitionist is presenting the aversive images to himself.

Hendrix and Meyer (1976) demonstrated that exhibitionism can be controlled through a multifaceted treatment approach that includes no aversive techniques. They used progressive relaxation to lower a client's tension-anger pattern and cassette tapes and autogenic training to further the relaxation response. Psychotherapy uncovered the suppressed anger and fear of interacting with females, and assertiveness training was used to control these situations. This was combined with increased self-verbalizations designed to heighten self-esteem and confidence. At that point, standard sexual counseling helped in the attainment of adequate heterosexual relationships. Also included was systematic desensitization, which was used to dissipate a phobic fear of being rebuffed by females. In addition, Dr. Hendrix accompanied the exhibitionist to in vivo situations, such as the campus snack shop (being introduced as his friend, if necessary). Dr. Hendrix monitored the situation and then later counseled the client on his socialization patterns.

Wickramasekera (1976) proposed a then-unique treatment. He required the patient to undress and dress several times before a mixed-sex audience of therapists who had the subject explore associated affect, bodily sensations, and fantasy during exposure. The patient was asked such questions as "What do you think we see (feel/think) as we look at you right now?" in an objective, noncritical yet unempathic manner. During the second part of the session the patient was again required to undress and dress several times (at his therapist's direction) and was asked questions to facilitate comparison of present feelings with antecedents, moods prior to and during exposure, and consequent moods and events. Video taping (to be reviewed later by patient and therapist) and having the patient observe himself in a mirror are also part of this procedure. The treatment induces a high degree of anxiety in patients for whom it is appropriate (those who are nonpsychotic, nonpsychopathic, and somewhat anxious), which appears critical to the success of the treatment. In persons who do not experience the required level of anxiety, it could be increased by bringing into the audience either victims or people close to the exhibitionist (wife, mother, daughter) or even by chemically increasing anxiety, for example, by injections of sodium lactate prior to the sessions (Liebowitz et al., 1985).

Wickramasekera offers several explanations for the treatment's effectiveness: It involves (1) extinction of the exhibitionist's private fantasies, since the female or mixed-sex audience does not react with shock or fear; (2) punishment by the connection of aversive visceral consequences (profuse sweating, headache, rapid heartbeat) to other internal cues or self-disclosure; and (3) cognitive dissonance, which predicts maximum attitude and behavior change with voluntary participation, minimal reward, and maximal effort (all of which are involved in the treatment).

No matter what technique is used or how effective it appears to be with any individual client, periodic "booster" sessions are worthwhile because of the high level of recidivism.

Voyeurism (302.82)

Voyeurs continually search for situations in which they can view individuals or groups of individuals in the nude or in some form of sexual activity in order to obtain sexual arousal. Like pedophiles and exhibitionists, voyeurs have a high recidivism rate (Levin and Stava, 1987). Virtually all cases of voyeurism reported to the authorities involve males, but there is no evidence that this behavior never occurs in females. Our society is organized to respond differently to exhibitionistic and voyeuristic behavior by females.

Approximately one-third of voyeurs are married. Even though the age of the voyeur at the time of the first voyeuristic act is the middle to late twenties, there has usually been a significant history of sexual and other offenses throughout adolescence. As with exhibitionists, there is a large history of broken homes and marital distress. Voyeurs seldom maintained close relationships with sisters or other girls when they were young.

Most voyeurs are not markedly disturbed, and the simple act of obtaining arousal from looking is of course a normal part of many sexual experiences. Triolism, or the sharing of a sexual partner while one observes, is a major reinforcement in group-sex experiences and is not classified as voyeurism.

Only a small proportion of voyeurs pose a serious physical danger to their victims (Hollin and Howells, 1991). They are psychopathic in personality and show the following specific behavior patterns: They are most likely to enter a building in order to carry out their voyeuristic behaviors, and they draw attention to themselves in some way while they are watching.

DSM-IV

To make the DSM-IV diagnosis of voyeurism, the clinician must establish that the behavior, that is, observing an unsuspecting person in the nude or while disrobing or engaging in a sexual act, meets Criterion A and B for the paraphilias.

DIAGNOSTIC CONSIDERATIONS

Like the exhibitionist, the voyeur does not show extensive psychopathology on psychological tests and has similar personality test patterns. Lachar (1974) suggests that the prototypical MMPI-2 pattern for a voyeur shows elevated scores on 3, 4, and 5, with the elevation on 3 or 4 being the highest, and with a T score seldom being above 70. On the average, the score on scale 9 tends to be lower for the voyeur than for the exhibitionist. That very small subgroup of voyeurs who pose a danger to others has diagnostic patterns parallel to those of primary psychopaths, although they show more elevation on scale 5.

On the 16 PF, voyeurs are relatively close to the pattern of exhibitionists, but voyeurs average a bit higher on scales L and Q_3. This reflects their more circumspect patterns of pathology, which is usually accompanied by feelings that they would like to retain control of events in their worlds. Those with the detached personality characteristics indicated by elevations on 1 and/or 2A on the MCMI-III may be more predisposed to engage in this behavior.

TREATMENT OPTIONS

All of the techniques noted for the treatment of exhibitionists are virtually equally appropriate to the treatment of the voyeur. In particular, the aversion therapies have often been used. However, the treatment of one voyeur by a colleague of the senior author brought home the point that it is critical to be accurate regarding which stimuli are to be eliminated by the shock. This client had been administered shock on presentation of the hypothesized arousal stimuli: a clear view of the nude bodies of a couple through a window. This treatment was ineffective until the shock was eventually paired with slides of open windows as they would appear from a distance of about thirty feet. This unique scene had become the initial discriminative stimulus for the arousal pattern, and the voyeurism decreased markedly when these slides were paired with shock in an aversive therapy procedure.

Frotteurism (302.89)

Frotteurism is generally defined as the act of rubbing up against the body of a stranger, usually the stranger's buttocks, in order to achieve sexual arousal or even orgasm, if feasible. The act is usually carried out in a crowded public place, like a subway, swimming pool, or dance floor. In the traditional literature, frotteurism was often not distinguished from fetishism or partialism, although there are fundamental differences. The fetishist becomes aroused by and attached to a particular nonliving object that symbolizes the desired love object, and, unlike frotteurs, who make attempts at heterosexual life and fail, the fetishist rarely attempts heterosexual encounters. Partialism is differentiated from frotteurism in that the partialist is attracted to and can only achieve arousal from a specific part of the body, whereas the arousal for frotteurs is generated more generally and is not tied to a specific body part (Schmidt, 1995).

Not unlike many voyeurs and exhibitionists, the frotteur usually has evolved a series of coverup plans to avoid the embarrassment of being caught and publicly humiliated. The violation of the taboo of sexual behavior in a public place is arousing, but the humiliation one could experience if caught is aversive enough to generate these coverup behaviors.

DSM-IV

In order to apply this diagnosis, the DSM-IV requires the fulfillment of Criterion A and B for the paraphilias, by rubbing against or touching a nonconsenting person.

DIAGNOSTIC CONSIDERATIONS

Freund et al. (1983) note that the great majority of frotteurs also show other deviant behaviors, for example, voyeurism and exhibitionism, rather than a pattern of frotteurism alone. Hence, many of the diagnostic responses and therapeutic considerations noted for voyeurism and exhibitionism also apply here. Like exhibitionists, elevations on MMPI-2 scales 4, 5, and 8 can be expected, although frotteurs could be expected to be higher on scales 9 and 0.

On the 16 PF, 0 and Q_4 are likely to be elevated to the degree the frotteur labels his (virtually all frotteurs studied have been male) behavior as ego-alien. Scales A, G, H, and Q_3 are likely to be moderately depressed—especially G and Q_3, because they indicate a disregard for social norms and a lack of control over impulsive behavior. On the MCMI-III, scales 1 and 8A should be moderately elevated, 2A moderately to significantly elevated, and scales 4 and 7 likely lower, the latter reflecting the usual introverted personality style and the impulsive behavior pattern, respectively. With frotteurs who have sought therapy, scales A and D on the MCMI-III are often elevated.

On the Rorschach, one would expect a number of texture responses denoting a passively expressed need for affection, a higher incidence of shading and achromatic responses, a higher E–B ratio reflecting any introverted personality characteristics, and a high number of flexion-movement responses (toward the center) (Exner, 1986).

TREATMENT OPTIONS

The techniques applicable to voyeurs, exhibitionists, and fetishists are all applicable here, depending on which components are paramount in the individual case. Shame aversion therapy (Wicksramasekera, 1976, 1988) would be especially useful here. For example, the frotteur would be required to perform his frotteurism on a woman in front of an audience of several women who were particularly selected for similarity in appearance to the type of woman the frotteur normally seeks out. During the act the frotteur would be required to conduct a dialogue with himself discussing what he is thinking, describing physical sensations, predicting how the observers and the victim are perceiving him, and what their opinions of him may be. The observers and victim could be instructed to show no emotion and to stare at the frotteur for the duration or to spontaneously generate aversive emotions, such as laughter. As with exhibitionists, periodic "booster" sessions will likely be required to maintain any therapeutic effect, and social-skills training will be necessary in most cases.

■ Sexual Masochism (302.83)

Sexual masochism has traditionally been considered as a need to engage in fantasy or actual behavior in which the experience of having pain inflicted on oneself is necessary to gain sexual arousal. The term "masochism" was coined in 1896 by Richard von Krafft-Ebing and was taken from the works of Leopold von Sacher-Masoch (1836–1895), whose novels focused on the theme of men being dominated by women. Sacher-Masoch actually obtained excitement from the fantasy that his wife might be unfaithful to him and flaunt the fact to him.

Sexual masochism predominantly occurs in males and has its beginnings in childhood experience where the infliction of pain in some way becomes tied to sexual arousal (Hollin and Howells, 1991). Crystallized behavior patterns are usually evident by late adolescence. In some cases there is an increased need for pain over a period of time. In extreme cases a bizarre form of sexual masochism originally referred to as "terminal sex" occurs. A male (typically) hangs himself by the neck with a noose while masturbating, in order to increase sexual pleasure. Releasing the noose just before the loss of consciousness theoretically increases the pleasure. This practice has increased in recent years and occurs most commonly among 14- to 25-year-olds. Miscalculation is thought to cause as many as two hundred deaths in the United States every year.

☐ DSM-IV

A diagnosis of sexual masochism is applied if the person fulfills Criterion A and B of the paraphilias, involving the act (not simulated) of being humiliated, beaten, bound, or otherwise made to suffer.

☐ DIAGNOSTIC CONSIDERATIONS

Masochists seldom come to the attention of legal authorities, or even therapists, unless they have been a victim of extreme sadism that requires medical treatment, and this is uncommon (Janus and Janus, 1994). In many respects they have the personality characteristics of the dependent personality disorder, except with a greater emphasis on a disordered sexual identification and a higher level of intrapsychic distress. Hence, higher elevations on scales 5 and 7 occur. Scores on scales 6A and 9 are substantially lower than would occur in sadism, which reflects the masochist's passivity and apathy, as well as the subtle defensive quality that may be hidden from others.

Again, the 16 PF profiles should be similar to those of a person with the dependent personality disorder, with some specific exceptions. Hypothetically, scale N should be significantly higher, as should scores on Q_1 and, to a lesser degree, Q_2. L is not usually as low as one might expect, since the submissiveness and adaptation to another is balanced by a subtle paranoid element, usually resulting in scores that are not extreme on this variable. A lower G score also reflects the unconventionality of this behavior, and in those individuals with guilt and a punitive conscience a high O score is obtained. Scale B is relatively low. An elevated 3 on the MCMI-III, indicating dependent submissiveness, is likely. The self-condemnatory and dependency aspects of the borderline (scale C) may predispose toward masochistic behavior. Some components of the avoidant personality may be present, indicated by elevation on 2A. The masochist may well give Rorschach responses that clearly indicate a submissive control behavior pattern, such as being "yoked" or "chained." Small or passive animal responses may also be noted.

TREATMENT OPTIONS

Sexual masochism, to the degree that it is motivated by a need for sexual arousal, can be treated with the aversion therapies (see the section on exhibitionism). In most cases this deviant arousal pattern involves interpersonal inadequacy, and both compulsion and pathologic dependency pervade the relationship. In that regard, the reader is referred to the next chapter on treatment options for the obsessive-compulsive and dependent personality disorders.

The therapist can help the masochist focus on the quality of the relationship by a neoanalytic technique used by Kirman (1980) in which he has the client write letters to the significant other. This helps to focus the feelings and bring to consciousness the many aspects of the relationship that often remain out of awareness. One might also use the "empty chair" technique made famous by Fritz Perls. Rather than writing out his feelings, the client addresses the fantasized other in the empty chair in an oral dialogue; this is aided by its being done in a group. In either case, these feelings are used as a stimulus for new behavior patterns.

Covert extension can also be employed. Here the client is asked to imagine the masochistic behavior pattern and then immediately imagine that the reinforcement that is expected to follow does not occur. Assertiveness training or psychotherapy with an Adlerian focus (since Adlerian therapy so directly focuses on inferiority issues) could complement and aid the development of a repertoire of more positive behaviors.

Sexual Sadism (302.84)

Sexual sadism is a condition wherein a person obtains sexual excitement from inflicting pain, injury, or humiliation on another (Fedora et al., 1992). It differs from the sadistic personality disorder, described in Chapter 9, which is an optional category in the DSM-IV (Schwartz, 1995). The term "sadism" is taken from the writings of the Marquis de Sade, whose works focused on sexual pleasure gained from inflicting pain and even death on others.

Most sadists show evidence of this pattern by early adolescence (Kernberg, 1992). The condition is chronic and is seen far more frequently in males than females. Sadism overlaps the concept of rape (Calhoun and Atkeson, 1991), although not all rapists are sadists, and vice versa. However, the reader is referred to the section on rape (Chapter 14) since there are parallel diagnostic considerations.

DSM-IV

A DSM-IV diagnosis of sexual sadism is appropriate if Criterion A and B of the paraphilias are fulfilled, involving acts (real, not simulated) in which another person suffers (physically or psychologically) or is humiliated.

MMPI-2

Unlike the sexual masochist, the sadist shows significantly disturbed patterns on the MMPI-2, with one or more scores above 70 T. This usually indicates a lack of impulse control, specifically on scales 4 and 8A (Hall et al., 1986); scale 9 is also usually elevated. The high scores on 8A and 8B show the unusual attitudes, thought patterns, hostility, and aggression inherent in this disorder.

Most male sadists present a macho image, with stereotypical male behaviors. Physical prowess and aggressive thrill-seeking behaviors are often evident. This can result in a low score on scale 5, except that confused sexual identification may counterbalance this, particularly if the person is oriented toward homosexual sadism. Females involved in sadistic behaviors tend to score high on scale 5.

16 PF

Sadists are likely to show high scores on scales E and H, emphasizing the dominant and aggressive components of this disorder. In addition, their distance from standard moral systems results in a low score on G and high scores on M and Q_1. Scores for L and Q_3 are also likely to be moderately high. A is usually low, reflecting the lack of any true interest in interpersonal relationships.

OTHER TEST-RESPONSE PATTERNS

A score of 85 or higher on the MCMI-III scale 6B is common here, with elevation on 6A and 5 likely. Some paranoid qualities may be present, causing relative elevation on P. The impulsivity present in these persons may cause some elevation on N. In addition to Rorschach Content responses that directly portray a sadistic element, such as hammers, explosions, and needles, figures that symbolize controlling authority, such as eagles, are occasionally noted. Mutilation content is also thought to be indicative of sadistic fantasy and possible sadistic behavior (Shafer, 1954).

TREATMENT OPTIONS

Since sexual sadism more often focuses on deviant sexual arousal than does sexual masochism, the aversive therapy techniques are appropriate (Fedora et al., 1992) (see the section on exhibitionism). This approach could be aided by some of the cognitive approaches, such as covert sensitization. The person should also somehow be made aware of the psychological effect on the "victim," and "couple" therapy with the victim could be instituted. Other techniques for teaching more appropriate interpersonal behaviors, such as those noted in the section on exhibitionism, would also be helpful because sadism is often a reaction to inadequacy and/or modeling from early training where physical abuse was common.

Zoophilia

Although this disorder was included in DSM-III, it has since been dropped as a formal DSM diagnostic category, probably because of the rarity of its occurrence (Schwartz, 1995). The essential variable in zoophilia is the use of animals as the means of producing sexual arousal. This label is most appropriate when such behavior or fantasy is consistently preferred even though there are other outlets reasonably available. Zoophilia, which occurs primarily in males, is very rare. It may occasionally be a sign of schizophrenia.

The traditional term, "bestiality," referred primarily to having sexual intercourse with animals, whereas "zoophilia" refers to *any* type of sexual contact with animals. The preferred animal is usually one with which the person had contact during childhood, such as a pet or farm animal. Zoophilia is a moderately common theme in pornography and usually involves a female having a sexual experience with a pony or a dog. This theme is common because the usual consumer of pornography is male, and this appears to be an exciting theme for males. In actuality, the data of Kinsey et al. (1948, 1953) suggest that such patterns are extremely rare in females and only a bit more common in males, at least where the pattern has clinical significance.

DIAGNOSTIC CONSIDERATIONS

In the typical person who shows clinical zoophilia, the major features are significant depression, problems in interpersonal skills, and anxiety. Hence, we would expect MMPI-2 elevations on scales 2, 7 and 0, respectively. Also, the disordered sexual life could cause at least a mild elevation on scale 5.

In the 16 PF the shame, anxiety, lack of interpersonal skills, and social isolation should result in high O and Q_4 scores and relatively low A, C, and F scores. Scale B is low in these individuals, and similarly, N is expected to be low and Q_2 moderately low. One may, again, expect 1 and/or 2 as a prominent feature of the MCMI-III profile, although the behavioral apathy of the asocial type may make a prominent score on 1 less likely here. Any depression and anxiety will be indicated by elevations of at least 75 on scales A and D.

☐   TREATMENT OPTIONS

There are few reports in the literature concerning the treatment of zoophilia. Aversive conditioning procedures would be helpful regarding any fetishistic components. Since immaturity and inability to make adequate heterosexual contacts are often a factor, social retraining and the techniques of rational-emotive therapy (Ellis and Dryden, 1987) might also be applied.

■   # Gender Identity Disorder

Gender identity disorder (GID) has traditionally been differentiated from trans-sexualism only in that in GID there is no persisting preoccupation with changing (via medication or surgery) into the sexual characteristics of the opposite sex (Schwartz, 1995). To qualify for a DSM-IV diagnosis of Gender Identity Disorder, with usual onset usually between age 2 and 4, there must be evidence of a persistent and significant cross-gender identification, not just a perceived cultural advantage for being the opposite sex. In adolescents and adults, the required behaviors are unspecified, but children must show at least four of the following: (1) repeatedly stated desires to be, or insistence one is, the other sex; (2) in boys, preference for simulating female attire or cross-dressing and in girls, for stereotypical male clothing; (3) cross-sex preference in fantasy or play; (4) intense desire for participation in other sex's play or pastimes; or (5) strong preference for opposite sex playmates. Also required is impairment in an important life area, no concurrent physical intersex condition, and evidence of persistent discomfort with one's sex or that sex's gender role (e.g., in adults, this may be manifest in a desire for transsexual surgery). The diagnosis is specified by age, that is, GID in Children (302.6), in Adolescents or Adults (302.85), and if sexually mature is specified by "Sexually Attracted to Males," . . . "Females," . . . "Both," . . . "Neither."

GID is a chronic disorder, and a disturbed parent–child relationship, particularly the absence of a model of the same sex, predisposes a child to this disorder. Also, any other characteristics, either physical or psychological, that cause identification of a child by others as one of the opposite sex (such as long hair and soft features in males) also facilitate GID.

Clinicians have an important role not only in diagnosing GID in standard clinical settings but also in the psychological screening of such persons as appropriate for sex-change surgery. It is controversial whether this surgery is necessary. However, because such surgery is likely to continue, it is most important that people be thoroughly screened. Most reputable surgeons who deal with these problems mandate a team assessment, for example, by a psychologist, psychiatrist, and an endocrinologist. The early success rate of this surgery, about 90% in male or female sex reassignments (Pauly, 1968), undoubtedly reflects the thorough psychological screening techniques that were employed. As this procedure becomes even more commonplace, screening will probably become more lax and individuals who are inappropriate candidates will have an increasing chance of being operated on. For example, certain schizophrenics have a delusional belief that they are of the opposite sex, and some disturbed homosexuals and transvestites who cannot deal with the demands of their perceived role conflicts may unconsciously view a sex change as an escape from these conflicts. The clinician involved in such procedures should especially consider indicators for schizophrenia, paranoia, transvestism, and homosexuality when dealing with potential transsexual candidates (Schwartz, 1995).

MMPI-2

One would expect the GF score to be elevated in male-to-female GIDs and the GM scale elevated for the reverse pattern (Gentry and Meyer, 1991). Tsushima and Wedding (1979) found the MMPI profiles of GIDs, to be surprisingly within normal limits. Of course, scale 5 is high in males due to nonidentification with the traditional male role, along with the conflicts about sexual identity. While presurgical males-to-females were found by Fleming et al. (1981) to be high on 5, 6, and 8, presurgical females were high on 5 and relatively high on 6, 7, and 8. Postsurgical females (those who had been male) were high on 5 and relatively high on 6 and K. Postsurgical males were high on 5 and relatively high on 6. Fleming et al. note that the tendency to peak on 5 and 6 is consistent with the early research literature about MMPI profiles of transsexuals.

On occasion, scale 1 and, to a lesser degree, 3 may be slightly elevated, reflecting preoccupation with body structure. In accordance with the preceding, scale F may be elevated. On the other hand, if GIDs perceive the need to present themselves as healthy to pass the screening, scale K would be quite high and signs of pathology would be suppressed. If they are anxious and ambivalent about the identity issue, scales 4 and 8 may be slightly elevated; and if this has generated depression, scale 2 is raised.

16 PF

As with the MMPI-2, the pattern is generally within reasonably normal limits. However, the mode of sexual adjustment results in slightly higher I scores and slightly lower E, H, and N scores in most males, with the converse being true in most females. Scale B should reflect the average or above-average intelligence in most GIDs, and, since they endorse attitudes that differ from the average, they are likely to be higher on M and Q1 and moderately low on G.

OTHER TEST-RESPONSE PATTERNS

On the Rorschach test, GIDs (compared to normals) displayed significantly more intense levels of aggression, a lower level of object relations, poorer reality testing, and impaired boundary definition, being in this way similar to a borderline personality. Certain TAT cards, for example, 1, 5, 13 MF, 17 BM, and 18 BM, often elicit themes relevant to sexual identity (Bellak, 1993).

On the MCMI-III, the distress and confusion about gender identity may cause elevations on A and D to 75 or higher, and very likely on C as well. Although no clear-cut pathological indicators are typically present, some generalizations may be possible. Males who seek to be females may be more likely to have personality types that are more commonly characteristic of females, so the prominent scale indicator may be 3 or 4. Conversely, females wishing to be males may have personality characteristics traditionally thought of as male, so scale 6A may be prominent.

TREATMENT OPTIONS

A classic option for the GID has been surgery to change the genitalia to that of the opposite sex. The first sex-change operation occurred in Europe in 1930. There is good evidence (Pauly, 1968) that in certain individuals this is now an effective procedure, although psychotherapy for the social adjustment to the new sex is an important adjunct. In general, the surgical success is higher when the change is from male to female. In large part, this reflects the much more complex surgery required when the change is from female to male, as well as the accompanying higher probability of problematic side effects and outright failure.

In some cases, surgery is an unnecessary intervention, as psychotherapy and the passage of time can deal effectively with these identity concerns. This is particularly true when therapy is combined with aversive sexual-reorientation training and other techniques of psychosocial conditioning (Abel et al., 1986; Money, 1987). Also, covert modeling to retrain more appropriate sex-typed mannerisms and behaviors is helpful for all clients. The clinician might also take note that well-known attorney Melvin Belli (1979) once argued persuasively that therapists can come under tort liability for taking a person through transsexual surgery, and it can possibly be considered under "criminal mayhem" statutes if there is any lack of clarity about the person's consent or ability to consent. Belli argues that adequate consent is problematic in most cases because the "compulsive" quality of the need to change sex is contradictory to the law's requirement that consent be "an affirmative act of an unconstrained and undeceived will" (p. 498). However, could not this concept of being compelled into treatment be applied to almost any disorder?

Sexual Dysfunctions

As with the paraphilias, the sexual dysfunctions come in varied forms. It is generally estimated that most people have at least occasionally experienced some form of sexual dysfunction, and more enduring sexual dysfunction may affect as many as 50% of marriages (Janus and Janus, 1994; Seidman and Rieder, 1994). Overall, the determinants of sexual dysfunctions are psychosocial, interpersonal, and/or neurophysiological.

In the DSM-IV the Sexual Dysfunctions are differentiated into four subcategories, based on phases of the sexual response cycle: (1) Desire—Hypoactive Sexual Desire Disorder (302.71), Sexual Aversion Disorder (302.79); (2) Arousal—Female Sexual Arousal Disorder (302.72), Male Erectile Disorder (302.72); (3) Orgasm—Female (302.73) and Male (302.74) Orgasmic Disorder, Premature Ejaculation (302.75); (4) Resolution—Dyspareunia (302.76), Vaginismus (306.51). All of the following require causation of "marked distress or interpersonal difficulty" as a result of the condition, with additional specific requirements. All of the Sexual Dysfunctions are further specified as "Lifelong" versus "Acquired Type," "Generalized" versus "Situational Type," and "Due to Psychological (or Combined) Factors." "Clinician's judgment" is emphasized much more in DSM-IV than in prior DSMs.

Hypoactive Sexual Desire is simply consistently deficient sexual fantasies and desire for sexual activity, as defined by the clinician's judgment. Sexual Aversion Disorder is defined as persistent or recurrent extreme aversion to sexual contact with a partner.

Female Sexual Arousal Disorder is defined as persistent or recurrent inability to maintain an adequate swelling-lubrication response; Male Erectile Disorder by persistent or recurrent inability to obtain or maintain an adequate erection. Female Orgasmic Disorder is defined by recurrent or persistent delay in (or absence of) orgasm following normal sexual excitement phase. It's interesting that "the adequacy of sexual stimulation she receives" is a factor in this disorder whereas no similar factor is mentioned for Male Orgasmic Disorder, although the criteria are otherwise similar. Premature Ejaculation requires unwanted and persistent or recurrent ejaculation before, at the time of penetration, or shortly thereafter.

Dyspareunia can occur in a male or female and requires recurrent or persistent genital pain associated with sexual intercourse. Vaginismus refers to recurrent or persistent involuntary spasms of the outer third of the vaginal musculature that is not due to a medical condition and interferes with sexual intercourse.

Other diagnoses that may be employed are the various sexual patterns noted above that are "Due to . . . [indicate the General Medical Condition]" and "Substance-Induced Sexual Dysfunction," which requires that the disorder first occur within a month of use of the substance and be "fully explained" by the use of the substance. Of course, there is also a category "Sexual Dysfunction Not Otherwise Specified" (302.70).

Since the problems and patterns of individual clients with these disorders are inherently dominated by that client's anatomical-psychological sexuality, this chapter separates the discussion by sex. Since, overall, female sexual disorders tend to reflect less psychological impairment, and because male psychosexual dysfunctions have received more attention in the literature, we'll focus on these first.

■   # Male Psychosexual Dysfunction

As noted, Male Erectile Disorder (302.72) and Male Orgasmic Disorder (302.74) refer to a disruption (at different points) of attempts to attain orgasm. The major organic factors to be ruled out are spinal cord disorders, nondominant-hemisphere parietal-lobe dysfunction, significant circulatory problems (often found in severe diabetics, but also not that uncommon in otherwise normals), and consistent alcohol or drug use (Schnarch, 1992; Masters et al., 1991, 1994).

The research literature refers to male erectile disorder as "erectile dysfunction," and most people simply term it "impotence." The latter term is undesirable for several reasons, primarily because it connotes general personality inadequacy and weakness of character. It is interesting to note that weakness in the male and coldness in the female, as connoted by the terms "impotence" and "frigidity," respectively, are opposites of the characteristics most commonly prescribed for sexual roles in our society: power and competence for males and sensitivity and warmth for females. Most erectile dysfunction is partial; that is, a man can attain erection but either cannot reach orgasm or does not maintain the erection for very long. Total erectile dysfunction over a significant period of time is not that common in young to middle-age males and suggests a biological cause. It is noteworthy that at least 25% of erectile dysfunction cases include both a significant organic and psychogenic component (Mohr and Beutler, 1990).

Hypoactive Sexual Desire occurs relatively rarely as a separate disorder, and organic dysfunction should always be ruled out. It is often a reflection of disorder in a marital relationship rather than evidence of significant individual pathology, and in that sense, a more extreme variation is the Sexual Aversion Disorder.

Masters and Johnson (1970) define premature ejaculation as a clinical problem if the orgasm occurs involuntarily more than half the time before the partner's orgasm. Premature ejaculation can be further subdivided into primary premature ejaculation (related to inexperience in the sexual area): a chronic, high state of arousal, possibly accompanied by fear of dealing with intimacy. As might be expected, it is most often a disorder of the young (indeed, the great majority of males may have such an experience in one of their first interpersonal sexual experiences), and it does not correlate with any significant pathology. In secondary premature ejaculation, it is common that a disturbance in the relationship with a partner results in conflict expressed through premature ejaculation. The trouble is in the relationship, although individual personality factors of the partners may contribute (Masters et al., 1994).

☐   ## DIAGNOSTIC CONSIDERATIONS

Much of the literature has focused on diagnostic issues in males with erectile dysfunction. One major question is whether the dysfunction stems from organic or psychological factors. The following cues are suggestive of erectile dysfunction in which organic factors play a major part:

- Gradual onset
- Sequentially deteriorating erections
- Normal libido
- Ability to initiate but not to maintain erection
- Loss of nocturnal and masturbatory erection

The following are generally indicative of psychogenic erectile dysfunction:

- Episodic history
- Sudden onset
- Acuteness, brought on by life stresses
- Normal morning and nocturnal erections
- Loss of libido

If there is any good indication that an organic factor may be part of the picture, a comprehensive exam is in order, which should include: interview and psychological testing, interview with spouse or partner, hormone assay (testosterone, prolactin, estradiol, luteinizing hormone), relevant venous and arterial function and nerve function tests, glucose tolerance test, and a nocturnal penile tumescence (NPT) exam.

Most researchers agree that persons with erectile dysfunction—indeed, virtually all of the psychosexual dysfunctions—do not show markedly deviant profiles on standard psychological tests. There are some trends and differences, depending on whether the dysfunction is psychologically or biologically generated. Beutler et al. (1975) report a 90% success rate in using the MMPI to differentiate psychogenic versus biogenic erectile dysfunction, by two rules: (1) In psychogenic erectile dysfunction, scale 5 is typically higher, that is, above 60, than if it is biogenic; and (2) there is no consistency in the scores that are above 70 (65 in MMPI-2), but those scales that are elevated are usually the ones that reflect the sexual role problems (i.e., scale 5, a histrionic denial of problems as in scale 3, or depression on scale 2).

Another factor that often effectively differentiates psychologically generated dysfunction from biogenic cases is the occurrence of NPT, or erections that occur during sleep. Just as most females show clitoral arousal while sleeping, most (but not all) sexually normal males experience a number of NPTs every night during sleep. Almost all NPTs occur during REM sleep, and NPTs decrease, slowly, in frequency and duration with age. Although rigidity slowly decreases with age, circumferential increases during the tumescence period typically do not (Mohr and Beutler, 1990). Those individuals with biogenic erectile dysfunction tend to have few if any NPTs while sleeping, whereas those whose dysfunction is psychogenic show a number of NPTs—although the "hit rate" of diagnostic accuracy with this technique can be as low as 65% (Mohr and Beutler, 1990). For example, various medications and clinical depression can suppress NPTs. The initial problem with this diagnostic cue was getting someone to stay awake all night to watch. The solution is to put a measurement device around the penis during sleep. Two widely used methods are the potentest (perforated gummed stamps placed around the penis) and the snap gauge. The snap gauge, which consists of three plastic bands, each of which breaks at different degrees of expansion of the penis, has the advantage of measuring both rigidity and circumferential expansion.

The urologist's traditional technique in this area, the Doppler ultrasound, provides the Penile Brachial Index (PBI), a contrast of blood pressure in the arm and the penis. Unfortunately, this is not always a reliable measure, in part because it is administered when the penis is flaccid and also because it cannot consistently distinguish between the deep arteries (those most critical to erection) and the superficial arteries. A much more reliable measure is obtained with the Rigi-Scan. The Rigi-Scan is a portable device that stores more information, e.g., duration of erection and rigidity at both the base and on the shaft. Measurements need to be taken for more than one night, ideally with a device, such as the Rigi-Scan, that measures strength and persistence of erection in addition to simple occurrence. Several methods (such as, covernography, a radiologic procedure) can assess vascular involvement, and vascular factors have been increasingly recognized as implicated in "gray area" cases (Mohr and Beutler, 1990).

On the 16 PF, persons with erectile dysfunction are likely to show higher than average scores on Q_4 and O, reflecting anxiety and insecurity. Their scores on E and Q_3 will vary depending on whether they have coped with the dysfunction by resorting to even more stereotypical masculine behaviors (resulting in high E and Q_3 scores) or have become more submissive in relationships and see themselves as unable to control their worlds (low scores). If they experience guilt over failing in their relationships, scores on O are likely to be raised. A high level of performance anxiety is likely to correlate with at least an average or moderately elevated M score. They show more reproductive anatomy responses on the Rorschach, as well as more emphasis on pelvic anatomy and more use of the internal white space.

A scale 4 score of 85 or higher on the MCMI-III may show a predisposition toward this disorder. To the extent that performance anxiety, guilt, and depression are present, elevations of 75 or higher on A and D should occur. Scale 3 may also be elevated. High scores on B and/or T should alert the clinician that the dysfunction may be caused by organic factors.

The Derogatis Sexual Functioning Inventory is one of the more sophisticated and useful self–report instruments available for providing information about sexual functioning (Mohr and Beutler, 1990).

☐   TREATMENT OPTIONS

A number of physical, chemical, and psychological techniques have been developed to treat erectile and orgasmic dysfunctions (Masters et al., 1994, 1991; Woody, 1992; Lo Piccolo, 1993; Mohr and Beutler, 1990). Penile artery bypass surgery can be used, although a specific circulatory problem is rarely the issue. Various forms of revascularization are more likely to be useful. Certain prosthetic devices can be used for organically based cases and occasionally for severe psychogenic cases as well. One is a semirigid rod that is implanted in the corpora cavernosa, the parts of the penis that engorge with blood in an erection. The consequent permanent erection can be an embarrassment, and it interferes with urological diagnostic procedures. An alternative is a hydraulic inflatable device. Clients are generally satisfied with those, although many report less frequent intercourse than expected; indeed, some seem content to just have the device, and don't use it much.

It is noteworthy that the idea of a prosthesis is not necessarily a product of our modern, high-tech culture, as is documented in this true anecdote reported by R. O'Hanlon in his book *Into the Heart of Borneo* (1984).

"But Leon, when do you have it done? When do you have the hole bored through your dick?"

"When you twenty-five. When you no good any more. When you too old. When your wife she feds up with you. Then you go down to the river very early in the mornings and you sit in it until your spear is smalls. The tattoo man he comes and pushes a nail through your spear, round and round. And then you put a pin there, a pin from the outboard motor. Sometimes you get a big spots, very painfuls, a boil. And then you die."

"Jesus!"

"My best friend—you must be very careful. You must go down to the river and sit in it once a month until your spear so cold you can't feel it; and then you loosen the pin and push it in and out; or it will stick in your spear and you never move it and it makes a pebble with your water and you die."

"But Leon," I said, holding my knees together and holding my shock with my right hand, "do you have one?"

"I far too young!" said Leon, much annoyed; and then, grinning his broad Iban grin as a thought discharged itself: "But you need one Redmon! And Jams—he so old and serious, he need two!" (pp. 82–83)

Endocrine treatments such as testosterone derivatives have been helpful in some cases (although these seem to inflate interest more than erections), but a hormone deficiency is seldom the critical issue. The oral drug Gingko biloba, derived from the leaves of the Gingko tree, available in the United States as an herb in health food stores, has shown promise in improving erections as a secondary result of its positive effect on periploral circulation. Injections into the penis, at the time sex is desired, of a vasodilator such as papaverine (although the maker, Lilly, disavows such use) or prostaglandin E, along with the alpha blocker phentolamine, is effective in providing erections in 65–80% of cases; those who do not respond are usually the very old, the very ill, and those with vascular impairment (so these administrations can have a diagnostic function as well). A small proportion of normal men do not respond to these injections when they are administered while lying down, but do respond if they are standing. Aside from the requirement of self-injection, other drawbacks are the high costs and, in some cases, accumulated scarring, priapism, decrease of effectiveness over time, and even abnormal liver functioning.

The vacuum construction device (VCD) is a moderately effective, non-invasive technique. The VCD is a cylinder that is placed over the penis and pressed against the body to produce an airtight seal. A vacuum is created, which engorges the penis, and rubber bands are slipped off the end of the device, retaining the erection for up to thirty minutes. VCD-produced erections are less rigid although slightly larger than normal and are especially helpful with erectile dysfunction where vascular insufficiency is a critical factor (Mohr and Beutler, 1990).

However, the safest and generally most effective treatments for both arousal and orgasmic disorders are the "sensate focusing" psychological techniques pioneered by Masters and Johnson (1970) and the more sophisticated cognitive therapies, which are both used to help the client stop spectatoring (becoming too distanced from the act). These are particularly effective if carried out with a stable partner from the client's natural world. Sensate focusing is not a totally modern development: Sir John Hunter, a physician practicing around 1750, would advise his clients to go home and lie in bed "a fortnight and caress and fondle." His only reported difficulty was that "no one ever completed the treatment" (Lo Piccolo, 1985). Cognitive therapy and sensate focusing can be aided by systematic desensitization for specific phobias that might hinder erection, such as vaginal odor. In many cases, problems in the interpersonal situation are major contributors to the erectile and orgasmic dysfunction, so marital (or couple) therapy, including an emphasis on improving both social and communication skills in the primary client, is necessary to eliminate these precursors to the dysfunction sequence (Masters et al., 1994; Schnarch, 1992).

Treatment for sexual aversion and inhibited sexuality components (whether with males or females) is difficult primarily because a low desire for sex predicts a low desire for sex therapy. Also, a low sex drive, in an otherwise healthy adult, is a paradoxical disorder in that people are "hard-wired" rather than "programmed" for sex and a low interest in sexuality runs so counter to society's cultural values. In addition to couple therapy and sensate focusing, therapy here usually needs to focus on helping the person become more aware of both general affect and body states and also to include some sexual-drive induction techniques (Woody, 1992). The latter could include training the person to use sexual fantasies (have the client write them out, but make it clear you only want to know that the task was carried out; you are not going to cause embarrassment by checking the content). Very likely, this will need to be amplified by the use of erotica and instruction in masturbatory techniques and the control of masturbatory fantasy.

Most individuals (male or female), or couples who have any of the psychosexual dysfunctions often need to be challenged on common underlying problematic cognitive assumptions, such as (1) sex should be "perfect," "special," "ecstatic," "novel," "routine," et cetera; (2) sex should occur "in bed," "in the dark," "somewhere exciting," "after a show of romance," "with all our clothes off," et cetera; (3) without intercourse, it's not "real" sex; and (4) without both of us having an orgasm, it's not "real" sex.

Compliance problems and relapse among people treated for sexual dysfunction or inhibited sexuality are commonly reported (Schwartz, 1995). Consistent monitoring and "booster sessions" are almost always helpful. Success is much better where specific coping strategies for relapse have been taught and monitored. Such skills include role playing a discussion with a partner subsequent to a dysfunction occurrence; articulating and then replaying specific behaviors learned in therapy; using specific cognitive "mantras" such as "I was told this would happen, but I know it will pass," "I'm loved and accepted whether these episodes occur or not," et cetera (e.g., recovering heart attack victims may need to add mantras such as "It's absurd to think I'd die because of intercourse, I'll feel better"); reading positive information books or pamphlets; and generating a sensual, romantic, and/or erotic mind-set (Schnarch, 1992).

Another major problem in males, premature ejaculation, is usually treated by the "squeeze technique." The couple is admonished to engage in sensate focusing without attempting intercourse. As ejaculation appears imminent, the partner squeezes hard just below the rim of the head of the penis, interrupting the cycle of pre-ejaculatory muscle spasms, and then the couple continues in the sensate focusing until control is gained (Masters et al., 1991). In many cases of premature ejaculation a very high sexual-drive level is operating, which counseling about increased frequency of masturbation can help alleviate.

■ Female Psychosexual Dysfunction

Some of the same treatment issues, as well as most of the diagnostic considerations, noted about the male psychosexual dysfunctions apply equally well to the problems of female psychosexual dysfunction, and the reader is referred to these immediately prior sections. There is no significant personality pathology correlated with most cases of female psychosexual dysfunction, although scales reflecting depression and immediate anxiety are likely to be raised, just as they are in premature ejaculation and in erectile dysfunction.

□ DIAGNOSTIC CONSIDERATIONS

It is generally agreed that most female sexual dysfunctions are less likely to reflect allied pathology, either generic or situational, than male sexual problems (Woody, 1992; Masters et al., 1994). In part, this is because the female can perform adequately in spite of inhibited responses in different phases or activities of sexual arousal.

The 2-3/3-2 MMPI-2 code is often found in these cases, but the elevations are not usually above 70 T. This reflects an overcontrolled individual, one who is denying responsibility for problems and yet is experiencing depression from them. An anxious and introverted woman with psychosexual dysfunction is more likely to have a 1-2/2-1 profile, again without the scales being markedly elevated.

To the degree that anxiety and guilt are a result of the psychosexual problems, high I and Q_4 scores are likely on the 16 PF. The other scales do not vary in any consistent manner. In that small subgroup of females with psychosexual dysfunction who have been traditionally labeled as hostile and castrating, high scores on E, L, Q_1, and, to a moderate degree, on H and Q_3 are found.

Scale 4 on the MCMI-III is likely to be high. The superficial flirtatiousness and seductiveness of the histrionic may be a predisposing factor toward psychosexual dysfunction. As psychosexual problems serve a psychological function, scale N will be elevated. As with male psychosexual dysfunction, elevations on A and D may indicate anxiety, depression, and guilt concerning dysfunction.

Elevations on the MCMI-III scales A, H, D, 8A, and C correlate most highly with coexisting conditions. Elevations of A, H, or D indicate conditions especially likely to foster or coexist with sexual dysfunction. Those with personality patterns represented by scales 1, D, and C may be more likely to experience inhibited sexual desire.

TREATMENT OPTIONS

Just as with the male, the sensate focusing technique pioneered by Masters and Johnson (1970) is often effective and can be similarly aided by systematic desensitization of specific fears and phobias. Use of cognitive-behavioral techniques to deal with cognitive distortions from past training or trauma and counseling-education about issues such as tolerating arousal, partner functioning, body image and self-stimulation are both useful. Masturbatory training is emphasized more in the treatment of female dysfunction than in male dysfunction (Masters et al., 1991). The woman is advised to masturbate regularly (a vibrator is often helpful here) with fantasies of intercourse, with the male gradually taking his place in the masturbatory experience and then literally in the vagina while masturbation still takes place to facilitate orgasm.

Some nonorgasmic or weakly orgasmic women have improved their ability to experience orgasm through exercise of the pubococcygeal muscle. To perform these exercises, referred to as the "Kegal exercises," the woman contracts the pubococcygeal muscle as though she were trying to keep from urinating. This is performed in sets of ten, several times a day. Various companies market electronic devices that act to stimulate the muscles of this area through electrotherapy. These devices are purported to tone and condition, involuntarily and quickly, the pelvic muscles and thus to facilitate orgasm, although it is clear they are not effective with all women (Chambless et al., 1984). As regards Female Sexual Arousal Disorder (302.72), medication and menopause are common causes of insufficient lubrication, as are negative attitudes from trauma or taboos. A water-soluble lubricant can often take care of the situation, and cognitive-behavioral techniques are used in more difficult cases. In some cases, testosterone-estrogen compounds have helped with arousal problems in women.

The other major female psychosexual dysfunctions, vaginismus and dyspareunia, are usually the result of involuntary spasms of the vaginal musculature. Vaginismus has been most effectively treated by the insertion of graduated catheters into the vagina. The first one used may be as thin as a pen, and only when it can be tolerated comfortably for a period of time is one of somewhat larger dimension inserted. Eventually a catheter the size of an erect penis is used. The technique is most efficient when the partner participates in the insertion of the catheters, then transfers this to fingers, then to insertion of the penis. It is also advised (Masters and Johnson, 1970) that the partner witness a pelvic examination, since this helps to dispel any irrational fears that may have developed. Possibly more important, it helps to reassure the partner that the physical responses are not specific to his overtures for intercourse. Cox and Meyer (1978), as well as others, have found that various forms of relaxation training, sensate-focus exercises (prepped by cognitive training), and general sexual counseling have also been helpful with dyspareunia. (Although psychological factors—guilt, taboos, trauma—can be causal, the primary causes are usually painful childbirthing, abrasion by pubic hair, and inadequate lubrication for intercourse.)

CHAPTER 9

The Personality Disorders

■ **Overall Concepts**

Personality disorders are probably the most common pattern of disorder, yet these disorders have seldom been given the research and clinical attention they deserve. In addition to the many clients who receive only a personality disorder diagnosis, the great majority of clients with an Axis I diagnosis, no matter what it is, also receive (or at least deserve) an Axis II diagnosis. And if we count the subclinical patterns (see Table 9.1), which often are a critical focus in the therapeutic enterprise, a great majority of the population could be included (Widiger and Costa, 1994; Costa and Widiger, 1994).

The personality disorders are chronic, pervasive, and inflexible patterns of perceiving and responding to the environment that are sufficiently maladaptive to cause disruption in functioning and environmentally generated subjective distress. In DSM-IV the personality disorders are listed on Axis II. Even if a prominent personality pattern does not warrant a formal diagnosis of personality disorder, it can still be listed on Axis II, but without the relevant code number that formally designates it as a disorder.

Most individuals in need of a personality disorder diagnosis do not originally think there is any compelling reason for changing themselves (Turkat, 1990; Benjamin, 1993). Any such realization comes only when they move into situations that require higher levels of intimacy or more flexible behavioral adaptations. The fact that they cannot meet these requirements results in coercion from the environment, or at least feedback that they cannot ignore, resulting in referral for therapy.

The clinician needs to decide whether the personality disorder pattern is an outgrowth of another disorder, such as a major depressive disorder. For that reason, the clinician needs to assess carefully the issues of chronicity and pervasiveness of behavior. In many cases an individual client will require personality disorder diagnoses. The DSM-IV does not list a specific time or duration necessary to warrant a personality disorder diagnosis, except when a personality disorder is diagnosed in children. In that instance, duration of at least

TABLE 9.1 Personality Types and Correlated Traits and Disorders

PERSONALITY TYPES	TYPICAL BEHAVIORS	INTER-PERSONAL PATTERNS	THINKING STYLES	MOOD-AFFECT EXPRESSION	VIEW OF SELF	PROBABLE PERSONALITY DISORDERS
Controlling	Manipulative	Authoritarian	Calculating	Disapointment	Unappreciated	Paranoid, antisocial, sadistic
Aggressive	Bold, initiating	Confrontive	Dogmatic	Anger	Assertive	Passive-aggressive, antisocial, sadistic
Confident	Poised	Unempathic	Focused	Calm	Self-assured	Narcissistic, paranoid, antisocial
Sociable	Animated, engaging	Demonstrative	Superficial	Dramatic	Charming	Histrionic, borderline, narcissistic
Cooperative	Docile	Compliant	Open	Tender	Weak, helpful	Dependent, compulsive, avoidant
Sensitive	Erratic	Unpredictable	Divergent	Pessimistic	Misunderstood	Passive-aggressive, borderline, avoidant
Respectful	Organized	Polite	Hierarchical	Restrained	Reliable	Compulsive, paranoid, passive-aggressive
Inhibited	Watchful	Shy	Threat-sensitive	Uneasy	Lonely	Avoidant, schizotypal
Introverted	Passive	Withdrawn	Vague	Bland	Placid	Schizoid, schizotypal, compulsive
Emotional	Energetic	Flamboyant	Distracted	Intense	Interesting	Borderline, schizotypal, histrionic

Adapted in part from T. Millon (1981).

one year is required, and even then, the DSM-IV still forbids the application of the term "antisocial personality disorder" before the age of 18.

The personality disorders have traditionally been grouped into three clusters in the DSMs. The first includes the paranoid, schizoid, and schizotypal personality disorders, as these are denoted by peculiar or eccentric behavior. The second cluster focuses on dramatic and emotionally labile behavior: It includes the histrionic, narcissistic, antisocial, and borderline personality disorders. The last cluster, which emphasizes chronic fearfulness and/or avoidance behaviors, includes the avoidant, dependent, and obsessive-compulsive disorders. There is of course a catch-all category termed Personality Disorder NOS (301.90), used for individuals who do not fit any of the criteria for a specific category, yet clearly fall within the overall patterns of the personality disorders.

SPECIFIC TESTS

The reader is referred to Chapter 13 for a discussion of the 16 PF-5 and related tests, as such tests are specifically designed to assess personality factors. Ben-Porath (1994) and his colleagues have developed a set of MMPI-2 scales specifically designed to measure the individual personality disorders. The scales are based in part on those designed for the original MMPI by Leslie Morey. The MMPI-2 scales have differing numbers of items ranging from fifty-seven for the Borderline Personality Disorder to sixteen for the Histrionic and Narcissistic categories. Not surprisingly, these latter two categories appear to be the weakest as far as some validity aspects. There is some item overlap, which Ben–Porath argues is necessary, since some symptoms still overlap categories. The high overlaps are Schizoid-Avoidant, fourteen items; Histrionic-Avoidant, nine; Narcissistic-Dependent, seven; Paranoid–Schizotypal, seven; Histrionic-Schizoid, five; all the rest only having two, one, or none. Using 82 males and 111 females from the original MMPI-2 sample, they obtained generally good test-retest reliabilities after one week, with the lowest on Paranoid (males = .76; females = .82) and highest on Avoidant (males = .91; females = .92). There is little evidence yet available to make definitive conclusions about acceptable validities for the scales.

TREATMENT OPTIONS

By definition, individuals with the personality disorders are not likely to seek therapy out of a perception of intrapsychic deficit or conflict. Their presence in therapy has usually been stimulated by some social or legal coercion (Benjamin, 1993; Winston et al., 1994). For the clinician in private practice, this coercion is most likely in the form of distress generated among the client's intimate others. When forced by dire circumstances, for example, possible loss of a needed relationship or their freedom in society, they may pledge to change. But they will usually say something like, "I will try really hard to . . ." rather than "I will do it." At such times, keep in mind the adage "trying is lying."

Some form of marital therapy or family therapy is often required. A variety of family-therapy options are available. A frequent approach, in which the nuclear family members are seen together or in various combinations by two or more therapists during the sessions, is called "conjoint family therapy." It is the type most likely to be effective with the personality disorders, as it provides the multiple perspective, duration and intensified focus that are important here. Kin network therapy brings close friends, neighbors, and more distant family members into therapy. It is particularly useful in the schizophrenic disorders or allied disorders where the person has deteriorated socially, but it can also be useful in the schizoid, avoidant, and dependent personality disorders.

In some instances a trial of a low dose of antipsychotic medication may mute those symptoms such as anger, resentment, mistrust, or anxiety that are commonly found in persons with severe or several personality disorder diagnoses.

■ Paranoid Personality Disorder (301.00)

The paranoid personality disorder (PPD) can be thought of as anchoring the other end of the continuum of paranoid disorders from the most disturbed and fragmented pattern, paranoid schizophrenia (Oltmanns and Maher, 1988). However, since there is neither thought disorder nor even a well-formed minor delusional system in the PPD, it is not listed under the paranoid disorders and is not a psychotic condition. Like the other personality disorders, it is a chronic, pervasive, and inflexible pattern of behavior that typically has been in evolution since childhood and is already recognizable in adolescence. Modeling of parental or other significant others is possibly even more important in this disorder than in the psychotic paranoid conditions.

It's been said that paranoids are "just people who have been able to get all the facts." Since paranoid personality traits more easily develop in such groups as immigrants, the elderly, prisoners, and the hearing-impaired, it may be more accurate to say they are "just people who have all the facts they are able to get."

PPDs manifest hyperalertness toward the environment and have a chronic mistrust of most people. They see themselves as morally correct, yet vulnerable and envied, and see others as morally inferior and/or malicious. As a result, their information base is continuously distorted and their affect is constricted. Consequently, they find it difficult to adapt adequately to new situations or relationships, which is paradoxical because of their hyperalertness to their environment. As Turkat (1990) has pointed out, they will frequently be correct in assuming that other people are against them. Yet the paranoia is usually a disabling overreaction to a low initial level of scrutiny by others.

Unless they have almost absolute trust in another person, PPDs cannot develop true intimacy and are continually seeking various ways to be self-sufficient. They avoid the emotional complexities of working out a meaningful relationship and tend to be litigious. For example, they may write negative letters to public figures or bring lawsuits on minimal grounds. It is rare for them to come into therapy without significant coercion from others. The disorder is more common in men.

☐   DSM-IV

The DSM-IV's desire for an operational definition for PPD results in clumsy criteria. The DSM-IV requires evidence of chronic, pervasive, and unreasonable mistrust of others, such that the motives of others are perceived as malevolent, beginning by early adulthood as indicated by at least four of the following behaviors: (1) unreasonably expects exploitation or deception, (2) is preoccupied by unreasonable doubts about loyalty or truthfulness of friends or associates, (3) is reluctant to confide in others due to fear that what is said will be used maliciously against him or her, (4) perceives demeaning or threatening messages without any good evidence they are, (5) persistently carries grudges and is unforgiving, (6) perceives character attacks on characters that are not there and reacts quickly in anger and/or counterattack, and (7) has recurrent and unjustified suspicions about spouse or partner's fidelity. Finally, the occurrence must not be exclusively during the course of schizophrenia or a psychotic mood delusional disorder.

☐   ## MMPI-2

As with the other paranoid-type disorders, it might be expected that the PPD will be high on scale 6. However, this is not always the case, as such individuals are hyperalert about being perceived as paranoid and may guard against this (Turkat, 1990). Hence, there is a wide range of scores for the PPDs on scale 6, although on the average it is well above the mean. Blacks score higher on scale 6 throughout the range of both normal and paranoid patterns.

PPDs will occasionally use some kind of random or devious answering scheme with the MMPI-2, so the reader is referred to the section on malingering in Chapter 16. They are easily irritated at the forced-choice format, especially since they are only allowed a binary decision. They also become irritated at the significant self-disclosure required in many of the MMPI-2 items.

The scales that tend to be highest in PPDs are 3, 6, 1, and K. This reflects the use of denial and projection, the inclination to focus on physiological concerns when in treatment, and the need to present a facade of adequacy. Since the clinician is not likely to see paranoid personality disorders unless persons have somehow been coerced into treatment (as in marital therapy), there may also be a mild elevation on scale 8, reflecting immediate distress and the dawning awareness that the personality system is maladaptive. A moderately elevated scale 4 is also expected, but it is typically not as high as in many other disorders. They usually score high on the CYN content scale.

☐   ## 16 PF

Just as on the MMPI-2 scale 6, PPDs do not always score as high as might be expected on the L scale. This is another disorder where it is particularly worthwhile to score for faking-bad on the 16 PF (Winder et al., 1975; Krug, 1981) to assess the extremity of the response patterns.

The suspiciousness, guardedness, and disintegrating delusional system suggest that Q_3 will be high and scales Q_1 and N will be low. Q_4 can be expected to be low, although if persons are seen for testing in a mental health situation, that score is raised.

The moralistic nature of the paranoid-personality attitude system (Turkat, 1990) predicts a higher G score. The need for dominance combined with a fear of vulnerability suggests high E, low I, high N, and high H scores. Scale A is likely to be lower than might be expected from overt behavior, reflecting an inner reluctance to be self-disclosing and to exchange intimacy. These people are usually higher on scale B than are most other psychopathology groups.

OTHER TEST-RESPONSE PATTERNS

The most typical features of the MCMI-III profile are an elevation on scale 6B and P (Choca et al., 1992). Because PPDs often sense themselves incapable of judging safe from unsafe, experiences of apprehension may be present and reflected in an elevated A scale. Paranoid-personality styles are more likely to occur with the antisocial personality (elevations on 6A and P), the narcissistic personality (elevations on 5 and P), and the passive-aggressive personality (elevations on 8A and P).

PPDs respond to the WAIS-R with the same argumentativeness and even condescension that are consistently seen in the other tests (Allison et al., 1988). Their meticulous approach results in many details, which aids their score on such tests as comprehension and similarities. At the same time, their rigidity, suspiciousness, and peculiar information systems can detract slightly from the comprehension score, so the highest score in the profile is on similarities. These factors can result in good scores on both arithmetic and picture completion, as well as some peculiar picture arrangement sequences. If they become too meticulous and detailed, they do poorly on digit symbol.

On the Rorschach, they are prone to resent the ambiguous stimuli and hence respond with condescending criticism, occasional rejection, flipping of the cards, and a focus on detail responses. F% and F+% are high, and there are relatively few M responses (particularly in light of their intellectual level) and few Color responses. The more grandiose they are, the more likely they are to have W responses. Animal and Popular responses are common, and the record is generally constricted. Suspiciousness on certain TAT cards, for example, 9 GF, 11, and 16 (Bellak, 1993), is likely.

TREATMENT OPTIONS

The reader is referred to the earlier section on the paranoid disorders, since most of the comments there relate to this disorder as well. PPDs often had early experiences wherein they were punished for any violation of family myths or revealing family "secrets." They were also often punished for showing "hurt" or dependency but may have been rewarded for (1) keeping out of the way; (2) any signs of family loyalty, especially in repudiating attacks from others; and/or (3) keeping grudges. As a result, they expect attack or at least rejection or slights from others and assume support from significant others even though they often are unable to provide these others with reinforcement for same, or much in the way of emotion or overt support.

As with other disorders in which there is a paranoid issue, it is essential to gain the trust of such clients through empathy, but not through participation in the disorder patterns (Benjamin, 1993). It is especially necessary to empathize with and articulate the consequences of the clients' behavior, such as the sense of being isolated and not understood or the interpersonal rejection that appears unfair to them. If there is any positive change because of these approaches, catharsis techniques may be helpful to get at the conflicts that are causing the avoidance patterns. Then the therapist can begin to build in more appropriate socialization patterns.

Overall, the following guidelines are usually helpful with PPDs:

1. Openly accept the clients' mistrust as a "reasonable first strategy (sometimes), and be careful not to violate that trust.

2. Focus on the least sensitive issues at first, acknowledging that self-disclosure and/or self-critique is painful and a bit risky.

3. Understand that a basic horror of feeling inadequate underlies the paranoid system. This is often combined with the fact that emotions (especially positive, complex emotions such as love) are difficult, or sometimes virtually incomprehensible to such individuals. Emphasize real personality strengths and work to bolster accessible but less competent patterns, e.g., appropriate assertiveness, stress management, etc. Model and reward any glimmers of humor, especially any self-deprecating humor.

4. Be willing to collaborate on issues such as time of sessions or number of sessions per month. While this behavior would feed the pathology of the histrionic, it bolsters the sense of adequacy of the paranoid. Avoid techniques such as hypnosis that emphasize a client's vulnerability.

5. Help PPDs develop "tests" of their hypotheses that others are generally malevolent, e.g., in small tasks and commitments. Follow up with any exercises that build empathy toward others' feelings.

6. Realize PPDs often have spouses and significant others who have a covert investment in their partners' paranoia; i.e., consider referral or ancillary family sessions.

7. Challenge the underlying beliefs that: (a) I am unique and others are jealous; (b) others will exploit my mistakes; (c) it always pays to be wary, accusatory, and adversarial (some paranoids do make good trial lawyers); (d) people who are trusting or content are fools—i.e., I can't be that way; or (e) negative events are generated purposefully by others.

■ Schizoid Personality Disorder (301.20)

The essential feature of schizoid personality disorder (SPD) is impairment of the ability to form adequate social relationships. As a result, SPDs are shy and socially withdrawn or, as Joan Didion states in *The White Album* (p. 121), "only marginally engaged in the dailiness of life." They have difficulty expressing hostility and have withdrawn from most social contacts. However, although some schizoids do vacillate between desiring and not desiring social contact, the behavior is usually ego-syntonic (unlike that of agoraphobia).

If, in addition to inadequate interpersonal skills, SPDs show peculiarities and difficulties in communication, the appropriate diagnosis is the next disorder to be considered: the schizotypal personality disorder. Schizotypals are more likely to have a family history of schizophrenia (Knable et al., 1995). Thus, that category predicts more consistently to the eventual emergence of a schizophrenic disorder than does the SPD (Widiger et al., 1986, 1994). Those schizophrenics who carry an earlier SPD diagnosis have a poorer prognosis.

The temperament of SPDs is such that they gravitate into jobs that require solitude, such as work as a night guard. As they age or become vocationally dysfunctional, they are likely to move into a "skid row," particularly if they are males. Even though they excessively fantasize and also communicate in peculiar ways, they show no loss of contact with reality (Zimmerman, 1994).

DSM-IV

According to the DSM-IV, although SPDs have few if any friends, they show no communication disturbance. It is required that SPD—which is marked by social-relationship detachment, introverted behavior, and constriction of expression or emotion in social settings—causes vocational or social disruption by at least four of the following: (1) does not desire or enjoy close relationships, including with family; (2) almost always seeks solitary pursuits; (3) has little or no interest in sexual experiences with another; (4) takes pleasure in only a few activities, at most; (5) lacks close friends-confidants, other than first-degree relatives; (6) appears indifferent to praise or criticism; (7) is detached, cold or flat emotionally.

MMPI-2

When the SPD is reasonably well integrated and is not disturbed by pressures from the environment to change, a predominantly normal MMPI-2 profile is attained. As Lachar (1974) points out, a high score on the O scale is obtained, but the other scores are not usually consistently elevated. If SPDs become more disturbed by the environment and begin to question the appropriateness of their functioning, a raised scale 2 occurs. As upset increases, a rise on scales F and 8 is likely, with a lesser rise on scale 9. They tend to score high on the SOD content scale.

The 1-8 profile has been labeled as that of a nomadic individual in whom there is little clear evidence of emotional lability. Attempts at interpersonal interaction are sporadic, and significant problems occur in dealing with persons of the opposite sex.

☐   16 PF

The social isolation of SPDs is evident in low scores on scales A, E, F, and H. They are high on Q_2 and, to a lesser degree, on Q_3. To the degree that they fit the characteristics of the SPD, they are lower on M, O, and I and higher on C, whereas these scores move in the opposite direction as the criteria fit the schizotypal personality disorder more closely.

☐   OTHER TEST-RESPONSE PATTERNS

The most salient indicator in the MCMI-III profile is elevation on scale 1. Low scores on scales 4, 5, and N are likely. To the degree this pattern is closer to the schizotypal, elevations should be higher on 2A, 7, and 8A (Edell, 1987). Depersonalization can occur, which may cause elevation on S. When decompensation occurs or during periods of great stress, elevation on SS may occur, although SS is more typically in the low range of scores.

SPDs, as is true of most of the character disorders, show somewhat higher WAIS-R performance scale scores than verbal scale scores (Maruish, 1994). The interpersonal problems of both the schizoid and the schizotypal affect the verbal scales more directly. Within the verbal subtests, higher arithmetic and digit-span scores are characteristic of this and other groups that tend toward an interpersonal-detachment syndrome (Keiser and Lowy, 1980). Within the performance subtests, lower picture arrangement and picture completion scores occur. Golden (1979) states that such individuals demonstrate a constricted use of space on the Bender-Gestalt test.

Both the SPD and the schizotypal, particularly the former, provide a constricted response record on the Rorschach, as well as some rejections. A high percentage of animal content responses and few Color responses are expected. Few H responses or poor-quality H responses can be expected. Occasionally there is a vague response that cannot be pinned down, or even an occasional oddly supported FC response. Exner (1978, 1986) asserts that such individuals are likely to have a higher Experience Potential than Experience Actual and that their M production is usually high relative to the overall quality of the protocol. They are also likely to show slow reaction times to many of the cards. A constricted response record along with a blandness of theme and character portrayal is a common performance on the TAT.

☐   TREATMENT OPTIONS

Like people with an avoidant personality disorder (discussed later in this chapter), SPDs have inadequate interpersonal relations. But, unlike those with an avoidant personality disorder, SPDs do not care, for the most part, so therapy is quite difficult (Winston et al., 1994). In fact, SPDs are not likely even to enter into therapy because such a relationship is the magnification of what is usually avoided. If for some reason they do become involved in therapy, the therapist must help them develop trust in that relationship and not overwhelm them with initial confrontations. The therapist can facilitate the therapeutic relationship by initially going with the direction of the SPD pathology, that is, accepting some interpersonal distance and de-emphasizing "relationship," de-emphasizing the need for insight, and focusing more on practical matters. Understand that in the childhood of SPDs, abuse and/or intrusions provided unpredictability and anxiety control was associated with intrusion, with aloneness and separateness providing a safe haven.

Thus, the therapy process is analogous to gaining the trust of the paranoid personality. If that trust *is* obtained, the source of avoidance can possibly be located and dealt with via systematic desensitization, client-centered therapy, or some other means to dissipate withdrawal patterns.

Covert extension may even be useful here. SPDs would be asked to imagine their distancing patterns vividly and then immediately complete the image by envisioning that the usually occurring reinforcing events do not occur. Since in many ways the SPD is trying to develop a completely new response pattern, covert modeling may also be used. In this the client repetitively imagines the desired behavior, probably an interpersonal pattern, and reinforces it by imagined positive outcomes.

Overall, the following strategies may be helpful with an SPD:

1. Understand that SPDs show a significant reluctance to use their therapists as a coping resource, as they have never learned to use other people for social support, so it is unwise to stress them in this dimension, especially if early in therapy.

2. Understand that your relationship with SPDs may be their most in-depth social connection. But they still won't value you very much, on a relative basis to other clients, and will tax your empathy and warmth.

3. If a comfort level is reached, consider "bridging" (i.e., continue your individual sessions) the client into a therapy group that you are sure will be supportive and not too demanding initially.

4. Help the client toward "collecting" pleasurable memories and events that involve others.

5. Role play social skills and verbalize "emotional responses" one might expect to emerge over time in someone having such adventures. Remember that a social relationship of any duration is as much an adventure for SPDs as is Mt. Everest for novice climbers.

6. Conversely, help the clients tie negative emotions, e.g., depression, to the schizoid pattern. It's amazing how well SPDs can dissociate the two.

7. Contract for periodic (actually, reasonably often for SPDs) booster sessions to help them avoid a relapse.

8. Challenge underlying assumptions such as (a) Any disruption of my emotional routine (however minimal the emotions are) is scary and messy—in that sense the SPD's experience is analogous to the obsessive-compulsive's fear of disruption of external routines; (b) people don't really mean anything to me; (c) I can survive alone (maybe not optimally, but at least predictably) and need space to do that; or (d) it's necessary to be free and independent—other people are like Brer Rabbit's "Tar Baby," if you relate to them, you get stuck to them.

■ Schizotypal Personality Disorder (301.22)

The reader is referred to the previous category, the schizoid personality disorder, since many of the features of that disorder are found here. The essential difference is that, in addition to the disturbances in social functioning, the schizotypal personality manifests peculiarities in communication. Schizotypal individuals are much more likely than the schizoids to show dysphoria and anxiety, and because of the odd thinking patterns, they are more likely to have developed eccentric belief systems and become involved in fringe religious groups. The schizotypal personality is also more likely to be emotionally labile, overtly suspicious, and hostile of others than is the schizoid (Costa and Widiger, 1994). Many schizotypal individuals also meet the criteria for the borderline personality disorder, to be discussed in a subsequent section. In that case, both diagnoses should be given.

☐ DSM-IV

A diagnosis of schizotypal personality disorder is marked by pervasive socio-interpersonal deficits and discomforts and cognitive or perceptual distortions and behavior eccentricities. It can be supported by establishing at least five of the following: (1) ideas of reference; (2) evidence of magical thinking or odd beliefs that are not subculturally determined; (3) unusual perceptual experiences, including bodily illusions; (4) odd thinking and speech; (5) suspicions or paranoid ideation; (6) inappropriate or constricted affect; (7) odd, eccentric, or peculiar behavior or appearance; (8) lack of close friends or confidantes other than first-degree relatives; (9) excessive, nonhabituating social anxiety that tends to be associated more with paranoid fears than with negative judgments about self.

It is not rare to find some evidence of schizophrenia in family members. If blatant schizophrenic symptoms begin to occur, the schizophrenic diagnosis takes precedence and the schizotypal label is designated "pre-morbid."

☐ MMPI-2

Edell (1987) finds the 2-7-8 code to be especially likely to be manifest in the schizotypal personality disorder. As with the schizoid, scale O is typically raised. Because of the more pervasive disorder reflected in communication problems and labile emotionality, scales F and 4 also are relatively high, in addition to 2, 7, and 8. If depression is not a major factor, 2 and 7 will be lower. If the person is more inclined to be nomadic and to have flat affect and somatization in addition to the communication problems, a pattern with a moderately elevated F and higher scores (in order) on 8, 1, 2, and 3 can be expected. They tend to be high on the B12 scale, as well as on SOD.

16 PF

To the degree the schizotypal shows aspects similar to the schizoid, the profile will resemble that discussed in the previous subsection. However, if, as is more likely, emotional lability, confusion, and suspiciousness are present, scores on B, C, and Q_3 would be lower and scores on Q_4, E, A, and L will be somewhat higher. Also, the score on O is typically higher than in the classic schizoid personality disorder.

OTHER TEST-RESPONSE PATTERNS

As is evident, there are some similarities to the test patterns of schizoids. However, in many respects the schizotypals are closer to the schizophrenic and the borderline personality disorder, particularly in their performance on such tests as the WAIS-R and Rorschach (Swiercinsky, 1985). The patterns noted previously for the acute or less disturbed schizophrenic are applicable here.

TREATMENT OPTIONS

Since, phenomenologically, this is a somewhat polyglot diagnosis, and individual schizotypals will show differing primary and secondary patterns, the comments noted in the subsections on the schizoid, paranoid, and borderline personality disorders apply to a degree to the schizotypal personality disorder. The section on schizophrenic disorders is also useful because the schizotypal individual is seen as predictive of later schizophrenic functioning (Knable et al., 1995). Hence, the therapist's attention must be directed not only toward the interpersonal withdrawal processes, but also to the emergent disturbances in affect and thinking that are common. Family therapy may be useful in preventing the emergence of a full-blown schizophrenic disorder (Griffin, 1993). These individuals have great difficulty in group therapy because they are quickly perceived as "weird" and may be scapegoated or even directly attacked by the group. A low dose of an antipsychotic medication, such as haloperidol, can be helpful.

Histrionic Personality Disorder (301.50)

The histrionic personality disorder (HPD) is commonly encountered in clinical practice (Zimmerman, 1994). HPD is marked by dramatic and intense behavior, problematic interpersonal relationships that others perceive as superficial and shallow, and problematic sexual adjustment. These persons seek attention and are overreactive, with the responses being expressed more dramatically and intensely than is appropriate—hence the term "histrionic." This category has traditionally been labeled the "hysterical personality." However, as noted earlier, "hysteric" wrongly suggests a disorder that parallels the causes and symptoms of what has been previously labeled "hysterical neurosis."

HPDs may elicit new relationships with relative ease, as they appear to be empathic and socially able. However, they turn out to be temperamentally and emotionally insensitive and have little depth of insight into their own responsibilities in a relationship (Johnson, 1994). They quickly avoid blame for any difficulties in interpersonal relationship and, in that sense, show a degree of the projection that is characteristic of paranoid disorders. Even though they may be flirtatious and seductive sexually, there is little mature response or true sensuality. If their apparent sexual overtures were to be accepted, the HPDs may act as if insulted or even attacked.

There has been a continuing controversy as to whether HPD occurs with any frequency in males. This is not surprising, since the meaning of the Greek root term *hystera* is "uterus." Ancient explanations for HPD blamed an unfruitful womb, which became distraught and wandered about the body. Hippocrates thought marriage would cure hysteria by anchoring the womb. Even Freud suggested marriage as a cure. Since conflict over expressing sexual needs may be a factor, such "medicine" might even work at times. But just as often, this "medicine" brings on iatrogenic problems that are worse than the "disease."

It is clear that HPD is found in males (Turkat, 1990), but because the symptoms are a caricature of the traditional role expectations for women, it is more common in women (Millon, 1981). There is evidence that the same developmental patterns in females that eventuate in histrionic behavior lead to more antisocial behavior patterns in males (Zimmerman, 1994), and this would fit with the role expectation theory.

☐ DSM-IV

In general, HPDs show attention–seeking and overly emotional behaviors, beginning by early adulthood, as evidenced by at least five of the following: (1) discomfort when not the center of attention; (2) interactions often marked by inappropriate sexually seductive or provocative behavior; (3) rapidly shifting and shallow emotional expression; (4) consistent use of physical appearance to draw attention to self; (5) impressionistic, non-detail speech style; (6) self–dramatization, theatricality and exaggerated emotional expression; (7) suggestibility; (8) perception of relationships as more intimate than is actually the case.

☐ MMPI-2

The 2-3/3-2 profile is the one most commonly encountered in an HPD. When the HPD is seen in the clinical situation, distress and upset are usually evident, possibly accompanied by manipulative suicide gestures. Thus, an elevation on scale 2 of greater than 70 T can be expected. When distress is not so marked, the expected elevation on scale 3 takes precedence. The elevation on scale 3 often signals the histrionic's monstrous lack of insight. The rare 3-9/9-3 profile is also indicative of histrionic functioning (Kelley and King, 1979a), as are the more common 3-4/4-3 and 4-9/9-4 patterns (Graham, 1993).

Scales 4, 7, and 8 are also likely to be moderately elevated. Scale 4 reflects the HPD's tendency toward egocentricity, overdramatization, and shallow interpersonal relationships. The underlying self-doubt and anxiety raise the 7 score, and the tendency toward impulsive emotionality and self-dramatization elevates scale 8.

Scales L, F, and K usually fall within normal limits. If the individual has begun a defense by focusing on somatic complaints, scale 1 may be elevated. Scale 5 is likely to be elevated in males, reflecting the association of hysteria with traditional feminine role behaviors; it is usually quite low in females. Scale O is not usually markedly elevated; *any* elevation, however, is surprising because these people make a first impression on the unsophisticated that they are highly sociable. If controls are breaking down and the HPD feels that he or she is losing control, a higher score on scale 9 is expected, although it is usually within normal limits.

OTHER TEST-RESPONSE PATTERNS

Elevation on scale 4 would be expected on the MCMI-III. Because HPDs are often seeking attention and validation from others, scales 1 and 2A should be relatively low. The somatization factor may be used as an attention-getting device, in which case one would expect an elevation on scale H. Other scales that may be periodically elevated because they serve as methods for dramatic attention-getting devices include N and S. Anxiety may be experienced when needs for dependence are not being met, resulting in elevated A, although typically the HPDs' style is quite ego-syntonic.

The WAIS–R verbal score is typically less than the performance score for HPDs. Within the verbal scales the information subscale is usually low, as is the arithmetic subscale (particularly in females). HPD females are prone to make complaints about the arithmetic test or to make comments like "I've never been able to do math at all." Digit span is expected to be moderately high, and comprehension is often the highest subscale. HPDs are occasionally inclined to moralize in response to some of the items, particularly in the comprehension subtest.

Within the performance subtests, those that tap speed and visual-motor coordination (such as digit symbol) are high, as is picture completion. Block design is sometimes surprisingly low compared to the other tests of similar skill requirements.

On the Rorschach, HPDs often provide what may be an initially surprisingly low number of responses and blocked responses and/or a low number of Color or shading responses, considering their apparent intensity and involvement. But this relates directly to their lack of introspection and insight. There is a low W% and there is an emphasis on easy, obvious details. They may portray some of the cards as scary or ugly. They may see monstrous or frightening animals and give responses involving sexual innuendo. At the same time, they deny dysphoric content in the cards. There are a relatively low number of W and M responses, relative to intelligence. Occasionally HPDs will make "blood" responses to the color cards.

TAT stories often contain dependency and control themes, and they may even become personalized and generate some affective display. Blocking occasionally occurs to "sexual" or "aggressive" pictures, and some cards may be called "ugly," "sickening," or the like. As with borderlines, "primitive splitting," presenting characters as all good or all bad, or in an incongruous juxtaposition, is occasionally seen (Bellak, 1993).

TREATMENT OPTIONS

Being prone to dramatic and exaggerated patterns, HPDs are most responsive, at least initially, to a dramatic therapy approach, and they are one of the personality disorders that can show some reasonable improvement with relatively short-term approaches (Winston et al., 1994). Hypnosis, some of the consciousness-raising techniques, and even dramatic placebos can be useful here. Low-key or nonintense therapy approaches may be seen as invalid by HPDs simply because of the lack of intensity.

HPDs have often been raised in households where "showy love" and "act as if we love each other" ethics were primary, appearance was reinforced, and indeed may have been the only means effective in eliciting attention from and/or controlling the caregiver. Sickness, or weakness, as long as it was not too repulsive, often was similarly effective. Hence, to gain an initial relationship, the therapist may need to be more emotionally evident and offer frequent demonstrations of support, while allowing them to be a positive center of attention—for example, accepting their recitation of "Let me tell you the ways how I've been done wrong" without too quickly pushing them to take responsibility for their present status.

Once there is any engagement in the therapy process, a shift has to be made to an approach that deals with the disturbed interpersonal relationships and avoidance of responsibility. Group therapy can eventually be helpful because it provides the consensual data so important to convince HPDs of their disorder. However, unless there has been some trust and dependency generated in the group and/or with the therapist, the group will quickly perceive the HPD as shallow and deceptive. Denial and flight from therapy will be quick, and the critically necessary confrontation with the fear and anxiety that have been kept out of consciousness is avoided.

Over time, the following guidelines for therapy with HPDs are usually helpful:

1. Reward their product, not their presentation—the opposite of their behavioral history.

2. Reward any attention to reflective thoughts or efforts toward systematization or routine behaviors—again, a real change.

3. Emphasize appropriate assertiveness and mastery behaviors as therapy goals.

4. Avoid the role of rescuer, understanding that you will be guided toward that role and toward feeling frustrated and/or responsible for any of the clients' failures.

5. Avoid the demands that the clients be treated as "special," e.g., an unwarranted break on fees or seeing them for longer periods or at hours you don't normally see clients.

6. Consider an up-front financial fee contract that gives greater rewards for staying in therapy to at least an agreed-on point, e.g., a high up-front fee that can be credited to later (or more productive) sessions.

7. Use writing assignments to develop analytic and problem-solving thought patterns (usually sorely lacking) and attention to detail.

8. Challenge such common underlying beliefs as (a) Unless my emotions at least appear intense, they won't mean anything to others (and eventually, even to me); (b) being responsible or attending to details means the loss of "zest for life"; (c) rejection is disastrous; (d) people won't love me for what I do but what I pretend to be, or what I present to entertain/entice them; or (e) being "special" means never having to say "I'm sorry" (or at least I don't have to feel it or mean it), or provide restitutions or repair.

■ Narcissistic Personality Disorder (301.81)

The narcisstic personality disorder (NPD) category, first seen in the DSM-III-R, centers on individuals who are to a degree products of our modern social-value systems. NPDs are "flattery-operated"; more specifically, they manifest arrogant, haughty behaviors and/or attitudes, an unrealistic sense of self-importance, exhibitionistic attention seeking, an inability to take criticism, interpersonal manipulation, a lack of empathy, and a sense of "entitlement" that allows them to break the rules (Raskin and Novachk, 1991), resulting in substantial problems in interpersonal relationships.

No doubt such people have always existed, but it appears that this pattern has become more common in recent years. It is not a surprising development when there are advertisements about "The Arrogance of Excellence" and self-help seminars unequivocally urging people to live out the axiom "I'm number one" (with little evidence that there is much room for a number two or three close behind).

The NPD pattern is usually personally evident in adolescence, and the disorder is chronic. As with other personality disorders, NPDs only come to the attention of a clinician when coerced by circumstances (Kernberg, 1984). The prognosis for major change is moderate at best. NPDs are similar to antisocial personalities, except that NPDs are not so aggressive or hostile and their value systems are more asocial and hedonic than antisocial.

□ DSM-IV

According to DSM-IV, the essential diagnostic feature of the NPD—which is a pervasive pattern of grandiosity, need for admiration, and lack of empathy, beginning in early adulthood—must include five of the following: (1) grandiose self-importance; (2) preoccupation with fantasies of unlimited success, power, brilliance, beauty or ideal love; (3) belief in one's specialness or uniqueness and consequent belief in only associating with or being understood by certain others; (4) a need for excessive admiration; (5) a sense of entitlement; (6) interpersonally exploitive behavior; (7) lack of empathy; (8) envy of others or beliefs that others are envious of him or her; (9) arrogant and haughty behavior or attitude.

NPDs naturally have a rather fragile personality integration and may on occasion manifest brief psychotic episodes. As a character in Peter de Vries's novel *Consenting Adults* (1980, p. 183) so aptly puts it, "I have this crush on myself—but the feeling is not returned."

MMPI-2

Lachar (1974) finds that individuals who can develop only superficial relationships score low on scale O. Since NPDs are so interpersonally exploitative (Raskin and Novachk, 1991), an elevation on scale 4 is also expected. They often fit a stereotypical sexual role, so males are usually low on scale 5. Not surprisingly, they are usually quite low on the LSE content scale.

If their patterns are ineffective in coping with the environment, they show situation-generated depression, so a rise on scales 2 and 9 can be expected. If, instead, they become suspicious and irritable, a rise on scale 6 occurs. If they begin to descend emotionally into a brief psychotic disorder, scale 8 should reflect this.

NPDs with a 4-9 profile are not uncommon—they blame their problems on the world and want quick-fix solutions in therapy. They will be impatient for therapy results, and this can quickly generate interpersonal and countertransference therapy issues.

16 PF

Their inflated sense of worth and extroverted assertiveness are expressed in high scores on A, E, and H, while the asocial value system is evident in a low score on G. NPDs also score moderately high on Q_1, and they also tend to be high on Q_3. They are variable on scales C, O, and L, depending on the degree of personality integration and whether or not they are moving toward a brief psychotic episode, suspiciousness, or depression.

OTHER TEST-RESPONSE PATTERNS

The most prominent indicator on the MCMI-III is elevation on scale 5. Scales 4 and 6A and 6B may also be elevated. Because NPDs do not like to admit personal weaknesses or admit psychic distress, elevations on scales A, D, and S are rare, although when they do occur, they may be used as rationalizations for being unable to live up to their inflated self-image. During periods of stress, elevations on P and PP may occur (Choca et al., 1992).

Throughout the testing situation, NPDs are prone to avoid tasks that demand introspection and/or persistent problem solving, particularly if they can use wit or charm to distract the clinician. If the charm does not work effectively, they occasionally feign inadequacy to avoid a task. NPDs are also likely to produce some pedantic, almost condescending, responses. They occasionally will assert that they only guessed when they sense that they have missed an arithmetic solution, even when the evidence shows that they did not guess.

As a result of these tendencies, they do more poorly on WAIS-R tasks that demand persistence and detailed responses, such as object assembly, arithmetic, vocabulary, comprehension, and block design. The picture arrangement subtest occasionally elicits personalized comments that reflect the narcissism. Overall, they do a bit better on the performance scales than on the verbal scales.

On the Rorschach, NPDs are inclined to give "to me" responses. If they feel the clinician is positively attending to them, they provide more responses than do histrionic individuals, yet seldom in accurate detail, particularly in the M and W responses. As a result, these responses show poor quality. In a related fashion, the F+% is not high. If they are at all distressed, they produce constricted records that focus on Popular and Animal responses and may provide "pair" or reflection responses.

NPDs have a higher number of C responses than individuals with the obsessive-compulsive disorder, and those that occur in the obsessive record are better integrated into the overall response pattern. They seldom respond directly to shading, but often make texture responses that are apparently suggested by form or outline. If the narcissism is channeled into direct body expression, responses such as "People exercising" may be noted. Responses that have an ornate or flashy quality are found. Responses focusing on fancy food or clothing, particularly exotic forms of clothing, or gem or perfume responses are also thought to be indicative of the narcissistic personality disorder (Shafer, 1954). Also, an emphasis on both CF and pure C responses is indicative of narcissism.

TAT stories are often void of meaningful content, and the NPD may detract from the essence of the story by a "cute" ending or a related joke. Cards that demand a response to potentially anxiety-inducing fantasy, such as 13 MF, may result in either a superficially avoidant story or one with blatantly lewd or shocking content, again reflecting an avoidance of the essential features of the cards (Bellak, 1993).

TREATMENT OPTIONS

The NPD may be even more difficult than the antisocial personality to engage in therapy, in large part because the therapist seldom has as much coercive control (Benjamin, 1993). For example, one of the few times NPDs enter therapy is when they fear the loss of a dependency role, as in a marital situation. It also may occur when there is a marked discrepancy between expectations (usually fueled by fantasy) (Raskin and Novachk, 1991) and reality. Psychoanalytic therapy appears well suited to confront the pathology of narcissism, and transactional analysis within marital therapy may be of help because it can give both spouse and client a way of more positively conceptualizing the narcissism, that is, the "child" in the personality. Groups can be initially "seduced" by the NPDs, but with time they are viewed as exploitative and self-centered, often resulting in anger and rejection from the group.

NPDs often had periods in childhood when they received "total-indulgent" love (a bit different than unconditional acceptance), sometimes with a component of submissive nurturance (hence allowing a presumptive control of others), and were taught that imperfection could be a cause for rejection. To gain a relationship, a therapist may initially need to allow some dominance, to accept them as a "great client" (but not a "great co-therapist" as they often assume), and be judicious in providing negative feedback.

To the extent the pattern can be more easily accepted, feedback should be followed by some modeling of new behaviors (first, by channeling the psychopathology into "productive narcissism"), either in role playing with the therapist, in a multiple marital-group setting, or in imagination. Role playing and quid pro quo behavioral contracting are useful adjuncts in attempting to change these behaviors, although they require helping the NPD to articulate needs, a difficult step.

Overall, the following guidelines may help:

1. Set clear therapy relationship limits, e.g., schedules of visits and payments, amount of fees, behavior with staff and people in waiting room; smoking rules, or any other indications of "elite" status. When the rules are broken—and they will be—use it as fodder for the therapy hour.

2. In this same vein, expect your counter-transference reaction to be very negative at times; track your thoughts in response to this response and bring them into the therapy session. The critical point is communicating how these negative thoughts were generated, without kicking off such clients' easily elicited humiliation or rejection fantasies.

3. Expect to have NPD clients occasionally make you feel very good. When this happens, realize you have just succumbed to one of their most powerful manipulations and use that in the session. Conversely, a therapist may sometimes "go the extra mile" to get this type of approval. Ultimately, maintain a stable, objective response to attempts to either devalue or flatter your work.

4. Be cognizant that NPDs are often involved in allied hidden patterns such as drug abuse (especially high-status drugs), abusive patterns (after all, the victims are lesser mortals), or financial and vocational irresponsibility. Allied psychopathic and/or histrionic patterns are common.

5. Eventually challenge such underlying beliefs as: (a) I am special (unique, elite); (b) I like to challenge or compete with others, but because of both (a) and the fact it is psychologically necessary for me to prevail, I may play by other rules (usually known only to me); (c) any defects I have come from my bad parents and/or background; (d) recognition, admiration, and respect are necessary, and others exist to provide it, and indeed, promote it; or (e) sharing, serving others, or selfless behaviors are signs of weakness and signal disintegration of self.

■ Antisocial Personality Disorder (301.70)

The essential characteristic of the antisocial personality disorder (ASP) is the chronic manifestation of antisocial behavior patterns in amoral and impulsive persons. They are usually unable to delay gratification or to deal effectively with authority, and they show narcissism in interpersonal relationships. The pattern (see Table 9.2) is apparent by the age of 15 (usually earlier) and continues into adult life with consistency across a wide performance spectrum, including school, vocational, and interpersonal behaviors (Loeber, 1990; Hare, 1986; Hare et al., 1991; Kaplan, 1995). Hare et al. (1991) point out that this category has too many criteria and includes too many diverse personalities, but, unfortunately, his criticisms and concepts were not integrated into DSM–IV. This category as it is formulated in DSM-IV is probably best conceptualized as "a deviant child grown up."

TABLE 9.2   Paths to Various Antisocial Patterns

AGGRESSIVE/VERSATILE PATH, LEADING TO "CAFETERIA-STYLE" OFFENDING, INCLUDING VIOLENT, PROPERTY, AND/OR DRUG OFFENSES/ABUSES	NONAGGRESSIVE ANTISOCIAL PATH, LEADING TO MORE SPECIALIZED OFFENDING, INCLUDING PROPERTY, DRUG OFFENSES/ ABUSES
Characteristics of the aggressive/versatile path	**Characteristics of the nonaggressive path**
Higher rate of genetic, prenatal, and birth disorders	Lower rate of genetic, prenatal, and birth disorders
Onset of conduct problems in the preschool years	Onset in late childhood or early to middle adolescence
Aggressive and concealing problem behaviors	Mostly nonaggressive conduct problems
More hyperactive/impulsive/attention problems as children	No appreciable hyperactive impulsive/attention problems
Poor social skills	Capable of social skills
Poor peer relationships	Association with deviant peers
Academic problems	Sporadic or minimal academic problems
High rate of instigation of offenses	Low rate of instigation of offenses
Low remission rate	Higher remission rate, at least for delinquency
More males than females	Higher proportion of females than in the aggressive/versatile path
Higher rate of drug abuse	Lower rate of drug abuse
Higher rate of stimulation seeking	Lower rate of stimulation seeking

Adapted in part from Loeber, 1990.

Although the DSM-IV discusses only the overall category of ASP, there is good evidence that it can be further subdivided into categories of primary psychopath and secondary psychopath (Lykken, 1957; Zuckerman et al., 1980; Hare et al., 1991). Primary psychopaths are distinguished by the following characteristics: (1) They have a very low level of anxiety and little avoidance learning; (2) they are significantly refractory to standard social-control procedures; and (3) they are high in stimulation-seeking behaviors, particularly the "disinhibition" factor that refers to extroverted, hedonistic pleasure seeking. It is advisable to delineate the consequent ramifications of the differences in primary and secondary psychopaths in a clinical report, since such discriminations are glossed over by the use of the overall term "antisocial personality disorder."

DSM-IV

The DSM-IV term "antisocial personality disorder" has evolved through a variety of terms and now supersedes the terms "psychopathic" and "sociopathic," at least in formal diagnostic labeling. Pritchard's (1835) term "moral insanity" is considered by many to be the first clear forerunner to the present "antisocial personality disorder" label. "Psychopath" first emerged in the label "psychopathic inferiority," introduced by Koch late in the nineteenth century (Cleckley, 1964).

Terms incorporating "psychopath" were common until the DSM-I, published in 1952, used "sociopathic personality." The DSM-II, in 1968, introduced the term "antisocial personality," which is used in the DSM-IV.

In spite of this evolution (or possibly because of it), there have been significant data indicating that this diagnostic grouping is a meaningful concept to clinicians (Hare, 1986). In an early study on the diagnostic reliability of the standard categories, Spitzer et al. (1967) found the highest level of agreement ($r = .88$) when clinicians assigned persons to the "antisocial personality" category, with the lowest index of agreement ($r = .42$) found with psychoneurotic reactions.

To apply the ASP diagnosis, the DSM-IV requires that the individual be 18 years old with a pervasive pattern of disregard or violation of others and evidence of Conduct Disorder with onset before the age of 15, as supported by evidence of at least three of the following: (1) failure to conform to socio-legal norms as denoted by repeated acts that are grounds for arrest; (2) irritability and aggressiveness, as seen in repeated fights or assaults; (3) consistent irresponsibility in work or financial obligations; (4) impulsivity or failure to plan ahead; (5) deceitfulness, as indicated in lying or conning; (6) reckless disregard for one's own or other's safety; or (7) lack of remorse.

RELATED DIAGNOSTIC CONSIDERATIONS

A recent conceptualization views psychopathy as composed of two main factors (1 = Affective-Cognitive Instability, 2 = Behavioral-Social Deviance) (Hare et al., 1992; Hare et al., 1991). This view has helped generate and, in turn, has been facilitated by Hare's PCL-R (Psychopathy Checklist-Revised), a twenty-item assessment technique that uses self-report and interview observation data, which is then cross-checked with collateral information. A score of 30 or higher (out of a potential 40) is considered a good cut-off for indicating psychopathy. There is a newer twelve-item "screening" version, which has less validation data but which has an "r" of approximately .80 with the full PCL-R and which is more applicable to nonforensic populations. A score of 18 or more (out of a possible 24) on the shorter version is considered a good cut-off for indicating psychopathy.

The following components contribute to the Affective-Cognitive Instability factor (#1): glibness, a grandiose sense of self, pathological lying, conning-manipulative behaviors, lack of remorse, shallow affect, callousness and lack of empathy, and failure to accept responsibility. Components of the Behavioral-Social Deviance factor (#2) are a higher need for stimulation, a parasitic lifestyle, poor behavioral controls, early behavior problems, lack of realistic goals, impulsivity, irresponsibility, having been adjudicated delinquent, and a history of violating supervision or probation. Factors 1 and 2 show an average "r" of about .50.

In general, recent research on the psychopath (much of which includes use of the PCL) indicates:

1. While there is a dropoff in criminal activity for psychopaths at about age 40–45, this effect holds primarily for nonviolent crimes. There is only a slight dropoff for violent crimes, so "normal life does not begin at 40" for psychopaths.

2. Concomitantly, while the Behavioral-Social Deviance factor starts to drop off at age 40–45, the Affective-Cognitive Instability factor only lessens slightly with age.

3. Similarly, while the Behavioral-Social Deviance factor (#2) is a good predictor of general criminality and recidivism, is highly correlated with criminality, and is negatively correlated with SES and, to a lesser degree, I.Q., factor 1 is a better predictor of violence but is virtually uncorrelated with SES and I.Q.

4. Factor 1 is negatively correlated with neuroticism and trait anxiety and is positively correlated with narcissism and dominance. Conversely, factor 2 is positively correlated with trait anxiety, psychoticism, and a higher Pa-Ma index from the MMPI.

5. While treatment may effect a positive change in the average criminal, it seldom does so with psychopaths, especially to the degree they are strong on factor 1. Indeed, there is evidence that psychopaths who are high on factor 1 may get worse with treatment, i.e., group and individual psychotherapy can be a "finishing school" for psychopaths. True to their nature, they seem to learn little about themselves in therapy but learn more about others and then more boldly use such information. At least in part, this is because they are language-disordered in the sense that the affective components of language are weak or missing, voiding the likelihood of empathy or remorse.

6. In general, while socioeconomic and family background variables are good predictors of general criminal behavior, they are relatively nonpredictive for psychopathy, especially where it is loaded on the Affective-Cognitive Instability factor. However, since psychopaths are good learners of violence, positive family and socioeconomic factors somewhat lessen the probability of violence in psychopaths.

☐ ## MMPI-2

The 4-9/9-4 profile has been considered the classic ASP profile. The 9 component can be conceptualized as the activator/energizer, a catalyst for behavioral acting-out of the more basic cognitive components of the psychopathy. As Megargee and Bohn (1979) demonstrated, distinct bimodality indicates an amoral psychopath who fits most of the classic descriptors of the ASP yet is not particularly hostile. Not surprisingly, most ASPs score high on the Antisocial Practices (ASP) content scale.

When the profile contains a definite spike-4 profile with only a secondary moderate elevation on scale 2, it is more likely to be a primary psychopath who in addition is easily provoked to violence. The primary psychopath who is prone to violent behavior commonly scores high on scales 8, 6, and 4. Such individuals appear to be especially dangerous if they have a high scale 9 score in addition to high scores on scales 8, 6, and 4. Within a psychopathic population the level of scale 6 is an indicator of whether hostility is overt or suppressed.

The bimodal 4-9/9-4 profile, noted earlier, is more indicative of secondary psychopathy, as is another common code, the 2-4/4-2 profile with moderate elevations on the other scales. In the 4-9/9-4 group, to the degree that 9 is greater than 4, one is likely to observe a higher level of tension and more somatic concerns. The rare spike-9 profile (when not under treatment because of a spouse's complaint of marital difficulties) is indicative of a primary psychopath who has also abused drugs heavily.

A high F scale is more characteristic of the secondary psychopath and/or the younger psychopath than the primary psychopath and/or the older psychopath. When there is a 4-8/8-4 profile and most other scales are low, a hostile, cold, and punitive psychopath who borders on schizophrenia should be considered (Lachar, 1974). If the 4-8/8-4 elevation is accompanied by elevations on the Bizarre Mentation and Family Problems content scales, consider psychosis; but if elevations are on the Cynicism and Anger content scales, consider a diagnosis of aggressive psychopathy. The expression of aggression in the psychopath appears to be inhibited to the degree that scales 2 and 3 (and 5 for males) are high. Aggression is much more likely, as noted earlier, when scales 6, 8, and 9 are high. When psychopathic individuals are seen in a hospital setting rather than as outpatients, they are more likely to score higher on scales F, 1, 2, 3, and 7, reflecting their greater situational distress.

☐ ## 16 PF

The modal 16 PF profile for primary psychopaths finds high scores on scales O, L, and M, with average high scores on Q_4 and A. They obtain low scores on

Q_3 and G, with moderately low scores on C and B. They generally score high on E, although this fluctuates rather wildly, with some primary psychopaths scoring very low. Since low I predicts to roughness and insensitivity, this is likely, especially in more aggressive psychopaths.

Golden (1979) also suggests that logically, a high N score is typical of the psychopath, because shrewdness and manipulation of others are characteristic of this pattern. Those psychopaths who are particularly high on the stimulation-seeking variable should score low on G and Q_3 and high on Q_2 and L. Within all subgroups of the antisocial personality disorder category a high M score is thought to predict recidivism.

The modal profile for secondary psychopaths shows high scores on scales Q_4, O, and A, with low scores on C, Q_3, and H. They are also moderately low on G and Q_1 and tend to be average or below on N (in contrast to the primary psychopath), although again they also vary widely on N. On the average, they are not as low on scale B as are the primary psychopaths.

OTHER TEST-RESPONSE PATTERNS

The highest MCMI-III elevations are expected on 5 and 6A and often 6B. When the 5-6A code is highest, B, T, and PP also tend to be somewhat elevated, and P, S+P, and C+P are high as well. Because ASPs are generally not highly distressed, marked elevations on A, D, and H are not likely; however elevations on A may occur, especially just prior to acting-out. Because alcohol and drug abuse are common here, elevations on B and/or T are likely.

On the WAIS-R, ASPs, especially those more inclined toward primary psychopathy, generally have a performance IQ higher than the verbal IQ, sometimes by 10 points or more. If they have had school-related problems, as is almost always the case, their low scores in the verbal subtests are on information, arithmetic, and vocabulary, reflecting their lack of adequate achievement in academic subjects. On the comprehensive subtest the "marriage," "bad company," and "laws" items can bring out relevant content. Some explanations of the picture arrangement subtest include similar material. Picture completion and block design usually give two of the higher scores, and these persons usually do reasonably well on object assembly. Digit symbol and digit span are also often quite high (Keiser and Lowy, 1980).

In certain older individuals (with a mean age of 44), probably best viewed as secondary psychopaths, Heinrich and Amolsch (1978) found an unusual WAIS-R pattern consistently associated with persons who have poor work and marital histories, show drinking problems, are assaultive while drinking, and are inclined toward somatic concerns and situational depressions. They show a verbal IQ greater than a performance IQ by 6 to 21 points; high vocabulary and comprehension scores; low digit-symbol, block-design, and object assembly scores; and an average picture completion score.

Gacono and Meloy (1994), using the Exner system, found the following variables to be prototypical of the psychopath: (1) approximately twenty responses; (2) core characteristics—Lambda > .99, D = 0, Adj D = 0; (3) affect—

FC: CF+C = 1:4, Afr is < .50, Pure C > 0, T = 0, Y = 0, Space is > 2; (4) interpersonal—Pure H = 2, (H)+Hd+(Hd) = 2.5, COP = 0, Ag = 0, Sx = 1; (5) self-perception—Rf = 1, Per > 2, W:M > 3:1; (6) cognitive—X+% and F+% both about 55%, X – % is 22, M– is 1, WSum6SpecSc is 17.

On the Rorschach, ASPs usually present casual yet alert facades (Hare, 1986), which is in contrast to their at least moderately constricted and shallow protocols. If they are defensive, the record will be quite constricted, and they may reject cards that they can clearly handle cognitively. Otherwise, a low to average number of responses is provided. Vague percepts may be seen at first and then developed flamboyantly, possibly accompanied by "cute" although hostile comments. There may be guarded rejections of cards, and there is usually a delayed response to the color cards. They do respond to color (particularly the primary psychopath), although more often in fairly primitive and impulsive ways, with pure C responses (Gacono and Meloy, 1994). While there is a low number of M and W responses, an absence of shading, and a low F+%, there are a high number of Popular responses. There is a high number of Animal responses, rather than human responses, and weapons are occasionally noted (Wagner and Wagner, 1981; Shafer, 1954).

The TAT stories are often somewhat juvenile in theme, and although the protagonist may be caught in a negative act, there is little mention of deserved punishment. If, on the other hand, they perceive the social demand of the situation as requiring some commentary on punishment, they will so comment, yet with superficial shallowness (Karon, 1981).

As noted, one of the better measures of psychopathy is the Hare PCL-R (Hare et al., 1991; Serin et al., 1990). Iacono (1991) points to a number of physiological markers for psychopathy that could be built into specialized evaluations; for example, they show relatively attenuated electrodermal responses to a "countdown" threat of predictable but noxious stimuli—smaller anticipatory skin conductance increases but high anticipatory heart rate changes.

TREATMENT OPTIONS

The treatment problem with all the personality disorders—getting the client into therapy and meaningfully involved—is acute with the ASP. To the degree the person shows primary psychopathy, the chances become poorer for any meaningful change, no matter what treatment is used, or, as the British prime minister William Gladstone (1809–1898) put it, "The disease of an evil conscience is beyond the practice of all the physicians of all the countries in the world," and this seems to include psychologists as well. Most effective are controlled settings, with personnel who are firm and caring and sophisticated in controlling manipulations, in which the ASP client resides for a significant period of time. Confrontive therapies can also be moderately effective, depending upon the degree of psychopathy (Winston et al., 1994), but they require some form of coercion, such as institutionalization, to keep the person in therapy.

Any inpatient treatment program should include four major components: (1) supervision, manipulation of the environment, and provision of education by the staff to facilitate change; (2) a token economy system that requires successful participation for patients to receive *anything* beyond the basic necessities; (3) medical and psychiatric treatments to deal with ancillary psychopathology, for example, neurological disorders and depression; and (4) a system of necessary social cooperation to maximize conformity and encourage development of the group ethic. This last component is seldom a consideration. In such a program every possible task that can reasonably be performed by another and which is not essential to health will be *required* to be performed only by one inmate *for* another. For instance, no inmates are allowed to go to the soda machine for themselves; they must get someone else to do so for them. Again, this encourages cooperation and reciprocation and may help inmates to internalize some mores. If some inmates are left out by others. it may become necessary to assign "partners" who will fulfill these functions for one another.

Aside from institutional settings, the chief time a therapist is likely to see an ASP is in a disturbed family situation. Marital and family therapies that work on a quid pro quo rather than on a good-faith contracting approach are of most help.

Various medications can be of help with certain components of the ASP. For example, antipsychotics can be helpful with various paranoid components, especially when there are additional indications of seizures. Carbamazepine, some antipsychotics, lithium, or beta blockers can be helpful for various dimensions of lack of control or violent tendencies (Young and Hillbrand, 1994), but benzodiazepines (e.g., Valium or Xanox) may be counterproductive.

Attention should also be paid to the stimulation-seeking nature of these clients (Zuckerman et al., 1980). This need can be interpreted as similar to that of the alcoholic, in that the ASP needs somehow to fulfill this drive or be inclined to indulge in deviant patterns. Therapists can work with psychopaths to develop means of gaining stimulation in less self-destructive ways. A consistent pattern of engagement in sports and other strenuous and/or exciting activities and jobs that provide for a high level of activity and stimulation are helpful. The paradoxical effect of stimulant drugs (as with hyperactives) can be helpful with a small subgroup of the more manic psychopaths, but much care must be taken in management.

Overall, the therapist working with an ASP generally needs to

1. Expect resistance to entering therapy, and then to staying in therapy. Since these clients are easily bored and, as just noted, are highly stimulation-seeking, this must be considered in planning for general rehabilitation as well as specifically for the therapy hour.

2. Expect such clients to be deceptive about their history and present status. To the degree feasible, independently corroborate any critical questions about history or present behaviors. Contract ahead of time that if you feel it necessary, you will obtain such data from significant others or other appropriate persons.

3. Turn their competitiveness (which easily moves to control, even cruelty) into a plus. For example, show them they are not competing well (they are not considerate of others, don't do socially sanctioned behaviors, e.g., church). The trick is increasing prosocial behaviors without just building a better psychopath.

4. In line with 2 and 3, clearly confront the individual's psychopathy and any record of deviant behavior. The presentation of "objective" profiles from tests like the MMPI-2 or 16 PF can be effective here. Confront the psychopathology as a lifestyle disorder that will require treatment of a significant duration (and cost)—thus, one might contract for some financial penalty for early withdrawal. At the same time, avoid the role of judge and stay as much as possible in the role of collaborator. Maintaining a degree of adequate rapport is critical. Any exercises that help to develop empathy or social sensitivity are useful.

5. Challenge the following underlying beliefs as delineated by Beck et al. (1990): (a) rationalization—my desiring something justifies whatever actions I need to take; (b) the devaluing of others—the attitudes and needs of others don't affect me, unless responding to them will provide me an advantage, and if they are hurt by me, I need not feel responsible for what happens to them; (c) low-impact consequences—my choices are inherently good, and, as such, I won't experience undesirable consequences or, if they occur, they won't really matter to me; (d) I have to think of myself first—I'm entitled to what I want or feel I need and, if necessary, can use force or deception to obtain those goals; (e) rules constrict me from fulfilling my needs.

Conduct Disorder

Conduct disorders (CDs) are marked by a persistent pattern of behavior that violates major age-appropriate social norms or the rights of others for at least six months. To earn the diagnosis of CD, at least three of the following factors should be in evidence: (1) often bullies, intimidates, or threatens others; (2) often starts physical fights; (3) has used a dangerous weapon; (4) has stolen, with victim confrontation; (5) has been physically cruel to people; (6) has been physically cruel to animals; (7) has forced someone into sexual activity; (8) often lies or breaks promises for manipulative purposes; (9) often stays out at night, over parental objection, beginning before age 13; (10) has stolen items, of nontrivial value, without victim confrontation, including within the home; (11) has set fires with intent to cause damage; (12) has deliberately destroyed property (excluding fire setting); (13) has run away from parental home, overnight, at least twice, or once for a lengthy period; (14) has often been truant, beginning before age 13, or has high work absence if employed; (15) has broken into someone's house, building, or car. Items 1 and 13 were added in DSM-IV in order to make this category more gender-equal.

The diagnosis can be retained beyond age 18 if the diagnosis of Antisocial Personality Disorder is not met. If at least one conduct problem appeared before age 10, it is childhood onset type; otherwise it is adolescent onset type. Since it's hard to find a child who by age 10 has not at least been physically cruel to other children or to an animal, it's hard to see how this differentiation, as stated, is useful. Severity of the CD can also be denoted as mild (i.e., few, minor problems), moderate, or severe.

A full evaluation of the family is essential for adequate diagnosis of the conduct-disordered child (Gomez and Samson, 1994) (also see Figure 9.1). Young children who show evidence of an oppositional defiant disorder are at clear risk for a later CD diagnosis to the degree they show aggression and lying, and there is associated family pathology.

Because it has been found useful by some diagnosticians and therapists, the discrimination from earlier DSMs, that is, on the dimensions of introversion and aggression, is continued here in the discussions of diagnosis and treatment.

FIGURE 9.1 Evolution of Aggressive Delinquency

MMPI-2

Overall, scales 4, 8, and 9 have been "excitatory" in regard to acting-out in adolescence, whereas scales 0, 2, and 5 have been seen as "suppressor" scales. A moderately elevated 4-9 code, with most of the other scales not particularly high, is typical of the peer group-oriented CD. A combination of the 4-8-9 scales with generally elevated scales throughout would be more consistently found in the solitary-aggressive conduct disorder. A caret-shaped profile on the validity scales (low L, high F, and low K) typifies the most severely emotionally disturbed subgroup of this disorder.

The 8-4 profile, with an elevation on 6 as well, is likely to be found in the solitary-aggressives who also have a paranoid component. They often show an incredible amount of alienation from self and others, usually directed in the Harris-Lingoes subscales. But the 8-4 profile without a high 6 would be more likely with individuals who are acting-out aggressively but are at least somewhat more socialized. The 2-4/4-2 profile, with a distinctive slope to the right and possibly a mild elevation on scale 6, is characteristic of those who are more likely to be undersocialized and nonaggressive—they are usually placed in the undifferentiated category. In general, though, scales O, 2, and 5, if high, predict lower rates of delinquency.

16 PF

On the 16 PF a group-oriented CD should score somewhat higher than the solitary-aggressive type on scales A, B, G and, to a moderate degree, N and Q_3. They are likely to be lower on L and Q_1 and, to a moderate degree, on E. The aggressive continuum is reflected in several scores: likely higher on E, H, and L; lower on B, C, G, I, and M, and moderately lower on N and Q_3. Q_4 particularly reflects the anxiety experienced in the evaluation situation, as well as other environmental conditions. The more socialized the individual, the more situational anxiety and thus a higher score on Q_4.

OTHER TEST-RESPONSE PATTERNS

To the degree that the client is socialized and more likely to be a group-type CD, WAIS-R and WISC-R scores will be more even between and within the verbal and performance tests, and the differences are more pronounced with the WISC-R than the WAIS-R (Grace and Sweeney, 1986). To the degree that the client is more aggressive and undersocialized, performance scores are likely to be higher than verbal scores. To the degree that avoidance of school is a factor, scores would be lower on information, arithmetic, and vocabulary than on other subtests. The ability to abstract has been hypothesized as important in curbing physical aggression; hence, aggressive individuals may be lower on similarities, all other variables being equal.

Solitary-aggressive CDs are more likely to be resistant to the testing process itself and to show negativism throughout both this test and the Rorschach. To the degree they are undersocialized, they should do somewhat less well on comprehension and picture arrangement than clients who are more aware and attuned to social norms. From a general perspective, individual CDs who are more involved with passive or status offenses are more likely to have higher intelligence overall than those who are involved in more aggressive acting-out behaviors (Kronenberger and Meyer, 1996).

On the MCMI-III the group-type CD may experience more distress related to associated behaviors, producing more frequent elevations on A and D, while the solitary-aggressive type may show relatively higher elevations on 1, 2A, 5, and 6A. To the degree the person is undersocialized yet nonaggressive, elevations on 1, 2A, 6A, 8A, S, B, and T and low scores on 4, 7, and N can be expected.

On the Rorschach, solitary-aggressive CDs are likely to reject cards, to avoid the task in a variety of ways, to give more personalized (PER) responses, and to show more direct manifestations of violent and bizarre content than more socialized and/or less aggressive clients. Those tending to be undersocialized, solitary, and aggressive are also likely to show the following characteristics: lower F percentage, lower W percentage, lower M percentage, more pure C, CF greater than FC, more Animal responses, higher white-space responses, and more emphasis on D and Popular responses in an overall protocol with a low number of responses (Quevillon et al., 1986).

On the TAT (Quevillon et al., 1986), young male CDs typically make more mention of parents, give more aggressive stories, and give responses that involve materialistic objects and a need for achievement. Aggressive youths in general give stories in which the hero was aggressive but received little punishment for his actions, as well as themes that include vivid and instructive stories about murder, burglaries, and hold-ups. These youths tend to ramble on without any clear themes and often have difficulty describing card 2. Stories that are superficial and have an absence of empathy or sympathy are common. Some youths give stories that are evasive, and they frequently mention that the stories are not autobiographical. Human figure drawings can be useful with this group, as it is a task they are more receptive to (at least in one-on-one testing), and some norms have been developed for them (Marsh et al., 1991).

TREATMENT OPTIONS

Early intervention is critical, and, indeed, children first arrested at a young age are more likely to commit a greater number of and more serious crimes (Kernberg and Chazan, 1991). If the individual is more solitary, undersocialized, and aggressive, there is a need for a highly controlled living system that includes all aspects of functioning (Hillebrand and Pallone, 1995). Token economy programs, combined with an emphasis on basic academic and vocational skills, will likely be necessary, along with a focus on the control of behavior. The more subtle strategies designed for the primary psychopath and the paranoid may also be appropriate. In response to the group-type CD, especially when nonaggressive, the requirement of a highly structured and supervised residential program is lessened. An emphasis on a group-living model comes to the fore, and in some cases, outpatient treatment with such approaches as reality therapy, support groups, and the more traditional psychotherapies can be useful (Lyons and Woods, 1991; Johnson, 1994). A focus on parent training and classroom control using time-out procedures, contracting, and reinforcement structuring would also then be appropriate. Family therapy is usually necessary, and community-based interventions (e.g., setting up sports activities, scouting programs, and other positive group experiences) can also be effective (Gomez and Samson, 1994; Loeber, 1990).

Borderline Personality Disorder (301.83)

At first glance this disorder may seem to overlap with the schizotypal personality disorder, as both at least imply an easy transition into a schizophrenic adjustment. However, individuals with borderline personality disorder (BPD) are neither as withdrawn socially nor as bizarre in symptomatology as are schizotypals or schizophrenics. Although the DSM-IV does not specifically mention it, this category seems to be in part a resurrection of an old term at one time much favored by clinicians: "emotionally unstable personality." Persons in the BPD category show significant emotional instability, are impulsive and unpredictable in behavior, are often antisocial, are irritable and anxious, often show "soft" neurological signs, and try to avoid being alone or experiencing the psychological emptiness or boredom to which they are prone (Stone, 1990). There is some evidence that as BPDs improve, they show more predictable behavior patterns, yet this is combined with increasingly evident narcissism. Ironically, a number of BPDs who appear to be very disturbed in their twenties look much better in their thirties, although much of the underlying psychopathology is still there (Stone, 1990).

An occasional additional feature of BPD is pseudologia phantastica. Snyder (1986) reports several case studies in which pathologic lying is a cardinal feature. This lying may reflect an attempt to control or to enhance self-esteem. Some borderline individuals may be aware of their lying, while others may not be. In clinical cases where the individuals were confronted with their inaccuracies, they quickly dropped or changed the stories.

DSM-IV

To diagnose BPD—a pervasive pattern of mood, self-image, impulse control, and interpersonal instability beginning by early adulthood—at least five of the following are required: (1) frantic efforts (excluding those behaviors in #5) to avoid actual or imagined abandonment; (2) an unstable and intense interpersonal relationship pattern, with extremes of idealization and devaluation; (3) persistent and markedly disturbed or unstable identity or sense of self; (4) two impulsive self-damaging behaviors (excluding #5); (5) recurrent suicidal behaviors, gestures, or threats or self-mutilation; (6) affective instability due to marked mood reactivity, usually a few hours, not more than three days;

(7) chronic feelings of emptiness; (8) inappropriate, intense anger or lack of anger control; (9) transient, stress-related paranoid ideation or severe dissociation.

BPD is thought to be relatively common (approximately 1–2% of the general population), and it is one of the most consistently diagnosed personality disorders. Yet, it may be a confusing diagnostic category for clinicians. A diagnosis with at least schizotypal and histrionic components is often seen.

MMPI-2

In many respects, BPD parallels schizophrenia, without the distinct emphasis on delusions or hallucinations and with a higher level of responsiveness toward other persons. Hence, along with general elevation of the profile, particular elevations on scales 8, 2, and 4 should be expected (Trull, 1991; Edell, 1987). While the F scale should be lower, scales O and K should be higher than in schizophrenia. Scale 6 should show elevation if problems in management of anger are involved, although manipulative borderlines, especially young adults, will sometimes exaggerate responses contributing to this scale. The rare 2-6/6-2 type is likely to receive a diagnosis of borderline personality disorder or a similar one (Kelley and King, 1979a). If mood instability is involved and the person is in a manic phase, a rise on scale 9 and a drop on scale 2 are likely, with the opposite expected in the converse mood situation. BPDs are usually quite high on the ANX, DEP, and/or ANG content scales.

16 PF

If BPDs avoid being alone, even though there is instability in interpersonal relationships, A should be high and Q_2 should be low. Overall, scales C, H, and Q_3 should be low, with high scores on Q_4, O, and I. Mood at the time of the testing will determine the score on F, and the degree of suspiciousness will be reflected in the height of the L scale. On the average, moderately low scores on M and N can be expected, but these can fluctuate markedly.

The variable self-assertion and avoidance exhibited by BPDs emerge on scale E, although BPDs can be docile and passive in order to fulfill their dependency needs. At other times they are aggressive, paranoid, and manipulative, particularly when they are rejected. Also, since their social instability and irritability disrupt their social functioning, probable rejection results in their occasionally appearing at the more assertive end of the E continuum.

OTHER TEST-RESPONSE PATTERNS

From an overall perspective, the inadequate insulation of intellectual abilities from the intrusion of emotion can be observed in the connotations of the BPD's language (Stevenson and Meares, 1992). It often becomes colored by personal concerns, although it usually stays within the bounds of appropriateness. For example, an explosive BPD client, when asked to define "terminate," replied, "To murder or kill someone—say, for revenge" (Swiercinsky, 1985). While some of these impairments may suggest organic dysfunction, BPD clients do not usually show such features as perplexity, concreteness, perceptual failure, constriction, oversimplification, or psychomotor retardation.

The most likely elevation of the BPD profile on the MCMI-III is on scale C. These individuals are subject to most of the clinical symptom syndromes at some time or another, so periodic and variable elevations on A, H, N, R, and D are to be expected. Elevations on scale 8 may be present, in that the moodiness and behavioral unpredictability that characterize the passive-aggressive are often present in a more extreme form in BPDs. Those with high scores on 3, 4, and 7 and/or 8A are at risk with respect to this pattern in that these types are more prone to borderline functioning as they deteriorate.

On the performance subtests of the WAIS-R, in particular object assembly and block design, the increasing difficulty of the tasks often elicits haphazard trial-and-error efforts that are laced with noticeable displays of frustration and impatience. The BPDs' inclination to resort to arbitrary solutions is often evident in the arithmetic subtest, especially when these clients are requested to reveal the way they came to the incorrect response. Requests as to how they arrived at their response on other subtests can often be similarly useful. On the Rorschach, illogical and fabulized combinations occur, but when actual contaminations occur, it more likely bodes a schizophrenic disorder (Swiercinsky, 1985). On tests like the TAT, "primitive splitting," an oft-cited characteristic of the BPD, is seen in characters that are all good or all bad, for example, angels or devils, in characters in which only one side of the personality is portrayed or even admitted to or good-bad characteristics are juxtaposed incongruously. Inappropriately extreme effect portrayals, separation-anxiety themes, and acting-out rather than delayed gratification themes are common (Bellak, 1986).

TREATMENT OPTIONS

BPDs have typically been the target of and/or witnessed a chaotic, soap opera early life, often mixed with some form of abuse wherein love was equated with pain and loss of control (Kroll, 1993). Attempts at self–definition received random reinforcement, at best, and crises and sickness were the keys to attention and nurturance.

Reflecting such chaos, BPD is truly a polyglot syndrome and will therefore require equally variable treatment responses (Kroll, 1993; Stevenson and Meares, 1992; Stone, 1990). The impulsivity demonstrated in BPD suggests that the reader should refer to comments regarding the antisocial and narcissistic personality disorders, as well as those regarding substance abuse or possibly one of the sexual deviations. The comments on the antisocial personality regarding stimulation seeking are also relevant, since boredom is common in BPDs. Also, borderlines show a high rate of suicide attempts and "successes"; Stone (1990) reports a 9% rate of eventual suicide. Schizotypal and histrionic components are also not uncommon and require the treatment responses noted in those categories.

Multiple hospitalizations are not uncommon. Medication may be necessary, for example, for any depressive components, and fluoxetine has been useful to generally calm and stabilize extreme response patterns. Since there is usually some disordered autonomic-emotional functioning, biofeedback and relaxation training may be appropriate. If there are a number of neurological "soft" signs, treatment will have to take probable CNS involvement (see Chapter 11) into account. Group therapy can be helpful if the BPDs will allow the development of trust in the group, but such clients are often unwilling to share the attention of the therapist and are so emotionally unpredictable that they are difficult to work with. They can exert such a high cost on the progress of the group that they make it unwise to include them.

From an overall perspective, the therapist needs to:

1. Provide a stable and predictable overall framework for therapy, and discuss necessary deviations. At the same time, give clients a sense of control over the emotional aspects of the therapy relationship. In contrast to therapy with narcissists, allow BPDs as much input as feasible over such issues as therapy schedules, seating arrangements, topics to be discussed, whether to use homework assignments and what types, etc. Be prepared to tolerate and explore negative transference issues.

2. Help them to establish a clearer sense of identity. Realize that BPDs have extreme but poorly organized views of relationships with caretakers and thus bring odd and dysfunctional expectancies into interpersonal relationships. They tend to remember significant others as having destabilized and/or left them at crisis times, and they need to have these memories healed and eventually replaced.

3. BPDs are intense and labile emotionally and are stressful to significant others (and therapists). Yet, paradoxically, they need to understand that they avoid facing any intense negative emotions, so find it hard to grieve the many relationship losses they generate. They maintain a facade of competence and independence, yet desperately want various types of help, then react negatively when it is not forthcoming. They need to role play expressing their emotions as they develop and also role play how to ask for help in more appropriate ways.

4. BPDs need to be helped to understand that they are prone to "dichotomous thinking"; i.e., they perceive issues, persons, etc., in extremes, or in black-and-white terms. When people fail them somewhat, they perceive the failures as total.

5. Understand that BPDs consistently generate "crises," so clear guidelines for responding need to be formulated early on and communicated to the clients. Teach them to communicate affect verbally, rather than through behavior.

6. Challenge, although more subtly than with other personality disorders, the following beliefs: (a) I'm afraid I'll be alone forever, as no one who really gets to know me will stay with me or love me; (b) if I ignore my own needs, I can entrap some people into relationships, but, since I can't control my feelings and I need the relationships, I'll be very unhappy; (c) although I need people, they will eventually hurt or reject me, so I must protect myself; (d) people and/or relationships are usually all good or all bad, and the same relationship can offer both at different times; (e) I deserve any bad things that happen to me; or (f) my misery (and/or "badness") is how people recognize me as a unique self.

◼ Identity Disorder

This traditional diagnosis, while incorporated into the thinking of both lay-persons and mental health professionals, was not included in the most recent DSM. However, many professionals still find it useful. The essence of the concept is uncertainty about identity in the following areas: career choice, sexual patterns, friendship choices and behavior, moral values, religious identification, peer group loyalties, and long-term goals. This disorder naturally occurs most commonly in late adolescence, when people are forced by society to make choices and face changes in these areas.

☐ TREATMENT OPTIONS

Therapies that are effective here are similar to those usually applied to the depersonalization disorder and to some of the more neurotic disorders. With some of these clients a low dose of antidepressants—for example, 25–50 mg of imipramine or its equivalent—may be of significant help. The client-centered therapy of Carl Rogers is especially appropriate, since he initially developed this while working with young ministerial and graduate psychology students who were going through various identity conflicts.

If the client has moved too far in avoidance of choices, the reality therapy of William Glasser may be more appropriate. An existential perspective is important in whatever therapy takes place. Clients need to face the choices that they are avoiding and to envision and accept the consequences. An adolescent therapy or support group is often useful here because it gives such clients awareness that others are moving through the same choices and it provides feedback about new choices and initiatives (Duncan et al., 1995).

◼ Avoidant Personality Disorder (301.82)

People with Avoidant personality disorders (AVD) are shy and inhibited interpersonally, yet at the same time they desire to have interpersonal relationships, which distinguishes them from those with the schizotypal or schizoid personality disorders. They also do not show the degree of irritability and emotional instability seen in the borderline personality disorder.

A major feature of AVD is a chronic unwillingness to tolerate risks in deepening interpersonal relationships (Millon, 1981). They resonate, negatively, to this refrain from the poetry of W. B. Yeats:

Only God, my dear
Can love you for yourself alone
and not for your yellow hair

These persons are extremely sensitive to rejection and seem to need guarantees ahead of time that relationships will work out (Johnson, 1994). Naturally, such guarantees are seldom available in healthy relationships. Thus, the friends they manage to make often show a degree of instability or are quite passive.

In many ways, AVD is close to the anxiety disorders, since there is a degree of anxiety and distress, and low self-esteem is common (Eysenck, 1985). However, the behaviors that produce the distress are relatively ego-syntonic. Their depression and anxiety are more related to their perceived rejection and criticism by others.

This common disorder is seen more often in women. Any disorder in childhood that focuses on shyness predisposes one to AVD.

DSM-IV

To diagnose an AVD, the clinician must observe a combination of social inhibitions, feelings of inadequacy, and hypersensitivity to negative evaluation in a persistent pattern starting from early adulthood, and evidenced by at least four of the following: (1) avoidance of occupations with significant social contact because of hypersensitivity to negative evaluation; (2) avoidance of interpersonal involvement unless sure of being liked; (3) restraint in intimate relationships because of fear of shame or ridicule; (4) preoccupation with social criticism or rejection; (5) inhibitions in new interpersonal situations as a result of feelings of inadequacy; (6) belief one is socially inept, personally unappealing, or inferior; (7) unusual reluctance, because of potential embarrassment, to engage in personal risks or new activities.

MMPI-2

A 2-7/7-2 profile is common, reflecting depression about assumed rejection and apprehension and self-doubt about the ability to deal with others. To the degree that this has resulted in social withdrawal, a high score on scale O is expected, as well as a moderate decrease on scale 9. Since AVD often appears in females who are strongly identified with the traditional feminine role, a low score on scale 5 occurs. If the AVD still has energy that is being channeled into anger, a 3-4 profile can be expected, with allied mild elevations on 2, 7, and 6. Indeed, a 6-7/7-6 profile is indicative of this disorder (Graham, 1987). If functioning is beginning to go to pieces as a result of the rejection and social withdrawal, an elevation on scale 8 occurs. AVDs are usually very high on the SOD content scale.

16 PF

Low scores on scales E, C, and H are consistent with this syndrome, reflecting shyness, threat sensitivity, passivity, and emotional upset. High scores on Q_4

and O are evidence of the expected tension and insecurity, and a moderately high score on I reflects fear of rejection and sensitivity. Social clumsiness is balanced by a hyperalertness in social situations, hence particularly deviant scores on N are not too common. The self-perception by AVPs that they should automatically be accepted interpersonally may result in a higher than average A score. However, actual experience, of which they are somewhat aware, keeps this from being very high and will even temper it to average or below in some profiles. AVPs tend to be moderately low on Q_3 and M, although this is highly variable. The L score, usually low, will depend on whether they have begun to channel their rejection into anger and suspiciousness of others.

OTHER TEST-RESPONSE PATTERNS

To the degree AVPs feel accepted by the examiner, they do better on the verbal subscales of the WAIS-R than on the performance subscales. Since they are often females with strong traditional role identities, low scores on arithmetic are common. Dependency may be reflected in some of the content of the comprehension items, as well as in the picture arrangement subtest, which is low in introverted clients. Blocked or relatively inactive M responses on the Rorschach are common. A high number of Popular responses occurs, and content may focus on more passive animals, such as rabbits and deer (occasionally being hurt or killed), or on passive interactions in the M responses.

The most prominent characteristic on the MCMI-III is an elevation of 85 or higher on scale 2A, with depressed scores on scales 4 and 7. Generalized anxiety, a common symptom in this pattern, is evidenced by elevation on A. The ego-dystonic detached style of the AVP causes elevation on D. Moderate elevations (75–85) may occur on scales 8B and C, in that characteristics of these disorders are likely to occur concurrently. The higher the elevation on S, the more decompensation has occurred.

TREATMENT OPTIONS

AVPs often received plenty of early nurturance, but also received rejection-humiliation for failure and were told to expect even worse from others. Restraint and self-effacement around others were rewarded, and family loyalty and the inability to count on others (rather than the malevolent deceit the paranoid expects) were family mores. To effect an initial or short-term relationship with an AVP, which can be effective (Winston et al., 1994) one should minimize negative comments, offer frequent reassurance, and model a more "laid-back," relaxed interpersonal style. Similarly, programmatic relaxation training should be helpful.

Training in social skills is critical here. Have them develop a hierarchical list of social events to be dealt with in stepwise fashion, combining systematic desensitization and assertiveness training. The need for assertiveness training is often as great in AVP as it is in the dependent personality (see the following subsection for suggestions equally applicable here). In addition, since the AVP is more concerned with the risk in relationships, existential and confrontive therapy approaches are useful adjuncts. Rational-emotive therapy (Ellis and Dryden, 1987) is especially useful because it was worked out on a population that had these kinds of concerns. Since the Adlerian therapies focus on issues of inferiority, there may be special applicability here. Also, since there is a neurotic-like component to the AVP (Eysenck, 1985), paradoxical-intention approaches may be useful. AVPs may elicit "protective responses" within a group-therapy setting, but an unwillingness to self-disclose may eventually lead to rejection by the group.

Another helpful treatment for dependent and avoidant personality disorders is covert negative reinforcement; this technique is most useful when the client cannot easily envision the desired behavior and would not be highly responsive to covert positive reinforcement. In covert negative reinforcement the client imagines a highly aversive event and then imagines this event is terminated by the performance of a new set of desired behaviors. It is critical that there be as little time lapse as possible during the switchover in images.

Also, see the following discussion of the next disorder, as many of those techniques are equally applicable to AVPs.

■ Dependent Personality Disorder (301.60)

People with the dependent personality disorder (DPD) have a pervasive need to cling to stronger personalities who are allowed to make a wide range of decisions for them. They are naive and show little initiative. There is some suspiciousness of possible rejection, but not to the degree found in the avoidant personality disorder.

In one way, DPDs can be seen as successful avoidant personality disorders. DPDs have achieved a style that elicits the desired relationships, but at the cost of any consistent expression of their own personality (Johnson, 1994). They show elements of agoraphobia, not crystallized, and they lack any real self-confidence.

Since DPD is an exaggeration of the traditional feminine role (Widiger and Costa, 1994), it is not surprising that it is far more common in women. If the individual is not in a dependent relationship, anxiety and upset are common. Even if enmeshed in a dependent relationship (and many DPDs also often show some borderline personality disorder characteristics as well), there is still residual anxiety over the possibility of being abandoned. The borderline is more likely to show rage or other frenetic behaviors at the prospect of abandonment.

☐ DSM-IV

The essence of the DPD diagnosis is a need to be taken care of leading to submissive-clinging behaviors and fears of separation, evident by early adulthood. To make a formal diagnosis of DPD, five of the following are required:

(1) inability to make everyday decisions alone; (2) allowing others to assume responsibility for major life areas; (3) difficulties in expressing disagreements with others, from a fear of loss of support or approval; (4) difficulties in self-initiation, from self-image problems rather than deficits in motivation or energy; (5) excessive efforts to gain support or nurturance from others, to the point of doing things he or she finds unpleasant; (6) feeling of discomfort when alone, related to fears of being unable to care for him- or herself; (7) quick replacement of relationships to get care and support; (8) unrealistic preoccupation with fears of having to care for oneself.

MMPI-2

The 2-7/7-2 profile is characteristic of individuals who are experiencing anxiety and depression, who are passive-dependent and docile, and who present a picture of severe dependency. A high 3 scale and a mildly elevated K scale are common. Naiveté and passivity are reflected in a surprisingly elevated L scale, but the F scale is usually in the average range. Some DPDs (and avoidants) elevate the "naive" Harris-Lingoes subscales, for example, on Hy and Pa. These people are afraid to acknowledge any faults in others for fear that they may be rejected. DPDs are usually very low on the LSE content scale.

The acceptance of the stereotypical feminine role shows up on a low scale 5, and the lack of resistance to coercion from authority is reflected in a low 4 scale. There is a subgroup of DPDs who are a bit more aggressive and manipulative, and they tend to show the 2-4/4-2 profile (Anderson and Bauer, 1985). Scale 9 is also low, reflecting passivity and lack of initiative. Scale O tends to be elevated, although this is variable, depending on emerging concerns about their own behavior and their sense of comfort about the permanence of their dependency relationships. If anger is beginning to develop as a result of any consistent rejection of the dependency, some elevation on scale 6 occurs. Otherwise, this is rare.

In young men an interesting and rather rare profile, the 1-9/9-1 type, with both T scores greater than 70, has been found to indicate passivity and dependency. However, there is a hostile component directed toward females that is associated with this profile, so the dependency relationship would probably be directed toward males. Thus, one would look to the 5 scale for elaboration on the issue of sexual identity and possible preference.

16 PF

The DPD should obtain scores quite low on the classic 16 PF dependency factors: scales E, L, M, Q_1, and Q_2 (Karson and O'Dell, 1976). In addition, the I score should be high in females. In males, moderately low scores on Q_4 may be noted and A is high. There are probably low scores on Q_3 and N and a high score on O. Surprisingly, there is not a particularly low H score—it may even be above average. It is also noteworthy that a low score on L is not consistently found in DPD, which may reflect not only a high threshold for jealousy but also the unconscious anger alleged to be a result of the submergence of one's personality to another.

OTHER TEST-RESPONSE PATTERNS

A high score on scale 3 of the MCMI-III would be expected, along with an elevation on A when any insecurity about having placed their welfare in the hands of others occurs. DPDs often adopt physical problems to further the pattern of requiring help and care, resulting in an elevation on H. An elevated D may appear during periods when they are not getting needed nurturance and security. Because elements of the avoidant and histrionic personality disorders are often present, elevations on scales 2A and 4 may occur.

On the WAIS-R the performance scale score may be higher, although this is not as consistent as in some of the other personality disorders. Arithmetic and information seem to be consistently low, relative to other scores, reflecting a withdrawal from a problem-solving approach to the world. Within the performance subtests, lower scores on object assembly occur and odd responses indicating a need for support are occasionally found in picture completion.

A constricted use of space is a common feature in the drawing of the Bender-Gestalt figures.

The Rorschach record is often highly reflective of the attitude of the examiner. A DPD who feels accepted in the testing situation and believes that the examiner desires a high number of responses will produce an extensive record. Otherwise, a record with a less-than-average number of responses can be expected. As with the avoidant personality, passive Animal and passive M responses are found, as well as a high number of Popular responses. There is also a tendency toward use of color rather than form in determining responses, relative to other personality disorders, and there is a likelihood of perceiving small-detail responses. Dependency and compliance themes are often elicited in card 2 of the TAT (Bellak, 1993).

TREATMENT OPTIONS

The abuse plus dominance equals love equation is seen in the backgrounds of many DPDs. Yet even in some of these DPDs, there was often an experience of sufficient, even excellent early nurturance. However, weaning from such nurturance was often delayed too long. A dearth of reinforcement for competence or autonomy was followed by isolation, even mockery, by many peers. Compliant, "out of sight (but still close by), out of mind" patterns were rewarded. Thus, to facilitate the initial relationship the therapist may have to offer more dominance, sense of protection, and nurturance than he or she normally would.

Assertiveness training is eventually needed in the treatment of DPDs. It may need to be preceded by methods that help clients gain a greater awareness and articulation of their dependency, via consensual feedback from a group, from catharsis, or from other consciousness-raising techniques.

In the response acquisition stage of assertiveness training, modeling is carried out with audio- or videotaped demonstrations by same-status, -age, and -sex models. Covert modeling is particularly helpful where persons are trying to develop a whole new behavior style. Clients imagine another person performing the assertive behaviors that they wish to have in their repertoire. After response acquisition, there is response reproduction, in which behavior rehearsal, role playing, and even directed practice are useful. After this, response consolidation is effected through clear feedback, again possibly using audio- or videotape. Changes are crystallized into the ongoing personality through cognitive self-reinforcement and by requests and contracting for increasingly widening the range and targets of the assertive behavioral responses. Since DPD often occurs in the context of family or marital difficulties, attention will have to be paid to the partner, who may view any change as threatening.

Overall, the therapist needs to:

1. Present the goal of therapy as "controlled freedom," since DPDs have a strong underlying fear of "independence"; independence signifies isolation and loss of self.

2. A totally nondirective approach, especially at first, is too threatening for these clients. Move as soon as feasible into a Socratic type of "guided discovery" when the DPD requests what to do, which will inevitably happen. Guided imagery can help nurture embryonic independence behaviors, but change is often slow, and a goal of "total independence" is often unrealistic.

3. Be careful to avoid the authoritarian or "benevolent guru" role. This role is tempting to assume with any dependent clients, as they will quickly reward you—understand that they have finely honed skills in eliciting such patterns and intuiting what will be rewarding to each individual in that role. While "rescuing" can be frustrating with borderline personality disorders, it feels good with DPDs.

4. Set clear limits in areas where dependency can emerge. DPDs easily "fall in love" with the therapist and make the therapist vulnerable to a variety of dual-relationship behaviors, including sexual intimacies.

5. Remember that DPDs may be getting many rewards for their behaviors, in the midst of the negatives that have led them into therapy, e.g., abusive relationships. Very often significant others only want very circumscribed changes, so once changes begin, they and their partners will likely subvert progress. At the same time, the eventual termination of therapy is always threatening to DPDs. Group therapy can sometimes help as a sort of weaning process.

6. Work on activities that indirectly foster independence. Joining clubs, taking cooking and car- and home-care classes, and developing an exercise plan (even better, at a health club), all help.

7. Challenge such underlying belief systems as: (a) I am perpetually at risk of being alone in a cold and dangerous world; (b) I will destabilize and/or suffer if I'm alone; (c) I'm not able to cope with and/or enjoy life without a supportive other; (d) a loss of self is a fair price to pay in order to obtain a relationship with a supportive other, even if I am periodically abused in some fashion; or (e) I need constant access to this other, with as much intimacy as I can elicit, so I'll be as subservient and inoffensive as I need to be.

■ Obsessive-Compulsive Personality Disorder (301.40)

Obsessive-compulsive personality disorder (OCPD) is occasionally confused with the obsessive-compulsive disorder, but there are significant differences between the two syndromes. First, OCPDs seldom become obsessed about issues. Second, the term "obsessive-compulsive" here refers to a lifestyle in which obsessive-compulsive features are pervasive and chronic; it does not refer to a specific behavior. Third, the obsessive-compulsive lifestyle is ego-syntonic for the most part, and OCPDs only come to treatment when coerced.

OCPDs are preoccupied with rules and duties, are unable to express warmth and caring except in limited situations, are highly oriented toward a lifestyle marked by productivity and efficiency, are temperamentally and emotionally insensitive, and are generally distant from other individuals. They can be described as workaholics without warmth. An associate once commented that this is the type of person who can obtain a complete physical exam from a proctologist.

It is true that a degree of compulsivity is effective, particularly in our society. It becomes a problem when it overwhelms the rest of the personality. Paradoxically, OCPDs are often indecisive and poor planners of their time, a result of their narrow focus and concern with precision, even when precision may be irrelevant (Johnson, 1994). They are inclined to be excessively moralistic, litigious, and hyperalert to criticism and perceived slights from others. Traditionally, males tend to more often show this disorder, probably because it is often concerned with exaggeration in the domain of work, whereas, for example, the histrionic is concerned with exaggeration in the domain of love.

☐ DSM-IV

To diagnose an OCPD, the DSM-IV requires a pervasive pattern of preoccupation with orderliness, perfectionism, and control, at the expense of flexibility, openness, and efficiency, evident by early adulthood and indicated by at least four of the following: (1) preoccupation with details, to the exclusion of an overall perspective (they see the trees rather than the forest, and not even all of the trees); (2) perfectionism that interferes with tasks; (3) excessive devotion to vocation and productivity; (4) overconscientiousness, scrupulousness, or inflexibility in matters of morality or values (and not accounted for by subcultural or religious factors); (5) hoarding worthless objects that are without sentimental value; (6) reluctance to delegate or cooperate as a result of control issues; (7) miserliness toward self and others, to avoid future catastrophes; (8) rigidity and stubbornness.

MMPI-2

OCPDs attain a moderately high K scale and seldom have highly elevated MMPI-2 profiles because they are not inclined toward self-disclosure. They often attain elevations on scales 3 and 1, the latter particularly so if physical complaints have become a focus for their distress. They find it more comfortable to see themselves as having a physical rather than a psychological disturbance. The 9 scale is also elevated; in large part, this elevation reflects how autocratic and dominant OCPDs are in personal relationships. Litigiousness and developing paranoid concerns are reflected on scale 6. A moderately high 7 score may occur if there is a querulous and complaining attitude, although scale 7 usually reflects obsessionalism rather than compulsive factors. Not surprisingly, OCPDs tend to score high on the OBS content scale. To assess their level of unacknowledged anger, check the O-H supplementary scale and the TPA content scale.

16 PF

OCPDs also typically present a reasonably normal profile here. Since there is denial of anxiety, Q_4 is low, and the need for control of intrapsychic processes leads to a high Q_3. Isolation from other people results in a high Q_2 score, and the rigidity and possibly developing paranoia lead to a high L score. Scale A is also lowered for the same reasons. Scores are not particularly low on C or high on O. They tend to be high on E, the degree depending on the orientation toward dominance in interpersonal relationships. Scores are moderately high on G or N and moderately low on I and F. Since the coping systems of OCPDs result in better academic performances and intellectual achievements, they attain one of the higher scale B scores.

OTHER TEST-RESPONSE PATTERNS

On the MCMI-III, a high score on scale 7 is expected. Elevation on A is rare, as anxieties are usually controlled. Occasionally anxieties are expressed as psychosomatic or physical complaints, represented by elevation on H. Characteristics of the dependent or paranoid personalities may be present, causing elevations on scales 3 or P, respectively.

As a result of an emphasis on achievement and productivity, adequately functioning OCPDs score at least in the average range—usually above—on the WAIS-R. They will give overly precise and detailed answers, which helps on comprehension and similarities. But in tests based on speed, such as digit symbol, block design, object assembly, and picture arrangement, the same traits can lower the scores. Their interpersonal and problem-solving rigidity causes difficulties with the more complex puzzles in picture arrangement. Generally, they attain a higher verbal IQ than performance IQ.

On the Bender-Gestalt test, OCPDs are inclined to count the dots or small circles in the cards, may orient all the figures in a precise arrangement, and generally approach the task systematically and methodically.

On the Rorschach there is an emphasis on Dd and D responses, with a high F+% and fewer W and Color responses. Some responses are described in overly specific detail, and they make criticisms of the blots. Relative to those with the other personality disorders, OCPDs provide a high number of responses overall. TAT stories are often lengthy, with varied themes offered. Occasionally the primary theme is lost in a focus on details, especially as elicited by certain cards, for example, card 2 and 13 MF (Bellak, 1986).

TREATMENT OPTIONS

OCPDs have often experienced backgrounds wherein adequate caregiving and even sufficient nurturance were mixed with (1) "performance" as a condition of love-attention; (2) judgments of failure and/or invidious comparisons with siblings or peers; (3) rules presented as impersonal abstracts; and (4) demands for persistence even where success (at least as defined by parents) is unlikely, and then punishment for "mistakes." Hence, to initially facilitate a therapy relationship, the therapist needs to provide consistent though not "overly emotional" support, accept their hierarchical view of the world, and provide a diagnosis by logic and schemata (they love to follow the DSM-IV diagnosis, as it provides a sense of mastery and some evident goals).

Developing rapport can be difficult, as OCPDs usually lack emotionality and a sense of humor. Often they only allow rapport after a base of competence-based behaviors have been "produced" by the therapist. Since therapists are often subclinical MMPI-2 4-9s and want to "get on with it," they easily become impatient with the details and periodic tediums OCPDs engender. So, appropriate monitoring and constructive use of counter-transference responses are important (Bongar and Beutler, 1995).

Cautela and Wall (1980) suggest the use of covert conditioning procedures to counteract the compulsivity; in particular, they recommend the use of the covert sensitization technique. As described elsewhere, this technique involves the imagination of a highly aversive event or contingency immediately after developing the imagery of the undesired behavior—in this case, the compulsive pattern to be eliminated. The technique is effective not only for this pattern but for a number of the habit disorders.

In another useful technique, paradoxical intention, clients are simply instructed to do the very acts they have been resisting (Seltzer, 1986). As this proceeds, clients are told, by a number of apparently absurd instructions, to vary the circumstances and quantity of the behaviors produced. As this occurs over time, they develop a greater sense of control over their behaviors and may then choose to give them up. Group therapy can be a helpful followup because OCPDs are likely to regress into their cold and distancing compulsive behaviors if the changes are not thoroughly incorporated into their lifestyles for some length of time. However, groups can be impatient with OCPDs' judgmental behaviors and condescension.

In general, therapists should consider the following when working with OCPDs:

1. OCPDs tend to set higher expectations for themselves than others; these expectations may be only at the overt level, as they usually harbor much anger (the expression of which they fear) toward others for not working as hard as they do. Consider having them develop written charts comparing themselves with specific others, and use the contrasts as access to the anger and as a means of helping them toward concretely lowering their standards.

2. Humor is a natural antagonist to obsessive-compulsive patterns. Model humor for them or consider showing and discussing humorous tapes or books. ("Saturday Night Live" 's classic vignettes of The Anal-Retentive Gardener, Fisherman, etc. are excellent.)

3. Consider bibliotherapy assignments (an assignment they usually take to easily), not only in books with humor, but those that describe and thus model a more relaxed lifestyle, e.g., Thoreau's *Walden,* Zen, Taoist, and other Eastern religion literature, mystery books about laid-back detectives such as John MacDonald's Travis McGee series, etc. Participation in classes on meditation, yoga, or tai chi can be beneficial. Relaxation training is also helpful.

4. Monitor for ancillary patterns often found in OCPDs, i.e., depression, psychosomatic disorders, sexual inhibition, substance abuse (occasionally rationalized as self-prescribed medication), etc. They are more inclined to hide these "defects" than are some other clients.

5. Challenge common underlying beliefs such as (a) To err, or worse, to fail (even early in the game) is anxiety-provoking, will allow others to criticize me, and makes me feel less than a whole person; (b) to lose control or to face uncertainty is anxiety provoking; (c) my obsessiveness and/or compulsivity is powerful enough to avoid anxiety, errors, failure, or finding myself with nothing to do, i.e., the existential void; (d) yet, as regards meaningful decisions, rather than "Better to have tried and failed than to never have tried at all," my motto is "Better to have not tried at all, than to have tried and failed"; (e) details are important—if you can see trees, no need to look for the forest; (f) feelings or emotions interfere with thinking, and I must always depend on logic for control; (g) love and relationships involve too much chaos and unpredictability, so control and possessiveness are necessary to retain love; (h) I am responsible for myself and others; or (i) I hate others when they don't follow "the rules," i.e., my rules, and especially if they get by with it.

▪ Passive-Aggressive (Negatavistic) Personality Disorder

The passive-aggressive personality disorder (PAPD), which was included in all prior DSMs, was not included in DSM-IV. This is apparently because (1) its origins in the military lexicon still haunt it; (2) in DSM-III-R, it was available as a diagnosis only after ruling out all other personality disorder diagnoses, the only such diagnosis with that caveat—not surprisingly, few diagnoses of PAPD occurred; and (3) as one diagnostician has commented, "the best way to conclude to a PAPD diagnosis is to live with the person for a month"—an effective, although costly method, as many ex-spouses have found out. This exposure over time is more discriminating for diagnosing PAPD than it is for the other personality disorders. Hence, therapists know the disorder well; screening diagnosticians don't. PAPD is still available as a "criterion set" or optional diagnosis in DSM-IV.

The essential behavior pattern in the PAPD is indirectly expressed resistance to social and occupational performance expectations that results in chronic ineffectiveness. The core disorder is hostility that is not directly expressed, so "double messages" to others result. The underlying hostility affects significant others, yet the PAPD denies, often as if insulted, any aggressive or hostile motivation. The actual behavior expressed may be either passive or aggressive, but physical aggression seldom occurs (Volavka, 1995).

Most parents have had the experience of a child pushing them to the limit of their control and then backing off. Like that child, the PAPD becomes acutely sensitive to such limits and is consistently able to go so far but no further (Benjamin, 1993). When this pattern becomes an integral part of a social and vocational lifestyle, a PAPD exists. Although these patterns are commonly modeled and learned in childhood, such a family usually reaches a state of mutual détente. The pattern causes severe problems when it is transferred into any new intimate, consistent contact relationship, such as marriage.

The PAPD takes the standards and belief systems of significant others and turns them around to immobilize the others effectively. The strategy (which is not thought to be a conscious behavior) is to present the "enemy" (often a person depended on) with a choice that forces the other either to capitulate or to violate an individual belief system. That person is thus immobilized, with no adequate reason to justify retaliation.

DSM-IV

As noted earlier, this is not an official DSM-IV diagnosis but is available as a criterion set or optional diagnosis, which requires evidence of negativistic and passive resistance to demands for adequate performance, evident from early adulthood, and manifest in at least four of the following: (1) passive resistance to fulfilling social and occupational tasks, (2) complaints of being misunderstood or unappreciated, (3) sullen argumentativeness, (4) unreasonable criticism and scorn of authority, (5) envy and resentment toward those who appear more fortunate, (6) exaggerated and persistent complaints of personal misfortune, (7) alternation between hostile defiance and contrition.

MMPI-2

The 3-4/4-3 combination is commonly seen in PAPDs (Graham, 1993). Where scale 3 is greater than 4 and both scales are relatively high, they are oriented toward the passive mode. When scale 4 is higher than 3, accompanied by a moderate to high elevation on scale 6, the aggressive mode predominates. If both scales 3 and 4 are high, there is a tendency toward dissociative responses (Lachar, 1974).

Elevation on scale K is also probable since PAPDs will downplay their faults and show a lack of insight about intrapsychic dynamics. An avoidance of responsibility, possibly through somatic complaints, produces mild to moderate elevations on scales 1 and 7. Scale 9 is average to low in this pattern, except when hostility is a counterphobic defense against dependency, when the rare 3-9 profile may be given. Also, when a man is being seen as a result of his wife's complaint of marital problems, a spike-9 profile has been found to be indicative of passive-aggressive functioning (King and Kelley, 1977). Graham (1987) also notes that a 1-2/2-1 profile may be indicative of this disorder.

The "Scarlett O'Hara" V on scales 4–5–6 for women is a marker for significant and often very destructive (though passively) personality traits. The PAPD who is closest to actual loss of control of aggression shows a 4-6/6-4 profile, with high F and 8 scales, as well as a low scale 2 score. Persons with this profile have much cross-sex hostility. If the scores here are very high, consider an emerging paranoid schizophrenic adjustment.

16 PF

The 16 PF profile of PAPDs is generally not remarkable. The E score fluctuates, depending on whether the passive (low E score) or aggressive mode is operative. The apparent dependency of many PAPDs would suggest a low Q_2 score. However, this is balanced by underlying hostility and resistance, which raises the score into the average range and occasionally to an above-average score. PAPDs are usually moderately low on G, although not markedly low on C. The interpersonal manipulation inherent in this pattern results in a high N score and at least an average L score. The L and H scores are higher in the aggressive mode, with the I score being lower.

OTHER TEST-RESPONSE PATTERNS

An MCMI-III scale 8A score of 85 or higher suggests a PAPD, and 6B is also likely to be elevated. During stressful periods, elevations on A and D are likely to occur. Psychosomatic complaints may occur, causing a raised H score. Moderate to high elevations on scales 4 and especially C are possible since these disorders occur relatively frequently in conjunction with 8A.

Golden (1979) found passive-aggressive individuals to be high on the comprehension scale of the WAIS, but in general, the performance scale score is slightly higher than the verbal scale score. They do well on visual-motor tasks such as digit symbol, block design, and object assembly. They also do well on digit span but are only average on arithmetic. Elaboration of responses on picture arrangement and comprehension may cue the passive-aggressive orientation.

On the Rorschach a long response latency and a high percentage of FC and Space responses are noted, as well as a relatively high number of Texture and

Popular responses. Occasional odd combinations of aggressive and passive content may occur, such as children and guns, or there may be rather arbitrary assignments of color or content to a space (Wagner and Wagner, 1981). PAPDs may produce responses that directly suggest their pattern of relating, such as people passively manipulating others or arguing or animals sneaking around.

Many authors have asserted that the use of white space suggests the negativistic tendencies that are characteristic of PAPDs. An aggressive-content response, such as bombs, fire, scissors, or volcanoes, is more likely to be evident in PAPDs who are inclined to actually threaten aggression on occasion. Phillips and Smith (1953) assert that a rough-texture response is also characteristic of this pattern.

TREATMENT OPTIONS

PAPDs usually experienced adequate nurturance as a young child, but often experienced weaning from such nurturance as abrupt and/or harsh. Caretaking in later childhood and adolescence was less predictable and often neglectful in one or more dimensions. Punishments were occasionally harsh (especially for initiatives toward autonomy or expressions of anger), and, like OCPDs, they often were subject to unreasonable demands for performance. To facilitate a degree of relationship, initially avoid telling such clients what to do and setting too many limits (i.e., don't get between the dog and the hydrant), avoid demonstrations of anger, and tolerate and interpret the clients' mood responses.

The eventual critical task for the clinician treating PAPDs is to set up feedback situations so that they can no longer effect their interpersonal controlling patterns and yet cannot deny their existence (Benjamin, 1993). Some form of family or marital therapy that confronts the underlying belief system is often indicated (Baucom and Epstein, 1990).

Also, any form of effective data presentation about personality patterns is helpful, especially if it can be stored for future use (Cattell, 1986). For that reason, audio- or videotapes of different sessions are useful in confronting PAPDs with their patterns. Consensual feedback from a group is also useful in overcoming avoidance mechanisms, although some PAPDs may be too sophisticated for some groups and, as a result, will absorb too much of the therapist's psychic energy. Since inadequacies are often at the core of this pattern, assertiveness training may be appropriate. If anger is the focus, assertive training is still helpful, but it may need to be embellished with methods that focus on catharsis.

From an overall perspective, a therapist working with a PAPD client should:

1. Remember that since the most common reason PAPDs enter therapy is because of complaints they are not meeting expectations, e.g., in job or relationships, you can assume they will act similarly with you. They can be deceptive, but of course not directly so; rather, they often give partial or misleading information, or just don't bring forth relevant facts.

2. The automatic thought "I don't have to get there on time—nobody can tell me what to do" is common to PAPDs. Thus, they are inclined to be late for payments, sessions, etc., so clear contracts with detailed consequences are necessary.

3. PAPDs are also often late within a much longer perspective—the developmental tasks of life, e.g., establishing a career or getting married or having children. This stems not only from their "you (in this case, society) can't make me do it" attitudes but also from an impaired ability to tie responsibilities to time and the fact that responsibility per se is often aversive because it is interpreted as a "society should." This is an area that most therapists usually ignore but one that is critical to any long-term change (Oates, 1987).

4. Analogously, there is often passive refusal to accept the disciplines and sacrifices needed to develop either vocational or interpersonal "careers." Attaining the required credentials and "putting in time" in order to gain the payoff of an accrual process is seen as too restricting and demanding. Asking them to sketch past histories of "critical choices," to keep diaries of present choices, and to project desired life goals (followed by means to attain them) may open up this area for discussions and possible changes.

5. These clients quickly test a therapist's "unconditional positive regard," as they tend to whine and project blame onto others, or, as one colleague put it, "They don't quite have the guts to be truly paranoid." Whining behaviors can be addressed by talking to them about the "Help me . . . yes, but" syndrome in which they implicitly ask for help (by whining), then passively refuse intervention.

6. Getting them to take responsibility for their life circumstances is difficult. One book that deals effectively with this general issue is *Rapid Relief from Emotional Distress* (actually a somewhat misleading title) by Gary Emery and James Campbell, New York: Rawson Associates). The exercises they discuss are very useful for such clients.

7. In addition to challenging the beliefs embedded in the prior points, the therapist must look at these central beliefs of the PAPD: (a) I know I can really be self-sufficient, but I apparently do need others, at least now, and I resent that; (b) any control by others is aversive; (c) straightforward confrontation or resistance is dangerous and doesn't work; (d) while I apparently have to accept some subjugation of my desires and/or loss of control, they'll pay a price for making me do so; (e) if the conditions were right (and/or I really tried), I would be outstanding; (f) following rules, expectations, deadlines, etc., makes me less of a whole person; and (g) no one, including me, really deserves to have authority.

■ Oppositional-Defiant Disorder (313.81)

The DSM-IV notes that the oppositional defiant disorder (ODD) shows a negativistic, hostile, and defiant pattern for at least six months, with evidence of at least four of the following symptoms occurring *often*: (1) loses temper, (2) argues with adults, (3) defies or refuses to comply with adults, (4) deliberately annoys others, (5) blames others for own mistakes or misbehavior, (6) is easily annoyed, (7) is angry or resentful, (8) is spiteful or vindictive. This behavior is typically carried out toward significant others, such as teachers and parents, and it may persist into various self-destructive social interactions. Such children and adolescents may show a degree of conformity and usually resist any interpretation that they are oppositional, just as passive-aggressives do (Kronenberger and Meyer, 1996).

DIAGNOSTIC CONSIDERATIONS

Scales 4 and 6 on the MMPI-2 are more likely to be high. On the 16 PF, scale E would typically be somewhat higher, reflecting stubborn aggressiveness, and G would be quite low, reflecting rebelliousness. Since ODDs are likely to be more naive socially, N would be lower than in the PAPDs, and Q_1 and Q_2 would probably be a bit higher. A more overt anti-establishment attitude is probable, so persons would be more resistant to taking the tests. An MCMI-III profile similar to that of PAPDs is likely, with some elements of scale 6A present, as minor acting-out is more likely to be present here. On the Rorschach, more pure C and fewer Popular responses can be expected than with PAPDs. They express avoidance and negativism on both the Rorschach and TAT (Quevillon et al., 1986).

TREATMENT OPTIONS

Behavioral interventions are often helpful here (Bellack et al., 1990), and family therapy and/or parent support group participation may be necessary to strengthen the parents' resolve to stick to a behavioral plan. Overall, treatment is similar in many respects to that for the PAPD. Considerations expressed in the section on the paranoid disorders regarding the development of trust are also relevant here. Since ODD is often evidence of a systemic family disorder, family therapy should be considered for that reason as well.

Sadistic Personality Disorder

As noted in Chapter 1, the term "sadistic personality disorder" does not officially appear in the DSM-IV, although the concept has a long history (Kernberg, 1984, 1992). Kernberg terms the sadistic personality the "malignant narcissistic" and places it between the antisocial and the narcissistic personalities on this continuum. The sadistic personality might also be thought of as an antisocial pattern, but with better socialization and a more prominent quality of revenge.

The dominant trend is a love of cruelty and an absence of remorse (Kernberg, 1984). Extreme cases are described in the literature, including the torture and murder of innocent victims with knives, garroting, or flagellation (Volavka, 1995). The motive for these actions is described as an irresistible urge, the fulfillment of which produces strong satisfaction for the sadist. The sadist is most often male and his behavior is described as being both coercive and yet seductive, frequently promising children amusement, candy, or gifts and attracting women by posing somehow, for example, as a scout for a modeling agency.

There is a noteworthy distinction between sexual sadism, which is a paraphilia and thus appears on Axis I of a DSM-IV diagnosis, and the sadistic personality disorder. While sadistic sexual patterns are common in the sadistic personality disorder, it is not a necessary part of the pattern. In essence, the sadistic personality disorder is marked by a very assertive lifestyle based on power motives, commonly accompanied by gender dominance, the inflicting of pain for pleasure, and extreme aggression with or without sexual motivation. The sadistic behavior is well rationalized, and the individual may even present a very self-righteous air. Two childhood patterns of behavior are often noted (Johnson, 1994; Kernberg, 1984, 1992). One is similar to that of the antisocial personality, that is, inordinate lying, gross disrespect for authority, impulsive anger, temper tantrums, and excessive truancy. The other involves a shy, introverted child who shows few or only subtle early signs of aggression, with sadism later used as a method for covering feelings of inferiority.

☐ MMPI-2

The primary elevation in the sadistic personality disorder is commonly on scale 4, reflecting the aggressive hostility, interpersonal exploitiveness, and lack of respect for social norms found in such individuals. Scale 6 should be at least moderately elevated, reflecting the paranoia mentioned earlier. Scale 3 may also be elevated due to the narcissistic elements of the disorder. Scale 9 is often above average, although not usually as high as in the antisocial personality. The 9-3 or 9-4 profile, which is found in the narcissistic and aggressively competitive person who inflates his or her own self-esteem by the devaluation of others, would apply here. This pattern of sadistic behavior is occasionally found in athletes, who may receive significant reinforcement for such attitudes.

Scale K is commonly higher than F. Low scores should be expected on scales 2, 0, and 7 because these individuals are generally socially adept, if somewhat superficial, and because the sadistic behaviors and attitudes are typically ego-syntonic. In males, scale 5 is usually low, just as this scale is generally low in narcissistic and antisocial individuals. As noted earlier in this book, punitive or interpersonally destructive people who go about in the guise of a helpful role often show elevations on 4 and 8 and could fit this pattern.

☐ 16 PF

Sadistic personalities should score quite high on E, reflecting their aggressive dominance; on N because of their manipulativeness; and on H because of their usual interpersonal boldness (Golden, 1979). Scales A and F should also be moderately high, reflecting the extroversion and level of socialization that would be high, yet usually not so clearly pronounced as in narcissistic individuals. The lack of respect for social norms is usually reflected in a low score on G and a high score on Q_1. The lack of remorse and guilt and the inflated self-esteem of such individuals should show up in higher scores on C and Q_3 and lower scores on I, O, and Q_4. L should be at least moderately high, reflecting the lack of trust in the world in general.

MCMI-III

On the MCMI–III, persons with sadistic personality disorder are most likely to score high on scale 6B, as well as on 6A, antisocial (aggressive), and on scale 5, narcissistic, because of the similarities they share with these patterns. A high score on scale P, paranoid, is also likely. Drug and alcohol abuse are frequent complications of this pattern, so there may be elevations in scales B and T as well. Low scores should occur on scales 3, dependent; 7, compulsive (conforming); A, anxiety; and D, dysthymia. These scales reflect anxiety and a low sense of self-efficacy and self-esteem, seldom problems for sadistic personalities. Scale H, hypomania, is elevated in some sadistic individuals, although usually not to the extent found with antisocial persons.

OTHER TEST-RESPONSE PATTERNS

Sadistic personalities usually give constricted and guarded responses to the Rorschach. As with antisocial and narcissistic individuals, F+% can be expected to be low, but not quite as low as with the antisocial because of often greater sophistication and integration (although a distorted form) of the personality (Hare, 1986). The number of W responses is indicative of the grandiose rationalizations and sense of entitlement (Exner, 1986). M should be low, as it is in the case with the antisocial personality. But, when it *is* present, it is likely to be active and, quite frequently, aggressive. Animal and Popular responses should be common as well, reflecting guardedness. An analysis of the content of responses may show some ostentatious and flamboyant responses, reflecting grandiosity.

Responses to the TAT are not likely to manifest much overtly aggressive content in more socialized and sophisticated subjects. Since many sadistic personalities rationalize their behaviors, they are often quite frank about their violent proclivities. Many statements they make will be interpreted by others as jokes when they are actually quite earnest. Some of this ideation may appear in responses to the TAT. Sexually aggressive stories would not be surprising in response to many of the cards representing male–female interactions, and perhaps to other cards, depending on the sexual orientation of the sadist or the degree to which others are reduced to external objects (Kernberg, 1984). Intimidation through shocking stories would not be surprising in such persons. Sadists are likely to denigrate the task here, as well as in other projective tests. Answers are also likely to be short and constricted, reflecting the more suspicious orientation of some of these individuals, especially if they feel unable to gain a sense of control over the task.

Many of the comments regarding the Rorschach and the TAT apply as well to the production of drawings. The sadistic personality will either try to shock the clinician with an overtly grotesque drawing or will draw overly simple pictures to avoid disclosure of any intrapsychic content. In either case, the sadistic personality is likely to approach the task with contempt. The human figure he or she identifies with is likely to be complete and to seem powerful and confident, reflecting the feelings of superiority. When the sadistic personality draws others, they are likely to be smaller and less detailed and to have a generally inferior aspect. Drawings of trees and houses are also likely to be large, powerful, and indicative of a well-defended self.

TREATMENT OPTIONS

As with any disorder of personality, and especially with a sadistic personality disorder, the problem is to bring clients into therapy in the first place and then to get them to participate in a meaningful way. In addition, their behavior and threats of violence represent a significant danger to the clinician and others. Direct financial or other exploitation is to be expected. As one clinician facetiously (we think) commented, "This is the type of client you refer to a colleague you never liked."

Kernberg (1984, 1992) offers some helpful suggestions: Eliminate the possibilities and potential implements of harm to the client or therapist, establish honesty, confront the inability of the client to depend on the therapist, and confront the client's desire to destroy the therapist because he or she represents an autonomous nurturing person and generates resentment. Any confrontations should be calculated to cause the sadistic personality to project dishonesty and attempts at sadistic control onto the therapist, a process Kernberg calls "paranoid regression in transference." Yet there is an emphasis on maintaining a consistent affirmation of reality. The core belief that "inflicting pain brings me control, and/or sexual arousal, and/or escape from boredom" has to be at least nullified if any success is to be attained.

When the syndrome is accompanied by a paraphilia or a disorder of impulse control, behavioral therapies could prove helpful. Risky and/or competitive sports or strenuous physical activity can be useful as socially acceptable outlets for the clients' aggressive impulses (Zuckerman et al., 1980). Marital counseling is in order when individuals are involved in a long-term dominance-submission relationship. Overall, a strong emphasis on the concrete consequences of destructive behaviors is important, and although long-term therapy is almost always required, it is not often effective.

CHAPTER 10

Impulse Control and Eating Disorders

■   **Overall Concepts**

This section in DSM-IV is in part a catch-all grouping for those patterns that are not efficiently classified elsewhere. The essential features of a disorder of impulse control are a buildup of tension prior to the act, failure to resist the impulse, an experience of pleasure or release on carrying out the act, and consequent harm to others and/or oneself. Even though there may be some guilt after the act, it is essentially ego-syntonic, and there may be little conscious resistance to the impulse (Kaplan, 1995; McCrown et al., 1993).

The subcategories of impulse control disorders in DSM-IV are pathological gambling, kleptomania, trichotillomania, pyromania, and intermittent-explosive disorder. There is also a residual category: Impulse-Control Disorder (NOS) (312.30). The subcategories of the eating disorders are anorexia nervosa and bulimia nervosa.

☐   OVERALL TEST-RESPONSE PATTERNS

On the MMPI-2 a lack of impulse control is generally reflected in elevations on scales 4, 6, 8, and 9. The MAC score is likely to be elevated. On the 16 PF, high scores are usually obtained on F and Q_1, and often on A, whereas low scores on Q_3 and G are typical. Performance scale scores are higher than verbal scale scores on the WAIS-R. Within the verbal scale, arithmetic and information are usually two of the lower scores. Response times to the Rorschach are short, and the record may often have a lower-than-average number of responses. F and F+% are lower than normal, and there are more Color responses than in most disorders.

Oas (1984) found that certain variables in drawing tasks, particularly the Draw-A-Person and Bender-Gestalt tests, predicted to a general trait of impulsivity. Oas studied samples of adolescents, but the experience of a number of clinicians suggests that many of these variables apply equally well to adults.

The variables that Oas found to discriminate impulsive from nonimpulsive individuals are as follows: (1) quick completion time, (2) obvious aggressive content, (3) poor overall quality, (4) discontinuity, (5) obvious omissions, and (6) lack of proportion. Nonimpulsivity is indicated by the (1) degree of overall detail, (2) amount of sketching, (3) eye emphasis, (4) mouth detail, (5) amount of shading, and (6) absence of omissions and discontinuities.

■ ## Pathological Gambling (312.31)

The characteristics of pathological gambling are a progressive and chronic pre-occupation with the need to gamble and a consequent disruption in some area of the individual's world. Because so many states have moved toward legalized gambling in various forms, especially lotteries, making gambling increasingly accessible to people, the number of pathological gamblers is bound to continue to rise (Kaplan, 1995). During the 1980s nationwide lottery sales increased fivefold to over twenty billion dollars. Sales are still rising, though at a slower pace; however, more states are now legalizing many forms of gaming. If the trend continues, a high level of gambling, and even pathological gambling, will, like smoking in the 1930s and 1940s, seem like a natural part of life rather than a disorder, especially since virtually all of our governments "for the people" have a high and increasing financial stake in its spread and continuance.

Compulsive gamblers, like antisocial personalities, are stimulation-seeking, and both specifically show "disinhibition," or the inability to control impulses (Zuckerman et al., 1980). The initial streak of compulsive gambling is usually set off by a first big win.

Many compulsive gamblers report that they only feel alive when they are gambling and may refer to the rest of their lives as boring. They are generally nonconformists and are narcissistic and aggressive (Walker, 1985). A number of compulsive gamblers work only to make enough money to gamble heavily when they get to a spot like Las Vegas. Others have a more normal outward appearance, especially those who gamble in more legitimate outlets like stock and commodities markets.

Most gamblers are extroverted, competitive and, at least occasionally, impulsive individuals (McCrown et al., 1993). They are brighter than average, yet, surprisingly, they often experienced learning difficulties as they grew up. Many had placed their first bet by the age of 15. Other factors that predispose to pathological gambling are an overemphasis in early family life on material symbols, with little value placed on financial planning and savings; an absent parent before the age of 16; and availability in the family of a gambler as a model (Meyer, 1992a; Walker, 1985).

☐ ### DSM-IV

To diagnose pathological gambling, the DSM-IV requires that an individual show recurrent and persistent maladaptive gambling, as evidenced in at least five of the following ways: (1) is preoccupied with gambling; (2) increases gambling in order to obtain the desired excitement; (3) has made repeated unsuccessful efforts to stop; (4) becomes restless or irritable when attempting to stop; (5) gambles to avoid problems, for example, dysphoria; (6) gambles to recoup losses; (7) is deceptive to cover gambling activities; (8) has violated the law to finance gambling; (9) jeopardizes or voids a personal or vocational opportunity as a result of gambling; (10) relies on money from others for gambling.

MMPI-2

There are few data on the modal test patterns for this group, although the variables just noted correlate with the personality descriptors associated with the bimodal, moderately elevated 4-9 profile. Another type of pathological gambler shows scores more consistent with major depression. When pathological gamblers are seen by a clinician, they have already begun to experience substantial distress and hence are likely to score higher on scale 2. The stimulation-seeking quality is reflected on scale 9 and the MAC scale, and the extroversion characteristic of this pattern is seen in a low scale 0. At the point of referral they would also probably be agitated and distressed, which in combination with their impulsiveness should result in an elevation on scale 7. A moderate elevation on scale 3 can also be expected since the tendency to reject responsibility for changes and forces in their worlds is reflected here. F or K scale elevations will depend on the situation in which the gamblers are being tested. If for some reason they are defensive about gambling, the K scale would be elevated. On the other hand, there are situations in which being labeled "disturbed" would help them avoid some of the consequences of their behaviors. As a result, a high F scale would occur, which in turn would also elevate a number of the other scales.

16 PF

On the 16 PF the extroversion, stimulation seeking, and lack of self-control that characterize this pattern are reflected in high A and H scores and a low Q_3 score. Q_1 and, to a slightly lesser degree, C and O will be dependent on the characteristics of the testing situation, that is, on whether the subjects have reasons to be defensive or open about the pathological gambling. They are also likely to be higher on E in particular, as well as on B, F, N, and L. A lower score is obtained on I.

OTHER TEST-RESPONSE PATTERNS

The nonconforming, narcissistic, and aggressive components present in the personality of the pathological gambler are likely to be evidenced by MCMI-III elevations of 75 or higher on 5 and 6A, with low scores on 7. Elevations on A and D are likely when the lifestyle of the pathological gambler begins to create significant problems within the family or with financial status. Alcohol abuse may coincide with this disorder, producing an elevated B.

☐   ## TREATMENT OPTIONS

Since the disorder of pathological gambling is very likely to surface first in family problems, family or couples therapy is often necessary. Also, many pathological gamblers need to be treated for an underlying depression. In addition, the following phases of intervention, similar to those used in the treatment of other addictions, are useful here (Walker, 1985).

1. Elimination of immediate opportunities to gamble by way of inpatient hospitalization

2. Immediate initiation of an educational process about pathological gambling and the insidious role it takes in every individual's life

3. Individual and group psychotherapy to help the individual explore attitudes and beliefs that have supported his or her gambling behavior over a period of years

4. Economic counseling for living within a set income

5. Discussion of the person's understanding of the odds they are confronting, e.g., using David Spanier's (1994) excellent book, *Inside the Gambler's Mind* (University of Nevada Press), as a reference point

6. Possibly preventive periodic inpatient hospitalization as a preventive measure once every six to eighteen months

7. Regular attendance at Gambler's Anonymous

8. Confronting the pathological gambler's underlying cognitive distortions such as (a) "The credo 'If at first you don't succeed, try, try again' applies to my life only when I'm gambling, and it always does there," and (b) "I really deserve a better break from life than I've received," along with their memory distortion of more easily recalling wins than losses—normals remember each equally well

Since stimulation seeking (with concomitant disrupted norepinephrine levels) is often a critical variable in the reinforcement pattern for pathological gambling, the comments regarding fulfilling the need for stimulation seeking detailed in the section on the antisocial personality disorder are relevant here.

For the over-aroused, the anxious and harried type, the following additional treatment procedures would appear indicated:

1. Relaxation training—particularly important as a self-control device to combat symptoms of nervousness and related discomforts

2. Various forms of meditation and stretching techniques for achieving relaxing, mind-altering states

3. The regular use of exercise—particularly walking, jogging, and swimming

4. The short-term use of tranquilizing medications to help the client through a particularly stressful period, such as dealing with the legal/financial con-

sequences of past excessive gambling (Great care has to be exercised here because of the potential for addiction-dependency.)

5. "Taking a vacation"—an idea that should not be dismissed out of hand (Time away allows a temporary escape from impending stressors, which in turn short-circuits a buildup of stress to an unbearable level.)

Managing a case involving hypo- or under-arousal is more problematic. In general, the strategy is one of helping clients find some source of stimulation and challenge that does not involve gambling. Some possibilities to consider are:

1. Hobbies or sports that give the needed amount of excitement—gamblers, like alcoholics, tend to be deficient in recreational skills, and the counselor may find referral to a university physical education department or a YMCA helpful.

2. A challenging activity like taking a course or undertaking a project such as building a boat.

3. Vocational assessment and guidance—pathological gamblers may need help in finding a job in which more of their needs are met. It's possible that an assembly-line worker would find gambling no longer necessary after switching to work as a private investigator.

Participation in Gamblers Anonymous (213-386-8789; P.O. Box 17173, Los Angeles, CA 90017) is helpful for many such clients. Spouses can get information about the support group Gamanon at P.O. Box 157, Whitestone, NY 11357.

Kleptomania (312.32)

Most authorities agree that thievery in various forms has been on the rise in our society. For example, statistics annually compiled by the U.S. Department of Commerce suggest that about 150 million instances of shoplifting occur every year, accounting for almost 25% of business losses. They suggest that about one in every twelve shoppers is a shoplifter, although no more than one in thirty-five shoplifters is ever apprehended.

Certainly, many people steal simply because it seems so easy to get something free, for a lark, or to be one of their crowd (Meyer, 1992a). However, a small proportion of these individuals show actual kleptomania. They are distinguished from typical thieves in that kleptomaniacs seldom have any real need for the objects they steal and may even throw them away. They usually prefer to steal while alone, there is usually a lack of planning, and there is a quality of "irresistible impulse" in their behaviors.

Kleptomania often begins in childhood, primarily through stealing small items or sums of money from parents or friends. Stealing as a means of being accepted into an adolescent peer group is another common feature in the backgrounds of kleptomaniacs. There is usually evidence of depressive features (McElroy et al., 1991), reflecting an inability to control the behavior, as well as some problems in interpersonal relationships. For example, many older women who show a kleptomaniac pattern are widowed or emotionally neglected by their husbands; the behavior gives them a thrill, sometimes sexually tinged, although they often pay for it with remorse. In fact, many show a clear sense of relief when apprehended. Some kleptomaniacs are not significantly disturbed psychologically in areas other than this lack of specific behavioral control (McCrown et al., 1993). Yet, the condition is often chronic and is commonly associated with significant depression, anxiety, and/or eating disorder problems (McElroy et al., 1991).

☐   ## DSM-IV

The DSM-IV requires fulfillment of the following diagnostic criteria for this pattern: a recurrent failure to resist stealing unneeded objects or those of little value; rising tension before the act; the actual stealing behavior accompanied by a sense of release, pleasure, or gratification; no apparent need for the item or important monetary profit; and the act is not committed to express anger or vengeance, or as a response to a delusion or hallucination, and is not better explained as an Antisocial Personality or Conduct Disorder Manic Episode.

☐   ## DIAGNOSTIC CONSIDERATIONS

Consistent with the fact that some kleptomaniacs are not often significantly disturbed psychologically, their MMPI-2 and 16 PF protocols are also usually unremarkable. If persons are being seen in the criminal justice system rather than the mental health system, they are likely to show a higher K score on the MMPI-2 and, to the degree they are unsophisticated, a higher L score. If they are being seen in the mental health system or if they are viewing psychopathology as a means to avoid criminal sanctions, F will be higher. However, since many are significantly depressed, scale 2 is typically raised, reflecting the situationally generated depression, as well as an ongoing underlying depressive component. In that regard, scale 7 is also likely to be raised. Scale 9 is average or low, and scale 0 is usually a bit elevated, reflecting their propensity for being alone with their conflicts.

Similarly, on the 16 PF they tend to show elevation on scales C, Q_4, and O and are usually not high on scale A. Scale Q_3 will vary depending on whether it directly reflects their inability to control impulses, which would result in a low score, or whether they are counterphobically trying to control their impulses, which would raise Q_3.

☐   ## TREATMENT OPTIONS

Since schizoid behaviors and/or depression are common precursors to kleptomaniac behavior, treatment approaches for those patterns are often important here. Thymoleptic medication is often useful (McElroy et al., 1991). For the specific behaviors of kleptomania the aversive therapies are often used. Kellam (1969) employed a particularly ingenious aversive procedure to control shoplifting in a chronic kleptomaniac. Kellam required this person to simulate his entire shoplifting sequence, which was filmed. As the film was played back, the client was asked to participate with internal imagery in what was going on, and a painful shock was administered at crucial points. Such a technique could be amplified by having a person take a portable shock unit and self-administer shock whenever the impulse arose. If the shock unit is clumsy, the person could be instructed to hold his or her breath until discomfort ensues, since this acts as an aversive cue.

An alternative aversive technique is to have such clients go into a store and when their impulses become so severe that they feel they will not be able to resist, they are to take an expensive and fragile object and drop it on the floor. Embarrassment, the need for a coping response with store employees, and the need for restitution all act to create a very aversive moment.

Other clinicians have treated kleptomania by systematic desensitization, hypothesizing that the behavior will subside if one can decrease the tension in the sequence of anxiety arousal-completion-release. As anxiety then lessens, better coping behaviors for dealing with anxiety are developed. Cognitive behavioral techniques and/or existential approaches that deal with the loss of interests and meaning evident in some kleptomaniacs, particularly older females, may also be necessary.

■ ## Pyromania (312.33)

As with thievery, deliberate fire-setting behavior appears to have increased substantially in modern society. Of course, most cases of arson are not really indicative of pyromania. It is now estimated that as much as 80% of business property fires are caused by arson. In these cases the perpetrator is far more likely to be an antisocial personality who is doing it for hire—a "paid torch." Cases of arson in which there is no clear reward for the individual who started the fire could indicate pyromania, but mental retardation or a psychotic episode should also be considered.

Pyromaniacs, like kleptomaniacs, experience a buildup of tension prior to the behavior and a release of tension after performing the fire setting (McCrown et al., 1993). The behavior is often first seen in childhood or adolescence, and it is seldom the only antisocial behavior displayed. Hyperactivity, problems in school, poor peer relationships, and stealing are commonly associated behaviors. It has been found that fire setting in childhood, when combined with enuresis and/or cruelty to animals, is somewhat predictive of assaultive crimes in adulthood, although these crimes may not include fire setting (Meyer, 1992a).

Pyromania is much more common in males than in females and is often found in individuals who have had trouble in making transitions through developmental stages. There are analogous data showing that peaks in the incidence rate of arson occur around the ages of 17, 26, 40, and 60 in males. If there is a problem with alcohol, pyromaniacs show patterns of alcohol abuse rather than addiction, and they often show an inordinate interest in fire-fighting paraphernalia. Pyromaniacs may be indifferent to a fire's destruction or stimulated by it.

☐ DSM-IV

The DSM-IV requires evidence of at least more than one deliberate fire setting, with a buildup of tension or affective arousal before the setting of the fire; fascination with or interest in fire and its situational contexts; continuing inability to resist the impulse; and pleasure, gratification, or a release of tension when setting the fire or when witnessing-participating in the aftermath. There should also be an indication that neither profit, anger, or vengeance, covering illegal activity, nor some sociopolitical belief system is the basic motive for the fire setting, and that the behavior is not better explained by an Antisocial Personality or Conduct Disorder or Manic Episode.

☐ DIAGNOSTIC CONSIDERATIONS

Like kleptomania, there is not much consensual clinical literature or hard data to indicate the patterns one can expect here. However, on the average, pyromaniacs are more disturbed than kleptomaniacs. They are likely to score high on scales 4 and 8 of the MMPI-2, but not usually at a psychotic level. They will probably also score higher on scales 6 and 9 and, to the degree the impulses are denied, scale 3. The F and the 4 scores are elevated to the degree there is an antiauthority component. Moodiness, a sense of alienation from others, and inability to control impulses are reflected in any elevations on scales 8, 0, and 6.

On the 16 PF, pyromaniacs show more evidence of disorder than do kleptomaniacs. Pyromaniacs will likely be low on scales C, G, and Q_3 and higher on scales L and Q_4. They are also likely to show some elevation on scales E and H, reflecting their destructive and controlling orientation toward the environment. Analogously, this latter component as well as the distancing from others may raise scale Q_1 and lower scale A. Scale B on the average is low, reflecting their usual less-than-average intelligence.

Pyromaniacs may show labile and impulsive affect responses, as indicated by a number of uncontrolled reactions to the color cards of the Rorschach. In fact, it is suggested that when children with borderline psychosis provide "blood," "fire," or other similarly destructive associations to the Rorschach color areas, potential dangerousness in general, and possible fire-setting behavior in particular, should be suspected (Armentrout and Hauer, 1978). MCMI-III elevations of 75 or higher on scales 5 and especially 6A are probable. Hypomania (elevated N) is more likely to be present in this disorder, although, as with anxiety, it may vacillate, depending on whether testing is done before or after pyromanic activity occurs.

TREATMENT OPTIONS

The significant disturbance, often characterological, that usually accompanies pyromania suggests that a wide variety of treatment options may have to be considered, depending on the trend of the overall pathology (Kernberg, 1992). Since these individuals are often adolescents or young adults, family therapy is especially warranted (Brown, 1991), and since schizoid patterns are typical, the reader is referred to that section of this book. A low level of serotonin is occasionally noted, so chemotherapy may be of help.

Two specific behavioral techniques are appropriate for the fire-setting behaviors. Overcorrection requires the individual to make a new, positive response in the area of specific disorder. For example, public confession and a restitution of damages through working for the individual who is offended would be one application for pyromania. Negative practice has also been used, wherein the pyromaniac is required to perform a behavior ad nauseam until it takes on aversive qualities. For example, the client is required to strike thousands of matches in a row, over several sessions. These techniques would be embedded in an overall treatment program.

Trichotillomania (312.39)

The term "trichotillomania" was first introduced into the clinical literature in 1889 by the French dermatologist Hallopean (Krishnan et al., 1985). However, it was not until the DSM-III-R that it was designated as a DSM diagnostic category. Trichotillomania is traditionally defined as recurrent, irresistible impulses to pull one's own hair, usually from the scalp. It is more common in females and usually first starts in childhood or early adolescence, although it can occasionally erupt in a mature adult.

This behavior can persist for many years, often recurs after spontaneous remission, and is marked by efforts at concealment (Christenson et al., 1991). Bald spots (alopecia) often appear, in some cases leading to total baldness, so wigs are frequently used.

DSM-IV

To warrant a DSM-IV diagnosis of Trichotillomania, there must be noticeable hair loss resulting from the recurrent inability to resist impulses to pull out one's hair; an increasing tension experienced when resisting or before giving in to the impulse to pull out the hair, with a sense of relief or pleasure or gratification experienced when doing it; and with impairment in a life area. The diagnosis is not made when it is better explained by another mental disorder or by a general medical condition, for example, a preexisting skin disorder.

DIAGNOSTIC CONSIDERATIONS

Scalp biopsies can be useful, as atrophic anagen hairs and bulbar inflammation are not found, though traumatized hair bulbs, catagen hairs, and pigment casts are likely to be found. Since the literature suggests a connection between trichotillomania and obsessive-compulsive disorders and that in some cases it is a mask for depression (Krishnan et al., 1985), a 2-7/7-2 profile or a 7-8/8-7 profile with some elevation on 2 is to be expected on the MMPI-2. In those cases with a strong hypochondriacal element, scales 1 and 3 should be affected and, to the degree denial and secretiveness are involved, K and 6 should be elevated.

On the MCMI-III, the commonly reported dependency-family conflict (Krishnan et al., 1985) should generate a high scale 3, with the compulsive components raising scale 7. In clients who are closer to the borderline personality disorder, scale C should be high. On the 16 PF, scales C and Q_3 should be low. And the dependency issues should generate low scores on Q_2, L, and E. Similar parallels to obsessive-compulsive, depressive, and dependency-oriented profiles should be noted on the Rorschach and TAT.

□ TREATMENT OPTIONS

For child and adolescent trichotillomaniacs, a central focus for the therapist will be the dependency issue within a standard psychotherapy format, as well as efforts at response prevention (Christenson et al., 1991). Chemotherapy (especially clomipramine) can be useful, not only to quell secondary itching and skin problems, but (in older children and adults) to deal with the obsessive-compulsive and depressive components that are common to this disorder. Hypnosis and certain behavioral techniques (e.g., thought stopping and aversion therapy) have proven useful as well.

■ Intermittent-Explosive Disorder (312.34)

The distinguishing feature of the intermittent-explosive disorder is a sudden eruption of aggressive impulses and the loss of control of these impulses in an individual who normally inhibits or does not experience them (Huesmann, 1994). It is typically affect-driven, that is, often manifested in "rage." The individual often sees it as a "loss of control" or "temporary insanity," and certain cases of physical abuse no doubt reflect this disorder. Regret and guilt are common, and the behavior is disproportionate to any environmental stressors (Maiuro, 1993). The disorder appears most commonly in late adolescence or early childhood.

Occasionally both prodromal physiological or mood symptoms and consequent partial amnesia for the behavior are reported; hence, the pattern was traditionally referred to as "epileptoid." A concomitant clear diagnosis of organic epilepsy is not common. However, in a number of these cases there are some nonspecific EEG abnormalities or minor neurological signs. The presence of such signs is not so rare, even in a sample of apparently normal individuals, but clear evidence for a physiological contribution should be thoroughly considered.

☐   ## DSM-IV

The DSM-IV requires (1) several discrete episodes of loss of control of aggressive impulses, as in property destruction or assaultive acts; (2) aggressiveness clearly out of proportion to any precipitating event; and (3) no better explained for the episodes by another psychological or general medical condition or by use of a substance.

☐   ## MMPI-2

As noted in the section on aggression potential, persons who are continually assaultive and without guilt tend to score high on scales F, 4, and 9, with secondary elevation on 8 or 6. However, although the continuity factor does not fit with the descriptors of the intermittent-explosive disorder, Fowler (1981) notes that high 4 and 6 scores can be expected here. The degree of guilt and rumination over this behavior is reflected in the elevation on scale 7.

The 4-3 profile, as described by Davis and Sines (1971), would be more likely to call for the explosive disorder diagnosis. In this profile there is a peak on 4, a secondary peak on 3, and little significant elevation elsewhere. This profile, mainly seen in males, is particularly characteristic of individuals who maintain a quiet ongoing adjustment but are likely to demonstrate occasional hostile-aggressive outbursts. Such behavior may or may not warrant the diagnosis of intermittent-explosive disorder, depending on the characteristics previously described. This profile is applicable to females and occurs quite generally.

To the degree that both 4 and 3 are highly elevated, the likelihood of aggressive episodes increases. In general, when scale 3 is greater than 4, the potential for control and inhibition of the aggression is increased, whereas to the degree that 4 is greater than 3, control dissipates.

Lachar (1974) suggests that the rare 3-9 code is indicative of persons who are emotionally labile and show recurrent hostility and irritability. Since they naturally suppress the hostility in clinical assessment, they could be diagnosed as having an explosive disorder. However, it is more likely that they have a passive-aggressive personality disorder, a histrionic personality disorder, or both.

There is a derived scale on the MMPI-2, termed the Over-Controlled Hostility Scale (Megargee et al., 1967), composed of thirty-one MMPI-2 items. Although some studies have not been positive, many have supported the validity of this scale in predicting persons who show outbursts of aggression (Greene, 1991). Hence, they could easily fit the DSM-IV diagnosis of explosive personality. The scale has been an accurate predictor in incarcerated adult populations, but it has sometimes been weak in the normal population. Nevertheless, it is one of the most well-researched scales and is worthy of consideration.

☐   ## 16 PF

Since these individuals generally show regret over their behaviors and see them as ego-alien to a degree, a low score on G is not likely, as it would be in most cases of aggressive behavior. Also, C is not usually low nor are Q_4 and N high, as would be common in psychopaths. Q_3 is usually high, reflecting the attempts at control that are characteristic of these individuals, and Q_1 is usually moderately low. In spite of their passivity, they do not score markedly low on E or H, but neither are they very high. Scores are average or lower on M and N, reflecting the general denial of the aggression and the lack of introspection about motives and conflicts.

OTHER TEST-RESPONSE PATTERNS

In cooperative subjects the Brief Anger-Aggression Questionnaire (BAAQ), a six-item measure, allows a good rapid assessment of violence-prone individuals (Maiuro, 1993). There is some evidence that quiet but potentially explosive persons attain lower picture arrangement scores on the WAIS-R than do more extroverted and consistently aggressive types. Comprehension and similarities subtests are usually relatively lower here. Rorschach patterns are quite constricted, and there is less abstraction content. M responses are not that uncommon, and when they do occur, they tend to be more passive. Responses with content like "blood" or "explosions" or responses indicating inner tension and turmoil occur in a number of explosive disorders. Color responses tend to have poorer form than otherwise expected. Minor neuropsychological signs on a variety of tests are often associated with this disorder, and it is a reasonable axiom that there is some impaired brain functioning, although seldom any gross brain damage.

TREATMENT OPTIONS

The overall goals should be to (1) increase awareness and accountability; (2) enhance emotions and cognitions that precede and accompany the propensity to violence; (3) increase support and social contacts; (4) decrease hostile-dependent relationships; and (5) develop conflict-resolution, anger-management, and appropriate assertiveness skills (Maiuro, 1993). It is critical in treating this disorder to get the clients in touch with their ongoing anger responses, usually suppressed, and at the same time to teach them more effective ways either to abort the anger or to deal with it productively (Huesmann, 1994). Psychoeducational and cognitive behavioral approaches are useful in this regard (Maiuro, 1993). Awareness and anger-management techniques can put them in touch with the anger that is typically not evident in their usual functioning. Group therapy can provide the feedback essential to breaking down their defenses against seeing themselves as having chronic anger (Ellis, 1992). The keeping of a diary or the writing of (undelivered) letters to significant others who may be a factor in generating the anger (Kirman, 1980) also helps clients get in better touch with their anger (Ellis, 1992).

Once this is accomplished, the therapist could attempt to use the development of a controlled relaxation response to abort the anger. Similarly, biofeedback training to develop an overall relaxation response could be useful to mute or abort anger (Hillebrand and Pallone, 1995). Assertiveness training or analogous procedures could then be used to structure more effective ways to cope with the ongoing frustration and anger. Lithium treatment has been found effective with that subgroup of persons with intermittent-explosive disorders who show evidence of a latent or cyclical manic component. Clients in this category also occasionally respond well to ethosuximide, and those with a CNS lesion causing the rage have been helped by propranolol (Yudofsky et al., 1981).

In relationships with significant others, training in a specific time-out procedure can be useful (Maiuro, 1993). When violence training has progressed enough that cues are recognized, the client assertively tells the significant other he or she needs a "time-out," or signals for same with a "T." Then the client uses an agreed-upon allowance to leave the scene, for example, for an hour, to go somewhere he or she enjoys, without any drinking. The client returns home as promised and makes overt efforts to make contact and to calmly state and discuss the issues related to the anger.

Anorexia Nervosa (307.10) and Bulimia Nervosa (307.51)

The essential requirements for a diagnosis of anorexia nervosa, according to DSM-IV, are a refusal to maintain body weight at or above 85% of expected minimum normal weight for age and height, or failure to meet that 85% minimum during periods of growth; intense fear of gaining weight or being fat, even though underweight; related body-image distortion or denial of seriousness of current low body weight; also, for post-menarcheal females, amenorrhea (absence of three consecutive periods) or period only stimulated by hormone administration. The diagnosis can be further specified as "Restricting Type," diagnosed by excluding the other type, "Binge-Eating/Purging Type," which requires regular binge-eating or purging during the current episode.

Anorexia nervosa, meaning a "nervous loss of appetite," is an apparently "voluntary" self-starvation that is seen primarily in middle and upper socioeconomic classes of women (Fornari et al., 1994; Bruch et al., 1988; Agras, 1987). It typically occurs first during puberty as a young woman becomes more conscious of her self-image. Over 75% of cases originate between age 13 and 18, about 1 in 200–250 females in this age range can be expected to develop the disorder. There is an irrevocable (even with calcium supplements), loss of bone mass, and followup studies estimate long-term mortality rates at between 5% and 15% (Vitousek and Manke, 1994; Fornari et al., 1994). Sexuality may be channeled into the eating area, as these women usually avoid sexual acting-out. After the "sin" of eating, they may resort to self-induced vomiting and laxatives to "cleanse" the body of food. Although anorexia nervosa is rare in males, when it does occur, there are systematic differences from female anorectics. Males are less likely to use laxatives, are often less conscientious about school, are less likely to have had large appetites premorbidly, are more likely to have had enjoyable sexual experiences, and are less likely to die from the condition. Anorectics who also show episodes of bulimia (binge-eating), in general are more disturbed than anorectics who do not.

The parents of the anorectic are typically very controlling, yet caring, individuals. As a result, the anorectic appears to use the disorder as a statement of independence from the family in the narrow area that she can control. The salient personality characteristics are excessive dependency and sensitivity, introversion, perfectionism, yet subtle but persistent selfishness and stubbornness (Vitousek and Manke, 1994; Bruch et al., 1988).

The converse pattern is bulimia nervosa, a chronic pattern of binge-eating. Bulimia (from the Greek words for "hunger of an ox") is known as the "gorge-purge syndrome." The essential features, according to DSM-IV, are recurrent binge-eating, denoted by a sense of lack of control of eating, *and* eating in a discrete time period much more than others would normally eat; a minimum of two binge episodes a week for at least three months; recurrent, inappropriate compensatory attempts to control weight, for example, by diets, laxatives, or vomiting; and body and/or self-image distortion from weight or shape. Further specification can be made to a "Purging Type" if in the current episode there is regular misuse of diuretics, laxatives, or enemas or self-induced vomiting. If not, then it is the "Nonpurging Type."

Blouin et al. (1992) found significant seasonal variations in bulimia. They found a high correlation of binge behaviors, but not of purging behaviors or severity of depression, with number and occurrence of dark hours within the month, and an overall much higher rate of binging and purging in the winter months.

Although anorectics are typically shy, they are passively controlling and stubborn. Those bulimorectics who are also anorectic are more likely to be extroverted, industrious perfectionists who attempt to control their peers in direct ways. Many bulimorectics weigh in at normal levels, while others are obese; anorectics are almost always cadaverously thin. Both groups come from families in which food is a focus, as in socialization or recognition. Anorectics will often cook exotic meals for others, although they may eat only a small portion themselves. Bulimorectics do not usually like to cook because they are afraid they will eat all the food before the guests show up.

There is increasing support for the addition of a DSM diagnostic category of "binge-eating" which refers to the compulsive overeater who does not engage in such self-destructive behaviors as purging (Friedman and Brownell, 1995; Wilson and Walsh, 1991). Many of the treatment recommendations at the end of this section will apply to them as well. This is a "criteria set" diagnostic option in DSM-IV, and along with other, severe patterns of eating disorder, can be included under the diagnosis of Eating Disorder (NOS) (307.50).

DIAGNOSTIC CONSIDERATIONS

From an overall perspective, the diagnosis of anorexia or bulimia is relatively easy in a motivated, cooperative client who is reporting honestly—with this disorder a rare client. Differential diagnosis should consider possible organic factors or medical conditions like Crohn's disease or Simmond's disease and evaluate whether commonly accompanying psychological disorders, such as depression, are correlated or causal. Physical tests, for example, for thyroid dysfunction and elevated cortisol levels in anorectics and for elevated serum amylase levels in bulimics and anorexics, are useful. Other signs often noted in anorexia are skin changes such as dryness or scaliness, and cardiovascular changes like bradycardia and hypotension. In bulimics, and in anorexics who also have a bulimic component, one should look for (1) hypertrophy of salivary glands; (2) dental erosion, particularly on the lingual surface of the upper teeth; (3) lesions over the dorsum of the dominant hand; (4) fluid or electrolyte abnormalities; and (5) petechial hemorrhages and a flushed appearance if recent vomiting has occurred.

Where the anorectic pattern is similar to other adolescent patterns that emphasize rebelliousness, distress, and family discord, a 2-4-8 MMPI-2 pattern can be expected. In the more classic anorectic patterns the combined dependency and perfectionism of the anorectic are likely to elevate scale 7, while the general psychopathology should elevate scales 6 and 8 (Small et al., 1981). The subtle selfishness, self-centeredness, and stubbornness should elevate scales 1 and 3 somewhat. The interpersonal avoidance and sensitivity would tend to elevate scale 0. At the same time, all of the patterns are influenced by the denial of pathology, so scales L and K tend to be elevated while F is depressed, although less so to the degree the client is an adolescent rather than an adult. The anorectic who also shows episodes of bulimia is more likely to score higher on scales 2, 3, 4, 6, and 7 than the anorectic who does not also manifest bulimia, and scale 7 is most often elevated in bulimorectics (Kirkley and Janick, 1987).

Bulimorectics are more likely to be extroverted and should therefore show a low 0 scale, as well as a higher scale 8, reflecting the sense of loss of control. Since they are more overtly self-disclosing, all scales should be more highly elevated, on the average, particularly scales 2 and 4.

On the 16 PF the anorectic tends to score low on scales A, F, H, and Q_1 and moderately low on M, while the bulimorectic tends to score high on these scales, particularly A, H, M and Q_1. The anorectic is higher on Q_3 and Q_2; the bulimorectic tends to be in the middle on these scales. The anorectic also scores quite high on G, whereas the bulimorectic scores toward the middle. Surprisingly, the anorectic is toward the middle on scales I and L, reflecting the subtle stubbornness and selfishness that are not apparent in initial interactions (Yager et al., 1991). Both usually score quite high on scale B, reflecting their tendency to be in the upper range in intelligence and socioeconomic status. Both also tend to be reasonably high on O.

Personality patterns most likely to develop anorexia or bulimia nervosa include those patterns represented by MCMI-III elevations on scales 3, 7, 8A, 1, E, and C. Passive-aggressive controlling tendencies are evidenced by elevations on 8A, while high scores on 3 indicate shyness and dependency and high scores on 7 point to compulsivity and perfectionism. Elevated scores on 1 and E are more likely in the anorectic than in the bulimic.

Higher intelligence and socioeconomic status predict overall high scores on the WAIS–R, with verbal scores usually being a bit higher than performance scores. The perfectionism and compulsivity evident in anorectics, combined with their conservative and production orientation to school situations, usually result in elevations of information and vocabulary scores. Their stubborn perfectionism usually slows them down somewhat on the digit symbol, block design, and object assembly tests, yet they seldom make the errors of impulse that are more often noted in the bulimorectic.

There has been little research on Rorschach patterning in anorexia nervosa (Wagner and Wagner, 1978), although there are some detected commonalities. Reflecting the perfectionism and denial of pathology, the total number of responses is low, there is a low proportion of movement (M) to detail (D) responses (reflecting an individual who is making an economical use of constricted or limited resources), and response latencies are slow. There is a high F and F+%, with closely integrated Color responses and subtle sexual and anatomical responses occasionally included. Not surprisingly, responses that focus on food are common. Wagner and Wagner (1978) conclude that in most other respects they resemble those with the conversion disorder.

We believe bulimorectics to have a higher number of responses and a more adequate W:M ratio, although content that focuses on food is similarly present. If W:M is high, then they are striving beyond their resources. There is much greater use of integrated color, although the F+% is lower, and overall there is less use of form.

The Bulimia Test (BULIT) (Smith and Thelan, 1984) is a thirty-two–item, self-report multiple-choice scale that has been found to be a reasonably valid and reliable predictor of bulimia in a nonclinical population. A revised version with improved items and validity is available (Thelan et al., 1991). The Eating Attitude Test is an effective measure of attitudes toward eating (Koslowsky et al., 1992).

TREATMENT OPTIONS

General goals include weight restoration, treatment of physical complications, and "a change in the relentless pursuit of thinness." Since anorexia nervosa often results in a very severe—even life-threatening—weight loss, hospitalization combined with forced and/or intravenous feeding may be necessary. Nutritional counseling may be helpful, but one has to be careful to avoid moving back into the anorectic's favorite battleground—food. Noradrenergic-blocking medications, such as chlorpromazine, are effective with those anorectics who have high anxiety, peripheral vasospasms, and little appetite. Those who seem to show early satiety, rather than little appetite, may respond to low dosages of dopamine blockers. At this stage a behavior modification program to develop feeding behaviors may be helpful, although the critical issue is deriving the reinforcements that can build up the feeding behavior (Fornari et al., 1994; Agras, 1987).

A more psychodynamic approach has been found to be useful as clients move into more normal functioning, with a focus on the ambivalence over dependency, the high need for perfectionism, and, as trust develops, the subtle selfishness and narcissism that emerge. Family therapy is also likely to be necessary since so much of this pattern is related to the interactions over dependency and control in the family.

Bulimorectics can respond to many of the same therapy techniques noted for the anorectics (Fornari et al., 1994; Blouin et al., 1992; Freeman, 1991; Agras, 1987). Those with an electrolyte imbalance from intense vomiting will need medical intervention, for example, for a depletion of potassium. Antidepressants may be indicated in some cases of bulimia. In addition, group therapy and/or a support group may be helpful. This provides both a sense of control and a source of feedback. Adolescent group therapy can be useful for anorectics, too, but only after they have made substantial improvements through other techniques.

As noted, a diary is part of an effective therapeutic regimen for persons with virtually any type of eating disorder. In addition, the daily report form in Figure 10.1 (adapted from Freeman, 1991) is useful as part of the diary and is an efficient reporting device to give the therapist a better feel for what is happening with the client. It is specific to bulimia nervosa but can easily be modified to be useful with any eating disorder.

Relapse prevention is critical with both disorders. Clients should receive exposure training for high-risk situations, as well as cognitive training to eliminate negative self-talk and learn to discriminate lapses from relapse.

Any person with an eating problem needs counseling regarding diet facts and simple control of eating behaviors, counseling of the type used with the more common problems of binge-eating without purging, general obesity, and persistent-eating disorders (Friedman and Brownell, 1995; Agras, 1987). Facts such as the following could be presented via a handout and supplemented by an oral amplification that is modified to the specific eating disorder involved.

1. Changing exercise amounts and energy-burning patterns in general is more critical in generating weight loss than changing diet amounts and patterns. But don't use this as an excuse to ignore the quality and quantity of your diet.

2. There is a biological drive toward high-fat and very sweet foods, so control should be directed toward "what" as much as "when" and "how much."

3. Weight loss is not hard to attain; keeping weight off is. Understand this is biologically as well as psychologically driven. It takes a long time for the body to reset to a lower weight.

4. It is more difficult to lose weight during the second diet than the first.

5. Most diets are broken in the late afternoon.

6. Persons trying to lose weight must keep fluid intakes high. The body needs a *lot* more water and other fluids when undergoing weight loss.

7. If the activity level remains the same and there is a cessation of smoking, there will be a weight gain.

FIGURE 10.1   Daily Report Form for Eating Disorder Clients

	Date	Day			Comments:
		Vomit	Lax	Other	
NAME_____					
Your next appointment is on:	Breakfast				
at:					The desire to not eat today has been:
Please call extension if you cannot keep your appointment	_____				
	_____				Not there at all As strong as it possibly could be
Please record daily everything that you eat and drink, the number of binges that you have, the number of times that you vomit, and the number of laxatives you take	Lunch				
	_____				Today's urge to overeat has been:
	_____				Not there at all As strong as it possibly could be
NUMBER OF BINGES_____ PLEASE BRACKET ALL BINGES	Evening meal				
	_____				Today in general I have felt:
	_____				Not emotionally upset at all Extremely emotionally upset
	Totals				
	_____				

8. For women, food cravings often increase in the days before their menstrual periods, so they are more vulnerable to lapses during these times.

Also, it is highly recommended that any person with an eating disorder of any significance implement and monitor, via a diary, a day-to-day program based on general diet tips such as the following:

1. Drink six to eight glasses of water each day, *at least*. This may be the single most effective technique of all.

2. Eat a high-carbohydrate breakfast and avoid eating anything at least two hours before going to bed.

3. Eat a salad or have a low-calorie beverage or a cup of soup before a meal, then delay eating any main meal for an extra five minutes. Hot tea is very effective for a number of people.

4. Slow down while you eat, chew longer, and savor flavors.

5. Don't eat standing up, in front of the television, while talking on the phone, in the car, or on the run. Try not to eat alone.

6. Try to eat two or three main meals and two small snacks every day at predetermined times so that you develop a feasible routine. Don't wait until you are extremely hungry to eat.

7. Avoid drinks with alcohol or sugar.

8. Be creative. For example, visualize yourself eating slowly before you even sit down for dinner.

9. Use thought control. About to binge? Yell "Stop!" although, admittedly, this may not be practical in a public place.

10. Avoid keeping food around, other than planned food.

11. Brush your teeth after every meal; you'll be less likely to snack.

12. Identify times when you are prone to binge or overeat and plan alternative activities that are not compatible with eating.

13. Avoid weighing yourself unless it is specifically prescribed. Don't look for weight loss when you are learning normal eating patterns.

14. Develop an exercise program that is effective and that you can comfortably integrate into your life. Make a decision to walk rather than drive whenever possible.

15. If you find youself thinking too much about food or body image, this may be because you have a conflict you haven't dealt with and/or you are anxious or depressed. Try to identify what's going on and take some positive, coping measures.

16. Plan ahead as to how you will handle "tough" situations like being in a supermarket, at a party, etc. Drink a lot of water and a high-fiber snack one–half to one hour before you go.

17. Set aside some time each day to reflect on how you are doing in this area and in life in general. Decide what you are doing well, affirm yourself for that, and visualize how you can improve in areas where you are not doing as well.

18. Recruit help from family and friends and any other source of help that has meaning or usefulness to you. Be open about your decision to lose weight, ask them to help you, and then spell out how they can help.

Over-the-counter diet medications have typically been effective in the short run but not always in the long run, and may result in a rebound to a point higher than the original level. Some significant success has been found with a combination of the prescription drugs fenfluramine and phentermine, which also produces such positives as a drop in blood pressure, cholesterol, and blood sugar levels. Yet, again, it's not clear if these gains can be maintained without long–term or lifetime use of these drugs. Mild stimulant drinks like tea can be helpful; for some people, hot tea can be both an energizer and a diet suppressant. Consider becoming a tea gourmand rather than a food gourmand.

CHAPTER 11

CNSI, ADHD, and Retardation

Most fighters have some type of trauma. Hey, we're in the traumatizing business.

James "Bonecrusher" Smith
—after being denied a boxing license in England in April 1994 because of trauma to his brain

■ Central Nervous System Impairment

Clinicians often face the issue of whether or not there may be central nervous system impairment (CNSI) in a client (Zeidel, 1995; Anderson, 1994; Margolin, 1992). Earlier in this book we used the traditional and less accurate terms like "organic dysfunction" and "organic brain damage" because they are so commonly used by clinicians; throughout this chapter we'll simply refer to it as CNSI. The specifics of a broad yet thorough CNSI evaluation will not be discussed here because this would require more material than is appropriate for this book. If there is reason to think there is CNSI and there is a request or need for a more certain and/or localized diagnosis, it is important to have a full evaluation carried out by a clinical neuropsychologist and/or a neurologist with specific, supervised speciality training who, preferably, is board-certified.

For an initial conceptualization of a client's problems from an anatomy-behavior perspective, consult Table 11.1. The types and range of information needed for a full neuropsychological assessment are embedded in the model report format in Chapter 16. It is evident from that format that a good history is always critical. Sudden onset of symptoms, whatever their nature, should alert the clinician to possible CNSI. Changes in functioning of any sort are important data, so information from family and friends is helpful.

Close observation of speech quality and problems, dress, grooming, gait and coordination while walking to and from the office, and affect can all provide clinical signs to help the clinician (Anderson, 1994). For example, the number

TABLE 11.1 Anatomic Localization Associated with Behavior Dysfunctions

FRONTAL LOBE LESIONS

MOTOR ABNORMALITIES

May vary from total paralysis to problems with coordination and integration of movement
Apraxias, especially reflecting conceptual problems
Spastic contralateral hemiparesis

EXPRESSIVE LANGUAGE DYSFUNCTION (PRIMARILY WITH DOMINANT-SIDED LESIONS)

Aphasia—nonfluent[a]
[Broca's] (Comprehension often intact)

BEHAVIORAL DYSFUNCTION

Overall difficulties in starting and stopping behaviors, and in the organization of behavior
Decreased spontaneity and initiative
Perseveration and difficulty in shifting behavior and attention
Decreased judgment in social situation
Loss of abstracting ability or conceptually based insight
Amotivation, apathy, and/or flat affect
Release phenomena (e.g., primitive reflexes)
Figure–ground problems
Perseveration, if one can get started at all
Involuntary tactile movements on self
Concreteness; stimulus-boundedness
Emotional incontinence; unpredictable impulsivity; emotional lability

PARIETAL-TEMPORAL-OCCIPITAL LOBE LESIONS, LEFT [a] AND RIGHT [b]

SENSORY-INTEGRATIVE ABNORMALITIES

Agnosias
Defects in stereognosis and graphesthesia
Visual agnosias[f]
Visual field defects[f]
Visual distractions and inattention[f]
Visual perceptual distortions[f]
Disrupted immediate memory[e]
Remote memory dysfunction[e]
Disrupted rhythm sense[e] (often more right)
Receptive speech dysfunction[e] (usually more left)
Disrupted auditory interpretation of data[e]
Spatial dysfunction[d]

Construction/synthesis disorder
Serial ordering deficits
Disrupted pressure, touch, temperature perception[d]
Prosopagnosia,[ef]

BEHAVIORAL DYSFUNCTIONS

Body image disruption[d] (often more right)
Denial of illness[d] (often more left)
Mood swings[e]
Anger-control problems; rage reactions[e]

PARIETAL-TEMPORAL-OCCIPITAL LOBE LESIONS—LEFT [b]

SENSORY-INTEGRATIVE ABNORMALITIES

Dyslexia[d]
Dyscalculia[a,d]
Dysgraphia[a]
Finger agnosia[a]
Ideomotor apraxia[c,d]
Ideational apraxia[c]
Right-left agnosia[d]
"Angular gyrus syndrome" (anomia, apraxia)

LANGUAGE DYSFUNCTIONS

Fluent aphasias (Wernicke's); transcortical sensory aphasia

BEHAVIOR DYSFUNCTIONS

Verbal memory

PARIETAL-TEMPORAL-OCCIPITAL LOBE LESIONS—RIGHT [b]

SENSORY INTEGRATIVE ABNORMALITIES

Pain asymbolia[d]
Amusia[e]
Left hemispatial neglect and autotopagnosia
Constructional apraxia (visuo–spatial agnosia)
Dressing "apraxia"
Spatial acalculia

BEHAVIORAL DYSFUNCTION

Anosognosia (denial of illness)[c]

(Continued)

TABLE 11.1   *(Continued)*

Defective recognition and recall of complex auditory and visual stimuli (music, etc.)
Anosodiasphoria—indifference toward deficits, despite awareness

BASAL GANGLIA (CONTRALATERAL TO LESION)

Movement disorder—Parkinson's, athetosis, chorea, hemiballismus, dystonias, dyskinesias
Tremor
"Emotional incontinence"—the hallmark symptom of pseudobulbar palsy in bilateral basal ganglia damage

BRAIN STEM

Cranial nerve palsy with contralateral hemiparesis, hemisensory loss—ipsi or contralateral ataxia
Ophthalmoplegia
Nystagmus
Bulbar palsy

CEREBELLUM

Tremor or intention
Impaired rapid attending movements
Ataxia
Scanning speech

SPINAL CORD

Para or quadraparesis; flaccid paresis
Sensory loss (at specific levels)
Bladder, bowel, sexual dysfunction

[a] Function usually localized to dominant lobe
[b] Function usually localized to nondominant lobe
[c] Many of the so-called parietal lobe "apraxias" may actually be at the perceptual-organization integrative levels constituting "agnosias."
[d] Usually primarily parietal
[e] Usually primarily temporal
[f] Usually primarily occipital
Adapted in part from Doerr and Carlin, 1991.

of hesitations of two seconds or longer in an ordinary sentence is a cue to the possibility of Alzheimer's disease. Whereas normals seldom make more than one such hesitation every thirty seconds, persons with Alzheimer's will make about four in a thirty-second period. Any signs of asymmetry should particularly be noted. For example, one client with visual-field deficits neatly shaved one side of his face, but only roughly and sloppily shaved the other side. Obtaining some subject-as-own-control data is also useful, such as grip strength, performance on finger-tapping tasks, or having the person touch various body parts with either hand with the eyes closed. Deficits may be especially meaningful if a short-form measure of I.Q., such as the Shipley Institute of Living Scale (Jacobsen and Tomkin, 1988), indicates average-or-better general intelligence. In addition to these specific performance tasks there are also normative or test data, the focus of this section. Test-retest data—say, at six-month intervals—can also be useful.

Dementia, the central feature of many organic brain dysfunctions, may sometimes be confused with depression (referred to as "pseudodementia"). The following, adapted from C. Wells and G. Duncan (1977), *Neurology for Psychiatrists* (Philadelphia: Davis), presents clinical features that help to differentiate the two:

DEMENTIA

1. Recent memory is more disrupted.

2. Memory gaps for specific events is unusual.

3. Symptoms are of long duration.

4. Complaints of cognitive loss are infrequent and typically imprecise.

5. Clients often appear unconcerned.

6. Attention and concentration are usually faulty.

7. "Near-miss" answers are frequent.

8. Clients conceal disability.

9. Clients struggle to perform tasks, and often delight in accomplishments, however trivial.

10. Clients rely on notes, calendars, etc., to keep up.

11. Clients show consistently poor performance on tasks of similar difficulty.

12. Affect is labile and shallow.

PSEUDODEMENTIA

1. Long- and short-term memory are equally disrupted.

2. Memory gaps occur for specific periods and events.

3. Symptoms are of short duration.

4. Complaints of cognitive loss are frequent and often detailed.

5. Clients usually communicate distress.

6. Attention and concentration are often well preserved.

7. "Don't know" answers are typical.

8. Clients emphasize disability.

9. Clients make little effort to perform even simple tasks, and may highlight failures.

10. Clients do not try to keep up.

11. Clients show significant variability in performing tasks of similar difficulty.

12. Affective change is often pervasive.

13. Clients often retain social skills.

13. Loss of social skills is often early and prominent.

14. On tests of orientation, clients mistake unusual for usual.

14. On tests of orientation, clients often give "don't know" answers.

15. Behavior is usually compatible with severity of cognitive dysfunction.

15. Behavior is often incongruent with severity of cognitive dysfunction.

16. Nocturnal accentuation of dysfunction is common.

16. Nocturnal accentuation of dysfunction is uncommon.

17. History of previous psychiatric dysfunction is uncommon.

17. History of previous psychiatric dysfunction is common.

If the clinician is to carry out a substantial neuropsychological assessment, extensive methods of obtaining normative data, such as the Halstead-Reitan, Luria-Nebraska, or Smith-Michigan batteries, are appropriate here. It is worth noting that for many years the Halstead-Reitan battery, which includes a WAIS-R or WISC-R and requires four to five hours test time, was seen by clinicians as the "benchmark" battery. Much more diverse batteries that have recently emerged, however, are prognostic as well as diagnostic and can be extremely useful in other applications, such as evaluating the effects of drug trials. A good intermediate-level screening battery for CNSI might include a WAIS-R (or a validated short form such as the Satz-Mogel), MMPI-2, specific tests for lateralization (such as grip strength), the Purdue Pegboard and/or tapping tests, tests for sensory response, and at least some of the other tests that help cover the required variety of modalities and functional domains (e.g., Reitan Aphasia Screening Test, Word Finding Test, Indented-Paragraph Reading Test, Benton Visual Retention Test, Wechsler Memory Test, Trail-Making Test Part B, Boston Naming Test, Rey Auditory Verbal Learning Test, Symbol Digit Modalities Test) (Lezak, 1995; Zeidel, 1995; Margolin, 1992; Orsini et al., 1988).

A clinician might consider including a test like the Reitan Aphasia Screening Test, a shortened version of Halstead and Wepman's Aphasia Screening Test (Reitan and Wolfson, 1986), in a routine test battery. It takes only about ten minutes to administer and is a rough assessment of spatial and verbal factors, as well as aphasia. It is a good gross screening measure for significant cerebral impairment, as normals seldom make errors and perform effortlessly. It is very important to elicit the best possible performance the person can honestly give, to the point of allowing extra trials, and to never immediately accept "I don't know" responses. If a client then makes even two or three errors, it is worthwhile to take a deeper look for more signs of cerebral impairment. An excellent item on the Reitan Aphasia Screening Test is the request for the client to produce a Maltese cross. Clinicians could add some version of the Maltese cross in conjunction with a few other figures, perhaps similar to cards A and 7 of the Bender-Gestalt, to the routine self-administered battery in Appendix B. Some specific measure of memory is also useful.

The Trail-Making Test Part B is one of the most sensitive indicators of CNSI in the Halstead-Reitan Battery. For young to middle-age adults, a time of 0–26 seconds is considered normal, 27–39 seconds is in the mild range, 88–120 seconds is moderate, and over 120 seconds is in the severe range. On Trails B, age is a factor in performance. Respective borderline deficit and critical deficit performance in seconds, for the following ages, are: age 40 (+95, +125); 40–49 (+100, +150); 50–59 (+135, +175); 60–69 (+170, +280); and 70+ (+250, +375), although an important confounding variable is number of errors, I.Q., and responsiveness to the test situation (see Table 11.1).

The following screening technique for CNSI developed by Elbert Russell uses Trails B as a starting point:

A. If Trails B scale score is ≥ 3 (Age and Time Norms)

Age   49 –   ≥ 195
Age   50–59 ≥ 215
Age ≥ 60   ≥ 225

Assume a full evaluation is necessary; otherwise go to B (below).

B. If any 3 of these criteria are met, assume a full evaluation is necessary; otherwise assume normal client.

1. Trails B scale score is ≥ 2 (Age Norms)

Age < 50   85 sec.
Age 51–59   115 sec.
Age ≥ 60   135 sec.

2. Digit Symbol: Age norms, 8 or less (.≤8)
3. Block Design: Age norms, 8 or less (.≤8)
4. WAIS Block Design: 4 Age norm scale points ≤ than Vocabulary
5. WAIS Block Design: 1 Age norm scale points > than Vocabulary
6. Non-dom hand: ≥ Taps than Dominant (N ≥ D)
7. Non-dom hand: 10 or < taps than Dominant (≤ 10) taps
8. Dom hand: Scale Score ≥ 3
9. Non-dom hand: Scale Score ≥ 3
10. Wechsler Memory Scale–Revised (WMS–R): Verbal 1/2 hr. scale score ≥ 3.
11. WMS-R Figural: 1/2 hr. scale score ≥ 3

A major concern has to do with how emotional ("functional") status affects performance on these tests. To the degree that psychiatric problems impede performance, they may lose their value as "indicators" of CNSI. The WAIS–R is more problematic in this respect than are many other neuropsychological tests, even when controlled for education. For example, two of the most sensitive tests to organicity on the WAIS-R—arithmetic and digit symbol—are also commonly affected by psychiatric disturbance. On the other hand, Trails B and many of the Halstead-Reitan tests tend to be fairly resilient to the affects of emotional disturbance (Gass, 1991a). Also, pattern analysis is important in diagnosing CNSI using neuropsychological tests, since it is common for psychiatric patients to have a few scores within the impaired range in a battery of tests. In fact, experts often accept the guideline that even normals are "allowed" to "blow" one test.

The CNSI literature often discusses the value of fixed versus flexible batteries. In many ways this is a false issue because one can simply use one of the fixed batteries, for example, the Halstead-Reitan, and then supplement it with whatever other specific tests are viewed as helpful in a particular case. In clinical situations it is certainly arguable that an individualized battery might be optimal, as it is more directly tailored to the referral question, and should be more flexible and cost-efficient. However, a major disadvantage of the flexible battery is that, although it seems to adequately address the specifics of the referral question, it may miss something important or even critical. The classic example is finding "ability X" to be intact but neglecting the fact that executive functions, which initiate and guide ability X in daily living, are impaired. A second disadvantage is that pattern analysis is much more difficult and less definitive in cases involving more subtle lesions. Also, a minor advantage of the fixed battery, norms for the battery as a whole, is not available for a flexible battery, and this cost has to be factored into the decision. In forensic situations, some clinicians may feel the defensibility and protection of fixed-battery norms may tip the scales in this decision.

More importantly, any diagnostician must be aware of the common signs of CNSI in the standard tests and in behavior, particularly in the event that no one has yet asserted the possibility of CNSI (Anderson, 1994). For example, the interaction of type of symptoms with rapid-versus-gradual onset can distinguish between cerebral impairment and such psychopathology as the affective disorders. When a syndrome with a gradual onset of a wide range of affective symptomatology is accompanied by neurological and cognitive deficits, along with aphasia and agnosia and/or a loss of sphincter control, irreversible CNSI is probable, although reversible conditions such as normal-pressure hydrocephalus could cause this. If the affective symptomatology is unaccompanied by the latter symptomatology and the depression and/or mania is severe and possibly accompanied by persistent delusions, an affective or bipolar disorder is more probable, although CNSI later in life can produce such symptoms.

If instead there is a rapid onset of symptoms focusing on confusion, agitation, attention problems, and disrupted sleep patterns, along with problems in self-care (including impaired sphincter control) and a focus primarily on visual hallucinations, there is a high probability of acute CNSI, such as delirium. If death does not occur, recovery is often reasonably rapid. But if symptoms do not include such evident self-care problems and instead include delusions or auditory hallucinations, then an affective or schizoaffective disorder is probable.

SPECIFYING CNSI LOCATION BY TEST

Specifying location via test data is always challenging—and often impossible— because of the nature of most brain-disorder patterns and the variability of brain–behavior relationships. However, the following schema (Table 11.2) suggests various tests that may aid in locating site of disorder by test or subtest performance.

The discrimination between right and left cerebral hemisphere impairment has fascinated clinicians for a long time. As an overall rule, by far the best and most reliable neuropsychological tests for discriminating between right and left hemisphere lesions are the sensory and motor tests (e.g., Reitan-Klove Sensory-Perceptual examination, Finger Tapping, Grip Strength, Grooved Peg-

---

TABLE 11.2 Tests to Aid in Locating Site of Disorder

FRONTAL LOBE DISORDERS

Milan sorting test, Halstead category test, and Wisconsin card-sorting test, as tests of ability to abstract

The Porteus Maze Test, Reitan Trail Making Test, the recognition of figures in the Figure of Rey as tests of planning, regulating, and checking programs of action

Benton's Verbal Fluency Test for estimating verbal skill and verbal regulation of behavior

TEMPORAL LOBE DISORDERS

Figure of Rey, Benton Visual Retention Test, Illinois Nonverbal Sequential Memory Test, Recurring Nonsense, Figures of Kimura, and Facial Recognition Test as modality-specific memory tests

Milner's Maze Learning Task and Lhermitte-Signoret amnesic syndrome tests for general retentive memory

Seashore Rhythm Test, Speech-Sound Perception Test from the Halstead-Reitan battery, Environmental Sounds Test, and Austin Meaningless Sounds Test, as measures of auditory perception

PARIETAL LOBE DISORDERS

Figure of Rey, Wechsler Block Design and Object Assembly, Benton Figure Copying Test, Benton Judgment of Line Orientation, Hooper Visual Organization Test, Halstead-Reitan Tactual Performance Test, and Fairfield Block Substitution Test as tests of constructional praxis

Several mathematical and logicogrammatical tests as tests of spatial synthesis

Cross-modal association tests as tests of suprasensory integration

Benson-Barton Stick Test, Cattell's Pool Reflection Test, and Money's Road Map Test, as tests of spatial perception and memory

OCCIPITAL LOBE DISORDERS

Color naming, color form association, visual irreminiscence, as tests of visual perception; recognition of faces of prominent people, map drawing board, and Tactual Performance tests). Right versus left differences on these tests—unlike verbal versus visuospatial differences—are much more definitive for diagnostic and localization purposes. Nevertheless, specific deficits in spatial orientation and perceptual and/or organizational functions point to right hemisphere disorder, whereas specific problems in language, motor, and executive functions suggest left hemisphere or frontal impairment. Right hemisphere impairment is more likely to be manifest in a disruption of emotion-laden knowledge and a disruption of the nuances of speech. Difficulties in right-left spatial orientation problems have traditionally been seen as suggestive of disorder in the right hemisphere. But language is a critical factor in such discriminations, and so attention to the quality of a client's difficulty may lead to a hypothesis that there is left hemisphere disorder instead.

Benton (1980) has commented on the ability to make facial recognitions as a diagnostic sign. His data, as well as those of others, suggest that specific facial agnosia, prosopagnosia (the loss of ability to recognize familiar friends and family), is a good indicator of a bilateral lesion that has damaged a small number of cells in the lower rear portion of both sides of the brain. Damage to only one side appears to result in only partial prosopagnosia: The patient is able to identify familiar faces in photos, but not in real life, and makes "close mistakes" in identification. Consistent problems in facial discrimination, such as in identifying new acquaintances, usually indicate right hemisphere impairment, and, again, if the lesion turns out to be even more localized, it is probably posterior rather than anterior.

The clinician can also include a finger-tapping test, using a simple event counter. The general assumption is that performance will be about 10% better with the dominant hand (thus the opposite hemisphere), so any substantial deviation from this pattern can be suggestive of disorder in one hemisphere. A grip-strength test is also advised. A result in these tests, wherein the left hand is 20% or more deficient in comparison with the right hand in right-handed clients or the left hand is no better than the right in a left-handed client is suggestive of right cerebral damage. If performance on these tests has the reverse results, this is suggestive of left cerebral damage. The Indented-Paragraph Reading Test (Caplan, 1987), a test with an uneven left border, has proven effective in helping pinpoint right-hemisphere damage. With syndromes in which dementia is suspected, especially in older individuals, the Boston Naming Test is useful, as language-naming deficits are often an early sign. Van Gorp et al. (1986) provide normative data on this test for individuals over 59 years of age. When testing older individuals, the data on normal, healthy older adults, provided in Table 11.3, should be of help.

MMPI-2

In general, the MMPI-2 scales that are most commonly affected by neurologic symptom-item endorsement are scales 1, 2, 3, 7 and 8. However, there is no modal MMPI-2 profile for CNSI, and for good reason: There is no modal CNSI pattern of deficit, and the following needs to be read in light of that caution. In

TABLE 11.3 Normative Data on Neuropsychological Tests for 156 Healthy, Well-Educated ($\overline{X}$ = 14–15 Years), Elderly People

	VERBAL I.Q.	PERFORM-ANCE I.Q.	WMS* LOGIC PROSE IMMED	WMS VISUAL REPRO-DUCTION	WMS LOGIC PROSE DELAY (45 MIN.)	VISUAL REPRO-DUCTION DELAY (45 MIN.)	TRAILS A	TRAILS B	BOSTON NAMING TEST
58–85 (N = 156) Mean	117.650	110.617	8.925	7.633	6.233	4.733	48.700	107.550	54.017
STD DEV	13.527	13.493	2.752	3.498	2.733	3.741	14.468	45.631	5.391
58–65 (N = 28) Mean	117.200	109.200	9.750	9.600	7.800	6.600	41.500	84.400	55.500
STD DEV	11.331	11.555	2.395	2.757	2.163	2.459	7.832	24.600	4.528
66–70 (N = 45) Mean	114.800	111.467	8.467	8.667	5.733	6.333	43.200	105.200	55.467
STD DEV	17.034	16.831	2.649	3.811	2.235	3.830	14.982	43.432	3.944
71–75 (N = 57) Mean	122.875	115.083	9.271	7.792	6.313	4.375	50.083	97.791	53.875
STD DEV	11.380	11.938	3.148	2.992	3.158	3.932	12.884	30.404	5.728
76–85 (N = 26) Mean	110.545	101.000	8.045	4.091	5.318	1.636	59.727	153.090	51.000
STD DEV	11.246	8.775	2.185	2.256	2.483	1.690	15.950	62.603	6.356

*Wechsler Memory Scale
Table adapted from Van Gorp, W., Satz, P., and Mitrushina, M. (1990), Neuropsychological processes associated with normal aging, *Developmental Neuro-psychology, 6(4),* 279–290.

this area the dominant axiom should be that individual differences are determinative (Gass and Russell, 1986, 1991). Yet there are a number of patterns that should alert the clinician to pursue a consideration of possible CNSI. An obvious first sign is not a code type but an examination of how the person completed the form. For example, persons with visual-field deficits may neglect portions of the answer form, thus invalidating the profile. Extremely erratic profiles will show up in the validity scale elevations; confusion or dementia may be causal, although the reader should also consult the section on malingering for relevant information.

An alternative approach is to identify the most common (approximately 25% of patients) and discriminating MMPI-2 items in samples with specific CNSI patterns such as closed head trauma (CHT) and stroke (Gass, 1991b, 1992). In closed head injury the affected scales are scale 8 (ten items), scale 7 (six items), and scales 1, 2, and 3 (five items each), though the impact is usually greatest on 8 and 2. The pattern is fairly different with stroke and probably with other focal lesions (e.g., hematoma, tumor, infection, etc.) as well. In Gass's sample the affected scales were scale 3 (thirteen items), scale 1 (twelve items), scales 2 and 8 (seven items each), scale 9 (four items), and scale 7 (three items), with the most impact on 3 and 1. As a result, in stroke the "conversion V" is a common artifact arising out of bona fide physical symptoms of stroke. For that reason, a correction factor can be helpful in analyzing the MMPI-2.

Gass (1992) has published separate corrections for use with CHT and stroke patients. It should be emphasized that the correction is applied in a way that reflects the uniqueness of the patient's responses to the relevant MMPI items. It should not be used with patients who were emotionally disturbed prior to their brain impairment, that is, with patients for whom these items are as likely to have psychopathologic significance. The correction has a tabular format, with the MMPI-2 item numbers in the left-hand column and the scored direction of each item listed under each MMPI-2 scale in subsequent columns *(See Tables 11.4 and 11.5)*. Application requires the following steps:

1. Inspect the answer sheet to determine which of the correction items were endorsed in the scored direction. Using the table, circle each of the endorsed items each time it appears across the entire row.
2. Determine the raw score contribution for each scale by counting in each column the number of times a scale-related item was circled. Record this number on the bottom line of each column.
3. Compute the corrected raw score by subtracting the number obtained for each scale in Step 2 from the raw score of that scale.
4. Determine the profile impact by plotting the new (corrected) raw scores on the MMPI-2 profile sheet and contrasting this with the original profile.
5. Interpret the corrected profile using the standard approach (outlined above), including profile correlates.

A number of individuals with a left hemisphere dysfunction (especially to the degree that this is the dominant hemisphere) will show a "catastrophic

TABLE 11.4 Correction Table for Use in Computing Adjusted Minnesota Multiphasic Personality Inventory-2 (MMPI-2) Raw Scores

ITEM	MMPI-2 SCALE								
	F	1	2	3	4	7	8	9	0
31	___	___	31T	31T	31T	31T	31T	___	31T
101	___	101T	___	101T	___	___	___	___	___
106	___	___	___	___	___	___	106F	106F	106F
147	___	___	147T	___	___	147T	147T	___	___
149	___	149T	___	___	___	___	___	___	___
165	___	___	165F	___	___	165F	165F	___	___
170	___	___	170T	___	___	170T	170T	___	___
172	___	___	___	172T	___	___	___	___	___
175	___	175T	175T	175T	___	175T	___	___	___
179	___	179F	___	179F	___	___	179F	___	___
180	180T	___	___	___	___	___	180T	___	___
247	___	247T	___	___	___	___	247F	___	___
295	___	___	___	___	___	___	295F	___	___
325	___	___	___	___	___	325T	325T	___	___
Totals	___	___	___	___	___	___	___	___	___

response" pattern on the MMPI-2 (although numerous individuals with a right frontal trauma also show the same pattern); those with right-hemisphere dysfunction are more likely to appear "indifferent" or depressed. Lachar (1974) notes that the relatively rare 1-9/9-1 code, with a low scale 2, is found in a number of persons with acute CNSI. This most commonly occurs where there is a dawning awareness in clients that they have suffered a loss of function and where they are dealing with it counterphobically. As they lose the will to fight in response to the loss and as depression emerges, a 2-9/9-2 code is relatively common. When their personality functions begin to fall apart, and activity levels are raised against their phobia, the 9-8/8-9 profile may occur (Gynther et al., 1973a). While scale 8 is often the highest scale in epileptic patients, scales 1, 2, and 3 are more likely to be elevated in clients with multiple sclerosis. Scale 8 is also often elevated as aphasic clients begin to withdraw.

Persons with CNSI from a toxic substance are likely to show a generally elevated MMPI-2 profile with a particularly high score on scale 8 and scores on most other scales (excluding the 5 scale) at about 70 T. Scales that tend to be higher in this profile are 1 and 2. When CNSI occurs as a result of senility or a neurological degenerative process, elevations are more likely on scales 2 and 8, both around the 70 T mark. The senile group tends to have a slightly higher elevation over all in the other scores, with scale 1 being particularly higher than in the neurological degenerative group (Pennington et al., 1979).

TABLE 11.5   Correction Table for Computing Adjusted MMPI-2 Raw Scores for CVD Patients

ITEM	0	F	1	2	3	4	7	8	9
10	___	10F	10F	10F	___	___	___	___	___
31	___	___	31T	31T	31T	31T	31T	___	31T
45	___	45F	45F	45F	___	___	___	___	___
47	___	47F	___	47F	___	___	___	___	___
53	___	53T	___	___	___	___	___	___	___
106	___	___	___	___	___	___	106F	106F	106F
141	___	141F	141F	141F	___	___	___	___	___
147	___	___	147T	___	___	147T	147T	___	___
148	___	___	148F	148F	___	___	___	___	___
152	___	152F	___	152F	___	___	___	___	___
164	___	164F	___	164F	___	___	___	___	___
168	168T	___	___	___	___	___	168T	168T	___
172	___	___	___	172T	___	___	___	___	___
173	___	173F	___	173F	___	___	___	___	___
175	___	175T	175T	175T	___	175T	___	___	___
177	___	___	___	___	___	___	177F	___	___
182	___	___	___	___	___	___	182T	182T	___
224	___	224F	___	224F	___	___	___	___	___
229	___	___	___	___	___	___	229T	229T	___
247	___	247T	___	___	___	___	247T	___	___
249	___	249F	___	249F	___	___	___	___	___
Totals	___	___	___	___	___	___	___	___	___
Scale	F	1	2	3	4	7	8	9	0

According to Lachar (1974), the chronic CNSI patients are more likely to have scores elevated above 65 T on scales 8, 6, 4, and 2. Scales 1 and 3 are usually lower, except with those who have multiple sclerosis and similar disorders. In one sample of neurological clients, scales 1, 2, and then 4 were the highest (Dahlstrom et al., 1986). Watson et al. (1978) find that the scale 1 to scale 7 ratio is much higher for CNSI clients than for other groups with psychopathology. Also, the F scale is high, particularly if damage is severe. In chronic CNSI the 9 scale is often a barometer of the person's reaction to it; a lower 9 score indicates either acceptance or a lack of reaction to it, while a high 9 suggests an attempt to cope, although poorly at times. When scales 8 and 6 are very high and there are other solid indications of CNSI, the CNS disorder is possibly accompanied by schizophrenia.

When dealing with possible CNSI cases, particularly in the aged, the MMPI-2 may have to be administered over several sessions because of fatigue and/or attention problems, or it may only be possible to use a short form.

☐ ## Specific Scale Indicators

Certain scales offer specific data that may be of help in CNSI diagnosis.

Scale K: On scale K, high scores (T > 60) sometimes occur in neurologic patients who have not been properly prepared to take the MMPI, who are unclear about the reasons for being evaluated with the MMPI, and who want to avoid "looking crazy." High scores also occur in inpatients who believe that openness in disclosing problems may thwart their plans for being discharged. To the degree that K exceeds 60 T and is higher than F, consider profile invalidity due to a defensive attempt to appear well adjusted. However, any clinical scale elevations that exist can be interpreted.

Scale 2: This scale has five clear CNSI-related items. Moderately elevated scores on scale 2 sometimes reflect the physical and cognitive sequelae of brain injury in the absence of depression. In this case, elevated scores (T > 65) on content scale DEP provide clearer support for the presence of depression. Also, note evidence of low self-esteem (LSE). If scale 2 (T = 60–70): Is the neurologic patient depressed? This is doubtful if the prominent contribution lies in subscales D3 (Physical Problems) or D4 (Mental Dullness).

Scale 3: If T = 60–70: Does the potential neurologic client have hysterical features? This is doubtful if the prominent contribution lies in subscales HY3 (Lassitude-Malaise) or HY4 (Somatic Complaints).

Scale 4: This scale is seldom strongly affected by CNSI-related symptom endorsement. It has heterogeneous item content; in a valid profile the presence of antisocial attitudes and behaviors can be clarified by considering content scale ASP (Antisocial Practices). Poor anger control can be assessed using ANG.

Scale 7: This scale has six CHT-related items. Interpretation of this scale can be refined by noting evidence of generalized anxiety (ANX), obsessional thinking (OBS), and irrational fears and phobias (FRS).

Scale 8: This scale has ten clearly CNSI-related items. In evaluating the possibility of psychosis, elevated scores should be viewed in conjunction with a more homogeneous measure of a psychotic thought process (Bizarre Mentation, BIZ). In evaluating the interpersonal correlates of scale 8, consider the social discomfort scale (SOD). If scale 8 (T = 60–70): Does the neurologic patient have schizoid or psychotic features? This is doubtful if the prominent contribution lies in subscales SC3 (LEM, Cognitive), or SC6 (Bizarre Sensory Experiences). Note: In psychiatric patients these two subscales are often the most important for inferring the presence of a thought disorder. However, in any patient population, content scale BIZ often provides a more definitive basis for assessing psychotic thinking.

Other content scales include measures of areas of importance to treatment planning with brain-injured patients. Negative work attitudes (WRK) has implications for an individual's potential for successful involvement in rehabilitation, employment, or other productive activity. Family problems (FAM) assesses the patient's perspective on the quality of the home or family environment. Negative treatment indicators (TRT) provide information about a patient's attitudes toward personal change and the value of psychological services. The marital distress scale (MDS) is sensitive to marital problems that could potentially affect symptom presentation and aftercare. Periodic violent or explosive behavior can be assessed using the over-controlled hostility scale (O-H). Critical-item sets may provide clues to special problems. Individual items may be used as "red flags" for further investigation of problems such as suicidal ideation or intent, hallucinations, or delusional thought content.

Cognitive Complaint Index

In neuropsychological patients a set of cognitive complaint items (CCI) from MMPI–2 may be helpful in assessing patients' beliefs and concerns regarding their own cognitive efficiency (Gass et al., 1990). The degree of concern can be evaluated in relation to actual performance on tests of attention and memory:

31. I find it hard to keep my mind on a task or job.
165. My memory seems to be all right (F).
168. I have had periods in which I carried on activities without knowing later what I had been doing.
229. I have had blank spells in which my activities were interrupted and I did not know what was going on around me.
299. I cannot keep my mind on one thing.
308. I forget right away what people say to me.
325. I have more trouble concentrating than other people seem to have.
341. At periods my mind seems to work more slowly than usual.
472. I am greatly bothered by forgetting where I put things.
533. I forget where I leave things.
565. It takes a great deal of effort for me to remember what people tell me these days.

If there is a relatively high level of complaints and generally intact test performance: Hypothesis 1: The patient may overestimate problems with attention and memory. Hypothesis 2: Despite having intact attentional and memory *capacity*, emotional factors may interfere with cognitive functioning in daily living. If there is a low level of complaints and poorer test performance: Hypothesis: The patient may have limited awareness of cognitive deficits and may overestimate his or her abilities.

16 PF

Because of the variety of reactions subsumed under the term "central nervous system impairment," a modal 16 PF profile for CNSI is not available. However, persons with CNSI are generally high on scales O and Q_4, reflecting their sense of insecurity and anxiety. Those individuals who have moved into depression would probably not score so high. Q_3 is low, reflecting the degree of personality disintegration, and scale B is lowered, indicating the correlated loss of intellectual functioning. Moderately low scores on Q_2, F, and H are also standard. The scores on scale E vary markedly, depending on the reaction to the awareness of loss. If persons have become depressed and submissive to a hospital environment, E is low, whereas if they are attempting counterphobic mechanisms, it is elevated. G tends to vary markedly as well, but usually is at least moderately high.

OTHER TEST-RESPONSE PATTERNS

Before looking at possible cues from specific WAIS-R subtests, several overall perspectives that can aid the clinician in this type of assessment must be stated.

1. On the WAIS-R the general rule has been that low verbal scales relative to performance scales indicate left hemisphere lesions (if it has been determined that the left hemisphere is the dominant one), and with a lesser degree of applicability, low performance scores relative to verbal scores indicate a right hemisphere lesion, especially to the degree that this discrepancy is determined by low scores on picture arrangement and block design. Unfortunately, these discrepancies are not always clear-cut or perfectly correlated. Indeed, a number of normals show a significant VIQ-PIQ split, and patients with acute right hemisphere damage and diffuse bilateral degenerative conditions (e.g., Alzheimers) show a low VIQ to PIQ ratio. Chronic hemisphere lesions often fail to show any pattern unless they are large enough and strategically located. Nevertheless, these are good first rules of thumb. Left hemisphere damage may produce a very low profile, and such clients may be difficult to differentiate from those with mental retardation. Persons with right hemisphere damage do better on comprehension, similarities, and vocabulary than on other verbal tests, and better on picture completion within the performance tests. Those clients with relatively acute but diffuse CNSI do somewhat better on verbal tests than on performance tests, particularly on vocabulary and information, but they also do well on picture completion in the performance tests. They do particularly poorly on digit symbol, as do most CNSI groups, as well as on arithmetic, and usually on block design. Over all, it is reasonable to assert that a low-performance/high-verbal pattern is more suggestive of overall CNSI than is the high-performance/ low-verbal pattern. Also, it is worthwhile to remember that traumatic head injuries clearly to one side produce patterns more similar to diffuse CNSI than one would find in unilateral CNSI produced by processes other than acute trauma.

2. In general, marked verbal-performance splits are likely to indicate intracerebral tumors or cerebrovascular accidents. Clients with cerebrovascular accidents are then more likely to show disrupted differential performance on grip strength and tapping tests than do clients with tumors.

3. In verbal subtests that require a high level of verbal precision and identification (the vocabulary scale), expressive speech problems are suggested by hesitating and circuitous speech—the patient cannot find the precise word.

4. The picture completion subtest can also be helpful in assessing the difficulties in expressive speech. It is important that the clinician create very specific demands. If the clinician's style is to accept approximate answers easily, or pointing rather than naming, for example, the client is not adequately pressed to make the precise designation.

5. The similarities subtest and the proverbs on the comprehension subtest test general intellectual and abstracting abilities, and thus identify more diffuse cerebral impairment or at least cerebral trauma that leads to a wide range of impairment.

6. The overall range between lowest and highest WAIS-R subscales is a good indicator of general impairment. When the range between scale scores is greater than 5 in persons without another handicap (such as lack of education), the clinician should consider the possibility of CNSI.

7. The highest WAIS-R subscale scores provide a reasonably good index of premorbid intellectual functioning in cases of cerebral impairment, but only when they are scales that correlate reasonably well with the full-scale WAIS-R, as in the vocabulary subtest. When digit span is the highest postmorbid scale, it would not be an especially efficient predictor.

8. Within-subtest scatter (consistently missing easy items while answering hard ones accurately) is an important indicator of the ability to maintain set. Clients with certain cerebral impairments find it hard to keep the program in mind and to process the data at the same time. For example, they may keep in mind the general problem on the arithmetic subtest but forget the exact numbers in the process—or the reverse.

Digit symbol is commonly low in all brain-injured persons. Arithmetic is almost as consistently low, especially in those with left hemisphere injuries. In combination with digit span, arithmetic is an excellent measure of the degree of transient anxiety and depression, although the CNSI can affect digit span as much as or more than depression can. Information may be low in persons who are suffering early CNSI in the left hemisphere, but it remains reasonably high in most CNSI cases, as do comprehension and similarities. Picture arrangement most often reflects right hemisphere disorder (often the right anterior temporal lobe—the frontal lobe is also a strong possibility as well), as do object assembly and block design. The diagnostician may see unusual placements in block design and object assembly, placements that the client finds difficult to explain. Picture completion and similarities are rarely affected, except in chronic CNSI. Most schizophrenics do better on information than on similarities; this can be one cue to distinguish between them.

Block design also helps in the discrimination between CNSI and schizophrenia. It usually remains relatively high in schizophrenia, whereas it is virtually always affected to some degree in CNSI. It is consistently low in diffuse brain injuries and in injuries involving the right temporal and parietal lobes.

In another important discrimination, object assembly is often one of the higher scores in mentally retarded persons, whereas both CNSI and schizophrenics, as well as depressives, are prone to do poorly (Golden, 1979).

Fuld (1984) has provided further validation data of a marker of dementia of the Alzheimer type that was occasionally noted earlier in the literature. This WAIS-R subtest profile marker, indicating the probable presence of this dementia, is defined by the following formula:

$$A > B > C < D, A > D$$

in which A is the mean of the information and vocabulary subtest scores, B is the mean of the similarities and digit span scores, C is the mean of the digit symbol and block design scores, and D is the object assembly score. All subtest scores are age-corrected. This marker was positive in approximately 50% of actual Alzheimer-dementia cases, but in only 11% of non–Alzheimer-dementia cases, in two separate studies (Fuld, 1984). A further validation (Satz et al., 1987) found the marker gives an equally effective discrimination between Alzheimer-dementia cases and the normal elderly.

An abbreviated form of the WAIS-R can be very useful with the elderly, considering the possible attention and fatigue factors. One of the best abbreviated versions was developed originally by Satz and Mogel (1962). This short form, now applied with the WAIS-R, uses every third item on information, vocabulary and picture completion, all items on digit span and digit symbol, and odd items on the remaining subtests. Mitrushina and Satz (1991) found test reliabilities between .81 and .83 for verbal, .70 and .72 for performance, and .79 and .83 for full scale sum of scaled scores in an elderly population ($\overline{X}$ age = 70.4; SD = 5.0); compared to .86 (verbal), .85 (performance), and .90 (full scale) found in earlier research on a normal adult age sample. The slightly lower reliabilities are apparently due to the lower number of items presented. Lowest reliabilities were found on picture arrangement and object assembly. These authors conclude the Satz-Mogel form can be very useful as a screening device with the elderly, especially using the verbal scales.

On the Wide-Range Achievement Test-Revised (WRAT-R), disorders in reading ability should cue the clinician toward the possibility of temporal-occipital left hemisphere disturbance or long-standing learning disability in the presence of average or above-average I.Q. A significant loss of spelling ability should suggest the possibility of parietal and/or occipital dysfunction (Cantwell and Baker, 1987).

The classic signs of CNSI on the Bender-Gestalt are perplexity, impotency, distortions, perseveration, significant rotation of designs, and peculiar sequencing. Impotency, or statements indicating dissatisfaction with one's performance, is common throughout all the tests when such a client runs into difficulty. Also common is the element of perplexity, wherein a person overtly indicates confusion and uncertainty about handling the task given.

On the Benton Visual-Retention Test, signs similar to that on the Bender-Gestalt are evidence of CNSI. More specifically, Golden (1979) states that persons with CNSI are most likely to make three types of errors here: the omission of a peripheral figure, rotation, or size error (a loss of the size relationship between the major and peripheral figures). It is important to note that even though rotations do occur in normals, they are more likely to be stabilizing errors: when a figure that is presented as at an angle is then rotated so that it sits flat. Alexias or aphasias may be involved if the client has difficulty recognizing previously learned configurations (e.g., circle, square) (Bender, 1938).

As with the other drawing tests, distortions, perplexity, impotency, and perseveration in response to the Draw-A-Person Test are classic signs of cerebral impairment. The clinician might find it useful to have clients routinely write their name as well as a novel sentence (e.g., "The shed is next to the house") on the same pages with the persons they have drawn. In general, clients with left hemisphere impairment can often do the overlearned task—that is, write their name—reasonably well. But at the same time, they have marked difficulties with the novel sentences. Also, as a general rule, if the drawing is adequate but the writing is bad, the left hemisphere may be impaired, whereas if the drawing is poor and the writing is acceptable, the localization, if any, may be in the right hemisphere. Differences in the general style of drawings between those with right hemisphere CNSI and left hemisphere CNSI are reflected in the following contrasts:

RIGHT-HEMISPHERE CNSI	LEFT-HEMISPHERE CNSI
Loss of adequate gestalt relationships	Sequential relationships impaired
Scattered and fragmented individual responses	Simple and coherent individual responses
Loss of adequate spatial relationships	Spatial relationships adequately retained
Corrective lines are added	Gross lack of detail
Drawings are made energetically, almost driven	Drawings are made slowly and laboriously, haltingly at times
Orientation to the general task is faulty or lost	Orientation to the general task structure is reasonably accurate

It is important to look for perseveration in the drawing tests, as well as in a wide range of performance areas. One cerebrally impaired client kept doing an infinite division problem almost to a point of exhaustion, at which time he simply said, "There's too much of this."

On the Rorschach, perplexity, repetition, and impotency are also common, which is not surprising in light of the ambiguity of the stimuli. There is often a delayed reaction time to the cards, and persons may turn the cards in a confused manner, indicating an attempt to cope with a task in which they lack confidence (Exner, 1986).

Overall, there are a low number of responses, with the average time per response quite high, and a deterioration of the response quality as clients proceed through the cards. Constriction, being bound to stimuli (e.g., "This is where some ink has been splashed"), fragmented responses, and a high need for more structure are common. Positional responses are more common than normal. Occasional perseveration of content occurs, sometimes even to the point where there is a repetition of automatic phrases. In particular, there may be a perseveration of CF responses in the last three cards. "Color naming" and crude CF and C responses are given, in contrast to a low number of M responses and a low F+%. Vague W responses, with good form Dd responses, may be found. Responses about anatomy content and those in which humans or animals are mutilated reflect the client's concerns about his or her own deterioration.

Bellak (1993) points to the following consistent features found in the TAT stories of persons with CNSI (some of these apply equally well to other tests, such as the Rorschach):

1. Use of fewer ideas and words
2. Longer response times, often with punctuating pauses
3. Concrete, simple descriptions; occasionally a listing of items in the picture
4. Trite stories with little action
5. Confusions and misinterpretations
6. Proportionately fewer common themes
7. Perseveration of themes; repetition of words and phrases
8. Difficulties in providing adequate responses (especially to more complex or vague cards) or in changing inadequate response
9. Expressions of self-doubt
10. Missing the most salient objects in a card, e.g., the violin in card 1 of the TAT
11. Stereotypical stories from TV or popular stories
12. Inability to focus on one central character throughout
13. Problems in developing any parallel plot or bringing the story to a reasonable conclusion
14. Lack of coordinated plot or action sequences
15. Themes of problems in learning, dependency on others in everyday behaviors, being isolated from peer situations, or of impulsive unplanned actions

The potential treatments for CNSI are so broad and diverse, and yet have to be so individualized for each client (Zeidel, 1995; Anderson, 1994), that it would not be reasonable to even try to outline them here.

■ Attention-Deficit Hyperactivity Disorder

Current recognition of attention-deficit hyperactivity disorder (ADHD) in the DSM-IV reflects the belief of physicians, teachers, and psychologists over the years that persisting problems in regulating both attentional processes and motor behavior are part of a distinct syndrome frequently seen in clinical settings (Wender, 1995). Originally, terms such as "hyperactivity," "hyperkinesis," and "minimal brain dysfunction" were used to characterize the condition, which was believed to involve various forms of mild central nervous system impairment. So strong was the association between excessive activity and underlying brain impairment that the corresponding diagnostic terms were used interchangeably for years. In practice, the nature of this deficit was seldom specified, owing to the wide range of disorders and conditions that may have hyperactivity as an associated symptom. This caused endless confusion among professionals and considerable anxiety on the part of parents whose children were labeled as having "minimal brain damage" or the "hyperkinetic syndrome."

More recent research, however, strongly suggests that neither attentional problems nor hyperactivity should *necessarily* be assumed to involve CNS damage (Gomez and Sanson, 1994; Silver, 1992). Current research has amply documented the fact that genetic (especially), physiological dysfunction, nutritional, motivational, social, and environmental factors all may play important roles in the regulation and allocation of attentional capabilities.

INDIVIDUAL HISTORY VARIABLES OFTEN NOTED IN HYPERACTIVE CHILDREN

Family history of hyperactivity or learning disability	Poor coordination	Disturbed by loud noises
	Difficulties with speech, writing, reading, spelling	Mirror writing
Mother's trauma or illness during pregnancy		Letter reversals
Mother's substance abuse	Conduct problems in general, especially if little evidence of guilt or remorse	Visual disturbances
		Severe headaches
Oxygen disruption during delivery		Fainting
	Preference for very bland or overly spiced foods	Impulsivity
Problems or trauma during delivery		Aversive to peers and/or caretakers
	Tendency towards food "addictions" and/or allergies	
Perceived from early on as "overactive"		Migraines
	Transfixed by high-action TV or movies	Convulsions
Slow development		
High fevers	Behavior problems in school	Epilepsy

Head banging, knee-elbow rocking	Left-handedness	EEG abnormality, or if "normal" some non-specific abnormalities
Hyperkinesis	Easily distracted	
Reduced attention	Disturbed by bright lights	

ADHD occurs at an apparent consensus rate of about 3–8% (3–5% by DSM-IV estimates) with about a 5:1 ratio of males to females, and with an even higher ratio for the more active and aggressive forms (Silver, 1992; Robe, 1987). Approximately 25% of first-degree relatives of children diagnosed with ADHD also have this disorder.

The DSM–IV defines two alternate criteria sets for ADHD—fulfilling Criterion A1, along with the standard criteria for the diagnosis, that is, (1) some of the symptoms had to be present before age 7; (2) some impairment from symptoms in at least two settings; and (3) clear evidence of impairment in social, academic, or occupational functioning results in the diagnosis of Attention-Deficit/Hyperactivity Disorder, Predominantly Inattention Type (314.00)). Fulfilling Criterion A2 plus the standard criteria is required for the diagnosis of Attention-Deficit/Hyperactivity Disorder, Predominantly Hyperactive-Impulsive Type (314.01). If both Criterion sets A1 and A2 as well as the standard criteria are met, the diagnosis is Attention-Deficit Disorder, Combined Type (314.01).

To fulfil Criterion set A1, at least six of the following must have persisted for six months, they occur "often," are maladaptive, and are inconsistent with developmental level: (1) carelessness with details or making careless mistakes; (2) difficulty in sustaining attention in tasks or play; (3) difficulties in organizing tasks and activities; (4) avoidance, aversion to or reluctance to be in tasks requiring sustained mental effort; (5) frequent loss of things necessary for tasks or activities; (6) easy distraction by external stimuli; (7) forgetfulness.

Criterion set A2, with the same prerequisites (e.g., "often," six months' duration, etc.), is fulfilled by six of the following (the first six are sublabeled Hyperactive, the second three as Impulsive, but this does not really affect the diagnosis): (1) fidgets with hands or feet or squirms in seat, (2) leaves seat when expected to stay, (3) runs or climbs excessively (in adolescents or adults, a subjective feeling of restlessness is enough), (4) has difficulty in staying in quiet play or leisure, (5) is always "on the go" or appears "driven by a motor," (6) talks excessively, (7) blurts out responses before question completed, (8) has difficulties in awaiting turn, (9) interrupts or intrudes on others.

☐ ## RELATED DIAGNOSTIC CONSIDERATIONS

In many ADHD cases a neuropsychological evaluation (see preceding section) and/or an evaluation for possible retardation (see upcoming section) are indicated (Anderson, 1994). In any case a thorough assessment for ADHD includes an evaluation of the following factors: (1) the client's overall behavioral repertoire and patterns of interactions with the environment, (2) patterns of motor activity, and (3) how the person typically approaches and works through tasks. Evaluations should include a multimethod assessment that includes structured and unstructured interviews with parents and the adolescent, direct observation in the natural setting, self-report measures, completion of behavior rating scales by parents and teachers, intelligence and achievement tests, and specific assessments such as a continuous performance test (CPT) (e.g., the Gordon Diagnostic System, the Porteus Maze, Jumbled Numbers Game, the Child Behavior Checklist [CBCL], the Connors Parent-Rating Scale-Revised (CPRS-R), etc.) (DuPaul et al., 1991). By the time an evaluation has been completed, a person with ADHD may well have been assessed by pediatricians, teachers, psychologists, and parents. Each of these individuals has relevant information to the overall decision.

TYPES OF HYPERACTIVITY

Of course some cases will not fit neatly into any category, but an alternative and helpful conceptualization is that there are four major types of hyperactivity (Robe, 1987; Silver, 1992). The least common is environmentally generated hyperactivity, about 5–10% of all hyperactive children. This type may even be labeled "pseudohyperactivity," as it has no significant biologic component, unlike the other three forms of hyperactivity.

The two major causes of environmentally generated hyperactivity are a severe stress, such as loss of a parent or child abuse, and the child's having been spoiled in such a way that he or she has never learned to deal with limits on activity. Not surprisingly, the parents of the latter type of hyperactive child do not see the behavior as nearly the problem that teachers and day-care workers do.

A common characteristic of such children is an absence of hyperactivity before the trauma or hyperactive behavior only in certain situations, for example, where limits are not clear or are not enforced. Treatment for such children includes anxiety-reduction techniques if stress is involved and school consultations and family therapy to teach the teachers and parents how to more effectively set limits.

A second pattern is stimulant- or food-facilitated hyperactivity. Some people have argued that certain foods or food additives cause the majority of hyperactive cases. It soon became apparent to most experts that this was erroneous, but many experts do agree that these factors can be a significant facilitator in about 10–15% of hyperactive cases. Such children often manifested food allergies as early as infancy and may show standard allergy patterns.

Such children also show more unpredictable outbursts of hyperactivity than do the other forms of hyperactivity, although they are especially likely to increase their hyperactivity after certain meals. Commonly suspected culprits here are foods high in simple sugars, foods high in additives and preservatives, chocolate, and milk, egg, or wheat products. It's important to note that the range of foods that could be the cause of such behavior is wider than originally imagined.

Naturally, the focus of treatment is to eliminate those foods that facilitate the hyperactivity. However, this should only be done after an exhaustive survey of food intake and related behaviors. For example, for a minimum of two weeks, and often longer, parents should keep a log of all foods the child eats, including the lists of ingredients. An hourly behavior chart is also kept. These are very time-consuming tasks, but if they are not diligently carried out, the problem substance will escape discovery. All of this should be done in consultation with the child's pediatrician.

If the hyperactivity is food-facilitated, certain consistent patterns should become clear. Those foods can then be systematically eliminated, and the hyperactivity should diminish. If the hyperactivity does not lessen, one of the other and more common hyperactivity patterns should be considered—overstimulated (overactive) hyperactivity, which accounts for about 30% of all cases of hyperactivity, or understimulated (underactive) hyperactivity, which accounts for approximately half of all cases of hyperactivity.

In spite of the opposite labels, children in both of these patterns show high levels of activity and distractibility. Also, unlike environmentally generated hyperactivity, both patterns start becoming evident even in early childhood. Table 11.6 highlights the characteristics and differences between these two major hyperactive patterns.

OTHER TEST-RESPONSE PATTERNS

For a young adult who is still diagnosable as ADHD, elevations on the MMPI-2 scales 4, 6, 8, and 9 are probable. The expectations for those in the population that would come to clinical detection would be that about half would fit in the category of conduct disorder. If there is a lack of reported violent behaviors, expect a 4-9/9-4 profile. A 2-4/4-2 profile would also be a possibility. The high 9 should be especially prominent in those patients who are still experiencing an active episode.

Scale 4 often co-varies with the degree of resentment over constraints on overactivity, and their score also indicates how they will react to later constraints and rules. As 2 rises, indicating a whining, dissatisfied component over constraints, a lack of activity/emotion outlets is more likely.

On the 16 PF (or more likely the HSPQ, since this type of referral question is more likely to occur in adolescents), low scores on Q_3 and B are most probable, with high scores on O, L, and M also being likely. On the MCMI-III, scale N is most likely to be high, with V high to the degree the attention span is actually limited. To the degree an antisocial component has developed, scale 6 would be high.

On both the Rorschach and TAT, ADHD clients are likely to show the general affects of impulsivity and distraction (see Chapter 10). They may end out with long response times, show a confused sequential analysis of the blot or picture, and tend to stay with Popular responses or stories. Boundary/containment response issues are common. Parts may be missed: For example, Bellak (1986) noted that the failure to even identify the violin in TAT card 1 has been

TABLE 11.6   Characteristics of Major Hyperactive Patterns

OVERACTIVE (OVERSTIMULATED) HYPERACTIVITY (30%)	UNDERACTIVE (UNDERSTIMULATED) HYPERACTIVITY (50%)
Child carries a high level of neuro-physiological arousal, so is highly "stimulation-respondent"	Child carries a low level of neuro-physiological arousal, relative to psychological needs, so is highly "stimulation-seeking"
Responds reasonably well to "quiet time" or stimulus-reduction methods; responds to standard "time-out" wherein stimuli are highly restricted	Has difficulty calming down at "quiet time"; needs some structured activity even during "time-out" or will quickly be disruptive or destructive; liable to be excessively spanked, as shows little response to it.
Becomes somewhat calmer as evening progresses; will usually fall asleep easily enough, but is a restless sleeper, and hard to awaken.	Has difficulty going to bed and to sleep—"the tireder they get, the worse they are"—but usually sleeps soundly. Often awakens early and is ready to go right away.
Likes TV, but can be easily over-stimulated by it; often has to do other things while watching TV.	Likes TV, especially highly stimulating programs, but can sit for hours in front of such programs, as if hypnotized.
Is overstimulated and has difficulty "coming down" from periods of physical activity.	Can be calmed by long periods of intense physical activity.
Is finicky eater. Doesn't like green vegetables or strong-flavored foods, like broccoli, curry, etc. Favorite foods are bland, like macaroni and cheese, meat, potatoes; often will use cheese or sauces to mask flavors.	Usually enjoys a number of strong-flavored foods; will quickly over-season and oversugar foods. Loves colorful, oversweetened, novelty breakfast cereals. (These children are the perfect target for the Saturday morning cartoon advertisement.)
Often shows hyperactive response in new situations or to changes in routine. The more consistent, structured, and calm the home and school environment, the better the child behaves.	Often is well behaved in new situations, but gets progressively worse as newness wears off (so clinicians may need to schedule several sessions in order to see the problem behavior emerge). Constantly seeks more stimulating environment.
Stimulant medications (e.g., Ritalin, Cylert) are seldom markedly effective, and moderate to high doses may make matters worse. Small doses of mild tranquilizers or sedatives help in some cases. May show sedation from over-the-counter medications containing codeine or antihistamines.	Stimulant medications are usually effective (such children may even be calmed by coffee or tea) as preparation for therapy and retraining. When high doses are needed to control behavior, ability to learn effectively may be impaired.

observed in numerous ADHD cases. On the Rorschach a higher number of Animal responses and delayed responses to the color cards are expected.

ADHD adolescents are likely to attempt performance drawings brusquely and rapidly (Oster and Gould, 1987). Where there is an associated spatial dyslexia, drawings of a face tend to be "neolithic" (there is no separation of the nose from the forehead and no suggestion of a nose bridge). To the degree they are also emotionally disturbed, they are likely to show a confused order of drawings, overly large drawings, and boxed figures (Rossini and Kaspar, 1987). Watching them attempt the drawings may be at least as instructive as what the drawings actually produce. They may be distracted easily and may make this apparent by glancing around the room, investigating distracting objects, fidgeting, or drawing objects that are different from those requested. Because ADHD tends to result in a lower school performance, related concerns may lead such individuals to draw figures that reflect strong feelings of inadequacy and guilt, and they sometimes describe their drawings as stupid or crazy.

TREATMENT OPTIONS

Therapy of some sort is critical for these cases as the long-term effects of hyperactivity on both academic and social adjustment are negative. Hyperactivity is, of course, a precursor to academic failure (hence, a skill-building package is essential to any treatment program), but hyperactivity can also be a precursor to a wide variety of other patterns, such as schizophrenia and criminality. Both family therapy and parent-training techniques are necessary for most cases (Gomez and Sanson, 1994; Dangel and Polster, 1986). Part of the family therapy should be directed toward helping parents and siblings reduce the stress, guilt, and wear-and-tear these children generate in these families. The parents of such a child are apt to heartily agree with the following classic quip: "Life begins when the children leave home and the dog dies."

Approximately 70–80% of school-age ADHD children do respond with at least some improvement to stimulant medications. The quantity and quality of a child's response are "rate-dependent"; that is, the higher the drug-free rate of the child's problem behavior(s), the more effective the medication is beyond the effects of regression to the mean. Amphetamine was first employed for the treatment of hyperactivity in 1937. Chemotherapy with methylphenidate (Ritalin), introduced into common usage in the 1960s, and related substances (e.g., Cylert) is now a common approach (Sylvester and Kreusi, 1994). Clonidine, an alpha-adrenergic stimulating agent whose action consists of inhibiting noradrenergic activity, has been increasing in popularity. All of these medications have significant side effects, including inhibition of growth in height and weight, if used for any significant length of time. Yet, they do lead to improvement in many ADHD children and adolescents, which leads to some difficult cost–benefit clinical questions. Imipramine is now often used in ADHD cases where there is evidence of a depressive component. There are also ADHD cases where a genetic defect related to thyroid hormone regulation is apparently a significant factor, and thyroid regulation will be a primary treatment here.

A variety of behavioral and cognitive behavioral techniques have proven helpful for ADHD (Silver, 1992; DuPaul et al., 1991). The main drawbacks with these techniques are the high cost in personnel time and the problems of generalization of effects. If there is a neuropsychological problem, specific rehabilitative efforts are usually required (Anderson, 1994). For older children and adolescents with ADHD, a support therapy group can be helpful.

■ Mental Retardation

Mental retardation is another common referral problem for the clinician; it has traditionally been agreed that about 1% of the population falls into this category (Borthwick-Duffy, 1994; American Association on Mental Retardation, 1993; Berk, 1989). The DSM-IV requires indication of significantly subaverage intellectual functioning (Criterion A) (an I.Q. of 70 or below, although testing measurement error, approximately 5 points, would allow a diagnosis up to an I.Q. of 75) in a standardized, individually administered test, and onset before the age of 18 (Criterion C). Also required (Criterion B) is evidence of significant limitation in adaptive functioning in at least two of the following skill areas: communication, self-care, home living, social/interpersonal skills, use of community resources, self-direction, functional academic skills, work, leisure, health, and safety. It's good that an I.Q. score is required, as it appears that the majority of the population would qualify on Criterion B. The criteria for severity and descriptors and interventions, by age, are found in Table 11.7.

If there is good reason to believe that significant intellectual retardation is present with functioning at least below an approximate I.Q. of 70, and for some reason the individual is untestable, the term Mental Retardation, Severity Unspecified (319) is used. The diagnosis of Borderline Intellectual Functioning (V62.89), encoded on Axis II requires evidence of problems in adaptive coping and an I.Q. of 71 to 84.

Since the MMPI-2 requires approximately an eighth-grade reading level, it is seldom administered to most mentally retarded persons, although the taped version can be used effectively, or it can be read to the client (the reader is referred to the initial portion of Chapter 12 on the clinical correlates of the MMPI-2). Regardless of which method of administration is used, such clients sometimes respond with a random response pattern (Sabine and Meyer, 1992) (see the section on malingering).

Aside from the overall scores obtained on the WAIS-R, there are certain trends in the subtest patterns of mentally retarded individuals. First, they score relatively high on object assembly, whereas persons with CNSI score low. Performance subtests may exceed the verbal subtests, but this is not always the case. Academically oriented tests, such as information and arithmetic, are usually low. Also, the similarities test is relatively low, while comprehension, picture completion, and digit span are higher.

TABLE 11.7 Criteria for Severity of Mental Retardation, by Age

LEVEL	PRESCHOOL AGE (BIRTH TO 5 YEARS)	SCHOOL AGE (6 TO 12 YEARS)	ADULT (OVER 21 YEARS)
Mild Retardation (I.Q. of 50–55 to 70—by DSM-IV) (about 85% of retarded persons)	Can develop social and language skills; less retardation in sensorimotor areas. Seldom distinguished from normal until older. Referred to as "educable."	Can learn academic skills to approximately sixth-grade level by late teens. Cannot learn general high school subjects. Needs special education, particularly at secondary school levels.	Capable of social and vocational adequacy with proper education and training. Frequently needs guidance when under serious social or economic stress.
Moderate Retardation (I.Q. of 35–40 to 50–55) (10% of retarded persons)	Can talk or learn to communicate. Poor social awareness. Fair motor development. May profit from self-help; can be managed with moderate supervision.	Can learn functional academic skills to approximately fourth-grade level by late teens if given special education.	Capable of self-maintenance in unskilled or semiskilled occupations. Needs supervision and guidance when under mild social or economic stress.
Severe Retardation (I.Q. of 20–25 to 35–40) (3–4% of retarded persons)	Poor motor development. Speech is minimal. Few or no communication skills. Generally unable to profit from training in self help.	Can talk or learn to communicate. Can be trained in elemental health habits. Cannot learn functional academic skills. Profits from systematic habit training.	Can contribute partially to self-support under complete supervision. Can develop self-protection skills to a minimally useful level in a controlled environment.
Profound Retardation (I.Q. of 20–25 or below) (1–2% of retarded persons)	Minimal capacity for functioning in sensorimotor areas. Needs nursing care.	Some motor development present. Cannot profit from training in self-help. Needs total care.	Some motor and speech development. Totally incapable of self-maintenance. Needs complete care and supervision.

Adapted in part from J. M. Sattler, *Assessment of Children's Intelligence and Special Abilities* (Boston: Allyn and Bacon, 1982), p. 426.

On the Rorschach a low number of overall responses is usually obtained, containing a low F+%, a high F%, few or poor M responses, and a high percentage of Animal responses. When W responses are made, they are of poor quality. Repetitive and perseverative content occurs, and apparently impulsive inferences to content from the stimuli of the blots are common. On the Bender-Gestalt, changes in angulation, closure difficulty, irregular use of space and sequence, a probability of rotations, and collision tendencies are noted. Simplistic drawings, such as attachment of the appendages to the head, are seen on the Draw-A-Person Test in more severely retarded persons.

A wide variety of interventions are necessary to effectively deal with mental retardation and its associated problems (Borthwick-Duffy, 1994; American Association on Mental Retardation, 1993). Those with less impairment profit most from psycho-educational and social-skills interventions, and the greater the degree of impairment, the more necessary are the various behavioral interventions (Matson and Gardner, 1991).

CHAPTER 12

Clinical Correlates of the MMPI-2

Collecting the classical descriptors and correlates of such tests as the MMPI-2 has been carried out throughout the years by numerous authors, mainly through an accrual process. Those authors and the senior author of this volume owe much to many other clinicians and researchers who have contributed their ideas and data. In this section on the MMPI-2 I have taken material from my own experience and integrated it with both the classical and recent sources of clinical interpretation of the MMPI-2, primarily those noted earlier (see Table 1.1 in Chapter 1).

■ MMPI-2

The Minnesota Multiphasic Personality Inventory, published in its original form in 1943, was then revised into a second edition that was first published in 1989 (MMPI-2). MMPI-2 is composed of 567 (as opposed to 556 in the original form) self-reference statements that cover topics from physical condition through social history, emotional states, social attitudes, and moral belief systems. Clients are encouraged to answer every question, though they often skip a few, and their only answer options are true or false.

The MMPI test was originated by Starke Hathaway, a medical psychologist, and Jovian McKinley, a neuropsychiatrist, who at the time were working at the University of Minnesota Hospitals. Hathaway and McKinley accumulated a large collection of self-reference statements from textbooks, psychological reports, and other tests. They eventually limited their pool of statements to the 504 they thought were relatively independent of one another. They hoped that they could develop a test that would substantially aid in the routine psychological examinations given there, though, ironically, Hathaway has stated that he only expected it to be used locally.

Hathaway and McKinley first administered the test to groups of normals and to patients in the following clinical groups: Hypochondriasis, Depression, Hysteria, Psychopathic Deviant, Paranoia, Psychasthenia, Schizophrenia, and

Hypomania. They performed an item analysis in order to detect which items significantly differentiated these groups. In the second stage the scales derived from that item analysis were administered to groups of normals and patients who had those specific clinical diagnoses already assigned, and after adequate cross-validation, the scales were accepted into the test. It was only later that the Masculinity-Femininity (Mf) scale was added, with the original purpose of differentiating heterosexual males from homosexual males. The final addition to the basic scales, the Social Introversion (Si) scale, was initially used to distinguish female college students who were socially retiring from those who were active in a number of extracurricular activities. Only later was this scale generalized to males.

The original MMPI was the most widely used personality test in the world, as is MMPI-2 now. The revised MMPI, MMPI-2, published in 1989, was improved by rewriting dated, difficult, and sexist items. Religious items, sixteen repeated items (originally included only to facilitate machine scoring), and approximately fifty items found to be useless were eliminated. Yet, over all, only relatively small changes occurred in the items that contribute to the three Validity scales and the ten basic Clinical scales, which can be scored if the client completes the first 370 items. This was fortunate, as it left the essence and great bulk of all the research concerning these scales directly applicable to MMPI-2 (Ben-Porath & Butcher, 1989; Graham, 1993; Harrell et al., 1992; Clavelle, 1992).

In the latter part of MMPI-2, items 371 to 567, substantial changes were made (Graham et al., 1991; Butcher et al., 1990; Ben-Porath & Butcher, 1989). This allowed the development of new scales and provided information in areas not directly tapped by the original form, for example, suicide, orientation to therapy, attitudes toward work, mental and eating disorder items, and others.

The most significant early criticism of the MMPI-2 normative group (2600 individuals) was that it was more highly educated than the general population. The criticism was technically correct, except that it was made in comparison to 1980 census data. Census data in 1990 revealed a marked increase in the educational level of the populace, and that trend was predicted to continue. So, the original difference in 1989 was much smaller than critics apparently realized, and (possibly inadvertently), the MMPI-2 is well designed in this dimension for the long run. In any case, a major virtue of the MMPI-2 is that the normative data show that education level has been virtually eliminated as a variable in the interpretation of the basic scales. Post-graduate males average about 5 points higher on scale 5 (they averaged much higher on the original scales), and more educated individuals certainly score lower on L. But these are the only major differences.

Also, in the MMPI-2 normative sample, from the perspective of the accuracy of clinical and behavioral inferences, the highly educated and blacks do not score significantly differently than does the general population, so separate norms are not needed. Differences by sex are found, but these are incorporated into the scoring and then in the clinical interpretations. Females are a bit more likely to show peaks on 3 and 6, and males on 1, 4, and 7.

Sabine and Meyer (1994) collected data on lower-class persons, including a substantial portion of homeless persons, a group underrepresented in the MMPI-2 normative group. This disenfranchised, lower-class group showed much more pathology, almost approximating a "fake-bad" profile. No doubt this reflects a greater level of pathology per se. However, we believe it also reflects a response set in this group, that is, putting your worst foot forward does not result in the same negative societal reinforcements that occur when a middle-class individual takes this approach. Not using the K correction may give a truer portrayal of such a lower-class individual on MMPI-2.

Concomitantly, MMPI-A was developed for use with adolescents age 14–18, and according to Archer (1992) can also be used with 12- and 13-year-olds who show adequate maturity. A seventh-grade reading level is required for the written version; an I.Q. of 70 and a third-grade education level for alternate administrations. Supervision of the testing environment is even more important than with adults. MMPI-A has 478 items, and the first 370 must be completed to score the basic scales. Taking developmental issues into account, most of the interpretive commentary generated from the MMPI and MMPI-2 research literature can be applied to MMPI-A (Archer, 1992; Butcher and Williams, 1992).

The MMPI-2 can be administered individually or in a group and can be hand or machine scored. There are a number of short versions of the MMPI-2, but they have many drawbacks in reliability and validity. National Computer Systems (NCS), by agreement with the University of Minnesota, has the copyright to the MMPI. Only they, or their leasors, have a legal right to sell a program to score the MMPI. There is some indication that computerized administration may produce lower overall profiles, yet, using T scores, clinicians may develop their own computerized *interpretation* program. However, it is clear that any clinician who then uses such a program is ultimately responsible for its use—its report should be used as a guideline, and the clinician is responsible to know how adequate the program is that he or she is using, and, outside of NCS's service, that is hard to know.

NCS, although it says it does not desire to do so, is required by state laws to market to nonpsychiatric physicians. Unfortunately, virtually all of them (and numerous mental health practitioners, for that matter) have little or no training beyond a couple of weekend workshops, if that. Use by such individuals without a consult by someone more expert is unethical. The only recourse to control such use is through a civil liability suit, or a complaint to the appropriate state licensing agency or professional association.

A number of clinicians use a computer terminal. The client may take the test at the terminal or the answer sheet can be directly fed into the terminal; in either case, the results are quickly provided to the clinician. No significant differences have been found between taking it by hand or at a computer. (See also the comments on computer-generated reports in Chapter 18.) Any computerized interpretation of an MMPI-2 protocol should always be first routed through a clinician who has had *substantial* training in MMPI-2 interpretation, since that clinician can consider the profile in light of the many and often subtle particulars of an individual case that are not fed into the computer.

The raw data from the MMPI-2 are translated into T scores. These are the scores that are eventually coded onto the profile sheet. Separate norms are available for males and females. After any initial scoring, a K correction is added to the raw scores obtained for scales Hs (1), Pd (4), Pt (7), Sc (8), and Ma (9), although there is some evidence that this can lead to more false positives and fewer false negatives in diagnosis (Hsu, 1986).

There are two major coding systems for use with the MMPI-2. Hathaway's (1947) was the original system, although the more complete system developed by Welsh (1948) is far more commonly used. The reader is referred to Graham (1993) for a detailed discussion of his adaptation of this method. As an example of his adapted Welsh code, the following profile has been coded from the T scores:

$$7^* \ 2'' \ 1' \ 8\text{-+} \ 46/\text{:}\underline{35\#} \ 0 \text{ to the right of } \#9$$

What this actually says is that:

7*	Scale 7 is 90 T to 99 T
2"	Scale 2 is between 80 and 89
1'	Scale 1 is between 70 and 79
8-	Scale 8 is between 60 and 64
46/	Scales 4 and 6 are between 50 and 59
/:	The juxtaposition of two break symbols (/ and :) indicates no score was in the T range of the one to the right—in this case, 40–49 range
35#	# indicates scales 3 and 5 are between 30 and 39 T; the underlining states that they are within 1 T-score point of each other

To the right of #9 indicates that scale 9 is 29 T or less

If a scale(s) was in the 100–109 T range, those scale numbers would be preceded by **; if in the 110–119 range, by '; if above 120, by ".

While there is no inherent upper age-level limit for the MMPI-2, only individuals with at least an eighth-grade reading level and 18 years of age can validly complete the MMPI-2 (Paolo et al., 1991). Those with less than an eighth-grade reading level take the test by having someone read the items to them or by listening to an audiotape. However, they must also be able to comprehend the items.

One might ask why a sixth- to seventh-grade reading level was deemed appropriate for the original form, but an eighth-grade level is the rule of thumb for MMPI-2, especially when an attempt was made to reduce problematic language and concepts. Quite simply, it reflects an overall drop in reading skill in the populace. Hence, an eighth-grade reading level today is about the same level of skill as a sixth- to seventh-grade reading level twenty-five years ago.

Average reading difficulty was computed for the 567 items and 61 sub/ special scales of the MMPI-2 (Paolo et al., 1991). The mean for all items was

600.02 (SD = 304.57), which essentially corresponds to a fifth-grade reading level. Approximately 90% of the items require less than a ninth-grade reading level; three items require a high school education or more. The Amorality (Mal) subscale has the highest requirement, an average reading level greater than eighth grade. The scale 9 subscales were the most demanding. For persons with low reading ability, interpretation of the nine subscales should be made cautiously, and use of the taped version is recommended (Sabine and Meyer, 1992).

Both the normal and abnormal profiles of adolescents differ from those of adults; when dealing with adolescents, the adolescent form of the test (MMPI-A) should be used (Archer, 1992; Butcher and Williams, 1992). As noted, the MMPI-A is for use with adolescents in the 14–18 age range, whereas MMPI-2 is appropriate for 18-year-olds and up. With an 18-year-old, I'm inclined to use the MMPI-2, because of the more extensive data accumulated on it, but one might consider whether that person has started to drop an adolescent lifestyle and is beginning to accept some primary responsibility for taking care of adult-level needs, and only use the MMPI-2 in such cases.

Clinicians have often used "critical items" on the MMPI-2, and the best set, the Koss-Butcher items, is scored by NCS. Critical items are usually single items whose content is used to cue the clinician to further inquiry in that area or to indicate a problem because of the face validity of the item. The problem with using any one of them is that each is a one-item scale and consequently has extremely low reliability. A number of sets of these critical items have been used historically, but most have not consistently predicted the behavior they seem to reflect. Additionally, most of them are loaded with items to which the deviant response is "true," which leaves them open to a "yes-saying" bias. In addition, many of them overlap too highly with the F scale and may reflect a tendency to fake-bad.

If the clinician uses them, a perusal of critical items marked by the client is worthwhile. For one thing, clients who admit to these face-valid items usually feel that they have communicated directly to the clinician and may be quite surprised if the later content of a clinical contact indicates a lack of awareness about these issues. An extremely high level of endorsement of critical items may be indicative of malingering.

In proceeding through the individual scales of the MMPI-2 here, there will be descriptions of each scale, along with overall behavior correlates, correlates of high and low scores on each scale, some patterns the clinician can expect from the scale interrelationships, and guidelines for developing and using code types.

In the traditional clinical interpretation approach to the MMPI-2, authors referred to the basic clinical scale name rather than its number. As the years passed, however, it became clear that the actual behavioral correlates of a scale have not always matched the originally applied scale name. Therefore, the scale numbers, rather than names, are used throughout this text. The traditional names are listed here for the sake of convenience.

SCALE NUMBER	TRADITIONAL SCALE NAME
1	Hypochondriasis (Hs)
2	Depression (D)
3	Hysteria (Hy)
4	Psychopathic Deviant (Pd)
5	Masculinity-Femininity (Mf)
6	Paranoia (Pa)
7	Psychasthenia (Pt)
8	Schizophrenia (Sc)
9	Hypomania (Ma)
0	Social Introversion (Si)

It is common to hear persons experienced in the use of MMPI-2 referring to individuals as, say, "a high 4" or "4-8." These shorthand descriptors are helpful as an abbreviated communication of various behavioral descriptions. In general, a high score on the MMPI-2 (and MMPI-A) is one above 65 T; moderately high is a score of from 60 to 65 T; moderately low is from 40 to 45 T; and low is below 40 T.

A more precise understanding is gained by periodically referring to Table 12.1. While MMPI-1 was plotted in linear T scores, in MMPI-2 the basic clinical scales, with the exception of the validity scales (L, F and K) and scales 5 (MF) and 0 (Si), are plotted in uniform T scores. Also, the MMPI-2 Content scores are in uniform T scores. Thus, a T score of 65, whether it is on scale 2 (D) or 4 (Pa), or one of the content scales like ANX (Anxiety) or BIZ (Bizarre Mentation), indicates that approximately 8% of the MMPI-2 normative group scored at this point or higher. With a T score of 40, no matter which of these scales it is

TABLE 12.1   Percentile Equivalents for K-Corrected T-Scores
(Applies to the basic Clinical scales, except L, F, K, 5 (MF) and 0 (Si), and also to the Content scales)

UNIFORM T SCORE	PERCENTILE EQUIVALENT
30	<1
35	4
40	15
45	34
50	55
55	73
60	85
65	92
70	96
75	98
80	99

Source: Auke Tellegen, Department of Psychology, University of Minnesota, Minneapolis, MN 55455; data from MMPI Restandardization Project.

on, you know that approximately 15% of the normative group scored lower than this. Note that the supplemental scales, for example, Anxiety (A), Repression (R), Ego Strength (Es), and the Harris-Lingoes subscales are *not* in uniform T scores. Thus, a T score of 65 will tell you nothing about the percentage of persons in the normative sample scoring above or below this point on that scale; *however,* whatever the distribution, the concept of the T score—that is, that this is clinically high or low or whatever—does apply.

The traditional conceptualization of the MMPI-2 scales depicted below gives a schema that many clinicians find useful. It should never be applied in a hard-and-fast manner, but as a guideline.

Similarly, two other overall guidelines may be helpful. First, a "positive slope" on the clinical scales—that is, distinctly lower on 1, 2, 3, and 4, relative to 6, 7, 8, and 9—suggests an individual with poor day-to-day functioning, to the point where institutionalization or other forms of external control may be necessary. "Negative slope," the opposite phenomenon, suggests significant emotional turmoil and dissatisfaction with life; yet the ability to maintain day-to-day functioning is usually maintained. Second, if two of the traditional clinical scales (1, 2, 3, 4, 6, 7, 8, and 9) are above 65 T, or if one scale is above 70 T, some form of intervention often is or will be necessary.

■ Individual Scale Interpretations

This section gives the correlates of 1-point codes. It is followed by a section that delineates 2-point codes, as well as the rarer data available on 3-point codes, and information on how these codes are affected by scores on the other basic scales.

Several guidelines for interpretation are suggested:

1. Use a "well-defined" breakpoint to establish a code type, that is, at least a difference of 5 points or more between the two scales. The greater the differ-

FIGURE 12.1 Traditional Conceptualization of MMPI-2

	SOCIAL DEPENDENCY		HOSTILITY; ACTING-OUT
Self-Blame **(Neuroticism)**	D (2) ←	Activity Level → Ma (9)	**Self-Aggrandizement** **(Psychopathy)**
	Pt (7) ←	Behavioral Control → Pd (4)	
Somatic and/or Self-Pity **(Psychophysiological)**		Compliance Trust	**Reality Contact** **(Psychosis)**
	Hs (1) ←	→ Pa (6)	
	Hy (3) ←	Attachment, Thought Clarity → Sc (8)	

ence, the more confidence you have in making a code-type interpretation. The more well defined the code type, the more likely it is to be predictive of that individual over time.

2. For your primary interpretation, use the most complex well-defined code type for which data are available. For example, presume there is at least a 5-point T score difference between the highest and the second-highest T scores (which gives you a well-defined 1-point code, that is, the top score). Presume also a 5-point T score difference between the second- and third-highest scores (which gives you a well-defined 2-point code, that is, the top score and then the second highest). If there are interpretive data available for the 2-point code, which is likely, make your primary interpretation from that information base, and then supplement it with data from the well-defined 1-point code, that is, the top score. If there was also a well-defined break between the third- and fourth-highest T scores, and data were available on that 3-point code, that would provide your primary interpretive base.

3. If there is a well-defined break between the third- and fourth-highest scores, that is, a 3-point code, but no data is available for interpreting that 3-point code, use the code type of the two highest scores for your primary interpretation, whether or not there is a 5-point break between these two top scores.

4. If there is no well-defined code type with an available interpretation information base, go to individual scale interpretation, although you will also likely find it useful to check with the most clearly defined (as close to 5 T score points as feasible) 1-, 2-, or 3-point code type(s), and integrate these to the degree feasible, realizing you have to place less confidence in the available interpretations to the degree a code type cannot be differentiated.

5. Within some clinical scales (i.e., 2, 3, 4, 6, 8, and 9) the Harris-Lingoes scales (discussed at greater length later in this chapter) can be used to analyze the relative weights of factors contributing to any elevated score. These scales derive from a systematic analysis of subgroups of related construct and content items within those clinical scales. This analysis was refined during the development of MMPI-2. These scales are especially useful to (a) resolve inconsistencies within the MMPI-2 (see #6), (b) analyze why a client receives an elevation that was not expected from history or observation data and (c) help interpret scores that are marginally elevated (T = 60–65).

6. To resolve apparent inconsistencies (e.g., high on 2 and 9, or even 2 and 4), use the following decision rules in sequence: (a) Presume the inconsistency really is only apparent, and analyze the data from that perspective; (b) if one prong of the inconsistency comes from a code-type interpretation and one from a single-scale interpretation (e.g., a Harris-Lingoes subscale), accept the code-type interpretation as it is based on more data; (c) when the inconsistency derives from two scales, give greater weight to the higher score; (d) give greater weight to the better researched scales—e.g., clinical scales over content scales, the MAC over scale 4 if the question is specific to addiction; (e) if all else fails, accept the inconsistency as unresolvable from these data, and look to other data.

7. Use the following table when reading the individual scale interpretations (yet remembering that all 1-point differences are comparable, that is, a 65 T is no more different from a 64 T than a 62 T is from a 61 T).

INTERPRETATION	T SCORE
Very Low	38 and below
Low	44 and below
Normal	45–57
Moderate	58–64
High	65 and above
Very High	75 and above

8. Because of better norming procedures, the test taker is more likely to obtain a low or very low score on an MMPI-2 scale than would have been the case with the MMPI. Hence, one should be more cautious in applying the specific interpretation for low scores detailed in the following pages (many of which evolved from work with the original MMPI). The very conservative approach is that low scores in apparent normals simply indicate better functioning on the variables measured by that particular scale.

THE ? SCALE

On the ?, or "cannot say," scale, it is generally considered that within the first 370 items a raw score of 30 or more renders the profile invalid (although elevated scores may be interpretable), and a score of 20–30 within the first 370 items suggests the profile should be interpreted with considerable caution (Butcher, 1990). Also, consider whether any particular scale is affected by omissions. The ? scale is not actually a scale because it accounts only for the number of items to which the individual has not responded. If a client obtains a high ? score, a reading difficulty should first be considered. If this can be ruled out, gross impairment in the decision making required to give an answer should be considered. If this is not the problem, then obsessive, paranoid, or blatant avoidance issues should be considered. Obsessive clients may feel constrained by the either-or dichotomy in the MMPI-2; rather than commit themselves, they may skip items. Paranoids naturally fear the self-disclosure involved in a number of items and may avoid them.

Obviously an ounce of prevention is the most logical cure for this problem. To the degree you have established some rapport with individuals before they take the MMPI-2, you are more likely to obtain a valid and interpretable profile. Also, clients should be clearly instructed ahead of time to fill out all the items or leave, at most, only a few blank. One has several options in the face of a high ? score. In most instances where many items have been skipped, the clients can be persuaded to answer more questions, which leads to a valid profile. Some clinicians score the items that have been skipped in the direction they feel the clients would have answered them, while other clinicians score them in the significant direction. Such scoring reflects the finding that a nonresponse can refer to either controversial content or decisional ambiguity. In either case the profile should be compared with that obtained by the original scoring.

☐   ## THE L SCALE

The L scale is composed of fifteen items, such as "I do not always tell the truth," that are scored only if they are answered "false." High L scales are seen as more important as a validity indicator in MMPI-2 than in MMPI-1, especially for men (Graham et al., 1991a). Graham argues a T > 60 suggests probable invalidity; others accept a T > 65 or T > 70 cutoff. These face-valid items identify people who, in a naively defensive fashion, present an overly idealistic and perfectionistic portrayal of themselves, especially in areas that bear on moral character or impulse control. Interestingly, high L scores do not totally negate the validity of the profile since they are generally independent of elevations on most other scales. L scales tend to be a bit higher among the elderly. Sophisticated or psychologically minded or well-educated people seldom score high on this scale, as the items are quite transparent. When well-educated clients do score high, they are likely to be repressed and rigid in their personality structure, tense with stereotypic stress-coping styles, and conforming in behavior. Oddly enough, high scores actually seem to predict to underachievement.

A clinician should naturally consider possible deception any time a high score is obtained, although this is usually true only when test takers are not well educated. After considering demographics, the clinician should note that people with high scores generally are naive and defensive about their conflicts, are often unable to perceive the effects of their behavior on others, are inflexible in problem solving, are rigid in thinking, use denial, and have a low tolerance for stress. Persons in occupations where there is a strong demand to present a "good person" image (e.g., a minister) score higher on this scale, whatever their educational level. A high L score is also associated with a denial of any need for help and with an unwillingness to be honest about deficiencies, admit guilt about behavior, or admit to alcohol abuse (Hedlund, 1977). Thus, the groups most likely to score high on this scale are saints, priests, ministers, rabbis, and some prisoners—the prisoners because they are trying to present themselves as "normals." (Prisoners, however, have a poor feel for what normal is since neither they nor their associates are in that range.)

Highly sophisticated individuals who are manipulative and defensive may score low on the L scale, although a low score usually indicates a fairly relaxed and independent individual who has responded openly to the items. A very low score (0–1 raw score) may occasionally be associated with wariness and cynicism, but a moderately low score (2–4) primarily reflects a person who is not particularly defensive, is willing to admit some deficiencies in the self, and is able to communicate reasonably well with others. Finally, a very high score suggests a pathological confusion that may be either organic or functional.

☐   ## THE F SCALE

The F scale consists of sixty items chosen because they were answered as true by fewer than 10% of a normal adult population. They were originally used to pick up on people who didn't read the items with attention and/or ability.

High to very high T scores suggest either marked confusion, significant errors in scoring, inability of the client either to read the items or to understand the directions, random responding, a false claim of negative symptoms, hostility toward the examiner, or for other reasons a clearly invalid profile (Butcher, 1990, 1995). If a reading problem is suspected, simply having the client read the first ten items out loud may clarify the situation. If a reading problem is noted, the use of a tape-recorded version (one available from the Psychological Corporation) is suggested. Extremely high T scores (above 90) may indicate that item response was random or that the client answered true to all questions, was faking-bad, or, if an inpatient, was psychotic. The clinician should rule out organic brain dysfunction in these clients. Gynther et al. (1973a) have shown that high F scores in an adult inpatient population may warrant the term "confused psychotic." If the F is high and K is low, the F score has been pulled up by the schizophrenia scale items (8). In an outpatient population a high F is more likely to indicate some form of an invalid profile. Giving clearer instructions to or confronting and accepting of any hostility in an apparently intact client who produces a high F profile usually results in a subsequent valid test. Since the F scale is highly correlated with scales 6 and 8 (reflecting item overlap), a 6-8/8-6 profile with a high F score may be directly interpreted, though with some caution. If TRIN and VRIN are within acceptable limits and F is > 65 T, at least consider exaggeration or embellishment of problems secondary to acute distress, a plea for assistance, malingering, or other forms of noncompliance. However, generally, F in the T range of 65–80 is more reflective of psychopathology than invalidity.

Moderate T scores (in the range of 58–64) are associated with mild confusion; some significant emotional problems marked by moodiness or agitation; and unconventional and sometimes very deviant religious, social, or political views. Antisocial (acting-out) and withdrawn behaviors are commonly, and paradoxically, associated with these moderate scores in adolescents. But psychotics and those labeled as severe neurotics often have F scale scores in this range, so severe psychopathology must be ruled out. If there are other indications of anxiety, a score in this range may be a plea for help.

Normal to low scores on the F scale are associated with normal response sets, a calm demeanor, and conventional behavior patterns. If the score becomes very low, a denial of psychopathology and even more rigid and conforming personality patterns are likely. Faking-good should also be considered.

In general, to the degree one can rule out an invalid profile (Berry et al., 1991), elevation of the F scale can be considered indicative of overall psychopathology. The higher it is, the more likely it is that there is general psychopathology. Conversely, the lower the F scale, the more likely it is that any existing problems are focused and under control.

THE K SCALE

The K scale consists of thirty items obtained by comparing the responses of disturbed individuals who had normal profiles with normals who also had normal profiles, and it is now generally used to identify faking-good cases, though this should be done with caution (Graham et al., 1991b). Over all, it is easier to identify faking-bad than faking-good. K scale items correlate well with social-desirability scales, by measuring more subtle defensiveness than the L scale. In that sense, they function as a suppressor variable in the other scales (Meehl and Hathaway, 1980). The amount of K contributing to the T scores of other scales should always be considered. K scores are inversely related to elevations on scales 8, 7, and 0.

There is usually a negative correlation between scores on F and K, although certain clients, especially inpatients, may score moderate to high on both. These persons are likely to have a reason for avoiding responsibility for psychopathology, such as in a criminal case. At the same time, they feel the need to be honest, possibly from the urging of an attorney or from a need to use an admission of specific psychopathology to excuse behavior. Well-educated and/or sophisticated individuals score higher on this scale, although the positive deviation from the mean is usually not as marked as it is in the opposite direction on L.

If K > 70, there is a good chance that the profile is invalid. High K (60–70) scores are generally associated with attempts to deny vulnerability and psychopathology. Such persons are unwilling to admit to psychological or physiological deficit, are inclined to blame others for their problems, and as a result are not likely to cooperate in an intervention attempt. They have little insight into their own patterns and are intolerant toward deviant or disturbed behavior in others. A high K indicates resistance to intervention, whereas a normal to moderate elevation (50–60) indicates a good prognosis for treatment change and a good balance in the test-taking approach. In fact, a rise in K is often found with improvement through treatment. Education and income effects are less on K in MMPI-2 than in the original MMPI. The only strong relation with education, K, and clinical scales is with scale 5. The post-graduates show only 5–8 T score points over a low-educated group, and this probably reflects better mental health rather than a validity difference. A high K score generally contraindicates delinquency in adolescents, especially in females, and, indeed, contraindicates antisocial acting-out in general. A generally "false-responding" set will elevate K as twenty-nine of the thirty items are scored by marking "false."

Low K scores suggest possible faking-bad, confusion, and conformist and/or critical and suspicious attitudes. It may indicate weak emotional-behavioral controls and that the person is hurting and/or is feeling vulnerable. Such individuals have low self-esteem, may be surprisingly harsh or clumsy in dealing with others, and thus usually have marked interpersonal problems. Low scores may also represent an exaggeration of problems as a plea for help, excessive openness to the point of masochistical confession; very low scores may indicate a confused state that may be either organic or functional.

The F-K index, long a popular indicator with clinicians (Woychyshyn, 1992), is discussed later with regard to several diagnostic categories. In particular, the reader is referred to the section on malingering for qualifications of the interpretation of this index. It has been traditionally asserted that when the index (in terms of raw scores) is negative and is greater than 12, it indicates a deliberate effort by the client to be seen as emotionally healthy and without vulnerability, and when F-K is positive and more than 11, faking-bad should be considered. Most clinicians now feel that wider differences should be allowed and that the index is more effective in assessing faking-bad than faking-good (Graham et al., 1991b).

It is often worthwhile to consider the profile in both its K-corrected and uncorrected forms. Also, some experts believe that the K correction in its standard form does not always gives a true picture of the pathology. A third perspective is to compensate by K across the board, that is, to consider the clinical scales as being as much too low, in T score points, as K is above 50 T. Thus, if K is at 60 T, look at all clinical scales with an addition of 10 T score points. The standard K-corrected form is most often the best option, but using the other perspectives can generate some interesting hypotheses in cases where one is at a dead end.

TREATMENT PREDICTIONS WITH L, F, AND K COMBINATIONS

In general, if L and K are high and F is low, these persons are poor candidates for psychotherapy. Both conscious and unconscious denial are usually present—problems are perceived as the fault of another person or fate. There may be some acceptance of a strictly biological explanation of disorder. If F is very high and L and K are below average, these clients are saying they are overwhelmed and are not sure they can continue to "hang on." They need "first aid" and/or hospitalization. When F is about 65 and L and K are a bit below 50, these clients admit to having problems but are not in dire need, yet they are reasonably receptive toward therapy. If F is high and L and K are above 60, there is a significant degree of confusion in several directions. This confusion can be functional, organic, or toxic in origin.

THE BACK SIDE F SCALE (F[B])

MMPI-2 includes an additional forty-item validity measure, F(B), the Back Side F scale, to detect deviant responding in scales that trap items after the first 370 items. If the F scale indicates an invalid profile, the F(B) is probably not needed because the whole profile is likely to be invalid. If the F is in the valid range and F(B) is below T = 90, validity is established for the whole set of responses. But if the T score for F is considered valid and F(B) is at a T score greater than 90, cautious interpretation of even the clinical and validity scales is indicated and interpretation of scales based on back-side items can only be made with great caution, as so many of these scales are filled with face-valid items.

Like the F scale, the Back F consists of items (forty in this case) that no more than 10% of the population sample would endorse. Item 281 is the first item to appear in the test.

Most of the interpretive comments that apply to the F scale apply to the Back F as well. Extreme scores (raw score of 23 and above) suggest an invalid profile, psychosis, and/or an adolescent in the midst of an identity crisis. A raw score of 16–22 Back F is comparable to an interpretation of a high score on F, 8–15 to a moderate F score, 3–7 to a normal F, and 2 or less to a low F score.

SCALE 1 (Hs)

Scale 1, traditionally referred to as the Hypochondriasis scale, is composed of thirty-two items that focus on bodily functions and disorders, although in a number of ways it is more of a characterological scale. This scale is relatively unidimensional, the items are reasonably obvious in content, and the complaints embedded in the items are not very specific. Symptoms, if specific, tend to be epigastric. Thus, persons with actual physical disorders are generally below 65 on this scale and are more likely with time to score higher on scale 2 as a reaction to the disorder. Scale 1 is a good indicator of overall pessimism—the higher the score, the more pessimistic the view of the world—and correlates particularly with the channeling of pessimism into somatic concerns and complaints. Higher scores seem to correlate negatively with intellectual ability; those who score high on this scale are often described as dull, unambitious, unenthusiastic, and lacking ease in oral expression (Graham, 1993). Clients with high 1 scores (65 T and above) may be using physical symptoms to focus tension, to express hostility, or to control others. They are nonpsychologically minded and as a result, often are consulting a physician. These individuals can be very frustrating for a physician to deal with. High scores are also associated with clinical depression (usually exogenous rather than endogenous), although this correlation with depression does not usually hold for blacks. High scores on scale 1, unless found in the relatively rare 1-8/8-1 profile, seldom correlate consistently with extreme psychotic processes. T scores greater than 80, however, may indicate somatic delusions. Even moderate scores (T score 58–64) on this scale are likely to be associated with a degree of somatization (as well as actual physical handicap and illness), and since this is combined with the narcissism, immaturity, lack of ambition, and stubbornness that are also characteristic of this group, the clinician's patience is sorely tested. As might be expected, such individuals are demanding and critical regarding intervention attempts and are particularly resistant to psychological interpretations of their disorder. As a result, they seldom respond positively to psychotherapy, instead demanding support, attention, and concrete physical explanation for their disorder. Therapists may find it a helpful technique with such clients to allow a focus on physical complaints for a set period of time in the therapy hour (sort of an "organ recital"). This procedure can facilitate a later uninterrupted discussion of the other critical issues that are often avoided. Shorter sessions are also helpful with such clients (Fowler, 1981). Placebos can be useful; however, clients who are high on scale 1 are at risk for dependency if medicated.

If scales 1 and/or 3 are significantly elevated, especially if they are the only ones elevated, such clients are not usually tolerant of psychological intervention. If they feel the need for treatment, they expect it to be traditionally medical. They particularly don't want to make the connection between psychological factors and their overt symptoms. One approach is to overtly avoid the apparent connection at first, for example, with interpretations such as "I can't tell you why your stomach distress occurs" (though you may actually have a very good idea why), "so let's talk a bit about what's going on with your life." Later you may speculate on possible connections, although the client may only stay at the level of everyday problem solving and never be willing to make that connection.

Persons who are low (below 45 T) on scale 1 are usually adjusting adequately to their worlds and are usually cognitively insightful, although some may appear moralistic and may have problems with the warmth and sharing demands of intimate interpersonal relations. Persons who are very low (T score of 38 and below) on scale 1 have deinvested in their bodies and may act as if they don't care what happens to them, for example, riding a motorcycle at high speed (which, along with the gun, is the neuropsychologist's most dependable referral source).

SCALE 2 (D)

Scale 2, subtitled the Depression scale, consists of fifty-seven items. It is the most frequent peak scale in psychiatric clients, and it clearly measures what it purports to: the degree of contentment with the world, level of self-esteem, and the view of the future. People who score high on scale 2 are clearly distressed. Comparison with the DEP content scale may allow differentiation between distress and depression. High 2s are usually depressed and withdrawn and show psychomotor retardation; they may be schizoid. There is a good chance they may harbor suicidal ideation if 2 is elevated above the 80 T mark, or if 2 is the only scale elevated above 65 T. Adolescents score somewhat lower than the general population, whereas the elderly score higher on the average, probably reflecting the different range of options available in these age groups, as well as their different sense of optimism about the future.

Unless they are attempting to fake-bad, persons with a very high score on scale 2 consistently show a clinical level of depression, and they probably warrant the potentially psychotic-depressive diagnosis. If the elevation is moderate, it may reflect either a depressive episode, a neurotic-depressive component, a state of mild chronic dissatisfaction, or depression from an accompanying maladaptive personality style that cannot cope with changes in the world.

People with high scale 2 scores are at least moderately withdrawn and show a low activity level, whereas persons low on scale 2 are typically comfortable with their worlds and are reasonably gregarious, active, and alert. In some cases a very low 2 score may reflect a lack of impulse control and possible conflict with societal mores, yet this has not usually brought the person into legal difficulties. Hedlund (1977) asserts that there is no strong correlation of scale 2 with psychotic symptomatology.

Persons high on scale 2 (and scale 7 as well) initially show a moderate to marked interest in therapy. However, this can be a direct result of their situational distress; when the crisis passes, they may terminate therapy, even though pathological patterns remain. If there is no elevation, it is probably difficult to do intrapsychic psychotherapy. Some elevation on 2 is a good prognostic sign for psychotherapy. Contracting for behaviors that increase activity level is helpful here.

Although there is no definitive suicidal profile on the MMPI-2, it appears that scale 2 is more indicative of suicidal ideation than of actual suicide attempts, and factors tapped by other scales, for example, scale 9, appear to act as catalysts for actual behavior in this regard.

As noted, persons low on 2 are usually reasonably well adjusted, active and alert; they are even enthusiastic, although they may be perceived by others as too flamboyant and uninhibited. Healthy adolescents often show low 2 scores. Very low scores here may reflect the manic phase of a cyclothymic process.

Using the Harris-Lingoes scales (especially helpful with a score between 60 to 80 T), high scorers on D1 (Subjective Depression) show classic depression commonly marked by agitation and nervousness, although they may complain of lack of energy. They lack the focus to cope with everyday tasks; they are inadequate and insecure and show low self-esteem. They also ruminate, cry, and show appetite and sleep disturbance. Low D1 scorers lack these symptoms and are usually happy, extroverted and self-confident. High scorers on D2 (Psychomotor Retardation) are immobilized, socially nonparticipating and even avoidant, and slowed motorically and deny hostility. Low D2's are active, initiating, and admit hostility when appropriate. High D3's (Physical Malfunctioning) are preoccupied with and report many physical symptoms; low D3's report good health. High D4's (Mental Dullness) communicate hopelessness, helplessness, energy depletion, and problems in memory and/or concentration; low D4's deny such symptoms and see life as interesting and within their mastery. High D5's (Brooding) ruminate, see themselves as unable to control their thought processes, are irritable and easily hurt by criticism, and feel life lacks meaning. Low D5's show opposite patterns.

SCALE 3 (Hy)

Scale 3, termed the Hysteria scale, is composed of sixty items that tap two overall constructs: (1) a denial of problems or vulnerabilities in one's emotional or interpersonal world, and (2) complaints of reasonably specific somatic problems. Naïveté, narcissism, neurotic defensiveness, and a lack of awareness of intrapsychic issues are characteristic of persons high on scale 3. Like those with the avoidant personality disorder, they may demand attention and caring responses, although they avoid committing themselves in this way.

Scale 3 is only moderately correlated with the development of conversion symptomatology, the initial construct that it was thought to tap, and it shows a low correlation with psychotic complaints. However, a T score above 80 is suggestive of a conversion reaction. Rather than evidencing the hypochondriasis so characteristic of scale 1, scale 3 is more likely to tap depression-generated somatic complaints, as well as ego-alien anxiety and agitation. Thus, sophistication is a factor in the score obtained on scale 3. Those who are brighter or higher in socioeconomic class tend to score higher on scale 3; women are more likely than men to be high. Persons with a spike on 3 often show problems with authority and feel unaccepted by their social group. They often show their rebellion passively or via somatic symptoms, but, in some cases they will blatantly act out in a sexual or aggressive mode.

Persons high on scale 3 are usually still interpersonally adequate, although they may be rather manipulative. The naïveté, anxiety, and need for attention result in an initially high level of apparent interest in psychotherapy. They love advice; they simply do not follow it. When these persons realize that they cannot manipulate their therapist to feed their egos, they may stop in a huff or attempt to maneuver the therapist into a physical or medical interpretation of their difficulties. They consistently seek "medical" reassurance. Yet they are also quite suggestible and usually responsive to hypnosis. When 3 and K are both elevated and F and 8 are low, the individuals are often overly conventional and affiliative, with an exaggerated need to be liked. They have problems with assertion and avoid the exercise of power.

Persons with a moderate elevation on 3 tend to be very optimistic. They are also likely to be cognitively and socially superficial and are extroverted, even exhibitionistic.

Persons low on scale 3 may be tough-minded and cynical. They usually have a relatively low need for involvement with people, may even be misanthropic, and have a narrow range of interests. Generally, these people are conforming to social mores and show little affect.

Referring to the Harris-Lingoes Scale, high Hy1's (Denial of Social Anxiety) are socially skilled and extroverted and accept criticism; low Hy1s are socially introverted and conforming. High Hy2's (Need for Affection) seek attention and affection, are trusting and nonconfrontational, and avoid or deny unpleasant situations or feelings; low Hy2's are inclined to be self-absorbed and are suspicious and critical of others. High Hy3's (Lassitude-Malaise) report general weakness and fatigue rather than specific symptoms. They report sleep and concentration problems. They seek reassurance and attention. Low Hy3's do not show such symptoms. High Hy4's (Somatic Complaints) report multiple specific somatic symptoms, such as, chest pains, dizziness, or nausea. They deny affect and convert conflict into symptomatology. Low Hy4's do not show such patterns. High Hy5's (Inhibition of Aggression) say they are decisive and sensitive to others and deny hostility or depictions of crime or aggression; low Hy5's show opposite characteristics.

SCALE 4 (Pd)

Scale 4, traditionally termed the Psychopathic Deviate, has fifty items that generally tap the following factors: (1) an angry rebelliousness against recognized rules and mores, (2) shallow and often hostile and manipulative interpersonal relationships, (3) inability to profit from experience or to plan effectively for long-term future contingencies, and (4) anger at family and a belief that one was victimized as a child.

Behaviorally, scale 4 shows a high correlation with antisocial behavior, moodiness, characterological patterns, substance abuse, and sexual immorality. A high scale 4 indicates potential for hostile and aggressive outbursts, as well as possible depressive ideation (not necessarily accompanied by psychomotor retardation). Whether or not they act out their problems in some fashion depends on whether scales 8 and/or 9 are high and K is low. "Normals" who are high on 4 (i.e., showing no demonstrable psychopathic behaviors and possibly benefiting from a technique like the PCL-R) are unconventional, rebellious, immature, sometimes exhibitionistic, and seldom popular. Blacks and late adolescents score higher on this scale, on the average. Indeed, a reasonably high scale 4 is "normal" in many adolescents. Yet, especially in adults, T scores above 75 are commonly associated with asocial/antisocial patterns. High Pd's are usually extroverted, maybe even energetic and creative, yet don't empathize well with others' needs; they are also angry and dissatisfied, impulsive, and lacking in social poise. They do not usually have blatant psychotic symptoms or high intrapsychically generated anxiety. Women in this range are very likely to have had trouble with the law, as have men, who may have shown some substance abuse.

Individuals who show a moderate score on 4 may be responding to social and/or authority conflicts, so the score should lessen as the conflict lessens (perhaps they are college students—about 10% of college students will be above 65 T on 4)—or they may show chronic but not extreme social conflicts or concerns.

Persons who are normal on scale 4 usually show adequate interpersonal relationships and are perceived by other people as sincere and concerned. If their scores are low, they are more likely to be conforming and even rigidly responsive to the dictates of authorities, to be manipulated by others, to tolerate boredom and mediocrity, and may lack enough energy to actuate plans. Males who score very low often have a lack of interest in if not a deep-seated mistrust of females.

Whereas persons who are low on scale 4 can become dependent on the therapist's advice and recommendations and will even seek out a therapist who will give such direction, persons high on scale 4 are likely to be manipulative in any quest for or response to therapy. They may seem to be good candidates because they are usually articulate and socially sophisticated. However, they subtly project blame onto other persons or situations and are inclined to use therapy to avoid problems of the real world, such as coercion from legal authorities or from intimate others. They are likely to terminate therapy as soon as they have obtained the goal of their manipulation or if they perceive the therapist as either unresponsive toward that end or able to confront their manipulations effectively.

Using the Harris-Lingoes scales, a high score on Pd1 (Familial Discord) reflects an experience of present family and/or family of origin as distressing, lacking in warmth or support, controlling, and possibly abusive. Low Pd1's see their families in opposite terms. If Pd1 is the clear major source of variance in an elevated scale 4 score, there may be little true psychopathy. High Pd2's (Authority Problems) are assertive, opinionated, resentful and rebellious against authority or social demands, and have often been in trouble in school or with the law. Low Pd2's are conforming, suggestible, and self-effacing. High Pd3's (Social Imperturbability) seek and are skilled in social interactions, sometimes to the point of trying to be the center of attention (or conversely, show managed blandness), deny dependency, and are assertive in their opinions. Low Pd3's are clumsy in and avoidant of social situations, quiet, and conformist. High Pd4's (Social Alienation) feel lonely and estranged socially, are self-centered and inconsiderate, and express regrets about life but externalize conflicts and project responsibility to others. Low Pd4's have a sense of "belongingness," like routine, and like and trust others but are not especially suggestible. High Pd5's (Self-Alienation) feel agitated and unhappy, have a sense of guilt and a lack of self-integration, have problems in concentration, and are inclined toward alcohol abuse. Low Pd5's see life as stimulating and enjoyable, seek predictability and deny excessive use of alcohol.

SCALE 5 (Mf)

Scale 5, the Masculinity-Femininity scale, is composed of fifty-six items that tap vocational preference, aesthetic interests, sexual-role interests, and an activity-passivity dimension. In general, low scores indicate a person who fits closely with traditional role expectations of his or her sex, whereas high scores reflect a person who in some way has moved away from the traditional role. For both sexes a T score above 80 suggests a serious sexual problem. Scale 5 is highly correlated with education and intelligence, with an r of up to .25 with intelligence often being reported.

Men who are low on scale 5 are usually perceived by others as bland, insouciant, and/or macho. They are not likely to be introspective, they are self-indulgent and overly independent (but actually rather conforming), they disdain intellectual and artistic pursuits in favor of active outdoor interests, and they often delight in being coarse and adventurous and may see themselves as "good old boys." They avoid psychotherapy.

Men who are high on scale 5 may have a homosexual identification and/or show a lack of identification with activities associated with the traditional male role. However, a more precise understanding of sex-role orientation is gained by looking at the supplemental scales GM and GF (Gentry and Meyer, 1991). High scale 5 males tend to be more passive, dependent, and submissive in interpersonal relationships. They are peace-loving and usually avoid confrontations. They are usually sensitive, sophisticated, and higher socioeconomically and intellectually and may have interests in the humanities and arts. They usually do well in therapy, especially group therapy. Ambitious and intrapsychically introspective individuals also tend to score higher on scale 5. If combined with a low 4, it suggests a very passive man, a "milquetoast." By contrast, low 5, high 4 males show an exhibitionistic, almost compulsive, masculinity, often as a counterphobic reaction to issues of tenderness or vulnerability. High 5 males in a psychiatric population are dependent and insecure, may show identity ambivalence, and are socially sensitive and passive. Depression, guilt, and anxiety are common.

Women who score low on scale 5 are likely to be passive and submissive, but sometimes petulant. They prefer to be involved in dependent interpersonal relationships, and, if they exert any control in the relationship, it is through passivity and stubbornness. Low-score women who are well educated are more positive and assured about themselves and their sex role. They may not be stereotypically feminine, but they often have many feminine characteristics. They may view themselves as plain (Graham, 1987). A very low 5 suggests some masochism, but they are also usually self-pitying, fault-finding, and appear (and may be) helpless. Women high on scale 5 have rejected many aspects of the traditional female role. They perceive themselves as extroverted and content with their world, but they can be emotionally insensitive and others may see them as unfriendly or even aggressive. As a result, they easily elicit aggression in others, including therapists.

Women with a high 5 more often are interested in sports and other outdoor activities than are women low on this scale. High scoring, normal females are independent but adventurous. In psychiatric populations, high 5 females are usually perceived as competitive, dominating, and irritating. A high scale -5 score in a hospitalized woman has in a number of cases been associated with underlying psychosis; such clients may exhibit hallucinations, delusions, and suspiciousness, although acting-out is uncommon (Graham, 1987).

☐   ## SCALE 6 (Pa)

Scale 6, termed Paranoia, includes forty items, and a high score comes from paranoid or unusual ideas or even delusions, feelings of being wronged, actual persecution, or complaints about others. At the same time, a low score does not rule out similar ideation. In fact, people who are sophisticated, integrated, and defensively paranoid may score quite low on this scale. In general, there are few false positives, but true positives may be missed. Very high scores are relatively uncommon, but to the extent that T is greater than 75, look for frank psychosis, clear paranoia, or paranoid schizophrenia as a possible diagnosis.

High scorers are seen as hostile, externalizing, overly sensitive, suspicious, and egocentrically self-righteous. As scores drop into the moderate-to-high range, more integrated paranoid ideation and hypersensitivity are probable and sexual deviation or preoccupation is a significant possibility. Anger toward others for a deprived or punitive childhood or toward authority also elevates this scale into at least the moderate range. However, moderate scores are usually obtained by individuals who are perceived by others as cooperative and intelligent and without any psychological disturbance, although they may be overly sensitive interpersonally. As a result, it is worthwhile to examine responses to individual items on this scale. High scores here with female psychiatric patients are more likely to reflect suspiciousness and emotional withdrawal than they do in male psychiatric patients; the male's high score is more likely to reflect odd thought content.

As noted, a person with a low score on scale 6 may well be a very sophisticated and guarded paranoid, although it's more probable that he or she is a generally optimistic and productive individual. They are often interpersonally insensitive and usually underachievers. In a psychiatric population a low scale 6 is associated with subtle defensiveness and stubbornness; when a score of less than 40 T is present, frank paranoid disorder is possible, and controlled anger and suspicion are likely.

Individuals high on scale 6 seldom become meaningfully involved in psychotherapy. They are much more concerned with "Who did that to me?" than with "How could I have done that?" At best, they are intellectualized and rigid. Some success can be attained over time if the therapist is able to give adequate feedback, maintain integrity as a therapist, and gradually develop in them at least a modicum of trust.

Using the Harris-Lingoes scales, persons high on Pa1 (Persecutory Ideas) show classic paranoid symptoms, that is, perceive threat from others, possibly at a delusional level, and feel misunderstood, are suspicious, blame others, and project conflict and responsibility onto others. Low Pa1's do not show these patterns and generally trust others. High Pa2's (Poignancy) perceive themselves as more sensitive and more intense in their feelings than others, feel misunderstood and/or lonely, are subjective and "thin-skinned," and can be stimulation- and risk-seeking. Low Pa2's show the opposite characteristics. High Pa3's (Naiveté) are trusting toward others; deny hostility or negative motives in self and others; and see themselves as nonhostile, noble, and/or moral. Ironically, *low* Pa3's show some paranoid components as they are suspicious, self-centered, and hostile. They are untrustworthy, yet see others as dishonest.

SCALE 7 (Pt)

Scale 7, called the Psychasthenia scale, consists of forty-eight items that include factors of (1) general discontent with one's world; (2) obsessional concerns; (3) anxiety, and (4) indecision, poor concentration, and self-devaluation. Scale 7 primarily taps the obsessional, rather than the compulsive, features of the obsessive-compulsive disorder. The primarily compulsive personality is not that consistently high on this scale, presumably because the compulsive's rigidity and denial ward off feelings of insecurity or low self-esteem. People high on this scale anxiously ruminate about problems in their worlds and have perfectionistic standards of performance that they seldom feel they actually meet. As a result, they show feelings of inferiority in many areas and have a negative self-image. A T score over 75 suggests excessive fear and apprehension, even panic. With high T scores, generalized physical complaints, such as fatigue, exhaustion, and insomnia, are commonly reported, as well as more specific complaints involving the heart or the gastrointestinal or genitourinary systems (Graham, 1993). They are described as being anxious and indecisive. These features not surprisingly lead them into psychotherapy, but the obsessiveness and perfectionism often cause initial problems. They are not likely to give in, so they continue to introspect and ruminate when changes in behavior would be more productive. They usually do best with structured therapies, at least in the initial stages, as they can think themselves to death in unstructured situations. If the therapist can be patient and keep such clients involved beyond this initial stage of resistance, the prognosis becomes more positive. An abrupt involvement in therapies that quickly knock out repression and denial, such as confrontational therapies and encounter groups, can be dangerous to high 7 clients, since they may be attempting to hold onto control of very high anxiety or self-destructive impulses.

Hedlund (1977) found the presence of phobias to be correlated with a high scale 7 score for white samples only. In female patients there is a significant negative correlation of irritability and delusions with high scale 7 scores. In general, when a high 7 is found in a psychotic client, it points to a more acute onset. High T scorers who are apparently normal are described as verbal and idealistic (if male, unemotional and responsible but sentimental; if female, emotional, "high strung," and having self-discontent).

Persons with a moderate score on 7 are conscientious, punctual, and not that anxious (unless faced with uncertainty or a disruption of schedule). Persons low on scale 7 are perceived by others as contented and satisfied with their lives, self-confident and emotionally stable, and yet also ambitious and status-seeking. They are generally content and are at least relaxed toward responsibilities.

SCALE 8 (Sc)

Scale 8, traditionally termed the Schizophrenia scale, is the longest subscale on the MMPI-2, made up of seventy-eight items that focus on factors of (1) confused thought processes, (2) hallucinations and other indications of formal thought disorder, (3) social and interpersonal alienation, and (4) depression and dissatisfaction. Scale 8 correlates most highly (approximately .75) with scale 7 and moderately (approximately .50–.55) with F, 4, and 2. It is a difficult scale to interpret since a person who has an average K score need only endorse any subset of twenty items on 8 to gain a T score of 65. Comparison of 8 with the BIZ content scale facilitates a symptom differentiation.

Persons high on scale 8 are usually significantly disturbed, although a subsample of individuals may be faking-bad, especially when the T score is over 90. As noted, confusion, bizarre thought processes, and social alienation are characteristics of high 8 scorers. Most who have a high score feel as if they are out of phase with the world. It is interesting that a score over 100 T here is not necessarily indicative of schizophrenia; it is more likely to reflect acute, situational distress and/or an identity crisis. Agitated neurotics and people who are severely emotionally unstable, and yet only borderline with respect to psychosis, may also score extremely high on scale 8. Schizophrenics are more likely to score between 70 and 90 on the T score. Persons in the high T score range may show problems in attention and staying with tasks, with accompanying agitation and anxiety, even if not schizophrenic. They often have high standards that they feel unable to meet, are inclined toward guilt, and have low self-esteem. When under stress, they are prone to become irritable and stubborn.

Persons very low on scale 8 are perceived as happy and reasonably productive individuals, accepting of authority and yielding in interpersonal relationships. Yet they have rigid and conventional thought patterns and are unable to come up with abstract or creative solutions to interpersonal and vocational problems, particularly if scale M on the 16 PF is also low.

Persons with high scores on scale 8 are enigmatic for the therapist. They are often willing to discuss their problems openly, but it is hard to pin them down about concrete ways to change their behavior. They are prone to discussions that distract from the focus on the problem and are unstable in their trust of the therapist. Nevertheless, they are likely to remain in some form of contact with the therapist over a long period of time, and if a degree of trust can be generated, modest and steady progress may occur.

Referring to the Harris-Lingoes scales, individuals high on Sc1 (Social Alienation) feel alienated, misunderstood, and mistreated. They have had few love relationships, are socially avoidant, feel their family has rejected and/or patronized them, and lack rapport with others. Low Sc1's show an absence of such responses and feel accepted by their families. Persons high on Sc2 (Emotional Alienation) lack self-rapport and show marked depression and despair and/or flat affect along with apathy; they may be masochistic and/or sadistic. Low Sc2's deny such patterns. High Sc3's (Lack of Ego Mastery, Cognitive) show a pattern expected in schizophrenia, that is, thought disorder. They report odd and/or confused thoughts and feelings of unreality and/or depersonalization. Low Sc3's report an absence of such symptoms. High Sc4's (Lack of Ego Mastery, Conative) see life as a strain and feel they can not cope. They show high levels of inhibition and "psychological weakness." They worry, withdraw, and show depression and despair. They may feel hopeless and wish they were dead. Low Sc4's do not show such symptoms and say they find life worthwhile. High Sc5's (Lack of Ego Mastery, Defective Inhibition) experience and are frightened by a sense of impending loss of control. Emotion and affect are ego-alien. They show hyperactivity, labile emotions and irritability and may report amnesic episodes. Low Sc5's do not admit to such symptoms. High Sc6's (Bizarre Sensory Experiences) report a variety of unusual physical symptoms, experience depersonalization; and admit to unusual thoughts, delusions of influence, and hallucinations. Low Sc6's report an absence of such experiences.

SCALE 9 (Ma)

This scale, termed the Mania scale, includes forty-six items that focus on a propensity for (1) high energy output, (2) distractibility and lack of persistence in tasks, (3) extroversion and stimulation seeking, (4) grandiosity, and (5) amorality. Scale 9 can be thought of as a force that drives whatever else is there, sort of a behavioral and emotional amplifier. Persons very low on scale 9 show little energy and may be depressed; most are lacking in self-confidence and a reasonable degree of optimism about the future. A high 2 with a low 9 suggests severe depression. The clinician should note that even when scale 2 is not elevated, a very low score on scale 9 is a cue for underlying depression. As 9 moves up toward the average range, the client is more likely to be quietly productive, reliable in most job situations, and possibly perceived as quiet and withdrawn.

This scale is age-driven, and elderly individuals on the average score up to 10 points lower on it; adolescents average up to 10 points higher than normal adults. Blacks also tend to score a bit higher here. In some females a high 9 may result from counterphobic attempts to deny dependency and/or passivity.

In general, people very high on scale 9 are likely to be significantly disturbed psychologically and show grandiosity and a high level of distractibility. A T score of greater than 80 may suggest a manic or psychotic episode; in some individuals a high 9 may reflect a counterphobic attempt to avoid an anticipated (at some level of consciousness) depression. As scores move into the moderate to higher ranges, these tendencies are muted, although the individuals still have problems organizing tasks. They may be creative, but they need others to carry their plans to the point of actualization. They tend to be extroverted and perceived by others as gregarious, occasionally as pushy.

High 9's are difficult for the therapist to work with because they are hyperactive and distractible, not inclined to view themselves as vulnerable or responsible for problems in their world, and not able to persist introspectively to connect contingencies between their behavior and the difficulties they are encountering. Also, high 9's often struggle with control issues with therapists and others. If confronted by the therapist, they are likely to intellectualize their problems, attempt to distract from the issue by acting out, or simply terminate therapy. Lithium therapy should be considered here.

A high 9 score, associated with moderate elevations on scale 4 and 3 and a moderate or greater elevation on K, denotes narcissistic and aggressively competitive persons. They do not tolerate vulnerability or dependency, and they raise their self-esteem by denigrating others. If this pattern is bolstered by real-world support for the narcissism, such as a high level of physical attractiveness or athletic skill, the personality style is reinforced in a vicious cycle. When these people enter therapy, the therapist hears various fascinating anecdotes and may even be entertained by dramatic self-confrontations. However, marked change cannot be expected unless the cycle of narcissism is broken in some way, such as aging or trauma resulting in a forced loss of attractiveness.

Persons with T scores in the moderate range usually show the ability to balance their resources and productivity reasonably well. They tend to manifest a pleasant, outgoing temperament but will respond with agitation to external restrictions. A low score on 9, especially when this scale is the lowest on the profile, usually suggests a somewhat lethargic individual. If 9 is very low, depression may be present, reflected in fatigue and physical exhaustion. Low 9 clients may occasionally be tense and anxious, yet are usually reliable, dependable, and responsible and may confront their problems with perseverance and practicality. Low-scoring males often have home and family interests and are willing to settle down. The prognosis is more favorable for hospitalized patients with low 9 scores.

Using the Harris-Lingoes scales, persons high on Ma1 (Amorality) use their perception of others as dishonest and self-centered to rationalize similar patterns in themselves and enjoy manipulating and exploiting others, often with a veneer of disarming frankness. Low Ma1's trust others and see them as caring. High Ma2's (Psychomotor Acceleration) report classic manic symptoms; have accelerated motoric, thought, and speech patterns; display labile affect; are highly stimulation-seeking and/or hyperactive; can revert to boredom if unsatisfied; and experience impulses to shock and/or harm others. Low Ma2's deny such patterns and are calm and risk-avoidant. High Ma3's (Imperturbability) deny social anxiety but feel impatient and irritable toward others and say they are seldom influenced by the arguments or opinions of others. Low Ma3's are suggestible yet uncomfortable with others. People high on Ma4 (Ego Inflation) can be grandiose, certainly have a streak of narcissism, and resent demands from others, especially if the other is somehow perceived as an underling. Low Ma4's accept most demands from others as reasonable and make reasonably objective self-appraisals.

SCALE 0 (Si)

Scale 0, subtitled Social Introversion, contains sixty-nine items. It was developed later than the other scales and as a result does not have as much consensual clinical experience or data supporting it. Subscales are now available for this scale; Si1—Shyness/Self-Consciousness, Si2—Social Avoidance, Si3—Self/Other Alienation (Ben-Porath et al., 1989). These subscales can help considerably in the clinical interpretation of the Si scale. Persons high on Si1 show classic shyness and social discomfort and avoidance, both with individuals and groups. Si2's especially avoid group interactions. Si3's are more "neurotic"; that is, they have low self-esteem, lack self-confidence, and are nervous and indecisive.

Scores on 9 are usually quite stable over time and may represent biologic and constitutional factors that contribute to an introversion-extroversion component and feelings of social discomfort.

This scale was designed to assess the propensity for avoidance of social responsibilities and contact with others. While it seems to assess this factor, it also may tap psychomotor depression, particularly when associated with social insecurity. Such individuals would score high on scale 0 and are usually perceived by others as oversensitive and touchy. Charles Manson, certainly a touchy person at best, had a 0 score above 80 T, along with scores over 80 T on 4, 8, and 9. A T score over 70 occasionally signifies a well socialized and controlled but basically psychotic personality who has not been identified by the other scales. Individuals scoring low on scale 0 are likely to be seen as happy-go-lucky and extroverted but also as opportunistic and manipulative, and they may occasionally manifest problems in impulse control. Yet, a low score on 0 often mutes the pathology suggested by elevated scores on other scales; it indicates the person may be able to vent pathology in socially acceptable ways or in a reasonably non–self-destructive manner. Very low scorers are very superficial, and often manipulative, in relationships.

Elderly individuals score a bit higher on this age-driven scale. Persons high on scale 0 are often initially resistant in therapy because they fear rejection in interpersonal relationships and are insecure about increased vulnerability. Yet, if they can deal with this issue in the initial stages of therapy, the prognosis is reasonably positive, for they are inclined to work productively in dealing with their symptoms. Social-skills training is useful here. Marital couples with a T score difference of 20 or more have a strong chance of experiencing marital difficulties.

■ MMPI-2 Interrelationship Interpretations

The reader should use the guidelines for interpretation delineated at the beginning of the previous section on individual scale interpretations. Since there is a small number of MMPI-2 three-point codes with valid correlates, they are discussed within the first relevant two-point code, for example, the 2-4-7/2-7-4/4-7-2 code is discussed within the section on the 2-4/4-2 code.

Note that one of the most frequent code types in psychiatric settings is a WNL (Within Normal Limits). These clients describe themselves in a variety of positive terms. If this is not consistent with the data, consider the possibility you may have a person with a chronic, severe personality disorder or possibly a psychotic individual who can cover and/or deflect attention from his/her symptomatology.

Spike 1's have a long somatization history that they use to control others (even if they have some actual symptomatology). They are not at all psychologically minded and are refractory to intervention.

The 1-2/2-1 combination is consistently indicative of somatic disturbance, accompanied by a degree of irritability, agitation, pain, and anxiety. These individuals do "hurt" in one way or another. Unfortunately, they have often learned to live with their complaints (and their complaining), so even when they change through intervention, a return of symptoms is probable. Somatic complaints (especially digestive problems) are common. The 1-2 code is relatively infrequent and, without associated elevations, points to the somatoform disorders. If 7, 8, and F are also elevated, schizophrenia should be considered. The 2-1 code is a more frequent combination, particularly in males. Men here show somatic tension along with pessimism and depression, and there is usually little physical basis for their disorders. Women who score 2-1 show more classical hypochondriacal patterns, with an emphasis on restlessness and tension, while adolescents are tense and shy and often have academic problems, sometimes school phobia. When the pattern is 2-1 rather than 1-2, there is a greater emphasis on tension-anxiety and depression.

When one is assessing an inpatient sample, particularly male, alcoholism and depression should be considered, especially episodic forms of alcoholism accompanied by somatic concerns. Persons with the 1-2/2-1 code are generally passive-dependent in interpersonal relationships, are concrete in their thinking, and are not likely to take responsibility for their behaviors, especially if 3 and 4 are also elevated. This passivity, combined with a general avoidance of responsibility, makes them at best a moderate risk in therapy. They need very directive and structured therapy targeted at overt symptoms, and do not do well in traditional psychotherapy. They can become medication-dependent, but an antidepressant like imipramine can help restore disturbed sleep patterns (Lewak et al., 1990).

Scales 1, 2, and 3 are commonly referred to as the "neurotic triad" because elevations on these scales are found in most neurotic disorders, although "chronically hypochondriacal" may be the most applicable term when all three scales are elevated. These clients often exhibit an exaggerated need for affection. When scales 1 and 3 are elevated, with a valley (10 T score points or more) on scale 2 (the conversion V), these clients are prone to use somatic disorder as a projection channel for personal difficulties. The function is hysteroid and/or hypochondriacal rather than classically psychophysiological, and they strongly resist psychological interpretations of their disorders. Persons with an acute illness tend to have high scale 2 scores, often without remarkable elevations on other scales. Persons with a clear, stepwise 1-2-3 code (in that order) are indeed on a downward slope, that is, their functioning is often deteriorating. Acute clinical distress, with possible neurological involvement and/or masking of depression is signaled by 1-2-9 and 2-1-9 codes. Persons with 1-2-3-4 or 2-1-3-4 codes are commonly alcoholics, often with a strong hostility and/or acting-out component.

The 1-3/3-1 pattern is common in older people and in women, and when other scales are not particularly elevated, it reflects a combination of neurotic symptomatology and psychophysiological concerns. Consistent with the hysteric component, these persons have shallow interpersonal relationships, are narcissistic, resent others, and are either somewhat Pollyannaish or avoidant in reaction to their problems. They are resistant to psychological treatment; brief stress-innoculation treatment may be the most useful approach (Butcher, 1990). Males who show the 1-3/3-1 pattern may be feminine in orientation, particularly if the pattern is accompanied by an elevation on scale 5. When elevations on 1 and 3 are accompanied by a high 7, a panic disorder is quite possible. In adolescents this profile is often accompanied by somatic problems, attention-seeking behaviors, and possible eating disorders, and they are often referred because of school problems.

The 1-3/3-1 codes are common, and if 1 is greater than 3, there is more irritability, whining, and pessimism. When 3 is higher, there is more optimism, so a more long-suffering martyr-like complex may be in evidence. To the degree that scale 1 is close to the height of scale 3 and scale 2 is somewhat lower, conversion reactions are more likely, although true medical conditions (even though "real" symptoms may be exaggerated here too) also show this pattern. Such complaints as hypertension, low back pain, eating disorders (such as anorexia nervosa and obesity), and gastrointestinal disorders are common. These individuals are seldom truly incapacitated by their symptoms, and there is usually a neurotic component. They dissociate from anger, sadness, and/or grief. They fear being judged as "bad" by others. Persons who show a multiple personality are also likely to obtain a 1-3/3-1 code. The combination of passivity, resistance to responsibility in a psychological disorder, preference for medical explanations, and the suggestibility and high need for structure all predict problems in psychotherapy with 1-3/3-1 clients. They want to explain their psychopathology in somatic terms, prefer powerful and magical cures, and are inclined to terminate the therapy relationship prematurely if signs of concern by the therapist are not forthcoming. When a 1-3/3-1 is associated with a high K, and especially if F, 2, 7, and 8 are low, they are very defensive, almost "overly normal," helpful, and sympathetic. They cannot tolerate the role of "patient" and resist any interpretation of unconventionality or vulnerability (Butcher and Graham, 1988). They easily habituate to drugs.

When the 1-3/3-1 profile is accompanied by a marked elevation on scale 8 and an elevation on F, one must look for somatic delusions and/or psychotic paranoia. Types under the 1-3-8 code are commonly diagnosed as schizophrenic disorder, paranoid type, or paranoid personality disorder. They may appear as delusional, with bizarre symptomatology. Depression and suicidal ideation or behaviors may be present, and such individuals often are preoccupied with religion or sex. They are prone to substance abuse; are often loud, angry, anxious, restless, or bored; and are not particularly interested in forming personal relationships. Types under the 1-3-9 code are occasionally diagnosed as having organic brain syndrome or, more likely, somatoform disorder (especially conversion reactions). They tend to be impulsive, and if the organic brain syndrome is present, they will likely show spells of aggressiveness (Graham, 1993).

The 1-4/4-1-code type is relatively infrequent with inpatient groups, yet it occurs at least moderately often in outpatient clinical settings. In either case it occurs far more often in men; commonly indicates consistent problems in meeting the responsibilities of life, with resultant self-pitying and antiauthoritarian attitudes rather than classic psychopathy; is correlated with hypochondriasis; and is possibly focused on low back pain or headaches. With inpatients it is more often associated with a combination of somatization symptoms, narcissism, and alcohol problems, and there are correlated problems with the vocational and interpersonal areas, particularly with the opposite sex. The 1-4/4-1 adolescent is provocative, defiant, and pessimistic, with problems at both home and school, and may even make manipulative suicide attempts.

Persons of this type are most responsive to short-term symptomatic treatment, and even here, the response is up and down at best. There is often a high associated score on the L scale, and if so, such persons do poorly in psychotherapy because of their resistance, somatization, and possible problems with alcohol. A very low score on 1, combined with a high score on 4, suggests someone who has truly given up on his or her body and is likely to take high risks physically, possibly as a counterphobic reaction to early anxiety about bodily symptoms (Fowler, 1981).

The 1-6/6-1 code is also rare. It indicates somatic and hypochondriacal preoccupations, probably delusional if 8 is also high. It may indicate an attempt to stave off an emerging psychotic process, and it has the associated projected hostility. Adolescents with this code are emotionally insecure, defensive, and evasive, with family problems in general and father absence specifically occurring.

The 1-7/7-1 code, which occurs more often in males, generally reflects high somatic tension and many physical symptoms. Obsessive patterns, especially focused on somatic complaints and pain, and feelings of inferiority are typical. They may report sleep problems and depression.

The 1-8/8-1 code may be indicative of schizophrenia, especially acute schizophrenia, particularly if 8 is markedly elevated and F is also elevated. In general, 1-8/8-1's often have vague and even odd medical complaints, have trouble with the acknowledgment and expression of aggression, and may alternate behaviorally within a classic passive-aggressive pattern. Types under the 1-8/8-1 code may also feel socially inadequate (and often are) and lack trust in others. They become isolated and alienated from peers, which may lead to nomadic lifestyles and accompanying poor work history. They may show sexual-deviate patterns. They usually have some dissociative or schizoid components, especially if scale 0 is also high.

The 1-9/9-1 profile is a rare code, marked by a high level of agitation, irritability, and distress, yet they may report themselves as carefree and independent. Masked depression should be considered. Gastrointestinal symptoms and headaches also occur. Types under the 1-9/9-1 code may appear to be ambitious, but they often lack direction and experience and may become frustrated when their goals are not met. Such persons may be passive-dependent in actual functioning, yet maintain gruff exteriors. If a number of other scales, including F, are moderately elevated, the possibility of brain damage should be considered. This code is infrequent in adolescents. Males with this code are aggressive and evasive, while females are extroverted and tense.

An extremely rare code, the 1-0/0-1 pattern indicates high social discomfort, passive-avoidant patterns, conventional behaviors (out of fear of being caught), and numerous somatic complaints.

Since a spike (a marked elevation relative to all other scales) on scale 2 particularly taps symptomatic or reactive depression, it is unstable on repeat testing, compared to other scales. The spike-2 type is seldom described in clinical literature, but, when found, it is likely to be a depression in response to environmental stress. In some cases it is related to an ongoing depressive process that develops out of an inability to deal effectively with aggression, with a concomitant history of rage reaction (Kelley and King, 1979c). Spike-2 clients are usually introverted and reserved. If a person with a spike 2 denies depression, further evaluation for possible suicide risk is especially important (Butcher and Graham, 1988). They usually respond well to short-term therapy; if they do not, look for an emergence of elevations on 4, 7 and/or 8.

The 2-3/3-2 code is marked by apathetic depression, anxiety, and overcontrol, with depression predominating when 2 is higher than 3 and with anxiety and accompanying neurotic and somatic symptoms predominating when 3 is higher than 2. In both codes there is evidence of passive dependency and shyness, particularly when 2 is high and 9 is low. The emphasis here is more on inadequacy than on somatization, the latter being primary in the 1-2/2-1 code. Clients with a 2-3/3-2 profile are more likely to have accepted their psychopathology, as opposed to the 2-7/7-2 types, who are usually still struggling to cope with it. The 2-3/3-2 in females has more emphasis on sexual dysfunction and depression (and their depression may reflect a failure of histrionic defenses), whereas in males there is a bit more of a dependent yet driven component. When scales 4, 7, and 8 are also moderately elevated in a 2-3/3-2 type, histrionic components are probable, although actual acting-out may be muted to the degree 7 is high. The 2-3/3-2's seem to seek responsibility in vocational and interpersonal situations but then are stressed by and dislike the obligations of such commitments. They are usually inefficient rather than incapacitated. They are achievement- and power-oriented and are overcontrolled, but they are sensitive to rejections, so they do not get into situations where actual competition could take place. In this sense, they are "homebodies" and prone to agoraphobic or avoidant personality disorder patterns.

To the degree that 2 is greater than 3, success in psychotherapy is more probable. In fact, some elevation on 2 is almost a prerequisite for success in psychotherapy because it suggests an allowance for vulnerability that the therapist can work with. When 3 is greater than 2, there is a greater tendency to avoid intrapsychic introspection and more likelihood of projection. Hence, response to psychotherapy is poorer, and directive and dramatic therapies are more helpful. Medication can be helpful, although 3-2's are prone to quickly report "distressing" side effects (Lewak et al., 1990).

Moderate elevations on scales 2, 3, and 7 are characteristic of the phobic disorders and sexual dysfunctions. In addition to these types of problems, adolescents with this code type are clearly marked by poor peer relationships, especially with the opposite sex. They are loners, except for some subgroups in the school setting.

The 2-4/4-2 code is relatively common in inpatient populations, but not as likely to occur in outpatients. Since 2-4/4-2's are often both depressed and consumers of stimulation (Anderson and Bauer, 1985), alcoholism or other kinds of substance abuse are common. Other types of concomitant sociolegal and family problems (and some situational guilt) also occur; these people are often secondary psychopaths "in trouble." They are "personality-disordered"; often immature and egocentric and are ambivalent about whether to indulge in self-pity or projection. If scales 2, 4, 8, and 9 are all high, there may be evidence of schizophrenic disorder, and if 6 is also elevated, a possible paranoid component may be present.

Even though 2-4/4-2 types can often present a facade of confident behavior, they easily move into manipulative and impulsive behaviors, including suicide. In that same vein, they are likely to manifest a cry for help, possibly through manipulative suicide gestures. They verbalize a need for help; then, when help is proffered, they terminate therapy after soothing the situation but before fully dealing with the more basic aspects of the problem. In general, male alcoholics with these patterns show a long history of alcohol abuse that is associated with secondary psychopathic patterns. Female alcoholics in this code type are more likely to have depressive components, situational stress, and physical complaints. A disturbed family background is common, so family and/or marital background is usually necessary. Working on a series of small, specific goals is a good strategy. Adolescents with this code usually also have very disturbed families, school problems, runaway behavior, and drug abuse patterns.

The 2-4-7/7-4-2/4-7-2 pattern is common among passive-aggressive personalities and alcoholics (Graham, 1993), who tend to be fearful, worried, and high-strung. They avoid competitive situations and are conflicted about dependency, yet show anger, hostility, and immaturity. They tend toward phobic behaviors and may be ruminative or over-ideational. They may have problems with anxiety during treatment, but they seem to respond well to goal-oriented therapies.

The 2-5/5-2 code is very rare in females. Those few who do display it are usually from a lower social class, showing much interpersonal and social-role conflict. Males with this code are passive, noncompetitive, sensitive, and idealistic and often manifest chronic but mild depression. Conflicts are handled via fantasy and self-awareness.

The profile type 2-6/6-2 is rare and is primarily seen in females. They are likely to complain of physical symptoms first; on further examination, they often report a recent interpersonal stress, such as breaking up with a lover or spouse (Kelley and King, 1979a). They usually are more flat than depressed in affect, show paranoid ideation and anger, are openly hostile, have had relatives who have had problems with alcohol, and are concerned about potential alcoholism in their own lives. They are inclined to be dependent (although they feel trapped and resentful), are preoccupied with thoughts of suicide, and have often made manipulative suicidal gestures in the past. They are significantly disturbed characterologically and thus may earn the diagnosis of borderline or paranoid personality disorder. Medications that do not threaten their vigilance set or tap their addiction potential can be useful in the short run. To the degree 6 is high and is higher than an elevated 2, a psychotic paranoid pattern is possible. Therapy is difficult, although the elevated 2 makes it possible. Adolescents with a 2-6/6-2 are more inclined to be introverted and insecure, with strong conflicts over sexual feelings.

Scales 2 and 7 are the two best distress and turmoil scales, in that order. The 2-7/7-2 pattern is very common in outpatients, especially males. If both scores are very high, you can expect the presence of depression or dysphoria (probably with some agitation or rumination), difficulties in concentration, somatic complaints, and a high probability of suicidal thoughts. When scales 4, 8, and 9 are also elevated and 1 is low, the probability of acting out suicidal thoughts is raised; the elevation on 8 in particular gives a cue as to the lack of control and/or presence of psychosis. If 0 is high, interpersonal avoidance and fear of rejection can also be expected. Males who show this overall pattern are more likely to have concomitant obsessive-compulsive patterns (especially when 7 is higher than 2), as well as vague somatic complaints and insomnia.

Persons with moderate to high 2-7/7-2 patterns are generally passive and dependent, yet are tense and often somewhat depressed, are intropunitive but show little anger or hostility, and keep emotionally distant from most people. Further, 2-7/7-2 types may be rigid in their thinking and may be poor problem solvers. They may also be meticulous and perfectionistic and present themselves as extremely moral and religious people (Graham, 1993). The scale 7 component points more to anhedonia than to classical depression; if it is high in the 2-7/7-2 combination, it points more to a lack of ability to experience pleasure than to psychomotor retardation (Gynther and Green, 1980). As a result, the clinician should explore possible suicide ideation. When scale 1 is also elevated, the agitated anxiety of the 2-7/7-2 profile is channeled into marked somatization. A neurotic diagnosis is probable, and assertive training can be helpful.

In general, the prognosis for 2-7/7-2 types in psychotherapy is positive. Psychotherapy was designed for 2-7/7-2s, as they usually remain in therapy, especially to the degree 7 is elevated, since 7s persist in everything. If both 2 and 7 are very high, it is difficult to do therapy (especially if you are a 4-9 therapist and want to get on with things) as their problem-solving abilities are paralyzed. If 2 and 7 are below 50, it is difficult to do intrapsychic therapy. Anxilytic medications can be helpful but should be administered on a time-contingent basis (e.g., three to six months) to avoid habituation.

When scale 4 (rather than 1) is elevated (2-7-4), chronic alcoholism, family and marital problems, passive-aggressive patterns, and underachievement are probable. Individuals with the 2-7-4 code are self-deprecating and guilty, may be counterphobic to dependency, and show some chronic depression. They often show alcohol and family problems and are difficult to treat. When 2, 7, 4, and 5 are elevated (low 5 in females), the person often appears weak and self-effacing and elicits deprecation from others. The person seen as the "clown" or "silly egghead-intellectual" is often found here.

When elevations on 2 and 7 are associated with an elevation on scale 3 (the 2-7-3), one finds both high aspirations and high standards. There is often success in achievement, yet with a high cost in stress; paradoxically, the tendency toward passive dependency is even more marked, and they elicit "rescuing" in others (including therapists). They need firm confrontation. Passive behaviors accompanied by underlying anger and hostility are more probable when the elevation on scale 2 is predominant, associated with high elevations on scales F, 8, and 4 and only a moderate elevation on scale 7 (Carson, 1969). Fowler (1981) notes than when a high 5 is combined with a high 2-7/7-2, there is a paradoxically high probability of sexual acting-out.

The 2-7-8/2-8-7 three-point code types show features of both psychosis and neurosis. These clients are tense, phobic, depressed, and often suicidal, yet also may show brief psychotic episodes, somatic symptoms, and blunted emotional responses. They often need crisis intervention plus psychopharma-cology. They set high standards for themselves, yet feel inadequate and infe-rior. They often are schizoid and show interest in obscure subjects. Males with some high-point combinations of scales 2, 7, and 8 are more likely to be psy-chotic than are females, who are more likely to be neurotic (Kelley and King, 1979b).

The 2-8/8-2 code occurs infrequently, particularly in outpatient groups. A sense of having been deprived or hurt as a child is typical, as if one had been raised by one of Harry Harlow's "wire-mothers." Confusion, a sense of being "broken" or defective, concreteness, social awkwardness, dependency prone-ness, a high level of tension, and depression are common. Individuals may also have blackouts, nausea, or vomiting. If there is evidence of thought disor-der and scale 1 is also raised, then somatic delusions are probable. If 4 is also high, acting-out and fears of loss of control are common. Another common diagnosis is bipolar disorder: When 2 is markedly high and greater than 8, psychotic depression is likely; but when 8 is greater than 2 and particularly high, a schizophrenic or schizoaffective adjustment is more probable. In either case, there is often serious maladjustment, and there may be suicidal ideation, which is more likely to be associated with a specific plan than in the 2-7/7-2 profile. Even where the 2-8/8-2 code is associated with only mild elevations, inefficiency and problems in carrying out plans occur, they fear a (further) loss of control, and a sense of having been rejected by others, including therapists, is common. They need support and nurturance, but therapeutic relationships are stormy and not often successful. Reflecting their neurosensory experience base, epileptics are often elevated on 2 and 8, but typically are fairly low on the BIZ content scale. In general, this code type is more indicative of pathology in females, and with them particularly it should be a cue to look for substance abuse (Kelley and King, 1979c). In adolescents these same patterns equally apply, although a history of nonspecific brain disorder and/or hyperactivity is not uncommon.

The 2-9/9-2 profile incorporates a true paradox, since it is the manifestation of simultaneous energetic and depressive components. It may well represent an at-tempt through manic defenses to cope with underlying depression, although such a coping pattern is not often successful. If both 2 and 9 are very high, a bipolar affective disorder is suggested, although the possibility of a defense against de-pression caused by loss from organic brain damage should also be considered. Persons with this pattern are often self-centered, agitated, moody, and irritable. This pattern is occasionally found in male alcoholics who are agitated and also defending themselves against depression by increased alcohol abuse. Clients with the 2-9/9-2 profile may report anxiousness and somatic problems, particularly in the upper gastrointestinal tract. Medication is often necessary, but this requires a high level of monitoring as they are inclined to self-regulate their use. In adoles-cents the 2-9/9-2 profile can reflect tension, narcissism, separation anxiety, and problems in developing a distinct identity.

When 2 is low but K and 9 are elevated (the K-9 profile), the personality is organized around competitiveness and interpersonal power. These individuals are narcissistic and depend upon evidence of weakness in others for their self-enhancement—they like to "run up the score." Females may evidence exhibitionistic attractiveness—the Hollywood syndrome.

The 2-0/0-2 profile is obtained by shy individuals who are insecure about their introversion and as a result have chronic, episodic depression. It is also particularly common in women and in adolescents who are having social difficulties. In all age ranges it may manifest itself as a mild, chronic depression. Fowler (1981) reports that this pattern is notably common in parents (especially women) who bring their children to child-guidance clinics, and that 2-0/0-2's ultimately often beget 2-0/0-2's. Any training in social skills is helpful, as is psychotherapy to help these shy and socially inept people adjust to and accept the more stable components of the introverted pattern. Single doses of antidepressants at night can be helpful, as these clients often have sleep problems, don't like to take medications, and are sensitive to side effects (Lewak et al., 1990).

Spike 3's tend to be Pollyannish and conventional and deny any disharmony with others. They can be phobic toward assertion or anger. They are nonpsychologically minded and easily develop physical symptoms that carry secondary gain. Though others are likely to see them as "spacey," they see themselves as rational and logical. They can be almost phobic toward experiencing physical or emotional pain. They may elicit exploratory surgeries (Lewak et al., 1991), looking for the "cause" of their inner pain. They are not likely to change much in therapy, and usually quickly terminate once the referral crisis is past.

The 3-4/4-3 profile, a common code in outpatients (especially females), is associated with problems in impulse control, usually focused on chronic anger and hostility (often directed at family members or significant others). When 4 is greater than 3, there is a higher probability of acting-out behavior; this profile is often noted in female delinquents. The 4-3's are usually relatively passive, but they may show emotional or behavioral outbursts, as well as generally poor judgment. They are sensitive to, and project, any criticism. However, as Davis and Sines (1971) suggest, when 3 is greater than 4, the anger is more repressed and more likely to manifest itself in intermittent aggression. Diagnoses such as a dissociative reaction, intermittent explosive disorder, or passive-aggressive personality disorder are common, whereas a diagnosis that focuses on emotional instability and anger is more characteristic when 4 is greater than 3. Some 3-4/4-3 clients may exhibit sexual promiscuity. They may appear to be socially conforming, yet are inwardly rebellious. Suicidal ideation is possible following bouts of drinking and acting-out behaviors (Graham, 1993), reflecting an ongoing, unacknowledged depressive component (therapists must be aware of this or they will get nowhere). High conflict over dependency, denial, the antisocial aspects, and the tendency to avoid responsibility for behavior make great success in psychotherapy improbable. They are prone to misuse prescription medications.

When this code type is found in females, it often reflects marital problems associated with sexual difficulties and, as already noted, problems in dealing effectively with anger. These persons are usually overcontrolled but occasionally fly into rages (Kelley and King, 1979a). As a 3-4 client changes to a 4-3, divorce becomes more probable (Fowler, 1981).

The 3-5/5-3 code, moderately common in males and uncommon in females, usually manifests itself in a man who *appears* to be competent and even charming. However, narcissism, denial, immaturity, and essential passivity mean there is little productivity, persistence, or ultimate responsibility. The code is frequent among fathers of child clients. Adolescents with a 3-5/5-3 are moderately depressed and withdrawn, are affectively shallow, often have weight problems, and lack skills with the opposite sex.

The 3-6/6-3 code is characterized by overt anxiety, tension, and rigidity that cover a strong fear of criticism and a blandly manifested but deeply suppressed hostility. There is a denial of this hostility, especially of any of its results as it emerges in passive or episodic aggression. The hostility is often directed toward significant others, yet is denied or repressed, so marital, family, or social problems are common. But their hostility, egocentricity, and resistance to psychological causation make therapy difficult. Although adolescents with this code type often perform well academically, they may manifest drug abuse and/or suicide attempts and are oversensitive, evasive, and resentful.

People who score moderately high on these two scales are hypersensitive to criticism, suspicious, and hostile, yet they overtly promote themselves as naive and optimistic about the world. They often were—and sometimes still are—"model" children. They have significant difficulties in interpersonal relationships and perceive their problems as emanating from others. To the degree that these two scales are high, there is more likely to be a clear paranoid disorder. If there is distinct bimodality, paranoia is common, whereas a rise on scales F and 8 suggests paranoid schizophrenia as more likely.

The uncommon 3-7/7-3 person is an "anticipatory worrier." Although worrisome and prone to take (and seek identity in) responsibility, they are more denying and repressed (especially the 3-7) than their relatively high 7 would suggest. They strongly fear the loss of control of anger in themselves or others, possibly reflecting abuse situations in childhood. They manifest various physical and psychosomatic disorders (often including insomnia), especially if stressed. They may elicit elective surgeries but are likely to respond negatively to the direct outcome or the side effects. Assertiveness training and anger-management techniques are useful, as are behavioral procedures like thought stopping and relaxation training. They are prone to dependency on pain- or anxiety-reducing medications, but they respond well to them in the short run.

The 3-8/8-3 person (also an uncommon code) shows confusion, distress, and a high probability of anxiety attacks, which are occasionally channeled into either phobias or acting-out (depending on scale 4). Histrionic, narcissistic, and dependency features are common. Obscure, intractable somatic symptoms are often reported. If both scales are high and F is also high, certainly consider possible cognitive dysfunction, including organic involvement. When scores are more moderate, consider a diagnosis that includes dependency and dissociative and/or hysteroid defense mechanisms. This disturbed thinking may manifest itself in unclear thoughts, poor concentration, lapses of memory, unusual ideas, or loose and unclear ideational associations. Further, delusions and hallucinations, as well as incoherent speech, may be present. The most common diagnosis is schizophrenia, although somatoform disorder may also be present (Graham, 1993). If 2 is moderately elevated in this pattern, psychotherapy is usually effective. If it is low, a supportive and structured therapeutic orientation is more productive. When an elevation on scale 3 is accompanied by an elevation on K and concomitant low scores on scales F and 8, look for individuals who are conforming, constricted emotionally, and yet dependent on others without acknowledging their dependency because it signifies vulnerability.

The rare 3-9/9-3 profile is usually found in women rather than men. These extroverted, often dramatic individuals quickly draw attention to themselves in social settings. They crave approval and dread failure, but then resent the control this need transfers to others. These persons usually manifest acute medical distress and/or depression as a referral complaint, often episodically, but on closer examination they are likely to show evidence of a histrionic personality disorder or, less frequently, an actual brain dysfunction or a conversion disorder. Alcoholism is common. They are verbally aggressive and inclined to distort their perceptions easily, and they have particular difficulty dealing effectively with sexual relationships, especially communication in the relationship. At a secondary level they are likely to show headaches and a number of other somatic complaints (Kelley and King, 1979a). Adolescents show similar patterns and are often embroiled in family conflict.

A spike-4 profile commonly suggests problems with the law. Spike 4's are often classic psychopaths (or college students, who are often high). They are egocentric and impulsive and have difficulty in relationships of any depth, although they often relate well initially. As 0 approaches a T of 30, this is even more pathognomic; they easily show anger outbursts. They are emotional survivors who are unlikely to truly try again in a relationship. If both the I.Q. and K are high, calculated and more clever criminal behavior can be expected—for example, white-collar crime. They typically stay in therapy only because they have to, and medications are contradicted. The aging process is the most effective therapy.

The 4-5/5-4 code denotes an antiestablishment and antiauthoritarian personality, but the subtlety of expression of such attitudes is modulated by parental-cultural background, I.Q., and level of education. Although a rare code in females, if present, it may include a strong "masculine protest," as well as overt aggression. A common diagnosis for the 4-5/5-4 profile is passive-aggressive personality disorder.

Men with a 4-5/5-4 profile are often bohemian characters inclined toward various types of nonconformity. They are defensive and passively rebellious and report themselves as emotionally stable. Ambivalence over dependency and control, as well as regards sexual identity, is common. They may be overtly homosexual and flaunt this in a passive-aggressive manner. Males with a high

4 and a low 5 show stereotyped macho masculinity. Females with low 5 and high 4 scores, on the other hand, lean toward social masochism. They adopt an overly feminine posture but carry a significant degree of underlying hostility. They often generate hostility and then use guilt and/or legal sanctions to punish the aggressor. To the degree 6 is also elevated, there is a transfer of blame onto others. Females with both a high 5 and a high 4 are those who have adopted behaviors that do not fit with the traditional female role. If these scores are not markedly elevated, they suggest a woman who has developed an independent and competent lifestyle. Adolescents with this code type are more likely to directly rebel and act out. They are provocative, prone to abuse drugs, and often delinquent.

The 4-6/6-4 code is mildly similar to the 3-8/8-3 code, except that there are fewer anxiety and phobic components and the emphasis is on narcissism, immaturity, suspiciousness, and anger. These individuals report vague physical and psychological symptoms and often show very poor work and interpersonal histories. It occurs with some frequency in adolescents, where it does not signal the degree of pathology it does in adults, although they are likely to abuse drugs and have strong conflicts with parents and school. In both adolescents and adults there is often a transfer-of-blame mechanism, and others view them as obnoxious. To the degree scale 3 is also elevated, the pattern is more one of immaturity than obnoxiousness.

A passive-aggressive diagnosis is common, although paranoid schizophrenia must be considered if scales 4 and 6 are very high and scales 8 and F are high. Women with this pattern who are also high on 5 are hostile and angry and are effective at eliciting rage reactions in others, especially males. Women with a 4-6/6-4 and a low 5 are overly identified with the traditional female role but feel trapped as a wife or mother and react with passive-aggressive patterns. Persons with a 4-6/6-4 pattern seek attention and deny blame and are often bitter, obnoxious, and difficult to deal with. They expect others to change rather than themselves, and they quickly reject responsibility for any problems. They may abuse alcohol. Intermittent aggression and a prepsychotic adjustment are also probable (Fowler, 1981). They may present somatizations in the forms of asthma, hay fever, hypertension, headaches, blackouts, and cardiac problems (Graham, 1993). They avoid being involved in any therapy, if at all possible, and seldom make any significant and lasting changes even when they are involved. Little progress can be made unless there is some resolution of the dependency that underlies the more overt anger patterns. Low doses of a nonsedating phenothiazine can be useful if the individual is very paranoid and angry, but there is addiction potential.

Women with a high 4 and 6 and a low 5 (the Scarlett O'Hara V) are hostile and angry, but passive-aggressive in their expression. They bait others with their dependency and demands. Whereas a boat is a hole in the water you throw money into, this type of woman is a hole in a family you throw affection into. If 3 is also high, they are overtly social or warm. They still irritate, if not enrage others, but they are blithely unaware of how or why this happens.

The 4-7/7-4 combination presents the paradox of the insensitivity and social alienation connoted by scale 4, combined with the moodiness and excessive concern about the effects of one's behavior connoted by scale 7. As a result, such individuals, both adolescents and adults, may be involved in inconsistent or cyclical emotional responses and acting-out behavior in which damage to other people is followed by apparent regret—such as the alcoholic who goes on a spree and disrupts friends and family, then follows this with contrite pleas for forgiveness. The remorse may even be real, but they seldom change significantly. They easily dissimulate, yet there is good reason to believe that they are truly insensitive to the feelings of others, and family situations are usually very dysfunctional. Certain sexual-deviate patterns that are a counterphobic response to a fear of the opposite sex show a 4-7/7-4 profile. When the profile has high scores on 2-7 and 4-9, there is often a warring between these somewhat disparate elements. With age, both 4 and 9 tend to diminish, and the more obsessive and depressive elements of the 2-7 profile emerge. Clients with a 4-7/7-4 indicate a desire for change and will become involved in psychotherapy, especially to the degree 7 is higher than 4. Critical to success is their ability to see the link between their anxiety and consequent impulsive, self-destructive acting-out behaviors. At the same time, however, they are concrete in their thinking and not psychologically minded; thus, they are not easily responsive to most insight-oriented therapies and they prefer symptomatic support and structure.

The 4-8/8-4 code types are perceived by others as narcissistic, unpredictable, or weird, and these perceptions are accurate. They are inclined toward antisocial and schizoid behaviors, yet these are usually within a family structure and reflect some underlying dependency and a deteriorating loss of control. Very often, from an early age, they develop a set to perceive others as hostile and dangerous, and their consequent "striking-out" in turn reinforces their sense of alienation. In this vein, Scott and Stone (1986) found 4-8/8-4 profiles to predominate in a sample of adult and adolescent clients who had been victims of father–daughter incest as children.

They tend toward "black moods" and may have periods of obsessive suicidal ideations or even vicious aggression. And if both scales are very high, with 8 greater than 4, the likelihood of bizarre thinking, psychosis, and paranoid suspiciousness increases. In this case the clinician should consider the diagnosis of paranoid schizophrenia. Usual diagnoses include schizophrenia (paranoid type), antisocial personality, schizoid personality, or paranoid personality. Persons with a 4-8/8-4 code, especially when there is also a high score on 6, usually had very destructive family backgrounds and appear to feel as if the world is a jungle. As a result, they perceive their own acting-out as a matter of survival. Sirhan Sirhan, the assassin of Robert F. Kennedy, showed a clear 4-8-6 pattern, although his F was also almost as high (T = 80) (Fowler, 1981).

When 4 and 8 are high, such individuals may continually show antisocial behaviors (e.g., rape), they are prone to violence if cornered, and they prefer a nomadic and transient existence with few responsibilities. When elevations on 4 and 8 are accompanied by a high F and a low 2, one may find a punitive and interpersonally destructive person who goes about in the guise of a helpful person, such as a minister or guidance counselor. Punitive aggression, almost to the point of sadism, is directed into a good cause. In spite of an apparently caring role, they are often schizoid in their personal life. Adolescents of this type are extremely miserable and unhappy, show odd or even bizarre disorder patterns, and are immature and resentful. Therapy is difficult with 4-8's and includes constant "trust testing," if it happens at all.

The 4-9/9-4 code is a very common one; when high, it is frequently found to indicate a characterological-behavior disorder, most often an antisocial personality disorder, both in adults and adolescents. These individuals do not profit from experience, ignore social standards and mores, are seekers of a high degree of stimulation and may appear good-natured and charming. Yet they often become embroiled in sociolegal difficulties, are self-centered, and show deficient functioning in the interpersonal and vocational areas. At the very least, they show an enduring propensity to subvert the potential "good" of self and family. They are narcissistic and impulsive, and even though they may manifest a certain degree of energy and ambitiousness, they have many problems resulting from their transient lifestyle, narcissism, acting-out, and inability to follow through on plans. David Berkowitz, the notorious "Son of Sam" killer, presented a clear 9(T = 78)-4(T = 75) pattern.

Histories of alcohol abuse, notably episodic sprees, are common, especially if F is also high. Occasionally this pattern indicates a bipolar disorder (Graham, 1993). If the 4-9/9-4 profile is distinctly bimodal, these persons are not so consistently aggressive, but they are inclined toward deception. To the degree 8 and 6 are elevated, they are likely to be more directly aggressive. To the degree 0 is elevated, they are more likely to be slick and effective in their manipulations of others.

It is interesting that women who obtain a 4-9 profile that is not markedly high overall have been characterized as having high potential for sales positions. If 4 and 9 are only moderately elevated (in men or women) and there is an indication of psychological distress via scale 2, such persons can respond positively in psychotherapy, although initial sessions are generally replete with resistance and confrontation is often required. When 4 and 9 are quite high and 6 and/or 8 is elevated, success in psychotherapy is much less probable. Any 4-9's who appear in therapy (usually brought there somehow) want you to fix their worlds, not them; they intellectualize to excess, and they expect quick results.

Persons with a 4-0/0-4 code (usually females, as this is a rare code for males) carry much anger, but they are unable to express it directly because they are shy and evasive. They report little emotional distress and few health problems, but they easily develop resentments and hold grudges and can be destructive to others if this does not entail any direct confrontations. One male who did show this pattern, Charles Manson, also had virtually equal elevations, all over 80 T, on 8 and 9 as well.

A spike-5 profile is often indicative of transient situational disturbance. If not, it is usually a person who reports self-confidence and good physical and psychological health. It is commonly high in normal, liberal college males and in avowed homosexuals.

The 5-6/6-5 code type is uncommon. These individuals are aloof, abrasive, and/or politically or morally self-righteous. They see themselves as positive on virtually all dimensions, including being liked by others. They are especially inaccurate on the last facet so, not surprisingly, have substantial interpersonal difficulties, especially heterosexually.

Males with a 5-7/7-5 pattern are introspective, excitable, and interpersonally sensitive, with episodes of anxiety and/or depression, along with schizoid components if 0 is also elevated. Females show many interpersonal problems, especially with males.

The 5-8/8-5 person is likely to have a personal and family history marked by physical or sexual abuse, substance abuse, and/or psychiatric disorder. Although not usually psychotic, they have odd or intrusive thoughts, are shy and reserved, and have substantial difficulties in sexual and family adjustment.

Individuals of code type 5-9/9-5 actively seek stimulation and are easily bored; whether the consequent behaviors get them in trouble depends on 4, and also on 6 and 8. They like to be in control and see themselves in a very positive light. They relate easily, although their heterosexual relationships are usually stormy.

Males with a 5-0/0-5 code are introspective but, unlike 5-7/7-5's, are more schizoid and anxious than they are depressed. Both females and males with a 5-0/0-5 code show problems in heterosexual relationships, are easily embarrassed, but see themselves as happy and well-adjusted—which they are not. Females with this code often come from a lower education and/or socioeconomic background and appear passive, yet they show many social-role conflicts.

Spike 6's are rare; when it occurs the individuals are openly distrustful and suspicious and probably clinically paranoid. They need to develop trust, although this is a monumental therapeutic task.

The 6-7/7-6 code is uncommon, often associated with elevations on 2 or 8, and denotes anxious, tense, guilt-prone (especially to the degree 2 and/or 7 is high rather than 8), hypersensitive individuals. They typically use obsessive-compulsive defenses that are no longer effective in controlling anxiety and rumination. They misinterpret others, leading to distant or volatile relationships.

The 6-8/8-6 code type is closely associated with a prepsychotic or psychotic adjustment, especially if these scales are substantially elevated. There is much rebellion and anger and other persons are alienated, thereby creating a vicious cycle for their prophecy that they are persecuted. They can be episodically and inappropriately aggressive and, at best, appear unusual to others.

In general, 6-8/8-6's show underlying inferiority, fearfulness, and low self-esteem, which seem to be counterphobically defended against by an irritable and hostile veneer. They demonstrate poor judgment in a number of areas and are emotionally unstable. They naturally do not respond well to psychotherapy and, if at all receptive, are inclined toward fad treatments. Significantly elevated 6-8/8-6 profiles, with high L and F scores and relatively low scores on scales 3 and 7, suggest markedly disturbed persons who show paranoid ideation, although organic brain syndrome should also be considered. The degree of available psychological energy, often reflected in the degree of accompanying elevation on scale 9, is the determining factor in whether the underlying hostility evidences itself.

If both the 6 and 8 scales are quite high (above 75 T) and 7 is relatively low (65 T or lower), that is, a 6-7-8—the "paranoid (or psychotic) valley"—Gynther et al. (1973a) suggest looking for further evidence of paranoid schizophrenia associated with auditory hallucinations. This is especially true of psychiatric patients with this distinctive profile, as a diagnosis of schizophrenic, paranoid type, is common, but there should also be a thorough consideration of the validity of the profile. These individuals are likely to manifest psychotic behavior, autistic thinking, blunted affect, rapid and incoherent speech, and withdrawal into fantasy when stressed. Psychotropic medications should certainly be considered for this population. Even when 6 and 8 are not especially elevated, potential for insight is stunted, at best. Scales 2 and 0 are often above a T score of 60 in persons with 6-8 or 7-8 code types who have a thought disorder and below a 55 T score in clients with a manic mood disorder (Greene, 1991). The 6-7-8 pattern occurs with adolescents, in whom learning disabilities and nonspecific brain damage are also commonly noted, as well as violent temper reactions.

The hallmark of the high 6-9/9-6 profile is hostile excitement and a counterphobic response to underlying insecurity and dependency. Referral is often precipitated by a perceived rejection or attack by a loved or trusted other. A diagnosis of paranoid schizophrenia is common. The clinician needs to consider the possibility of organic brain dysfunction where the manic and suspicious adjustment may be a reaction to loss of functioning in a personality that finds loss unacceptable. At more moderate levels the 6-9/9-6 profile suggests strong dependency and affection needs that are usually not met. These individuals are overresponsive to emotional slights or threats, so often present angry or hostile reactions. Medication is usually necessary, although they will be distrustful of it, and especially of its side effects.

While shy and easily embarrassed, the 6-0/0-6 profiles, especially if 6 is not markedly elevated, are usually well adjusted and have pleasant yet sometimes distant relationships with others.

Spike 7's, an uncommon pattern, are quite shy and are fear-prone and uncertainty-phobic. They are tense and obsessive-compulsive, and phobic patterns are common. The pathology is commonly stable, and they are less successful in therapy than one might initially expect. Time-contingency (e.g., three-months) prescriptions of anti-anxiety medication are helpful.

The 7-8/8-7 pattern, in the moderate range, shows depressive and/or obsessive-compulsive features, often with much inner insecurity and turmoil (Butcher and Graham, 1988). If elevations are marked and accompanied by elevations on scales 0 and 2, severe depression, anxiety, and introverted behavior should be expected and deterioration into a more blatant schizophrenic adjustment is possible. Deterioration is marked by the use of neologisms, bizarre speech, depersonalization, and possibly catatonic stupor. Even in the less extreme range, these individuals show a low level of social skills, and if they are not diagnosed as schizophrenic, they are likely to have borderline personality traits (Kelley and King, 1979b). When initially seen, 7-8/8-7 clients may be confused and panicked, and they are typically tense, anxious, insecure, and shy. They may feel chronically insecure, inferior, and inadequate and have a difficult time making decisions. They will usually report problems, especially sexual ones, in interpersonal relationships, and as a result may ruminate or fantasize profusely. Suicide attempts are not infrequent, and, to the degree that scale 8 is high, they may have a bizarre quality. To the degree that 7 is greater than 8, these individuals usually retain better control in behavior adjustment, are less likely to be blatantly psychotic, and are still fighting deterioration. Unfortunately, a high scale 7 is soluble in alcohol and other drugs; fortunately, closely monitored medication can be of help.

If both scales 7 and 8 are elevated well above the 70 T mark and 8 is higher, schizophrenia is a strong probability, especially if scales 1, 2, and 3 are relatively low. This holds true even more for men than for women. Even if no psychosis exists, a significant and pervasive emotional disturbance of some sort is probable.

The 0-7/7-0 code is characterized by tension, insecurity, anxiety, and low self-confidence. This group is shy and has substantial difficulties in interpersonal relationships—especially adolescents with family members—and may be agoraphobic.

Spike 8's are odd, eccentric, and nonconformist, at best. Some are psychotic; most have odd sexual fantasies and often odd behaviors. They tend to be aloof, but unhappy in their aloofness. Their behavior is often disorganized, and they show poor judgment. Occasionally an intelligent, self-confident and creative (but aloof) individual will present a spike 8. Spike 8's usually need medication, the type of medication often depending on the relative elevation of 2 and 7.

The 8-9/9-8 type identifies individuals who are narcissistic and hostile, have difficulties relating effectively to others, and may at times manifest inappropriate surges of anger or exuberance. It is a more common code in adolescents and young adults, where it is often associated with self-centeredness and hyperactivity. They often have high needs to achieve, but performance is inefficient. The fear of relating is handled by distractibility techniques, so psychotherapy is extremely difficult. It is very hard for them to focus on any issue for any significant period of time. Medication is often necessary. They are usually responsive to medication, but because of the high 9 may need high dosages, or lithium. Even if the scores are only moderately high, there should be much concern about long-term adjustment. Multiple-drug abusers, particularly adolescents, may show this pattern. In adults a high 8-9/9-8 is associated with a schizophrenic adjustment with a poor prognosis, odd or pressed speech patterns, and delusions and/or hallucinations and confusion. The pattern probably represents either a disorganized or an agitated schizophrenic, depending on scales 6, 3, and K. If not psychotic, they are at least egocentric and dysfunctional in most life areas. There is often a history of delinquency, or at least of behavioral problems. A high 8-9/9-8 associated with elevation on scales F, 2, and 7 may be a schizoaffective disorder, depressed type. Even moderately high

8-9/9-8 elevations are symptomatic of a significant psychopathological process (Butcher and Graham, 1988).

The 8-0/0-8 code is a relatively uncommon one, especially in males and young adults. They are significantly socially avoidant, nonverbal, indecisive, and isolated. Often diagnosed as schizoid, they are not very comfortable with their adjustment and show some anxiety as well as a propensity to become lost in fantasies.

A spike-9 profile is likely to indicate drug abuse and/or antisocial personality disorder; in males it is also associated with aggressive acting-out (King and Kelley, 1977). In general, spike 9's are extroverted and sociable, but without intimacy. They have high energy levels and occasionally show manic or grandiose episodes. They are usually impulsive and rebellious, with scale 4 being an important modifier. They need to learn to avoid their anxious, striving perceived failure-frustration cycle. Guiding them to be "laid back" or to live in the "here and now" is a therapeutic challenge.

Although shy, 9-0/0-9's (a very uncommon code type) usually have adequate social skills and high energy and can be a bit manic. They are self-confident, occasionally to the point of grandiosity, and usually present themselves as happy and well adjusted.

The spike 0 on the MMPI-2 is suggestive of situational adjustment difficulties, such as marital problems and/or a schizoid adjustment; mild but chronic emotional distress also may indicate religiously oriented distress, perhaps an abrupt loss of faith in God (Kelley and King, 1979a). Spike 0's are shy and easily embarrassed, so are prone to phobias and fears, although usually not of major proportions. Their "affect starvation" and the need to positively cope with their characterological shyness will be foci in therapy.

■ Diagnosis Code Type Relationships

To facilitate the reader's use of the two-point codes, a list of first-consideration (not exclusive) diagnoses associated with specific two-point codes is presented in Table 12.2. This table is coordinated with the material in the previous section, as well as with that discussed in the later sections on the various clinical syndromes.

TABLE 12.2   First-Consideration Diagnoses and Two-Point Codes

CODE	FIRST-CONSIDERATION DIAGNOSES
1-2	Chronic Alcohol Intoxication, Anxiety Disorder, Female Psychosexual Dysfunction, Schizophrenia (rare), Somatization, Hypochondriasis, Depression, Passive-Aggressive Personality Disorder
1-3	Conversion Disorder, Hypochondriasis, Malingering, Faking-Good, Panic Disorder, Psychogenic Pain Disorder, Eating Disorders, Multiple Personality

(Continued)

TABLE 12.2 *(Continued)*

CODE	FIRST-CONSIDERATION DIAGNOSES
1-4	Hypochondriasis, Social Phobia, Chronic Alcohol Intoxication, Substance Abuse, Somatization, Affective Disorder
1-6	Somatization, Paranoid Schizophrenia
1-7	Somatization, Obsessive-Compulsive Disorder, Eating Disorders
1-8	Pedophilia, Schizoid Personality Disorder, Acute Schizophrenia (relatively rare), Affective Disorder, Borderline Personality Disorder
1-9	Masked Depression, Post-Traumatic Stress Disorder, Central Nervous System Impairment (rare), Dependent Personality Disorder (rare), Sexual Masochism (rare)
2-1	Anxiety Disorder, Conversion Disorder, Chronic Alcohol Intoxication, Female Psychosexual Dysfunction, Somatization
2-3	Female Psychosexual Dysfunction, Depression (especially for females), Generalized Anxiety Disorder, Histrionic Personality Disorder, Panic Disorder, Affective Disorder
2-4	Acute Alcohol Intoxication, Schizophrenia, Secondary Psychopathy, Antisocial Personality Disorder, Suicidal Potential, Unsocialized Nonaggressive Conduct Disorder, Adjustment Disorder
2-5	Passive-Aggressive Personality Disorder, Dependent Personality Disorder
2-6	Paranoid Personality Disorder, Major Depression, Paranoid Schizophrenia, Histrionic Personality Disorder, Borderline Personality Disorder (rare)
2-7	Agoraphobia, Avoidant Personality Disorder, Dependent Personality Disorder, Major Depression, Bipolar Disorder, Depressive Episode, Dysthymic Disorder, Chronic Alcohol Intoxication, Factitious Disorder, Generalized Anxiety Disorder, Identity Disorder, Obsessive-Compulsive Disorder, Psychogenic Pain Disorder, Possible Toxic Addiction to Pain Killers, Schizotypal Personality Disorder, Sexual Masochism, Stuporous Catatonic Schizophrenia, Suicide Potential, Zoophilia
2-8	Depressive Episode, Possible Bipolar or Cyclothymic Disorder, Suicidal, Central Nervous System Impairment, Post-Traumatic Stress Disorder, Generalized Anxiety Disorder, Panic Disorder, Explosive Disorder, Schizoaffective Disorder
2-9	Bipolar Affective Disorder, Central Nervous System Impairment
2-0	Depressive Episode, Possible Bipolar or Cyclothymic Disorder, Schizoid Personality Disorder, Avoidant Disorder
3-1	Compulsive Personality Disorder, Conversion Disorder, Hypochondriasis, Malingering, Faking-Good
3-2	Depressive Episode, Possible Bipolar or Cyclothymic Disorder, Female Psychosexual Dysfunction, Histrionic Personality Disorder

3-4	Histrionic, Borderline, Passive-Aggressive and Avoidant Personality disorders; Dissociative Disorder; Intermittent Explosive Disorder; Manic Episode (rare); Pedophilia; Psychogenic Amnesia; Voyeurism; Substance Abuse
3-6	Paranoia, Paranoid Personality Disorder, Paranoid Schizophrenia, Somatization, Affective Disorder
3-7	Depersonalization Disorder, Somatization, Anxiety Disorder
3-8	Multiple Personality, Pedophilia, Schizophrenia (rare), Somatization, Possible Psychosis, Affective Disorder
3-9	Somatization, Bipolar Disorder, Conversion Disorder, Explosive Personality Disorder (rare), Possible Psychosis, Histrionic Personality Disorder (rare), Panic Disorder, Passive-Aggressive Personality Disorder (rare)
4-1	Hypochondriasis, Social Phobia, Chronic Alcohol Intoxication, Somatization
4-2	Acute Alcohol Intoxication, Primary Psychopath, Antisocial Personality, Schizophrenia, Secondary Psychopath, Suicide Potential, Unsocialized Nonaggressive Conduct Disorder
4-3	Aggression Potential, Explosive Disorder of Impulse Control, Passive-Aggressive Personality Disorder, Pedophilia, Rape, Voyeurism
4-5	Narcissistic and Passive-Aggressive Personality Disorders, Exhibition-ism, Homosexuality, Opiate Abuse, Aggression (in females)
4-6	Substance Abuse (especially Amphetamine Disorder), Oppositional Personality Disorder, Chronic Alcohol Intoxication, Paranoid Schizo-phrenia, Passive-Aggressive Personality Disorder, Somatization (rare), Intermittent Explosive Disorder, Depression
4-7	Chronic Alcohol Intoxication, Bipolar and Cyclothymic Disorder, Substance Abuse
4-8	Exhibitionism, Pedophilia, Primary Psychopathy, Schizoid Personality, Antisocial Personality, Borderline Personality, Pyromania, Rape, Schizophrenia, Sexual Sadism, Unsocialized Aggressive Conduct Disorder
4-9	Amphetamine Disorder, Chronic Alcohol Intoxication, Pathological Gambling, Rape, Secondary Psychopathy, Antisocial Personality, Histrionic Personality, Narcissistic Personality, Sexual Sadism, Social-ized Nonaggressive Conduct Disorder
5-1	Transsexualism
5-3	Transvestism
5-7	Schizoid, Passive-Aggressive Personality Disorder, Anxiety Reactions
6-1	Paranoid Schizophrenia
6-2	Borderline Personality Disorder, Shared Paranoid Disorder
6-3	Paranoia, Paranoid Schizophrenia, Paranoid Personality Disorder, Somatization

(Continued)

TABLE 12.2 *(Continued)*

CODE	FIRST-CONSIDERATION DIAGNOSES
6-4	Chronic Alcohol Intoxication, Paranoia, Paranoid Schizophrenia, Passive-Aggressive Personality Disorder, Shared Paranoid Disorder
6-7	Obsessive-Compulsive Disorder, Multiple Phobias, Anxiety Reactions, Affective Disorder, Avoidant Disorder
6-8	Aggressive Acting-Out, Polydrug Abuse, Paranoid Schizophrenia, Central Nervous System Impairment, Borderline Personality Disorder, Schizoaffective Disorder
6-9	Central Nervous System Impairment, Paranoid Schizophrenia
7-1	Somatization
7-2	Agoraphobia, Avoidant Personality Disorder, Dependent Personality Disorder, Depressive Episode, Bipolar or Cyclothymic Disorder, Dysthymic Disorder, Chronic Alcohol Intoxication, Obsessive-Compulsive Disorder, Post-Traumatic Stress and Adjustment Disorder, Sexual Masochism, Suicidal Potential
7-3	Somatization
7-4	Chronic Alcohol Intoxication
7-8	Borderline Personality Disorder, Substance Abuse, Brief Reactive Disorder, Depression, Suicidal Attempts, Obsessive-Compulsive Disorder, Schizophrenia, Schizophreniform Disorder
7-0	Anxiety Disorders, Agoraphobia, Avoidant Personality Disorder
8-1	Pedophilia, Schizophrenia, Schizotypal Personality Disorder
8-2	Depression, Schizoaffective Disorder
8-3	Multiple Personality, Pedophilia, Somatization
8-4	Paranoid Schizophrenia, Pedophilia, Primary Psychopathy, Antisocial Personality, Rape, Unsocialized or Socialized Aggressive Conduct Disorder
8-6	Central Nervous System Impairment, Schizophrenia, Paranoid Schizophrenia, Primary Psychopathy, Antisocial Personality
8-7	Borderline Personality Disorder, Brief Reactive Psychosis, Depression, Obsessive-Compulsive Disorder, Schizophreniform Disorder
8-9	Acting-Out in General, Polydrug Abuse, Agitated Catatonic Schizopohrenia Central Nervous System Impairment, Depression, Schizoaffective Disorder, Disorganized Schizophrenia, Mania, Paranoid Schizophrenia
8-0	Schizoid and Avoidant Personality Disorders, Schizophrenia
9-1	Central Nervous System Impairment (rare), Dependent Personality Disorder (rare), Sexual Masochism (rare)
9-2	Central Nervous System Impairment, Bipolar Affective Disorder
9-3	Conversion Disorder, Histrionic Personality Disorder (rare), Panic Disorder, Somatization (rare)

9-4	Chronic Alcohol Intoxication, Secondary Psychopathy, Antisocial Personality
9-6	Central Nervous System Impairment, Manic Episode, Bipolar or Dysthymic Disorder, Paranoid Schizophrenia
9-8	Central Nervous System Impairment, Depression, Schizoaffective Disorder, Disorganized Schizophrenia, Mania, Bipolar or Dysthymic Disorder, Paranoid Schizophrenia
0-2	Depression
0-7	Agoraphobia

■ Additional Scales

Besides the traditional validity and clinical scales, the most widely used scales are the Content scales, the Supplementary scales, the Harris-Lingoes scales, and the Subtle-Obvious scales, scoring for which has been provided by NCS ever since MMPI-2 came out.

□ CONTENT SCALES

Most agree the Content scales have been very useful. From one perspective, they are scales composed of Obvious items, purified of any Subtle items. As noted earlier, in addition to the original clinical scales, they are the only scales plotted from the normative sample into uniform T scores; thus a particular T score, for example, 60, is comparable from a percentile standpoint (see Table 12.1) across all of these scales. They are psychometrically sound (Butcher et al., 1990; Graham, 1993) but have varying degrees of external validity. The major drawback is that they are easily faked, so a reasonably cooperative subject is required in order to assume that the following interpretations are accurate. At the same time, since they are face-valid, they can give you a sense of what your clients are trying to tell you about themselves or how they want you to see them. As with the clinical scales, a T score of 65 or above is high, and a score of 40 or below is low.

1. *Anxiety (ANX):* A high score suggests standard anxiety-related symptoms like difficulty in concentration, low self-confidence, apprehension, nervousness, sleep problems, and distractibility. Such individuals are likely to be pessimistic and feel stressed and/or depressed. Correlates highly with scale 7. Females are a bit more likely to show hostility and irritability. Low scorers are likely to be self-confident and show a low rate of these symptoms.

2. *Fears (FRS):* A high score indicates multiple fears and/or phobias; a low score the absence of same. Also correlates significantly with scale 7.

3. *Obsessiveness (OBS):* High OBS scorers are rigid, ruminative and indecisive; worry a lot; lack self-confidence; may be schizotypal in their ruminations about odd thoughts, and show various compulsive behaviors like hoarding unimportant things or counting. Low OBS scorers are adaptable and self-confident and show an absence of obsessive-compulsive patterns.

4. *Depression (DEP):* A purer measure of depression even than scale 2. High scorers report depressive thoughts, are indecisive and uninterested in life, and are sad and blue. They report feeling pessimistic, guilty, and lonely; they have health concerns and may be suicidal. Low scorers do not report such symptoms and usually have adequate energy and self-confidence.

5. *Health Concerns (HEA):* High scorers are preoccupied with bodily functions, report a variety of physical symptoms, and say they have little energy. Also may point to schizotypal and/or borderline propensities. True neurological disorder may be involved; e.g., clients with multiple sclerosis will report a wide variety of physical symptomatology. Low scorers report generally positive physical health. It can effectively discriminate chronic pain patients from psychiatric patients or normals.

6. *Bizarre Mentation (BIZ):* High scores here reflect reports of psychotic symptoms, i.e., thought disorder, hallucinations, delusions, or depersonalization. Correlates significantly with 8 and F. Low scores reflect an absence of these symptoms.

7. *Anger (ANG):* High scorers are openly admitting feelings of anger, hostility, and irritability. They feel they may lose control of their feelings physically or verbally. Low scorers claim to not experience these feelings or to sense that they might lose control of their feelings.

8. *Cynicism (CYN):* High scorers are classic misanthropes. They expect the worst from others, even from those close to them and from fate. They resent any demands from others, although they may set high demands for themselves. Low scorers report trusting, liking, and helping others and are generally not seen as pushy or hostile.

9. *Antisocial Practices (ASP):* Those high on this scale also tend to be somewhat misanthropic, but they use their misanthropy as a basis to rationalize antisocial patterns. They have problems in school or with the law, resent authority, and vicariously enjoy other's criminal antics. Males are especially likely to swear, curse aggressively, posture, and/or exhibit temper tantrums when irritated. Low scorers report an absence of trouble with or distrust of others and can accept authority.

10. *Type A (TEA):* This scale was included because it was a "hot" topic when MMPI-2 was being developed. High scorers reflect the refrain from *Alice in Wonderland:* "I'm late, I'm late for a very important date." They are competitive and become easily irritated, annoyed, or impatient. They are often direct but insensitive in interpersonal relationships. Low scorers don't usually feel competitive, pressed for time, or easily irritated and are usually seen by others as easy-going.

11. *Low Self-Esteem (LSE):* A high score here reflects feelings of unattractiveness, incompetence, guilt, and failure. They are passive, sensitive to criticism and tend to worry and be indecisive. Low scorers report self-confidence, can accept criticism, report few fears, and are usually decisive.

12. *Social Discomfort (SOD):* High scorers are shy and introverted. They are interpersonally avoidant. Low scorers report being comfortable in initiating interpersonal contact, like being in social groups, and are extroverted.

13. *Family Problems (FAM):* Persons with high scores report a high level of discord in their present and/or past families, perceive and resent intrusion from family members, and have a pessimistic view of marriage. They may have been physically abused as children. Low scorers value family life and see their own experiences in that realm as positive.

14. *Work Interference (WRK):* High scorers have attitudes that predict to poor work performance. Such behaviors include questioning their career choices and the value of work to their life, as well as obsessiveness, indecisiveness, low self-confidence, or tension and pressure relevant to work performance. Low scorers report an absence of work-disruptive attitudes and behaviors and are likely to be self-confident and at least reasonably ambitious.

15. *Negative Treatment Indicators (TRT):* This is probably best construed as a measure of compliance in treatment, rather than probable success. Persons who score high here believe they can't be helped, both as a result of the magnitude of their problems and their sense of inadequacy, as well as their hostile and/or avoidant attitudes toward treatment procedures and/or personnel. They tend to show poor judgment and poor problem-solving ability. Low scorers believe they can be helped, are willing to cooperate in that process, and show good judgment and problem-solving skills.

SUPPLEMENTAL SCALES

There have been many scales constructed out of the MMPI-2 item pool, and no doubt more will be constructed in the future. All are scored in linear T scores rather than uniform T scores. They have varying levels of reliability and validity. Of the scales recognized by the architects of MMPI-2 from the time of its revision, the following have both (1) consistent relevance to clinicians and (2) sufficient reliability and validity.

1. *Anxiety (A):* This scale is a less pure measure of anxiety than the previously described Anxiety (ANX) Content scale. Indeed, it is actually a pretty good measure of general maladjustment. High A clients are anxious, socially inhibited and awkward, compliant and conforming, cautious and cool, and defensive. They prefer a slow life pace and function poorly under stress. Low A individuals are not anxious, are confident, resourceful, vigorous, interpersonally friendly, and assertive. They are sometimes dominant, can

be inclined toward status and/or power, are sometimes unable to delay gratification or impulse, and prefer action to thought.

2. *Repression (R):* High R people are conventional and conforming but usually clear-thinking. They internalize conflict and can be slow and even compulsive in productive work. They resonate to formality and manners. Low R's are emotional, enthusiastic, and occasionally eccentric. They eschew detail or decorum, can be impulsive, daring, and generous, but also at times can be selfish, shrewd, sly, and sarcastic.

3. *Ego-Strength (Es):* This scale was originally designed to predict the response of "neurotics" to one-on-one psychotherapy. High scores still predict a good response to the degree those conditions hold. Otherwise, a good rule of thumb is that a high Es score in a person who is (1) admitting problems and (2) asking for help predicts a good response. If the person is not admitting problems and/or indicating an interest in help, a high Es does not predict that well in either direction. High Es's basically have better psychological resources and are reasonably well adjusted. Although admitting they have problems, they report fewer stressors. They are generally reliable, sociable, and not prejudiced toward opinions or people (except possibly authority figures). They can be manipulative, pushy, and even cynical. Low Es's lack self-confidence, do not persist psychologically or vocationally, feel (and usually are) inadequate, may be confused, and are inclined toward chronic physical or psychological disorder.

4. *MacAndrews Alcoholism-Revised Scale (MAC-R):* See Chapter 2 for a discussion of this scale.

5. *Overcontrolled-Hostility Scale (O-H):* See Chapter 14 for a discussion of this scale.

SUBTLE-OBVIOUS SCALES

Scoring for Subtle-Obvious items has been available since the inception of MMPI on scales 2, 3, 4, 6, and 9, reflecting the development of these scales by Weiner in the mid-1940s. John Graham articulates one clear perspective on the value of the Subtle-Obvious scales, occasionally saying, "They suck real bad and you shouldn't use them." Others see them as having more value (Greene, 1991). There are two foci in the research literature. The first is to assess whether subtle or obvious items predict to external correlates, for example, depression. It is not surprising that Obvious items predict better to such external correlates as admitted depression. The real issue is the second research trend, that is, to assess whether people who are instructed to (or actually do) fake one way or another can be detected. The evidence is mixed (Butcher, 1995; Graham, 1990; Greene, 1991). But many clinicians report it is a useful approach to point to possible faking when there are only a few prior indicators. Also, in some instances where an overall faking set is apparently not present, a major discrepancy between Subtle and Obvious items on one scale, for example, scale 4, may point to an important area for further scrutiny.

CHAPTER 13

Clinical Correlates of 16 PF Test

This chapter discusses the Cattell Sixteen Personality Factor Test (16 PF), specifically the fifth edition (herein referred to as 16 PF-5) as a personality measure. Certainly other tests are available—for example, traditional ones such as the California Psychological Inventory (CPI), the Myers-Briggs Type Indicator and the Personality Research Form, and somewhat newer instruments like the Multidimensional Personality Questionnaire (MPQ) and the NEO Personality Inventory-Revised.

Each has its good points (and drawbacks) and can be very helpful in various research or clinical situations. However, the 16 PF-5 is recommended for consideration both as a test in its own right, and as a complementary test to the MMPI-2 because (1) the 16 PF for the most part measures ongoing personality traits, a number of which are important but are not measured in MMPI-2; (2) it has an impression management score that aids in the interpretation of the test and in the battery as a whole; and (3) the 16 PF is well designed, has good validity and reliability data, requires only a fifth-grade reading level in the fifth edition, and has accrued substantial clinical and research data (Conn and Rieke, 1994; Russell and Karol, 1994; Cattell, 1993). We'll first examine individual scale correlates and then turn to data based on scores of related factors.

■ **Cattell's 16 PF Test**

The 16 PF-5, developed primarily by Raymond Cattell and Herbert Eber, was devised to tap a wide range of a client's ongoing personality functioning. It was designed more for personality traits and conflicts than is the MMPI-2 (Cattell, 1989), which is oriented primarily toward categories of dysfunction and psychopathology. The 16 PF-5 gives scores on sixteen dimensions that Cattell derived through a factor analysis of a huge number of personality descriptors; they were then validated on a wide variety of abnormal and normal client groups.

Traditionally there were six available forms of the original test. The first five forms are designated by the letters A through E. The sixth is a short form (128 items), which is Part 1 of the original form of the Clinical Analysis Questionnaire (Krug, 1980). Form A was the one most commonly used. It is composed of 187 items; the 16 PF-5 has 185. This means there are approximately ten items for each of the sixteen scales in 16 PF-5, except for B (fifteen items) and Q_1 (fourteen items). The client's response to an item affects only one scale on the 16 PF-5, whereas in the MMPI-2 a single response may affect more than one scale.

The 16 PF-5 was made available in 1994, in effect replacing the prior forms of the 16 PF. Of course, the continued usage of the earlier forms still has validity.

Improvements asserted for the 16 PF-5 are (1) item content has improved readability and lessened ambiguity, and "bias" items have been revamped; as a result, a fifth-grade reading level is usually adequate, whereas at least a sixth-grade level was required for Form A; (2) normative data now reflect U.S. Census (1990) data; (3) test-taking time has been reduced to thirty-five to fifty minutes, from forty-five to sixty minutes for Form A; and (4) psychometric properties are better. Average test-retest reliabilities are .80 at two weeks and .70 at two months. Internal consistency reliabilities average .74, with a range of .64 to .85. New response set indices are available; Impression Management (IM) replaces the Faking Bad and Good scales, and the Acquiescence (ACQ) and Infrequency (INF) scales are new. Some new criterion scores, self-esteem and empathy, are available.

The 16 PF-5 standardization sample is 2500 (49.8% male, 50.2% female), stratified from an original sample of 4449. Age is 15 to 92, with a mean of 33.3 years. Whites made up 80.4% of the stratified sample; blacks, 12.8%; Asian-Americans, 3.0%; Native Americans, 2.3%; and Hispanics, 9.0%. The Hispanic sample crosses racial groups; thus, the total sample exceeds 100%. The sample is also adequately stratified by geographic region.

One reasonable criticism of the standardization sample for the 16 PF-5 is that it is overeducated (M = 13.6 years of education; S.D. = 3.30) relative to the general population, a criticism noted in MMPI-2 as well (see Chapter 10). However, since the trend is for the general population education level to rise over the years, this criticism will gradually lose its relevance, and eventually the "defect" may prove to be fortuitous.

Another reasonable criticism is that it is much more complicated and time-consuming to hand-score a 16 PF-5 protocol than it was in prior versions of the test. This may in part be driven by the demands of the test. However, it's probably more directly related to the fact that purveyors of tests are well aware they make much more money on those customers who use on-line computer or marketer-produced scoring reports than when a clinician hand-scores his or her own protocols.

As with the evolution of MMPI to MMPI-2, one has to be concerned whether or not the 16 PF has been changed so much in 16 PF-5 that it is now just a new test with an old name. The changes here are greater than they were with the MMPI. However, the available data indicate that (1) enough of the old test remains (of the 185 16 PF-5 items, 88% are from previous 16 PF forms, al-though many were rewritten to some extent), (2) many of the changes were only in wording, and (3) neither the wording changes nor the new items changed the scale meanings (indeed, in many instance, they apparently improved scale integrity); as a result, the research on interpretation using the prior forms can be usefully applied to 16 PF-5 (Conn and Rieke, 1994; Russell and Karrol, 1994; Cattell, 1993).

The 16 PF allows three response choices, with "uncertain" or "cannot de-cide" as a question mark on the answer sheet, available on all items except those on Factor B (Reasoning). The Infrequency Scale is composed of 32 "?" responses. This, along with the fact that it is much shorter and does not ask questions that are quite so unusual or personal, makes the 16 PF more accept-able to most clients than the MMPI-2. As with the MMPI-2, it is helpful to encourage test takers to give the most accurate responses they can and to an-swer every question, if possible. If more than twelve questions go unanswered, the protocol is invalid. Test takers should also be warned against spending extensive time mulling over an answer and be asked to give their first clear responses.

Like prior editions, the 16 PF-5 uses "sten" (a range of 1–10 superimposed on a normal curve) scores to transform raw data into a comparable format; scores in the 4–7 range are considered "average," with "4" designated as low average, "7" as high average. Low scores are 1–3, and high 8–10, although interpretation may make use of the real differences available in those ranges.

In spite of this terminology, extreme scores (i.e., outside of the 4–7 range) are relatively common. Indeed, 69% of the population produce from three to seven extreme scores, 85% produce two to eight extremes, and only about 1% show no extreme scores.

Three factors (Warmth, "A"; Dominance, "E"; and Sensitivity, "I") exhibit significant gender differences in the distributions. Therefore, separate-gender norms as well as combined-gender norms are available for these factors.

In addition to the primary sixteen factors, five "global factors" (termed "secondary factors" in earlier editions) are also scored. These five factors (Ex-traversion, Anxiety, Tough-Mindedness, Independence, and Control) bear a close resemblance to the "Big Five" personality factors that have received so much attention in the research in recent years (Extraversion, Neuroticism, Open-ness, Agreeableness, and Conscientiousness).

■ 16 PF Factors

□ SCALE A

Scale A—referred to as "Warmth" (Warm vs. Reserved)—is considered the major factor, by variance scores, in personality prediction. It generally differ-entiates between people who are reserved and aloof (low on scale A) and those who are sociable and warm. Degree of warmth is considered to be a relatively fixed trait, and women score a bit higher here than men. High A's are more gregarious, adaptable, and trusting, sometimes to the point of being too emotionally needy and/or Pollyannaish; less prone to cyclical moodiness; and less vulnerable to criticism. However, very high A scores may be associated with mania and/or difficulties in impulse control. Also, high A's are gullible and avoid being alone, sometimes at the cost of compulsive and/or self-defeating behaviors. They are successful (and like to work) in arenas that require social contact, for example, families or organizations, but underachieve where working alone is a critical task component. Their clinical conditions reflect their potential flaws of gullibility, need for approval, and emotional dependency.

Most of the adjectives associated with low A's are fairly negative, although such persons are often more compulsive and precise and therefore more productive in certain areas. They easily find the negative in people or situations. They are often more effective in tasks that require working alone and/or generating their own structure, especially if they are also high on B (intelligence). They are only self-disclosing and generate rapport if they feel comfortable in a particular relationship and, even then, are inclined to withdraw from requests for intimacy. Very low A's tend to remain flat in their emotional lives and aloof in relationships, and Heather Cattell (1989) sums it up well, saying, "Communicating a desire for intimacy to an A-person is often like describing color to the congenitally blind" (p. 24). Persons who score very low are likely to earn adjectives like "schizoid" and "introverted," as well as "obnoxious," and frequently display the "burnt-child" syndrome (especially if scale E is also low) in interpersonal relationships.

SCALE B

Scale B, the second-largest 16 PF factor by variance, was originally labeled "High General Intelligence (appropriately enough, the high end of the scale) versus Mental Defectiveness." It is now termed "Reasoning" (Abstract vs. Concrete), with three types of reasoning being tapped—verbal, numerical, and logical. It is probably best thought of as reflecting the ability to reason and to discern relationships, classify events, and form typologies. In actuality, low scores do not necessarily indicate low mental ability. For one thing, there are only fifteen items on this scale, so any precise assertions of validity of predicting intellectual level are unrealistic, especially where issues of distraction, emotional disruption, and reading or language difficulties apply. There is no good evidence for gender or race bias.

Low scores may be associated with random or distorted answering sets, attentional difficulties, impulsiveness, or a lack of ability to persist on a task. Low scores should only be a major concern if there is good reason to believe the person was trying to do well. High scores (8–10) generally indicate at least average—probably higher—intellectual ability.

SCALE C

Scale C is termed "Emotional Stability" (Stable vs. Reactive). It is considered to reflect dissatisfied and labile emotionality (the low end of the continuum), as opposed to emotional stability or ego strength. It taps emotional stability, maturity, and a low threshold for irritability and upset and consequent neurotic fatigue. Over all, scale C is probably the single most important predictor in the 16 PF for the ability to cope with, adapt to, and/or solve the broad range of life's problems. Most neurotics show low C scores; criminals are only relatively higher here. Persons low on C may be faking-bad, while those scoring high may have a high impression-management score. This scale loads most highly on the Self-Esteem global factor, and also highly on Anxiety, but, surprisingly, not much on the Self-Control global factor, which is most highly related to Rule Consciousness (G+) and Groundedness (M−).

High C persons have a somewhat stoic (although not necessarily passive) philosophy, are able to formulate problems concretely and specifically face problems without procrastination, are usually good time managers, are seldom perfectionistic, and accept limitations in self and life. They are good colleagues-companions, although they can sometimes seem too invulnerable, like Mr. Spock from "Star Trek." They tend to prepare effectively for anticipated stressful events and are usually reliable in emergencies. Often they learned these skills in difficult childhoods, but in difficulties they were able to cope with. However, Cattell (1989) suggests that a person with a high C score who also reports a difficult childhood is prone to "burnout," that is, less ego strength later in life.

Low C's tend to react to challenges or crises with more rigid emotional responses and cognitive solutions, may discount information and other persons' feelings, may respond too slowly or too impulsively, and are more likely to feel emotionally distressed by these situations. They are often disruptive interpersonally and are likely to report physical problems, anxiety, depression, and/or on, rarer occasion, psychosis.

Low C scorers need to have their self-esteem improved and some control over their emotional lability generated before they can make any strides with insight therapy. If there is no distortion, a higher C score offers a good prognosis for psychotherapy. There is some evidence that C will rise following a successful therapeutic intervention. In general, high C's have learned to channel their emotionality into productive and integrated behaviors, as opposed to impulsively dissipating it.

SCALE E

(The reader might wonder why there is no scale D in the 16 PF. In Cattell's original list of factors, D was referred to as "Excitability," and it was not thought to be a major differentiating issue in adults, so it is only found on the Cattell tests for children.)

Scale E primarily is termed "Dominance" (Dominant vs. Deferential). It includes lesser contributions from assertiveness and a willingness to conform to authority. Scores on E decrease with age, and, reflecting both hormones and society, males tend to be higher on E. Dominance (E+) is the major contributor to the Independence global factor. Scores on E increase with situationally positive events and decrease with negative ones (e.g., chronic illness).

A high score on E would indicate dominant and tough individuals who have strong needs to be independent (which may mask real feelings of inferiority) yet wishe to gain status and control over others (possibly as a form of self-protection), and they may be quite manipulative in their quest. However, probably because of the conflicts over role expectations, high scores in females have extra factor loadings from attention-getting, social poise, and possible hypochondriacal aspects. A high E score connotes an assertive (sometimes "abrasive" if it is very high—although a high E score does not inherently connote aggression) personality style, and, although it is not always associated with leadership ability, established leaders do tend to be higher on this score. Indeed, the more technologically advanced the society, the more intelligence is correlated with dominance. However, thought patterns can be rigid in high E's—these people not only know what's good for them; they know what's good for you as well. They feel little discomfort about their behaviors, but at an organismic level, these behaviors exert a cost in higher stress levels. They cope poorly with loss, especially irrevocable loss such as death, so grief is very difficult for them. Also, if they are ever forced to confront their own powerlessness, they are often devastated. Interpersonally, high E's can be vigorous and forceful, but they are just as likely to be conceited, sarcastic, quarrelsome, and/or opinionated.

Low E's tend to be acquiescent, submissive, self-effacing, and dependent. Over the long run, they tend to be perceived as a bit boring. Persons who are shy are low on E, whereas those who are narcissistic, chronically angry, or inappropriately assertive are higher on E. Low E's are prone to be neurotic and self-defeating and often feel vulnerable to and frustrated by the control of others. They often react with resentful depression and/or passive-aggression. Alcoholics tend to be low on E.

SCALE F

Scale F, which is highly loaded on genetic factors, is denoted as "Liveliness" (Lively vs. Serious). This may be better described as an alert, enthusiastic, and even happy-go-lucky style versus sober, introspective seriousness (the low end of the scale). Along with scale A, and also H, N and Q_2, scale F is an important predictor of extroversion-introversion. Persons who show bipolar affective disorders may swing markedly on this factor. Success in psychotherapy raises F, as does the initial effect of substance abuse. Hysteric individuals and those with sexual, personality, and impulsivity disorders usually score higher on this scale, whereas persons with depression, phobias, and introverted patterns score lower. A low score on F, along with a high O, suggests depression.

The F score drops rather markedly between the ages of 18 and 35 years, and there is some indication that F rises slightly with an increased metabolic rate. Although there is a slight correlation of an above-average F score with the holding of a leadership position, this does not necessarily connote *effective* leadership because the higher the F score, the more impulsivity is found. Persons in leadership positions who are high on F often need associates who can take the plans they generate and bring them to fruition.

High F's resonate to the poet Walt Whitman's phrase "I celebrate myself"; they "do what comes naturally" and enjoy novelty and variety. They enjoy social and sexual expression and are attention-seeking, and they may be overly attracted to the opposite sex. They are true "party animals." They are socially and physically mobile and are prone to dilettantism and narcissism (although it's a rather benign narcissism as it is not a retreat from the full self); hence, relationships are volatile when they persist for any duration. They are not likely to be effective in enterprises that require persistence. Unlike low C persons, whose failures are due to weak egos, such failures by high F's reflect the faddish, associative style of their interests. High F's can be flighty, even manic at times.

Low F's are often dour, with constricted emotionality but possibly a dry sense of humor, if there is any sense of humor. They behave and think ponderously, but if they are highly intelligent, they can be both creative and productive. Their sober demeanors, however, seldom lead to popularity. Although not inherently shy, they avoid "high-energy" social gatherings. Their responsible, conventional patterns reflect inhibitions rather than weak superegos. Low F's are prone to depressive episodes, and their periodic gloomy, "wet-blanket" attitudes don't support much marital happiness (although they may have marital status).

SCALE G

Scale G is termed "Rule Consciousness" (Rule-Conscious vs. Expedient). It denotes a person who is demanding, casual within the usual moral standards, and potentially undependable (the low end of the continuum) versus a conscientious and responsible individual. High G individuals are guardians of the moral order, group-conforming, cautious in decisions, and set in their thinking and biases. High G's are conscientious but also potentially staid and dogmatic. They are responsible workers and usually high achievers. They do have difficulties in "understanding" the irresponsible person; hence, they are especially stressed when parenting teenagers. "Women who love too much" are often high on G, but have elicited a series of relationships with low G men. Very high G scores are often obtained by professional moralists, for example, priests or ministers, and there is a significant correlation with the Impression Management score. The triad of high G and Q_3 and low Q_1 is the solid, stable citizen who can be a "stick in the mud."

Heather Cattell (1989) sees four major variants in low G persons: (1) faking-bad; (2) amorality, not necessarily psychopathy, which has additional components of inability to profit from experience and a lack of response to standard punishment stimuli, but more of a primitive egocentricity; (3) moral immaturity—cued by a low C as well as other components such as low H and high L and Q_4—a morality based on concrete reciprocity and avoidance of punishment; and (4) nonconventional morality — often cued by high C and Q. Markedly low scores may suggest a self-disclosing psychopath, and even moderately low scores suggest a person who is likely to disregard obligations. However, since this measures adherence to subgroup standards as well, certain criminals do score high here. Rebellious adolescents particularly score low. Scale G measures the more overt, standard, culturally accepted aspects of morality (rather than internalized guilt as tapped by O+), and other scores, such as on O, would further indicate whether this was a bona fide personality trait. There is a definitive correlation with age and socioeconomic class; the older the person and the higher the socioeconomic status, the higher the score on scale G.

SCALE H

Scale H is termed "Social Boldness" (Socially Bold vs. Shy). It denotes a person who is shy, constricted emotionally, and threat-sensitive (the low end of the continuum) versus one who is more adventurous, thick-skinned, and pushy but friendly. Cattell suggests that this is largely an innate (genetically determined) factor. High H scorers imply boldness-dominance, self-exhibition, a high interest in the opposite sex, and a high need for environmental stimulation. They may enjoy feeling fear—for example, love horror movies, roller coasters, dangerous events, and challenges. H+ delinquents respond far better to Outward Bound programs than to psychotherapy. A higher H person is more likely to be seen as intellectually and emotionally lazy, especially during the developmental years. One might be able to contact them with an ad in *Soldier of Fortune* magazine. High Hs are prone to sociopathic patterns. They can be thick-skinned and inconsiderate in relationships and easily opt for "open" marriages, although they don't always communicate this choice to their partners.

A low H score indicates a person with an overresponsive sympathetic nervous system. Low H's become self-absorbed, yet they are jealous when attending to others. They fear "doing the wrong thing" socially and can be friendly and polite so as not to draw attention to themselves, yet are basically shy. They live out the motto "Nothing risked, nothing lost." Their constricted worlds make for marital difficulties, and they do poorly outside of routine jobs. Very low H scores are found in introverted personalities, and alcoholics who use alcohol either for disinhibition or "to steady my nerves" are low on H. This is one of the factors that predict a basic schizoid temperament as well as, on occasion, a chronic schizophrenic adjustment. Since H connotes threat sensitivity, it should be low in such disorders as agoraphobia, panic disorder, and PTSD. There is some evidence that low H individuals are more likely to suffer ulcers.

☐ SCALE I

Scale I is labeled "Sensitivity" (Sensitive vs. Utilitarian). Common connotations have to do with individuals who take a tough and realistic view of life, are inclined to be self-sufficient, and are not highly responsive to vulnerability, pain, or conflict (the low end of the continuum), as opposed to people on the high end (an I+), who are sensitive and empathic and base judgments on personal tastes and aesthetic values. They can also be dependent, and possibly effeminate or demanding. Sensitivity (I+) is the major contributor to the Receptive aspect of the Tough-Mindedness global factor.

Factor I is seen as one pole (i.e., two functions) in the set of four operations or functions (feeling, thinking, sensation, intuition) by which people respond to their environment and which form the basis of the "trendy" test of the Myers-Briggs Inventory. I–, or low I, is seen as reflecting the feeling dimension, high I the thinking function. A low score on M, discussed later, apparently taps the sensation function; a high score taps the intuition. There is overlap, as high I's are often intuitive.

High I's base judgments on subjective and emotional responses, that is, feelings as opposed to the objective logic and abstraction of low I's. High I's are more likely to be romantic, empathic, repulsed by crudity, occasionally indecisive, sentimental, and artistic. Unfortunately, like Felix of "The Odd Couple," they expect the same sensitivity and empathy in others, but when paired with a low I—Oscar—they are not likely to receive them. They are prone to romantic fantasy and often have difficulty distancing themselves from their feelings. They can be prone to stress-based anxiety and psychosomatic disorders (especially if E is also high).

In general, this continuum reflects William James's traditional distinction between tough-minded and tender-minded people; those people in the tender-minded subgroup (high on I) generally wish to avoid conflict and have high aesthetic interests. Being low on I does not necessarily help a person adapt to conflict, however, possibly because the tough-minded continuum is a more brittle adjustment and therefore less adaptive to certain types of stress.

Low I's lack such sensitivity; are inclined to be rough and crude; and they are not inclined to self-analyze or to indulge vulnerability, either in others or themselves. They are not psychologically minded and usually have repressed rather than absent emotions. It is difficult for them to become aware of when they (or anyone else) are at the end of their emotional ropes, at which point they are emotionally brittle. Although scale I has not been found to be highly associated with psychopathology, psychotics on average are slightly lower than normals on this factor. Low I's have repressed emotions and difficulties with intimacy. They are unable to accept their tender or vulnerable sides and are usually unprepared for any interpersonal crises that their distancing patterns do not take care of.

There is a high genetic loading here, and there are age and sex differences on I: Older people tend to score higher than the very young, and women consistently score higher than men. At the extreme high point the clinician finds women who have stayed within the traditional female role, almost to a stereotypical degree. Macho men score very low on I.

SCALE L

Scale L is termed "Vigilance" (Vigilant vs. Trusting). It is often interpreted as suspicious jealousy and emotional distancing (an L+) as opposed to a relaxed trust and openness to the world (the lower end of the continuum). High L's expect to be misunderstood and/or taken advantage of, and if L is very high, paranoid concerns may be noted. Persons high on the scale tend to be cynical and defensively project their negativism and suspicions. Some take elitist views and arrogant postures and insist that their ideas be heard; in the latter respect they reflect some of the dominance characteristics also attributed to scale E. Others with high L appear more furtive and frustrated, with low self-esteem and constricted life view. Cattell (1989) sees the jealousy characteristic of high L's as consistently including the sequence of a sense of deprivation, an unfavorable comparison between self and others, a sense of impotence and/or falling behind in any prospect of righting the perceived imbalance, and defensive projection to restore self-esteem directed toward individuals or "fate." They are ever on the lookout to add more injustices and perceived deficits in others to their "collections." Persons high on L are not primarily schizoid, although their personalities easily result in rejection by others, so interpersonal isolation occurs and is a cause of distress and jealousy.

A major issue is how a person channels these traits into vocational and interpersonal interests. For example, eminent researchers often score higher on L because the characteristics of cynicism, isolation, and confidence in their intellectual superiority serve them well. But the typical high L person is at risk of being rejected, has too high a level of inner tension, has defenses that may be too brittle, and may not have enough access to other persons as emotional resources. Paranoid disorders commonly include a high L. Also, high scores predict general illness, especially coronary artery disease and psychosomatic concerns like low back pain.

On the other hand, low L persons in general are emotionally healthy, easily make others feel accepted as they feel at one with other people and the human race, and are usually noncompetitive, although they are subject to interpersonal manipulation and conning and can become heavily involved in dependency (from others) relationships. When the L score is not reflective of an individual's malingering or misperception, it is an indicator of good emotional health.

SCALE M

Scale M is labeled "Abstractedness" (Abstract vs. Grounded). It can be conceptualized as conventional practicality versus less conventional imagination (the high end of the scale). As noted earlier in the discussion of factor I, low M is seen as tapping the sensation pole of the Jungian sensation-intuition dimension, also a major component of the Myers-Briggs Inventory. Slightly less directly, high M taps the intuition dimension. Whereas high I's are intuitive in the sense of suddenly apprehending a hitherto unrecognized insight without apparent effort, that is, "out of the blue," high M's are intuitive in the broader sense of the word, that is, as "a habitual tendency to focus on the higher ratio of ideas, associations, and other internal mental processes, rather than to focus on external stimuli" (Cattell, 1989, p. 191).

Persons high on M have well-developed imaginations, tend toward intellectual narcissism, do poorly in detail work, and easily dissociate. They are open to unconventional options—when they act them out, they may be labeled "ahead of their time," eccentric, or possibly criminal. One way of conceptualizing high M's is to contrast them to factor traits they are commonly confused with. For example, high M's may be thought of as socially withdrawn, like low A's. But, rather than being truly schizoid, they are simply self-absorbed. It is also common to misinterpret the propensity of high M's to fail to make ordinary observations or forget important information as indicating lower intelligence than they actually possess. Also, their inclination toward offbeat styles, naive projections, and obtuseness in the face of social cues move toward impulsive acting-out when G is low (expediency—lower superego strength). Clinically, M's tend to be found in substance abusers, schizophrenics, and depressives and are prone to job dissatisfaction. There is some evidence that very high M's alternate between outbursts of rumination-generated activity and rather placid periods when they seem to be totally wrapped up in themselves. In that sense, this scale is a measure of a type of introversion. High M is also significantly and somewhat paradoxically correlated with both creativity (at least the generation of ideas and insights) and accident-proneness (e.g., the absent-minded professor).

Whereas high M's are prone to see a forest where there are only a few trees and shrubs, low M's tend to see a lot of trees and miss the forest. From a philosophical perspective, Plato, with his view that perceptions can be misleading and have to be anchored to an internal theory, would be a high M, whereas Aristotle, who believed truth came directly through the senses, would be a low M. Low M's are not psychologically minded and avoid introspection. They "call a spade a spade," prefer the routine and familiar, have good memories and like details, seldom are able to innovate, and can be a bit boring and frustrating in relationships (including therapy or marriage). They often like to work with facts and things, rather than ideas or people. They are prone to obsessive and compulsive patterns. Persons with somatoform disorders are lower on M than are those with anxiety-based disorders. The assumed explanation for this difference is that persons with anxiety-based disorders are keeping their conflicts in higher levels of consciousness, thereby experiencing anxiety, whereas the somatoform disorders reflect a denial of inner conflict.

SCALE N

Scale N is termed Privateness (Private vs. Forthright). Persons on the high end (N+) are socially alert, although a bit calculating and aloof, and may show sophisticated anxiety or concerns about success in relation to high internal standards. They tend to present and/or value social barriers, or at least facades. At very high levels, individuals are Machiavellian (or are faking-good), whereas if scores are too low, they manifest extreme naiveté about other people's motives (or, occasionally, the person who manipulates through naiveté—"I just let it all hang out. I'm ok, you're ok. Could you do this for me?"). Moderately high scores on N generally (and a bit more so in males) indicate a good family upbringing and positive character integration. Clinically, high N's are hard to read, and all other response-distortion indices should be closely appraised. Clinicians need to be alert to cues that differentiate some high N's who are "second-nature shrewd" (reflecting a long-term character) from those who are "second-thoughted shrewd" (who later in life adopted the pattern as a coping strategy) (Cattell, 1989).

Low N's "put all their cards on the table." Yet, as noted, a subgroup of low N's can be interpersonally dominant, in a straightforward manner, and tend to present a "transparent self." They are low in social ambition and can be conned or manipulated but seem to recover relatively easily from disappointments. They also tend to be socially clumsy and overtrusting and have rather simplistic interests. They tend to prefer animals, plants, young children, and the like over adults. Clinically, they are prone to immaturity, sometimes exhibit very poor judgment, and are usually a bit insensitive to others' feelings if they are not directly presented with them. Psychotics and neurotics on the average score lower on N.

☐ SCALE O

Scale O is generally labeled as "Apprehension" (Apprehensive vs. Self-Assured). It suggests a placid confidence (the low end of the scale) versus an insecure proneness to guilt (primarily reflecting a sense of inadequacy rather than a violation of internalized moral standards). A high O score is probably best thought of as reflecting lower self-worth or self-esteem, often accompanied by feelings of shame and doubt. Persons high on this scale are "worriers," which can be a positive coping strategy at times but tends to distance others. High O's can also be avoidant of stimulation and oversensitive, show a strong sense of morality and duty, and are prone to anxiety-based disorders, such as phobias or hypochondriasis. A high O score occasionally reflects situational rather than trait-based low self-esteem and/or depression, especially if F is low. Whether characterological or situational, persons suffering from negative feelings about themselves are likely to score low on O. This makes them vulnerable to taking dependent and/or masochistic roles if they do enter relationships.

Moderately low O scores suggest self-confident, generally cheerful, relaxed, and resilient individuals. They can accept blame, but they don't appear to really "feel" sorry. Very low O's often manifest an unshakable confidence; again, this can be a positive coping strategy. But it also means they miss opportunities for feedback; thus self-evaluation and improvements are less likely. Very low O's may also be psychopathic, may be more likely to act out their conflicts, or may have well-ingrained defense mechanisms. Low O's may verbalize guilt, but there seem to be no true feelings of it nor any restitution efforts. They have trouble with intimacy because of their lack of empathy. Along with scale G, O taps what Freudians have referred to as "superego."

SCALE Q_1

Scale Q_1 is termed "Openness to Change" (Open to Change vs. Traditional). It indicates a cautious conservatism (the low end of the scale), with a strong attachment to the past and present versus individuals who enjoy novelty and change from a purposeful perspective, with a free-thinking, future-oriented, and experimenting approach to life. Liberal (high Q_1) versus conservative political beliefs also affect this scale. Like the other Q scales, this factor has not been totally validated in all types of data collection, yet most clinicians find the Q scores to be extremely helpful. The interested reader is referred to Cattell (1973) for the subtle distinctions he used to discriminate the Q scales from the previously mentioned scales.

Persons high on the Q_1 scale are somewhat impatient and want to change whatever they perceive as the "status quo" in persons or situations. They are often somewhat critical of others but tend to be analytical and liberal in thought patterns, representing an intellectualized form of anger. They seek the "interesting" and are bored by the familiar and the routine. In males, high Q_1 is often correlated with anger toward authority. Depending on vocational and interpersonal situations, high-Q_1 persons can have difficulties with authority figures or establishment rules and hence can be disruptive in highly structured environments. They can be viewed as intellectualized aggressors, with an implicit potential for loss of impulse control. High Q_1's are future-oriented and see change as good, but fear being controlled by others or archetypes of their past. They are often viewed as "troublemakers" in job settings. They manage adequately in marriage if control issues are settled but seem to soon see greener grass if dissatisfied.

Low Q_1's are cautious and uninvolved politically and anticipate changes with trepidation, but they often adapt and resign themselves to negative circumstances. Their "cost-benefit" decision is usually "any gains from change are likely to be offset by the distress of change." They don't like people who are "different." They are dependable and loyal and are often highly attached to their families of origin, but, unfortunately, in many instances because of dependency rather than affection. They want to stay with what they know. They are prone to conversion hysteria, psychosomatic disorders, obsessive-compulsive patterns, and adjustment disorders and are prone to being used or abused. People quite low on this scale are colorless individuals who, rather than being rejected by others, are often simply ignored. Very low O's endure situations that are distressing, even when it seems to others they could or ought to leave those situations. They are prone to stress-based disorders, obsessive-compulsive patterns, and of course to adjustment disorders.

SCALE Q₂

Scale Q_2 is called "Self-Reliance" (Self-Reliant vs. Group Oriented). It taps basic dependency (the low end of the scale) as opposed to a self-sufficient resourcefulness, as well as a "proximity to others" variable. High Q_2's value privacy and freedom of choice. They are not schizoid per se or even shy but are content to spend substantial amounts of time alone and rarely feel lonely. They are likely to neglect (rather than manipulate) the interpersonal aspects and consequences of their actions. They are often rugged individualists and seldom seek advice or reassurance, yet they show at least a moderate degree of "neuroticism," which is probably why they have higher-than-average rates of coronary artery disease (which may be why the "Marlboro Man" is an archetypal high Q_2), hypertension, and peptic ulcers. As such, they are well advised to maintain at least one confidante, or even a beloved pet. A nondirective therapy approach (paradoxically, sometimes with bibliotherapy assignments) is the most effective approach with high Q_2's. High Q_2 males place a high value on sex, possibly because it allows a covert gratification of any unfulfilled intimacy needs (without any of that messy "touchy-feely" stuff).

Low Q_2's have a high need to "belong," often have strong family attachments, and in general show high rates of proximity-seeking behaviors. But at times they lack initiative or "character" and thus are prone to be exploited. They need much social approval, actually like to work on committees, are chronic "joiners," but easily move into dependent roles in relationships. Very low Q_2's may have problems due to their lack of initiative, their tendency to be exploited, or the weakening of their sense of self. They often develop strong transference relationships, à la the movie *What About Bob?* In that sense, Q_2 reflects a more basic dependency factor than scale G, as G taps more of an adherence to group standards.

SCALE Q₃

Scale Q_3 is titled "Perfectionism (Perfectionistic vs. Tolerates Disorder)." It points to a low self-concept integration (the low end of the scale) versus a controlled approach to life (Q_3+), with an emphasis on a strong, controlling will and a desire to retain the respect of self and others. High Q_3's like predictability, and "control" is often an issue. High Q_3's want to "do the right thing." They constantly monitor the appropriateness of their behaviors in relation to standards or ideals (which are often set too high). They take pride in typically fulfilling (at least that's their perception) these goals, but they don't report high joy in life and show little spontaneity. They actually have a deficit of unconditional self-acceptance, feel they are valued for what they do or will do, rather than for what they did do or just the fact that they are, and thus show perfectionism. They are generally trustworthy and reliable, so are perceived as good co-workers but not as fun companions. People high on scale Q_3 are ambitious, persist in tasks, and keep their commitments, yet they are also inclined toward inflexible judgments, smugness toward others, suppression of anger, and obsessive and compulsive concerns. They are also predisposed to paranoid and narcissistic patterns and to schizophrenic and dissociative disorders. In clinical terms, high scores on Q_3 can reflect a great need to control conflict and anxiety that threaten to break through brittle modes of coping; that is, they are wound too tight or, as Karson and O'Dell (1976) so aptly point out, there is a high need to bind anxiety into symptomatology or avoidance patterns.

Low Q_3's, on the other hand, tolerate disorganization and disarray, especially in their own "self." Also, a low score may reflect a lack of impulse control, a diffuse identity, or a lack of ability to structure one's psychological world effectively. Low Q_3's generally do as they please and care little how they are perceived by others. They are fickle in relationships and are not the best employees, as they do not persist on tasks, prepare well ahead of time, or take significant pride in their performances. Hence, they are high consumers of vocational and relationship counseling. They are prone to both antisocial patterns and the more "neurotic" personality and anxiety disorders. Q_3+ should cue to the issue of suicidal concern if there are other indicators of depression.

SCALE Q_4

Scale Q_4 is labeled "Tension" (Tense vs. Relaxed), that is, low anxiety and tension (the low end of the scale) versus high tension and anxiety. Q_4 is the best 16 PF-5 measure of situational anxiety; hence, there may be reasonable fluctuations over time. However, Cattell (1989) asserts that it "usually indicates that tension is a trait; therefore the examinee is characterologically a tense, volatile and easily upset individual" (p. 294). The client can often tell you whether the tension is a trait or a state. This scale is also the largest contributor to the global Anxiety factor. High Q_4's are behaviorally fidgety and "hyper"; are impatient and don't tolerate disruption well; and report feeling "pressured," "nervous," or "on the edge." However, Q_4 items are largely face-valid, so the scale is subject to impression management. High Q_4's are found in profiles of "neurotics"; bipolars; alcoholics; some psychopaths; and persons with impulsive, violent, or suicidal tendencies. If scale O is also high, it suggests an insecure and anxious quality that persists beyond the situational parameters. People quite high on Q_4 are likely to have experienced rejection by others, are oversensitive in various dimensions, and have a high level of frustrated sexuality. Once emotional disorder crystallizes into an obsessive or psychosomatic pattern, Q_4 is lower. Biofeedback, relaxation training, a vigorous exercise program, and anti-anxiety medication are good antidotes for the high Q_4.

Very low Q_4's have a phlegmatic temperament, lack vigor and drive; and are tranquil, relaxed, and unfrustrated. They are seen as laid back (and they are) and do a pretty good job living out the Zen admonition "sitting quietly, doing nothing." They show few strong passions or drives and not a great deal of motivation. To the degree Q_4 is more moderate, they are more relaxed but effective in most dimensions, although they are seldom mistaken for overachievers.

■ 16 PF-5 Scale Interrelationship Interpretations

The "global factors" noted earlier on the 16 PF-5 reflect those interactions of primary traits found to most clearly and consistently reflect a personality propensity. When using these second-order factors in a clinical analysis, it is of course important to consider the differential contribution of each individual component. We'll now turn toward general interrelationships among the individual 16 PF-5 factors.

If a person is high on scale A, it is important also to consider the score on Q_2; if that is low, the person has a particularly high need for interpersonal feedback and may be petulant and querulous if it is not provided. High scores on both A and F show a gregarious and friendly extrovert, whereas low scores on A and F point to a sober, serious personality, with a high score on L further indicating a hostile and suspicious introvert pattern. Low A and low H indicate a very shy and timid person, and low A and high Q_2 suggest a resourceful and independent person. When low A is combined with the sensitivity of a high I, expect a sensitive and reserved person, à la poet Emily Dickinson.

When a high scale B is combined with high scores on scales E and Q_3, there is likely to be much intellectualized hostility, with consequent rejection by others. It is also worthwhile to look at scale M in relation to scale B because this suggests to what degree intellectual competence is channeled into imaginative, creative activities rather than into more practical and immediate plans. High B's who are low on A are very vulnerable to being conned and to being used by others.

C+ and Q3+ point to a controlled, sometimes compulsive personality. C+O–individuals have very strong egos and are placid and serene, although sometimes frustratingly complacent. In contrast, C+H+ persons are "competent adventurers" in life. When C+ is combined with very low O and high L, distortion to protect a more fragile ego strength is suggested.

C–I– persons appear stoic, but their stoicism is based on an absence of personal reflection and a suppression of feelings, rather than a functional philosophy of life. C–F– persons show constricted thinking, consequently cope poorly with novelty, and naturally hunger for routine. C–I+ persons vacillate in decisions and relationships, apparently in hopes of avoiding the harsher realities of life. C–Q_3– individuals cannot maintain behaviors that generate social approval and seldom carry through with whatever good intentions they can generate. C–E– persons tend to be masochistic. C–O+ individuals are insecure worrywarts, C–Q_4+'s are tense and "stretched to the breaking point," and C–L+'s are usually quite paranoid in some dimension.

If a low scale C is found with a high H and lower G and Q_3 scores, a psychopathic quality is likely. When scales C, F, and A are low, particularly if associated with a moderately low H, look for a withdrawn, shy, and fearful individual. In general, a high O combined with a low C points to a deterioration in competency to adapt to environmental stressors, with Q_4 indicating the degree of concomitant anxiety.

As noted earlier, a high I score combined with a high E score predicts the development of stress-based disorders, especially if L and Q_4 are also high. A conflict arises in that the individual is both sensitive and dominant and is torn between the need to look assertive and yet to actuate a desire to reach out emotionally to other people. The competitiveness inherent in the high E blocks the needs of the high I. While E–H+'s are deferent out of a desire to be liked, E–H–'s are deferent to avoid attention. Cattell (1989) observes that high E's, along with F+, C–, G–, and Q_3–, persons, are especially prone to violent responses when threatened with loss. Low E, along with F–, Q_1–, O+, and Q_4+, should raise concerns about possible suicide. She also reports on data that divides low E individuals into five subgroups:

1. With low G = The Sufferer—Good Boy/Good Girl—Martyr. These individuals are willing to subordinate their self, but expect to be appreciated for it and seldom are—they "keep count."

2. With low C = The Uninvolved (but emotionally labile and tense). These people are conciliators who "walk on egg shells" to avoid conflict yet may have occasional uncontrolled outbursts of anger to "let off steam"—and they usually carry a lot of steam.

3. With high L = The Passive-Aggressive or Saboteur. Persons here assume others will resent their self-expressions, then see themselves as compromised; thus they become angry but fear their anger will be detected, so express it covertly.

4. With low E, high C, and high N = The Seducer or Shrewd Manipulator. This type "gets even, not angry." If such individuals also show high L (pattern 3), they are prone to violent discord in relationships, à la *Fatal Attraction*.

5. With low A and low F = The Wet Blanket, or whiny "sour grape." These individuals turn away from people and life, but take a piece of flesh on the turn.

High scores on E, L, and Q_1 particularly predict hostility, and the clinician should look to scores on scales B, M, and Q_3 to see whether this aggression is likely to be intellectualized or to manifest itself in controlled plans or actualized retribution.

A high F and low G combined with a high Q_1 and low Q_2 may indicate a young adult in severe conflict over identity development. When F+ is accompanied by A– and Q_2– scores, expect a detached, highly self-serving personality; here the Q_2– is not an inherent attachment to others, but the using of others. When F+ is found with lower C, G, and/or Q_3, asocial behavior can be expected.

Low G combined with high O is found in persons who portray themselves as rebellious and free-thinking but who experience much guilt whenever they act out this behavior. This is different from the pattern of low G and low O, consistently found in psychopathic individuals who show little if any guilt. Low G and F accompanied by high O suggest possible depression.

When high H is not balanced by high A or I, look for an especially insensitive individual who is very likely to bore or irritate people. High H and low B predict poor judgment and impulsive action, a bad combination. High H and low C predict poor reality testing, some impulsivity, and low frustration tolerance. Very low H and E scores predict a "doormat personality," often showing masochism and/or dependency. Persons with high H in combination with high Q_1 are critical in interpersonal relationships yet avoid the risks of taking responsibility for or acting on their criticism. When the isolated suspiciousness of the high L is combined with low scores on H and A, a paranoid-schizoid component is probable and warrants further scrutiny.

As noted, high I and high E are related to stress-based disorders. Conversely, low scores here predict an individual who appears passive yet may be tough at the core and able to resist stress reasonably well. Very high I and F scores suggest narcissism and histrionic tendencies. High I, H, A, and F suggest an activist, personally and socially. High I with low F and H points to intense but bottled-up feeling states. Low I, high A's are dangerous interpersonally as their extrovert components are perceived as sensitivity, but they never "come through" with that sensitivity and often hurt or disappoint others.

When both L and O are high, a furtive, apprehensive, and very emotionally constricted individual is likely; when L is high and O is low, expect patterns of arrogance and grandiosity. When L and B are high, A low, and O at least a bit low, expect less projective defensiveness as these highly intelligent, high self-esteem individuals are basically indifferent to others. Their suspiciousness is channeled toward more abstract phenomena, so they can be productive in areas that require analytic thinking and skepticism, like research. When L is low and other apparently contradictory scores occur, for example, high N or E or low G, at least consider more subtle forms of faking. If L is low and I and M are high, look for a person who avoids interaction with the world by escaping into fantasy, whereas if I and M are low and L and N are high, look for a shrewd, cold, and pragmatically plotting individual. If a low L is accompanied by a low E, one may have an individual who is both very dependent and manipulative—a person who takes on a "poor me" role and yet manipulates other people in a passive-dependent fashion.

High M's who have more indicators of introversion are likely to be deep thinkers but to have trouble sharing their ideas. More indices of extroversion indicate a persuasive and effective doer. The more common combination of M+ and I+ predicts to a rich inner life but also a lack of objectivity, whereas a person with the combination of M+ and I– can be creative in the sphere of objective facts, for example, the physical sciences. High M and low C suggest withdrawal in the face of emotional distress; M+ and G– suggest a person with unorthodox views in many areas and with the potential to act them out. M–, I– persons are ultra-realists, while M–, I+ persons are practical, giving (although sometimes boring or obtuse) doers. M– and F– together suggest a very difficult therapeutic endeavor. Interestingly enough, a high M score generally predicts to recidivism in criminal populations.

High N's, particularly when they also score low on Q_1, are interpersonally provocative, and if scale B is also high, this provocativeness may be used intellectually. High scores on N along with a low score on G and high scores on E and H predict a con artist, a person who manipulates others through a combination of assertiveness and shrewdness. The quality of the conning may be predicted by scores on M and B. Persons high on N, E, and Q_1 and low on G are particularly difficult to work with and cause a variety of troubles in interpersonal relationships. If they are also high on B and L, their disruption is more difficult to detect. When high N is found with high B (intelligence) and L, an apparently amicable demeanor may cover venomous jealousy and/or suspicion.

When low N is found with low B, a gullible "Simple Simon" is likely; if low N is with high I, high romantic expectations and sentimentality make them vulnerable to relationship manipulation. Low N and high M are seen as odd or "weird" and often elicit social rejection.

When both O and G are high, guilt embedded in low self-esteem is common, and the guilt is often neurotic rather than real. When the G is low (with high O), often found with young adults, there is guilt about not endorsing standard moral standards. High O and Q_3 reflect guilt from failing to meet a level of aspiration rather than moral guilt. When O is high and F is low but other anxiety indicators are not marked, consider depression.

Persons high on Q_1 and F and low on C tend to be disorganized and impulsive in both thought and behavior. High Q_1 and Q_3 scores, along with a moderately high G score, predict to compulsiveness; this is amplified into obsessive-compulsiveness to the degree that B is high and M is at either extreme (high—obsessive or low—compulsive).

When high Q_2 is combined with low B, expect a "closed (and ineffective) mind." If E and L are also high, the individual can be dangerous if crossed. High Q_2, low A people have given up on others, often reflecting a disappointing loss. High Q_2 and L reflect severe mistrust and a tendency to project insecurities and conflicts. High Q_2 and O are found in individuals who have withdrawn out of a belief they would be rejected if others knew their "real" selves. Low Q_2 and high E create conflictual relationships as they seek both dominance and emotional reassurance. The avoidance conflict of low Q_2, high L's is analogous; they are suspicious yet yearn for dependency.

High Q_3, E, and O predispose one to a traumatic response to any perceived failure. High Q_3 and G and low C and/or H set the stage for various dissociative disorders and responses. Low Q_3, C, and H with high L, O, and Q_4 are typical of individuals who see themselves as stupid and inadequate (and often are at least the latter) and are highly prone to anxiety responses. Low Q_3, O, and Q_4, on the other hand, show relaxed and self-accepting persons who appear sloppy and have a high level of "body hedonism." As noted, low Q_3's with low G and C are individuals highly prone to acting-out, have low impulse controls and a propensity for characterological disorders; the problem is compounded if C is also low but may be muted by the fear of punishment if F is also low. Q_4, the measure par excellence of present anxiety, takes on more ominous connotations if it is found along with high O and low C scores, as this predicts a more long-term disorder. When high Q_4 is associated with high M and I and low G and Q_3 scores, substance abuse is probable. When an individual is in a very difficult or stressful situation and is showing low Q_4 and O, look for defensiveness to the point of distorting reality. When low Q_4 is in combination with high L, look for someone who is out of touch with his or her bodily sensations. When low Q_4 and high O are seen together, look for evidence of fatigue and depression.

Over all, profiles that clearly slope right (low A through a high Q_4) are more indicative of psychopathology. Those that clearly slope left (higher A, B, and C down through lower Q scores) are more indicative of psychological health (Krug, 1981).

It should be noted that, on occasion, the 16 PF-5 and MMPI-2 profiles on an individual client may appear to be somewhat contradictory. It is rare that any direct contradictions occur, as the two tests do not measure exactly the same areas. However, if there is an apparent contradiction, the validity scores for each test should be checked. If all is in order, the secondary adjective in the 16 PF-5-scale descriptors should be given more weight to see if that produces a better meld. If there is still no resolution, which is unlikely, greater weight should be given to the MMPI-2 because it has been more thoroughly researched and has more items per scale.

CHAPTER 14

Aggression, Rape, Child Abuse, and Suicide

■ Overall Concepts

One of the most difficult situations for a clinician is dealing with an assessment of a prediction of danger toward self or others. The Tarasoff (1976) decision and its spawn haven't made things easier. From an overall perspective, one must (1) clarify the threat, (2) assess the severity and actuality of any danger to self or others, (3) identify potential victims(s) and specific plans relating threat to victim, (4) assess the imminence and overall time-frame of the threat, and (5) identify both short-term and long-term control and intervention options.

Before proceeding into the discussions of the specific patterns (i.e., aggression, suicide, etc.), consider the following assessment-management strategy for use with any client in whom there is the possibility of any dangerous behavior (to others or self):

1. Obtain a thorough history and directly question the client on thoughts about past behavior issues (including medical and psychological history variables) and about any present or recent thoughts of hurting oneself or others. Assess for such critical factors as history of impulsive and/or destructive behaviors, a history of affective disorder or bizarre behavior, head injury or toxic states, substance abuse, command hallucinations, etc.

2. Document critical data. To resolve specific uncertainties, check with collateral sources (with appropriate permissions) such as family, friends, and co-workers, and review all prior relevant records. Deal with milieu issues that may encourage acting-out.

3. If you feel uncomfortable about the client's ability to control such behaviors, seriously consider hospitalization, including the possibility of involuntary civil commitment (see Chapter 17).

4. In those cases where the client would not qualify for involuntary commitment, but you are still concerned, strongly encourage a brief voluntary

hospitalization. However, be careful how you word and record such episodes. For example, on September 14, 1989, Joseph Westbecker, upset over perceived grudges, went to a plant in Louisville where he had been employed, carrying 5 guns and 1200 rounds of ammunition. Using a semi–automatic AK–47 assault rifle, he went on a rampage, killing 8 people and wounding 12, then killed himself. Three days before, he had seen his psychiatrist who recorded his suggestion that Westbecker voluntarily check into a mental hospital; a behavior that would look reasonable under a routine peer review, but one this psychiatrist might reconsider in retrospect.

5. Develop a plan, in concert with a secondary monitor, e.g., a spouse, to keep guns and/or drugs away from the client.

6. Communicate your limits to the client, at the same time expressing a wish to help. In this vein, urge your client to refrain from using alcohol and/or nonprescribed drugs. Consider the use of a secondary monitor if risk warrants it.

7. Express your personal concern for and commitment to the client in a direct fashion; this may reduce feelings of violence to self or others.

8. Help them to recognize and label the underlying emotions (commonly anger and/or depression) and help them to make the link to acting-out. Help the client to develop alternative means of catharsis, e.g., words and artistic expression.

9. Provide concrete avenues of access to you outside the therapy session, encourage their use, and/or increase the frequency of the therapy contact.

10. Consider the initiation or adjustment of a medication regimen to control symptoms such as depression or anxiety.

11. Periodically review your treatment plan and your client's mental status. Provide assurances about confidentiality, but in the context of a discussion of your special duty (under the law and/or ethics code, etc.) to design a plan that protects specific others and/or society as a whole if clinical interventions are unsuccessful. Consider putting some or all facets of this plan in a form of contractual agreement (see the related discussion of this approach in the section on suicide later in this chapter).

Aggression Potential

Given the low base rates of severe aggressive behaviors (and suicide as well), making a highly accurate prediction to specific actual behavior is virtually impossible (Monahan, 1981, 1984). Monahan has pointed to the eight most critical demographic predictor variables for aggression. It is more common if the potential perpetrator (1) is young (this variable correlates strongly up until the 30–35 age range, after which the correlation is random); (2) is male; (3) is of a lower socioeconomic class; (4) is from a disadvantaged minority; (5) is less educated; (6) has a lower intellectual level; (7) has an unstable school and/or vocational history; and (8) has a history of juvenile violence and/or alcohol and/or drug abuse. Other demographic indicators of a potential for violence that have been noted throughout the literature are (1) a prior history of violent behaviors; (2) a prior history of suicide attempts; (3) a history of family violence; (4) soft neurological signs; (5) a discharge diagnosis that includes mania or command hallucinations; (6) evidence of noncompliance to treatment; (7) has weapons; fascination with weapons; (8) narcissistic, antisocial, or histrionic personality traits; (9) a pattern of cruelty to animals as a child or adolescent; (10) a rejecting, abusive or depressed father; and (11) recent stress, especially if associated with low levels of serotonin (Volavka, 1995; Bongar, 1991; Geen, 1990; Monahan, 1981, 1984). In addition to these predictors, assaultiveness on the ward by inpatient psychiatric patients is correlated with hallucinatory behavior, emotional lability, and a high level of activity.

There is even solid empirical evidence for specific imitative violence; for example, homicide rates increase consistently and significantly on the third day after a heavyweight championship fight, the most publicized type of prizefight (Miller et al., 1991). There is also increasing evidence of "bio-vio" indicators. For example, Virkkunen and Linnoila (1991) studied violent offenders and found that low cerebrospinal fluid 5-hydroxindoleacetic acid levels and a low blood glucose nadir in a glucose tolerance test predicted to aggressive acts, with the latter factor being the most predictive.

Additionally, there are test data that can help the clinician make predictions at a higher level than that allowed by impressionistic data or chance, as discussed in the following subsections.

MMPI-2

There are several indicators of potential for aggression against others in the MMPI-2 (Butcher, 1995; Kalichman, 1988). As in all areas of psychopathology, certain scales have been developed specifically to assess aggression potential. Ironically, in the general testing situation the examiner would have to know the "answer" already, at least to a degree, to employ some of these scales. They are of help when there are prior cues, and it is worthwhile for the clinician to keep a range of specific tests available for such situations. The classic Overcontrolled-Hostility (O-H) scale, devised and refined by Megargee and his colleagues (Megargee and Cook, 1975); is especially useful since it is embedded in a commonly used test, the MMPI-2. This scale is a subset of thirty-one MMPI-2 items. It effectively identifies a subgroup of assaultive criminals who are generally overcontrolled in their responses to hostility but who sporadically are extremely assaultive. The scale is less useful to the degree one strays from this population. It has been generally correlated with a reported lack of overt anxiety or depression, denial or repression of interpersonal conflict, and rigid control of emotional expression (Butcher, 1990). Blacks and females tend to score higher on this scale, so this should be accounted for in any interpretation.

The type of individual discovered in this scale is similar to the one with the 4-3 profile type described by Davis and Sines (1971). The profile peak is on scale 4, the second-highest elevation is on scale 3, and there is little significant elevation elsewhere. This profile is characteristic of men who maintain an ongoing quiet adjustment yet are prone to hostile, aggressive outbursts. They may or may not fit the criteria for the intermittent-explosive disorder. Davis and Sines hypothesize that those with the 4-3 profile type are constitutionally predisposed to this behavior by some kind of a cyclical internal mechanism that occasionally causes acute emotional outbursts. Later research (Butcher, 1990; Graham, 1993), for the most part confirmed the validity of this profile as suggestive of aggression potential across a number of settings, and among females as well as males.

To the degree that both 4 and 3 are highly elevated in a typically nonaggressive person, the likelihood of an occasional aggressive outburst increases. In general, when scale 4 is greater than scale 3, control decreases. Conversely, as scale 3 increases over scale 4, potential for more ability to control and inhibit aggressive impulses increases. In females the 4-3 pattern has also been commonly associated with promiscuity. This is probably true with males, but because of traditional sex role expectations, such behavior in males is not as commonly a focus in assessment.

Consistently assaultive individuals, whose overt interpersonal patterns are more consistent with this behavior, have high scores on scales F, 4, and 9, with secondary elevations on 6 and 8. All five of these scales have been classically regarded as scales that suggest a lack of impulse control. Persons with high scores on these scales combine social resentment and hostility, a lack of moral inhibitions, suspiciousness of and resentment toward authority and the world in general, and a lack of impulse control. Such a combination easily engenders hostility, even with minimal environmental stimulation. General problems in social adjustment also occur and combine with social resentment and envy of others to elevate the 0 scale. A high scale 5 score is generally indicative of ability to suppress aggression, although Graham (1987) notes that the 4-5/5-4 profile in women is correlated with aggression.

A specific criminal subgroup, "Charlie," with elevations on these scores, has been described by Megargee and Bohn (1979). Charlie's—who are hostile, paranoid, and dangerous—showed characteristic elevations on scales 8, 6, and 4, in that order, with distinctly low scales on 1, 2, and 3. From an overall perspective, high scores on F, 6, 7, and 8 predict to violent incidents in a prison setting.

The subgroup "How," also studied by Megargee and Bohn (1979), seeks interpersonal contact but is consistently rejected and builds up much anger, hostility, and anxiety. In that subgroup, scale 8 is usually highest, followed by scales 2, 4, and 1. The overall profile is distinctly elevated, with higher elevations on these scales in a distinctive jagged pattern.

The "double-M profile," with distinct elevations on 2, 4, 6, and 8, refers to individuals who are very unstable and dangerous to themselves or, more likely, to others. It is hard to bring them into a therapy situation, and if they appear, they are difficult to change.

16 PF

There has not been as much research on the prediction of aggression with the 16 PF as there has been with the MMPI-2. However, several scales considered together do modestly predict aggression. Scales that tap aggression potential per se are E, L, and Q_1, and in each a high scale is predictive. General impulsiveness is reflected in high scores on F and H. Low scores on G, O, and Q_3, along with a high score on F, are thought to be predictors of low ego control and thus to contribute to a prediction of acting–out.

OTHER TEST-RESPONSE PATTERNS

Persons who are inclined toward easy aggression seem less able to deal with their concerns by articulating them verbally (Huesmann, 1994; Megargee and Bohn, 1979); this may be reflected in the WAIS-R, since they usually obtain a verbal score that is lower than the performance score. Clients who act out aggressively tend to score lower on the similarities, vocabulary, and block design subtests.

Problems in aggression control are usually correlated with present or previous difficulties in adjusting to school. Hence, within the verbal section of the WAIS-R, scores tend to be lower on information, arithmetic, and vocabulary relative to the other three scales taken as a whole. Quiet but hostile and explosive individuals attain low picture arrangement scores, relative to the more extroverted and consistently aggressive type.

An elevation on MCMI-III scales 6A or B of 85 or higher should alert the clinician to aggression potential. The 5-6/6-5 codes also occur frequently in the context of the antisocial personality diagnosis and may therefore be predictive of aggression. The deficient social conscience and interpersonal exploitiveness of a high 5 (narcissistic), combined with the hostile affectivity and interpersonal vindictiveness of a high 6 (antisocial), would seem to be indicative of a potentially dangerous individual. To the extent that elevations on B and/or T occur, in conjunction with elevated 6, aggression potential increases. As P and PP become more elevated, aggression potential may increase.

Persons who exhibit patterns of intermittent-explosive behavior certainly have potential for aggression, although predicting these episodes may be considerably more difficult (Monahan, 1984). (See Chapter 10 for discussion of disorders of impulse control.)

On the Rorschach, individuals who are prone to aggressive behavior typically show short reaction times, do not provide extensive response records, and may give quick responses to card I and the color cards (Beck and Beck, 1978). They tend to be low in the number of FC responses and high in C, CF, and Popular responses (Phillips and Smith, 1953). Responses associated with fighting (swords, guns, blood) or aggressive animals (crabs, tigers) are expected from those assaultive psychopaths, who consistently act out aggressively. The explosion-oriented response is more characteristic of the explosive personality, individuals who are making an attempt to control aggression. Over all, elevated Rorschach special and content scales of Aggressive Movement (Ag), Explosion (Ex), and Morbid responses (MOR) raise the probability of aggression. Conversely, the potential for assault is contraindicated by a high number of F+, D, and FC responses, a high amount of abstraction content, and/or a higher number of Popular and Original responses (Gacono and Meloy, 1994; Exner, 1986; Phillips and Smith, 1953).

A number of specific contents on the Rorschach are often considered signs of aggression. On card I, in reference to the central light-gray detail on the midline, the responses "tomahawk" or "hammerhead" are given mainly by aggressive psychopaths. A response on card II like "two bears fighting with blood splashed around" is significant for the type of psychopath who entertains aggressive fantasies and is hostile toward the outer world. When the lower central light-gray detail of card III elicits a response like "jaws closing" conjoined with "blood," there is a possibility of latent hostility and sadistic aggression.

Potential for aggression is occasionally seen in frank, unsublimated expressions of aggressive impulses (Geen, 1990). More subtle clues are drawings that seem to press out against the edges of the page, heavy pencil pressure, short and/or jagged strokes, transparencies, unrelieved areas of white space, teeth, long spikelike fingers, and a same-sex person depicted in an explicitly aggressive posture (Oster and Gould, 1987).

The reader is referred to the previous sections on the antisocial personality disorder, conduct disorder, and the passive-aggressive personality disorder, since these disorders in particular contain the potential for ongoing aggression, and the criteria described there are applicable here as well. With regard to periodic aggression, the reader is referred to the sections on the explosive personality and on the paranoid disorders.

Ironically, the term *violence* stems from the Latin *vis*, meaning "life force." There are numerous potential causes of violent behavior. The following outline gives an overview of these causes, along with consensus intervention strategies:

A. Violence as an inherent part of human nature

    1. Traditional psychotherapy to modify basic personality patterns
    2. Medications to diminish anxiety and minimize inappropriate reactions
    3. Psychosurgery to change or interrupt patterns of brain functioning

B. Violence as a consequence of social learning

    1. Family therapy to change home environment or facilitate coping in the family setting
    2. Group therapy to enhance appropriate coping in social situation
    3. Assertiveness training and social-skills training to give concrete training in self-assertion without violence
    4. Systematic desensitization (SDT) to desensitize client to the precipitating stimuli, so as to diminish inappropriate or excessive reactions

5. Token economy, time-out, and social isolation to extinguish violent behavior through removal of environmental reinforcers as well as to
   strengthen appropriate responses
6. Classical conditioning to extinguish violent behavior, as in aversive conditioning
7. Parent effectiveness training such as Parents Anonymous to enhance
   adequate coping skills and provide a supportive peer group

C. Violence as a consequence of frustration and other situational factors

1. Traditional psychotherapy to release frustrations and to change coping
   patterns
2. Family therapy; see B1
3. Group therapy; see B2
4. Assertiveness training, social-skills training; see B3
5. Token economy to provide opportunities for positively reinforcing experiences while extinguishing the violent behavior
6. Parent effectiveness training; see B7

D. Violence as a means of communication

1. Expressive therapies to substitute alternate means of expression of feelings underlying violent acting-out
2. Assertiveness training, etc.; see B3
3. SDT; see B4
4. Parent effectiveness training; see B7

E. Violence and aggression as protection of territorial integrity and body space

1. SDT; see B4
2. Assertiveness training; see B3

The reader is also referred to Chapter 15 for a discussion of possible pharmacological interventions.

■ Rape

Rape does not appear directly as a diagnostic entity in DSM-IV, but this most
important syndrome is often an impulsive behavior and shows certain diagnostic correlates. There are a number of classification systems for rape, one of
the most influential being the pioneering work of Cohen et al. (1969). The following discussion reflects their concepts.

Aside from the rapes that occur as an incidental result of such disorders as
severe organic brain dysfunction or schizophrenia and those that are an impulsive and ritualistic gesture (the plunder of war), there is reasonable agreement that there are three major rape patterns. The first occurs where aggression is the major component and sexual satisfaction is somewhat irrelevant in
the motivational system. These rapists are hostile toward females and in general

carry a high level of aggression potential. The upcoming section on aggression potential deals with the diagnostic considerations relevant to such persons.

The second type of rapist needs to administer pain to another person to obtain sexual satisfaction. The pain is requisite, so this type of rapist is classified under the psychosexual disorder of sexual sadism (see Chapter 8).

A third major category of rapists is that which the aggression is an avenue to sexual contact and satisfaction, yet also in some ways to interpersonal contact; most cases of date-rape fit here. This is the individual whose diagnostic correlates are presented here. This sexually motivated rapist fits the pioneering results of Barbaree et al. (1979), who found that, in most cases, forced sex for this person fails to inhibit arousal, although it does so in most normal individuals. Incidentally, Abel et al. (1986) found that some rapists (the aggression subtype) are especially aroused by stimuli that connote a woman who is aggressive or manipulative or by sexual images that include aggression.

CHARACTERISTICS OF RAPE

Rape has traditionally been defined as the unlawful penetration of a female's vagina by a man's penis, reinforced by some form of coercion and without the consent of the victim. However, it is absurd to require penile penetration to define rape. Homosexual rape occurs, as does rape of men by women (although very rarely). Statutes have been rewritten in states to reflect this.

Rape is a common crime and is said to account for approximately 5% of all crimes of violence. Each year about one in every 2,000 women is a reported rape victim. However, it is estimated that only about 10% of victims of rape ever report it to the police. Also, only about two in twenty rapists are ever arrested, one in thirty prosecuted, and one in fifty convicted. More than 50% of reported rapes take place in the victims' homes, and in about 40% of the cases the rapist is known to the victim (Calhoun and Atkeson, 1991; Abel et al., 1986).

THE RAPIST

Most rapists are married, and a great percentage of married rapists have regular sexual relations with their wives. However, their sexual performance is often impaired during the rape. Like most other antisocial personalities and criminals, rapists are generally lower than average in intelligence.

A few researchers (e.g., Rada et al., 1976) have found elevated levels of plasma testosterone in some samples of the most violent rapists. In general, however, there is not much correlation between rape and physiological measures. An impossible problem is obtaining such measures at the critical predictive point, the time just before the rape, as many of these physiological variables differ markedly for any one individual depending on when they are assessed. However, measurements of penile response to sexual imagery may be useful here, as well as in making at least some tentative predictions about future behavior when that is important in disposition.

While any one rapist may show a combination of motivations, the following identifiers point to the predominant emotional patterns.* Those who are sadistic rapists will show characteristics of sexual sadism, discussed in Chapter 8.

ANGER RAPE

1. Aggression: uses more physical force than is necessary to overpower the victim.
2. Offender's mood state is one of anger and depression.
3. Offenses are episodic and are generated more impulsively.
4. Language is abusive: cursing, swearing, obscenities.
5. Dynamics: retribution for perceived wrongs, injustices, or "put-downs" experienced by the offender.
6. Assault is of relatively short duration.
7. Victim suffers physical trauma to all areas of her body.

POWER RAPE

1. Aggression: uses whatever force or threat is necessary to gain control of victim and overcome her resistance.
2. Offender's mood state is one of anxiety-agitation.
3. Offenses are premeditated, are repetitive, and may show an increase in aggression over time.
4. Language is instructional and inquisitive: giving orders, asking personal questions, inquiring as to victim's responses.
5. Dynamics: compensation for deep-seated insecurities and feelings of inadequacy.
6. Assault may be of an extended duration with the victim held captive for a period of time.
7. Victim may be physically unharmed; bodily injury would be inadvertent rather than intentional.

SADISTIC RAPE

1. Aggression: physical force (anger and power) is eroticized.
2. Offender's mood state is one of intense excitement.
3. Offenses are calculated and ritualistic, typically involving bondage, torture, or bizarre acts, and are interspersed with other, nonsadistic sexual assaults.
4. Language is commanding and degrading.
5. Dynamics: symbolic destruction and elimination.

*Adapted in part from W. Groth and J. Birnbaum (1979), *Men Who Rape: The Psychology of the Offender* (New York: Plenum).

6. Assault may be of an extended duration in which the victim is kidnapped, assaulted, and disposed of.

7. Victim suffers physical trauma to sexual areas of her body; in extreme cases she is murdered and mutilated.

☐   ## MMPI-2

It has been generally found that rapists are more disturbed across the board on such tests as the MMP-2 than are assaultists per se or exhibitionists (Levin and Stava, 1987). In many ways, rapists correlate with the dimensions of the antisocial personality (the reader is referred to that section). The 4-9/9-4 is the most common (Erickson et al., 1987). The 8-4/4-8 is also found, with the 8-4 being characteristic of rapists of adults, while the 4-8 is more characteristic of rapists of children (Armentrout and Hauer, 1978).

Kalichman et al. (1989) found five rather distinct MMPI-2 patterns in their sample of rapists. Those occurring most commonly were a subclinical 4-9 and a second group with a spike-4 profile. The next most common group showed elevations above 70 T on F, 4, 8, and 9, with moderate elevations on 5, 6, and 7. The last subgroup, a very disturbed group, showed elevations at about 100 T on 8, elevations above 80 on F, 4 (barely), 6, and 7, with elevations of 70 or above on most other scales except L, K, 5, and 0.

Rapists may obtain a high K score, reflecting the fact that they are typically under scrutiny for a criminal offense (see the section on malingering). Scale 5 is usually low in these individuals if there is a strong identification with the stereotypical male role. Scale 0 is mildly elevated if there is general ineptitude in interpersonal skills. This type of behavior, along with an inclination to deny responsibility for it, is seen in an elevation of scale 3.

Rader (1977) has suggested that the 4-3 profile characterizes the more repressed rapist, who is inclined toward significant violence. In this case, scale 6 is also likely to be elevated, although this depends on the degree of hostility allowed into awareness. Scales F and 8 are elevated to the degree the individual is losing control of impulses and is degenerating into more fragmented pathology, but faking-bad must also be considered.

☐   ## 16 PF

Rapists, if they are at all self-disclosing, score away from the average on a number of personality dimensions (Masters et al., 1991). The primarily sexually motivated rapist is more likely to score toward the average profile than is the aggression-motivated rapist. However, both types are likely to have a low score on C, reflecting their emotional instability; low scores on Q and G from their inability to control impulses and urges; and a high score on O from their insecurity. The sexual rapist who is more naive, suspicious, interpersonally open, and less aggressive is likely to score low on N, moderately low on H, and moderately high on Q_4 and I. Aggressively motivated rapists will score low on A and moderately low on I, but high on E, H, and Q_2. Both types are less than average on scale B.

OTHER TEST-RESPONSE PATTERNS

The hostile affectivity and interpersonal vindictiveness typical of the rapist predict MCMI-III scores of 85 or higher on scale 6B. To a lesser extent, the exploitiveness of the narcissist may predispose toward rape behavior, so an elevation of 75 or higher could occur on 5. Scale C and 6A are also high.

TREATMENT OPTIONS

Castration has been a time–honored approach for dealing with the rapist, and is still used in some cultures. Nonetheless, chemocastration, via drugs that lower the serum testosterone level, is still used (Abel et al., 1986). These drugs lower the likelihood of sexual arousal, but side effects are substantial and the drugs are not consistently effective. Suggestions for the legal disposition of the rapist may even include some irony: Fersch (1980) states that in rape "the criminal act ought to be brought under assault and battery with a dangerous weapon. Then the attention could be focused on whether or not the accused possessed a dangerous weapon" (p. 14)—albeit occasionally an impotent weapon.

The aversive therapies have been commonly used here and have shown moderate success (Calhoun and Atkeson, 1991). More effective ways of coping with anger are also necessary, possibly introduced by modeling or role playing. Marital therapy may be indicated, since for many rapists the initiation of the rape sequence immediately follows a marital battle. Refer to the program for sex offenders in Chapter 8.

Child Abuse

*I was coming home from kindergarten—
well, they told me it was kindergarten. I
found out later that I had been working in
a factory for ten years. It's good for a
kid to know how to make gloves."*

Ellen DeGeneres

The physical and sexual abuse of children has been clearly documented throughout history across cultures (Finkelhor and Dzuiba-Leatherman, 1994; Friedrich, 1991; Nelson, 1984). Although such abuse is frequently abhorred, few actual preventive measures have been taken. It is ironic that the first formal legal intervention in a child abuse case, that of Mary Ellen in New York in 1875, had to be prosecuted through animal protection laws and with the efforts of the Society for the Prevention of Cruelty to Animals. However, in the spectacularly short time of about five years, child abuse in the United States went from being virtually a nonissue to being the focus of national political concern (Nelson, 1984). All fifty states, partly spurred by the federal Child Abuse Prevention and Treatment Act, have established legal routes to identify and intervene in abusive families. Yet, because of the private nature of abuse and the reluctance of both perpetrators and victims to reveal its occurrence, clearly identified cases of child abuse are generally believed to represent only a portion of the actual cases. The difficulty of legislating in this area is highlighted by the research of Berlin et al. (1991) that suggests that mandatory reporting statutes for mental health professionals may, in light of the emphasis on full informed consent, impair the probability of an abuser seeking or remaining in treatment. DSM-IV has several "V" codes that may be applicable: Physical Abuse of Child (V61.21), Sexual Abuse of Child (V61.21), and Neglect of Child (V61.21).

There are few more daunting tasks than assessing issues related to possible child sexual or physical abuse. Before dealing with specifics, consider the following overall strategy, as adapted in part from an unpublished paper by Catherine Morrow (1994):

OVERALL ASSESSMENT STRATEGY FOR EVALUATING CHILD ABUSE

I. General Principles

    A. Task is to document the chronology context and consistency of complaint

    B. Must establish your role, including:

        1. external independence—refrain from allying yourself with any individual involved in the complaint

        2. internal independence—know your own biases and resist their interferences relative to the allegations

    C. Gather uncontaminated details and data for the court system

    D. Record all information, including use of audio or video tape if feasible

II. Requirements for the Interviewer

    A. Skillful management of parental behaviors, emotions, and reactions

    B. Knowledge of child development principles, especially cognitive and language development

    C. Skillful management of wide range of child behaviors, emotions, and reactions; comfort with children

    D. Current information with regard to child abuse literature

III. Avoiding Role Confusions

    A. Maintain interviewer stance rather than engage in therapeutic or advocacy procedures

    B. Avoid transmitting emotional interpretations of events to a child

    C. Remember that the judge/jury is the trier of fact; the interviewer gathers data and may be asked for expert opinions

IV. Preparatory Intake Considerations

    A. If possible, get court-appointed status

    B. Learn the legal issues at stake, clarify required time frames and financial considerations

    C. Review copies of pertinent medical reports, autopsies, police investigations, eyewitness statements, and other court information

    D. Obtain copies of and assess quality of any previous evaluations; consider any evidence of prior contamination

    E. Keep records of referral framework and all requests for interviews

V. Interviews

    A. Arrange for separate parent interviews if desired and always if complaint is incest

    B. Obtain data from following three areas:

        1. abuse-related info: where, when, how, frequency, duration, level of force, number of perpetrators, emotional closeness to alleged perpetrator, etc.

        2. child factors: developmental levels, school performance, extent of knowledge regarding adult sexual behavior, medical history, behavior problems, psychological status (especially a temporal change in status since alleged abuse), presentational style with which child tells story, child's understanding of the alleged abuse and disclosure sequelae

        3. family factors: marital status of parents, quality of parent–child relationship(s), parental reaction to the allegation, parental history of child abuse, parent's medical and psychiatric histories, parental teachings about sex, child-rearing practices of the family, child's access to sexually explicit information

    C. Inform parent of need to see child alone and note parental reaction

    D. Use the specific interviewing techniques described below. Consider the use of anatomical drawings and dolls only if they can be employed in a systematic basis that allows the use of some normative data framework

VI. Ancillary Services

    A. Psychological testing, e.g., intellectual, achievement, visual-motor, adaptive skill testing is often indicated

    B. Refer for medical exam if not already done

VII. Assess Level of Contamination

    A. Review any tapes to assess your own agenda relative to use of:

        1. leading questions

        2. disconfirmation (caution with repeated questioning)

        3. coercive techniques

      4. differentially reinforcing or punishing verbal and nonverbal behaviors on the part of the interviewer

  B. Judge extent of other possible sources of contamination
      1. technical—child intimidated by taping equipment
      2. system—child's friend placed in foster care after an allegation
      3. parental—intensive questioning may lead to unintentional distortion by child

The following are specific interviewing techniques:

1. The interview should begin with a period of free play, which is designed to achieve several goals: to allow the child and interviewer to become comfortable in the room and with each other, to establish a positive rapport, and to allow the interviewer to informally assess the child's developmental levels.

2. The interview should proceed from free recall to later prompting for detail. Leading questions, in which the interviewer introduces specific material that the child has not previously revealed to that interviewer, should be avoided.

3. Children are more likely to make errors of omission than commission; their narrative reports are usually accurate but sparse. To enhance retrieval, the interviewer can consider use of props or cues.

4. To maximize communication, the interviewer should listen to the child's use of spontaneous language and try to match his/her own sentence length and complexity to the child's.

5. Ask children to define terms rather than merely asking if they know what words mean.

6. To enhance participation, determine the child's fund of information and beliefs about the legal system, record this, and correct any misinformation.

7. Where feasible, avoid repeated questioning as children tend to interpret such repetition as feedback that their original responses are incorrect and may tend to change their answers.

8. Try to minimize the interviewer's high status role to decrease children's natural inclination to want to please adults in authority.

9. Because young children cannot understand sequential or temporal concepts well, use matching techniques to assist young children (e.g., Did that happen before lunch? Was it as long as Barney is on TV?).

10. Young children often pay more attention to peripheral details of an event than do adults. Children under 7, particularly, tend to encode the sensory characteristics of stimuli. These developmental differences in memory processes, coupled with sequencing difficulties, frequently produce disjointed reports with seemingly odd comments about a noise or smell. An adult, on

the other hand, is more likely to focus on characteristics of an alleged perpetrator. As a result, reports that seem to defy the developmentally appropriate memory and cognitive skills of children may alert the interviewer to attempts at adult coaching. On the other hand, precocious reports can, in some instances, reflect superior cognitive abilities.

RELATED DIAGNOSTIC CONSIDERATIONS

In the vast majority of cases the first diagnostic cue emanates from the child. There are a number of common physical signs of physical abuse. A way of remembering them are the "four Bs": unexplained or unusual bruises, burns, bald spots, or bleeding.

Look for bruises around the head or face or in easily protected areas, such as the abdomen; multiple bruises, especially if spread over the body; or bruises in the shape of an object, such as a hand or a belt. Likewise, burns of all types should cause concern, especially cigarette burns; burns with a specific shape, such as an iron; and burns that suggest that a hand has been immersed in liquid. Concern should be heightened if the child provides an explanation that does not fit the injury.

Behavioral signs of physical abuse include accident-proneness, problems with schoolwork and peers, shrinking from physical contact, and wearing clothes that seem more designed to cover the body than to keep one warm. Be especially on guard if any of these symptoms represent a change in the behavior pattern of a child. Over and above these signs, delinquency, drug abuse, anorexia nervosa, and excessive avoidance of parents may reflect an abuse situation in older children and adolescents.

Along with physical abuse, there has been increasing attention to the sexual abuse of children (Friedrich, 1991). The behavioral signs just noted also are found in cases of sexual abuse. Additional signs include extreme secrecy, excessive bathing, indications of low self-worth, provocative or promiscuous sexual patterns, appearing more worldly than friends, or suddenly possessing money or merchandise that could have been used to bribe the child to keep quiet. Precocious sexual behavior (especially under the age of 7) or precocious sexual understanding is a common cue. Certainly any clear, consistent report of explicit and progressive sexual abuse is a very red flag.

Specific physical signs of sexual abuse are pain, rashes, itching or sores in the genital or anal areas, enuresis, frequent urinary infections, or frequent vomiting.

On the MMPI-2, women who are at risk for child abuse tend to show a 4-8-9 pattern (Engleland et al., 1991). The 4-8 code has been shown to be predominate in the victims of father–daughter incest, when they are either later adolescent or adult clients (Scott and Stone, 1986). Adult victims may have significantly elevated 1, 2, and 5 scales, suggesting that depression is a feature. Adolescents show higher elevations on scale 9, suggesting acting-out behaviors.

One of the better measures for physical child abuse assessment is the Child Abuse Potential (CAP) Inventory, developed by Joel Milner (1991) (c/o Family

Violence Research Program; Dept. of Psychology; No. Illinois Univ.; DeKalb, IL 60015-2892). The CAP is a 160-item, self-administered, forced-choice questionnaire with a third-grade readability level, and it includes three validity scales. It shows classification rates, based on discriminant analysis, in the mid-80% to low 90% range, and unlike several other scales, produces more false negatives than false positives.

General diagnostic considerations flow from an understanding of the many factors that contribute to the ultimate emergence of an episode of physical and/or sexual child abuse (Finkelhor and Dziuba-Leatherman, 1994; Finkelhor, 1985). These factors are found within three contributing systems: sociocultural, familial, and individual. To the degree these factors are present, the probability of an occurrence of child abuse is increased. At the most basic level are the following *sociocultural factors* that facilitate an increase in child abuse episodes:

1. Lack of affirmation and support of the family unit
2. Lack of emphasis on parent–training skills as a prerequisite to parenting
3. Acceptance of and high media visibility of violence
4. Acceptance of corporal punishment as a central child-rearing technique
5. Emphasis on competition rather than cooperation
6. Unequal status for women
7. Low economic support for schools and day-care facilities

These sociocultural factors heighten the probability of abuse in conjunction with the following *familial factors:*

1. Low socio-economic and education levels
2. Little availability of friends and extended family for support
3. Single-parent or merged-parent family structure
4. Marital instability
5. Family violence as common and traditionally accepted
6. Low rate of family contact and information exchange
7. Significant periods of mother absence
8. High acceptance of family nudity
9. Low affirmation of family member privacy
10. "Vulnerable" children (to the degree they are young, sick, disturbed, retarded, or emotionally isolated)

The probability of abuse in a specific instance is in turn increased by the following *individual factors:*

1. History of abuse as a child
2. Low emotional stability and/or self-esteem

3. Low ability to tolerate frustration and inhibit anger
4. High impulsivity
5. Lack of parenting skills
6. High emotional and interpersonal isolation
7. Problems in handling dependency needs of self or others
8. Low ability to express physical affection
9. Unrealistic expectations for child's performance
10. Use of corporal punishment as a primary child-rearing technique
11. Presence of drug or alcohol abuse

In most cases, many (although not all) of these factors are found. Some predict more to physical abuse and some to sexual abuse, but most factors predict to either type. Other specific diagnostic considerations (including test correlates) and treatment considerations can be found in the prior section on aggression potential in the sections on pedophilia and incest (see Chapter 8) and the personality disorders (see Chapter 9).

TREATMENT OPTIONS

In addition to individual psychotherapy, there are three core approaches that are potentially useful in almost all such cases (Friedrich, 1991; Marshall et al., 1991):

1. *Family therapy.* Since the family is virtually always disrupted, family therapy is necessary. Even where the family system eventually changes, family therapy can help to mute the damage to all concerned.

2. *Parent training.* When the abuse comes from a parent, parent training is necessary to deal not only with the problems that led to the abuse, but to those generated by the abuse as well. Parent training to deal with this latter factor is also important when the source of abuse is external to the family.

3. *Support systems.* Abuse often comes where there has been a sense of emotional isolation. In this vein, a community-based counseling and support group is available to abusing parents in Parents Anonymous. This organization works the same way as Alcoholics Anonymous or Gamblers Anonymous. A similar group is Parents United. Contact with other abusers and the opportunity to share problems with sympathetic and understanding others are helpful for parents for whom abusive behaviors are triggered by psychosocial stressors and a sense of emotional isolation. There are also support groups for the victims of child abuse, which are especially useful with older abuse victims.

These approaches can be supplemented by other interventions, for instance, attempts to change the person's employment possibilities or social skills and cognitive behavioral interventions (Marshall et al., 1991). Where there is a couple involved, marital therapy is likely to be necessary if the marriage is to continue.

Children who have been sexually abused are more likely to show negative effects, both short-term and long-term, if (1) the abuse occurred over a substantial time span; (2) there were many episodes of abuse during that time span; (3) the child was abused by several, separate perpetrators; (4) the child was physically hurt; (5) the child was threatened or psychologically traumatized in or around these episodes; (6) the abuse was by the natural father or mother or by a loved parental figure, especially if that person is still loved and is separated from the child as a result of the abuse; (7) the child had to go through aversive confrontations in the legal process, especially if the perpetrator is found not guilty; (8) the child was old enough to experience some normal guilt and yet continued to participate; (9) the child does not have access to a loving, secure, and stable family structure; (10) therapeutic response was delayed or was of poor quality; or (11) the child was somehow made to feel responsible for whatever family disruption took place. A variety of treatment modalities will be needed; for example, there is often a post-traumatic stress component to the abuse and its aftermath, so something like systematic desensitization to prepare for and/or recover from the court appearance may be needed.

While treatment may help in a specific case, the greatest changes will come with efforts at prevention (parent training *before* becoming parents, reduction of the percentage of very young and/or single parents without skills or resources, educational programs in schools) or cultural change (efforts to reduce the acceptance of physical discipline) (Nelson, 1984; Finkelhor and Dziuba-Leatherman, 1994; Finkelhor, 1985). As recommended by the U.S. Advisory Board on Child Abuse and Neglect, programs should be designed to have health workers visit new parents in the home to discuss health care, make sure parents know how to care for the child, offer advice, and provide access to continuing support groups where needed.

■ Suicide Potential

As with aggression, the clinician is often called on to make predictions about suicide potential, and it is an equally difficult task (Chiles and Strosahl, 1995; Bongar, 1991; Apter et al., 1991). Although suicide is still an issue of concern in legal areas, it is no longer considered a crime. Only in recent times has our legal predecessor, England, stopped responding to a suicide attempt with an eminently practical solution, hanging. But hanging had superseded an even more flamboyant approach: driving a stake through the heart of one who attempted suicide. Edward Phillips claimed in his 1662 dictionary to have invented the word *suicide,* but the British poetry critic Alfred Alvarez reported in 1971 that he had found the word used even earlier, in Sir Thomas Brown's *Religio Medici,* written in 1635 and published in 1642 (Schneidman, 1985).

The combined suicide rate in the United States during this century has remained at about 12 per 100,000 population and accounts for about 1% of deaths per year. However, suicide appears to be increasing among the elderly and among young adults; at present, it is the second highest cause of death for white males age 15 to 19 (approximately 88 per 100,000). More men than women actually kill themselves (at an approximate a ratio of 3:1); in psychiatric patients it is only about a 1.5:1 ratio, although it seems that more women than men *attempt* suicide. The basic risk factors for suicide completion have remained relatively consistent over the years: old, male, white, lives alone, medically ill, alcoholic, schizophrenic, depressed. More recently, add AIDS, panic attacks, and borderline personality disorder. The majority of suicides, approximately 90%, are committed by whites (in both absolute numbers and per capita rate) as opposed to blacks, and most of the data about suicide is based on whites.

Suicidal individuals tend to give clues to those around them, and these areas should be the focus of any evaluation (Chiles and Strosahl, 1995). Seriously suicidal individuals tend to perceive life negatively and associate many attractive concepts with death; the reverse is true for those who are not so intent on self-destruction. Such measures as the semantic differential could be helpful in this regard. Approximately 80% of those who have made a suicide attempt discussed their intent to do so with persons around them, and they are usually open to discussing their suicidal concerns with clinicians. Also, for those who have made an attempt, the rate of suicide is about 1% per year over at least ten years following the first attempt.

In addition to being depressed, with a low threshold for emotional pain and with a proneness toward feelings of hopelessness *and* helplessness, a loss of a sense of continuity with the past and/or present, and loss of pleasure in typical interests and pursuits, suicidal persons are more likely to (1) have a history of self-damaging acts, often previous suicide attempts (in this context, the first axiom of psychology could well be "Behavior predicts behavior," and the second axiom could be "Behavior without intervention predicts behavior"); (2) have a personal history and/or family history of suicide, or depression, especially if it is a major endogenous depression, or of psychosis; (3) have panic attacks or manic episodes; (4) have had a parent or other important identity figure who attempted or committed suicide; (5) have a history of family instability and/or parental rejection; (6) be socially isolated; (7) have a chronic physical illness; (8) show a preoccupation with death and/or make statements of a wish to die, especially statements of a wish to commit suicide; (9) manifest consistent life patterns of leaving crises rather than facing them (in relationships: "You can't walk out on me—I'm leaving you"; or in jobs: "You can't fire me, because I quit"); (10) show a family history of self-damaging acts; (11) show a personal or family history of addiction patterns; (12) live alone or are involved (married or similarly occupied) with a loved mate who is competitive and/or self-absorbed; (13) show sudden cheerfulness after a long depression; (14) are noted to be putting their affairs in order, for example, giving away favorite possessions and revising wills; (15) present command suicidal hallucinations in some fashion, especially in the context of a history of related behaviors; (16) show some abrupt atypical behavior change, for example, withdrawal from family or friends (Chiles and Strosahl, 1995; Fawcett, 1992; Bongar, 1991; Schneidman, 1985).

At the biological level, depressions marked by low levels of 5-HIAA hydroxyindoleacetic acid, a metabolite of serotonin; a blunted thyroid-stimulating hormone (TSH) response to a thyrotropin-releasing hormone (TRH) stimulation; high levels of plasma cortisol (20 mcg % or higher); low platelet MAO, low platelet serotonin, high platelet serotonin-2 receptor responsivity; and a high ratio of adrenaline to noradrenaline have all been associated with an increased probability of suicide attempts. Also, suicide completers' brains show one-half to two-thirds the number of receptical, or "binding," sites for the chemical imipramine then do normal brains. The initiation of the suicidal event is especially likely to be triggered by a major life stress or, for example, the experience of a chronic debilitating illness or the loss of an important social support, such as a confidante (Schneidman, 1985).

The following factors can increase this potential and increase the probability that an attempted suicide will be completed (there is about a 15% probability that a serious attempt will be successful) (Schneidman, 1985; Bongar, 1991):

1. A cognitive state of constriction, that is, an inability to perceive any options or way out of a situation that is generating intense psychological suffering

2. The idea of death as a catalytic agent for the cessation of distress

3. Acute perturbation–high distress/agitation/depression/excessive perfectionism/rigidity

4. An increase in self-hatred or self–loathing

5. Perception of self as a source of shame to significant others.

6. Fantasies of death as escape, especially if there are concrete plans for one's own demise

7. Easy access to a lethal means, e.g., as in physicians, who show high suicide rates. Evidence of a plan

8. Absence of an accessible support system (family and good friends)

9. Life stresses that connote irrevocable loss (whether of status or of persons), such as the relatively recent death of a favored parent, even something like retirement (This factor is particularly important if the person at risk is unable to mourn the loss overtly.)

10. High physiologic responsiveness: cyclical moods, a propensity toward violence, and a high need for stimulation seeking in spite of suicide thoughts. (Ironically, in previously violent psychiatric patients, sadness showed a low correlation with suicide attempts, whereas it was consistently correlated with attempts by previously nonviolent patients [Apter et al., 1991].)

11. Serious sleep disruption and/or abuse of alcohol or drugs

12. Lack of a therapeutic alliance and/or constructively supportive friendship alliance

13. Persistence of secondary depression after remission of primary disorder and/or recent discharge from psychiatric hospital (last three months)

14. A history of panic attacks and even more importantly, evidence of recent panic attacks (as allegedly occurred just before White House aide Vincent Foster's suicide in July of 1993)

Fawcett (1992) finds that various factors are differentially predictive of suicide attempts, depending on whether the attempt is early (within one year) or later (one to five years). While panic attacks, alcohol abuse, loss of interest, psychic anxiety, diminished concentration, and global insomnia are more predictive of early attempts, expressed suicidal ideation, a sense of hopelessness, and prior suicide attempts are more predictive of later attempts.

In general, most people who are severely depressed and suicidal are more dangerous to themselves when they begin an upswing out of the depths of depression. If successive testings by an MMPI-2 or specific depression scale reveal an initial upswing in a depressive who has discussed the possibility of suicide, precautions should be emphasized at that time. There are various types of suicide, as listed next, and type of intervention will depend on the motivation for the suicide in the individual case (Schneidman, 1985).

□ TYPES OF SUICIDE

1. *Realistic:* These are suicides precipitated by such conditions as the prospect of great pain preceding a sure death.
2. *Altruistic:* The person's behavior is subservient to a group ethic that mandates or at least approves suicidal behavior, like kamikaze pilots in World War II.
3. *Inadvertent:* The person makes a suicide *gesture* in order to influence or manipulate someone else, but a misjudgment leads to an unexpected fatality.
4. *Spite:* Like the inadvertent suicide, the focus is on someone else, but the intention to kill oneself is genuine, with the idea that the other person will suffer greatly from consequent guilt.
5. *Bizarre:* The person commits suicide as a result of a hallucination (such as voices ordering the suicide) or delusions (such as a belief the suicide will change the world).
6. *Anomic:* An abrupt instability in economic or social conditions (such as sudden financial loss in the Great Depression) markedly changes a person's life situation. Unable to cope, the person commits suicide.
7. *Negative self:* Chronic depression and a sense of chronic failure or inadequacy combine to produce repetitive suicide attempts, eventually leading to death.

A dimension that is especially useful to most clinicians is the concept of manipulative versus "genuine" suicide (Schneidman, 1985). "Parasuicide" is another term used to designate suicide attempts designed to impact or change the environment, without any significant intent to take one's own life. Unfortunately, it is hard not to provide immediate reinforcement for a parasuicide, thus heightening the probability of its repetition. Genuinely suicidal persons see their psychic pain as inescapable, intolerable, and interminable. Both of these latter types will be discussed.

MMPI-2

Greene (1991) notes that any time that scale 2 is the only scale above 65 T, a careful evaluation of suicide risk is indicated, particularly if there are no overt signs of depression. However, the prototypical pattern for a suicidal individual is the 2-7/7-2 combination. This code particularly reflects suicidal ideation, and any time 2 is elevated above 70 T, the clinician should pursue the question of possible suicidal ideation. Reflecting the dictum that "If you want to know something specific about clients, you should ask them about it," the critical items concerning suicide (especially 150, 506, 520, and 524) should always be checked. The likelihood of this ideation's being actualized increases as scores on scales 4, 8, and 9 rise. Such a rise reflects an increasing loss of control over impulses, a rise in the energy available for behavior, and an increasing sense of isolation and resentment toward other people. A rise in scale 8 also reflects poor judgment; hence, suicidals who are not totally genuine in their suicide motivation may actually kill themselves whether they want to succeed or not, as poor judgment may bring inadvertent "success."

Some people are suicidal for only short periods of time, usually when there is a severe loss in their psychological worlds that has not yet been integrated (Bongar, 1991). Such people are temporarily suicidal, and if they can be restricted during these periods and treated, they are likely to reintegrate and move away from the suicidal ideation. A high spike on scale 2 is characteristic here.

The 2-4/4-2 code is more likely to reflect a manipulative suicide. Where both scales 4 and 6 are elevated, in addition to at least a moderate elevation on scales 2 and 7, repressed anger and interpersonal hostility are basic to the suicide attempt as manipulation. It is an attempt to inflict punitive guilt and consequent behavior control on another.

Several observers have noted that an additional pattern, at least in women, has been associated with suicide attempts. The major features are a low K scale and a high 5 scale (both suggesting a strong, almost counterphobic rejection of femininity); a paradoxically high score on scale 3, indicating a histrionic component; and a high score on scale 0, reflecting a sense of social isolation and rejection. These women feel alienated and disturbed in their self-identities, yet they have no sense of possible alternatives to deal with their distress. Since they are impulsive as well, the potential for an acting-out behavior is heightened.

16 PF

On the 16 PF, attempters consistently show themselves to be more tense, expedient, shy, suspicious, emotionally unstable, apprehensive, self-sufficient, extremely anxious, and somewhat introverted. Translated into 16 PF scales, this means high scores on Q_4, 0, 1, Q_2 and lower scores on G, H, and C. Furthermore, repeated attempters typically score lower on scales Q_3 and C than do first-time attempters, indicating less stability and more impulsivity.

OTHER TEST-RESPONSE PATTERNS

Exner (1978, 1986) has provided the most elegant and effective research on the use of Rorschach in the prediction of suicide. In 1978 he offered eleven variables that together form a prediction for suicide potential. The variables he first cited as important are as follows:*

1. FV + VF + V + FD is greater than 2.
2. An occurrence of a color-shading blend response.
3. Zd is greater than $\pm$ 3.5.
4. 3r + (2)/R is less than 0.30.
5. Experience Potential is greater than Experience Actual.
6. CF + C is greater than FC.
7. S is greater than 3.
8. X + % is less than 0.70.
9. Pure H is less than 2.
10. P is greater than 8 or less than 3.
11. R is less than 17.

In addition to the eleven criteria used in the original constellation, two new criteria have been established (Exner, 1986). The addition of an upper range to the egocentricity scale (3r + (2)/R is greater than 0.45 or less than 0.30) and the incorporation of the Morbidity index (MOR is greater than 3) have significantly improved the accuracy of the index. The original criteria (eight of eleven variables) could accurately predict 75% of suicides, categorizing 20% of depressed inpatients and 12% of schizophrenics as false-positive errors. The new criterion (eight of thirteen variables) can predict 83% of suicides accurately, classifying only 12% of depressed inpatients and 6% of schizophrenics as false-positives. Neither of the two scales made false-positive errors in classifying nonsuicidal controls as suicides. This change represents a significant increase in power.

Other authors have supported Exner's concepts that the number of responses is low in suicidals, especially when they are depressed; that less integrated Color responses are more common, and that the number of Popular responses is either very high or low (Swiercinsky, 1985). Also, there is some

* J. Exner, *The Rorschach: A Comprehensive System*, Vol. 2: *Current Research and Advanced Interpretation* (New York: Wiley, 1978, p. 204). Used with permission of the publisher.

indication that transparency responses (such as light bulbs) or cross-sectional responses (such as X rays) are found more commonly in potential suicides than in other persons, and the greater the number of vista and shading responses, the greater the depression-based suicide potential.

Phillips and Smith (1953) state that content suggesting decay or geographic depression (e.g., canyons) is indicative of suicidal ideation. Others have argued that landscape or serenity associations are indicative of suicides who have not yet communicated their intent. Responses that suggest hanging or drowning or other direct means of suicide should obviously alert the examiner to further consideration.

McCann and Suess (1988) examined 131 psychiatric inpatients to conclude that a 1-2-3-8 MCMI-III code type reflects an affect/mood disturbance, with prominent depressive features and a blend of schizoid, avoidant, dependent, and passive-aggressive personality traits. One-fourth of their patients obtained this code type, which they see as offering a significant suicide risk.

As might be expected, elevations on the MCMI-III of 85 or higher on D and CC, and a high score on the Desirability scale would be indicative of suicide potential (Coca et al., 1992). If N begins to increase and a very high D begins to decrease on repeated testing, the patient may be acquiring the necessary resolve and energy to complete the act; thus, suicide potential may be high. Those personality patterns most likely to exhibit suicide potential are indicated by elevated scores on 2, 8A, 5, and/or C. These patterns are the most inconsistent, and they are particularly susceptible to poorly developed support systems. High scores on scale 8A are particularly associated with manipulative suicide potential.

Since completed suicides are more often psychotic, while attempters are more often neurotic, greater elevations on the pathologic personality scales S, C, and P than on scales 1 to 8, along with greater elevations on SS, CC, and PP, are found in those who are more likely to complete bizarre suicide gestures.

Beck et al. (1983) found that a score of 10 or more on the Hopelessness scale, devised by Beck, correctly identified 91% of later actual suicides. Also, the pessimism item of the Beck Depression Inventory was asserted to be predictive of later suicides.

Bongar (1991) discusses a number of scales specifically designed to assess suicide risk, for example, Beck's Scale for Suicide Ideation (SSI) and Suicide Intent Scale (SIS), the Reason for Living Inventory, Suicide Probability Scale (SPS), Index of Potential Suicide, et cetera. All have validity problems and are primarily research and/or minimal screening tools, but as such, they can be useful in certain specific situations.

Extra data may be available if an individual has already attempted suicide but has been prevented from completing it: the suicide note. The work of Edwin Schneidman and Norman Farberow (Schneidman, 1985) over many years has found that people who attempt suicide and genuinely mean to kill themselves write notes that are matter-of-fact and practical in their content. They may ask the target of the note to pay back small debts or return small items, or show other seemingly trivial concerns, and they do not show much emotional content. It is as if they have already integrated the idea that they will be dead, so emotion is no longer directly tied to living relationships. Those individuals who attempted suicide, but apparently had no real intent to kill themselves left romantic, emotion-laden notes, attempting to institute guilt in others and pressure them to change their behaviors. Obviously, they believed they would be around to reap the fruits of those changes.

PREVENTION

Suicide prevention techniques have been developed at both the societal and individual levels, but implementing them is not always easy. The following dialogue from the old television show "Mary Hartman, Mary Hartman" shows the difficulty most people have in responding effectively to a potential suicide's questions.

HEATHER (Mary's 12-year-old daughter): I have nothing to live for.

MARY: Sure you do.

HEATHER: Like what?

MARY: Well . . . wait and see.

INDIVIDUAL INTERVENTION AND PREVENTION

The clinician should be aware of and follow the general-practice principles discussed in Chapter 16. Also, facilitate ventilation of feelings and emotional responses. Help to reframe the issues and develop a different perspective. Assess the intensity or seriousness of the ideation, as well as the seriousness of any emotional disorder. Set up hospitalization and/or medication if needed. Help to reestablish positive relationships and personal practices. The clinician should be especially and immediately alert to the person's evidence of a plan and/or access to lethal instruments and take direct steps to change that situation. Respond with caution to any quick assurances that the crisis is past. Obtain collateral information without being demeaning or pejorative. Confrontation and exploration of any reported or inferred suicidal ideation are important. Generating the presence and active involvement by trusted therapeutic personnel and pertinent significant others is usually essential to such a process. The achievement of a time-limited no-suicide contract is a psychotherapeutic goal that many therapists choose to work toward. The client is asked if he or she will both agree to and verbalize a statement such as in Figure 14.1.

The "contract" in Figure 14.1 is helpful if responded to reasonably sincerely. It may serve to relax the client, who then has the burden of the suicidal decision temporarily taken off his or her shoulders. At the same time, because the agreement is not a permanent one, it allows the person to retain some level of suicidal ideation (which the client may feel is necessary). Finally, it usually offers the family and also the therapist a greater level of comfort with the overall therapeutic plan. Such an agreement, however, should not be used (or at

FIGURE 14.1   Sample No-Suicide Pact

I will not, for the next _____ days (up to at least the time of the next followup intervention) do anything to harm myself *or* anyone else, either on purpose *or* accidentally.

If, for any reason, I begin to feel that I might not be able to control thoughts or impulses to hurt or kill myself or others, I agree to immediately call

_____ at _____,
(phone number)

(optional — or _____ at _____).
(phone number)

If I am unable to reach _____(or _____), I

agree to go immediately and directly to _____ at
(hospital or agency)

_____ .

(address and phone number)

_____   _____
(Signature)   (date)

_____   _____
(Therapist)   (date)

_____   _____
(Witness)   (date)

least is not considered as having any controlling impact) with an individual who either does not understand its nature or who is known to be unreliable or quite impulsive.

It's also useful for the therapist and client to mutually prepare a "crisis card," which the client can keep with him or her in wallet or purse. If suicidal ideation occurs, the agreed-upon first line of defense is taken, for example, call a specific friend to talk, or go to the gym and exercise. Subsequent strategies, including calling the therapist and going to a crisis center or emergency room, are then listed in order of mutually agreed upon implementation.

Clinicians can be effectively involved in suicide prevention education by promoting and emphasizing those precautions that can be taken by their clients and which can be advised at the individual level by laypersons:

1. Attend seriously to people who voice a desire to kill themselves or "just go to sleep and forget it all."

2. Attend especially to depressed individuals who speak of losing hope and have difficulty projecting into the future, instead seeming fixated in the past.

3. Attend especially to persons with panic disorder or a history of panic attacks.

4. To the degree possible, keep lethal means (guns, large prescriptions of sedatives) away from suicidal individuals.

5. Generate a personal concern toward a suicidal person; a suicide attempt is most often a cry for help; for example, as O. J. Simpson wrote during his crisis immediately following the murders of his ex-wife and her friend, "Please think of the real O. J. and not this lost person." Suicidal individuals need a temporary "champion" who can point them toward new resources, suggest new options, and at least in a small way can diminish their sense of hopelessness.

6. Try to get the person to perform some of the following behaviors: (1) engage in regular physical exercise, (2) start a diary, (3) follow a normal routine, (4) do something in which he or she has already demonstrated competence, (5) confide inner feelings to someone, or (6) cry it out. Try to get the person to avoid self-medication and other people inclined toward depression.

7. Make every effort to guarantee that a suicidal person reaches appropriate professional help. Making an appointment is a good first step; getting a person to the appointment (and helping the person maintain that contact) is the crucial step.

SOCIETAL PREVENTION

Several things can be done on a societal level to lower the incidence of suicide (Phillips, 1986; Schneidman, 1985). Educating the public on the myths and facts of suicide is an important first step. Second, there is evidence that suicide prevention centers and telephone hotlines can slightly decrease the suicide rate. A third step in suicide prevention (and, analogously, in lowering the incidence of aggressive acts) may involve some restriction on media publicity about suicides (and violent aggression). Phillips (1986) documents the correlation between a rise and fall in suicide rates and the amount of newspaper publicity given to suicides in that locality. Such self-imposed restriction is a thorny ethical issue for newspapers and television, especially because rates of all externally directed violence (murder, rape) may also be increased by publicity about similar incidents (Miller et al., 1991).

CHAPTER 15

Psychopharmacology

■   **Overall Concepts**

Psychotropic medications can be a useful component in the treatment of numerous mental disorders (Buckley and Meltzer, 1995; Charmey et al., 1995; Wiesel, 1994; Riedlinger and Riedlinger, 1994). The introduction of the antipsychotic and antidepressant drugs in the 1960s revolutionized mental health treatment. Their use has resulted in decreased hospital stays, an increased emphasis on outpatient treatment, and an overall increase in the level of functioning for individuals with such disorders.

The term "psychotropic" broadly refers to medications that have an effect on the central nervous system to produce changes in aberrant behavior. These types of medications are divided into several groups based on their behavioral effects. However, psychotropic medications can have other uses, some of which will be discussed in this chapter, and there are drugs currently not classified as psychotropic medications that can also have behavioral effects. For example, Reserpine, developed as an antihypertensive in the 1950s, was routinely found to cause depression. In fact, Reserpine-induced depression in laboratory animals is often used as a model in the early development and testing of antidepressants. Ondansetron, currently undergoing clinical trials for use in the treatment of generalized anxiety disorder and social phobia, has been in use as an anti-emetic in chemotherapy-induced nausea. Drugs currently used in neurology can also be used to treat psychiatric disorders. Some of these crossover drugs will be discussed where appropriate.

As in many aspects of medicine, the early psychotropics were found by serendipity or were related to drugs that were being used for other purposes and refined for use as psychopharmacologic agents. Imipramine, for example, was originally being studied as an antihistamine. MAO inhibitors had originally been used as antituberculin drugs. From observations that patients on these or similar compounds improved their moods was born the field of psychopharmacology.

Familiarity with psychotropic medications is important for all mental health professionals in order to provide clients with the widest and most appropriate treatment range. It is important for all therapists to provide education to their clients about mental illness and possible treatment options.

Pharmacokinetics

The term "pharmacokinetics" refers to how the body handles a drug that has been administered. In other words, what happens to the drug once a person takes it? There are four major components to the concept of pharmacokinetics: (1) Absorption—where is the drug taken into the body, and how rapidly is it taken in? (2) Distribution—how does the drug get to its intended site of action, and exactly what bodily system does the drug affect? (3) Metabolism—where is the drug broken down in the body, and how rapidly does this take place? and (4) Excretion—how are the breakdown products from metabolism eliminated from the body? Let's now look at each of these four areas in more detail in order to understand how the psychotropic medications work.

Obviously, getting the drug into the body is the most important first step; this represents *absorption*. Most drugs are given orally. When taken by this route, the drug is swallowed and absorbed into the bloodstream somewhere in the gastrointestinal (GI) tract. Usually absorption occurs in either the stomach or the upper portion of the small intestine. A number of factors influence this process. The chemical composition of the drug, for example, will determine how rapidly it dissolves and also how quickly it passes through the gastrointestinal mucosa. The acid-base composition of the drug, referred to as its pH, will also affect rate absorption, as will the pH of the GI tract. Drugs that are *lipid soluble* tend to be absorbed more rapidly; lipid solubility simply refers to whether or not a given drug is chemically similar or dissimilar to most fluids and molecules in the body. The more similar it is, the greater its degree of lipid solubility and the faster its rate of absorption. Two other routes of absorption exist for psychotropic medications. One is the intravenous route, where the drug is injected directly into the blood system. This is the fastest route of absorption. Some psychotropic medications (such as the depot neuroleptics, described later in the chapter) are administered intramuscularly. They are injected directly into muscle tissue, where they bind with certain molecules and are released into the blood slowly over a period of days or weeks. This method has the advantage of eliminating the need for daily medication ingestion or injection. To summarize, absorption refers to how quickly a drug gets into the body. It is fairly obvious that the faster the absorption, the earlier the onset of therapeutic action.

Distribution refers to what happens to a drug after it gets into the bloodstream. In general, one of three things can happen: (1) The drug is freely dissolved in the blood, (2) it is bound to plasma proteins that circulate throughout the bloodstream, or (3) the drug is carried within the blood cells. How quickly the drug dissolves in the blood, binds to proteins, or gets absorbed and then released from the blood cells determines, in part, how quickly the therapeutic action of the drug begins. The psychotropic medications exert a large part of their actions on the brain. In order to reach the brain, however, these drugs must cross the *blood–brain barrier.* Not all of the blood vessels in the brain can release substances directly into brain tissue. In order for psychotropic medications to be effective in the brain, they must be able to gain access to those blood vessels that directly communicate with brain tissue. This requires that the drug molecules be of a certain size (i.e., very small), have a high degree of lipid solubility, and have affinity for certain neuroreceptors (more on these in the next section). If the drug has all of these characteristics, then it can pass through the blood–brain barrier. Once in the brain, the drug exerts its effects by acting on certain neurotransmitters and neuroreceptors, as described in the next section.

Once in the body, specifically in the brain, the drug begins to undergo a series of chemical changes that ultimately result in its degradation or breakdown; this process is referred to as *metabolism.* If metabolism did not take place, the drug would remain in its original form and exert its action indefinitely. In other words, there would be no way to control the action of the drug. The blood circulates throughout the body constantly, meaning that the drugs carried in the blood do the same thing. As a result, no psychotropic drug remains in the brain forever. One organ that the blood continually passes through is the liver, and it is here that most drug metabolism takes place. While some drugs are metabolized by other organs, the liver is of primary importance. Metabolism simply involves a series of chemical reactions, facilitated by enzymes in the body, that transform the drug into a number of related compounds. Some of these compounds retain the actions of the original drug and are called "active metabolites." Others lose the therapeutic action of the drug and become inactive. It is the rate of metabolism and the number of active metabolites for each drug that determine how long the therapeutic effect lasts.

The metabolic products from the drug are then eliminated, or *excreted*, from the body. For most drugs this occurs via the kidneys, with the drug metabolites being eliminated in the urine. Other routes of excretion include tears, saliva, sweat, feces, and breast milk. It is because of this latter route of excretion that many drugs are required to contain warnings against their use by women who are nursing. Excretion, then, is the final step in removing a drug from the body.

■ Classification

The psychotropic medications are typically divided into five groups based on their predominant behavioral effect: (1) antipsychotic agents, (2) antidepressants, (3) antimanic drugs, (4) antianxiety agents, and (5) sedative-hypnotics. Many of these drugs have secondary actions such as the control of violent and agitated behavior, and some are utilized as "truth serums." These uses will also be discussed later in the chapter.

Each group of drugs is useful in the treatment of specific mental disorders. For example, the antipsychotic drugs, often referred to as "neuroleptics," have their greatest application in the treatment of schizophrenia and other disorders accompanied by psychotic symptoms (e.g., psychotic depressions). Mood–altering agents such as the antimanic and antidepressant medications are useful in the treatment of severe depressions and bipolar (manic-depressive) illness. The antianxiety agents produce a generalized calming effect and are useful in the treatment of generalized anxiety. They have also been used in conditions in which anxiety is a prominent symptom (e.g., panic disorder or phobias), but then they generally require significantly higher doses. It should be noted, however, that true panic disorders are best treated with a group of drugs called selective serotonin reuptake inhibitors (SSRI), discussed in detail later in this chapter. The sedative-hypnotics tend to induce drowsiness and alter consciousness and are used in the treatment of sleep disturbances such as insomnia.

There is a large number of specific drugs within each of the groups listed. The proper selection of an appropriate class of drug and then within a classification—the selection of the specific drug for the actions desired as well as those to be avoided if possible—depends on the clinician's skills in a number of areas. Most importantly, it depends on the ability to understand the specific etiology of the behavior to be treated, the ability to accurately define behavior in terms of target symptoms, the need to understand how specific drugs can be used to affect specific symptoms, the ability to understand delay of onset and length of action, and an understanding of drug interactions as well as possible side effects. Each drug has both a trade name, assigned by the manufacturer, and a generic, or chemical, name. In the sections that follow, both names will be listed for each specific agent.

Because of their potential to alter behavior, and because some of these drugs are addicting, a number of the psychotropic agents are classified as controlled substances by the Drug Enforcement Administration (D.E.A.). Drugs are classified as controlled according to their potential for abuse; the greater the potential, the more limitations are placed on their use. Only the antianxiety agents and the sedative–hypnotics are presently classified as controlled. Table 15.1 lists examples of controlled substances and the D.E.A. classification system.

The clinician must be ever mindful that dependency and abuse are a function of personality factors as well as of the substance itself. This is especially true for the anxiolytic drugs. For example, individuals who use increasing dosages of anxiolytics as a way of "feeling better," "taking off the edge," or "getting through a tough day" or who have a history of drug-seeking behavior with abuse or dependency in other areas are likely to abuse anxiolytics. Such individuals need to be carefully monitored by the prescribing physicians, therapists, and dispensing pharmacies.

The senior author is reminded of a situation that occurred while leading a therapy group for substance abusers at the State Prison of Southern Michigan. One inmate had recently been returned to prison as a parole violator after it had been discovered that he had visited *every* emergency room in southern

TABLE 15.1   Controlled Substances

D.E.A. CLASS	CHARACTERISTICS	EXAMPLES
I	High abuse potential; no accepted medical use	LSD, heroin, marijuana
II	High abuse potential with severe physical and psychological dependence	Amphetamines, opium, morphine, codeine, barbiturates, cocaine
III	High abuse potential with low to moderate physical dependence and high psychological dependence	Compounds containing codeine, morphine (i.e., narcotic analgesics)
IV	Low abuse potential with limited physical and psychological dependence	Benzodiazepines, certain barbiturates, other sedative-hypnotics
V	Lowest abuse potential	Narcotic preparations containing nonnarcotic active ingredients (e.g., cough medicines with codeine)

Michigan presenting with symptoms of panic attacks and a host of other disorders. A physician who had just transferred hospitals recognized the patient as having been at his prior hospital the previous month, presenting with symptoms of chronic low back pain. A quick check of other emergency rooms turned up the fact that he had visited thirteen others within a two-month period!

A related concept is that of mind-altering versus mood-altering drugs. A mind-altering drug is a substance that will have a similar effect when given to a general population of individuals. Stimulants, for instance, if given to a hundred people at large, will have a stimulating effect to virtually all. Antidepressants (which are mood-altering), as an example, when given to a hundred people selected at random, are likely to have a positive effect only on those individuals suffering from an affective disorder. Even then, it may take weeks, and the effect of the drug is not superimposed over the existing mood; rather, it reestablishes a normal range of appropriate mood. Mind-altering drugs, on the other hand, limit the range of mood and superimpose the effect in almost anyone taking that type of substance.

■   ## Antipsychotic Drugs

The antipsychotic medications are a large class of drugs that are useful in the treatment of psychotic disorders, such as schizophrenia (Buckley and Meltzer, 1995). The characteristics of psychotic disorders are discussed in Chapters 3 and 4. A number of mental disorders in addition to schizophrenia may be accompanied by psychotic features. These include severe mood disorders such as psychotic depressions and mania. Transient psychoses may also be seen in certain of the personality disorders.

Antipsychotic medications are usually effective in correcting the thought disturbances, delusional thinking, and hallucinations seen in psychotic disorders. They are not directly effective with the apathy, social withdrawal, and blunted affects. A widely held theory asserts that many psychoses are caused by an overabundance of the neurotransmitter dopamine in the brain (Wiesel, 1994). Dopamine is believed to play an important regulatory role in thought and perception and is also important in coordinating fine motor movements. When imbalances in dopamine occur in the brain, the characteristic symptoms of psychosis (thought disorder, delusions, and hallucinations) are likely to occur. The antipsychotic agents appear to act by blocking dopamine receptors in the brain, thereby decreasing the functional availability of the neurotransmitter; these drugs correct the imbalance and thus restore thought and perception to their normal states.

In addition to their action on psychotic symptoms, most of the antipsychotic medications also cause some degree of sedation. This effect is useful in decreasing agitation that often accompanies a psychosis. As will be discussed later in the chapter, the sedating properties of these drugs also make them useful in the treatment of violent behavior. The phenothiazines (e.g., chlorpromazine and thioridazine), the largest group of antipsychotic drugs, tend to produce the most sedation.

In addition to their therapeutic properties, all medications have certain side effects and adverse reactions. As a group, the antipsychotics are noteworthy because of the large number of side effects that may occur. These are very potent drugs, and as such they affect a variety of systems in the body. One of the most common side effects is muscular stiffness and rigidity, referred to as "dystonia." These drugs may also cause a vague feeling of restlessness and the inability to sit still, referred to as "akathesia." The shuffling gait perceived by many as a hallmark behavior of the chronically ill patient who has been over-medicated is the result of akathesia. Some patients on high doses of these drugs for extended periods of time will develop involuntary movements of the face, mouth, and tongue; this syndrome is known as "tardive dyskinesia." All of the neuromuscular side effects are described under the general heading of "extrapyramidal symptoms." This term derives from the areas of the brain and central nervous system that control movement, the extrapyramidal tracts. These symptoms are also often referred to as "Parkinsonian" side effects because they clinically resemble the symptoms of Parkinson's disease.

The antipsychotic drugs exert an influence on other neurotransmitters in addition to dopamine. One of these is acetylcholine, a muscarinic transmitter that is involved in the regulation of many bodily functions. The antipsychotics block the action of acetylcholine, with the result that this group of side effects is often referred to as "anticholinergic" effects. Specific symptoms include dry mouth, intolerance to heat, constipation, and blurred vision. In extreme cases an anticholinergic delirium may occur, characterized by confusion, disorientation, and agitation. These drugs also may temporarily cause a drop in blood pressure, especially when arising from a sitting or supine position. This phenomenon, called "postural hypotension," may lead to dizziness. These symptoms complicate the already complex clinical picture and often require the administration of medication to offset the effects.

Other side effects noted with the antipsychotic medications include photosensitivity to sunlight, liver damage, cardiotoxicity, a depression of blood cell production leading to anemia (agranulocytosis), and seizures. A very serious and potentially life-threatening side effect is the neuroleptic malignant syndrome, characterized by high fever, convulsions, muscular rigidity, and rapid progression to coma and death. With such side effects as these, it is not surprising that the antipsychotics have a low potential for abuse, dependence, or addiction.

A large number of specific drugs are available in this group and are listed in Table 15.2. Despite their numbers, virtually all of these agents are thought to act primarily by blocking dopamine receptors in the brain, and many of the specific agents are chemically related to each other. The main features that differentiate the individual medications are dose range, degree of sedation,

TABLE 15.2   Antipsychotic Drugs

NAME (GENERIC/TRADE)	DOSE RANGE[a]
PHENOTHIAZINES	
Chlorpromazine (Thorazine)	50–1500 mg/day
Thioridazine (Mellaril)	50–800 mg/day
Fluphenazine (Prolixin)	5–40 mg/day
Fluphenazine decanoate (Prolixin D)	25–100 mg IM Q1–4 weeks
Perphenazine (Trilafon)	4–64 mg/day
Trifluoperazine (Stelazine)	5–40 mg/day
BUTYROPHENONES	
Haloperidol (Haldol)	5–100 mg/day
Haloperidol decanoate (Haldol D)	50–200 mg IM Q2–4 weeks
THIOXANTHENES	
Thiothixine (Navane)	5–60 mg/day
OTHER ANTIPSYCHOTIC DRUGS	
Loxapine (Loxitane)	20–250 mg/day
Molindone (Moban)	20–225 mg/day
Clozapine (Clozaril)	300–500 mg/day
Risperidone (Risperdal)	3–6 mg/day

[a] Average therapeutic dose range.
IM = intramuscular administration.

duration of action, and intensity of side effects. All of these drugs are metabolized by the liver, so caution is required in persons with pre-existing liver disease.

Three classes of antipsychotic drugs exist: (1) the phenothiazines; (2) the thioxanthenes, for example, thiothixine (Navane); and (3) the butyrophenones, for example, haloperidol (Haldol). Several other antipsychotics are also in clinical use that do not belong to any of these groups. For example, the substituted benzamides, sulpiride, remoxipride, and raclopride, as well as the D_2-receptor-blocking agent risperidone can be effective (Michels and Marzuk, 1993). The phenothiazines may be further subdivided into drugs with low potency that are used at relatively high doses (e.g., Thorazine and Mellaril) and those with high potency that are used at lower doses (e.g., Stelazine and Prolixin). As a general rule, the low potency–high dose drugs cause more sedation, whereas the high potency–low dose preparations have less sedation but more tendency to cause extrapyramidal reactions.

The two most commonly used antipsychotics are chlorpromazine (Thorazine) and haloperidol. There is some evidence that haloperidol is typically prescribed at higher dosages than is necessary to gain the desired effect (Rifkin et al., 1991). Long-acting (decanoate) preparations are available for haloperidol (Haldol D) and fluphenazine (Prolixin D). Both of these are given intramuscularly by injection and have a duration of action of from two to four weeks. The duration of action for orally administered antipsychotics ranges from four to twelve hours, depending in part on how quickly the drug is metabolized.

The first therapeutic effect that occurs, thirty to sixty minutes after ingestion, is a generalized calming effect, often accompanied by some degree of sedation. A person on antipsychotics is also likely to appear rather stiff and clumsy, due to the extrapyramidal effects mentioned previously. Although the person is fully alert while on these drugs, he or she may often appear emotionless and possess a rather blank stare, due also to the extrapyramidal effects. The full antipsychotic action on hallucinations and delusions may take from several days to several weeks to appear, depending on the severity and intensity of the symptoms. Unless the situation is acute, it is prudent to give low dosages in increasing frequency until one has titrated the dose of medication against behavior and side effects. Some psychotic patients do not respond significantly to these medications, for reasons that are not completely clear.

Two of the newer antipsychotics, clozapine (Clozaril), a dibenzodiazepene, and risperidone (Risperdal), seem to be effective with treatment-resistant patients (Buckley and Meltzer, 1995; Green and Salzman, 1990) and also have less potential for extrapyramidal side effects and tardive dyskinesia. Clozapine blocks a number of receptors in the brain: dopamine, serotonin, adrenergic, and muscarinic. Its specific mechanism of therapeutic action, however, is not known, although it is a weak D_2-receptor autogonist. Side effects include a potentially fatal agranulocytosis in 1–2% of patients receiving the drug (hence, consistent blood monitoring is necessary), as well as seizures, sedation, tachycardia, hypotension, hyperthermia, nausea, excessive salivation, and drooling. The dose range for clozapine is 300–500 mg/day (not to exceed 900 mg/day), but the risk of seizures increases dramatically at doses greater than 500–600 mg/day. Side effects for risperidone include insomnia, fatigue, somnolence, agitation and increased saliva.

■ Antidepressants

Depression, described in Chapter 4, is one of the most frequently encountered psychiatric symptoms. Most depressions occur in response to some trauma or loss that the individual can identify. In many cases this type of depression is self-limiting and does not require treatment. In those cases that persist, psychological treatments are usually effective in alleviating the depression. Some people, however, experience severe depressions that are seemingly unrelated to any external event and apparently reflect abnormalities in the neurotransmitters that regulate mood (Nathan et al., 1995; Riedlinger and Riedlinger, 1994).

The antidepressant medications consist of four broad groups of drugs: (1) the tricyclic and tetracyclic antidepressants (TCAs), which generally act on both serotonin and norepinephrine (examples are amitriptyline [Elavil] and imipramine [Tofranil]; (2) the monoamine oxidase inhibitors (MAOIs), which act primarily on norepinephrine; and (3) the nontricyclic antidepressants, a group consisting of drugs that act on serotonin and norepinephrine by unknown mechanisms and are structurally unrelated to the other antidepressants. This group includes bupropion (Wellbutrin), which is thought to act by blocking norepinephrine reuptake. Another member of this group is venlafaxine (Effexor), which acts on both norepinephrine and serotonin. Finally, (4) the selective serotonin reuptake inhibitors (SSRIs) act by blocking the reuptake of serotonin (5HT) into human platelet and inhibit neuronal serotonin reuptake (hence their name SSSIs), thus increasing the concentration at post-synaptic neuroreceptors, while having only weak effects on the uptake of other transmitters such as dopamine and norepinephrine. Drugs in this class include fluoxetine (Prozac), sertraline (Zoloft), paroxetine (Paxil), and trazodone (Desyrel).

For example, one of the newer antidepressants, the unicyclic bupropion (Wellbutrin), has an unknown mechanism of action, but is thought to act by blocking norepinephrine reuptake. It is not anticholinergic, but it can be too "activating" for some patients. Bupropion's release for use as an antidepressant was delayed when it was discovered, late in clinical trials, to have a higher seizure potential than the tricyclics to which it was being compared. Closer analysis of the data revealed that its increased seizuregenic potential was limited primarily to its use with a particular subgroup being studied—bulimic women.

Most of the antidepressants require a period of from ten days to two weeks before they begin to exert their therapeutic action (Charney et al., 1995). This poses a problem when a client presents with a high risk of suicide. Control and monitoring must be exerted until the medications or other treatments apparently take effect. During this lag period, blood levels of the drug are rising into a therapeutic range. These levels can be measured and the dose adjusted accordingly to obtain an optimal clinical response. Monitoring of blood levels also decreases the likelihood of toxic reactions. Amoxapine (Asendin), with a four-ringed structure, can be helpful because of its rapid onset of effect, sometimes within four to seven days.

Table 15.3 lists the antidepressant medications. The most commonly used tricyclics have traditionally been amitriptyline (Elavil), imipramine (Tofranil), and desipramine (Norpramin). Predictors of positive response to tricyclics include high socio-economic class, good treatment motivation, insidious onset, anorexia, weight loss, middle and late insomnia, and psychomotor disturbance. Predictors of poor response to tricyclics include hypochondriasis, hysterical

TABLE 15.3   Antidepressant Drugs

NAME (GENERIC/TRADE)	DOSE RANGE[a]
TRICYCLIC AND TETRACYCLIC ANTIDEPRESSANTS	
Amitriptyline (Elavil)	75–300 mg/day
Imipramine (Tofranil)	75–300 mg/day
Desipramine (Norpramin)	75–300 mg/day
Nortriptyline (Pamelor)	30–100 mg/day
Protriptyline (Vivactil)	15–40 mg/day
Doxepine (Sinequan)	50–300 mg/day
Maprotiline (Ludiomil)	75–150 mg/day
Amoxapine (Asendin)	50–300 mg/day
Clomipramine (Anafranil)[†]	150–250 mg/day
MAOI'S	
Tranylcypromine (Parnate)	20–60 mg/day
Phenelzine (Nardil)	60–90 mg/day
SELECTIVE SEROTONIN REUPTAKE INHIBITORS	
Fluoxetine (Prozac)	20 mg/day
Trazodone (Desyrel)	100–400 mg/day
Sertaline (Zoloft)[+]	50–200 mg/day
Paroxetine (Paxil)	20–60 mg/day
OTHER ANTIDEPRESSANTS	
Buproprion (Wellbutrin)	200–450 mg/day
Venlafaxine (Effexor)	75–225 mg/day

[a] Average therapeutic dose range.
[†] Used also for treatment of the obsessive-compulsive disorder.
[+] Used also for treatment of panic disorder.

traits, multiple prior episodes, and delusions. The MAOIs are used less often because of their side effects. The newer SSRI antidepressants, for example, fluoxetine, sertraline, and paroxetine, are rapidly becoming the most frequently prescribed drugs in the United States.

The initial effect experienced after taking many antidepressants is sedation. The severity of this effect varies with the drug; amitriptyline, for example, is very sedating whereas desipramine has relatively little sedation. Thus, a depressed patient with insomnia might benefit from amitriptyline. The drug would not be recommended, however, for a patient with prostate or bladder troubles because it can impede urination.

Antidepressants also can generate feelings of dizziness or lightheadedness. This occurs because norepinephrine exerts an effect not only on mood but also on other organ systems, such as the cardiovascular system. Most clients will also experience a calming effect, related to either the sedative effect of the drugs or to the direct action on serotonin. Depending on the degree of sedation and calming, the person may appear either drowsy or detached and disinterested; it is unlikely, however, that the person would appear intoxicated. Once the antidepressant action of the drug takes effect, the person will probably not notice any major effect from the medication; their mood will simply appear to be normal. In some persons, however, the mood will become somewhat agitated due to overstimulation of the norepinephrine system. In fact, persons with a bipolar disorder who take antidepressants may cycle into a manic episode.

The antidepressants have a number of side effects, many of which are potentially dangerous. Nearly all of the drugs in this class cause some degree of drowsiness and sedation. Like the antipsychotics, many also cause anticholinergic side effects. Other side effects include feelings of restlessness and agitation, sleep disturbances, nightmares, seizures, and exacerbation of psychosis in susceptible persons. The MOAIs may cause an interaction with certain foods and alcohol to produce a sudden rise in blood pressure (hypertensive crisis). Because of this effect, certain dietary restrictions (especially for foods containing tyramine such as beer, red wine, certain cheeses, liver, and pickled or smoked meats and fish) apply for MAOI use.

Several antidepressants, including maprotiline (Ludiomil) and bupropion, are associated with an increased risk of seizures, particularly when taken in high doses. The tricyclic antidepressants may cause a number of cardiac effects. At therapeutic doses these effects include tachycardia (rapid heart rate) and a decreased conduction time that causes electrocardiogram (ECG) changes. At very high doses, as seen in overdoses, these drugs cause cardiac arrhythmias, which may be potentially fatal, and slow heart rate. This effect presents a significant risk for persons with pre-existing heart disease or for those who overdose on these medications as part of a suicide attempt. Thus the tricyclics and tetracyclics should be prescribed in limited amounts to minimize the risk of overdose. Blood levels of the drugs should also be monitored to prevent toxicity. There is low potential for abuse or dependence in this group of drugs.

The Prozac Controversies

The most controversial newer-generation antidepressant, a serotonin reuptake inhibitor similar to sertraline and paroxetine, is certainly fluoxetine (Prozac). This versatile compound was initially accepted with great hopes for the treatment of depressed patients, but it quickly became highly controversial. Despite its demonstrated lack of toxic physiologic side effects, the drug was accused of creating some of the very conditions it was supposed to treat. Reports surfaced of individuals on Prozac increasing their suicidal or homicidal ideations, sometimes going so far as to act on those impulses. Many of these controversies continue despite the fact that there are only a few hundred reported cases of these kinds of behaviors in a population of almost five million people worldwide who have taken the drug. The latest controversy centers around the overprescribing of drugs like Prozac and its heirs; suggesting it is increasingly used in an Orwellian fashion to soothe the inherent anxieties of life.

Antimanic Drugs

Manic episodes often cycle with recurrent depressions, forming what is referred to as a bipolar disorder (previously called manic-depressive illness). Lithium, a psychotropic medication that functions as a mood-stabilizing agent, remains the first line of treatment for the manic phase of a bipolar disorder. Certain schizophrenic individuals may also respond favorably to lithium used in combination with an antipsychotic medication.

The exact mechanism of action for lithium is not clear. It is generally thought that manic episodes result from an excess of the neurotransmitter norepinephrine, just the opposite situation from depressive episodes (Nathan et al., 1995). Lithium is believed to act by stabilizing the membranes of neuronal cells in the central nervous system, resulting in a decrease in the amount of norepinephrine released from the cells. There is also a probable increase in the reuptake of norepinephrine by the cells, decreasing the overall concentration of the neurotransmitter. Lithium is metabolized and excreted by the kidneys.

Because it is a salt that occurs naturally in the body, unlike many of the other psychotropic medications, lithium has a therapeutic dose range that can be measured in the blood. Dosage of the medication, beginning with divided doses of 300 mg two to three times per day, is increased until the blood level reaches a range of 0.5 to 1.5 mEq per liter. Within seven to ten days on a therapeutic dose, the manic patient should be observed to become calmer and less agitated; have a general slowing of speech and thought processes; and return to a normal, or euthymic, mood.

The monitoring of lithium blood levels is necessary to prevent toxicity. Lithium toxicity is characterized by nausea and vomiting, muscle cramps, diarrhea, excessive thirst, and increased urination at blood levels between 1.5 and 2.0 mEq per liter. At levels above 2.0 mEq per liter, the individual experiences confusion, lethargy, tremor of the extremities, muscle spasms, ataxia (unsteady gait), slurred speech, convulsions, and ultimately coma. When maintained at therapeutic blood levels, however, lithium is notably free of day-to-day side effects. It is unlikely to cause sedation and has no potential for abuse or dependence. The most common side effects on therapeutic doses are fine tremor of the hand and skin rash. The long-term use of lithium virtually guarantees the eventual production of hyperthyroidism. Likewise, over time, there is a potentially reversible alteration of the basement membrane in the kidneys, which requires careful scrutiny.

When combined with certain other drugs, lithium can have problematic effects. Many diuretics (drugs that remove water from the body) increase the level of lithium and can cause toxicity. Other diuretics, like coffee and tea, can lower the level of lithium. Problems may occur when lithium is combined with hydroxyzine (Atarax, Vistaril), antipsychotic drugs, or methyldopa (Aldomet and others). Patients who are taking lithium should tell all the doctors they see about all other medication they are taking.

The evolution of lithium as an effective treatment is a good example of the driving force of the profit motive in pharmacological research. Lithium is a chemical element that was first isolated in 1817 by John Arfwedson, a young Swedish chemistry student. He named it lithium because he found it in stone (*lithos* in Greek). John Cade, an Australian psychiatrist, discovered the positive effect of lithium on mania by chance in the 1940s, while studying whether an excess of uric acid might be the cause of manic-depressive episodes. Cade injected humans with urea from the urine of guinea pigs. Expecting to learn that uric acid (a compound containing urea) increased the toxicity of urea, he added the most soluble salt of uric acid, lithium urate, and was surprised to find, instead, that the urea was less toxic as a result. Further experiments isolating lithium eventually indicated its curative properties.

However, it was a long time between initial discovery and the recent widespread marketing and use of lithium. In general, there had been surprisingly little research on lithium, while more exotic, less widely available compounds have received much attention. Two explanations for this seem plausible. First, there was warranted concern about the significant side effects of lithium. Second, since lithium is a naturally occurring element, it cannot be patented. Drug companies are much more interested in researching new synthetic compounds that they can patent, so that they can control the market and gain substantial profits.

Until the 1980s, mania was often misdiagnosed and, to some degree, is still misdiagnosed as schizophrenia since in its most virulent form it can be accompanied by delusions, hallucinations, and other psychotic behaviors. Commonly, in the acute manic state, lithium is given with a neuroleptic until the manic storm has passed. If the psychotic component of the mania begins to clear, the neuroleptic can be withdrawn, and the patient maintained only on lithium. Because many people with mania and hypomania miss the energized nature of the "high," compliance with the use of lithium tends to be low. Also, because it is a salt and is turned over fairly rapidly in the body, lithium has to be administered two to three times a day to maintain blood levels. There are some patients who are so precariously balanced with regard to their blood levels that missing one or two doses can be enough to initiate hypomanic behavior and thinking.

Until the 1970s there were no alternatives to the use of lithium and/or neuroleptics for the treatment of mania. In the 1970s, Robert Post first described the possible application of carbamazepine (Tegretol), an anticonvulsant previously used to treat temporal lobe epilepsy, for the treatment of mania. While carbamazepine does not produce the hypothyroidism common to lithium, it has significant side effects of its own; these include blood dyscrasias such as agranulocytosis and leukopenia, and it can also disturb iron metabolism. Therefore, like lithium, carbamazepine has a therapeutic dose level that needs to be carefully monitored.

Following the discovery of carbamazepine's value in the treatment of mania, other anticonvulsants used to treat temporal lobe epilepsy have been tried and found to be useful as well. These include valporic acid (Depakote) and clonazepam (Klonopin). Valporic acid has been effective with some cases of refractory mania, while clorazepam has been effective with bipolar patterns that have been resistant to other forms of treatment.

Clonazepam resembles a benzodiazepine in structure and, like the benzodiazepines, it is quite sedating with a potential for abuse. It has little or no antipsychotic properties and, also like benzodiazepines, mixes poorly with alcohol, suppressing CNS and respiratory functions. Since alcohol is commonly abused by bipolar patients in the manic phase of the illness, caution needs to be exercised in the use of this medication.

Unfortunately, as noted, lithium is not always effective with mania. About one-third of nonresponders show about a 50% lessening of symptomatology with divalproex sodium, and that 50% rate is comparable to the response to lithium. Some nonresponders to lithium have been found to respond to certain anticonvulsant drugs. Carbamazepine is the anticonvulsant that has been most widely used. Bipolars who cycle rapidly—that is, they change from mania to depression and back again over the course of hours or days, rather than months—seem to respond particularly well to carbamazepine. Valproic acid has been effective with some cases of refractory mania. Clonazepam has also been effective with treatment-resistant bipolar patterns.

■ Antianxiety Drugs

Anxiety is one of the most frequent complaints among persons requiring mental health consultation. The antianxiety medications exert a calming and sedating effect. Originally this class of drugs consisted primarily of the barbiturates, which had high potential for dependence and addiction as well as a variety of other side effects. Since the mid-1960s, however, a large number of drugs belonging to the benzodiazepine family have been introduced (Taylor, 1995). For the treatment of anxiety these drugs are more effective, safer, have less addiction potential, and generally produce less sedation than the barbiturates. Consequently, benzodiazepines have become some of the most frequently prescribed medications in the United States. In addition to their antianxiety effects, they are also useful as sedative-hypnotics. The introduction of chlordiazepoxide (Librium) and diazepam (Valium) heralded the benzodiazepine age. Both of these agents still have considerable clinical utility but they are often abused.

To understand the addictive nature or potential of these drugs, one must understand two important issues: the nature of anxiety and certain behavioral consequences of using the relatively short-acting benzodiazepines. Because anxious and fearful patients seek relief from very stressful feelings, any drug that brings about that relief has to be able to do so smoothly and continuously. Benzodiazepines, because of their varying half-lives, end up contributing to the problems they were prescribed to solve.

The term "half life" refers to the length of time it takes for one-half of a drug dose to be metabolized. Thus, half-life is a measure of how long a drug remains active in the body. The longer the half-life, the longer the overall duration of the drug's effect. The more recent benzodiazepines, such as alprazolam (Xanax), differ from those introduced earlier primarily in the length of their half-lives. Alprazolam has rapidly grown to be the most widely prescribed benzodiazepine and, consequently, the most widely abused.

As a result of having such short half–lives, these shorter-acting benzodiazepines can create what is referred to as "breakthrough anxiety states," or mini-withdrawal states, as their serum level in the body falls. For this reason, a behavioral paradigm can be created whereby individuals who are feeling anxious develop drug-seeking behaviors in an attempt to ameliorate these feelings. This drug-seeking behavior reinforces the further use of the drug and begins the process of abuse by putting the patient in a constant state of anticipatory anxiety and, therefore, anticipating the next dose of relief (the drug). Longer-acting benzodiazepines, or timed-release medications of this class, should theoretically have less abuse potential, but they may have no less potential for addiction since true physiological states of withdrawal are created when these drugs are used at therapeutic doses for extended periods of time. All of the benzodiazepines are metabolized by the liver. The currently used antianxiety agents are listed in Table 15.4.

The benzodiazepines exert their antianxiety activity by facilitating the action in the brain of gamma-aminobutyric acid (GABA), a neurotransmitter apparently responsible for modulating anxiety. The benzodiazepines bind to receptors in the brain and stimulate the release of GABA, which decreases anxiety. GABA, in turn, inhibits the firing of certain excitatory neurons that are responsible for many of the physiologic manifestations of anxiety.

In addition to their clinical action on anxiety and their sedative effects, the benzodiazepines also exert another effect: All members of this group are cross-tolerant with alcohol and other drugs such as the barbiturates. In other words, they may potentiate the effects of alcohol or other sedative drugs, making the concurrent use of antianxiety drugs and alcohol or other sedatives

TABLE 15.4   Antianxiety Drugs

NAME (GENERIC/TRADE)	DOSE RANGE[a]
BENZODIAZEPINES	
Diazepam (Valium)	2–40 mg/day
Chlordiazepoxide (Librium)	15–100 mg/day
Chlorazepate (Tranxene)	15–60 mg/day
Prazepam (Centrax)	20–60 mg/day
Halazepam (Paxipam)	60–120 mg/day
Lorazepam (Ativan)	2–6 mg/day
Alprazolam (Xanax)	0.5–6.0 mg/day
Oxazepam (Serax)	30–120 mg/day
Clonazepam (Klonipin)	0.5–6.0 mg/day
NONBENZODIAZEPINE	
Buspirone (Buspar)	5–20 mg/day

[a] Average therapeutic dose range.

contraindicated. The clinical benefit derived from this finding, however, is that the benzodiazepines can be used to detoxify and withdraw individuals who are addicted to either alcohol or the barbiturates. Chlordiazepoxide, for example, is often used to withdraw persons from alcohol and to treat alcohol withdrawal delirium (delirium tremens, or the "DTs"). Of course, one has to be careful with this population so that a secondary addiction to the benzodiazepines does not occur.

Because of the cross-tolerance with alcohol, a person who drinks while taking benzodiazepines will appear more intoxicated than a person using either drug alone. In fact, the sedating and tranquilizing effect of this class of drugs causes many persons taking them to appear drunk, even in the absence of alcohol consumption. Accompanying features sometimes seen with the benzodiazepines include slurred speech, ataxia, impaired coordination, slowed reflexes, and impaired judgment. As a result of these effects, persons taking benzodiazepines should exercise considerable caution when driving or operating machinery. These drugs have a relatively rapid onset of action, usually within thirty minutes. Their duration of action ranges from four to six hours for the short-acting preparations (e.g., lorazepam) to more than twenty hours for the longer-acting drugs (e.g., diazepam).

A new-generation antianxiety drug of the nonbenzodiazepine class, considered to be a partial serotonin agonist, was released in 1985. This drug, buspirone (BuSpar), has generated a good deal of controversy regarding its usefulness in the treatment of anxiety. Because of its extended onset of action, requiring up to two to three weeks to become effective, anxious patients previously disposed to the faster-acting benzodiazepines may be less tolerant of waiting for the drug to take effect. As a result, patients often discontinue use of this drug or fail to comply with its thrice-daily dosing requirement. Although its antianxiety effects are not as potent as the benzodiazepines, it has the advantage of having a very low potential for addiction or abuse.

The primary side effect of the benzodiazepines is excessive sedation, which is usually dose related. In other words, the higher the dose of the drug, the greater the degree of sedation produced. By themselves, however, the benzodiazepines are remarkably safe drugs. While overdoses of either the antipsychotics or the antidepressants are potentially life-threatening, this is not usually the case with the benzodiazepines. They may, however, interact with other drugs, such as the barbiturates, to depress respiration when taken at high doses. Tolerance, the need for progressively higher doses to achieve the same therapeutic effect, and addiction are potential risks. Because of this, these drugs are generally prescribed in the lowest effective doses for only brief periods of time. In general, tolerance and addiction are more likely at high doses taken over extended periods of time. Abrupt cessation of these drugs in an addicted person may cause seizures; thus, it is generally best to gradually reduce the doses over a period of several weeks before totally discontinuing these medications.

While the benzodiazepines and related compounds are used primarily in the treatment of anxiety disorders, other treatments such as biofeedback, relaxation training, and other forms of psychotherapy are also effective. Since such treatments are less intrusive and do not pose the problem of side effects, yet are still effective, they should be employed first.

A number of other drugs have been used to treat anxiety, although none is as effective as the ones previously described. Antihistamines, such as diphenhydramine (Benadryl) and hydroxyzine (Vistaril), have been used. Their antianxiety effect is largely a function of their sedating properties, and they are not thought to exert any direct effect on GABA. These drugs are also sometimes used to treat the extrapyramidal side effects associated with antipsychotic drug therapy. Propranolol (Inderal) acts to block receptors for beta-adrenergic neurotransmitters, a large group of transmitters that exert a number of effects throughout the body. Propranolol and the earlier mentioned SSSIs have been reported to be effective in the treatment of anxiety disorders like panic disorder.

Finally, clomipramine (Anafranil), a tricyclic antidepressant, has recently been emphasized as a treatment of obsessive-compulsive disorder. None of the other tricyclics has been found to be especially effective in the treatment of this condition, although an SSSI, sertraline, has also been found to be effective.

Sedative-Hypnotic Medications

Sleep disturbances are common complaints that in most cases are transient and thus do not warrant treatment. These difficulties may also be related to some other disease process, such as a medical condition or depression. Many individuals, however, have chronic problems with sleep. This has led to the development of a group of medications, the sedative-hypnotic drugs, whose primary action is the induction of sleep (Harsh and Ogilvie, 1995). Most of these agents act on serotonin and GABA in the brain, both of which exert a natural calming and sedating effect. Newer drugs, such as zolpidem tartrate (Ambien), target a specific receptor rather than a spectrum of receptors.

Most of the commonly used, commercially available sedative-hypnotic agents are actually antianxiety drugs whose sedating properties are stronger than their antianxiety properties. Thus, the antianxiety agents can theoretically be used to promote sleep. Those drugs marketed solely as sedative-hypnotics are ones whose antianxiety effects are relatively weak. As a result, most of the sedative-hypnotics currently available are either benzodiazepines or barbiturates. As with the other members of these groups, there is a definite potential for abuse and dependence. These drugs also tend to lose their effectiveness when taken for extended periods of time, a process referred to as tolerance, or habituation. The result is that higher doses are required over time to exert the same therapeutic effect, a consequence that facilitates addiction and dependence. Table 15.5 lists the sedative-hypnotic drugs currently in clinical use.

The side effects for these drugs are similar to those for the benzodiazepines and barbiturates. The most common side effect is excessive drowsiness on awakening. Persons taking these drugs will often complain of difficulty waking up and a "hangover" in the morning after drug use. In very high doses, respiratory depression may occur, particularly with the barbiturates. Tolerance and addiction, however, are the most serious long-term side effects of these drugs.

Chloral hydrate (Noctec) is a fairly "benign" hypnotic, with a wide margin of safety, that is unlikely to become addictive. An important point to make, however, with all hypnotics is their ability to alter the "architecture of sleep."

TABLE 15.5   Sedative-Hypnotic Drugs

NAME (GENERIC/TRADE)	DOSE RANGE[a]
BENZODIAZEPINES	
Flurazepam (Dalmane)	15–30 mg/day
Temazepam (Restoril)	15–30 mg/day
Triazolam (Halcion)	0.25–0.5 mg/day
Estazolam (ProSom)	1.0–2.0 mg/day
Quazepam (Doral)	7.5–15 mg/day
BARBITURATES	
Secobarbital (Seconal)	100–200 mg/day
OTHER SEDATIVE-HYPNOTICS	
Chloral hydrate (Noctec)	500–1000 mg/day
Zolpidem tartrate (Ambien)	10 mg/day

[a] Average therapeutic dose range.

Usually this takes the form of REM suppression (the dream state) that, upon discontinuation of the hypnotic, results in what is called "REM rebound." REM rebound is characterized by increased dream activity, often vivid, that frequently results in fitful sleep—the very reason the hypnotic was prescribed to begin with. While not addictive in the pure sense of the word, this drug, like most hypnotics—over-the-counter or prescribed—is habituative.

Zolpidem tartrate, while not a benzodiazepine in structure, shares some of the pharmacological characteristics of the benzodiazepine class of compounds. Zolpidem tartrate binds differentially to the GABA receptor complex; however, it appears to have minimal potentiating action with alcohol and does not produce amnesia at therapeutic doses, unlike the benzodiazepines. This class of hypnotics is new, and although the claim is made that there is little, if any, drug tolerance, the reader is cautioned that the very same claims were made about the methaqualones (e.g., Quaalude, Sopar) when they were first released. Several pharmaceutical companies have compounds similar to zolpidem under development.

Lately, trazodone (Desyrel) has been used, with fair success, as a sedative-hypnotic, with no suggestion of addiction or habituation. The drug is administered about an hour before bedtime at subclinical doses (about 25 mg) with efficacy often seen within three to four days. Trazodone may be especially beneficial in the patient who is depressed and presents with complaints of disturbed sleep and/or early morning awakening. It may be used alone or with another drug, typically an SSRI—which is nonsedating—in this type of patient.

There are several other drugs that have (1) a secondary sedative effect, (2) low addiction and abuse potential, and (3) a low ratio of side effects. One good example is the antihistamines, such as the over-the-counter medication diphenhydramine (Benadryl). Another is the group of drugs sometimes referred to as the ataraxics, such as hydroxyzine pamoate (Vistaril) and hydroxyzine hydrochloride (Atarax), which are primarily intended to reduce anxiety, especially where accompanied by physical conditions, for example, dermatological and/or gastrointestinal distress.

Generally, a good policy is to first try to cure a sleep problem with something like diphenhydramine. A trial of melatonin, a nonprescription natural hormone, is also worthwhile. Then, if these are unsuccessful, move to an ataraxic, especially if agitation from the stress of living is a factor. Then, if these are unsuccessful and manipulation or an addictive personality component is ruled out, one can move to the traditional sedative-hypnotics.

■ Anti-Parkinsonian Medications

Earlier it was mentioned that the antipsychotic medications cause a variety of extrapyramidal side effects characterized by muscular stiffness and rigidity, feelings of restlessness (akathisia), involuntary movements (dystonias), and a general slowing of movements (Parkinsonian effects). These occur most frequently in young, adult males and in persons recently started on antipsychotic medications. These effects are naturally quite bothersome to clients and are frequently responsible for poor medication compliance. Since the apparent mechanism of action is the blocking of dopamine, the same action that leads to a diminishing of psychotic symptoms also leads to neuromuscular disturbances.

Fortunately, several medications exist that have the ability to lessen the degree of these extrapyramidal symptoms. Collectively these drugs are often referred to as anti-Parkinsonian agents. The two most commonly used drugs in this group are trihexyphenidl (Artane) and benztropine (Cogentin). Both are administered orally in doses of 2 mg, up to three times a day. They may also be used either intravenously or intramuscularly. Both trihexyphenidl benztropin have strong anticholinergic effects, so their doses should be kept to a minimum. Although neither benztropin or trihexyphenidl causes classic addiction, they are frequently abused because persons taking these medications often experience a temporary "high" immediately after ingesting the drug.

■ Dementia Therapeutics

"Dementias" is a general term used to describe a group of symptoms reflecting the loss of intellectual capacities (such as thinking, remembering, and reasoning) of sufficient severity to interfere with an individual's daily functioning. Until recently, dementia was thought to be a normal part of the aging process; however, we now know it is not that simple. It has many causes: some untreatable, some treatable but not reversible, and some completely reversible. The most common cause of severe memory loss in the older population is Alzheimer's disease, accounting for approximately 50% of all cases of dementia. Strokes (multi-infarct dementia) are the second most frequent cause, accounting for another 10% of cases. Dementia associated with alcoholism and dementia related to depression rank together as the third most common causes.

This section offers an overview of some of the pharmacotherapeutics available. As with any area of clinical treatment, it is essential that a detailed and thorough workup be done to differentially diagnose the type or cause of the dementia presented. For example, the demtntia that results from major depression is both treatable and reversible. On the other hand, the depression that is often secondary to Alzheimer's disease is less amenable to treatment and does not usually play a significant role in the patient's loss of cognitive abilities.

Behavioral management is often a major problem in older patients with significant memory loss. The symptom picture may include agitation, visual and aural delusions, temper outbursts, hypersexuality, insomnia, and anxiety. For a number of reasons, drug therapy should be initiated at lower doses, and a "go slow" approach should be utilized. First, and foremost, is the fact that metabolism is generally much slower in this age group and, therefore, drugs may build to toxic levels if administered at higher dose levels or too rapidly. Also important is the ever changing symptom picture of the progressive dementias—by their very nature, what is present today may be absent tomorrow—as these patients "outgrow" their symptoms only to develop new ones at some later date.

It is important for the clinician to remember that, until very recently, the use of medications to treat dementia-related behavioral symptoms was done without the benefit of controlled trials demonstrating the efficacy of such treatments. At the time of writing, the authors could find no published data that consistently demonstrated the efficacy of one drug over another in controlling behavioral disturbances associated with dementia of the Alzheimer's type. Often it is necessary to try several drugs, in succession, allowing sufficient time for the onset of drug activity before trying another. There is no simple solution. It should also be remembered that often it is the patient who is medicated to treat the caregiver's stress!

Mild sedatives may be helpful for the agitated patient or the patient who wanders at night. Benzodiazepines have fewer side effects than the major tranquilizers or antipsychotics, especially in this age group, and are often tried first. Recent research has shown some positive correlation between the use of antipsychotics such as haloperidol and the increased frequency of accidents (resulting in broken arms, hips, etc.) in older patients.

A second area of medication to consider with the demented patient is treatment for the memory loss component. Patients whose progressive memory loss is due to cerebral vascular insufficiency may benefit from the ergoloid mesylate Hydergine. This is a relatively safe drug, free of the vasoconstricting properties that mark the ergot alkaloids often prescribed for migraine headaches. Hydergine's efficacy has never been established for improving cognition, despite its indication to treat this problem. Many physicians feel it is like chicken soup—"it doesn't hurt."

Dozens of compounds are in various stages of clinical development for the treatment of Alzheimer's disease. At best, treatments are palliative, in that it is the symptom (memory loss) that is being treated and not the underlying disease process. The course of the disease remains unchanged. Currently the only approved drug is tacrine (Cognex), a cholinesterase inhibitor, which has demonstrated mild to moderate memory improvement in some Alzheimer's patients. The drug has a side-effect profile that requires careful blood monitoring during the dose titration period. Drugs of this class work by inhibiting the breakdown of the neurotransmitter acetylcholine. Several other cholinesterase inhibitors, some without the side-effect profile of tacrine, are presently being tested.

Two other areas of drug development for the Alzheimer's patient are those aimed at slowing the progression of the disease and those aimed at stimulating nerve cell growth. Drugs that fall into either of these categories have yet to clearly demonstrate any efficacy other than in the laboratory and are still in the early stages of clinical trials.

Central Nervous System Stimulants

Certain central nervous system stimulants are effective in dealing with disorders such as hyperactivity and also in some forms of apathy-depression. For example, methylphenidate (Ritalin), one of the piperidyls, is commonly used to control hyperactive patterns, especially in children and adolescents. Other drugs that may be used to control these symptoms are diphenhydramine or diazepam, both of which are used intravenously in acute situations.

■ Medications for Control of Violent and Aggressive Behavior

Mental health professionals often deal with violent behavior when it occurs in association with mental illness. A variety of psychotropic medications have been found to be effective in controlling or diminishing this type of behavior (Young and Hillbrand, 1994; Huesmann, 1994). Such management is often complicated by the person's use of alcohol or drugs—both good intentions and inhibitions are soluble in alcohol.

Violence and aggression are generally caused by complex interaction of biological, psychological, and environmental factors (Volavka, 1995). The management of violent behavior with medication relies on an appreciation of the biological factors that underlie violence. As with other symptoms, the biological explanation of violence rests with the neurotransmitters. In general, violence is correlated with an interaction of three factors in the brain: (1) an overabundance of certain neurotransmitters (e.g., dopamine and norepinephrine), (2) a relative deficiency of other neurotransmitters (e.g., serotonin and GABA), and (3) excess electrical activity in the brain leading to seizures (Eichelman, 1988). Drugs that control violent behavior act by correcting the neurotransmitter imbalance or by decreasing the electrical activity in the brain.

It should be noted that violence occurring in mental health patients is not as common as often assumed (Teplin et al., 1994), although the rate is higher than in the normal population). Many clients with violent histories will also be found to have histories of drug or alcohol abuse. These substances promote violence by interfering with perception and judgment or by causing disinhibition of underlying aggressive tendencies. Clients who are intoxicated have much less control over aggressive impulses than do nonintoxicated persons. When violence is associated with a mental health condition, it is generally related to a psychotic episode, personality disorder, or an organic mental disorder (Teplin et al., 1994).

Table 15.6 lists the medications useful in controlling violent or aggressive behaviors. These drugs are members of several of the groups already described. When violent behavior is associated with a psychotic disorder, such as schizophrenia, the antipsychotic medications are clearly indicated. Violent tendencies in nonpsychotic persons may also be controlled by these medications because of their dopamine-blocking action. Antidepressants that increase the action of serotonin, such as trazodone (Desyrel), may also be useful. One of the actions of serotonin in the brain is a calming influence on behavior. Those drugs that increase levels of norepinephrine, however, may actually facilitate violent or aggressive behaviors. Lithium, through its action to decrease norepinephrine activity, may be useful in controlling aggression in some clients. Norepinephrine-blocking agents such as propranolol have also been shown to be effective.

TABLE 15.6   Medications Used to Control Violent Behavior

NAME (GENERIC/TRADE)	DOSE RANGE[a]
BENZODIAZEPINES	
Lorazepam (Ativan)	1–2 mg PO or IM Q2–4hr PRN
Oxazepam (Serax)	15–120 mg/day
MOOD-ALTERING DRUGS	
Lithium carbonate	300 mg in divided doses to attain a therapeutic blood level
Trazodone (Desyrel)	100–400 mg/day
ADRENERGIC BLOCKING AGENTS	
Propranolol (Inderal)	200–600 mg/day
ANTICONVULSANTS	
Carbamazepine (Tegretol)	200 mg in divided doses to attain a therapeutic blood level
ANTIPSYCHOTICS	
Haloperidol (Haldol)	2–5 mg PO or IM Q2–4hr PRN
Chlorpromazine (Thorazine)	50–100 mg PO or IM Q2–4hr PRN

[a] Average therapeutic dose range.
PO = oral administration.
IM = intramuscular administration.

The benzodiazepines, by increasing brain levels of GABA, which exerts a calming effect similar to that of serotonin, may also decrease violence. These drugs must be used cautiously, not only because of their potential for abuse but also because they cause a paradoxical increase in violence in some individuals.

Finally, carbamazepine, an anticonvulsant medication, is useful here (Young and Hillbrand, 1994), especially when violence occurs in association with seizure activity. Carbamazepine is an interesting drug because it seems to exert other effects independent of its anticonvulsant activity. Some psychotic or manic patients who fail to respond to other treatments have been found to improve on carbamazepine. This drug also appears to cause a decrease in impulsivity, which is often associated with violent and aggressive behavior.

■ Drugs Used for Assessment

Certain psychotropic drugs are used to induce a light sleep or trancelike state during which the person remains conscious and able to talk. This state closely resembles the altered level of consciousness achieved during hypnosis. During this period it is possible to interview the patient and obtain important diagnostic information. Previously repressed, or forgotten, memories may also be recalled. The drugs that promote such a state have often been referred to as "truth serum."

However, it is a common misconception that these drugs make people reveal information that they would otherwise withhold. This does not occur with legitimate medications. It is also not possible to be sure that the information obtained from such an interview is entirely factual.

Currently, two drugs are most commonly used for this type of interview, often referred to as narcotherapy or narcoanalysis. One of these is the short-acting barbiturate sodium amobarbital (Amytal). The other is a short-acting benzodiazepine, lorazepam (Ativan). The primary use of these agents is for diagnostic purposes, although lorazepam is also a frequently prescribed anti-anxiety agent when taken orally. Interviews using these drugs are useful for clarifying the diagnosis of catatonic schizophrenia, in which patients are often mute, and with certain disorders characterized by dissociative symptoms (see Chapter 7).

For this type of interview, both sodium amytal and lorazepam are administered intravenously. Small doses are injected at one- to two-minute intervals until the patient becomes drowsy but not completely asleep. Blood pressure and respirations must be monitored throughout the interview. Injection of the medication too rapidly will produce sleep, and using doses that are too high may cause respiratory depression or arrest. Therefore, this type of interview should only be performed by a qualified physician who is familiar with the procedure. As the person becomes drowsy, a series of generalized questions are asked, proceeding then to more specific questions. If the person appears to resist questioning, additional medication is gradually infused until the person becomes more open. Because the duration of action of these drugs is brief, additional medication must be infused periodically throughout the interview. At the close of the interview, medication is discontinued and the client is allowed to rest until fully alert and able to walk without difficulty. The client will be aware of information disclosed following the interview. How long this awareness remains depends on the underlying condition the client suffers from. Many neurotic individuals will remain aware of the contents of the interview, while catatonic patients are likely to lapse back into a psychotic state. As with all such procedures, this type of interview should only be conducted with the informed consent of the patient.

■ Other Drugs Used in Psychiatry

Many drugs from a variety of classes have been found to be effective for certain conditions where traditional drug therapy has been ineffective. One example of this is the calcium channel blocker verapamil (Calan, Isoptin). The calcium ion is an important intracellular messenger that exerts an effect on many neurons. An overactivity of this ion may result in signals being sent to neurons that are excessive brain activity. By blocking calcium in the brain, the neurons are restored to normal rates of firing. Verapamil has been found to be effective in the treatment of some types of bipolar disorder, tardive dyskinesia, and certain other movement disorders that are accompanied by psychiatric symptoms (e.g., Tourette's disorder).

Clonidine (Catapres) is an alpha-adrenergic receptor agonist (i.e., it facilitates the action of the alpha-adrenergic transmitters). This drug has been widely used to treat hypertension. The drug has also been found to be effective in treating Tourette's disorder and in helping patients to withdraw from opioids.

Legal Issues in the Use of Psychotropic Medications

Because the psychotropic medications exert powerful effects on behavior, mood, and thought, it is not surprising that a number of legal issues are associated with their use (see also Appendix D and Chapter 18). Specific issues include informed consent, malpractice, right to refuse treatment, the right to treatment, and the role of medications in criminal proceedings (Slovenko, 1995; Meyer, 1995).

One important legal concept involved in the use of psychotropic medications is informed consent. The basic principle underlying informed consent is that the patient has a right to determine what should be done to his or her body and cannot be forced to accept treatment that is not wanted. Informed consent requires that the client be apprised of the potential benefits and major risks of any proposed treatments, as well as all alternative treatments available. In order to give consent for treatment, the client must be competent, possess adequate information, and make the decision for treatment voluntarily. With respect to psychotropic medications, for example, the client must be informed about all potential major side effects and their relative risks, drug interactions, and any special precautions that should be taken. Common examples of risks that need to be explained thoroughly are tardive dyskinesia and the neuroleptic malignant syndrome associated with the antipsychotic drugs. It is often useful to start with low dosages of a medication to see if there is any negative response. If not, the dosage may be gradually "bumped up" until a therapeutic dose is reached.

Another related issue is malpractice, the negligent performance of a procedure. In order for malpractice to be proven, the following elements must be established: (1) The clinician owed a legal duty to the client; (2) the clinician breached that duty in the care rendered to the client; (3) the client suffered injury or damages, either physical or emotional; and (4) the damages resulted from the clinician's negligence (Wettstein, 1989). If a client suffers harm because of inadequate monitoring of medication, for example, the clinician may be held legally accountable. If a third party suffers harm as a result of a client's actions while under the influence of a psychotropic medication, the clinician may also be held accountable. Drug-induced reactions are responsible for about

20% of malpractice claims against psychiatrists (Wettstein, 1989). The major issues related to psychotropic medications include lack of informed consent, excessive dosage, lack of proper indications for medication, and tardive dyskinesia. A number of legal decisions have found psychiatrists and drug companies liable in cases of neuroleptic malignant syndrome. Suicide by overdosage of medication may also be grounds for a malpractice or wrongful death suit based on the argument that the clinician should have known of the potential for self-harm and taken proper steps to safeguard the client.

Related to the concept of informed consent is the right to refuse treatment. This concept basically says that a competent adult has the right to refuse treatment if the perceived risks or consequences are viewed as intolerable. However, both concepts have substantial limits in their actual application (Meyer, 1995). Even though the decision may be ill advised or have negative consequences for the person, the competent client retains the right of refusal. The question of competence, particularly in the psychotic client, becomes very important in this respect. It is interesting to note that almost all of the cases involving right to refuse treatment deal with the antipsychotic medications. Just as clients have a right to refuse treatment in most situations, they also (in varying degrees, depending on the situation) have a basic right *to* treatment.

CHAPTER 16

Malingering and the Factitious Disorders

■ Malingering (V65.2)

The issues of malingering (in truth, an act, not primarily a mental disorder) and distorted response sets are often a part of any clinical evaluation, but they are especially important in considering the categories of factitious disorder, antisocial personality disorder, substance dependence, schizophrenia, and the dissociative disorders. It is often appropriate to broaden the concept of malingering to any type of response that distorts the production of an accurate record; this is the context of the following discussion.

The focus of the DSM-IV criteria for malingering is the voluntary presentation of false or grossly exaggerated physical or psychological symptoms. DSM-IV notes that malingering should be suspected when there is (1) a medico-legal context, (2) discrepancy between objective findings and reported symptoms, (3) compliance problems, or (4) presence of an antisocial personality disorder. This is good advice, except that #4 should be considerably broadened; indeed, malingering can occur with virtually every DSM-IV diagnosis, or when no diagnosis is warranted. Malingering is often more understandable by the evident incentives and circumstances of the situation, rather than from the person's individual psychology.

Malingering is likely to occur in job screening, military and criminal-justice situations, or wherever a psychological or physical disability has a payoff (Pope et al., 1993; Rogers, 1988). It occurs more commonly in early to middle adulthood, is more common in males than in females, and often follows an actual injury or illness. Problematic employment history, lower socio-economic status, or an associated antisocial personality disorder are also common predictors of this disorder. The reader is advised to consult the section of Chapter 6 on the psychogenic pain disorder regarding the issue of chronic (actual) pain versus malingering.

□ OVERALL INDICATORS

Several overall patterns have been found to be characteristic of interview and test data from malingerers (Rogers, 1986, 1988; Ekman, 1985; Woychyshyn et al., 1992; Pope et al., 1993; Ganellan et al., 1993; Butcher, 1995). These characteristic patterns depend to some degree on the specific distorted response pattern that is being observed, that is, whether it is the result of malingering, defensiveness, disinterest, or some other source.

First, it is important to use your experience with the various patterns of mental disorder to evaluate the validity of symptoms presented by suspected malingerers. Also, any symptom reports should be rigorously questioned, at least at first, using open-ended questions such as, "What are those voices telling you?" rather than "Do those voices tell you to do anything?"

Overall, malingerers more often report relatively rare symptoms, as well as a higher total number of symptoms, than do honest respondents. Also, look for malingerers to present either very obvious and prosaic symptoms, improbable or absurd symptoms or symptom combinations, or symptoms of unprobable severity (e.g., being extremely high on 6, 8 and F). Malingerers are also more likely to be willing to discuss their disorder, especially how the negative effects of their disorder impact on rather narrow areas of functioning. They are more likely to report a sudden onset of the disorder; to report a more sudden cessation of symptoms if that has some functional value; to present more exaggerated behavior, more suicidal ideation, more visual hallucinations, and more symptoms that do not cluster; and to endorse the more evident, flamboyant, and disabling symptoms. They are more likely to give vague or approximate responses when confronted, to make inconsistent symptom reports, to take a longer time to complete a test or an interview response, to repeat questions, to use qualifiers and vague responses, to miss easy items and then score accurately on hard I.Q. items, and to endorse the obvious rather than the subtle symptoms usually associated with a disorder (hence, Obvious-Subtle item discriminations on the MMPI-2 can be helpful here). Malingerers tend to report the following less often than do true psychotics: disturbed affect, incoherent speech, poor personal hygiene patterns, concrete thinking or formal thought disorder, incoherent speech, or grandiose delusions or ideas of reference.

Delusions or hallucinations are commonly reported by individuals trying to feign psychological disorder. In general, the clues that lead one to believe that the reporting of a delusion or hallucination may be malingered are (Resnick, 1991):

☐ An abrupt onset or cessation

☐ If the person is eager to call attention to the delusion or hallucination or leads the discussion to this topic

☐ If the person's conduct is not consistent with the delusion (unless the person is a burned-out schizophrenic)

☐ If there is reported bizarre content without disordered thoughts or hallucinations

☐ If the delusion or hallucination somehow specifically reduces the relevant responsibility or culpability

Auditory hallucinations are the most common in schizophrenia, but the examiner should be suspicious of a report of auditory hallucinations if

☐ They are vague or if the person reports it is hard to hear them or to understand them

☐ They are reported as continuous rather than sporadic or intermittent

☐ The hallucination is reported as not being associated with a delusion

☐ Stilted language is reported as the content of the hallucination

☐ The content specifically exonerates the client from some blame or responsibility

☐ The person reporting the voices can give no strategy to diminish the voices

☐ The person says that he or she obeyed all command hallucinations

☐   ## MMPI-2

On the MMPI-2, interest is naturally centered on the validity scales as predictors of distorted response sets (Woychyshyn, 1992). Nevertheless, it appears that a number of other measures may be useful here—in numerous instances, *more* valuable than a direct reading of the validity scales.

One face-valid method is to compare differences on those items originally designated by Wiener and Harmon (1946) as Obvious and Subtle (see Chapter 12), although some experts (Graham, 1993) do not see much value in these items. Hovanitz and Jordan-Brown (1986) found that when diagnostic or drug-outcome criteria were used, the exclusion of the Subtle MMPI-2 items resulted in a statistically significant loss of predictive ability. The Obvious items, however, were found to be related to many diagnostic constructs within the scales. Woychyshyn (1992) finds the Subtle-Obvious scales to be more effective in detecting faking-good than faking-bad.

The standard validity scales do, however, provide much valuable information in this regard, and there is support for the use of the three validity scales excerpted from the test as a whole (Cassini and Workman, 1992). (The reader is referred to the discussion in Chapter 12 of the correlates of these scales.) The traditional rule of thumb has been that if the F-K ratio (the Gough Dissimulation Index) is +9, such people are trying to fake-bad, that is, to present a distorted picture of themselves that emphasizes pathology. If the score is 0 or less, the emphasis is on trying to look good and deny pathology. However, it is generally agreed that these axioms only hold if F and K are relatively low, and, even then, there are a high number of false positives and false negatives. For example, psychotic and other severely distressed individuals—those with a high level of anxiety—are likely to score in a T range of 65–80 on the F scale and so at first may appear to be malingering. It is also noteworthy that when there is evidence of a defensive profile—for example, a high K—elevations in the T range above 65 are usually of high clinical significance (Butcher and Graham, 1988).

The more recent and comprehensive data on faking-bad and -good on the MMPI-2 (Graham et al., 1991b) suggest the following guidelines. Remember, this is to gain maximum discrimination power in a statistical analysis; lower scores than those suggested may still suggest malingering, especially when combined with other MMPI-2 data or data from other sources.

To discriminate those consciously faking-bad within an essentially normal population (using raw scores):

1. Use a cutoff score of 18 on F, with those faking-bad being higher.
2. Use an F-K score of 17 for men and 12 for women, with higher scores indicating faking-bad.
3. Use a raw score Fb (Back Side F) of 19 for men and 22 for women—again, higher scores indicating faking-bad.

To discriminate those consciously faking-bad within a psychiatric population (again, using raw scores and assessing higher scores on all of these as suggesting faking-bad):

1. Use a cutoff of 27 for men and 29 for women.
2. Use an F-K of 27 for men and 25 for women.
3. Use an Fb of 23 for men and 24 for women.

Using these scales to assess faking-good has always been a somewhat difficult discrimination, and Graham et al.'s (1991b) data echo that admonition. Also, those solid findings that were obtained are confounded by the issue of whether one is trying to identify faked profiles or honest ones. Scale L proved to be the most effective scale for males: with an L score of 8 correctly classifying 93% of honest profiles, but only 67 percent of the fake-goods. To correctly classify 96% of the males faking-good, a cutoff of 4 on L was necessary. Scores of 8 and 5 produced similar respective discriminations in females. An L-K index of 23 was quite effective, in both directions, for females but did not work as effectively as L alone for males. The reader is referred to the extensive data and tables in Graham et al. (1991b) for information that will be useful in discriminations using a combination of variables in an individual case.

Borum and Stock (1993) suggest the use of a new index, Es-K, using T scores. Using this index was effective in discriminating law enforcement applicants identified as being deceptive from a comparison group for whom no deception was indicated, and this index was superior to all the standard indices. The deceptive group showed a mean Es-K index of −7.00 (SD = 4.31); the comparison group had a +2.22 (SD = 5.59), with a low false-positive rate.

Profiles with F scores that are in the T range above 90 are commonly associated with extremely disturbed individuals who manifest hallucinations, delusions, and general confusion. But such a T score finding in an outpatient or forensic client should suggest a possibility of malingering (Ganellan et al., 1993).

This is particularly so when dealing with an inpatient population. Also, individuals who have a T score of greater than 95 on the F scale have probably either responded randomly to the MMPI-2 or have answered virtually all the items "true." If all or the great majority of items are answered "false," the T scores are typically in the 75–99 range. Graham et al. (1991b) note that, in addition to the high F, the highest scales, in order, are typically 8, 6, with lesser but substantial elevations (i.e., a T score of 80–90) on 7, 1, 4, and 9 (slightly less on 9 for females, but in this range on 2), with elevations above 70 on 3, 2, and 0. A fake-good profile tends to have all scores well within the normal range, most near 50, with mild elevations on 5 and 9 in females and on 9 and 0 for men and occasionally on 2 in traditional females.

Malingering or other response distortion (or low comprehension or reading ability) may be reflected in an irrelevant (if not irreverent) and/or random response pattern. Since the Cannot Say scale is highly related to clinical profile stability and to item-change measures, there is good reason to limit the number of allowable missed responses.

The overall profile for a totally random response set is an L scale of approximately 60 T, an F scale of approximately 110, and K around 55, with an elevation on scale 8 being close to 95 T for females and approximately 110 for males. It is noteworthy that randomly generated MMPI-2's look very much like malingered fake-bad MMPI-2 protocols in many respects. Scale 6 is usually the lowest score. If there are all "true" responses, the F scale is practically off the top, the L scale is about 35, and the K scale is at 30 T. The profile peaks are on scale 8: 125 for males and around 105 for females, with a secondary peak on scale 6 of 90 T for both. It is worthwhile for the clinician to at least scan the response sheet quickly before turning it over for scoring. In cases where careless or random responding has occurred, it is often immediately evident, and the problem can be dealt with at that time.

By altering true and false responses, one obtains a T score of about 55 on L, 105 on F, and 65 on K, with a particularly strong peak on scale 8 (up to 120 T). Scores throughout the rest of the profile are high (Graham, 1977).

In general, when F and K are both high, look for deliberate faking. But if L is high and F and K are well within acceptable limits, first consider faking-good, but also consider that the individual is either naive or unsophisticated (or both) and at the same time is trying to look good. If K is high and L and F are within the normal range, a more sophisticated defensive system is probable and the profile can be considered as an indication of subclinical trends.

Another relatively common pattern that results from a form of malingering is the 1-3/3-1 pattern, with a high K scale and very low scores on 2, 7, and 8. Such an individual is quite defensive and unwilling to admit any faults, therefore will not tolerate the patient role and has a poor prognosis.

TRIN and VRIN

Two response inconsistency scales were developed for MMPI-2, TRIN (True Response Inconsistency) and VRIN (Variable Response Inconsistency), and there is good evidence that they are by far the best measures of random or inconsistent responding (Sabine and Meyer, 1992; Wetter et al., 1992).

TRIN is based on twenty item pairs for which a combination of two true or two false responses is semantically inconsistent, for example, the pair "I am happy most of the time" and "Most of the time I feel blue." In three pairs the response of either true or false to both indicates inconsistency; in eleven pairs, inconsistency is indicated only by a true response; and in six pairs, only by a false response. By subtracting the number of inconsistent false pairs from inconsistent true pairs and then subtracting from 9 (total number of inconsistent false pairs), an index score of 0 to 20 is obtained. A high score (Graham suggests 13 or higher) indicates indiscriminate "true" responding; a low score (less than 6) points to indiscriminate "false" responding.

VRIN is composed of forty-nine item pairs that produce one or two, out of four, possible configurations (true-true, true-false, false-true, false-false), again, where responses would be semantically inconsistent. Scores occur in a range of 0 to 49, with high scores pointing to random responding and/or confusion. The MMPI-2 research group at the University of Kentucky has accumulated evidence showing that while both random and malingered responding produced significant elevations on F and Fb, only random responding generated significant elevations on VRIN (Wetter et al., 1992).

MMPI-A

The development of the MMPI-A, with its four new validity scales (F1, F2, VRIN, and TRIN) and adolescent-based norms, has allowed greater precision in the assessment of malingering in adolescents. These four validity scales are included at the beginning of the MMPI-A basic scale profile and should be interpreted in conjunction with L and K. The validity scales were additionally reordered for the MMPI-A from L, F, K to F, L, K.

On "The Lie" (L) scale, Archer (1992) suggests the following interpretive suggestions: "45 and below—low—may reflect an open, confident stance among normal adolescents, "all-true" or "fake-bad" response sets are possible; 66 and above—marked—may reflect extreme use of denial, poor insight, and lack of sophistication, an "all–false" or "fake-good" response set may have occurred" (p. 113).

Although the K-correction procedure has become standard practice with adults, it is not utilized with adolescent profiles. Elevated T scores (those greater than 65) should alert the clinician to the possibility of a defensive test-taking attitude, and the TRIN scale should be used to determine if indiscriminate "nay saying," or false responding, accounts for such elevations.

According to Butcher and Williams (1992), TRIN scores of 75 and above are significant and indicative of profile invalidity because of indiscriminate "yea saying" (indicated by a T following the T score) or nay saying (indicated by an F following the T score). Additionally, elevations of L and K combined with an elevation on TRIN indicate an inconsistent nay saying response set and do not indicate defensiveness. The VRIN scale becomes elevated only when an adolescent responds to the test with carelessness and, thus, it can be used to clarify the meaning of an adolescent's elevated F score.

The MMPI-A F scale was created by the selection of items endorsed in a deviant direction by no more than 20% of the 805 boys and 815 girls in the MMPI-A normative sample. Archer offers the following interpretive guidelines for the F scale (1992): "45 and below—low—scores in this range may reflect very conventional life experiences among normal adolescents, and possible "fake good" attempts among disturbed adolescents; 90 and above—extreme—protocols with F scores in this range are likely to be invalid, if "fake-bad" and other response set issues are ruled out, may reflect severely disorganized or psychotic adolescents" (p. 109). Butcher and Williams (1992) further suggest the following as possible interpretations for elevated F scores: random responding, reading problems, faking-bad, exaggeration of symptoms, or serious psychopathology.

The F1 and F2 subscales for the MMPI-A are utilized similarly to the F and FB scales in the MMPI-2. The F1 focuses on the validity of the adolescent's responses to the basic MMPI-A scales; the F2 on the content and supplementary scales.

The following overall guidelines are for screening for faking-good on the MMPI-A: (1) Elevations are found on validity scales L and K, and (2) all clinical scales' T score values are 60 or less, but produced by adolescents with strongly suspected or established psychopathology. Screening criteria for faking–bad on the MMPI-A are: (1) the F scale is elevated to a T score of 90 or greater, and (2) a floating profile is evident, characterized by clinical scale elevations within the clinical ranges, with the exceptions of Mf and Si scale values.

16 PF

The older versions of the 16 PF are being rapidly supplanted by the fifth edition, first available in 1994. It contains an effective Impression Management scale, as well as an Acquiescence Scale (Conn and Rieke, 1994). For those who use the older versions, which are obviously still valid and are likely to remain in use for some time, the following data on faking-good and -bad scales are useful. The best data is on Form A of the 16 PF, as originally derived by Winder et al. (1975). The faking-good scale, often referred to as a "motivational-distortion" scale, is calculated by taking the sum of the responses that the individual gives to the following specific responses: 7-c, 24-c, 61-c, 62-a, 81-a, 97-a, 111-a, 114-c, 123-c, 130-a, 133-c, 149-c, 173-a, 174-c, and 184-a.

The faking-bad scale is calculated in the same way, by totaling how many of the specific marker questions an individual scores on the raw data sheet. The responses that are used to calculate this score are 14-a, 38-a, 42-c, 51-b, 52-c, 55-c, 68-c, 80-a, 89-c, 117-a, 119-a, 123-a, 143-a, 176-c, and 182-c.

Winder et al. (1975) assert that a cutoff score of 6 is useful for determining both faking-good and -bad. However, Krug (1978) obtained data on a much broader and more representative sample, and he finds one major difference in the cutoff scores. Krug's sample included 2579 men and 2215 women. On the faking-good scale, scores ranged from 0 to 15, with an M of 6.36 and an SD of 2.87 for men, while women's scores ranged from 0 to 14, with an M of 5.71 and an SD of 2.72.

Krug's data suggest that the cutoff score of 6 for the faking-good scales is much too liberal, since in using this cutoff score, almost 55% of people routinely screened would be labeled as faking-good, instead of the approximately 7% that Winder et al. (1975) report. Krug's data suggest that a raw score of 10 on the faking-good scale would be a much more appropriate cutoff point. Only about 15% of people taking the test would attain a score this high.

On the faking-bad scale, men ranged from 0 to 12, with an M of 2.45 and an SD of 2.27, while women scored from 0 to 11, with an M of 2.24 and an SD of 2.04. Winder et al.'s (1975) cutoff score of 6 for the faking-bad scale is supported by Krug. Both report that fewer than 10% of those taking the test will score above 6 on this scale.

It should be noted that, in general, college students show lower average scores than the adult population on both of the faking scores, and high school students score even lower than the college students; hence an age factor may be operating.

Those who are attempting to fake-good and deny anxiety score very low on O and Q_4, and in general, those who are faking-good score in the following directions: C+, H+, L–, O–, Q_3+, Q_4–, and G+. Those who are faking-bad tend to present a mirror image of these data.

Krug offers the following rules to be used for making the profile more accurately interpretable when scores range from 6 upward:*

FOR FAKING-GOOD

1. If the score is 7, subtract 1 sten score point from C and add 1 point to Q_4.
2. If the score is 8, subtract 1 point from A, C, G, and Q_3 and add one point to L, O, and Q_4.
3. If the score is 9, subtract 1 point from A, C, G, and Q_3 and add 1 point to F, L, O, and Q_4.
4. If the score is 10, add 1 point to F, L, and O, add 2 points to Q_4, subtract 1 point from A, G, H, and Q_3, and subtract 2 points from C.

FOR FAKING-BAD

1. If the score is 7, add 1 point to C.
2. If the score is 8, subtract 1 point from O and Q_4 and add 1 point to C.
3. If the score is 9, subtract 1 point from L, O, and Q_4 and add 1 point to C, H, I, and Q_3.
4. If the score is 10, subtract 1 point from L and Q_4, add 1 point to A, H, I, and Q_3, and add 2 points to C.

* S. Krug, "Further Evidence on the 16 PF Distortion Scales," *Journal of Personality Assessment, 42,* 1978, 513–18. Printed with permission of the Society for Personality Assessment and the author.

Individuals who randomly mark the 16 PF answer sheet show a very flat profile, with a low score on scale B.

RORSCHACH TEST

A major problem with the use of the Rorschach (as well as other projective techniques) in the detection of deception—the apparent susceptibility to fake psychosis on the test—is evident in a classic study by Albert et al. (1980). Results suggested that these experts were unable to discriminate the fakers (uninformed and informed college students) from the actual psychotic individuals, although they did discriminate all groups (fakers and true psychotics) from the normal group. The group most often seen by these experts as psychotic was the informed fakers. This study suggests that while the Rorschach is effective in pointing to psychotic psychopathology, reliable cues for distinguishing malingering from other psychopathology have not been found. The relatively small N in the study is noted. Other studies have generally supported the "fakeability" of the Rorschach, TAT, most neuropsychological tests, and figure drawings, especially by sophisticated and/or prepared persons (Rogers, 1986, 1988).

With this in mind, it is generally agreed that malingering clients (especially if unsophisticated) will respond to the Rorschach with a reduced number of responses and will also show slow reaction times, even when they do not produce particularly well-integrated or complex responses. They take a cautious attitude and thereby produce few responses, primarily determined by color. There are often high percentages of pure F and Popular responses. They easily feel distressed by the ambiguity of the stimuli and will subtly try to obtain feedback from the examiner as to the accuracy of their performance. Also, Seamons et al. (1981) note that if the F%, L, and X+% variables are in the normal range and there are a high number of texture, shading, blood, dramatic, nonhuman-movement, vista, or inappropriate-combination responses, malingering to cause a false appearance of a mentally disordered state should be considered. Granellan et al. (1993) found malingerers attempting to portray themselves as psychotic to provide more unusual percepts (Xu%) and more Dramatic Content responses, especially Morbid Content. A surprisingly high number of Level 2 or personal (PER) responses is similarly indicative.

OTHER STANDARD TESTS

The MCMI-III contains four modifier indices, three of which are designed to assess various forms of malingering. These are the Disclosure Scale (DIS), the Desirability Gauge Scale (DES), and the Debasement Measure (DEB). The fourth modifier, the Validity Index (VI), consists of four items with an endorsement frequency of less than .01. The DIS was designed to detect the degree to which respondents are inclined to be self-revealing and frank and is thought to be neutral to psychopathology. The DES is thought to essentially measure "faking-good"; the DEB measuring "faking-bad." However, Bagby et al.'s (1991) data suggest that all three scales are bidirectional indicators of dissimulation, that is, they tap both faking-bad and faking-good components—hence, they must be used with caution. When an individual is faking-bad, the Thought Disorder scale of the MCMI-III is easily elevated, as it is quite susceptible to faking (Jackson et al., 1991). Also, as noted earlier, since the MCMI-III is more of an "in-house" test than is the MMPI-2, it is still unclear how much of the research on the original version of the MCMI has any "carryover" to the MCMI-III, while it is quite clear there is a major if not virtually total carryover on the MMPI-2.

On intelligence and neuropsychological tests there is an overall tendency for malingerers to perform too poorly and inconsistently in relation to observed behavior or abilities as assessed by indirect methods. They produce abnormal scatter; give illogical, inconsistent, or "approximate" answers; produce odd or surprising "near misses"; miss easy items while they pass hard ones; and also sometimes give bizarre responses where intellectually slow individuals might give concrete responses. Remember to look for consistency between two tests that look different but which measure the same ability.

SPECIFIC TESTS FOR MALINGERING

Clinicians also need to look more to specific tests if there is any question of dishonesty (Schretlen et al., 1992). For example, scales that tap a social-desirability response set, such as the Marlowe-Crowne Social Desirability Scale (Marlowe and Crowne, 1964), give an idea of the direction of a client's response set. The Marlowe-Crowne test has shown good reliability and validity (Robinette, 1991). A validated short version of it (Zook and Sipps, 1985) can easily be included in a standard screening battery, such as the Meyer Information Battery found in Appendix B of this book. The Marlowe-Crowne scale and others like it—such as the M Test of Beaber et al. (1985) and the Structured Interview of Reported Symptoms, the SIRS (Rogers, 1988)—are also helpful in conjunction with the more standard detection scales built into such tests as the MMPI-2 and 16 PF. While Connell and Meyer (1992) found support for the use of the M Test and the SIRS in this respect, Gillis et al.'s (1991) data did not support the use of the M Test. Rogers et al. (1992) have improved the usefulness of the M Test with a two–step decision process that is helpful for anyone who consistently uses this test. The Personality Inventory for Children-Revised, Shortened Format, has been found to be effective in assessing deception in children (Daldin, 1985).

The Schedule for Affective Disorders and Schizophrenia (Spitzer and Endicott, 1978), a semistructured interview technique, is also of potential help here. A drawback of using it with malingerers is that it takes up to four hours to complete, although its length makes it easier to trip up a malingering client on inconsistent responses. Malingering is suggested if (1) sixteen or more of the "severe" symptoms are subscribed to, (2) forty or more symptoms are scored in the "clinical" range—a score of 3 or greater, or (3) four or more "rare" symptoms are subscribed to. These rare symptoms are each only found in 5% of a sample of 105 forensic patients, and only about 1% of this population showed five or more of these symptoms: (1) markedly elevated mood, (2) much less sleep in the previous week, (3) significantly increased activity level in the previous week, (4) thought withdrawal—something or someone is "pulling" thoughts from them, (5) delusions of guilt, (6) marked somatic delusions, (7) evident and recent loosening of associations, (8) incoherence at some point during the previous week, (9) poverty of speech, or (10) neologisms. These rare symptoms could probably be effectively included in a short screening procedure.

The Structured Interview of Reported Symptoms (SIRS) (Rogers, 1986) provides twelve strategies for the detection of malingered mental illness. In its current form the SIRS allegedly requires thirty to forty minutes for administration and consists of 150 structured inquiries that are rated X for no information, 0 for not present, 1 for qualified yes, and 2 for a definite yes. Scales exist for each of the twelve strategies. There is an additional scale to measure defensiveness, designed to reduce the overall transparency of the measure and provide some index of how willing subjects would be to endorse everyday problems. Thus, the thirteen components are as follows: (1) direct appraisal of honest (DA), (2) defensive symptoms (DS), (3) self-management of symptoms (SM), rare symptoms (RS), (4) improbable or absurd symptoms (IA), (5) symptom combination (SC), (6) overly specified symptoms (OS), (7) symptom onset and resolution (SO), (8) blatant symptoms (BL), (9) subtle symptoms (SU), (10) severity of symptoms (SEV), (11) selectivity of symptoms (SEL), (12) inconsistency of symptoms, and 13) reported versus observed symptoms (RO). In practice, the SIRS is more likely to take over an hour to complete, has a number of questions that may seem odd or even offend clients, and is of questionable usefulness since even its author has been consistently disinclined to offer cutoff point decision rules.

The M Test (Beaber et al., 1985) is a brief screening measure designed to identify the malingering of schizophrenic symptoms across a variety of settings. It is composed of thirty-three true-false statements measuring bizarre attitudes, false symptoms of mental disorder, and true symptoms of schizophrenia. The rationally constructed test items comprise three scales: The Confusion (C) scale consists of eight items unrelated to psychopathology that would be expected to be endorsed in a fixed direction irrespective of specific diagnoses (e.g., the item "I believe that cancer is a horrible disease"); the Schizophrenia scale (S) consists of ten items that are true indicators of schizophrenia defined in DSM-III; the M scale is composed of fifteen items that are not indicators of schizophrenia but include statements regarding bizarre and unlikely delusions, hallucinations, and behaviors uncharacteristic of those suffering mental illness (e.g., the item "I find myself bothered periodically by hearing a number of women's voices saying cooking instructions out loud when there is no one around"). The reliability of the M Test is quite favorable. Excellent internal consistency reliabilities (KR-20) were obtained in a diverse sample (N = 318) of community subjects, undergraduates, correctional inmates, and psychiatric patients (.87 for C, .87 for S, and .93 for M). In addition, principal components analysis of M Test items produced a three-factor solution that closely corresponded to the C, S, and M scales. Kurtz and Meyer (1994) report classification rates of simulated malingerers in correctional samples of 73% and 75%, respectively, although there was a problematic level of false positives. Various authors have offered alternative scoring procedures for the M Test in order to increase validity.

In 1964, Rey introduced a simple fifteen-item (three columns by five rows) visual memory test. Test-taking set is important, as the test is presented as being quite difficult, to enhance the malingerer's proneness to exaggerate symptomatology. It has since been adopted by others as a specific test for malingering. For example, Lee et al. (1992) administered the test to 56 outpatients with neurological disorders and 100 temporal lobe epilepsy inpatients. An error score of 7 was found to occur at or below the fifth percentile for both groups, suggesting 7 as a cutoff score to alert one to possible malingering of memory disorder. While correlated with intelligence, a consensus of the research is that, in the absence of significant psychiatric disorder, cognitive impairment or neurological disorder, persons with at least borderline intelligence should not recall fewer than eight or nine items or three complete rows.

The Balanced Inventory of Desirable Responding (BIDR-6) (Paulhus, 1991, available from the University of British Columbia) is a forty–Likert-item self-report measure of the tendency to give socially desirable responses. It has as yet had minimal clinical application but offers potential as a dissimulation measure. Factor-analytic investigations of socially desirable responding have consistently yielded two relatively uncorrelated factors represented by the BIDR subscales, Self-Deceptive Enhancement (SDE) and Impression Management (IM). The SDE scale measures the tendency "to give honest but inflated self-descriptions," with high scores associated with objective measures of overconfidence, overclaiming, and self-inflation, and a general positive association with self- and peer-reported measures of adjustment. The IM scale, which assesses the tendency "to give inflated self–descriptions in public settings," possesses minimal correlation with objective adjustment measures and has been demonstrated to be sensitive to situational demands for self-presentation (Paulhus, 1991). The reliability of both scales is favorable, with internal consistency values ranging from .70 to .82 for SDE and .80 to .86 for IM, across four samples (honest responders, fake-good, religious adults, and inmate psychopaths). Test-retest coefficients obtained in an undergraduate research sample (N = 83) over a five-week interval were .69 and .65 for SDE and IM, respectively. Evidence for the construct validity of the BIDR scales has been generally positive, and studies of dissimulation detection have found it to be sensitive to situational demand characteristics.

Schretlen et al. (1992) have provided interesting data to support the use of a recently developed Malingering Test (MgS), the Bender-Gestalt, and the MMPI in the detection of faked insanity. The MgS is a ninety-item, paper-and-pencil test, composed of simple questions in both open-ended and forced-choice formats, that takes about twenty-five minutes to complete. On the basis of earlier research, the following scoring criteria (Schretlen et al., 1992, p. 78) for the Bender-Gestalt were found to be effective in detecting faked psychosis:

(a) inhibited figure size, each figure that could be completely covered by a 3.2 cm square was scored +1; (b) changed position, each easily recognized figure whose position was rotated greater than 45 degrees was scored +1; (c) distorted relationship, each easily recognized figure with correctly drawn parts that were misplaced in relationship to one another was scored +1; (d) complex additions, each easily recognized figure that contained additional complex or bizarre details was scored +1; (e) gross simplification, each figure that showed a developmental level of 6 years or less was scored +1; and (f) inconsistent form quality, each protocol that contained at least one drawing with a developmental level of 6 years or less and at least one drawing with a developmental level of 9 years or more was scored +1. Scores for the first five of these features were then summed as a composite index of faking.

(A more detailed scoring manual for this use of the Bender-Gestalt and more information on the MgS are available from Dr. David Schretlen, Dept. of Psychiatry and Behavioral Science, Johns Hopkins School of Medicine, Meyer 218, 600 N. Wolfe St., Baltimore, MD 21205.)

The technique of explicit alternative testing (EAT) is effective for the detection of malingered memory deficits and has been employed in a number of studies. The forced-choice, two-alternative technique, also known as symptom validity testing, involves the assessment of reported deficit (usually reports of sensory or cognitive loss) by presenting a visual or auditory stimulus randomly over a number of trials with instruction for the patient to guess whether or not the stimulus is actually presented in a given time interval. Various specific tests such as the Portland Digit Recognition Test or the Test of Nonverbal Intelligence are available. Chance responding (generally set at ± 1.96 standard errors of 50% correct) is the expected performance of a genuinely sensorially impaired person. Performance below chance implies that the subject is aware of the stimulus but selectively denies its presence. Using an interference procedure, for example, having the client sort cards between requests for stimuli identification, increases effectiveness. The most common methods employed—choosing the opposite color, deliberate attempts to forget the present color, patterned responses—are rarely if ever sufficient for subjects to fool the statistical model.

The following are common faking strategies in Symptom Validity Testing: (1) While clients attempt to present realistic symptoms, their perception of what is realistic may be quite off; (2) fakers tend to distribute deliberate errors throughout the test rather than miss only difficult items. They usually do not guess randomly on items they know but, rather, try to control the percentage of errors; (3) fakers tend to perform at a crudely estimated fraction of their actual ability; and (4) fakers frequently protest that tasks are too difficult or feign confusion and frustration.

☐   OTHER METHODS

It is ironic that most clinicians have not become relatively sophisticated in methods other than psychological test measures of deception, and, even here, testing up until recent years was restricted to the MMPI-2. Only recently have clinicians shown an interest in adding physiological methods of deception assessment to their armory (Iacono, 1991). At the same time, most states are passing laws that permit use of the titles "polygrapher" and "lie detection examiner" only by individuals who have training specific to certain physiological tests. Unfortunately, some of the less efficient assessment modalities are often the ones used in the standard examination format and may even be mandated by state law.

One promising development is the use of event-related potentials (ERPs), that is, changes in brain wave activity, upon the presentation of various stimuli while minimizing conscious awareness. ERPs, for example, as measured by an EEG, can be either exogenous, dependent upon and varying with external stimulation, or endogenous, manifest when the subject must make a decision about the stimuli and occurring within the first 100–150 ms after the presentation. Of concern here are the endogenous type, whose amplitude, latency, and scalp distribution are relatively insensitive to changes in the physical properties of the stimulus and very sensitive to changes in the psychological demands of the task. They are considered by some researchers to be a more direct indicator of the cognitive act of stimulus processing, in view of their shorter latency. Of specific concern here is the P300, a positive-going ERP that usually appears 300 ms or more after a low-probability meaningful stimulus is presented to the subject. Variations in the P300 and other similar indices can be used to detect deception. Certain drugs, such as scopolamine, as well as distraction by a secondary task, persistent blinking, mandibular jaw muscle contractions, and gross body movements can obscure the ERP.

Several consistent behavioral cues have been noted in individuals who present a dishonest portrayal of themselves (Ekman, 1992; Bull and Rumsey, 1988). For example, on the average, such individuals nod, grimace, and gesture more than honest interviewees do; tend to tighten the eyebrow or lower the eyelid; and have less-frequent foot and leg movements. They also talk less and pause more often and speak more slowly, although they make more speech errors and smile more often. In addition, the dishonest interviewees tend to take positions that are physically farther from the interviewer. High voice pitch and many face and hand movements, relative to the individual's standard behavior, are also indicative of deception. Deceivers (1) manifest more nonwords, such as "ah" or "uh", (2) show more repetitions such as "I mean . . I mean I really," and (3) use more partial words such as "I cer-certainly did like it." Changes in pitch are the most accurate voice indicator of deception (Ekman, 1992).

Facial signs are not always reliable. But Ekman (1992) does note that the following facial movements are signs that an expression may be false: (1) Reliable muscles, that is, those not easily controlled (e.g., in forehead and upper eyelids), are not included as they would normally be; (2) facial actions are asymmetrical; (3) the expression is of longer duration (e.g., more than five sec.; with "surprise," a second or less) than is normal; (4) there is a false smile—that is, it is asymmetrical, it does not involve the muscles around the eyes, the duration seems inappropriate, or it only involves the actions of the lower face and the lower eyelids.

There is no real support for the idea that people who are deceiving will necessarily avoid eye contact (Ekman, 1992). There is some evidence that females will look longer into the eyes of male examiners while lying but usually not into a female examiner's eyes. These same cross-sex results hold for males as well, but not as clearly.

Research by Cody (1991) breaks down deceivers into those who tell "prepared" lies and those who tell "spontaneous" lies. Those who prepare ahead of time to deceive *tend* to (1) give the answer immediately after the question is asked; (2) provide very terse answers; (3) have speech microtremors; (4) nod their heads at the end of the lie; (5) rub some part of their bodies; and (6) lack enthusiasm and sound a bit as if they have rehearsed, which of course they have. On the other hand, people who tell spontaneous lies *tend* to (1) show odd grammatical errors; (2) provide brief but tentative answers; (3) show speech hesitations and silent pauses or pauses filled with "Ahhs"; (4) use meaningless phrases such as "like that" and "you know"; (5) employ "universal" words and phrases, for example, "always," "never," "certainly"; (6) completely freeze or scratch their heads or rub their hands together; and (7) fail to provide important or even obvious details.

Clinicians do not make much use of systematized interview observations or techniques that change the set of the person taking the test in order to gain a more truthful response. With reference to the set in which the test is taken, Macciocchi and Meyer (1989) told people that the test they were going to take had built-in scales to detect deception. These subjects provided more honest and less socially desirable response patterns than those who were told nothing except to be honest in their responses. Of even more importance, a group of subjects was told that if there was any hint in the psychological tests that they might have been deceptive, they would be given a lie detection examination. They were then even more honest and self-disclosing in their response patterns, compared to when the threat of detection was only by allegedly embedded psychological test scales designed to measure deception. More research in this area is needed to set test conditions more effectively so as to gain more honest responses.

■ Amnesia

Amnesia (see Chapter 7) is a commonly malingered symptom, probably because (1) it is seemingly easy to carry off, (2) it acts to void responsibility, yet (3) leaves the person fully functional in his or her world. True psychogenic amnesia is typically focused on personal memory, particularly those memories directly relevant to a traumatic event. Psychogenic amnesia can usually be differentiated from organic amnesia and faked amnesia by the sudden onset, shorter course, and sudden recovery, anterograde direction (continued ability to learn new information), recoverability under hypnosis, personal focus, and unimpaired ability to learn new information that are characteristic of psychogenic amnesia (Wiggins and Brandt, 1988; Rogers, 1986).

It is worthwhile for clinicians to first remember that vigor and/or apparent sincerity of presentation are not indicators of true amnesia. Indeed, there seems to be no clear correlation here. It's also worthwhile to remember that there may be both true and malingered amnesia in the same case. However, there are cues that indicate malingered rather than true amnesia:

1. True amnesia for situation is seldom either total or very specific. The manifestation of such patterns should cue one to possible malingering.

2. True amnesiacs have shown lower scores on MMPI-2 scales 1, 2, and 3 than malingering amnesiacs (Parwatikar et al., 1985).

3. Malingering amnesia often results in inconsistencies between reports, as well as with usual psychogenic or organic syndromes.

4. True amnesiacs rate themselves higher on the ability to recall information if they are told they will be given extra time or prompting, and, indeed, they do function better if primed. Malingerers are more likely to indicate the improbability of change in their amnesia; they then do not show much change even if prompted.

5. Malingerers show amnesia "as characterized by recall performance better than, and recognition performance worse than, that of brain-damaged memory-disordered subjects" (Wiggins and Brandt, 1988, p. 74). In addition, malingerers' serial-position pattern resembles that of normals rather than that of amnesiacs.

Factitious Disorders

"Factitious" means "not genuine" and refers to symptoms that are under voluntary control of the individual, a syndrome first clearly defined by Asher in 1951. At first this syndrome may sound like malingering (Spivak et al., 1994). The difference is that in a factitious disorder the goal or reinforcement sought is not obvious or inherent in the apparent facts of the situation. Instead, the motivation is often understandable only within the person's individual psychology. These patterns have been traditionally confused with the conversion disorders, but in both the somatoform and conversion disorders of DSM-IV the symptoms are not under voluntary control. Also, in a conversion disorder, symptoms seldom follow a pattern that is true to the factitious disorders: Although the symptoms are not under voluntary control, they are usually associated with a degree of anxiety and have occurred more frequently in the person's history.

Factitious disorders are rare, and, according to Spitzer et al. (1979), they are the most difficult DSM category to diagnose, in part because the feigned symptoms are often accompanied by a more subtle, yet actual, physical disorder. When diagnosticians become aware of what they perceive as deception, they are inclined to make a diagnosis of an antisocial personality instead of a factitious disorder and then give the person little attention. This is especially unfortunate, as such individuals present a substantial suicidal risk (Spivak et al., 1994).

The factitious disorders are subdivided into (1) Factitious Disorder with Predominantly Psychological Signs and Symptoms (300.16), (2) Factitious Disorder with Predominantly Physical Signs and Symptoms (301.19) (often referred to in the literature as Munchausen's syndrome), (3) Factitious Disorder with Combined Psychological and Physical Signs and Symptoms (300.19), and Factitious Disorder NOS (300.19). The general DSM-IV requirements in each syndrome are the intentional production or feigning of symptoms and motivation to assume the sick role. DSM-IV also requires an "absence of external incentives"; however this wording is unfortunate as it suggests an absolute status that is seldom found in the real world. There have also been increasing reports of "Munchausen's by proxy," now diagnosed under Factitious Disorder NOS, for example, where a mother has induced multiple hospitalizations in her child by administering laxatives. These mothers are preoccupied with medical terms and equipment and may even manifest some clear borderline personality disorder components. They also often initially present themselves as cooperative and then passively subvert or resist all interventions. In an also apparently increasing number of cases, a child is injured by the parent in order that the parent might gain the related attention.

In the predominantly psychological syndrome the symptoms are mental rather than physical and therefore are often less well defined. These people usually talk around a point or give approximate, evasive answers to direct questions, a pattern referred to as *vorbereiten*. For example, if asked an arithmetic question (such as "How much is 35 minus 12?"), they may respond with only an approximate answer ("20 or 25"). In that sense, they are not unlike persons with Ganser's syndrome, although that pattern usually lasts no more than a few weeks, even if treatment is no more sophisticated than supportive therapy. The factitious disorders, on the other hand, are chronic.

The factitious disorders are thought to be more common in males. This may only reflect a more ready acceptance of verbalizations of sickness from females, so that the diagnostician would be less inclined to recognize a factitious disorder in females.

Munchausen's syndrome was named after Baron Munchausen, an eighteenth-century German equivalent of our Paul Bunyan, both of whom are associated with tales of exaggeration. The all-time champion victim of Munchausen's syndrome appears to be Stewart McIlroy, whose path through sixty-eight hospitals (with at least 207 separate admissions) in England, Scotland, Ireland, and Wales was retraced by Pallis and Bamji (1979). Although McIlroy used false names and different complaints, he was eventually identified by scar patterns (i.e., the "gridiron stomach," a pattern seen in a number of these individuals) and other permanent medical characteristics. McIlroy is an excellent example of one who suffered mightily to satisfy his addiction. Over the years of his disorder he was subjected to thousands of blood tests and X rays, his spine had been tapped at least forty-eight times, and his abdomen and body parts were criss-crossed with many scars from exploratory surgeries. It is probable that he cost the British Health Services the equivalent of several million dollars.

The range of symptomatology is limited only by the client's imagination and degree of sophistication about medical information. Some experience with hospitals or medical situations, either through prior hospitalizations or through knowledge from family members involved in the medical profession, often contributes to this disorder. It is highly refractory to intervention (Spivak et al., 1994), in part because the person can often find another cooperative physician. Ironically, the disorder can take a high physical toll on the person, as seen in the case of Mr. McIlroy.

TEST-RESPONSE PATTERNS

The functional performance of individuals with these disorders is usually similar to that of malingering, although the psychology that generates the behaviors is somewhat different. Certainly the patterns and symptom picture described in the prior section on malingering are appropriate. It is unfortunate that clinicians have not paid more attention to the issue of the detection of deception, as it is relevant to so many disorders. The clinician is advised to depend on more than one test for indications of malingering. Also, the careful gathering and evaluation of past records, which are important in all disorders, are critical here (Rogers, 1988).

The factitious disorder with predominantly psychological symptoms generally parallels the classic signs of neurasthenia (Golden, 1979), in which the clinician can expect high 2, 7, 1, and 3 scales, in that order of elevation. The deception and sophistication found here would also suggest high 6 and 4 scales. A person with Munchausen's syndrome is more likely to show greater elevations on 1 and 3 than a person with psychological symptoms. The "Munchausen by proxy" mother often manifests a 1-3/3-1 pattern.

On the MCMI-III, elevations on 3 and C between 75 and 85 may occur. The submissive personality (elevation on 3) may use physical symptoms as a way to maintain nurturing and caregiving by others. Scale H may or may not be elevated, depending on the specific patterns of symptoms. The Rorschach and other projective tests are helpful because they present a situation in which it is hard to decipher the situational demands. Such tests disrupt the sophistication and polish of deceptive clients in their presentation of symptoms. For that reason, it is advisable to use a projective test early in the battery; disturbing their sense of surety about performance may spill over into the tests that follow.

TREATMENT OPTIONS

Biofeedback and other allied techniques are useful for any physiological disorder, regardless of the source, even including a physiological disorder that is a direct result of psychological conflicts (Schwartz, 1987). The factitious disorder is a different story, though, because the essential aspect is deception. Not surprisingly, such persons are going to be openly hostile and avoidant of treatment. Thus, unless they are coerced by a significant other, they are not likely to become involved in treatment. If they are coerced and are willing to participate, at least initially, many of the principles that hold for the paranoid disorders are applicable here.

Variations on the now traditional technique of reality therapy (Glasser, 1980) are also an appropriate therapeutic focus here. These emphasize that the person must accept responsibility for his or her behavior and, most importantly, for the consequences of that behavior. To the degree that reality therapy is effective, clients are more likely to come into contact with the conflicts central to their disorder. At that point, more mainstream psychotherapeutic modes are appropriate.

■   ## Ruling out Hypochondriasis, Factitious Disorder, or Malingering

There are three probable specific statuses that a clinician must invariably take into account where malingering or other distorted response sets are suspected. These three patterns are hypochondriasis (discussed in Chapter 6), factitious disorders, and true malingering. As noted, hypochondriasis is one of the somatoform disorders (along with the somatization disorder, conversion disorder, and psychogenic pain disorder), all of which are denoted by complaints of physical symptoms that have no identifiable physiological base and are not under voluntary control.

Clinicians are often called upon to determine if any of these three conditions exist. In order to facilitate this decision process, the following checklists for each of the three categories were developed by Elizabeth Salazar Jackson and the senior author. In the great majority of cases a high percentage (75% or more) of positive answers will occur on predominantly one checklist, indicating support for that pattern. If no condition clearly predominates, these three patterns can usually be ruled out. There are some cases in which two (or even, in very rare cases, all three) of these patterns will occur.

HYPOCHONDRIASIS CHECKLIST

1. Is there a morbid preoccupation with the body, or a part of the body, that is felt to be diseased or functioning improperly?

2. Is there a long-term pattern of social or occupational impairment?

3. Are normal bodily functions/fluctuations exaggerated as indications of disease?

4. Are beliefs about the issue sustained in spite of consistent medical information to the contrary?

5. Is there a general indifference to the opinions of people in the client's environment?

6. Is the client anxious, worried, and concerned about this "illness"?

7. Does the client dwell excessively on the symptoms, turning interviews into monologues—an "organ recital"?

8. Does the speech content consist almost solely of symptoms, their effect on his or her life, and the difficult search for a cure?

9. During conversation, does the client frequently point out afflicted areas of the body?

10. Is there an expression of obsessive-compulsive traits such as defensiveness, obstinacy, miserliness, or conscientiousness?

11. Is there an indication of narcissistic traits, such as egocentrism or oversensitivity to criticism or slight?

12. Is there a lack of sense of inner worth, self-esteem, or adequacy?

13. Does the client appear to have a preference for being ill, showing positive emotions if any real sickness is found?

14. Are there indications of an affective disorder, such as significant depressive tendencies?

15. Is there a history of frequent doctor visits, with one physician or through "doctor shopping"?

16. Is there an unusual and wide-ranging familiarity with psychological or medical terms and jargon?

17. Is there an apparent addiction to reading medical journals, health magazines, and other related materials?

18. Does the client follow unusual health fads, diets, or exercise plans?

19. Has the client often made appeals for extensive tests, examinations, and prescriptions?

20. Do the symptoms commonly deal with the head, neck, abdomen, chest, gastrointestinal system, or generally the left side of the body?

21. Are there indications of a dependent relationship in which affection is not effectively displayed outside of sickness situations?

22. Do the symptoms seem to fulfill an ego-defensive purpose?

23. Do the symptoms ease an intolerable personal situation, avoid anxiety or personal responsibility, or gain needed attention?

24. Do the symptoms appear to be an attempt to control a situation that seems to be getting out of the client's control?

25. Did the pattern appear to have an early onset?

26. Did the client grow up in an "atmosphere of illness," e.g., with a bedridden, chronically ill, or terminally ill family member or a family member in the medical field who brought work home in some fashion?

27. Were the client's parents, especially the mother, overprotective, strict, or overly sanitary in health tendencies?

28. Did the client grow up without parents for a substantial period, or was there a pattern of self-mothering?

FACTITIOUS DISORDER CHECKLIST

1. Is there an absence of evident or obvious gain that the client would achieve as a result of the presented disorder pattern?

2. Is there a gut-level sense that the client has been inducing the symptoms?

3. Could the problem fulfill a masochistic need, such as relieving guilt or a need to identify with the "sadistic" doctor?

4. Does the client show any counterphobic responses to other disorder patterns or syndromes?

5. Are there indications that deceiving others is a defense mechanism, e.g., against low self-esteem or a sense of powerlessness?

6. Are there indications that the presented disorder provides distance from frustrating objects, internal conflicts, or anxieties or provides a temporary identity while ego-dysfunctions are reorganized?

7. Is there any evidence that dependency needs are being gratified in the pattern?

8. Was childhood marked with institutional placement or sadistic, abusive, or rejecting parents?

9. Did the pattern apparently start in adolescence or early adulthood?

10. Is there a history of multiple hospitalizations?

11. Is there any evidence of multiple surgeries?

12. Do the symptoms appear to have symbolic meaning or to have been derived from a previously suffered disorder?

13. Does the client have a background in the health professions or some other access to medical knowledge?

14. Did the client grow up in an "atmosphere of illness"?

15. Is there any indication of wandering to many different hospitals or clinics?

16. Has the client accumulated diagnostic labels, medical biographies, radiographs, or thick hospital folders?

17. Is the medical history inconsistent with known pathophysiological courses?

18. Have there been any inconsistent lab or test results?

19. Have there been any unusual recurrent infections?

20. Has the client failed to respond to therapy as expected?

21. Has the client falsified his or her history in any way?

22. Does the client dramatically present one or more symptoms with elaborate stories, while interacting on a narcissistic level?

23. Is the client's attitude toward staff threatening, aggressive, hostile, and/or impatient?

24. Are there frequent requests for surgery, direct patient observation, or invasive procedures?

25. Does the client impassively or even eagerly submit to agonizing examinations and treatments, expressing high pain tolerance and/or exhibitionist traits?

26. Does the client show *pseudologia fantastica*, attention seeking, or restlessness?

27. Has the client ever discharged himself or herself or retreated indignantly when confronted?

28. Are there indications of any underlying histrionic, antisocial, and/or narcissistic personality disorder patterns?

MALINGERING CHECKLIST

1. Would the client obtain any obvious gain by being considered ill or disordered?

2. Does the client seem to perceive interviews as a challenge or threat?

3. Does the client appear to be annoyed at what he or she considers to be unusual tests?

4. Does the client appear suspicious, overly evasive, vague, or unusually lacking in comprehension of issues?

5. Are there seemingly exaggerated concerns for the symptoms?

6. Is there an easily expressed pessimism about recovery?

7. Is there a relative lack of concern about treatment for the presented disorder?

8. Is the client quickly or especially explicit in denying concern for financial (or other goal-oriented) matters?

9. Is there a focused rather than wide-ranging familiarity with medical or psychological terminology?

10. Does the client show an overly self-confident or assertive manner?

11. Are there any indications of antisocial or psychopathic personality traits?

12. Are there any indications that either of the parents showed manipulative or psychopathic patterns?

13. Do some symptoms seem to contradict symptomatology the client should have?

14. In cases that should supposedly show a long-term deficit or problem, is there an unusual lack of previous exams?

15. Are there other discrepancies, contradictions, omissions, or odd exaggerations?

16. Is there poor test-retest reliability in testing or interview patterns?

17. Whether or not there are discrepancies, exaggerations, etc., do some portions of the client's presentation just seem too "neat," as if coming out of a textbook?

■ ## Summary Contents

It would be useful if graduate training programs in the mental health professions emphasized more the use of physiological measures in detecting deception. For example, the psychologist's extensive background in the study of human behavior and expertise in interviewing and psychological testing could easily be supplemented by this specific training. This not only would facilitate the accuracy of general psychological testing; it would also provide our court system with a much more expert and effective effort toward the detection of deception than is available from the usually minimally trained polygrapher (Meyer, 1995; Rogers, 1988).

CHAPTER 17

Criminal Responsibility, Civil Commitment, and Competency

Forensic issues are becoming increasingly important to mental health professionals (Meyer, 1995) (see Table 17.1). The clinician can be brought into the forensic arena in a number of ways, as is evident in the list in the next section.

However, most of these roles only come about if the clinician chooses to enter the forensic arena, for example, helping to decide if parole should be granted, taking on child-custody or personal-injury cases, et cetera. Yet, any clinician, because of the status of one of his or her clients, can easily become involved in three of the broad, traditional areas on the interface of law and mental health: criminal responsibility, civil commitment, and competency.

Reply to a plaintiff who claims his cabbages were eaten by your goat: "You had no cabbages. If you did they were not eaten. If they were eaten, it was not by a goat. If they were eaten by a goat, it was not my goat. And, if it was my goat, he was insane." (I. Youngner; quoted by J. W. McElhaney, Trial Notebook, 2d ed. Chicago: American Bar Association, 1987, p. 49.)

■ Criminal Responsibility (Insanity)

The tests and standards used to assess insanity or, more broadly, criminal responsibility, vary somewhat from state to state (Steadman et al., 1993). The traditional formulation, referred to as the *M'Naghten* (1843) Test, is influential in many states and is the basic concept in the Federal Rules of Evidence. This in large part stems from John Hinckley, Jr.'s acquittal by insanity subsequent to his attempted assassination of President Reagan. The *M'Naghten* criterion is

TABLE 17.1 The Various Potential Roles of the Forensic Clinician as Fact Finder in the Legal Arena

CLIENT	ISSUE
Criminal defendant (client)	Criminally responsible or "insane"?
Witness to event	Adequate enough in perceptual and information-processing abilities?
Child witness	Mature enough to testify?
Rape victim	Credible or psychotic fantasy?
Offender	Dangerous to release?
Juvenile offender	Emotionally and cognitively mature enough to stand trial as an adult? Dangerous to be released?
Parole candidate	Rehabilitated? Dangerous to release?
Civil commitment (client)	Dangerous to community or to self?
Parent	Responsible enough to have custody of child?
Criminal defendant (client)	Competent to stand trial
Criminal defendant	Competent to be executed?
Testator (client)	Competent to make a valid will?
Contracting party (client)	Competent to make binding contract?
Guardianship/Conservatorship (client)	Able to make decisions on finances, etc.?

Adapted from W. Curran and S. Pollack, "Mental Health and Justice." In W. Curran, A. L. McGarry and S. Shah, Eds., *Forensic Psychiatry and Psychology.* Philadelphia: F. A. Davis, 1986.

whether or not a person committed an unlawful act as a result of "defect of reason" arising out of "a disease of the mind" that results in not "knowing the nature of the act" or, if the individual was aware of it, not knowing that it was wrong. This is often referred to cryptically as the "knowing-right-from-wrong standard."

In 1954 the *Durham* Rule, whose primary author was Judge David Bazelon, focused chiefly on the issue of whether the unlawful behavior was "the product of mental disease or mental defect" (*Durham v. United States*, 1954). Although this rule received initial acclaim, it has seldom been followed since.

A legal definition of insanity that has been especially influential on legal theorists—although to a somewhat lesser degree on state laws—was formulated by the American Law Institute (ALI) and is included in the Model Penal Code. It is comprised of two major sections:

1. Persons are not responsible for criminal conduct if, at the time of such conduct, as a result of mental disease or defect they lack substantial capacity

either to appreciate the criminality (wrongfulness) of their conduct or to conform their conduct to the requirements of law.

2. The terms ("mental disease" or "defect") do not include an abnormality manifested only by repeated criminal or otherwise antisocial conduct.

The rationale for the adoption of the ALI's definition is well articulated in the case of *People* v. *Drew* (1978):

First, the ALI test adds a volitional element, the ability to conform to legal requirements, which is missing from the *M'Naghten* Test. Second, it avoids the all-or-nothing language of *M'Naghten* and permits a verdict based on lack of substantial capacity. . . . (and) by referring to the defendant's capacity to "appreciate" the wrongfulness of his conduct the test confirms our holding . . . that mere verbal knowledge of right and wrong does not prove sanity. Finally, by establishing a broad text of nonresponsibility, including elements of volition as well as cognition, the test provides the foundation on which we can order and rationalize the convoluted and occasionally inconsistent law of diminished capacity. (p. 282)

Criticisms of the ALI Rule focus on its alleged extreme flexibility and the difficulties in determining what is specifically meant by "appreciate" and "substantial capacity." Also, some jurisdictions used the phrase "appreciate the criminality," while others used "appreciate the wrongfulness," and they seem to communicate different concepts (Rogers, 1986). As the court noted, the ALI Rule has both a "cognitive" arm ("appreciate the wrongfulness") and a "volitional" arm ("capacity to conform conduct to the requirements of the law"). The volitional arm is essentially an "irresistible impulse" test (discussed later); the question is whether the defendant could have controlled himself or herself. This question, of course, presents the difficult problem of distinguishing between an irresistible impulse and an impulse that is not resisted. Many states have dropped or ignored the "conform," or volitional element, thus rendering the ALI Rule very similar to the *M'Naghten* Rule. Unfortunately, the present Federal Rules of Evidence (the rules that apply to federal rather than state courts) offer what is basically a cognitive test similar to the M'Naghten Rule. (See Table 17.2.) Because the Supreme Court, on March 28, 1994, refused to overturn Montana's abolishment of an insanity defense more states may move to make the issue moot in their courts by not allowing such a defense.

Before proceeding, it should be pointed out that the expert witness, the clinician who offers an opinion in this area, does not make the ultimate decision, as stated in *United States* v. *Freeman* (1966):

At bottom, the determination whether a man is or is not held responsible for his conduct is not a medical but a legal, social, or moral judgment, . . . it is society as a whole, represented by a judge or jury which decides whether a man with the characteristics described should or should not be held accountable for his acts. (pp. 619–620)

TABLE 17.2 Comparison of Insanity Defenses

TEST	LEGAL STANDARD	FINAL BURDEN OF PROOF	WHO BEARS BURDEN OF PROOF
M'Naghten	"didn't know what he or she was doing or didn't know it was wrong"	Varies from proof by a balance of probabilities on the defense to prove beyond a reasonable doubt on the prosecutor	
Irresistible impulse	"could not control conduct"		
Durham	"criminal act was caused by mental illness"	Beyond reasonable doubt	Prosecutor
ALI— *Brawner*	"lacks substantial capacity to appreciate the wrongfulness of the conduct or to control it"	Beyond reasonable doubt	Prosecutor
Present federal law	"lacks capacity to appreciate wrongfulness of his or her conduct"	Clear and convincing evidence	Defense

Adapted in part from "Insanity Defense" by Norval Morris, *National Institute of Justice Crime File Study Guide*, 1986. Washington: U.S. Department of Justice, National Institute of Justice/Criminal Justice Reference Service.

This reflects the fact that "insanity" is not a psychological/medical term but is instead a legal term (Slovenko, 1995). Hence, the expert has the problem of transforming and explaining clinical data in such a way as to facilitate the jury's opinion about whether the individual is insane. Although the judge and jury ultimately decide the issue (and they rarely find anyone to be insane), it is not uncommon for the expert to be asked indirectly, and sometimes directly, whether the individual is "insane." Also, while "incompetency to stand trial" refers to the person's mental status at the time of the examination, there is an extra difficulty in that insanity requires an inference as to the mental status at the time of the alleged act.

Under the influence of the ALI standard, it seems reasonably clear that individuals with several conditions in DSM-IV can be considered to fit with the concept of insanity. First, the presence of delusions, hallucinations, or other significant interference with cognitive functioning should be enough to warrant an assertion of insanity. Hence, most of the schizophrenic disorders and those dissociative disorders in which the behavior is relevant to the criminal act would be considered appropriate. Also, in most instances the delusional (paranoid) disorders and some of the severe affective disorders, such as manic episode and depressive episode, would fit these criteria. Some juries readily accept the idea that hallucinations and delusions void criminal responsibility. However, a true connection has to be made between these phenomena and the alleged offense. Appropriate sections in this text deal with the specific diagnostic criteria commonly associated with these categories.

Juries are also usually more willing to see organic conditions that are coincident with the alleged offense as both more "real" and more causal, even when there is little reason to argue cause rather than correlation (Smith and Meyer, 1987).

Wettstein et al. (1991) asked four forensic psychiatrists to indicate whether they thought 164 defendants met any or all of four major insanity tests (the ALI cognitive test, the ALI volitional component, the American Psychiatric Association Test, and the *M'Naghten* Rule). These raters decided that 97.5% of the defendants met the ALI volitional criterion, 73.9% met the APA criterion, 70.3% met the *M'Naghten* Rule, and 69.5% met the ALI cognitive criterion. Nearly two-thirds of the defendants met all four insanity tests, and 24.4% met only the ALI volitional test. Few defendants met cognitive tests without also meeting the ALI volitional test. Thus, elimination of the volitional test for insanity reduced the rate of psychiatric recommendations of acquittal by about 25%. The authors conclude that the primary logical division between volitional and cognitive standards appears to be powerful but that distinctions between types of cognitive standards are not very potent.

Certainly some of the furor over the insanity defense is "overblown." Steadman and his colleagues (1993) studied forty-nine counties in a cross-section of eight states (though no southwestern states were included) between 1976 and 1987. He found that out of approximately 9000 felony cases, only 1% included an insanity defense. Of this 1%, about 25 percent were acquitted, and only 7% of those acquittals were by a jury. Also, looking at the median length of confinement on a murder charge, he found it to be 1828 days (about 5 years) when found guilty and 1737 days (4.7 years) when found not guilty by reason of insanity.

IRRESISTIBLE IMPULSE

Because of the narrow cognitive focus of the *M'Naghten* Rule, there have been a variety of attempts to establish "irresistible impulse" as an additional rule, essentially beginning with *State* v. *Thompson* in 1834 (Rogers, 1986) and then evolving in the United States in *Parsons* v. *State* (1887) and its federal counterpart, *Davis* v. *United States* (1897). As noted, the central problem for both courts and clinicians has been to differentiate between an impulse that is irresistible and one that has not been resisted. (In that regard, the reader is referred to Chapters 10 and 16.) One approach to pinning down this concept is to try to ascertain whether or not the perpetrator would have so acted with "a cop at the elbow." Only occasionally does one see a literal attempt here, as when attorney Daryl Blue, in December 1993, announced that he would appeal the conviction of his client who stabbed to death and decapitated an 81-year-old preacher in front of numerous people, including several police officers, as they attended a funeral in Bastrop, Louisiana. As Blue put it, "A rational man does not decapitate a man's head in the presence of a police officer."

In practice, this variation of criminal responsibility has not received strong support from either courts or clinicians, so it is recognized in only a few states. Federal courts have specifically curtailed its applicability to compulsive gambling (*United States* v. *Tonero*, 1984) and to the addictions (*United States* v. *Lions*, 1984), and, when it has received any support, it is usually with "command hallucinations" in schizophrenia and in severe obsessive-compulsive disorder cases. Courts and legislatures have had great problems with the notion of irresistible impulse. On the one hand, it presents both conceptual and practical difficulties. On the other hand, it does provide an insanity defense for a small group who (at least at the extreme) are severely emotionally disturbed and for whom criminal responsibility is problematic. The political acceptability of the volitional test/irresistible impulse has waxed and waned over the years, often depending on its use in some notable case. In recent years it has been at a low point.

EXCEPTIONS TO INSANITY JUDGMENTS

There are two major exceptions to a judgment of insanity. The first is condition resulting from substance abuse, particularly if the substance was voluntarily ingested. As asserted in *Barrett* v. *United States* (1977):

Temporary insanity created by voluntary use of alcohol or drugs will not relieve an accused criminal of responsibility even if that mental condition would otherwise meet the applicable legal definition of insanity. (p. 62)

However, there are occasions when this is not so clearly applicable. First, insanity may be argued if the substance abuse was *not* voluntary, that is, when caused by another person without the victim's awareness, for example, when someone "spikes" the victim's drink. Another instance is when "insanity" continues well beyond the actual effect of the drug use that was a catalyst for it, as stated in *State of New Jersey* v. *Stasio* (1979):

Insanity is available when the voluntary use of the intoxicant or drug results in a fixed state of insanity after the influence of the intoxicant or drug has spent itself. (p. 467)

The second exception to a judgment of insanity, under either the *M'Naghten* or ALI rules, is articulated in the secondary paragraph of the ALI Rule in stating there is no insanity defense available where there is an "abnormality manifested only by repeated criminal or otherwise antisocial contact." This would usually disallow the antisocial-personality syndrome (Wettstein et al., 1991).

Three of the other issues of criminal responsibility are guilty but mentally ill (GBMI), diminished capacity, and "syndromes." The relatively new GBMI, which essentially allows a finding of both insanity and guilt, has received much attention, probably because it gives the jury a way out of an especially difficult decision. Indeed, there is evidence that the availability of the GBMI defense substantially reduces the use of Not Guilty By Reason of Insanity pleas and verdicts (Roberts and Golding, 1991). But the criteria and techniques for the insanity decision component of the GBMI are often the same as in other insanity formulations.

Diminished capacity is a potential, partial defense to a criminal charge. It permits a reduction of the level of offense on a showing that the defendant is actually incapable of forming the required intent. Ironically, of the many and varied referrals to the Center for Forensic Psychiatry in Ann Arbor, Michigan, for consideration of this defense, it has almost never been found to be viable in practice (Clark, 1988).

"SYNDROMES" AND CRIMINAL RESPONSIBILITY

Syndromes, such as the "battered spouse syndrome," have been increasingly employed to mute (e.g., "diminished capacity") or void (e.g., some variation of insanity) responsibility for criminal acts. As a colleague quipped, "People used to say 'I didn't do it,' then they said 'maybe I did it' and/or 'I don't know why I did it,' now they say 'I did it, here's why.'" The dilemma in using something like the battered spouse syndrome as a defense is embedded in the "syndrome" component. A syndrome is defined in *Webster's Third New International Dictionary* as "1: a group of symptoms or signs typical of a disease, disturbance, condition or lesion in animal or plants, 2: a set of concurrent things: concurrence." Various other definitions of *syndrome* contain most of the same elements, with the general idea being that a syndrome is a group of behaviors or events that are reported or observed with consistency. For the specific issues here, syndromes are reported or observed patterns of behavior that are predictably precipitated by some event.

But there are difficulties conceptually. First there is the clear implication that somehow and/or in some degree, a consequent critical behavior has been compelled. For example, when establishing the battered spouse syndrome in an assault or murder case, the clear purpose is to void some degree or even all of the perpetrator's responsibility for the behavior. The standard argument, at least by implication, is that the establishment of the syndrome's existence de facto mutes or voids responsibility. At the same time, it is evident that (1) only a minuscule percentage of battered spouses ever criminally assault or murder their abuser; (2) there is no variable or set of variables that differentiates those who do from those who don't; and (3) if there is a valid case for the behavior as self-protection, the availability of the more legally acceptable self-defense claim negates the need for the establishment of a syndrome.

To highlight this in lectures and workshops, the senior author often argues for the validity of the "estranged spouse syndrome." One of the clearest, and most well-known examples demonstrating this syndrome is the case of O. J.

Simpson, as all of the essentials of the syndrome are allegedly found there: (1) One spouse (A) is evidently still in love with or emotionally dependent upon the other (B); (2) B is disengaging from A, but because of ambivalence, concern for A's feelings, fear of A, or some other reason, B provides mixed messages; (3) some event or series of events transforms A's intellectual understanding into an emotional or "gut-level" awareness; (4) A becomes severely emotionally disrupted by a sense of loss, often confounded by feelings of shame, humiliation, betrayal, or jealousy, and depression, anxiety, and anger grow in a variable admixture; (5) in some cases, personality predispositions of A (and to some degree B) combine with a catalytic event (possibly facilitated by easy access to means and the use of disinhibiting substances), and emotional arousal and disruption peak and in some cases spill into homicidal and/or suicidal ideation and behavior.

Why is this pattern more common in men? First, I believe the data clearly establishes a greater overall biological propensity toward aggression in males. Second, since, in our society, females are still much more likely to retain the majority of control and contact in child custody, the threatened and real loss is often far greater for males.

Why is this defense not available? Other than the fact nobody else has clearly conceptualized it as a potential legal defense, the answer seems to lie with our sociopolitical pressures and choices. Yet, relative to the battered spouse syndrome, the estranged spouse syndrome has at least equally predictable consistency and probably a statistically greater likelihood of cycle completion into homicidal or suicidal violence. In fact, a greater percentage of cycle completion along with the greater biological propensity toward aggression in males would support the argument that the behavior of a male who acts within the estranged spouse syndrome is actually more "compelled" than that of a female who acts within the battered spouse syndrome. Whether or not it would be acceptable as a legal defense, this does help to focus the issues inherent in the use of syndromes in the legal arena, such as the related sociopolitical issues, the voiding or mitigation of responsibility, and the concepts of concurrence and compulsion.

ASSESSMENT OF INSANITY

Kurlychek and Jordan (1980) presented an interesting study comparing the MMPI profiles of thirty male defendants who were found to be criminally responsible with those of twenty male defendants who were determined to be criminally not responsible. The modal code in the nonresponsible group was the 8-6 code. Six nonresponsibles obtained that code, and only two responsibles did. Three responsibles obtained 2-3 and 2-7 codes, but no nonresponsibles scored in that pattern. The modal code for the responsible group was 8-7 (six subjects), although three nonresponsible subjects also obtained that pattern. The high incidence of the 8-6 code in the nonresponsible clients suggested to the authors that highly delusional thought processes are a prevalent factor in nonresponsible defendants. The common codes in the responsible group (8-7, 2-3, 2-7, and 2-0) indicate that more neurotic and inhibitory effects on any psychotic tendencies are found in responsible individuals.

Since faking-bad is particularly likely to be an issue in a decision about insanity, the reader is referred to Chapter 16. All reasonable precautions should be taken to detect and prevent this. At the same time, clients should always be clearly told of the reason for the evaluation, what kind of decisions the information will be used for, and to whom it will be disseminated. A number of clinicians argue that, to buttress the credibility of testimony, it is helpful to have protocols scored and interpreted by computer. Although this generates only part of the information a clinician needs to interpret the profile, they assert this lends support and apparent credence to testimony. On the other hand, introducing computer-generated reports into court easily leaves one "locked into" many of the comments in the report that the clinician may disagree with, as well as the potential ploy then available to a cross-examining attorney of asserting that the clinician has to rely on such a report because of a lack of expertise with that test.

As yet, effective "tests" specific to the assessment of insanity have not been developed, in contrast to those tests used to efficiently evaluate competency to stand trial. However, there are data suggesting that the Rogers Criminal Responsibility Assessment Scale (R-CRAS) is useful as a decision tree (Rogers 1986, 1988). Twenty-three variables are rated to give scores on five discrete scales (the client's reliability, evidence of possible CNSI, psychopathology, cognitive control, and behavioral control). A hierarchical decision model, based on the ALI Rule, is then applied to these data.

Several studies have assessed the reliability and validity of the R-CRAS. Rogers (1986) reports that, over all,

Reliability findings indicated a moderate degree of reliability for the individual variables (mean reliability coefficient was .58) and much higher reliability coefficients for the decision variables (average kappa coefficient was .81). Most important, clinical opinion regarding sanity was in almost perfect agreement, with a 97 percent concordance rate and a kappa coefficient of .94. (p. 168)

Construct validity studies produced a .88 concordance rate, and a moderate degree of internal consistency (mean alpha of .60) was obtained. Grisso (1986) is generally positive about the value of the R-CRAS, only citing as negative the low reliability of several individual criteria and the absence of factor-analytic studies to statistically assess its structure.

Another scale, the MSE, devised by Slobogin et al. (1984), can be effective in one direction and in that sense is a good screening device. Those who are found on the MSE to have no significant mental abnormality almost uniformly are seen similarly in later court dispositions. However, a finding of mental abnormality on the MSE has little predictive validity to subsequent court decisions.

■ Civil Commitment

Clinicians are becoming increasingly involved in assessments of dangerousness to self or others (see Chapter 14) as this relates to civil commitment cases. During the 1970s and early 1980s the requirements for civil commitment were tightened considerably. Also, in the celebrated Donaldson case (*O'Connor* v. *Donaldson*, 1975), commitment without some form of treatment was held to be unconstitutional.

At present the basic requirements in most states for civil commitment are presence of mental illness or disorder leading to dangerousness. This dangerousness is usually further interpreted as being physically dangerous to others or unable to provide the basics of life for oneself. In addition (particularly following the *Donaldson* case), most states require that some form of effective treatment must be available where the client is to be committed, and a number of states require that the least restrictive alternative mode of dealing with the patient be used. There is now a clear trend toward expanding the scope of civil commitment, usually under doctrines that sound very much like *parens patriae.* These new statutes are often patterned after a proposal endorsed by the American Psychiatric Association to permit commitment of the "gravely disabled," who are defined fairly broadly as those who may deteriorate mentally without hospitalization. One problematic consideration in commitment is that, according to *Buchanan* v. *Kentucky* (1987), evidence gathered by clinicians during involuntary civil commitment evaluations may in some circumstances be used against the person in a related criminal proceeding.

The prediction of dangerousness is one of the most difficult assessment questions a clinician must face (Monahan, 1981, 1984) (see Chapter 14). The decision has to focus on reasonably immediate dangerousness to self or others, and the clinician must come to a decision under the standard of "reasonable probability." On the first point, the clinician could act on the most accurate available prediction of dangerousness by simply collecting all persons who had been incarcerated for a severe assault just as they left a penitentiary and then commit them, since in the long run it is reasonably certain that a high proportion of these individuals will endanger others. Of course, most of them do not provide an immediate threat of dangerousness—the issue at hand.

With regard to the clinician's prediction of dangerousness in an individual client, the reader is referred to the sections on aggression and suicide potential in Chapter 14. Also, assessments for mental retardation are appropriate, since in some cases there is an inability to provide for one's basic life care. Consideration of organic dysfunction (or CNSI) may also be relevant, as in the senile individual who is a diabetic. Such persons would probably not be able to take medication as required and in that sense would endanger their own lives. The clinician must recall, however, that the ability to predict specific dangerousness in any reasonably circumscribed period of time is very low and, in most cases, probably not at a level to warrant the cost, that is, the restriction of a person's freedom and civil liberties. A method that is useful in determining which patients should be involuntarily committed is the Three Ratings of Involuntary Admissibility scales (TRIAD) (Segal et al., 1986), which provides structured, reliable ratings on multifaceted scales related to the commitment decision.

■ Competency

"Competency" refers to a variety of legal doctrines—most notably, standing trial, managing one's own affairs (guardianship), and writing a will—and the criteria differ for each of these (Smith and Meyer, 1987). Competency even includes issues such as whether or not a person is competent to accept certain invasive treatments, such as ECT. Sometimes the evaluation need not be that extensive. For example, in December 1993 the Illinois Appellate Court postponed indefinitely the electric shock therapy that had been prescribed for Lucille Austwick, age 80. Lower courts had declared her mentally incompetent and had scheduled the therapy, but her guardian testified that, when informed of the therapy, she said, "That's ridiculous. If they want to do that, let them go shock themselves."

There is even an increasing interest in "competency to be executed," evolving from the Supreme Court case of *Ford* v. *Wainwright* (1986). With the exception of competency to stand trial, clinicians traditionally are not involved. However, some attorneys are now asking psychologists or other clinicians to assess their clients at the time they write a will if the attorney thinks there might be any future contesting of the will on the basis of competency. The clinician's report, made at the time of the writing of the will, is then filed with the will. This serves to make any later challenge rather absurd since the original assessment will be based on far more data than will be available following the individual's death. The procedure can be further strengthened by having the signing of the will and/or part of the evaluation videotaped as a record for later queries.

In general, competency to stand trial requires that a person has adequate mental ability to understand the charges and to participate in his or her own defense (Grisso, 1986). Insanity refers to the mental condition at the time the person committed the crime, whereas incompetency to stand trial refers to the person's mental condition at the time of the trial. In addition, and more specifically, the Supreme Court has stipulated that "the test must be whether he has sufficient present ability to consult with his lawyer with a reasonable degree of rational understanding—and whether he has a rational as well as a factual understanding of the proceedings against him" (*Dusky* v. *United States*, 1960). The individual has to understand the nature of the proceedings with which he or she is involved and the consequences of those proceedings and manifest an ability to cooperate with the attorney in defense preparation. Ironically, as held in *Colorado* v. *Connelly* (1986), severe mental illness (and apparently, incompetency to stand trial) does not necessarily make a confession involuntary and therefore inadmissible.

These are clearly different criteria from any of the notions relating to insanity. These are much more specific and more related to actual behavior than to inferred mental status. Yet, many clinicians who testify regarding incompetency do not realize this differentiation and as a result often confuse the issue of competency with that of either "psychosis" or "responsibility."

One of the major ways an individual can be incompetent is as a result of inadequate intellectual ability; the reader is referred to the portion of Chapter

11 on mental retardation. However, the clinician should not make a decision by using a strict transition from any particular I.Q. to an arbitrary cutoff point for competency. The I.Q. is a critical variable, but the final decision should also take into account other factors, such as history of adaptation, common sense (both in the client and in the clinician), and any already observed ability to cooperate with the attorney and discuss the issues of law. Most individuals with mild mental retardation can cooperate effectively, although not always. As one proceeds through the levels of moderate, severe, and profound mental retardation (see Chapter 11), the proportion of those persons who cannot competently assist in their trials rises quickly.

If clinicians do any significant number of competency screenings, it is strongly recommended that they become familiar with and use the various competency screening instruments that are available (Grisso, 1986), for example, the Interdisciplinary Fitness Interview (IFI), the Georgia Competency Court Test (GCCT), and the Competency Assessment Instrument (CAI). The IFI is ambitious in its attempt to integrate the perceptions of both a criminal lawyer and a forensic mental health expert. However, it is cumbersome, at times impractical, and difficult to apply, and its predictive validity has not yet been impressive. However, it is overwhelmingly cost-effective compared to the wasteful practice of placing individuals in a facility for as many as thirty days in order to obtain a competency evaluation. The GCCT employs the interesting feature of a visual display of the courtroom, but the tool has unfortunately not received much attention in either the research or clinical literature. Devised by the Laboratory of Community Psychiatry (1973) at Harvard, the CAI, along with the Competency Screening Test (CST), has received the widest attention. That group also attempted to develop a projective test for competency, similar in design to the TAT, but the instrument so far has not attained adequate reliability and validity.

The CAI attempts to standardize and structure the interview procedure; unfortunately, instructions for its use are not at all detailed. It is formulated as a set of thirteen areas of ego awareness, covering virtually all of the legal grounds required of defendants if they are to cope effectively with such proceedings. Some of the areas assessed by the CAI are awareness of available legal defenses, understanding of court procedures, appreciation of charges, range and nature of possible penalties, appraisal of possible outcome, capacity to inform the attorney adequately, and capacity to testify. The client is then evaluated on a scoring system of 1 (total incompetency) to 6 (totally competent) on the degree of ability in each area, based on an extensive interview as well as historic data. For example, in the ego function of "quality of relating to attorney," some of the suggested questions are: "Do you think your attorney is trying to do a good job for you?" and "Do you agree with his plans for handling your case?"

Interrater reliability on the scoring of responses to the items in the latest version of the CAI is .87, definitely an acceptable figure. The authors make the point that the efficacy and reliability of this instrument, as well as of the CST (unfortunately, developed on an inpatient population and not originally standardized on an outpatient population), are directly correlated with experience with the instrument and with the competency process itself. Reliability increased dramatically from the point of the clinician's first experience with the CAI to its fourth or fifth use. Before using these instruments, a test use with some colleague consultation is advised. Persons can obtain a full report of this project, entitled *Competency to Stand Trial and Mental Illness,* from the National Institute of Mental Health, Center for Crime and Delinquency, 5600 Fishers Lane, Rockville, MD 20852 or can get in touch with the Laboratory of Community Psychiatry at Harvard University.

The CST is a sentence-completion technique that has been copyrighted by the project's psychologists, Paul Lipsitt and David Lelos. It consists of twenty-two sentence items, such as "When Phil was accused of the crime, he . . . ," and the like. A handbook in the appendix of the report gives differently scored answers for each item, as they are scaled as either 0, 1, or 2, with higher scores indicating higher levels of competency.

The five items that were found to be particularly predictive of competency* are:

9. When the lawyer questioned his client in court, the client said . . .
13. When the witness testifying against Harry gave incorrect evidence, he . . .
14. When Bob disagreed with his lawyer on his defense . . .
19. When I think of being sent to prison . . .
22. If I had a chance to speak to the judge . . .

The scoring emphasizes degrees of legal understanding and psychological integration. For example, for number 9, answers such as "I am not guilty" or "I did not do anything" are assigned a 2, whereas an overspecific, vague, or hesitant response, such as "He had no knowledge of it" or "I don't know why—I guess I'm not guilty," brings the score down to 1. Irrelevant answers such as "He was too nervous to talk" or "The obvious thing" are scored zero. Similar scoring procedures are used with the other five items.

An impressive level of interrater reliability of .93 has been obtained for the CST, using standard Z scores. Also, the overall predictive accuracy of the CST "in agreement with subsequent court determinations of competency," ranges from 72.0 to 89.7%. The CST is especially effective in identifying persons who are unfit to stand trial; however, it is a bit less effective in its propensity to overclassify certain populations (e.g., the mentally retarded) as unfit. By combining the CST predictive information with the validity scales of the MMPI-2 and the female and male Draw-A-Person test, an accuracy rate approximately .90 is typically obtained.

There is some evidence that the CST screening was more valid than the highly structured and practiced judgments made by their trained raters. For

---

* P. Lipsitt and D. Lelos, *Competency Screening Test,* copyright 1970 by authors. Used with permission.

example, some persons who were eventually designated as incompetent by the raters, based on overall data, actually showed clear evidence of competence throughout all the tests. However, these particular individuals had a history of markedly aggressive behavior, and their crimes were repugnant to the community. Hence, the raters may have been swayed by those considerations.

Shatin (1979) found that a brief form of the CST (again, items 9, 13, 14, 19, 22) correlated .92 with the full-scale version in twenty-one female patients in a forensic psychiatric service examined for mental competency to stand trial, a result consistent with some data collected by the test's authors. This brief form also classified seventeen of the twenty-one patients in direct agreement with the results of a full clinical evaluation. Thus, there is good reason to believe that these five items will be useful and applicable to preliminary competency evaluations, possibly by incorporation into the Meyer Information Battery found in Appendix B.

An excellent competency examination would include the CAI as a means of structuring the interview, the CST, a WAIS-R (if necessary), an MMPI-2, and further assessments specific to potential malingering and personality functioning, such as the 16 PF and the Marlowe-Crowne Social Desirability Scale (Smith and Meyer, 1987; Grisso, 1986).

■ The Criminal Personality

Although the DSM-IV discusses the category of antisocial personality (see Chapter 9), it does little to distinguish the greater variety of individuals who are easily subsumed under the label "criminal personality" (Meyer, 1992a; Hare et al., 1991). There are a number of general characteristics of the criminal personality. The majority of offenses are caused by individuals age 21 or younger, and approximately 80% of adult chronic offenders were chronic offenders before age 18. Over all, criminals are male by about a 5:1 ratio—up to 50:1 in various categories of aggressive crime. With the rise in feminism, the ratio is increasingly closer to parity for "white-collar crime," but the high ratio of males persists for aggressive crimes. Both poor sociocultural conditions and heredity are major factors. Other more specific factors are low intelligence, especially verbal intelligence; mesomorphic body type; a history of hyperactivity; left-handedness; cold, harsh, and/or inconsistent parenting; psychopathy; and impulsivity.

■ Predictors of Criminal Recidivism

In addition to various psychological test-generated predictors of recidivism, the following reflect a consensus of literature about factors that predict that the individual will recidivate (return to a pattern of criminal behavior): (1) younger age, (2) male, (3) lower intelligence, (4) lower socio-economic status,

(5) lower educational level (not having a high school degree at the time of incarceration is one predictor; not having it at the time of release is a separate but highly related factor), (6) disadvantaged minority, (7) not being married at time of release (less so is not being married at time of arrest), (8) being younger at first arrest, (9) being older at time of release, (10) higher number of times incarcerated, (11) more time incarcerated, (12) having had a parole revocation, (13) lack of access to and/or use of job training or educational programs, (14) fewer financial resources at time of release, (15) lower job marketability, (16) crimes involving nonlethal violence, (17) crimes involving sexual assault or intrusiveness, (18) a property offense such as burglary or larceny, (19) history of sexual or physical abuse as child, (20) being raised in a dysfunctional family, (21) a history of hyperactivity, (22) indices of true psychopathy, (23) indices of brain disorder or dysfunction, (24) history of conduct disorder, peer rejection, or mental disorder as child.

CHAPTER 18

Professional Case Preparation

This chapter presents guidelines for more effective case preparation. By following these guidelines, the clinician will not only function more efficiently, but will significantly lessen the probability of being accused of malpractice. After the discussion of malpractice issues is the set of guidelines concerned with case preparation in general; this is followed by a model case report format that can easily be adapted to most clinical, neuropsychological, or forensic case situations. After that, we present guidelines for entering into a case as an expert witness, preparing for a deposition, and preparing for the actual courtroom appearance, if that is actually required. The chapter concludes with an examination of some of the major role conflicts a clinician often encounters in the legal arenas. Some of the major legal cases are specifically cited and discussed in Appendix D.

The authors were in part influenced by the notable contributions of such experts in the area as Shapiro (1984, 1991), Brodsky (1991), Grisso (1986), Melton et al. (1987), Monahan and Walker (1990), Slovenko (1995), and others, who will not be repeatedly cited throughout the chapter.

■ ## Malpractice

Malpractice considerations have been increasing for all mental health professionals. Claims are much higher against psychiatrists, in large part because they prescribe medication and use a number of intrusive techniques, such as ECT and psychosurgery. However, claims are increasing in every mental health sector. For example, during the first ten years (1961–1971) of the malpractice insurance program of the American Psychological Association, only a few malpractice claims were made, and none were paid. During the 1976–1980 period, however, 122 claims were processed, with estimated payments totaling $435,642, and both claims and payouts have continued to markedly increase since then.

While some malpractice claims have been based on intentional torts (e.g., battery, false imprisonment, or intentional infliction of mental distress), most are based on the torts of negligence and/or contract liability, that is, DDDD—Dereliction of Duty Directly causing Damage. Overall, claims commonly arise from concepts such as unfair advantage (e.g., sexual improprieties), incorrect or inadequate treatment or diagnosis, failure to obtain informed consent, breach of confidentiality, wrongful involuntary commitment, failure to prevent suicide, nonfulfillment of contract (implicit or explicit), defamation, or failure to refer and/or to avoid practicing in a specific area where competence is lacking. As regards actual claims, sexual impropriety claims—and payouts—are the most common for mental health practitioners in general.

Dual Relationships

Dual relationships, especially involving sexual intimacies, can occur with any client (Boyer, 1990). They are the primary malpractice risk issues for mental health practitioners as a whole. The clinician should be extra alert if the client (1) reports a history of sexual abuse; (2) reports "problems" with prior therapist(s); (3) has a history of being litigious even if "in the right"; (4) specifically sought treatment because of your "reputation" or particular treatment approach; (5) reports sexual affairs, especially if with authority figures; (6) seeks out physical contact of some sort or reports particular pleasure in coming to therapy; (7) brings you gifts or sends cards; (8) dresses or behaves seductively; or (9) attempts to control time or place for therapy, becoming upset if the clinician does not meet these demands.

If you do sense a developing problem in this regard, consider the following actions, as adapted in part from Boyer (1990):

1. Obtain permission from the client to consult regularly with a colleague, preferably one with hospital privileges. If the client needs hospitalization during the course of treatment, collaborate on the case. A team approach can help keep the client from overwhelming any single clinician.

2. Use a treatment plan that is rather traditional. Set clear limits on therapy sessions and phone calls as to place and time.

3. Avoid the appearance of a friendship by not giving cards or gifts to the patient. If small gifts or cards are given to you by the client, clarify that this is not expected. Do not accept large gifts.

4. Avoid touching or behaving toward the client in any way that could be interpreted as sexual. Do not meet the client in places or at times that could be misconstrued. It is not a good idea to provide social services to the client.

5. Place responsibility for the solving of reality problems on the client. Avoid interceding on the patient's behalf with her or his employers, attorneys, friends, or family.

6. As always, clearly document transference issues in the patient record. Records of any consultations on the patient should also be included in the record.

7. Refer the client to a colleague if you believe you may be vulnerable to dual relationship pressures. Sometimes even a competent clinician can fall into some form of dual relationship with such clients.

8. If, after all the preceding precautions are taken, the client complains about your actions to some authorized body, follow the suggestions offered shortly for responding to such actions.

As noted, the guidelines discussed throughout this chapter will help avoid the spector of malpractice, in addition to promoting their primary purpose: effective and efficient clinical functioning. Furthermore, several specific steps may be taken to lessen malpractice probabilities:

1. Think of records as eventual legal documents; know the record-keeping requirements of your profession and/or state—e.g., psychologists must keep a full record for at least three years after the last contact with a client, and a summary for twelve additional years.

2. Remember that courts can be very concrete in the assumption that "if it wasn't written down, it didn't happen."

3. Get written releases.

4. As noted, unless necessary, avoid touching clients, especially of the opposite sex.

5. Avoid dual relationships to the degree possible—especially avoid business relationships that involve clients because these easily lead to later lawsuits.

6. Don't collect overdue bills from clients whom you could reasonably expect to be litigious and/or who expressed disappointment with their treatment.

7. Avoid, to the degree feasible, high-risk clients—for example, paranoid, borderline, or narcissistic clients; chronic legal offenders; those having sexual problems in a fragmenting marriage; the seriously depressed and/or suicidals.

8. Ask new clients if they are currently involved or expect to be involved in litigation. Put this in any initial treatment contract or at least record it in your notes. Consider the cost-benefit of taking on someone expecting litigation.

9. If you are supervising students or other clinicians, make sure communication and insurance-liability issues are covered and clear. You should
    a. supervise only what you also know
    b. clarify responsibilities and boundaries
    c. have supervision in supervising others
    d. have adequate knowledge of the clients
    e. document your supervision

10. **R**emember that courts judge the "standard of care" from hindsight and from the expert testimony of your colleagues, so maintain and document colleague counsel and supervision where necessary (or, better yet, whenever there is a controversial client or issue, or, still better, as a consistent part of your practice), e.g., if you feel a client is attracted to you and/or vice versa.

11. Use any other professional or community resources whenever indicated, and be aware of the confounding and/or exacerbating effects of any psychotropic medications the client is taking.

12. Make an effective termination with any problematic client; i.e.;

    a. discuss fully the issues of why and when, transition, and financial arrangements

    b. if you feel further treatment is indicated, make that clear, provide some specific referral options, offer to do whatever would facilitate referral, provided needed contact during transition, and clearly state your perceived consequences of the client not seeking further treatment

    c. send a termination letter, with the relevant details just noted, in a form that requires a return receipt

If you become aware that a malpractice, ethics, or licensing complaint has become active, take the following actions, as suggested by professional activity groups in the various mental health professional organizations:

1. Consider the merits of the complaint. If the complaint is of minor nuisance value, it is possible (although we don't recommend counting on it) that you will not need legal assistance in responding to the complaint. If the complaint seems at all serious, you should most certainly seek the advice of an attorney.

2. Cooperate with the ethics committee or licensing board in their investigation of the complaint. Become familiar with their rules and procedures. Provide the ethics committee/licensing board with the documentation they request. Contact the chair of the committee/board if you have any questions regarding their investigation.

3. Gather all relevant documents and records, but do not show them to anyone except the ethics committee or licensing board and your attorney.

4. Do not destroy any documents.

5. Prepare additional documents, such as chronicles of events to refresh your memory.

6. Remember that professional case consultation with colleagues is not generally considered privileged information.

7. Be familiar with all the issues in your case.

8. Do not attempt to resolve or settle the case yourself.

9. Provide copies of your files, calendars, notes, etc., as advised by your attorney. Keep the originals.

10. Avoid any public comments and do not make self-incriminating statements. Remember, most professional liability policies do not cover ethics committee or licensing board complaints, since malpractice coverage is usually restricted to lawsuits. But consider a consult with an attorney before responding to an ethics committee or licensing board complaint.

Professional Liability Suits

If you become aware of the possibility that a suit may be filed against you, gather together all available information on the matter, meticulously follow all of the relevant steps noted previously, and, additionally, take the following steps:

1. Contact your insurance carrier. (Naturally, it's important to have adequate insurance in the first place.)
2. Do not attempt to resolve or settle the case yourself or with the plaintiff's attorney while not working with your own attorney.
3. Provide the insurance carrier with all the written information you have regarding the allegations.
4. Contact the attorney assigned to handle your case by the insurance company. Follow his or her advice. Remember, though, that you may additionally retain your own attorney on certain issues, if you wish.
5. Do not panic. Do not discuss the situation with anyone not directly representing your interests except for privileged conversations with your attorney.
6. Prepare any additional documents that could be useful in refreshing your memory.
7. Do not distribute any documents without your attorney's approval and refer all communications from the plaintiff or plaintiff's attorney to your attorney.

Response to Public or Media Inquiries

These kinds of issues often bring inquiries from the public and/or media. A good rule of thumb is to say, "No comment" and to keep in mind the words of the British dramatist Oscar Wilde (spoken in the late 1800s, so think what he would have said now): "In old days men had the rack. Now they have the press." If you fear that one or two of your comments will be taken out of context, and at the same time you do not want to be portrayed as avoiding making a comment, state that you would be willing to comment as long as it is stipulated that the interview as a whole will be broadcast or published. You could then challenge, as seems appropriate, a published statement suggesting or stating that you were unwilling to make any comment. But, if you do speak out (on this, or just in response to inquiries in general from the media), observe the following guidelines to minimize complications:

1. Try to make sure the reporter and the news organization are reputable.
2. Ask that quotes be read back to you as a condition of talking, if possible.
3. When reporters call, tell them you want to think over their questions and you will call them back.
4. Think about the context of your comments within the article and how controversial the topic is. Will your comments hurt anyone?
5. Ask the reporter what assurances can be given that he or she won't draw conclusions you are not making.
6. Ask yourself if you are violating anyone's confidentiality in speaking to the media and if you need a signed waiver.

In any case, using the specific steps already noted as well as the guidelines that follow should help you practice more effectively and avoid malpractice.

General Principles for Case Preparation

Clinicians can take a number of measures to ensure that their procedures are ethical, appropriate, and expert. This set of suggestions concerns general issues with which most professionals in these areas would concern themselves; later, we will discuss the preparation of reports, the preparation for depositions, and the active courtroom appearance. The general suggestions for case preparation are as follows:

1. Don't take on a case in which you do not have a reasonable degree of expertise. There are numerous examples of mental health professionals taking on cases in which they only have a passing awareness of the issues or the requirements of practice. If you are trying to branch into a new area, make sure that you receive appropriate background education and supervision. After all, even the best and most experienced clinicians continue to use colleague consultation throughout their careers. It is also appropriate to inform the client, in a nonthreatening way, if this is a new area for you and to tell the client what the limits are that can be expected from your participation.

2. Establish a clear contract with your client. At the very least, make a thorough oral presentation in a contractual manner of what the client can expect from you and also of what you will expect from the client. It is usually advisable to put this in writing. The contract should clearly cover the issues of confidentiality (especially when seeing a child or adolescent) and compensation.

3. Keep meticulous notes on your encounters with the client and on related events, especially in diagnostic cases, because these often will have

implications in the legal arena or in other decision-making agreements. Make sure that when you return after a lengthy absence from the case that you will be able to clearly reconstruct what occurred between you and the client and that you can report clearly what the client told you. Additionally, it is worthwhile to record your overall impressions at the time when you first summarized the data in your own mind.

4. Observe relevant guidelines in keeping records. The following are modeled on federal guidelines. A record should contain, at a minimum, identifying data, dates of services, and types of services and, where appropriate, may include a record of significant actions taken. Providers should make all reasonable efforts to record essential information within a reasonable time of their completion. If treatment is involved, a treatment plan must be included. The guidelines for retention of records are governed by state, federal, and professional regulations. From a conservative perspective, the full record should be maintained intact for three years after the completion of planned services or after the date of last contact with the user, whichever is later; the full record or a summary of the record should be maintained for an additional twelve years; the record should be disposed of no sooner than fifteen years after the completion of planned services or after the date of last contact, whichever is later. If those records are subsequently submitted to another professional or an agency, the records should be accompanied by an indication of whether or not the clinician considers the information (especially assessment data) to be obsolete.

5. Make sure your relevant history is a thorough one. Many cases have related issues that occur in the history of the client. The relevance of these issues may not be apparent at the time. Make sure that you have looked at all of the potential issues that are possibly relevant.

6. Use standard procedures and tests. Your results will be more acceptable to other professionals and to the courts. This does not preclude using some unusual techniques, but do so in a context of commonly accepted procedures and tests.

A Model Report Format

Whether the clinician is communicating with agencies, other professionals, attorneys, or the court, a formal report is often required. The following general outline has been found to be useful in such report writing. The clinician collects all relevant data and then goes through the sequence point by point as the report is dictated or written. Exclusion of subsections or inclusion of other information sections is easily accomplished to meet the requirements of an individual case and/or the court's request.

In order to be most effective here, the clinician should use a combination of information sources (Shapiro, 1991). These generally consist of (1) psychometric approaches, (2) observational approaches, (3) clinical interviews, (4) psychophysiological measures (possibly even polygraph examinations), and (5) peripheral methods such as hypnosis and sodium amytal. Documentation of those sources that were used is especially important if the clinician must take this report into the legal arena. As noted in the last chapter, there are numerous ways the clinician can be brought into the legal system.

The following is a model outline for a case report.

Name of Client:

Name of Examiner:

Date of Examination:

Date of Report:

A. Introductory Variables

1. Age
2. Sex
3. Educational background
4. Socioeconomic status
5. Occupational status, responsibilities

B. Referral Source and Related Information

C. Circumstances of Examination

1. Place of examination
2. Length of exam
3. Present medications and last time used
4. Tests administered

D. General Appearance

1. Physical characteristics
2. Dress and grooming
3. Unusual behavior or mannerisms

E. Level of Response

1. Answers questions fully?
2. Volunteers information?
3. Protocols adequate?
4. Attitude toward testing and examiner

F. Presenting Problem and Dimensions of that Problem

1. Duration
2. Pervasiveness
3. Severity
4. Frequency

G. Consequences and Implications of Presenting Problem

1. Functional aspects of impairment regarding
   (a) job
   (b) family
   (c) school
   (d) social milieu

    2. Legal status (e.g., pending litigation) of this incident or others

    3. Necessary changes in habits, roles (especially if acute)

    4. Adoption of coping skills or defense mechanisms, both healthy and unhealthy

H. Historical Setting

    1. Was the onset of any symptoms acute or gradual?

    2. Circumstances surrounding onset of symptoms

    3. Evidence of data re pre-morbid functioning in these areas

I. Other Historical Factors

    1. Level of adjustment as a child

    2. Level of adjustment as an adolescent

    3. Prior hospitalizations and diagnoses

    4. Parental relationships, then and now

    5. Sibling relationships, then and now

J. Other Present Situational Factors

    1. Marital relationship

    2. Children

    3. Job or school

    4. Other maintaining factors

K. Current Physical/Physiological Condition

    1. Medication, types and dosages

    2. Medical complications (e.g., removal of limb)

    3. Other factors not directly related to presenting problem

L. Type of Affect and Level of Anxiety

    1. Amount

    2. Appropriateness

    3. In-session versus ongoing functioning

    4. General mood

    5. Effects on testing and interview behavior

M. I.Q. Level

    1. Subtest variability

    2. Pre-incident vs. present level

    3. Educational preparation vs. inherent ability

    4. Potential functioning

    5. Personality inferences

N. Organic Involvement

    1. Any significant indicators

    2. Degree, if any

    3. Specific or global

    4. Cause: alcoholism, birth or prenatal factors, trauma

    5. Cause of or coincidental to other disorder

O. Thought Processes

 1. Hallucinations or delusions
 2. Paranoid traits
 3. Degree of insight
 4. Adequate social judgments
 5. Adequate abstracting ability
 6. Orientation to environment

P. Overall Integration and Statement of Personality

 1. Functioning—Diagnosis

Q. Evaluation of Patient's Current Overall Attitudes Toward His/Her Situation

 1. Expectancies about recovery
 2. Attitude toward disorder
 3. Motivation for treatment
 4. Understanding of status/condition
 5. Coping skills, responses to stress and crisis

R. Identification of Any Need for Further Referral or Consultation

S. Identification of Targets for Modification, Intervention

T. Treatment Recommendations

 1. Individual, family, and/or group therapy
 2. Chemotherapy
 3. Hospitalization
 4. Predictions of dangerousness to self or to others
 5. Interest in change
 6. Probability of maintenance in treatment

U. Priority of Treatment Recommendations (Including Reevaluation and Followup), Based on Available Resources

V. Judgment Regarding Prognosis, Based on

 1. Age at time of onset
 2. Phase of disease or disorder
 3. Known morbidity rates
 4. Severity of affliction
 5. Accessibility of family, other social-support systems
 6. Test results
 7. Patient's attitude

W. Other Summary Formulations and Conclusions

In a November 1989 interview, Jessica Hahn, the victim of a sexual assault by evangelist Jim Bakker, was quoted as saying, "If I weren't moving into show business right now, I would go to college and study law and psychology." (Expert Opinion, Vol. 3, no. 2, p. 10, 1990)

■ ## Expert Witness Case Preparation

While the suggestions and principles presented thus far are important for virtually any professional in the mental health area, there are several other suggestions that are important if you eventually become directly involved in the judicial process in a client's case.

1. Take some time to observe courtroom procedures in general and try to observe various mental health professionals in the role of expert witness. This will allow you to become familiar and comfortable with courtroom process.

2. Even though mental health experts who are called by one party should be an advocate for their opinions and not for that party, they still must operate within the adversarial legal system. Therefore, you should not discuss the case with anyone other than the court or the party for whom you have conducted an evaluation without the knowledge or permission of the court or that party.

3. Once the opinion has been formed, insist that the attorney who employs you provide the basic facts of the case and the relevant statutory and case law and that he or she explain the theory under which the case is to be pursued. Understanding of these issues is crucial to your preparation for the case, and reports and testimony should specifically address these legal issues.

4. Prepare your case in language that will be meaningful to the court. Remember that jurors are going to be put off by jargon, or they will misunderstand and, thus, not give proper weight to your testimony.

5. Prepare yourself to give a thorough overview of all the examination devices that you will be referring to. In the courtroom you may be asked about the reliability and validity of these devices, about how they were derived, or about what they are purported to measure. You should be ready to answer crisply and efficiently, in a language that people will find understandable and useful.

6. Make sure you are current on the relevant literature.

7. Make sure ahead of time of the role you will take in the courtroom situation and communicate this to the attorney who has brought you into the case. It's especially helpful if you can get the attorney to role play all of the questions he or she expects to ask you, with your answers, so that you both know what to expect. It's also helpful if the attorney will role play the questions he or she expects the opposing attorney to ask. Ask him or her to be a true "devil's advocate" in this process.

8. When you are close to actually presenting the case in deposition or in court, make sure you can be comfortable with your knowledge of the client. This may entail bringing the client in for visits shortly before the court testimony. In many court cases the professional may do the evaluation years before actually going into court. In such a case you really ought to see the client again, if at all possible, to check on prior data that was collected and to update your impressions and inferences.

Deposition Preparation and Presentation

In virtually every case that takes on a legal dimension there is a strong likelihood that the clinician will be deposed. Indeed, in many cases there may be no courtroom appearance after a deposition, either because the case is settled out of court or the material that came to light in the deposition eliminated the need or desire to have the clinician testify in person.

Many of the suggestions already mentioned as critical in general and in expert witness case presentation—or that will be mentioned shortly as important in preparing for a courtroom presentation—are relevant to the deposition as well. However, the following are more specific to preparation for a deposition.

1. Organize and review all materials pertinent to the case and request a predeposition conference with the attorney.
2. Bring to the deposition only those records, notes, etc. that you are willing for all involved parties to be aware of or, in many cases, to gain access to. Have a *vita* updated and available.
3. Be aware that there are two types of subpoenas. The first, the *subpoena ad testicandum*, is what most people assume, a summons to appear at court at a specified date and time. The second, the *subpoena duces tecum*, requires the clinician to bring specific materials to the court.
4. Remember that just because a particular set of records has been requested, or even subpoenaed, does not mean it must be released. If in doubt, the clinician should (a) insist that the attorney requesting the information provide a valid authorization from the affected person, (b) request a court order before releasing the information (in some jurisdictions, even a court order is not sufficient), and (c) seek independent legal counsel before acting.
5. Bring an extra copy of your curriculum *vitae*, as it is likely it will be incorporated into the record at this time.
6. Be courteous and speak in a voice that is audible to everyone, especially the stenographic reporter.
7. Be honest in all responses, but do not provide information that is not requested. Avoid any elaboration.
8. Think before you respond. You can take as much time as you wish to think out your response since there is no issue of conveying a confused or tentative image to a jury, as there is in the courtroom.

9. If an attorney objects, stop talking. It is best to let the attorneys deal with the point in question.

10. Remember that the opposing attorney will be evaluating you as a witness and may try many things in deposition that won't be used in trial.

11. Thoroughly read and check the deposition when a copy is sent to you for your signature; do not waive your right to sign it. Correct any errors in it as your attorney instructs. Keep a copy of the deposition with your other records pertaining to the case.

12. Prior to going to court, review your copy of the deposition and take it with you to the witness stand.

■ Courtroom Presentation

While all cases in which the clinician is deposed do not result in a court appearance, many do. The following suggestions are useful when it actually comes to presenting testimony in the courtroom.

1. First and foremost, be honest in all of your testimony. If you do not know the answer, say so, and offer to give related information that may clarify the question. But do not try to answer questions when you really do not know the answer. Aside from the ethical issues involved, it is very likely that you will be tripped up later in the cross-examination.

2. Leave your ego at the courtroom door. Don't be overly reluctant to admit limitations in your expertise or in the data that you have available. If the cross-examining counsel presents a relevant and accurate piece of data, acknowledge this firmly and clearly and do not put yourself into a defensive position.

3. Acknowledge by eye contact the person who has requested your statement, be it the judge or one of the attorneys. But at the same time, as much as possible, maintain eye contact with the jury.

4. Be aware of the classic errors of the expert witness: becoming (a) too technical, (b) too complex in discussion, (c) too simplistic, (d) too talkative and/or overdramatic, or (e) condescending and/or hostile. Any of these approaches is likely to lose the attention of the jurors and may also turn them against you and the content of your testimony.

5. Avoid long, repetitive explanations of your points. If at all possible, keep your responses to two or three statements, but occasionally vary the format of your presentation so that you do not come across as some sort of automaton. If you feel more is needed, try to point out that you cannot fully answer the question without elaborating. At the same time, avoid a simple "yes" or "no" without some added explanation if any is indicated.

6. Never answer questions that you do not really understand. If you are uncomfortable with the wording of the question, ask to have it restated and, if need be, describe your problems with the question as originally posed. Don't allow the attorney to hurry you into a response you're not sure you want to make.

7. Similarly, listen carefully to what is asked in each question before you answer. If there is a tricky component to the question, acknowledge that and then try to deal with it concisely. Try to avoid "Yes, but . . ." answers. If the attorney has made an innuendo that is negative to the case or to you, respond, if you feel it is appropriate, without becoming adversarial. Keep your response unemotional. This *may* be a good time to bring in a bit of humor. However, the use of humor requires *great* caution, as it can easily communicate hostility, which is usually counterproductive.

8. If you feel the attorney has misstated what you have just said, when he or she asks a followup question, take the time to unemotionally clarify what you actually did say and then go on and answer the next question.

9. Speak clearly, fluently, and somewhat louder than you would normally. Make sure the jury hears you. Speak when spoken to and avoid smoking or chewing. Avoid weak or insipid speech patterns, comonly marked by (a) hesitation forms, such as "Uh," "You know," or "Well,"; (b) formal grammar; (c) hedges, such as "sort of," "I guess," or "I think"; (d) overly polite speech; or (e) the use of a questioning form of sentence structure rather than straightforward sentences. Communicate a confident, straightforward attitude.

10. Avoid using any graphs, tables, or exhibits that are not easily visible, readable, and comprehensible by the average juror.

11. Be prepared for questions about journal articles, books, et cetera, relevant to issues in this particular case. This is more important now than it was at the deposition stage. You can't check up on all of the relevant literature, but by familiarizing yourself with some key recent articles, you can more easily blunt an attack.

12. Be prepared to be questioned about the issue of fees. Attorneys who know they can't impeach you any other way, and fear the truth value of your testimony, especially like to use this ploy, often ad nauseam. An attack here by an opposing attorney is especially common if the attorney recognizes the validity of the expert's credentials in general and fears the truth value and impact of the expert's expected testimony. Attorneys may ask questions like "How much are you being paid to testify for this client?" You need to correct that and state that you were asked to do an evaluation, then give your full and honest opinion to the best of your knowledge, and that it was then up to the attorney to decide whether he or she wanted to go ahead and use you in the courtroom. Also, clarify that you are not being paid for your testimony, but that you are being paid for the time that you put into this trial, no matter what testimony would emerge from the time spent. Attorneys are more likely to attack you for charging a flat fee for a case than if you charge by the hour, probably because most of them charge by the hour, a point they would like the jury to forget, especially when it's obvious to everyone that they are repeating points, using redundant witnesses, or using delay tactics. If you feel there is any residual implication that you are being biased by the fee, confront that directly.

13. Be professional in your dress and demeanor. Informal dress is seldom appropriate in a courtroom. Reasonably conservative attire makes a more positive impression on the jury. Similarly, your demeanor should be professional, and you should avoid becoming involved in any kind of tirade or acrimony.

14. Never personalize your interactions with an attorney who is attempting to discredit you. At times you may find it useful to call the attorney by name, but avoid any type of condescension. If you become emotional and make any kind of personal attack, you will likely taint the value of your testimony. There may be times when you do need to express some emotion in giving an opinion in order to emphasize that opinion. But make sure the emotion is properly placed on the opinion and not as a defensive or attacking response toward the court, jury, or a cross-examining attorney.

15. Be prepared to go beyond a simple, linear presentation of data. Jurors look for a "Gestalt," a scenario that integrates and explains the data. Develop the scenario in your own mind, ahead of time, that makes your data meaningful, one that fits with the other facts of the case.

Just as the clinician is organizing to make an effective presentation to the court, the attorneys are preparing to devalue any or all parts of the clinician's testimony. The well-prepared clinician keeps in mind the strategies that he or she is likely to encounter.

■   ## Anticipating the Cross-Examination

Cross-examination is designed to challenge or discredit those data and opinions that have been presented by the clinician that are inconsistent with that attorney's case. Severity of the attorney's cross-examination, including the use of techniques mentioned throughout this section, is often motivated by the quality of that attorney's case. The weaker the case, the more likely the cross-examining attorney is to resort to such ploys, as they may distract the jury from the content of the case. There are a variety of ways in which the cross-examining attorney may attempt to challenge your testimony. Many approaches are reasonable and straightforward. However, many attorneys will use whatever means they can, some of which would not be considered ethical in other professions, to distract the jury from the truth value of your testimony.

1. A primary target for examination is the expert's qualifications. Two kinds of questions concerning qualifications are (a) whether a witness is sufficiently qualified to be permitted (by the judge) to testify as an expert and (b) the "weight" that should be given (by the judge or jury) to the expert's opinion. Presumably, the more highly qualified the expert, the greater the weight should be given that professional's opinion. The expert's experience in the area and the level of relevant education are common targets. More often, the critique is directed toward the specialization that is important in this particular case. For example, an expert clinical psychologist may have had little involvement in the area of neuropsychology, and yet the critical point in the case may involve a neuropsychological issue. This, of course, would appropriately reduce the credibility of the expert.

2. If you have strong credentials, ask the attorney who brought you into court to avoid the "stipulation" ploy by the opposing attorney, that is, quickly stipulating that the expert is qualified in order to avoid having the jury hear the relevant information about expertise and credentials.

3. Some attorneys like to use the "original source," "historic martyr," or "stupid experts" gambits. In the original source ploy the expert is asked if he or she did the original work relevant to the issue or ever did any research in this area. Conversely, in the historic martyr gambit the witness is asked about those experts who went unrecognized in their own time for their brilliant findings in order to set a basis for criticizing the witness's testimony. In the stupid experts approach, studies are brought forth that purport to show that experts are quite often wrong or do no better than laypersons. Be prepared to handle these issues directly and straightforwardly.

4. Another common way to challenge the expert witness is through contradictory testimony from other experts in the field. These experts may testify in the trial, or the challenge may be in the form of a book or article submitted as written authority. A favorite approach is to attempt to lead the witness down the garden path by asking if such-and-such a source is authoritative, or the like, and then presenting contradictory testimony from that source. So, when an expert is asked if this book or person is authoritative, it is often appropriate to say something like "Dr. ____ does write in this field. Other experts might agree with some of the things he says, but he's not my authority (or the only authority)."

If you do accept the results of an article, you may wish to also reply to the effect that "There are many articles in this area; this is but one, and it would be inappropriate for me to comment on the findings you mention without looking at them in the context of the whole article. If the court wishes to grant a recess to allow me to do that, I'll be happy to comment on it." However the courts seldom like to grant extra recesses.

5. Cross-examining attorneys often try to attack the procedures used by the expert witness. A classic instance is the discovery that the expert spent a very short period of time in an evaluation of that client. An expert who so cavalierly comes to such an important decision should be vulnerable in cross-examination.

The particular tests used in an evaluation are also important. For this reason, most mental health expert witnesses prefer to use a variety of objective psychological tests in their examination. It is debatable whether having the tests scored and interpreted by computer adds something to the testimony (Garb, 1992). It can be argued that this adds a validation by an "apparently objective other." At the same time, sending off a test for scoring or interpretation can be construed, through the presentation of the cross-examining attorney, as dependency on outside opinions because of a lack of expertise. Also, one is prone to be "locked into" all of the statements made in the computer-generated report. Some may clearly not fit this individual case, and the clinician may disagree with a number of the statements.

Projective tests can of course be used in court, but they are much more vulnerable to cross-examination. A sophisticated attorney is likely to pull out an ink blot and ask for the expert's response or a typical response, and then try to get a statement from the expert as to what is the appropriate idea here or what can be made of a response the client made. This is one of those times when it is very critical for the expert witness to communicate that the opinions and inferences have been based on a variety of data and not from any individual piece of datum.

6. Another area in which the clinician can be impeached is through bias, for example, by attacking the expert witness as a "hired gun" and asking a variety of questions about how the individual has been paid. The expert should be prepared to note that it was his or her evaluation that was paid for, not any outcome or particular slant to the testimony, and that it was stated up front, "I will make my evaluation and give you my honest opinion."

7. Another possibility is to attack the expert as a "professional witness," one who spends virtually his or her entire career going from courtroom to courtroom. People who do a lot of forensic work are vulnerable to this characterization, and they need to be ready to present a picture of how they become involved in court cases and why they appear frequently.

8. Another potential point of attack is any special relationship to the client. If there is any sense in which the expert is a friend of the person being evaluated, is doing the client a "favor," or in turn is receiving "favors" for the testimony, the expert's testimony is likely to have little positive impact on the jury.

9. Expert witnesses are occasionally cross-examined on their personal vulnerabilities or deficiencies. Any general indications of instability or deviation in the history of the expert witness may be brought out if they can be discovered. Persons who have obvious vulnerabilities, possibly a history of alcoholism or hearing or vision problems (which may in some instances be relevant), should consider means of handling such an attack.

10. Just as attorneys will try to challenge the sources of an inference, they will also try to impeach the process of deriving the inference or opinion. They may try to introduce at least apparently contradictory data, or they may just simply ask, "Isn't this alternate idea *possible?*" It is important for the expert witness not to become too defensive here. There may be a reasonable admission that other interpretations are possible. The expert witness needs to define that we live in a world of probabilities, possibly stating something to the effect that: "Yes, almost anything is possible, for example, it's possible it will snow tomorrow, but it's really very improbable (this has more impact if you are testifying in Florida in summer than in Minnesota in winter). But I do want to emphasize that in my opinion the bulk of evidence supports the opinion I have rendered."

11. An excellent way to impeach an expert witness is to disclose prior reports or transcripts of court testimony given by the same expert that are apparently contradictory to the present testimony. More likely than not, there is no true contradiction. But, by taking things out of context, a cross-examining attorney may make it appear that way. The expert should be aware of this possibility; experts who publish a great deal are particularly vulnerable. They need to be able to explain this situation reasonably, for example, that opinions do change over time and that they may have made a statement some time before in a book with which they do not wholly agree now, or they need to point out why the earlier comments do not exactly apply here. Again, defensiveness is a bad strategy. Openness can be the best method of handling this type of attack.

Clinicians should remember that, at its root—and sometimes only in theory—cross-examination is a process of searching for the truth by challenging the ideas and conclusions of the expert. In this sense, it compresses into a short time the long process of challenge to publication and research. Cross-examination is not a perfect process of truth finding. It is often inefficient, and it is open to abuse. The presentation of information to a lay jury may, in a few instances, cause obfuscation through cross-examination. Some attorneys unfairly attack or even badger witnesses. The fact that some attorneys try these tactics, however, does not mean that they have succeeded; such tactics often backfire. Juries probably (we hope) resent trickery aimed at credible experts. If a mental health expert has drawn reasonable conclusions based on full examination and has avoided exaggerated statements and emotional responses to cross-examination, the expert will have succeeded in making his or her point to the jury.

A dry run, a practice cross-examination, can be helpful, particularly for the expert who has not testified before. It may also be instructional to review Ziskin and Faust (1988) or similar materials so that the approaches any sophisticated attorney may take in a cross-examination can be anticipated.

■ The Clinician's Role in Court

As an increasing number of clinicians enter the forensic arenas, they encounter ethical situations and practical problems that are seldom found in other areas of practice (Meyer, 1995). One of the most frequent dilemmas concerns being asked to take, in the same case, more than one of the following three roles: expert witness, consultant, advocate. Each has a different ultimate client focus: expert witness—court, consultant—client/attorney, and advocate—cause. Any one of these roles is proper for a clinician, but accepting more than one role in the same case, or even blurring the roles' boundaries, is inappropriate (Smith and Meyer, 1987).

Pressure to take more than one role in a single case may come from either the clinician or the attorney. Pressure from within the clinician often comes when there is a late call for help with the case. Demand characteristics of the situation, that is, the "pull to affiliate," can readily couple with personal needs to put the clinician in the classical role of "rescuer." In the extreme, the unsuspecting clinician may soon be agreeing to testify as an expert witness, to suggest theories of defense, to offer advice on how to make the client more presentable to a jury, and to help select a jury.

A closer look at the three roles will make clear the reasons why the roles should not be combined or blurred. The expert is present to assist the jury with questions that it does not have the required special knowledge to address by itself. In that sense, the "client" is the court. The designation "expert witness" refers not only to the qualifications and expertise of the person in the role, but especially to the rules that will govern the person's testimony. Unlike other witnesses, the expert witness may render an opinion. Further, the expert witness may incorporate "hearsay evidence" that other witnesses may not use, and opinions may be based on this evidence. As Shapiro (1984) notes:

Whenever one testifies in court, . . . one should not consider oneself an advocate for the patient, for the defense, or for the government. One is an advocate only for one's own opinion. When the expert witness allows himself or herself to be drawn into a particular position, because of a feeling that the patient needs treatment, that the patient should be incarcerated, or that society needs to be protected, the credibility and validity of one's testimony invariably suffers. (pp. 77–98)

It would be an abuse of process, as well as a way of diminishing the value of the testimony, for the expert witness to use his or her unique role in order to advocate anything other than a professional opinion.

The role of consultant in forensic cases is also one that clinicians are occasionally called on to take. The "client" in this case is the side that retained the consultant. Jury selection, preparation of direct- and cross-examination questions, review of treatment records, procurement of appropriate expert witnesses, recommendations for packaging and sequencing of evidence, courtroom jury monitoring, and other consultant functions may be performed. However, the forensic consultant must maintain some distance from the advocacy role taken by the attorneys.

Keeping professional distance from the advocacy process is one of the most challenging tasks faced by the consulting clinician. However, it is essential that this task be completed successfully. The consultant role, per se, requires that one "call it as one sees it" and not as the client wants it. It is possible that the client will perceive such professional detachment as coldness and lack of care about the case, but that risk must be taken. The focus must be, instead, on rendering the best possible consulting opinion, regardless of what effect it might have on the advocate's behavior or case. The consultant cannot be accountable for the use that the client makes of the opinion that is given, nor is the consultant accountable if the advocate fails to use the opinion.

The role of advocate is seldom a legitimate one for clinicians. This is fortunate, since this role is fraught with ethical implications. As an advocate the clinician is a member of the team and, like other team members, has the goal of winning. The sciences and arts of the mental health professions are here used to achieve an end that the advocate defines as worthy. This may include conviction, acquittal, or modification of sentences in criminal cases. It is possible, and perhaps likely, that an advocate in a case will have personal motives that are not necessarily related directly to the case. For example, advocates for or against capital punishment may be more concerned with the issue of execution than with presentation of the most complete or accurate possible case to a jury.

It is important for the clinician to make it clear when an advocate role has been taken. Otherwise, juries or the media may mistake statements intended only to advance a cause for a reasoned, responsible professional opinion. Use of such expertise to promote a particular view that is not scientifically supported generally would be considered unethical.

Thus, as an expert witness the clinician will find a primary allegiance to the opinion rendered to the court; as a consultant, to the best information rendered to the client; and as an advocate, to service to a cause or point of view. Again, it can be appropriate to take the role of expert, consultant, or advocate, but each of these roles has limits, and one should neither take more than one role per case nor blur the role boundaries. In difficult cases of this sort, colleague consultation can be especially helpful. But if doubt still persists, the old adage "If in doubt, don't" is the wisest course.

APPENDIX A: BIBLIOTHERAPY

KEY: R* = Recommended
C* = Classic

■ Abuse—Physical and Sexual

C*   *The Battered Woman* by Lenore Walker, 1980, Harper Collins.

The classic text on spouse abuse and the battered spouse syndrome. However, it is not really a scholarly work; there is not even one reference.

C*   *The Courage to Heal: A Guide for Women Survivors of Child Sexual Abuse* by Laura Davis and Ellen Bass, 1988, Harper Collins.

Causes, results and a program of hope and recovery are offered by pioneers in this area. However, the book should not be recommended unless there is a prior certainty that abuse occurred. The authors unfortunately reiterate the premises that (1) many standard psychological symptoms and/or (2) uncertainty that abuse occurred should be taken as proof that it did.

R*   *When the Bough Breaks: A Helping Guide for Parents of Sexually Abused Children* by Aphrodite Matsakis, 1991, New Harbinger.

A comprehensive guide to responding to a child's sexual abuse in a manner most conducive to healing.

R*   *Getting Free: You Can End Abuse and Take Back Your Life* by Ginny NiCarty, 1986, Seal Press Feminist. (Also on audiotape.)

Generally sound and helpful advice is offered by a director of one of the most respected battered women's shelters.

■ Abuse—Other

Abused No More: Recovery for Women in Abusive and-or Co-Dependent Alcoholic Relationships by Robert J. Ackerman and Susan E. Pickering, 1989, TAB Books.

The Verbally Abusive Relationship: How to Recognize It and How to Respond by Patricia Evans, 1992, Bob Adams.

■ Addiction—Alcohol and Drug

R*   *Alcoholics Anonymous: The Story of How Many Thousands of Men and Women Have Recovered from Alcoholism,* 3d ed., 1990, Alcoholics Anonymous World Services, Inc.

The "Big Book" of AA. It describes the methods used in the Alcoholics Anonymous program and provides personal accounts of alcoholics who have been helped. Comments on AA's approach are incorporated in several appendices.

R*   *Addiction, Change and Choice: A New View of Alcoholism,* V. Fox, 1993, Tucson, AZ, Sharp Press.

The 800-Cocaine Book of Drug and Alcohol Recovery by James Cocores, 1991, Simon & Schuster Trade.

Rational Recovery from Alcoholism: The Small Book by Jack Trimpey, 1992, Delacorte.

Trimpey is the founder of Rational Recovery, based on the psychological principles of Albert Ellis. This book discusses the RR program, provides information on forming groups, and discusses co-dependency in rational terms.

C*   *Twelve Steps and Twelve Traditions,* 1987, Alcoholics Anonymous World Services, Inc.

The twelve steps followed by AA members (and copied or modified by numerous other "twelve-step" groups) are amplified in this text. The twelve traditions of AA, which are part of its outreach, are also explained.

C*   *Adult Children of Alcoholics* by Janet Wotitz, 1983. Health Communications.

The all–time best seller in this area.

C*   *Kick the Drug Habit: The Basic Guide,* 3d ed. by C. J. Alexander, 1989, Tucson, AZ, Antler Publishing.

Written for drug users interested in release from addiction as well as their concerned others. Explicates factors at work in drug addiction.

■ Addiction—Sexual and Relationship

Co–dependence: Misunderstood, Mistreated, 2d ed. by Anne Wilson Schaef, 1992, Harper.

Discusses the co-dependency concept as well as recent criticism of the codependency movement.

C*   *Codependent No More—Beyond Codependency* by Melody Beattie, 1989, Harper. (Also on audiotape.)

A leading author identifies the characteristics of co-dependents and offers techniques for recovery.

R*   *Don't Call It Love: Recovering from Sexual Addiction* by Patrick Carnes, 1991, Bantam.

Part 1 of Carnes's book discusses the nature of sexual addiction. Part 2 outlines a twelve–step recovery process. The numerous statistics and charts (some of which should be taken with a grain of salt), resource lists, and bibliographies should prove useful to both the sexually addicted and the professionals who work with them.

C*   *Women Who Love Too Much* by Robin Norwood, 1985, Pocket Books.

Norwood was one of the first to discuss the pattern of addictive relationships formed by women from dysfunctional families.

R*   *Finally Getting It Right: From Addictive Love to the Real Thing* by Howard Halpern, 1994, Bantam.

Good practical advice, but addressed primarily to women.

■ Addiction—Other

R*   *Healing the Addictive Mind* by Lee L. Jampolsky, 1991, Celestial Arts.

An approach to changing dependency on addictive patterns by removing reliance on outside forces for peace of mind.

Working Ourselves to Death: The High Cost of Workaholism and the Rewards of Recovery by Diane Fassel, 1993, Harper.

An examination of factors involved in various types of workaholism, gender differences, the effect on the family, and approaches for recovery.

C*   *Confessions of a Workaholic* by Wayne Oates, 1971, Albingdon.

The pioneer book, still timely, and a most delightful read.

■ Aging

R*   *In the Middle of this Road We Call Life* by James Jones, 1995, Harper/Collins.

Helps in finding a return to meaning for those whose distress is in that direction.

R*   *Aging Well: A Guide for Successful Seniors* by James F. Fries, 1989, Addison-Wesley.

A comprehensive approach to the issues of growing old, from attitudes to dealing with the challenges of aging.

Growing Older and Wiser: Coping with Expectations, Challenges, and Change in Later Years by N. Billig, 1993, Lexington Books.

Emphasis on personal abilities and expectations of life in later years.

C*   *Vital Involvement in Old Age* by Erik H. Erikson, Joan M. Erikson and Helen Q. Kivnick, 1986, Norton.

A closer look at the eighth stage in the life cycle, enlivened by interviews with octogenarians.

Your Renaissance Years by Robert L. Veninga, 1992, Thorndike Press.

■ Agoraphobia

R* *How to Help Your Loved One Recover from Agoraphobia* by Karen Williams, 1993, New Horizon.

Very helpful, if the loved one is the client.

The House Without the Door: Emily Dickinson and the Illness of Agoraphobia by Maryanne M. Garbowsky, 1989, Fairleigh Dickinson.

An insightful portrayal of this famous poet's struggle with agoraphobia.

■ Alcoholic Addiction (see Addiction)

■ Anger (see also Mood)

Anger: Deal with It, Heal with It, Stop It from Killing You by Bill Defoore, 1991, Health Communications.

How to employ anger's positive power for mental and physical health.

R* *Anger Kills: Seventeen Strategies for Controlling the Hostility That Can Harm Your Health* by Redford Williams and Virginia Williams, 1993, Times (Random House).

Good ideas and exercises well presented.

C* *The Dance of Anger* by Harriet G. Lerner, 1989, Harper Collins.

An illumination of how anger (expressed or concealed) may work to protect the status quo in relationship dynamics and how, instead, it can be redirected.

■ Anxiety Disorders (see also Agoraphobia, Obsessive-Compulsive Disorder, PTSD, and Panic Attacks)

R* *An End to Panic* by Elke Zuercher, 1996, New Harbinger.

An excellent book offering good advice and exercises that help the lay person with all of the anxiety disorders, and especially with panic attacks.

What of the Night: A Journey Through Depression and Anxiety by Jeffrey Knowles, 1993, Herald.

An excellent first-person account.

R* *Straight Talk about Anxiety and Depression* by Michael Maloney, 1993, Dell.

Solid information presented in a readable manner.

C* *Anxiety Disorders and Phobias: A Cognitive Perspective* by Aaron T. Beck and Gary Emery, 1985, Basic.

The role of cognitive factors in anxiety disorders is presented along with techniques for dealing with them.

■ Assertiveness

R*   *Creative Aggression: The Art of Assertive Living* by George Bach and Herbert Goldberg, 1993, NAL-Dutton.

An enjoyable and up-to-date book by one of the pioneers (George Bach) of this area.

C*   *Pulling Your Own Strings: Dynamic Techniques for Dealing with Other People and Living Life as You Choose* by Wayne Dyer, 1991, Harper Collins.

Stick Up for Yourself by Gershen Kaufman and Lev Raphael, 1991, Schenkman Books.

Though targeted to children, the principles offered are useful to anyone who wants to improve self-esteem and learn how to exercise personal power.

When I Say No, I Feel Guilty by Manual J. Smith, 1985, Bantam.

One of the ten books most recommended by clinical psychologists, according to a national survey.

C*   *Your Perfect Right: A Guide to Assertive Living* by Robert E. Alberti and Michael L. Emmons, 1990, Impact.

Another of the ten books most recommended by clinical psychologists, according to a national survey.

■ Attention-Deficit Hyperactivity Disorder

R*   *Driven to Distraction* by Edward Hallowell and John Ratey, 1994, Pantheon.

An excellent overview of all issues, especially life management, for ADHD, ADD, and learning disabilities.

Attention Deficit Disorder by Thom Hartmann, 1993, Underwood-Miller.

A good book to help parents cope, as it emphasizes positives as well as explaining negatives.

R*   *Answers to Distraction* by Edward Hallowell and John Ratey, 1995, MHS.

Also excellent. A question-answer format.

R*   *Attention Deficit Disorder in Adults* by Lynn Weiss, 1992, Taylor.

Good practical help both for those who suffer from ADD and for their significant others.

C*   *Helping Your Hyperactive Child* by John F. Taylor, 1990, Prima.

A practical, comprehensive approach offering solutions and hope to parents.

■ Autism

R*   *Son Rise: The Miracle Continues* by Barry Kaufman, 1994, H. J. Kramer.

The journal of this father's (in concert with the mother's) arduous but successful attempt to reach and positively work with their "unreachable" autistic child.

Let Me Hear Your Voice: A Family's Triumph over Autism by Catherine Maurice, 1993, Alfred Knopf.

■ Bipolar Disorder (see also Mood Therapies or Depression)

R*   *A Brilliant Madness: Living with Manic-Depressive Illness* by Patty Duke and Gloria Hochman, 1992, Bantam.

Life on a Roller Coaster: Coping with the Ups and Downs of Mood Disorders by Ekkehard Othmer and Sieglinde C. Othmer, 1989, Psychiatric Institutes of America Press.

C*   *Manic-Depressive Illness* by Frederick K. Goodwin and D. R. Jamison, 1990, Oxford University Press.

Comprehensive summary of research and treatment issues with manic-depression.

■ Career Development

Shifting Gears: Planning a New Career for Midlife and After by Andrea Gross, 1992, Crown.

R*   *Upward Nobility: How to Rise High in Business without Losing Your Soul* by Owen Edwards, 1992, Crown.

Helpful advice on business ethics that can be readily applied, since it confines the ideal to limits of the practical.

C*   *What Color Is Your Parachute 1992? A Practical Manual for Job Hunters and Career Changers* by Richard N. Bolles, 1991, Ten Speed Press.

The career seeker's bible, updated annually. Also, one of the ten books most recommended by clinical psychologists, according to a national survey.

■ Codependence (see Addiction—Sexual and Relationship)

■ Depression (see Mood and also Suicide)

R*   *On the Edge of Darkness* by Kathy Cronkite, 1994, Doubleday.

An excellent book, with insights into and empathy with the experience of depression, especially in the many first-person accounts from the famous though not-so-happy.

R*   *Darkness Visible: A Memoir of Madness* by William Styron, 1991, Random House.

An articulate, first–person account of the experience of depression by a well-respected author.

R*   *Out of the Blue* by David Cohen, 1994, Norton.

A superb rendition of most of the issues regarding depression. Interesting and literate, it may put off the lower-functioning client, but will be much appreciated by many others.

Depression: The Mood Disease, rev. ed., by Francis Mark Mondimore, 1993, Johns Hopkins University Press.

Best on the physiological aspects.

C*
Depression: Causes and Treatment by Aaron T. Beck, 1972, University of Pennsylvania Press. A classic work by a well-respected authority on depression.

How to Cope with Depression: A Complete Guide for You and Your Family by J. Raymond De Paulo, Jr. and Keith R. Ablow, 1990, Fawcett.

When the Blues Won't Go Away: New Approaches to Dysthymic Disorder and Other Forms of Chronic Low-Grade Depression by Robert Hirschfeld, 1991, Macmillan.

How to Heal Depression by Harold Bloomfield and Peter McWilliams, 1994, Prelude. You'll probably find it a bit too simplistic, but a number of clients will respond well to it.

■ Divorce (see also Grief)

Answers: A Divorce-Separation Survival Guide by Divorce Support Services, Inc. Staff, 1991, Divorce Support.

R*
Boys and Girls Book about Divorce by Richard A. Gardner, 1992, Aronson.
One of the ten books most recommended by clinical psychologists, according to a national survey.
The Single Again Handbook: Finding Meaning and Fulfillment When You're Single Again by T. F. Jones, 1993, Nashville, TN, Oliver-Nelson Books.
A comprehensive post-divorce guide not only to recovery but also to fruitful living.

■ Drug Addiction (see Addiction)

■ Eating Disorders (see also Weight Control)

R*
Fat and Furious: Women and Food Obsession by Judi Hollis, 1994, Ballantine.
An up-to-date book that, in spite of the title, has some good information for men as well.
Inner Eating: How to Free Yourself Forever from the Tyranny of Food by Shirley Billigmeier, 1992, Nelson.

C*
When Food Is Love: Exploring the Relationship Between Eating and Intimacy by Geneen Roth, 1992, Plume.
Offers insights into the channeling of psychological issues into eating behavior.

■ Family—Dysfunctional (see also Therapy for the Consumer's Family)

C*
Adult Children of Alcoholics by Janet Woititz, 1990, Health Communications.
This book has brought national attention to the ACOA movement.

C*   *Bradshaw On: The Family: A Revolutionary Way of Self-Discovery* by John Bradshaw, 1988, Health Communications. (Also on audiotape.)

Discusses the psychological effects of the dysfunctional family; incorporates the topics of addiction, abuse, co-dependency, and more.

R*   *Homecoming: Reclaiming and Championing Your Inner Child* by John Bradshaw, 1992, Bantam.

Toxic Parents: Overcoming Their Hurtful Legacy and Reclaiming Your Life by Susan Forward with Craig Buck, 1990, Bantam.

■ Family—Normal

R*   *Back to the Family: Proven Advice on Building a Stronger, Healthier, Happier Family* by Ray Guarendi, 1991, Simon & Schuster Trade.

The Power of the Family: Strength, Comfort and Healing by Paul Pearsall, 1990, Doubleday.

When You and Your Mother Can't Be Friends: Resolving the Most Complicated Relationship of Your Life by Victoria Secunda, 1990, Delacorte.

■ Gender Issues—Men

Fire in the Belly: On Being a Man by Sam Keen, 1992, Bantam Books.

R*   *The Flying Boy: Healing the Wounded Man* by John Lee, 1989, Health Communications. (Also on audiotape.)

A story of male emotional growth: losing, finding, and expressing male feelings.

C*   *Iron John: A Book about Men* by Robert Bly, 1990, Addison-Wesley.

Through myth and commentary, helps men connect with their psychic roots and develop deeper emotional capacity by becoming more aware of their masculine nature.

■ Gender Issues—Women

R*   *Backlash: The Undeclared War Against American Women* by Susan Faludi, 1991, Crown.

A look at what women have gained, what still eludes them, and the overall cost of these gains.
Juggling: The Unexpected Advantages of Balancing Career and Home for Women and Their Families by Faye J. Crosby, 1991, Free Press.

A controversial look at the mental health–promoting aspects of the multiple roles women commonly take on as well as the challenges these roles pose.

C*   *Outrageous Acts and Everyday Rebellions* by Gloria Steinem, 1986, NAL-Dutton.
A collection of Steinem's writings that gives a personal voice to women's experience.

■   ## Gender Issues—Women and Men (see also Intimacy and also Marriage/Couples)

R*   *Men Are from Mars, Women Are from Venus* by John Gray, 1993, Harper/Collins.

An excellent book on communication issues.

■   ## Grief

Coming Back: Rebuilding Lives after Crisis and Loss by Ann K. Stearns, 1992, Ballantine.

R*   *How to Survive the Loss of a Love* by Melba Colgrove, Harold H. Bloomfield and Peter McWilliams, 1991, Bantam. (Also on audiotape.)

A step-by-step approach to the grief and rebuilding process appropriate to loss of any kind. One of the ten books most recommended by clinical psychologists, according to a national survey.

Talking about Death: A Dialogue Between Parent and Child by Earl A. Grollman, 1991, Beacon Press.

Helps children deal with death on their own level through an illustrative story that is followed by a guide for parents.

The Widow's Handbook: A Guide for Living by Charlotte Foehner and Carol Cozart, 1987, Fulcrum.

■   ## Intimacy

C*   *The Art of Loving* by Erich Fromm, 1956, Borgo Press. (Also available on audiotape from Recorded Books.)

R*   *The Dance of Intimacy: A Woman's Guide to Courageous Acts of Change in Key Relationships* by Harriet G. Lerner, 1989, Harper & Row.

A description of the steps required to strengthen good relationships and heal difficult ones. Clear advice integrated by case examples.

R*   *Mars and Venus in the Bedroom* by John Gray, 1995, Harper/Collins.

Effective advice on better lovemaking and communication between the sexes.

C*   *Loving Each Other: The Challenge of Human Relationships* by Leo Buscaglia, 1986, Fawcett.

Help with broadening our understanding of how relationships work, what meaning they hold, and how our actions can promote their growth or destroy them.

Why Men Don't Get Enough Sex and Women Don't Get Enough Love by Jonathan Kramer and Diane Dunaway, 1991, Pocket Books.

■ Learning Disabilities (see also Attention-Deficit Hyperactivity Disorder)

Classroom Success for the Learning Disabled by Suzanne Stevens, 1984, John F. Blair.

A good overall view of the issues.

R* *Learning Disabilities* by Jean Knox, 1989, Chelsea House.

An excellent introduction to the area. A good first book to read. Not great depth, but good on basics.

Disorders of Learning in Childhood by A. A. Silver, 1990, New York: Wiley.

A bit academic, but thorough and worthwhile for the client who already has basic information.

Making the Words Stand Still by Donald Lyman, 1986, Houghton Mifflin.

Very good source for the specific learning disability, dyslexia.

Mothers Talk about Learning Disabilities: Personal Feelings, Practical Advice by Elizabeth Weiss, 1989, Prentice Hall.

■ Marriage/Couples

R* *I Will Never Leave You* by Hugo Prather and Gayle Prather, 1995, Bantam.

Good help in finding and maintaining a permanent relationship.

The Art of Staying Together by Michael Broder, 1993, Hyperion.

Very readable, good advice, and while its "USA Today" style avoids depth, most clients relate to it pretty well.

R* *Getting the Love You Want: A Guide for Couples* by Harville Hendrix, 1990, Harper Perennial.

An evaluation of the "Unconscious Marriage" and description and guidance toward transforming your relationship into a "Conscious" one. Written by the founder and director of the Institute for Relationship Therapy.

Going the Distance: Secrets to Lifelong Love by Lonnie Barbach, 1991, Doubleday.

■ Meditation

Meditation Workbook: A Practical Guide to Doing It Your Way by G. Allica, 1991, Crossroad.

An effective how-to guide to numerous meditative techniques.

R* *Wherever You Go, There You Are: Mindfulness Meditation in Everyday Life* by J. Kabat-Zinn, 1994, Hyperion.

■ ## Men (see Gender Issues)

■ ## Mental Health (see Positive Mental Health)

■ ## Mental Retardation

R* *Down Syndrome: Growing and Learning* edited by Siegfried Pueschel, 1978, Andrews, McMeel and Parker.

Guidance to further the physical, emotional, mental and social development of a child with Down syndrome.

I Can Do It! A Guide for Those Who Know, Love and Counsel People with Mental Retardation by John Gerdtz and Mark McGarrity, 1992, Continuum.

C* *Improving the Personal Health and Daily Life of the Mentally Handicapped: A Caregiver's Handbook* by V. Shennan, 1984, Prentice-Hall.

■ ## Mood—Therapies (see also Depression)

C* *Cognitive Therapy and the Emotional Disorders* by Aaron T. Beck, 1979, NAL-Dutton.

Solid, straightforward description of Beck's cognitive therapy model from an original proponent of the cognitive perspective.

R* *Feeling Good: The New Mood Therapy* by David D. Burns, 1992, Avon Books.

Applies a cognitive therapy approach, primarily to depression. One of the ten books most recommended by clinical psychologists, according to a recent survey.

Getting Un-Depressed: How a Woman Can Change Her Life Through Cognitive Therapy by Gary Emery, 1988, Simon & Schuster Trade.

R* *Rapid Relief from Emotional Distress* by Gary Emery and James Campbell, 1987, Rawson Associates.

Offers varied cognitive behavioral techniques for a wide range of emotional-mood disorders. Very helpful for most clients.

Reinventing Your Life by Jeffrey Young and Janet Klosko, 1993, Dutton.

Focus on various negative cognitive "lifetraps" that cover most of the range of emotional disorders.

■ ## Motivation

Do It! Let's Get Off Our Buts by John-Roger and & Peter McWilliams, 1991, Prelude Press.

R*   *Feel the Fear and Do It Anyway* by Susan Jeffers, 1988, Ballantine Books.

A clearcut course of action teaches how to "unlearn" misconceptions about fear, replace them with attitudes of strength and conviction, and take action.

C*   *Overcoming Procrastination* by Albert Ellis & William Knaus, 1979, NAL-Dutton.

◼ Obsessive-Compulsive Disorder

Born to Spend: How to Overcome Compulsive Spending by Gloria Arenson, 1991, TAB Books.

R*   *Obsessive-Compulsive Disorders: Treating and Understanding Crippling Habits* by Steven Levenkron, 1991, Warner Books.

Stop Obsessing! How to Overcome Your Obsessions and Compulsions by Edna B. Foa and Reid Wilson, 1991, Bantam Books.

Getting Control: Overcoming Your Obsessions and Compulsions by L. Baer, 1991, Boston: Little, Brown.

A behavioral approach to self-treatment of OCD.

C*   *The Boy Who Couldn't Stop Washing: The Experience and Treatment of Obsessive-Compulsive Disorder* by J. L. Rapoport, 1989, Dutton.

OCD is described and delineated from "normal" excesses and its effective treatment is proposed.

◼ Panic Attacks and Disorder

R*   *An End to Panic* by Elke Zuercher, 1996, New Harbinger.

An excellent book offering good advice and exercises that help the lay person with all of the anxiety disorders, and especially with panic attacks.

R*   *The Panic Attack Recovery Book* by Shirley Swede and Seymour S. Jaffe, 1989, Signet.

Helpful strategies to manage panic. Written by a former agoraphobic and her doctor.

C*   *Panic: Facing Fears, Phobias, and Anxiety* by Stewart Agras, 1985, Freeman.

A classic and still highly informative examination of what we know about fears, phobias, and anxiety, aimed at demystifying them.

R*   *Panic No More: Your Guide to Overcoming Panic Attacks* by J. Carlton, 1994, Tulsa, OK, Stonehorse Press.

Coping with Panic: A Drug-Free Approach to Dealing with Anxiety Attacks by G. A. Clum, 1990, Pacific Grove, CA, Brooks/Cole.

◼ Parenting

Three Steps to a Strong Family by Linda Eyre and Richard Eyre, 1994, Simon & Schuster.

A bit short and a bit simplistic, but (possibly for those reasons) some clients respond well to it.

C*   *Between Parent and Child* by Haim G. Ginott, 1976, Avon.

One of the ten books most recommended by clinical psychologists, according to a recent survey.

C*   *Dr. Spock's Baby and Child Care* (6th rev. ed.) by Benjamin Spock and Michael Rothenberg. 1992, Penguin.

Thorough and encyclopedic. Better on physical than on psychological material.

If You Really Loved Me by Jordan Paul and Margaret Paul with Bonnie B. Hesse, 1987, CompCare.

From conflict to closeness in parent–child relationships.

C*   *P.E.T., Parent Effectiveness Training: The Tested New Way to Raise Responsible Children* by Thomas Gordon, 1975, NAL-Dutton.

A systematic alternative to either authoritarian or permissive child rearing. One of the ten books most recommended by clinical psychologists, according to a national survey.

R*   *Touchpoints: Your Child's Emotional & Behavioral Development* by T. Berry Brazelton, 1992, Addison-Wesley.

An excellent reference for information and advice about a child's emotional and behavioral development.

■ Personality Disorders

R*   *Without conscience: The Disturbing World of the Psychopaths Among Us* by Robert Hare, 1995, MHS.

An excellent sourcebook for information for laypersons who live with or are interested in the psychopath or antisocial personality.

Living with the Passive-Aggressive Man by Scott Wetzler, 1992. Fireside (Simon & Schuster).

Despite the sexist title, much of the material applies to both sexes.

R*   *Boundaries and Relationships* by Charles Whitfield, 1993, Health Communications.

An excellent treatment of critical issues for most with a personality disorder.

C*   *Narcissism* by Alexander Lowen, 1985, Collier.

A classic, and still one of the most helpful for clients.

C*   *Behind the Masks: Personality Disorders in Religious Behaviors* by Wayne Oates, 1987, Westminster.

Don't be put off by the religious connotation. This is well written, grounded in reasonable theory, and easily accepted by most clients.

■ **Physical Abuse (see Abuse)**

■ **Positive Mental Health (see also Self-Talk and Mood—Therapies)**

R*   *The Power of 5* by Harold Bloomfield and Robert Cooper, 1995, Rodale.

A good source for overall physical and psychological health strategies.

R*   *What You Can Change and What You Can't* by Martin Seligman, 1994, Knopf.

An excellent book by a noted researcher who spent his time in the trenches of research, but who also writes well.

Care of the Soul by Thomas Moore, 1992, Harper Collins.

Integrates spiritual and mental health components in a way that is meaningful to many clients.

R*   *Full Catastrophe Living* by John Kabat-Zinn, 1990, Delta.

Trained as a chemist, this author jumped fields and produced a superb book on coping with the stresses and challenges of life.

R*   *Healing and the Mind* by Bill Moyers, 1993, Doubleday.

Interviews on the mind's role in healing with medical experts in fields ranging from neurology to massage.

Necessary Losses: The Loves, Illusions, Dependencies and Impossible Expectations That All of Us Have to Give Up in Order to Grow by Judith Viorst, 1992, Fawcett Gold Medal.

Viorst describes how maturity, wisdom, and a deeper perspective can be gained through the course of our lives by letting go or losing those ideas that thwart our growth.

C*   *The Power of Positive Thinking* by Norman Vincent Peale, 1987, Fawcett.

A bible of positive thinking by one of the first to carry this message. More easily accepted by less "psychologically minded" clients.

The Protean Self by Robert Lifton, 1994, Basic Books.

Ideal for the subset of clients who respond to an academic, even metaphysical approach to this topic.

Revolution from Within by Gloria Steinem, 1992, Little, Brown.

R*   *The Road Less Traveled* by M. Scott Peck, 1988, Simon & Schuster Trade.

Presents a method for becoming more one's own person through confronting and resolving personal problems to enable greater personal growth. Readily applied to improving one's quality of parenting, freeing oneself from co-dependence, et cetera.

C*   *Success Through a Positive Mental Attitude* by Napoleon Hill and W. Clement Stone, 1985, Prentice-Hall.

A frequently cited book on positive thinking, one of the original works on this topic.

To Thine Own Self Be True by Lewis M. Andrews, 1989, Doubleday. (Also on audiotape.)

■ Post-Traumatic Stress Disorder (PTSD)

C*   *The Crime Victim's Book,* 2d ed. by Morton Bard and Dawn Sangrey, 1986, Carol Publishing Group.

Practical advice to traumatized victims as they work toward reestablishing control in their lives.

R*   *Post-Traumatic Stress Disorder: A Victim's Guide to Healing and Recovery* by Raymond B. Flannery, Jr., 1992, Continuum.

Prisoners of the Past: Overcoming Post-Traumatic Stress Disorder by Howard Levine, 1992, Psychiatric Institutes of America Press.

■ Premenstrual Syndrome (PMS) (see also Mood)

PMS: What It Is and What You Can Do about It by Sharon M. Sneed and Joe S. McIlhaney, Jr., 1988, Baker Books.

C*   *Pre-Menstrual Syndrome Self-Help Book* by Susan M. Lark, 1989, Celestial Arts.

Once a Month: The Original Premenstrual Syndrome Handbook by K. Dalton, 1990, Claremont, CA, Hunter House.

R*   *Unmasking PMS: The Complete PMS Medical Treatment Plan* by J. Martorano and M. Morgan, 1993, Evans & Co.

A simple approach to detecting PMS and suggestions for inexpensive, straightforward treatment.

■ Relaxation (see also Meditation and Stress)

R*   *Beyond the Relaxation Response* by Herbert Benson and William Proctor, 1985, Berkeley.

A classic in relaxation training, this book is one of the ten books most recommended by clinical psychologists, according to a national survey.

C*   *How To Meditate: A Guide to Self-Discovery* by Lawrence LeShan, 1984, Bantam.

A basic introduction to meditation.

Relaxercise by Mark Reese & David Zemach-Bersin, Sensory Motor Learning Systems. (Audiotape.)

The use of movement and motor exercises in relaxation-meditation.

■ Schizophrenia

R*   *The Family Face of Schizophrenia* by Patricia Backlar, 1994, Tarcher Putnam.

Good insights and advice are provided through the medium of numerous cases that clients can relate to.

Coping with Schizophrenia: A Guide for Sufferers, Family and Friends by Jacqueline M. Atkinson, 1989, Borgo Press.

R* *Surviving Schizophrenia: A Family Manual,* rev ed. by E. Fuller Torrey, 1988, Harper & Row.

Describes the nature, causes, symptoms, treatment, and effects on living from the point of view of the patient and the family.

■ Self-Talk (see also Positive Mental Health)

R* *Learned Optimism* by Martin E. Seligman, edited by Julie Rubenstein, 1992, Pocket Books. (Also on audiotape.)

An accessible, scientific explanation of the effect of explanatory style on our experience of life. Advice on how to deliberately transform our response to life's major and minor setbacks, offered by a leading authority on motivation.

C* *Your Erroneous Zones: Step-by-Step Advice for Escaping the Trap of Negative Thinking and Taking Control of Your Life* by Wayne W. Dyer, 1991, Harper Collins. (Also on audiotape.)

A frequently cited text on positive self-talk.

C* *Coping with Stress* by D. Meichenbaum, 1983, New York: Facts on File, Inc.

Stress illuminated and reinterpreted together with a battery of effective techniques, by the pioneer in self-talk research.

■ Sexual Abuse (see Abuse)

■ Sexual Addiction (see Addiction)

■ Sexuality

R* *Mars and Venus in the Bedroom* by John Gray, 1995, Harper/Collins.

Effective advice on better lovemaking and communication between the sexes.

R* *Heterosexuality* by William Masters, Virginia Johnson, and Robert Kolodny, 1994, Harper Collins.

Although the first two authors are no longer the Masters and Johnson family, they are still the masters of this subject. More than 500 pages, a ton of footnotes, and all quite good.

Dr. Ruth's Guide to Erotic and Sensuous Pleasures by Ruth K. Westheimer and Louis Lieberman, 1992, Shapolsky.

Gay, Straight, and In-Between: The Sexology of Erotic Orientation by John Money, 1988, Oxford University Press.

C*   *More Joy of Sex,* rev ed. edited by Alex Comfort, 1991, Pocket Books.
With its broad view of sexual behaviors, this updated "Joy" brings a welcome message in the era of AIDS.

When Someone You Know Is Gay by Susan Cohen and Daniel Cohen, 1992, Dell.

Shyness (see Social Skills)

Social Skills

C*   *How to Win Friends and Influence People,* rev ed. by Dale Carnegie and Dorothy Carnegie, 1981, Simon & Schuster Trade.

This update to Carnegie's classic still conveys solid, useful information. Therapists tend to overlook it, but many clients relate well to it.

Making Friends by Andrew Matthews, 1991, Price Stern.

R*   *People Skills* by Robert Bolton, 1986, Simon & Schuster.

A thorough approach to communication improvement. It includes identification of roadblocks to communication and explains the steps required for development of listening, assertion, and conflict-management skills.

C*   *Shyness* by Philip G. Zimbardo, 1990, Addison-Wesley.

The classic text for coping with shyness. Received very well by clients.

Stress (see also Relaxation)

R*   *The Power of 5* by Harold Bloomfield and Robert Cooper, 1995, Rodale.

A good source for overall physical and psychological health strategies.

The No-Gimmick Guide to Managing Stress: Effective Options for Every Lifestyle, 2d rev. ed. by E. Joseph Neidhardt et al., 1990, ISC Press.

C*   *The Relaxation and Stress Reduction Workshop,* 3d ed. by Martha Davis et al., 1988, New Harbinger.

In its third edition for good reason. It's excellent.

R*   *The Wellness Book: The Comprehensive Guide to Maintaining Health and Treating Stress-Related Illness* by Herbert Benson, 1992, Birch Lane Press.

A well-researched resource by a leader in mind/body medicine that explains specific techniques and serves to legitimize the mind/body connection in traditional medicine.

Your Emotional Health and Well-Being: How to Cope with Stress and Feel Better Fast by Prevention Magazine Staff, 1989, Longmeadow Press.

■ Substance Use (see Addictions)

■ Suicide

R*   *The Enigma of Suicide* by George H. Colt, 1992, Simon & Schuster.

An in-depth look at what is known about suicide, using psychology, anthropology, sociology, and biology's viewpoints and knowledge.

R*   *No One Saw My Pain: Why Teens Kill Themselves* by Andrew Slaby and Lili Garfinkel, 1994, Norton.

In addition to presenting families' stories and teens' journal material, a good overall discussion of depression and suicide is presented, along with guidelines for recognizing and working with this issue.

Suicide and Depression among Adolescents and Young Adults edited by G. L. Klerman, 1990, American Psychiatric Press.

■ Therapy (for the Consumer)

R*   *The Consumer's Guide to Psychotherapy* by Jack Engler and Daniel Goleman, 1992, Simon & Schuster.

C*   *If You Meet the Buddha on the Road, Kill Him! The Pilgrimage of Psychotherapy Patients* by Sheldon Kopp, 1976, Bantam.

Disclosure through stories, both ancient and near, of the path to growth each person must ultimately travel alone.

■ Therapy (for the Consumer's Family)

C*   *The Family Crucible: The Intense Experience of Family Therapy* by Augustus Y. Napier with Carl Whitaker, 1988, Harper Collins.

Scenarios from one family's therapy experience are presented and discussed both to elucidate the underlying dynamics and to demonstrate family therapy in action.

R*   *Family Healing* by Salvador Minuchin and Michael P. Nichols, 1993, Free Press.

Stories from actual family therapy cases are used to elucidate positive family life.

When Someone You Love Is in Therapy by Michael Gold & Marie Scampini, 1992, Hunter House.

■   ## Weight Control

R*

Eat More, Weigh Less by Dean Ornish, 1994, Harper Collins.

A more general approach than his earlier book, *Dr. Dean Ornish's Program for Reversing Heart Disease* (1992). This later book is more acceptable to most clients, offers substance rather than fad, and also some excellent and usable recipes.

R*

Love Hunger: Recovery from Food Addiction by Frank Minirth, Paul Meier, Robert Helmfelt, Sharon Sneed and Don Hawkins, 1990, Fawcett.

A complete weight-loss and maintenance program for compulsive overeaters. It incorporates addiction counseling, twelve-step recovery techniques, Christian teaching and diet guidelines and recipes.

Making Peace with Food: Freeing Yourself from the Diet/Weight Obsession by Susan Kano, 1989, Harper & Row.

Assistance in achieving freedom from diet, weight, and body image struggles from an eating disorders expert.

C*

The T-Factor Diet by Martin Katahan, 1990, Bantam.

■   ## Women (see Gender Issues)

APPENDIX B:
THE MEYER INFORMATION BATTERY

Name _____ Age _____ Sex _____ Date _____

Please finish each of the sentences. Say as much as you can about how you feel. Use your true feelings in your answers. Try to complete every one and say as much as possible about yourself. Thank you.

I am being evaluated now because _____

_____

_____

My favorite kind of job would be _____

_____

Men think I _____

_____

I could be a better worker if _____

_____

Women think I _____

_____

When adapting this battery, more space for responses should be included.

My school grades _____

_____

My father _____

_____

Failure _____

_____

Most bosses _____

_____

My blood boils when _____

_____

My biggest fear is _____

_____

The best way to control pain is _____

_____

The best way to control anxiety or depression is _____

_____

My mother _____

_____

I like best the kind of work that _____

_____

My proudest time is _____

_____

I wish I could forget _____

_____

If things go badly for you, do you get angry or depressed? _____

_____

    What do you then do about it? _____

_____

Above all, a good therapist _____

_____

The type of therapy or therapist that would *not* work for me is _____

_____

The type of therapy or therapist I do need is _____

_____

What do you think the future holds for you and why? _____

_____

At what time in your life were you closest to panic? _____

_____ Why? _____

When did you feel most guilty? _____

_____ Why? _____

What does marriage mean to you? _____

_____

Explain in some detail what death means to you. _____

_____

If I could be anything that I wished, I would choose to be _____

_____ because _____

_____

If I could have any three wishes in the world, I would wish _____

   1. _____

   2. _____

   3. _____

If I could make any one change in other people, it would be _____

_____ because _____

The very earliest thing that I can remember as a child is _____

_____

My most pleasant memory is _____

_____

My most unpleasant memory is _____

_____

Explain the four proverbs below. For example, the proverb *Large oaks from little acorns grow* means that great things may have small beginnings. Say as best you can what each of these proverbs means.

While the cat's away, the mice will play. _____

_____

It never rains but it pours. _____

_____

Don't cry over spilt milk. _____

_____

The burnt child dreads the fire. _____

_____

Have you ever seriously thought of killing yourself or hurting yourself, or have you ever made such an

attempt? _____ Please give details. _____

Have you ever had a strong desire to seriously hurt someone, or have you ever made an attempt to do so? _____ Please give details. _____

If the following people were asked to describe you in one word, what word would each probably use?

Mother _____Father _____

Brother(s) _____ Sister(s) _____

Your spouse or most intimate opposite-sex friend _____

Your boss _____

Your son(s) _____ Your daughter(s) _____

I would most strongly wish to raise my child to be _____

If there is one thing that I could go back and change about my life, it would be _____

Briefly describe your history of arrests and convictions (either felonies or misdemeanors), including any moving violations while in an automobile.

_____

_____

_____

Are you currently receiving treatment from any physician or mental health practitioner? Please give details, including their names.

_____

_____

_____

Briefly describe any history of psychological or psychiatric treatment (including treatment for alcohol or drug abuse).

_____

_____

_____

Has any blood relative ever had a problem controlling use of alcohol or ever been in significant trouble because of use of alcohol?

Yes _____   No _____ ; or has received psychiatric treatment? Yes _____   No _____ .

Please describe your relationship to this relative(s) and give details. _____

_____

_____

Has any blood relative ever been _arrested_ (not just convicted) for a felony? Yes _____   No _____

Please describe your relationship to this relative(s) and give details. _____

_____

_____

Have you ever been either warned, or disciplined, or have you ever lost a job because you violated some company rule, or because of missing work or being late for work?

Yes _____   No _____ (please circle one) If so, please explain _____

_____

_____

Have you ever been either warned, or disciplined, or lost your job because of sexual harassment, or fighting, or alcohol or drug use, or any related problem?

Yes _____   No _____ (please circle one) If so, please explain _____

_____

■   **Draw-A-Group**

Please draw a picture of any group scene that involves you and at least two other people. I know that many people are not artists and may seldom draw anything. However, simply go ahead and do your best. Use first names or role names (e.g., Jack, Sue, Amy, friend, father, sister, me, etc.) to label each of the figures in your drawing. Remember, I understand that not everyone draws well or even likes to draw. All I want is your best effort. Thank you.

■   **Drawing Explanation**

Use the space that follows to describe what is happening in the drawing you made. Describe what is going on, whether someone is talking to someone, what they are saying, or anything else that is important. Give all the details you can. Thank you.

What is your most serious physical problem at this time? _____

_____

What treatment are you receiving? _____

_____

What is your most serious emotional problem at this time? _____

_____

Why? _____

_____

Do you prefer to live in the city, the suburbs, or the country? _____

_____

Why? _____

_____

Which man of the past or present do you most admire? _____

Why? _____

Which woman of the past or present do you most admire? _____

Why? _____

Who has been more meaningful to you, your father or your mother? _____

Why? _____

What is your favorite movie of all time?_____

Why? _____

Who is your favorite male movie star? _____

Why? _____

Who is your favorite female movie star? _____

Why _____

Do you believe in God?_____ Why or why not? _____

_____

Do you practice a religion? _____ Why and in what way? Or why not? _____

_____

Has your sexual history been good or bad? _____Describe and say why it has been good or bad for

you. _____

_____

What has been the greatest injustice you have suffered? _____

_____What did you do about it? _____

_____

Thank you for your cooperation.

APPENDIX C:
TWO RELAXATION METHODS

This appendix provides two different techniques designed to help the client relax both physiologically and psychologically. The first is a brief and straightforward technique of relaxation training that has proven useful in crisis and short-term applications. The second method, autogenic training, which is focused on prolonged physiological relaxation, is designed to be practiced over a substantial duration.

■ Brief Relaxation Training

This particular technique is usually presented most effectively by a handout, as modeled in the following. It is best if you go through the procedure at least once in an office session. Taping your relaxation "patter" allows the client to replay it occasionally at home as a kind of booster. "A wide variety of simple relaxation-inducing techniques exists. While there is plenty of research and clinical support for the usefulness of such simple, straightforward relaxation techniques, there is little evidence that they differ markedly in effectiveness. Thus, you can vary the suggestions below in whatever ways are comfortable. You might proceed through the technique by attending to your own inner voice as it focuses on each area of the body.

Lie relaxed with your legs uncrossed and your arms comfortably beside you. First, focus mentally on your toes, imagining them to be limp, warm, and relaxed (you can vary this procedure by first flexing each muscle group before you proceed into a relaxation phase; some find that this increases the subsequent relaxation effect). Now, visualize your foot and then your ankles, and suggest that they relax and feel loose. Follow this pattern up your body, silently focusing on and identifying each part as you relax it (calves, knees, upper legs, hips). Then proceed through your lower torso, including the genital and anal areas. Suggest relaxation, calmness, and warmth. Proceed slowly but surely into the stomach area, again identifying each area, particularly if there is noticeable tension there. Suggest to yourself that your breathing is normal and calm (neither slowed abnormally nor fast). Go up through your chest, shoulders, and, part by part, down your arms to your fingertips. Then focus on the neck area, particularly noting the jaw muscles and even such small areas as the tongue and the tip of the nose. Focus next on the forehead, but suggest coolness here, for this is one body part where coolness is clearly associated with relaxation. Then suggest looseness in the scalp, and possibly finish off with a mental image of your whole body as relaxing calmly and serenely.

You might choose instead to work downward from the head to the toes or to develop other variations that feel more comfortable to you. Don't expect remarkable results in the first few days or so. But continued practice of a relaxation approach of some sort is one effective antidote and preventive measure in controlling many psychological and physiological disorders."

■ Autogenic Training (AT)

Autogenic Training (AT) is useful for those clients who are willing to commit to practice over a substantial duration. AT may seem like the product of a German academic who wants to Westernize yoga techniques, and, indeed, that's how it came about. The following discussion will focus on the best positions, the most effective training elements, and the exercises themselves. Again, the training effectiveness can be enhanced by practicing the technique with the client in the office, and reinforcing that with a handout incorporating much or all of the following material.

The basic ideas on autogenic training were developed in the early 1900s in Germany and subsequently received substantial research attention, particularly in Europe. The research on AT supports the idea that it can change processes such as the general stress syndrome as well as more specific psychophysiological processes in the body.

□ POSITIONS

Prone Position.   The great majority of people find that the most efficient way to learn and experience results from AT is to do the exercises while lying on a couch or a bed. (The following suggestions help most people maximize their results, but these comments are not to be read as hard-and-fast rules and can be modified to individual needs.) While lying down, the legs are usually slightly apart and relaxed so that the feet are inclined outward at a V-shaped angle. Some support (a folded blanket) under the knees helps many people to relax the muscles of both legs. The trunk, shoulders, and head are most easily relaxed when kept in a symmetric position. The arms should lie relaxed and slightly bent beside the trunk of the body. The fingers remain slightly spread and flexed and generally do not touch the rest of the body.

Particular attention should be given to determining the most relaxing position for the head, neck, and shoulders. It is advised to try different pillows to see which is most comfortable for these exercises. If there is a continuing of stiffness in the neck or shoulder muscles during the exercises, consider whether the head has been kept symmetrical and whether the pillow is in a reasonably comfortable position.

While doing the exercises in the prone position, it is advisable that the shoes be removed. When a blanket is used for cover, it should not be tightly wrapped around any part of the body since restriction or pressure may have a somewhat distracting effect during the exercises. Another point, and one frequently overlooked, is that certain people relax more completely and perform the exercises more effectively when given some support under the knees.

Reclining Chair Position.   The autogenic exercises can also be performed in a reclining chair that has a high enough back so that the trunk and head can rest passively and comfortably. Often reclining chairs provide postures that are not as comfortable as may first appear. Pillows and other means can be used to adjust them. There should be support throughout the length of the arms and the legs. Most of the suggestions made for the prone position are also relevant here.

Straight Chair Position.   Attaining some comfort and mastery of the straight chair position is helpful because it allows clients to practice the exercises in a great many places, including at work or even in public places such as airports.

In this posture the edge of the seat should not exert pressure on the legs, and the feet should rest solidly on the ground. In order to attain a position of maximal relaxation in this position, the client first straightens up completely while in a sitting position. Then, with both arms hanging down at the sides, he or she suddenly relaxes completely, which results in a kind of collapse of the trunk, shoulders, and neck, with the body supported primarily by the skeleton and ligament structure. It is best to keep the back relatively straight; in other words, the trunk collapses downward without bending forward. To the degree possible, the body should feel as if it is hanging loose. Most people find it ideal to have the underside of the forearms rest on the upper thighs. The head has dropped forward, and the arms, although touching the legs, generally feel as if in a loose position. One way to test the state of relaxation in this position is to lift one's hand and then let it drop of its own accord, or else have someone else do this.

TRAINING ELEMENTS

Passive Concentration.   Autogenic training proceeds most efficiently for people when they approach it with an attitude generally conceived of as passive concentration, which may best be explained by contrasting it to active concentration. The decisive difference between active and passive concentration is the attitude toward the functional results to be achieved. Passive concentration implies a casual attitude and a passivity toward the intended outcome of the autogenic exercises on that particular day. (This does not mean that there is no hope for positive results as an outcome of the exercises, but during the exercise there is no need to see results occurring.) Active concentration, on the other hand, is characterized by a concern and attention and even active efforts to try to make the result come about during that particular exercise. This attitude of active concentration often generates mild anxiety about performing well or achieving results, which is counterproductive to the overall training and should be avoided.

Autogenic training produces results over a gradual period of time. It is good practice to take the attitude, "During this particular session I really don't care whether my particular goal [such as warmth] happens. I know it will happen sometime, so I'm calm about it now." The client might be instructed to meditate on achieving passive concentration before actually going into the exercises and then, after finishing, look back to see if he or she achieved it. If not, the exercise can be viewed as a learning experience for the next time. Those who succeed can congratulate themselves and commit to trying to achieve the same attitude of passive concentration the next time.

Steady Flow of Images.   A second important element in AT is maintaining a steady flow of mental images, allowing no lapses of time to occur between repetitions. This steady flow may be provided by an "inner voice" or by visualizing the particular formulas as if they are in print or as if they are a neon sign in the mind that can be switched on and off at will. It is not particularly critical which modality or which method is used to maintain this steady flow of images other than speaking the words aloud. The form (inner voice, visual image, and so forth) that is most comfortable should be used throughout the later phases of therapy to enhance the conditioning effect.

Mental Contact.   "Mental contact" refers to putting the attention of one's mind in touch with the particular body part that is the focus of the particular formula that the client is imagining verbalizing at that time. For example, a client using the formula "my right arm is heavy" should try to imagine being mentally in touch with that arm. Some people even imagine themselves as being their arm. Whichever way works best is fine; what is important is to try to gain that mental contact over time while proceeding through the exercises.

From both experimental and clinical observations, it is clear that the functional value of these various formulas is markedly enhanced to the degree that the person not only maintains a steady flow of images but at the same time can gain mental contact with the part of the body that is the area of focus. This flow of images should be kept in pace with the formula being repeated.

Reduction of Stimuli.   AT is always most successful when external stimuli are reduced to the lowest possible level during the procedures. To the degree possible, the exercises should be practiced in a quiet room with very low lighting, if any, with all restrictive clothing (glasses, belt, girdle, or necktie, for example) loosened to a point of comfort or removed.

A further reduction of external stimuli is gained by closing the eyes. It is desirable to do this as soon as the posture is taken. A number of studies point to a functional relationship between the eye closure and more passive states of mental activity.

Preparing for the possibility of other types of external distractions is also helpful in facilitating exercises—for example, by taking the telephone off the hook so as to avoid having a call occur during the exercises. Nor should the exercise be performed when there is time pressure.

Time in Practice.   A practice period is generally made up of four or five subunits of practice. During the initial phases of autogenic therapy, each subunit of the exercises should take approximately one minute. That is, all of the formulas being worked on up to this point are practiced for approximately sixty seconds. After each subunit of the exercises, the trainee brings himself or herself back to a normal feeling by opening the eyes, flexing the arms and legs somewhat vigorously, and breathing deeply. Then he or she returns to the position chosen and carries out another subunit of the exercises, again for approximately sixty seconds. This is repeated until he or she has carried out four or five subunits to make up the practice for that day.

It is very important to practice at least once a day, if at all possible; in most situations, two times a day may be comfortable. It is best not to practice more than two times a day as this generally indicates a need to try to achieve results very quickly, and practicing much more than a couple of times a day does not seem to increase the efficiency of the exercises. After practicing the autogenic exercises for a month or so, some people feel comfortable in increasing the length of the subunits of exercises up to two to five minutes, while cutting down on the overall number of subunits of exercise. This is an individual decision.

■   The Exercises

The Overall Formula.   Most of the formulas gradually introduced into training are specific to a part of the body, but one overall formula such as, "I am at peace" or "I am calmness throughout" is interspersed throughout the repetition of the other formulas.

With this formula the mental contact is made with the body as a whole, possibly by the trainee's feeling as if he or she is in a "central core" of the body or up above the body looking down and watching it relax.

Standard Exercise 1: Heaviness.   The induction of a feeling of heaviness in the limbs is particularly conducive to overall relaxation. This exercise is carried out by the use of the following formula repeated in a steady flow while maintaining mental contact with each part: "My right arm is heavy," "My left arm is heavy," "Both arms are heavy," "My right leg is heavy," "My left leg is heavy," "Both legs are heavy," and finally, "My arms and legs are heavy." These need not always be repeated in the same sequence. Occasionally (possibly after three or four other repetitions), "I am calmness throughout" is used, while returning the mental contact to the overall body and person. After some months of practice, many trainees find that they gain a result relatively quickly by simply using the formula, "My arms and legs are heavy." But certainly in the initial stages it is important to use all of the formulas.

Standard Exercise 2: Warmth.   Just as with heaviness, the induction of warmth in most body parts induces the relaxation and restorative effect that is sought in AT. The formulas used in Standard Exercise 1 of heaviness are repeated but with *warm* substituted for *heavy*. During the initial training, these are interspersed with the formulas on heaviness—for example, "My right arm is heavy," "My right arm is warm," "My left arm is heavy," "My left arm is warm," and so forth. After some weeks of training, when the trainee notices consistent results upon repetition of the formulas, he or she can experiment with collapsing some of them and using phrases such as, "My right arm is heavy and warm," or even, "Both arms are heavy and warm."

Standard Exercise 3: Respiration.   Allowing oneself to breathe naturally is a critical step toward achieving the autogenic effect. The goal is not necessarily trying to achieve a slow and deep breathing pattern during the exercises but to let the breathing eventually take over at its own rate. The phrase used here, "My breathing just naturally happens," emphasizes that breathing happens regardless of the conscious control of the individual, which gives many trainees a sense of being in touch with the most basic forces in their body and in the world. Passive concentration is particularly important here, although most trainees find it initially difficult to avoid trying to breathe slowly and deeply. The goal, nevertheless, is to let it just happen. The mental contact in this exercise is usually with the general chest area, although some people find it helpful to allow mental contact with the overall body.

Standard Exercise 4: Abdominal Warmth.   The phraseology used in this exercise is, "My solar plexus is warm." The mental contact for this exercise is with that area approximately two to three inches below the navel. Attainment of warmth in this area effectively counteracts some of the internal disruption from anxiety and strongly furthers the autogenic aims. Many trainees find it difficult at first to visualize this area, but they gradually feel more comfortable with it and note the positive benefits when they achieve it.

Standard Exercise 5: The Cooling of the Forehead.   Whereas warmth is conducive to relaxation throughout most parts of the body, the induction of a sense of coolness is most helpful when focusing on the forehead. The phrase used in this exercise is, "My forehead is cool and smooth." The mental contact is usually made with the overall area an inch or so above the eyes up into the scalp.

The original exercises also included a training phase (and phrase that focused on the heart—"My heartbeat is calm and strong"). However, this technique is counter-productive more often than it is helpful.

In all of these exercises, trainees may occasionally note fleeting images related to the effect desired—for example, regarding the cooling of the forehead, they may fleetingly envision a cool breeze passing over the forehead. Such images can be helpful if they are not allowed to continue very long and disrupt the mental contact or the steady flow of the formulas.

A FINAL COMMENT ON AT

AT provides the benefit of being a technique clients can easily integrate into their lifestyle, similar to yoga or tai-chi. In fact, it was originally designed to be applied in this fashion. It is an effective long-term strategy to enhance immune responses, reduce situational tension, and lessen chronic anxiety.

APPENDIX D:
RELEVANT LEGAL CASES

In addition to the cases that cited and discussed in Chapter 17, there are numerous other cases that have some relevance to the practicing clinician. The following is a presentation of the major cases, important because they are either landmark cases, often older cases whose findings may now be modified to some degree, or they are more recent cases that have significant precedent value and/or present impact.

Consent and Control in Intervention

Schloendorff v. *Society of New York Hospital*—105 N.E. 92 (N.Y. 1914)
- First clear statement that informed consent requires that a client be apprised of the potential benefits and major risks of proposed treatments, as well as available alternative treatments.

Canterbury v. *Spence*—464 F.2d 772 (D.C. Cir. 1972)
- Defined the elements of modern informed consent, using the "patient criterion," i.e., what the typical patient would want to know.

Rivers v. *Katz*—495 N.E. 2d 337 (N.Y. 1986)
- Following precedent of *Rennie* v. *Klein* (1983), found a right to refuse treatment—state can only force treatment, e.g., medication, if not competent or if dangerous in the hospital.

Washington v. *Harper*—494 U.S. 210 (1990)
- Prisoners may be forced to take antipsychotic drugs, with only an institution-based due process review (as opposed to a full judicial review as required in the earlier precedent set in *Rogers* v. *Okin* [1979, 1986]), if (1) they suffer from "mental illness" and (2) are dangerous to self or others or are "gravely disabled."

Zinermon v. *Burch*—494 U.S. 113 (1990)
- Patient may have a cause of action against those who hold that person in a hospital, under a voluntary admission, when it is clear the person is incompetent to make such decisions.

Foucha v. *Louisiana*— H2 S.Ct. 1780 (1992)

- To hold an insanity acquitee who no longer manifests mental illness and is on an indefinite commitment until he or she is no longer dangerous violates the 14th Amendment's due process clause. Commitment could be continued if the person was *both* mentally ill and dangerous.

■ Privileged Communication/Confidentiality/Duty to Warn or Protect

Caesar v. *Mountanos*—542 F.2d 1064 (9th Cir. 1976)

- Ninth Circuit recognizes a constitutional right to privacy that includes a limited psychotherapist–patient privilege; recognizes the client owns the privilege and may waive the privilege.

Tarasoff v. *Regents of the University of California*—551 P.2d 334, (Cal. 1976)

- At first finds a "duty to warn" for clinicians; on appeal, amends it to a "duty to protect" identifiable third parties from dangerous clients.

In re *Zuniga*—714 F.2d 632 (6th Cir. 1983)

- Found a federal, limited common law psychotherapist–patient privilege.

Pennsylvania v. *Ritchie*—480 U.S. 39 (1987)

- Judge was allowed to subpoena a state agency's confidential mental health file, over defense objections, to decide which material would be revealed in a criminal case.

State v. *Szemple*—135 N.J. 406: 640 A. 2d 817 (1994)

- In 1975, Craig Szemple killed a 15 year old boy by gunshot. After the state had rested its case, it was asked to reopen it on basis of two alleged admissions of guilt: (1) a letter written to his wife, that her father inadvertently discovered, (2) he also admitted he killed "not one but three" to Mr. Bischof, a deacon operating as a Minister of Visitation by the Trinity Baptist Church, who also had a "certificate of organization." He in turn reported the admission to Mr. Szemple's sister and brother-in-law. By a 4-3 decision, New Jersey Supreme Court, marital privilege does not prevent disclosure, and also, that in the priest-penitent privilege, priest owns it.

■ Personal Injury

Dillon v. *Legg*—441 P.2d 912 (Cal. 1968)

- Recognized "zone of danger" concept in personal injury cases, with three criteria: (1) a close relationship to the victim, (2) close proximity to the accident, and (3) the emotional shock that is "sensory and contemporaneous" to the incident.

Molien v. *Kaiser Foundation Hospital*—616 P.2d 813 (Cal. 1980)

- Contrary to "zone of danger" concept, husband successfully sues physician who negligently misdiagnosed wife's condition as syphilis, leading to eventual divorce.

Meritor Savings Bank v. *Vinson*—477 U.S. 57 (1986)

- Found sexual harassment to be a violation of the victim's civil rights under Title VII of the Civil Rights Act.

TXO Products Corp. v. *Alliance Resources*—113 S.Ct. 2711 (1993)
- Although badly split on reasons, Supreme Court gives great latitude to states, as long as there are basic guidelines for juries, in awards of punitive damages.

Molzof v. *United States*—911 F.2d 18 (7th. Cir. 1990), rev'd 112 S.Ct. 711 (1992)
- Supreme Court rules that separate damages for loss of "enjoyment of life" are legitimate and recoverable if allowed under applicable state law. In effect, approves *Thompson* v. *National Railroad Passenger Corp.*, in which five types of damages were recognized: (1) expenses incurred, (2) pain and suffering and fright, (3) permanent injury (disability), (4) impaired earning capacity, and (5) impaired enjoyment of life. Loss of enjoyment of life was therein defined in terms of "the limitations on the person's life created by the injury," thus setting forth the distinctiveness of the loss of enjoyment of life for collecting damages.

Harris v. *Forklift Systems*—114 S.Ct. 367 (1993)
- Upheld a "hostile or abusive" standard under the "reasonable person" doctrine, unanimously holding that a person who was sexually harassed on the job need not prove she was psychologically damaged in order to recover damages, under aegis of Title VII of the 1964 Civil Rights Act, although in a later holding, *Saxton* v. *AT&T* (62 L.W. 1085 (1993)), a U.S. Appeals Court indicates seriousness or frequency must at least be established.

Child Custody

Finlay v. *Finlay*—148 N.E. 624 (N.Y. 1925)
- Firmly established the principle that custody decisions should reflect the "best interests of the child."

Painter v. *Bannister*—140 N.W. 2d 152 (Ia. 1966)
- Although involving an odd set of circumstances, it helped establish the concept of "psychological parent"; court allowed grandparents to keep custody of child over the claim of the natural father.

Santosky v. *Kramer*—455 U.S. 745 (1982)
- "Clear and convincing" is the standard of proof required to terminate parental rights.

Juvenile Proceedings

Kent v. *U.S.*—383 U.S. 541 (1966)
- Required due process in juvenile proceedings.

In re *Gault*—387 U.S. 1 (1967)
- Placed due process for juveniles within the 14th Amendment, requires (1) notice of charges, (2) right to have an attorney, (3) cross-examination and confrontation of witnesses, and (4) no self-incrimination.

McKeiver v. *Pennsylvania*—403 U.S. 528 (1970)
- Juvenile defendants have no constitutional right to a jury trial, although states may grant that right.

Parham v. *J. R.*—442 U.S. 584 (1979)

- As noted earlier, held that parents should be allowed to maintain a substantial, if not dominant, role in the decision to voluntarily admit their child to a mental hospital, absent a finding of abuse or neglect.

Stanford v. *Kentucky*—492 U.S. 937 (1989)

- States may execute children who were over 16 (i.e., in the disputed 16–18-year age range) when they committed the crime.

DeShaney v. *Winnebago County*—489 U.S. 189 (1989)

- There is no liability on a state for the failure of its child protective services agencies to protect a child and prevent the child's death at the hands of the child's parents, even when abuse has been repeatedly reported.

Maryland v. *Craig*—490 U.S. 836 (1990): *on remand, Craig* v. *Maryland*, 588 A.2d 328 (1991)

- Closed-circuit televised testimony of child abuse victim (with defense attorney present, but alleged perpetrator only watching televised testimony) is held to be constitutional in some circumstances.

White v. *Illinois*—112 U.S. 736 (1992)

- Supreme Court rules that defendants charged with molesting children have no *absolute* right to confront their young accusers at trial, thus admitting "hearsay" evidence.

■ Addictions

Robinson v. *California*—370 U.S. 660 (1962)

- It is unconstitutional to convict based on the "status" of being addicted.

Powell v. *Texas*—392 U.S. 514 (1968)

- May convict on behaviors stemming from addiction.

Traynor v. *Turnage*—485 U.S. 535 (1988)

- VA definition of primary alcoholism, i.e., defined as a type of alcoholism that is not the result of other psychological disorder, is "willful misconduct."

■ Professional Issues

Barefoot v. *Estelle*—463 U.S. 880 (1983)

- Mental health professional is allowed to testify to the dangerousness of the defendant in a capital case, even though the professional has not examined the defendant.

Shapero v. *Kentucky Bar Assoc.*—486 U.S. 466 (1988)

- Supreme Court recognizes right of attorneys (and by implication, other professional groups) to aggressively advertise to specific groups.

Edenfield v. *Fane*—113 S.Ct. 1792 (1993)

- Is a violation of 1st Amendment for a state or profession (in this case, Florida Board of Accountancy) to limit or prohibit direct, in-person and telephone solicitation of clients; a contrast to *Obralik* v. *Ohio State Bar Assoc.*, 436 U.S. 447 (1978) where such solicitation was forbidden for attorneys. It is likely that mental health professionals would come under *Obralik* (see 12/27/92 consent decree of Federal Trade Comm. with American Psychological Association that would allow virtually any type of advertising except direct, in-person, unwanted solicitation).

West v. *Atkins*—467 U.S. 42 (1988)

- Contractual mental health professionals, who are not full-time employees of the state, can be sued, while full-time employees performing the same tasks may be protected from suit.

Blue Shield of Virginia v. *McCready*—457 U.S. 465 (1982)

- Antitrust laws are successfully employed by mental health professionals, in this case psychologists, against practices limiting reimbursement through physicians.

Patrick v. *Burget*—486 U.S. 94 (1988)

- Professional peer review committees are not exempt from antitrust laws, e.g., regarding hospital privileges.

Supreme Court of Virginia v. *Friedman*—487 U.S. 59 (1988)

- A state may not require a professional to be a state resident to be admitted to practice by reciprocity.

Peel v. *Attorney Registration and Disciplinary Commission*—469 U.S. 91 (1990)

- State cannot prohibit professionals from advertising certification by a legitimate private organization, even if not the "best" or "highest" (or, in some cases, worth anything at all) certification available; permits lawyers and mental health professionals to claim to be "certified" or "boarded" by any "qualified" organization.

West Virginia University Hospital v. *Casey*—499 U.S. 83 (1991) (superseded by statute)

- Held that the award of attorney fees does not include the cost of expert witness fees the prevailing party paid in pursuing its claim.

Austin v. *United States*—113 S.Ct. 2801 (1993)

- Supreme Court gives great latitude to federal agencies, with limited review, in setting reimbursement policies to health care providers under Medicare, a probable prelude to its approach in universal health care.

■ ## Suicide

Meier v. *Ross General Hospital*—445 P.2d 519 (1968)

- Firmly established the basic duty of therapists to exercise adequate care and skill in diagnosing suicidality; it is a duty to protect the client from his or her own actions.

Dinnerstein v. *State*—486 F.2d 34 (2d Cir. 1973)

- Clearly establishes principle that clinician is held liable if treatment plan overlooks or neglects the patient's suicidal tendencies.

Bellah v. *Greenson*—146 Cal. Rptr. 535 (1st Dist. 1978)

- There is no *"Tarasoff* duty to warn" significant others of possible suicidality of client, especially as this refers to an outpatient setting.

■ Hypnosis

State v. *Hurd*—432 A.2d 86 (N.J. 1981)

- Establishes the still influential "Hurd rules" or "Orne criteria" for reviewing hypnotically refreshed testimony: (1) conducted by licensed psychiatrist or psychologist, (2) independent of prosecutor or defense, (3) prior information to hypnotist put in writing, (4) facts of case prior to hypnosis obtained and recorded, (5) session recorded (video desirable, not necessary), (6) only subject and hypnotist present at pre-sessions, session itself, and debriefing.

People v. *Shirley*—641 P.2d 775 (Cal. 1982)

- Applies a sweeping rule of inadmissibility of hypnotically refreshed testimony in California.

Rock v. *Arkansas*—483 U.S. 44 (1987)

- Supreme Court rules it is a violation of constitutional rights to arbitrarily exclude testimony of the *accused* about memories recalled during hypnosis in *criminal* cases.

■ Miscellaneous

Frye v. *United States*—295 F. 1013 (D.C. Cir. 1923)

- Procedure has to be generally accepted in the scientific community to be allowed into evidence.

Daubert v. *Merrell Dow Pharmaceuticals*—113 S.Ct. 2786 (1993)

- Overturns seventy years of "Frye rule" precedent (see preceding); supports Federal Rules of Evidence (1987) in that an expert need only have scientific evidence that will assist the trier of fact to understand or determine a fact in issue. Criteria courts should use are (1) used some accepted scientific methodology, (2) is subject to peer review and publication, (3) known or potential error rate still justifies use, (4) has achieved a degree of scientific community acceptance.

Landeros v. *Flood*—551 P.2d 389, 69 (Cal. 1976)

- Establishes basis for liability for failure to report child abuse.

State v. *Huss*—506 N.W.2d 290 (Minn. 1993)

- The Supreme Court of Minnesota overturns a father's conviction for criminal sexual assault, stating that the child's sex abuse allegations against her father were "improperly influenced" by "a highly suggestive book on sexual abuse," i.e., *Sometimes It's OK to Tell Secrets.*

Youngberg v. *Romeo*—457 U.S. 307 (1982)

- State has the obligation to provide the mentally retarded with "minimal services" that permit (1) the least restraint possible and (2) basic safety.

Wyatt v. *Stickney*—325 F.Supp. 781 (M.D. Ala. 1971), later preceding 344 F.Supp. 387 (M.D. Ala. 1972) affd in part, 503 F.2d 1305 (5th Cir. 1974) (*sub mom Wyatt* v. *Aderholt*)

- The most significant effort to define the right to treatment.

Griggs v. *Duke Power Co.*—401 U.S. 424 (1971)

- Tests that have the effect of discriminating are illegal if they are not directly relevant to measurement of job capability.

Detroit Edison v. *NLRB*—440 U.S. 401 (1979)

- The Supreme Court rules that privacy interests of test takers is a sufficient privacy interest to bar the union's requested access to scores. But the Court ignores the arguments that access to the test scores would ruin the validity of the tests, leading to the "truth in testing" movement on the legislative front.

Payne v. *Tennessee*—501 U.S. 808 (1991)

- The Supreme Court reversed its earlier decisions and held that states may present victim impact statements to juries in death penalty cases.

Cowan v. *State*—(1994) 112 S. Ct. 1371 (1994)

- Denied certiori in Montana Sup. Ct. decision in *State* v. *Cowan* (861 P.2d 869 (Mont. 1993) that abolition of the insanity defense violated 8th and 14th Amendments. Montana does have a mens rea requirement, but uses terms like "Knowingly", "purposefully," "with malice," and defendant could act purposefully and knowingly, and still not appreciate criminality of conduct nor be able to conform his behavior.

Farmer v. *Brennan*—62 USLW 4446 (1994)

- Supported the potential liability of prison officials, supporting an "deliberate indifference" standard, rather than a "reckless" standard, in denying humane conditions by failing to take reasonable measures to protect a transsexual inmate who was raped by fellow prisoners.

BIBLIOGRAPHY

Abel, G., and Rouleau, J. (1990). "Male Sex Offenders." In M. Thase, B. Edelstein, and M. Herson, Eds. *Handbook of Outpatient Treatment of Adults.* New York: Plenum.

Abel, G., Rouleau, J., and Cunningham-Rathner, J. (1986). "Sexually Aggressive Behavior." In W. Curran, A. L. McGarry, and S. Shah, Eds. *Forensic Psychiatry and Psychology.* Philadelphia: Davis.

Adler, M. (1988). "Milieu Therapy." In J. Lion, W. Adler, and W. Webb, Eds. *Modern Hospital Psychiatry.* New York: Norton.

Aganoff, J., and Boyle, G. (1994). "Aerobic Exercise, Mood States and Menstrual Cycle Symptoms." *Journal of Psychosomatic Research, 38,* 183–192.

Agras, W. (1987). *Eating Disorders.* New York: Pergamon Press.

Albert, S., Fox, H., and Kahn, M. (1980). "Faking Psychosis on the Rorschach: Can Expert Judges Detect Malingering?" *Journal of Personality Assessment, 44,* 115–119.

Allgulander, C., and Lavonri, P. (1991). "Excess Mortality among 3302 Patients with 'Pure' Anxiety Neurosis." *Archives of General Psychiatry, 48,* 599–602.

Allison, J., Blatt, S., and Zimet, C. (1988). *The Interpretation of Psychological Tests.* New York: Hemisphere.

American Association on Mental Retardation (1993). *Mental Retardation: Definition, Classification, and Systems of Support.* Annapolis Junction, MD: AAMR.

American Psychiatric Association (1952). *Diagnostic and Statistical Manual of Mental Disorders (DSM-I),* 1st ed. Washington, DC: APA.

_____ (1968). *Diagnostic and Statistical Manual of Mental Disorders (DSM-II),* 2d ed. Washington, DC: APA.

_____ (1980). *Diagnostic and Statistical Manual of Mental Disorders (DSM-III),* 3d ed. Washington, DC: APA.

_____ (1987). *Diagnostic and Statistical Manual of Mental Disorders (DSM-III-R),* 3d ed., rev. Washington, DC: APA.

_____ (1994). *Diagnostic and Statistical Manual of Mental Disorders (DSM-IV),* 4th ed. Washington, DC: APA.

Anastasi, A. (1987). *Psychological Testing,* 6th ed. New York: Macmillan.

Anderson, R. (1994). *Practitioner's Guide to Clinical Neuropsychology.* New York: Plenum.

Anderson, W., and Bauer, B. (1985). "Clients with MMPI High D-Pd." *Journal of Clinical Psychology, 41,* 181–188.

Apter, A., Kotler, M., Sevy, S., et al. (1991). "Correlates of Risk of Suicide in Violent and Nonviolent Psychiatric Patients." *The American Journal of Psychiatry, 148,* 883–887.

Archer, R. (1987). *Using the MMPI with Adolescents.* Hillsdale, NJ: Erlbaum.

_____ (1992). *MMPI-A: Assessing Adolescent Psychopathology.* Hillsdale, NJ: Erlbaum.

Armentrout, J., and Hauer, A. (1978). "MMPI's of Rapists of Adults, Rapists of Children and Non-Rapist Sex Offenders." *Journal of Clinical Psychology, 34,* 330–332.

Aronow, E., and Reznikoff, M. (1976). *Rorschach Content Interpretation.* New York: Grune & Stratton.

Bagby, R., Gillis, J., Toner, B., and Goldberg, J. (1991). "Detecting Fake-Good and Fake-Bad Responding on the Millon Clinical Multiaxial Inventory-II." *Psychological Assessment, 3,* 496–498.

Barbaree, H., Marshall, W., and Lanthier, R. (1979). "Deviant Sexual Arousal in the Rapist." *Behavior Research and Therapy, 17,* 215–222.

Barnett, P., and Gotlib, I. (1988). "Psychological Functioning and Depression." *Psychological Bulletin, 104,* 97–126.

Barrett v. *United States, 377* A.2d 62 (1977).

Barrett, C., and Meyer, R. (1992). "Cognitive Behavioral Therapy for Inpatient Alcoholics." In J. Wright, A. Beck, M. Thase, and J. Ludgate, Eds. *Inpatient Cognitive Therapy.* New York: Guilford.

Barsky, A., Wood, C., Barnett, M., and Cleary, P. (1994). "Histories of Childhood Trauma in Adult Hypochondriacal Patients." *The American Journal of Psychiatry, 151,* 397–401.

Baucom, D., and Epstein, N. (1990). *Cognitive-Behavioral Marital Therapy.* New York: Brunner/Mazel.

Bauer, M., Colabrese, J., Dunner, D., Post, R., et al. (1994). "Multisite Data Reanalysis of the Validity of Rapid Cycling as a Course Modifier for Bipolar Disorder in DSM-IV." *The American Journal of Psychiatry, 151,* 506–515.

Beaber, R., Marston, A., Michelli, J., and Mills, M. (1985). "A Brief Test for Measuring Malingering in Schizophrenic Individuals." *The American Journal of Psychiatry, 142,* 1478–1481.

Beck, A. (1976). *Cognitive Therapy and the Emotional Disorders.* New York: International Universities Press.

Beck, A., Freeman, A., and Associates (1990). *Cognitive Therapy of Personality Disorders.* New York: Guilford.

Beck, A., Steer, R., Kovacs, M., and Garrison, B. (1983). "Hopelessness and Eventual Suicide: A 10-Year Prospective Study of Patients Hospitalized with Suicidal Ideation." *American Journal of Psychiatry, 142,* 559–563.

Beck, A., Wright, F., Newman, C., and Liese, B. (1994). *Cognitive Therapy of Substance Abuse.* New York: Guilford.

Beck, S., and Beck, A. (1978). *Rorschach's Test: I. 1 Gradients in Mental Disorder. Third Edition of II. A Variety of Personality Pictures.* New York: Grune & Stratton.

Beck, S., and Molish, H. (1952). *Rorschach's Test: Advances in Interpretation,* New York: Grune & Stratton.

Bedrosian, R., and Bozicas, G. (1994). *Treating Family of Origin Problems.* New York: Guilford.

Bell, I. (1994). "Somatization Disorder." *Biological Psychiatry, 35,* 81–83.

Bellak, J. (1993). *The T.A.T., C.A.T. and S.A.T. in Clinical Use,* 6th ed. Orlando, FL: Grune & Stratton.

Belli, M. (1979). "Transsexual Surgery: A New Tort." *Journal of Family Law, 17*, 487–504.

Bender, L. (1938). *A Visual Motor Gestalt Test and Its Clinical Use.* New York: American Orthopsychiatric Association.

Benedikt, R., and Kolb, L. (1986). "Preliminary Findings on Chronic Pain and Post-Traumatic Stress Disorder." *American Journal of Psychiatry, 143*, 908–910.

Benjamin, L. (1993). *Interpersonal Diagnosis and Treatment of Personality Disorders.* New York: Guilford.

Ben-Porath, Y. (1994). "Assessment of the Personality Disorders with the MMPI-2." Kentucky Conference on Advanced Studies in Psychopathology. Lexington: University of Kentucky.

Ben-Porath, Y., and Butcher, J. (1989). "The Comparability of MMPI and MMPI-2 Scales and Profiles. Psychological Assessment." *A Journal of Consulting and Clinical Psychology, 1*, 345–347.

Ben-Porath, Y., Hostetler, K., Butcher, J., and Graham, J. (1989). "New Subscales for the MMPI-2 Social Introversion Scale." *Psychological Assessment, 1*, 169–174.

Benton, A. (1980). "The Neuropsychology of Facial Recognition." *American Psychologist, 35*, 176–186.

Berk, L. (1989). *Child Development: Theory, Research and Applications.* Needham Heights, MA: Allyn and Bacon.

Berlin, F., Malin, M., and Dean, S. (1991). "Effects of Statutes Requiring Psychiatrists to Report Suspected Sexual Abuse of Children." *American Journal of Psychiatry, 148*, 449–455.

Berry, D., Wetter, M., Baer, R., Widiger, T., et al. (1991). "Detection of Random Responding on the MMPI-2: Utility of F, Back F, and VRIN Scales." *Psychological Assessment, 3*, 418–423.

Beutler, L., Karacan, I., Anch, M., Salis, P., Scott, F., Williams, R. (1975). "MMPI and MIT Discriminators of Biogenic and Psychogenic Impotence." *Journal of Consulting and Clinical Psychology, 43*, 899-908.

Blatt, S., Baker, B., and Weiss, J. (1970). "Wechsler Object Assembly Subtest and Bodily Concern." *Journal of Consulting and Clinical Psychology, 34*, 269–274.

Bloom, B. (1992). *Planned Short-Term Psychotherapy.* Needham Heights, MA: Allyn and Bacon.

Bloom-Feshbach, J., and Bloom-Feshbach, S. (1987). *The Psychology of Separation and Loss.* San Francisco: Jossey-Bass.

Blouin, A., Blouin, J., Aubin, P., Carter, J., et al. (1992). "Seasonal Patterns of Bulimia Nervosa." *American Journal of Psychiatry, 149*, 73–81.

Bongar, B. (1991). *The Suicidal Patient.* Washington, DC: American Psychological Association.

Bongar, B., and Beutler, L., Eds. (1995). *Comprehensive Textbook of Psychotherapy.* New York: Oxford University Press.

Borthwick-Duffy, S. (1994). "Epidemiology and Prevalence of Psychopathology in People with Mental Retardation." *Journal of Clinical and Consulting Psychology, 62*, 17–27.

Borum, R., and Stock, H. V. (1993). "Detection of Detection in Law Enforcement Applicants." *Law and Human Behavior, 17*, 157–166.

Boyer, J. (1990). "Fatal Attraction: The Borderline Personality and Psychotherapy." *National Register Report, 16(2)*, 5–7.

Breier, A., Buchanan, R., Kirkpatrick, B., Davis, O., et al. (1994). "Effects of Clozapine on Positive and Negative Symptoms in Outpatients with Schizophrenia." *The American Journal of Psychiatry, 151*, 20–26.

Brodsky, S. (1991). *Testifying in Court.* Washington, DC: American Psychological Association.

Brown, F., Ed. (1991). *Reweaving the Family Tapestry.* New York: Norton.

Bruch, H., Czyzewski, D., and Suhr, M. (1988). *Conversations with Anorexics.* New York: Basic Books.

Bryer, J., Martines, K., and Dignan, M. (1990). "MCMI Alcohol Abuse Scales and the Identification of Substance Abuse Patients." *Psychological Assessment, 2*, 438–441.

Buchanan v. *Kentucky,* 483 U.S. 402 (1987).

Buckley, P., and Meltzer, H. (1995). "Treatment of schizophrenia." In A. Schatzberg and C. Nemeroff (Eds.) *Textbook of Psychiatry.* Washington, D.C.: American Psychiatric Press.

Bull, R., and Rumsey, N. (1988). *The Social Psychology of Facial Appearance.* New York: Springer-Verlag.

Burke, H., and Mayer, S. (1985). "The MMPI and the PTSD in Vietnam Era Veterans." *Journal of Clinical Psychology, 41*, 152–156.

Burrows, G. (1992). "Long-term Clinical Management of Depressive Disorders." *Journal of Clinical Psychiatry, 53* (Supplement), 32–35.

Butcher, J., Ed. (1979). *New Developments in the Use of the MMPI.* Minneapolis: University of Minnesota Press.

Butcher, J. (1987). *Computerized Psychological Assessment.* New York: Basic Books.

_____ (1990). *MMPI-2 in Psychological Treatment.* New York: Oxford University Press.

_____ Ed. (1995). *Clinical Personality Assessment.* New York: Oxford University Press.

Butcher, J., and Graham, J. (1988). "Clinical Applications of the MMPI." Workshop. February 5–6, 1988, Cincinnati, OH.

Butcher, J., Graham, J., Williams, C., and Ben-Porath, Y. (1990). *Development and Use of the MMPI-2 Content Scales.* Minneapolis: University of Minnesota Press.

Butcher, J., and Williams, C. (1992). *Essentials of MMPI–2 and MMPI–A.* Minneapolis: University of Minnesota.

Calhoun, K., and Atkeson, B. (1991). *Treating Rape Victims.* Elmsford, NY: Pergamon Press.

Cantwell, D., and Baker, L. (1987). *Developmental Speech and Language Disorders.* New York: Guilford.

Caplan, B. (1987). "Assessment of Unilateral Neglect: A New Reading Test." *Journal of Clinical and Experimental Neuropsychology, 9*, 359–364.

Carbonell, J., Megargee, E., and Moorhead, K. (1984). "Predicting Prison Adjustment with Structured Personality Inventories." *Journal of Consulting and Clinical Psychology, 52*, 280–294.

Cargonello, J., and Gurekas, R. (1988). "The WAIS-SAM: A Comprehensive Administrative Model of Modified WAIS Procedures." *Journal of Clinical Psychology, 44*, 266–270.

Carson, R. (1969). "Interpretative Manual to the MMPI." In J. Butcher, Ed. *MMPI: Research Developments and Clinical Applications.* New York: McGraw-Hill.

Cassini, J., and Workman, D. (1992). "The Detection of Malingering and Deception with a Short Form of the MMPI-2 Based on L, F, and K Scales." *Journal of Clinical Psychology, 48,* 54–63.

Cattell, H. (1989). *The 16 PF: Personality in Depth.* Champaign, IL: IPAT.

_____ (1993). "The Development of the Fifth Edition of the the 16 PF." American Psychological Association Annual Meeting, Toronto.

Cattell, R. (1965). *The Scientific Analysis of Personality.* Chicago: Aldine.

_____ (1973). *Personality and Mood by Questionnaire.* San Francisco: Jossey-Bass.

_____ (1979). *Personality and Learning Theory,* vol. 2: *The Structure of Personality in Its Environment.* New York: Springer.

_____ (1986). *Psychotherapy by Structural Learning.* New York: Springer.

Cattell, R., Eber, H., and Tatsuoka, M. (1970). *Handbook for the Sixteen Personality Factors Questionnaire.* Champaign, IL: IPAT.

Cattell, R., and Warburton, F. (1967). *Objective Personality and Motivation Tests.* Champaign: University of Illinois Press.

Cautela, J., and Wall, C. (1980). "Covert Conditioning in Clinical Practice." In A. Goldstein and E. Foa, Eds. *Handbook of Behavioral Interventions.* New York: Wiley.

Chambless, D. (1985). "The Relationship of Severity of Agoraphobia to Associated Psychopathology." *Behavior Research and Therapy, 23,* 305–310.

Chambless, D., Sultan, F., Stern, T., O'Neill, C., et al. (1984). "Effect of Pubococcygeal Exercise on Coital Orgasm in Women." *Journal of Consulting and Clinical Psychology, 52,* 114–118.

Charney, D., Miller, H., Licinio, J., and Salomon, R. (1995). "Treatment of Depression." In A. Schatzberg and C. Nemeroff, Eds., *Textbook of Psychiatry.* Washington, DC: American Psychiatric Press.

Cheek, D. (1965). "Emotional Factors in Persistent Pain States." *American Journal of Clinical Hypnosis, 9,* 100–101.

Chiles, J., and Strosahl, K. (1995). *The Suicide Patient.* Washington, DC: American Psychiatric Press.

Choca, J., Shanley, L., and Denburg, E. (1992). *Interpretative Guide to the Millon Clinical Multiaxial Inventory.* Washington, DC: American Psychological Association.

Christenson, G., Mackenzie, T., and Mitchell, J. (1991). "Characteristics of 60 Adult Chronic Hair Pullers." *American Journal of Psychiatry, 148,* 365–370.

Ciraulo, D., and Shader, R. (1991). *Clinical Manual of Chemical Dependence.* Washington, DC: American Psychiatric Press.

Clark, C. (1988). "Diminished Capacity in Michigan: Factors Associated with Forensic Evaluation Referrals." Mid-Winter Meeting, American Psychology-Law Society, Miami Beach, FL.

Clavelle, P. (1992). "Clinician's Perceptions of the Comparability of the MMPI and MMPI–2." *Psychological Assessment, 4,* 466–472.

Cleckley, H. (1964). *The Mask of Sanity,* 4th ed. St. Louis, MO: Mosby.

Cody, M. (1991). Personal communication.

Cohen, D. (1994). *Out of the Blue: Depression and Human Nature.* New York: Norton.

Cohen, S., Kessler, R., and Gordon, L. (1995). *Measuring Stress.* New York: Oxford University Press.

Cohen, M., Seghorn, T., and Calmas, W. (1969). "Sociometric Study of Sex Offenders." *Journal of Abnormal Psychology, 74,* 249–255.

Colligan, R., Morey, L., and Offord, K. (1994). "The MMPI/MMPI-2 Personality Disorder Scales: Contemporary Norms for Adults and Adolescents." *Journal of Clinical Psychology, 50,* 168–200.

Colligan, R., Osborne, D., Swenson, W., and Offord, K. (1983). *The MMPI: A Contemporary Normative Study.* New York: Praeger.

Colorado v. *Connelly,* 479 U.S. 157 (1986).

Conley, J. (1981). "An MMPI Typology of Male Alcoholics: Admission, Discharge, and Outcome Data." *Journal of Personality Assessment, 45,* 33–39.

Conn, S., and Rieke, M. (Eds.) (1994). *The 16PF Fifth Edition Technical Manual.* Champaign, IL: IPAT.

Connell, D., and Meyer, R. (1992). "Differential Validity of the SIRS and M Test." Unpublished paper.

Cooper, S., Perry, J., and Arnow, D. (1988). "An Empirical Approach to the Study of Defense Mechanisms: Reliability and Validity of Rorschach Defense Scales." *Journal of Personality Assessment, 52,* 187–203.

Corney, R., and Stanton, R. (1991). "A Survey of 658 Women Who Report Symptoms of PMS." *Journal of Psychosomatic Research, 35,* 471–482.

Costa, P., and Widiger, T. (Eds.) (1994). *Personality Disorders and the 5 Factor Model of Personality.* Washington, DC.

Costello, R. (1978). "Empirical Derivation of a Partial Personality Typology of Alcoholics." *Journal of Studies of Alcoholism, 39,* 1258–1266.

Cox, D. (1980). "Exhibitionism: An Overview." In D. Cox and R. Daitzman, Eds., *Exhibitionism.* New York: Garland.

Cox, D., and Meyer, R. (1978). "Behavioral Treatment Parameters with Primary Dysmenorrhea." *Journal of Behavioral Medicine, 1,* 297–310.

Craig, R. (1993). "Contemporary Trends in Substance Abuse." *Professional Psychology, 24,* 182–189.

———— (Ed.) (1993) *The Millon Clinical Multiaxial Inventory.* Hillsdale, NJ: Erlbaum.

Craig, R., Verinis, J., Wexler, S. (1985). "Personality Characteristics of Drug Addicts and Alcoholics on the Millon Clinical Multiaxial Inventory." *Journal of Personality Assessment, 49,* 156–160.

Craigie, F., and Ross, S. (1980). "The Use of a Videotape Pre-Treatment Training Program to Encourage Treatment-Seeking among Alcoholic Detoxification Patients." *Behavior Therapy, 11,* 141–147.

Crisp, A., Burns, T., and Bhat, A. (1986). "Primary Anorexia Nervosa in the Male and Female." *British Journal of Medical Psychology, 59,* 123–132.

Cromwell, R., and Synder, C. (Eds.) (1993). *Schizophrenia: Origins, Processes, Treatment and Outcomes.* New York: Oxford University Press.

Dahlstrom, W., and Dahlstrom, L., Eds. (1980). *Basic Readings on the MMPI.* Minneapolis: University of Minnesota Press.

Dahlstrom, W., Lachar, D., and Dahlstrom, L. (1986). *MMPI Patterns of American Minorities.* Minneapolis: University of Minnesota Press.

Dahlstrom, W., and Welsh, G. (1980). *An MMPI Handbook: A Guide to Clinical Practice and Research.* Minneapolis: University of Minnesota Press.

Dahlstrom, W., Welsh, G., and Dahlstrom, L. (1972). *An MMPI Handbook,* vol. 1: *Clinical Interpretation.* Minneapolis: University of Minnesota Press.

Dalack, G., Glassman, A., and Covey, L. (1993). "Nicotine use." In D. Dunner, Ed. *Current Psychiatric Therapy.* Philadelphia: Saunders.

Daldin, H. (1985). "Faking Good and Faking Bad on the Personality Inventory for Children-Revised, Shortened Format." *Journal of Consulting and Clinical Psychology, 53,* 561–563.

Dangel, R., and Polster, R. (1986). *Teaching Child Management Skills.* New York: Pergamon Press.

Daniel M'Naghten's Case, 8 Eng. Rep. 718 (1843).

Davis, K., and Sines, J. (1971). "An Antisocial Behavior Pattern Associated with a Specific MMPI Profile." *Journal of Consulting and Clinical Psychology, 36,* 229–234.

Dawood, M. (1985). "Premenstrual Tension Syndrome." *Obstetrics and Gynecology Annual, 14,* 328–343.

Dinwiddie, S., North, C., and Yutzy, S. (1993). "Multiple Personality Disorder: Scientific and Medicolegal Issues." *Bulletin of the American Academy of Psychiatry and the Law, 21(1),* 69–79.

Doerr, H., and Carlin, A. (Eds.) (1992). *Forensic Neuropsychology.* New York: Guilford.

Donnelly, E., Murphy, D., Waldaman, I., and Reynolds, T. (1976). "MMPI Differences Between Unipolar and Bipolar Depressed Subjects: A Replication." *Journal of Clinical Psychology, 32,* 610–612.

Duncan, M., Bregman, J., Weller, E., and Weller, R. (1995). "Treatment of Childhood and Adolescent Disorders." In A. Schatzberg and C. Nemeroff, Eds., *Textbook of Psychopharmacology.* Washington, DC: American Psychiatric Press.

Dunn, G. (1992). "Multiple Personality Disorder." *Professional Psychology: Research and Practice, 23,* 18–23.

DuPaul, G., Guevremont, D., and Barkley, R. (1991). "Attention Deficit-Hyperactivity Disorder in Adolescence." *Clinical Psychology Review, 11,* 231–245.

Durham v. *U.S.,* 214 F.2d 862 D.C. Cir (1954).

Dusky v. *U.S.,* 362 U.S. 402 (1960).

Eber, H. (1975). Personal communication.

_____ (1987). Personal communication.

Edell, W. (1987). "Relationship of Borderline Syndrome Disorders to Early Schizophrenia on the MMPI." *Journal of Clinical Psychology, 43,* 163–174.

Edinger, J. (1979). "Cross-Validation of the Megargee MMPI Typology for Prisoners." *Journal of Consulting and Clinical Psychology, 47,* 234–242.

Eichelman, B. (1988) "Toward a Rational Pharmacotherapy for Aggressive and Violent Behavior." *Hospital and Community Psychiatry 39,* 31–39.

Ekman, P. (1985). *Telling Lies.* New York: Norton.

Ekman, P., and O'Sullivan, M. (1991). "Who Can Catch a Liar?" *American Psychologist, 46,* 913–920.

Ellis, A. (1992). "Group Rational-Emotive and Cognitive-Behavior Therapy." *International Journal of Group Psychotherapy, 42,* 63–80.

Ellis, A., and Dryden, W. (1987). *The Practice of Rational-Emotive Therapy.* New York: Springer.

Ellsworth, R., Collins, J., Casey, N., Schoonover, R., et al. (1979). "Some Characteristics of Effective Psychiatric Treatment Programs." *Journal of Consulting and Clinical Psychology, 47,* 799–817.

Engleland, B., Erickson, M., Butcher, J., and Ben-Porath, Y. (1991). "MMPI-2 Profiles of Women at Risk for Child Abuse." *Journal of Personality Assessment, 57,* 254–263.

Erickson, W., Luxemberg, M., Walbek, N., and Seely, N. (1987). "Frequency of MMPI Two-Point Code Types among Sex Offenders." *Journal of Consulting and Clinical Psychology, 55,* 566–570.

Exner, J. (1974). *The Rorschach: A Comprehensive System,* vol. 1. New York: Wiley.

_____ (1978). *The Rorschach: A Comprehensive System,* vol. 2: *Current Research and Advanced Interpretation.* New York: Wiley.

——— (1988). *Rorschach: A Comprehensive System: Assessment of Personality and Psychopathology,* 2d Ed. New York: Wiley.

_____ (1993). *The Rorschach: A Comprehensive System,* vol. 1, 3d ed. New York: Wiley.

Eysenck, H. (1985). "Incubation Theory of Fear/Anxiety." In S. Riess and R. Bootzin, Eds., *Theoretical Issues in Behavior Therapy.* Orlando, FL: Academic Press.

Fabian, M., and Parsons, O. (1983). "Differential Improvement of Cognitive Functions in Recovering Alcoholic Women." *Journal of Abnormal Psychology, 92,* 87–95.

Fawcett, J. (1992). "Suicide Risk Factors in Depressive Disorders and in Panic Disorder." *Journal of Clinical Psychiatry, 53* (Suppl.), 9–13.

Fedora, O., Reddon, J., Morrison, J., Fedora S., et al., (1992). *Archives of Sexual Behavior, 21,* 1–16.

Feinberg, J., and McIlvried, E. (1991). "WAIS-R Intrasubtest Scatter in a Chronic Schizophrenic Population." *Journal of Clinical Psychology, 47,* 327–335.

Fenton, W., and McGlashan, T. (1991). "Natural History of Schizophrenia Subtypes." *Archives of General Psychiatry, 48,* 978–986.

Fersch, E. (1980). *Psychology and Psychiatry and Courts and Corrections.* New York: Wiley.

Finkelhor, D. (1985). *Child Sexual Abuse.* New York: Free Press.

Finkelhor, D., and Dziuba-Leatherman. (1994). "Victimization of Children." *American Psychologist, 49,* 173–183.

Fjordback, T. (1985). "Clinical Correlates of High Lie Scale Elevations among Forensic Patients." *Journal of Personality Assessment, 49,* 252–255.

Fleming, M., Cohen, D., Salt, P., Jones, D., and Jenkins, S. (1981). "A Study of Pre- and Postsurgical Transsexuals: MMPI Characteristics." *Archives of Sexual Behavior, 10,* 161–170.

Foa, E., and Kozak, M. (1986). "Emotional Processing of Fear: Exposure to Corrective Information." *Psychological Bulletin, 99,* 20–35.

Ford v. *Wainwright,* 477 U.S. 399 (1986).

Forgione, A. (1976). "Instrumentation and Techniques. The Use of Mannequins in the Behavioral Assessment of Child Molesters: Two Case Reports." *Behavior Therapy, 7,* 678–685.

Fornari, V., Kent, J., Kabo, L., and Goodman, B. (1994). "Anorexia Nervosa: Thirty Something." *Journal of Substance Abuse Treatment, 11,* 45–54.

Fowler, R. (1981). *Advanced Interpretation of the MMPI.* Guadaloupe, French W.I.: SEPA Workshops.

Freeman, C. (1991). "A Practical Guide to the Treatment of Bulimia Nervosa." *Journal of Psychosomatic Research, 35,* 41–49.

Friedman, M., and Brownell, K. (1995). "Psychological Correlates of Obesity." *Psychological Bulletin, 117,* 3–20.

Friedrich, W., Ed. (1991). *Casebook of Sexual Abuse Treatment.* New York: Norton.

Fuld, P. (1984). "Test Profile of Cholinergic Dysfunction and of Alzheimer-type Dementia." *Journal of Clinical Neuropsychology, 6,* 388–392.

Gacono, C., and Meloy, J. (1994). *The Rorschach Assessment of Aggressive and Psychopathic Personalities.* Hillsdale, NJ: Erlbaum.

Ganellan, R., Wasliw, G., Haywood, T., and Grossman, L. (1993). "Can Psychosis Be Malingered on the Rorschach?" American Psychological Association Convention, Toronto.

Garb, H. (1992). "The Debate Over the Use of Computer-based Test Reports." *The Clinical Psychologist, 45,* 95–100.

Gass, C. (1991a). "Emotional Variables and Neuropsychological Test Performance." *Journal of Clinical Psychology, 47,* 153–157.

_____ (1991b). "MMPI-2 Interpretation and Closed Head Injury: A Correction Factor." *Psychological Assessment, 3,* 27–31.

_____ (1992). Personal communication.

_____ (1994). Personal communication.

Gass, C., and Russell, E. (1986). "MMPI Correlates of Lateralized Cerebral Lesions and Aphasic Deficits." *Journal of Consulting and Clinical Psychology, 54,* 359–363.

_____ (1991). "MMPI Profiles of Closed Head Trauma Patients: Impact of Neurologic Complaints." *Journal of Clinical Psychology, 47,* 253–260.

Geen, R. (1990). *Human Aggression.* Pacific Grove, CA: Brooks/Cole.

Gentry, S., and Meyer, R. (1991). "A Validation Study of the MMPI-2 Sex Role Scales: An Analysis of the GM, GF, and MF Scales." Presented to Annual Convention of American Psychological Association, San Francisco.

Gilberstadt, H., and Duker, J. (1965). *A Handbook for Clinical and Actuarial MMPI Interpretation.* Philadelphia: Saunders.

Gilbert, J. (1978). *Interpreting Psychological Test Data.* New York: Van Nostrand Reinhold.

_____ (1980). *Interpreting Psychological Test Data-II.* New York: Van Nostrand Reinhold.

Gillis, J., Rogers, R., and Bagby, R. (1991). "Validity of the M Test." *Journal of Personality Assessment, 57,* 130–140.

Gilmore, J. (1991). "Murdering While Asleep." *Forensic Reports, 4,* 455–459.

Glasser, W. (1980). "Two Cases in Reality Therapy." In G. Belkin, Ed. *Contemporary Psychotherapies.* Chicago: Rand McNally.

Goldberg, L. (1992). "The Development of Markers for the Big-Five Factor Structure." *Psychological Assessment, 4,* 26–42.

Golden, C. (1979). *Clinical Interpretation of Objective Psychological Tests.* New York: Grune & Stratton.

Golden, R., and Meehl, P. (1979). "Detection of the Schizoid Taxon with MMPI Indicators." *Journal of Abnormal Psychology, 88,* 217–233.

Goldfried, M., Stricker, G., and Weiner, I. (1971). *Rorschach Handbook of Clinical and Research Applications.* Englewood Cliffs, NJ: Prentice-Hall.

Golding, S., Roesch, R., and Schreiber, J. (1984). "Assessment and Conceptualization of Competency to Stand Trial: Preliminary Data on the Interdisciplinary Fitness Interview." *Law and Human Behavior, 8,* 321–334.

Goldstein, A., and Stein, N. (1976). *Prescriptive Psychotherapies.* New York: Pergamon Press.

Gomez, R., and Samson, A. (1994). "Mother-Child Interactions and Noncompliance in Hyperactive Boys with and without Conduct Disorder." *Journal of Child Psychology and Psychiatry, 35,* 470–490.

Goodwin, F., and Jamison, D. (1990). *Manic–Depressive Illness.* New York: Oxford University Press.

Gottesman, I. (1991). *Schizophrenia Genesis.* New York: Freeman.

Grace, W., and Sweeney, M. (1986). "Comparisons of the P > V Sign on the WISC-R and WAIS-R in Delinquent Males." *Journal of Clinical Psychology, 42,* 173–176.

Graham, J. (1987). *The MMPI: A Practical Guide,* 2d ed. New York: Oxford University Press.

_____ (1993). *MMPI-2: Assessing Personality and Psychopathology,* 2nd ed. New York: Oxford University Press.

Graham, J., Timbrook, R., Ben-Porath, Y., and Butcher, J. (1991a). "Code-type Congruence between MMPI-1 and MMPI-2: Separating Fact from Artifact." *Journal of Personality Assessment, 57,* 205–215.

Graham, J., Watts, D., and Timbrook, R. (1991b). "Detecting Fake-Good and Fake-Bad MMPI-2 Profiles." *Journal of Personality Assessment, 57,* 264–277.

Green, A., and Salzman, C. (1990). "Clozapine: Benefits and Risks." *Hospital and Community Psychiatry, 41,* 379–380.

Greene, R. (1980). *The MMPI: An Interpretive Manual.* New York: Grune & Stratton.

_____ (1991). *The MMPI-2/MMPI: An Interpretive Manual,* 2d ed. Needham Heights, MA: Allyn and Bacon.

Griffin, W. (1993). *Family Therapy.* New York: Brunner/Mazel.

Grisso, T. (1986). *Evaluating Competencies: Forensic Assessments and Instruments.* New York: Plenum.

Gross, W., and Carpenter, L. (1971). "Alcoholic Personality: Reality or Fiction?" *Psychological Reports, 28,* 375–378.

Groth-Marmat, G. (1990). *Handbook of Psychological Assessment,* 2d ed. New York: Wiley.

Guertin, W., Rabin, A., Frank, G., and Ladd, C. (1962). "Research with the WAIS: 1955–1960." *Psychological Bulletin, 59,* 1–26.

Gynther, M., Altman, H., and Slettin, I. (1973a). "Replicated Correlates of MMPI Two-Point Types: The Missouri Actuarial System." *Journal of Clinical Psychology.* Monograph Supplement 39.

Gynther, M., Altman, H., and Warbin, W. (1973b). "Interpretation of Uninterpretable Minnesota Multiphasic Personality Inventory Profiles." *Journal of Consulting and Clinical Psychology, 40,* 78–83.

Gynther, M., and Green, S. (1980). "Accuracy May Make a Difference, But Does a Difference Make for Accuracy?: A Response to Pritchard and Rosenblatt." *Journal of Consulting and Clinical Psychology, 48,* 268–272.

Hall, G., Maiuro, R., Vitaliano, P., and Proctor, W. (1986). "The Utility of the MMPI with Men Who Have Sexually Assaulted Children." *Journal of Consulting and Clinical Psychology, 54,* 493–496.

Hammarberg, M. (1992). "Penn Inventory for Posttraumatic Stress Disorder: Psychometric Properties." *Psychological Assessment, 4,* 67–76.

Hare, R. (1986). "Twenty Years of Experience with the Cleckley Psychopath." In W. Reid, D. Dorr, J. Walker, and J. Bonner, Eds., *Unmasking the Psychopath.* New York: Norton.

Hare, R., Hart, S., and Forth, A. (1992). Workshop on the Assessment of Psychopathy. Biennial Meeting of the American Psychology-Law Society, San Diego, CA.

Hare, R., Hart, S., and Harpur, T. (1991). "Psychopathy and the DSM-IV Criteria for Antisocial Personality Disorder." *Journal of Abnormal Psychology, 100,* 391–398.

Harrell, T., Honaker, L., and Parnell, T. (1992). "Equivalence of the MMPI-2 with the MMPI in Psychiatric Patients." *Psychological Assessment, 4,* 460–465.

Harsh, J., and Ogilvie, R., Eds. (1995). *Sleep Onset: Normal and Abnormal Processes.* Washington, DC: American Psychological Association.

Hartmann, F., Poirier, M., Chantal-Bourdel, M., Loo, H., et al. (1991). "Comparison of Acetorphan with Clonidine for Opiate Withdrawal Symptoms." *American Journal of Psychiatry, 148,* 627–629.

Hathaway, S. (1947). "A Coding System for MMPI Profiles." *Journal of Consulting Psychology, 11,* 334–337.

Hathaway, S., and McKinley, J. (1967). *The Minnesota Multiphasic Personality Inventory Manual.* New York: Psychological Corporation.

Hauri, P., Ed. (1991). *Case Studies in Insomnia.* New York: Plenum.

Hecker, J., and Thorpe, G. (1992). *Agoraphobia and Panic.* Needham Heights, MA: Allyn and Bacon.

Hedlund, J. (1977). "MMPI Clinical Scale Correlates." *Journal of Consulting and Clinical Psychology, 45,* 739–750.

Heilbrun, A., Blum, N., and Goldreyer, N. (1985). "Defensive Projection: An Investigation of Its Role in Paranoid Conditions." *Journal of Nervous and Mental Disease, 173,* 17–25.

Heinrich, T., and Amolsch, T. (1978). "A Note on the Situational Interpretation of WAIS Profile Patterns." *Journal of Personality Assessment, 42,* 418–420.

Heller, J. (1974). *Something Happened.* New York: Knopf.

Hendrix, E., Thompson, L., and Rau, B. (1978). "Behavioral Treatment of an 'Hysterically' Clenched Fist." *Journal of Behavior Therapy and Experimental Psychiatry, 9,* 273–276.

Hendrix, M., and Meyer, R. (1976). "Toward More Comprehensive and Durable Client Changes: A Case Report." *Psychotherapy: Theory, Research, and Practice, 13,* 263–266.

Hewett, B., and Martin, W. (1980). "Psychometric Comparisons of Sociopathic and Psychopathological Behaviors of Alcoholics and Drug Abusers Versus a Low Drug Use Control Population." *The International Journal of the Addictions, 15,* 77–105.

Hillebrand, M., and Pallone, N., Eds. (1995). *The Psychobiology of Aggression.* Binghamton, NY: Haworth.

Hoehn-Saric, R., and McLeod, D. (1988). "Panic and Generalized Anxiety Disorders." In C. Last and M. Hersen, Eds. *Handbook of Anxiety Disorders.* Elmsford, NY: Pergamon Press.

Holland, T., and Watson, C. (1980). "Multivariate Analysis of WAIS-MMPI Relationships among Brain-Damaged, Schizophrenic, Neurotic, and Alcoholic Patients." *Journal of Clinical Psychology, 36,* 352–359.

Hollin, C., and Howells, K., Eds. (1991). *Clinical Approaches to Sex Offenders and Their Victims.* New York: Wiley.

Hovanitz, C., and Jordan-Brown, C. (1986). "The Validity of MMPI Subtle and Obvious Items in Psychiatric Patients." *Journal of Clinical Psychology, 42,* 100–108.

Hsu, L. (1986). "Implications of Differences in Elevations of K-Corrected and Non–K-Corrected MMPI T Scores." *Journal of Consulting and Clinical Psychology, 54,* 552–557.

Huesmann, L. R. (Ed.) (1994). *Aggressive Behavior.* New York: Plenum.

Iacono, W. (1991). "Psychophysiological Assessment of Psychopathology." *Psychological Assessment, 3,* 309–320.

IPAT Staff (1963). *Information Bulletin No. 8 to the 16 PF Handbook.* Champaign, IL: Institute for Personality and Ability Testing.

_____ (1972). *Manual for the 16 PF.* Champaign, IL: Institute for Personality and Ability Testing.

Jackson, J., Greenblatt, R., Davis, W., Murphy, T., and Trimakas, K. (1991). "Assessment of Schizophrenic Inpatients with the MCMI." *Journal of Clinical Psychology, 47,* 505–510.

Jacobsen, R., and Tomkin, A. (1988). "Converting Shipley Institute of Living Scale Scores to IQ." *Journal of Clinical Psychology, 44,* 72–75.

Janus, S., and Janus, C. (1994). *The Janus Report on Sexual Behavior.* New York: Wiley.

Jarvik, M. (1967). "The Psychopharmacological Revolution." *Psychology Today, 1,* 51–59.

Johnson, F., and Johnson, S. (1986). "Differences Between Human Figure Drawings of Child Molesters and Control Groups." *Journal of Clinical Psychology, 42,* 638–647.

Johnson, J., Klinger, D., and Gianetti, R. (1980). "Band Width in Diagnostic Classification Using the MMPI as a Predictor." *Journal of Consulting and Clinical Psychology, 48,* 340–349.

Johnson, M. (1966). "Verbal Abstracting Ability and Schizophrenia." *Journal of Consulting Psychology, 30,* 275–277.

Johnson, R., Tobin, J., and Cellucci, T. (1992). "Personality Characteristics of Cocaine and Alcohol Abusers." *Addictive Behaviors, 17,* 159–166.

Johnson, S. (1994). *Character Styles.* New York: Norton.

Kalichman, S. (1988). "Empirically Derived MMPI Profile Subgroups of Incarcerated Homicide Offenders." *Journal of Clinical Psychology, 44,* 733–738.

Kalichman, S., Syzmanowski, D., McKee, G., Taylor, J., and Craig, M. (1989). "Cluster Analytically Derived MMPI Profile Subgroups of Incarcerated Adult Rapists." *Journal of Clinical Psychology, 45,* 150–155.

Kaplan, H., Ed. (1995). *Drugs, Crime, and Other Deviant Adaptations.* New York: Plenum.

Karon, B. (1976). "The Psychoanalysis of Schizophrenia." In P. Magero, Ed. *The Construction of Madness.* New York: Pergamon Press.

_____ (1981). "The Thematic Apperception Test." In A. Rabin, Ed. *Assessment with Projective Techniques.* New York: Springer.

Karson, S. (1959). "The Sixteen Personality Factor Test in Clinical Practice." *Journal of Clinical Psychology, 15,* 174–176.

_____ (1960). "Validating Clinical Judgments with the 16 PF Test." *Journal of Clinical Psychology, 16,* 394–397.

_____ (1989). "The 16 PF." In C. Newmark, Ed. *Major Psychological Assessment Instruments*, 6th ed. Boston: Allyn and Bacon.

Karson, S., and O'Dell, J. (1976). *Clinical Use of the 16 PF.* Champaign, IL: IPAT.

Katon, W. (1993). "Somatization Disorder, Hypochondriasis, and Conversion Disorder." In D. Dunner, Ed. *Current Psychiatric Therapy.* Philadelphia: Saunders.

Keiser, T., and Lowy, D. (1980). "Heroin Addiction and Wechsler Digit Span Test." *Journal of Clinical Psychology, 36,* 347–351.

Keles, A. (1983). "Biopsychobehavioral Correlates and the MMPI." *Psychosomatic Medicine, 45,* 341–347.

Kellam, A. (1969). "Shoplifting Treated by Aversion to a Film." *Behavior Research and Therapy, 7,* 125–127.

Keller, L., and Butcher, J. (1991). *Assessment of Chronic Pain Patients with the MMPI–2.* Minneapolis: University of Minnesota.

Keller, M., and Baker, L. (1992). "The Clinical Course of Panic Disorder and Depression." *Journal of Clinical Psychiatry, 53*(Suppl.), 5–8.

Kelley, C., and King, G. (1979a). "Behavioral Correlates of Infrequent 2-point MMPI Code Types at a University Mental Health Center." *Journal of Clinical Psychology, 35,* 576–585.

_____ (1979b). "Behavioral Correlates of the 2-7-8 MMPI Profile Type in Students at a University Mental Health Center." *Journal of Consulting and Clinical Psychology, 47,* 679–685.

_____ (1979c). "Cross Validation of the 2-8/8-2 MMPI Code Type for Young Adult Psychiatric Outpatients." *Journal of Personality Assessment, 43,* 143–149.

Kellner, R. (1986). *Somatization and Hypochondriasis.* London: Praeger.

Kernberg, O. (1984). *Severe Personality Disorders.* New Haven: Yale University Press.

_____ (1992). *Aggression in Personality Disorders and Perversions.* New Haven, CT: Yale University Press.

Kernberg, P., and Chazan, S. (1991). *Children with Conduct Disorders.* New York: Basic Books.

King, G., and Kelley, C. (1977). "Behavioral Correlates for Spike-4, Spike-9, and 4-9/9-4 MMPI Profiles in Students at a University Mental Health Center." *Journal of Clinical Psychology, 33,* 718–724.

Kinsey, A., Pomeroy, W., and Martin, C. (1948). *Sexual Behavior in the Human Male.* Philadelphia: Saunders.

_____ (1953). *Sexual Behavior in the Human Female.* Philadelphia: Saunders.

Kirkley, B., and Janick, L. (1987). "Binge Eating in Obesity: Associated MMPI Characteristics." *Journal of Consulting and Clinical Psychology, 55,* 872–876.

Kirman, W. (1980). "The Modern Psychoanalytic Treatment of Depression." In G. Belkin, Ed. *Contemporary Psychotherapies.* Chicago: Rand McNally.

Kish, G., Hagen, J., Woody, M., and Harvey, H. (1980). "Alcoholics' Recovery from Cerebral Impairment as a Function of Duration of Abstinence." *Journal of Clinical Psychology, 36,* 584–589.

Kleinknecht, R. (1991). *Mastering Anxiety: The Nature and Treatment of Anxious Conditions.* New York: Plenum.

Klingler, D., and Saunders, D. (1975). "A Factor-Analysis of the Items for Nine Subtests of the WAIS." *Multivariate Behavioral Research, 10,* 131–154.

Klopfer, B., and Davidson, H. (1962). *Rorschach's Technique: An Introductory Manual.* New York: Harcourt Brace Jovanovich.

Kluft, R., and Fine, C. (1993). *Clinical Perspectives on Multiple Personality Disorder.* Washington, DC: American Psychiatric Press.

Knable, M., Kleinman, J., and Weinberger, D. (1995). "Neurobiology of Schizophrenia." In A. Schatzberg and C. Nemeroff, Eds., *Textbook of Psychiatry.* Washington, DC: American Psychiatric Press.

Koslowsky, M., Scheinberg, Z., Bleich, A., Mark, M., et al. (1992). "The Factor Structure and Criterion Validity of the Short Form of the Eating Attitudes Test." *Journal of Personality Assessment, 58,* 27–35.

Kozak, M., Foa, E., and McCarthy, P. (1988). "Obsessive-Compulsive Disorder." In C. Last and M. Hersen, Eds. *Handbook of Anxiety Disorders.* Elmsford, NY: Pergamon Press.

Kramer, J. (1990). "Guidelines for Interpreting WAIS–R Subtest Scores." *Psychological Assessment, 2,* 202–205.

Krishnan, R., Davidson, J., and Miller, R. (1985). "Trichotillomania: A Review." *Comprehensive Psychiatry, 26,* 123–128.

Kroll, J. (1993). *PTSD/Borderlines in Therapy.* New York: Norton.

Kronenberger, W., and Meyer, R. (1996). *The Child Clinician's Handbook.* Boston: Allyn and Bacon.

Krug, S. (1978). "Further Evidence on the 16 PF Distortion Scales." *Journal of Personality Assessment, 42,* 513–518.

_____ (1980). *Clinical Analysis Questionnaire Manual.* Champaign, IL: IPAT.

_____ (1981). *Interpreting 16 PF Profile Patterns.* Champaign, IL: IPAT.

Krug, S., and Johns, E. (1986). "A Large-Scale Cross-Validation of Second-Order Personality Structure Defined by the 16 PF." *Psychological Reports, 59,* 683–693.

Kurlychek, R., and Jordan, L. (1980). "MMPI Code Types of Responsible and Nonresponsible Criminal Defendants." *Journal of Clinical Psychology, 36,* 590–593.

Kurtz, R., and Meyer, R. (1994). The M Test, MMPI, and SIRS in assessments of malingering. American Psychology-Law Society. Albequerque, NM.

L'Abate, L., Farrar, J., and Serritella, D., Eds. (1992). *Handbook of Differential Treatment Addictions.* Needham Heights, MA: Allyn and Bacon.

Laboratory of Community Psychology (1973). *Competency to Stand Trial and Mental Illness.* Rockville, MD: National Institutes of Mental Health.

Lachar, D. (1974). *The MMPI: Clinical Assessment and Automated Interpretation.* Los Angeles: Western Psychological Services.

Lambert, M., Hatch, D., Kingston, M., and Edwards, B. (1986). "Zung, Beck, and Hamilton Rating Scales as Measures of Treatment Outcome." *Journal of Consulting and Clinical Psychology, 54,* 54–59.

Landman, J., and Dawes, R. (1982). "Psychotherapy Outcome: Smith and Glass's Conclusions Stand Up under Scrutiny." *American Psychologist, 37,* 504–516.

Lazarus, A. (1971). *Behavior Therapy and Beyond.* New York: McGraw-Hill.

Lazarus, A. (1987). "Discussion." In J. Zeig, Ed., *The Evolution of Psychotherapy.* New York: Brunner/Mazel.

Lee, G., Loring, D., and Martin, R. (1992). "Rey's 15-Item Visual Memory Test for the Detection of Malingering: Normative Observations on Patients with Neurological Disorders." *Psychological Assessment, 4,* 43–46.

Leff, J. (1994). "Working with the Families of Schizophrenic Patients." *British Journal of Psychiatry, 164* (Suppl. 23), 71–76.

Levin, S., and Stava, L. (1987). "Personality Characteristics of Sex Offenders." *Archives of Sexual Behavior, 16,* 57–79.

Levitt, E. (1980). *Primer on the Rorschach Technique.* Springfield, IL: Thomas.

Lewak, R., Marks, P., and Nelson, G. (1990). *Therapist Guide to the MMPI and MMPI–2.* Muncie, IN: Accelerated Development.

Lewy, A. (1993). "Seasonal Mood Disorders." In D. Dunner, Ed., *Current Psychiatric Therapy.* Philadelphia: Saunders.

Lezak, M. (1995). *Neuropsychological Assessment.* New York: Oxford University Press.

Liebowitz, M., Gorman, J., Fryer, A., Levitt, M., et al. (1985). "Lactate Provocation of Panic Attacks." *Archives of General Psychiatry, 42,* 709–714.

Lipsey, M., and Wilson, D. (1993). "The Efficacy of Psychological, Educational, and Behavioral Treatment: Confirmation from Meta-Analysis." *American Psychologist, 48,* 1181–1209.

Litz, B., Penk, W., Walsh, S., Hyer, L., et al. (1991). "Similarities and Differences Between MMPI and MMPI-2 Applications to the Assessment of Posttraumatic Stress Disorder." *Journal of Personality Assessment, 57,* 238–253.

Loeber, R. (1990). "Development and Risk Factors of Juvenile Antisocial Behavior and Delinquency." *Clinical Psychology Review, 10,* 1–42.

Lo Piccolo, J. (1985). "Advances in the Diagnosis and Treatment of Sexual Dysfunction." Convention Workshop. Louisville: Kentucky Psychological Association.

———— (1993). "Paraphilias." In D. Dunner, Ed., *Current Psychiatric Therapy.* Philadelphia: Saunders.

Lore, R., and Schultz, L. (1993). "Control of Human Aggression." *American Psychologist, 48,* 16–25.

Lorr, M., and Suziedelis, A. (1985). "Profile Patterns in the 16 PF Questionnaire." *Journal of Clinical Psychology, 41,* 767–773.

Love, A., and Peck, C. (1987). "The MMPI and Psychological Factors in Chronic Low Back Pain: A Review." *Pain, 28,* 1–12.

Lykken, D. (1957). "A Study of Anxiety in the Sociopathic Personality." *Journal of Abnormal and Social Psychology, 55,* 6–10.

Lyons, L., and Woods, P. (1991). "The Efficacy of Rational-Emotive Therapy: A Quantitative Review of the Outcome Research." *Clinical Psychology Review, 11,* 357–370.

MacAndrew, C. (1965). "The Differentiation of Male Alcoholic Outpatients from Nonalcoholic Psychiatric Patients by Means of the MMPI." *Quarterly Journal of Studies on Alcohol, 26,* 238–46.

Macciocchi, S., and Meyer, R. (1989). "The Context of Self–Disclosure, the Polygraph and Deception." *Forensic Reports, 4,* 51–59.

Maiuro, R. (1993). "Intermittent Explosive Disorder." In David L. Dunner, Ed. *Current Psychiatric Therapy.* Philadelphia: Saunders.

Maltzman, I. (1994). "Why Alcoholism Is a Disease." *Journal of Psychoactive Drugs, 26,* 13–31.

Margolin, D., Ed. (1992). *Cognitive Neuroscience in Clinical Practice.* New York: Oxford University Press.

Marlatt, A., Baer, J., Donovan, D., and Kiviahan, D. (1988). "Addictive Behaviors: Etiology and Treatment." In M. Rosenzweig and L. Porter, Eds. *Annual Review of Psychology*, Vol. 39. Palo Alto, CA: Annual Reviews.

Marlowe, D., and Crowne, D. (1964). *The Approval Motive.* New York: Wiley.

Marsh, D., Linberg, L., and Smeltzer, J. (1991). "Human Figure Drawings of Adjudicated and Nonadjudicated Adolescents." *Journal of Personality Assessment, 57,* 77–86.

Marshall, W., Eccles, A., and Barbaree, H. (1991). "The Treatment of Exhibitionists." *Behavior Research and Therapy, 29,* 129–135.

Mason, B., Cohen, J., and Exner, J. (1985). "Schizophrenic, Depressive, and Nonpatient Personality Organization Described Rorschach Factor Structure." *Journal of Personality Assessment, 49,* 295–303.

Masters, W., and Johnson, V. (1970). *Human Sexual Inadequacy.* Boston: Little, Brown.

Masters, W., Johnson, V., and Kolodny, R. (1991). *Human Sexuality,* 4th ed. Glenville, IL: Scott, Foresman, Little, Brown.

Masters, W., Johnson, V., and Kolodny, R. (1994). *Heterosexuality.* New York: Harper Collins.

Matarazzo, J. (1972). *Wechsler's Measurement and Appraisal of Adult Intelligence.* Baltimore, MD: Williams and Wilkins.

Matson, J., and Gardner, W. (1991). "Behavioral Learning Theory and Current Applications to Severe Behavior Problems in Persons with Severe Retardation." *Clinical Psychology Review, 11,* 175–183.

Maruish, M. (1994). *The Use of Psychological Testing for Treatment Planning and Outcome Assessment.* Hillsdale, NJ: Erlbaum.

McCann, J., and Suess, J. (1988). "Clinical Applications of the MCMI: The 1-2-3-8 Codetype." *Journal of Clinical Psychology, 44,* 181–186.

McCreery, J., and Walker, R. (1993). "Alcohol Problems." In David L. Dunner, Ed., *Current Psychiatric Therapy.* Philadelphia: Saunders.

McCrown, W., Johnson, J., and Shure, M. (Eds.) (1993). *The Impulsive Client: Theory, Research, and Treatment.* Washington, DC: APA Books.

McElroy, S., Pope, H., Hudson, J., Keck, P., and White, K. (1991). "Kleptomania: A Report of 20 Cases." *American Journal of Psychiatry, 148,* 652–655.

McNiel, K., and Meyer, R. (1990). "Detection of Deception on the Millon Clinical Multiaxial Inventory (MCMI)." *Journal of Clinical Psychology, 46,* 755–764.

Meehl, P., and Hathaway, S. (1980). "The K Factor as a Suppressor Variable in the MMPI." In W. Dahlstrom and L. Dahlstrom, Eds., *Basic Readings on the MMPI.* Minneapolis: University of Minnesota Press.

Megargee, E. (1992). "Impact of the Revised MMPI (MMPI-2) on the Megaree Based Offender Classification System." Report submitted to the National Institute of Justice.

Megargee, E., and Bohn, M. (1979). *Classifying Criminal Offenders.* Beverly Hills, CA: Sage.

Megargee, E., and Cook, P. (1975). "Negative Response Bias and the MMPI O-H Scale: A Response to Deiker." *Journal of Consulting and Clinical Psychology, 43,* 725, 729.

Megargee, E., Cook, P., and Mendelsohn, G. (1967). "Development and Validation of an MMPI Scale of Assaultiveness in Overcontrolled Individuals." *Journal of Abnormal Psychology, 72,* 519–528.

Meichenbaum, D. (1985). "Cognitive Behavior Modification." In F. Kanfer and A. Goldstein, Eds., *Helping People Change.* New York: Plenum.

Meister, R. (1980). *Hypochondria.* New York: Taplinger.

Melton, G., Petrila, J., Poythress, N., and Slobogin, C. (1987) *Psychological Evaluations for the Courts.* New York: Guilford.

Mester, R. (1986). "The Psychotherapy of Mania." *The British Journal of Medical Psychology, 59,* 13–20.

Meyer, R. (1992a). *Abnormal Behavior and the Criminal Justice System.* Lexington, MA: Lexington Books.

_____. (1992b). *Practical Clinical Hypnosis.* Lexington, MA: Lexington Books.

_____ (1995). *Preparation for Licensing and Board Certification Examinations in Psychology: The Professional, Legal, and Ethical Components,* 2d ed. New York: Brunner/Mazel.

Meyer, R. E. (1995). "Biology of Psychoactive Substance Dependence Disorders: Opiates, Cocaine and Ethanol." In A. Schatzberg and C. Nemeroff, Eds., *Textbook of Psychiatry.* Washington, DC: American Psychiatric Press.

Meyer, R., Landis, E., and Hays, J. (1988). *Law for the Psychotherapist.* New York: Norton.

Meyer, R., and Salmon, P. (1988). *Abnormal Psychology.* Boston: Allyn and Bacon.

Michels, R., and Marzuk, P. (1993). Progress in Psychiatry (2 parts). *New England Journal of Medicine, 329 (8&9),* 552–560, 628–638.

Miller, T., Heath, L., Molcan, J., and Dugoni, B. (1991). "Imitative Violence in the Real World: A Reanalysis of Homicide Rates Following Championship Prize Fights." *Aggressive Behavior, 17,* 121–134.

Millon, T. (1981). *Disorders of Personality, DSM-III: Axis II.* New York: Wiley.

_____ (1985). "The MCMI Provides a Good Assessment of DSM-III Disorders: The MCMI-II Will Prove Even Better." *Journal of Personality Assessment, 49,* 379–391.

Milner, J. (1991). "Physical Child Abuse Perpetrator Screening and Evaluation." *Criminal Justice and Behavior, 18,* 47–63.

Mitrushina, M., and Satz, P. (1991). "Test-Retest Reliability of WAIS-R. Satz-Mogel Short Form in a Normal Elderly Sample." *International Journal of Clinical Neuropsychology, 13 (3–4),* 1–4.

Mlatt, S., and Vale, W. (1986). "Performance of Agoraphobic Families Versus Nonagoraphobic Families on the 16 PF Questionnaire." *Journal of Clinical Psychology, 41,* 244–250.

Mohr, D., and Beutler, L. (1990). "Erectile Dysfunction: A Review of Diagnostic and Treatment Procedures." *Clinical Psychology Review, 10,* 123–150.

Moldin, S., Gottesman, I., and Erlenmeyer-Kimling, L. (1987). "Searching for the Psychometric Boundaries of Schizophrenia." *Journal of Abnormal Psychology, 96,* 354–363.

Monahan, J. (1981). *Predicting Violent Behavior.* Beverly Hills, CA: Sage.

_____ (1984). "The Prediction of Violent Behavior: Toward a Second Generation of Theory and Policy." *American Journal of Psychiatry, 141,* 10–15.

Monahan, J., and Walker, L., Eds. (1990). *Social Science in Law: Cases and Materials,* 2d ed. Westbury, NJ: Foundation Press.

Money, J. (1987). "Sin, Sickness, or Status: Homosexual Gender Identity and Psychoneuroendocrinology." *American Psychologist, 42,* 384–399.

Montplaisir, J., and Godbout, R. (1991). *Sleep and Biological Rhythms: Basic Mechanisms and Applications to Psychiatry.* New York: Oxford University Press.

Nathan, K., Musselman, D., Schatzberg, A., and Nemeroff, Eds., *Textbook of Psychiatry.* Washington, DC: American Psychiatric Press.

Nelson, B. (1984). *Making Child Abuse an Issue.* Chicago: University of Chicago Press.

Nelson, L., and Cicchetti, D. (1991). "Validity of the MMPI Depression Scale for Outpatients." *Psychological Assessment, 3,* 55–59.

Netter, B., and Viglione, D. (1994). "An Empirical Study of Malingering on the Rorschach." *Journal of Personality Assessment, 62,* 45–57.

Newmark, C., Ed. (1985). *Major Psychological Assessment Instruments.* Boston: Allyn and Bacon.

_____ (1989). *Major Psychological Assessment Instruments,* vol. 2. Needham Heights, MA: Allyn and Bacon.

Newmark, C., and Hutchins, T. (1980). "Age and MMPI Indices of Schizophrenia." *Journal of Clinical Psychology, 36,* 768–769.

Nietzel, M., Bernstein, D., and Milich, R. (1994). *Introduction to Clinical Psychology,* 4th ed. Englewood Cliffs, NJ: Prentice-Hall.

Oas, P. (1984). "Validity of the Draw-A-Person and Bender-Gestalt Tests as Measures of Impulsivity with Adolescents." *Journal of Consulting and Clinical Psychology, 52,* 1011–1019.

Oates, W. (1987). *Behind the Masks: Personality Disorders in Religious Behaviors.* Philadelphia: Westminster Press.

O'Connor v. *Donaldson,* 422 U.S. 563 (1975).

Ogdon, D. (1977). *Psychodiagnostics and Personality Assessment: A Handbook.* Los Angeles: Western Psychological Services.

Oltmanns, T., and Maher, B. (1988). *Delusional Beliefs.* New York: John Wiley.

Omer, H. (1994). *Critical Interventions in Psychotherapy.* New York: Norton.

Oren, D., Brainard, G., Johnston, S., Joseph-Vanderpool, J., et al. (1991). "Treatment of Seasonal Affective Disorder with Green Light and Red Light." *American Journal of Psychiatry, 148,* 509–511.

Oren, D., Moul, D., Schwartz, P., Brown, C. et al. (1994). "Exposure to Ambient Light in Patients with Winter Seasonal Affective Disorder." *American Journal of Psychiatry, 151,* 591–593.

Orsini, D., Van Gorp, W., and Boone, K. (1988). *The Neuropsychology Casebook.* New York: Springer-Verlag.

Osgood, C., Luria, Z., Jeans, R., and Smith, A. (1976). "The Three Faces of Evelyn: A Case Report." *Journal of Abnormal Psychology, 85,* 247–286.

Oster, G., and Gould, P. (1987). *Using Drawings in Assessment and Therapy.* New York: Brunner/Mazel.

Pallis, C., and Bamji, A. (1979). "McIlroy Was Here. Or Was He?" *British Medical Journal, 6169,* 973–975.

Paolo, A., Ryan, J., and Smith, A. (1991). "Reading Difficulty of MMPI-2 Subscales." *Journal of Clinical Psychology, 47,* 529–532.

Parsons v. *State,* 81 Ala. 577, 2 So. 854 (1887).

Parwatikar, S., Holcomb, W., and Menninger, K. (1985). "Detection of Malingered Amnesia in Accused Murderers." *Bulletin of the American Academy of Psychiatry and the Law, 13,* 97–103.

Patalano, F. (1980). "Comparison of MMPI Scores of Drug Abusers and Mayo Clinic Normative Groups." *Journal of Clinical Psychology, 36,* 576–579.

Pato, M., Pigott, T., Hill, J., Grover, G., et al. (1991). "Controlled Comparison of Busiprone and Clomipramine in OCD." *American Journal of Psychiatry, 148,* 127–129.

Patrick, J. (1988). "Concordance of the MCMI and MMPI in the Diagnosis of Three DSM-III Axis I Disorders." *Journal of Clinical Psychology, 44,* 186–190.

Paulhus, D. L. (1991). *Balanced Inventory of Desirable Responding* (unpublished manual). University of British Columbia.

Pauly, I. (1968). "The Current Status of the Change of Sex Operation." *Journal of Nervous and Mental Disease, 147,* 460–471.

Penk, W., Woodward, W., Robinowitz, R., and Parr, W. (1980). "An MMPI Comparison of Polydrug and Heroin Abusers." *Journal of Abnormal Psychology, 89,* 299–302.

Pennington, B., Peterson, L., and Barker, H. (1979). "The Diagnostic Use of the MMPI in Organic Brain Dysfunction." *Journal of Clinical Psychology, 35,* 484–492.

People v. Drew, Sub., 149 Cal. Rptr. 275 (1978).

Petraitis, J., Flay, B., and Miller, T. (1995). "Reviewing Theories of Adolescent Substance Abuse." *Psychological Bulletin, 117,* 67–86.

Phillips, D. (1986). "The Effects of Mass Media Violence on Suicide and Homicide." *Newsletter of the American Academy of Psychiatry and Law, 11,* 29–31.

Phillips, L. and Smith, J. (1953). *Rorschach Interpretation: Advanced Technique.* New York: Grune & Stratton.

Piotrowski, C., Sherry, D., and Keller, J. (1985). "Psychodiagnostic Test Usage." *Journal of Personality Assessment, 49,* 115–120.

Piotrowski, Z. (1979). *Perceptanalysis.* Philadelphia: Ex Libris.

Pitman, R., and Orr, S. (1993). "Psychophysiologic Testing for Post-Traumatic Stress Disorder: Forensic Psychiatric Application." *Bulletin of the American Academy of Psychiatry and the Law, 21(1),* 37–52.

Pope, K., Butcher, J., and Seelen, J. (1993). *MMPI, MMPI-2 and MMPI-A in Court: A Practical Guide for Expert Witnesses and Attorneys.* Washington, DC: American Psychological Association.

Potkin, S., Albers, L., and Richard, G. (1993). "Schizophrenia." In D. Dunner, Ed., *Current Psychiatric Therapy,* Philadelphia: Saunders.

Prien, R., and Klupfer, D. (1986). "Continuation Drug Therapy for Major Depressive Episodes: How Long Should It Be Maintained?" *American Journal of Psychiatry, 143,* 18–23.

Prochaska, J., DiClemente, C., and Norcross, J. (1992). "In Search of How People Change." *American Psychologist, 47,* 1102–1114.

Propkop, C., Bradley, L., Margolis, R., and Gentry, W. (1980). "Multivariate Analysis of the MMPI Profiles of Patients with Pain Complaints." *Journal of Personality Assessment, 44,* 246–252.

Quevillon, R., Landau, S., Apple, W., and Petretic-Jackson, P. (1986). "Assessing Adolescent Conduct Disorders and Oppositional Behaviors." In R. Harrington, Ed., *Testing Adolescents.* Kansas City, MO: Test Corporation of America.

Rabin, A. (1964). Lectures and personal communication.

_____, Ed. (1968). *Projective Techniques in Personality Assessment.* New York: Springer.

_____(1981). "Projective Methods: A Historical Introduction." In A. Rabin, Ed., *Assessment with Projective Techniques.* New York: Springer.

Rada, R., Laws, D., and Kellner, R. (1976). "Plasma Testosterone Levels in the Rapist." *Psychomatic Medicine, 38,* 257–268.

Rader, C. (1977). "MMPI Profile Types of Exposers, Rapists and Assaulters in a Court Services Population." *Journal of Consulting and Clinical Psychology, 45,* 61–69.

Rapaport, D., Gill, M., and Schafer, R. (1968). *Diagnostic Psychological Testing.* New York: International Universities Press.

Rapee, R. (1991). "Generalized Anxiety Disorder: A Review of Clinical Features and Theoretical Concepts." *Clinical Psychology Review, 11,* 419–440.

Raskin, R., and Novachk, J. (1991). "Narcissism and the Use of Fantasy." *Journal of Clinical Psychology, 47,* 490–499.

Reitan, R., and Wolfson, D. (1986). *Traumatic Brain Injury: Recovery and Rehabilitation.* Tucson: Neuropsychology Press.

Rennie v. *Klein.* 462 F. Supp. 1131 (D.N.J. 1978), later proceeding 476 F. Supp. 1294 (D.N.J. 1979), modified, 653 F.20 836 (3d Cir. 1981), vacated, 458 U.S. 1119 (1982), on remand, 720 F.2d 266 (3d Cir. 1983).

Resnick, R. (1990). Personal communication.

Reuter, E., Wallbrown, F., and Wallbrown, J. (1985). "16 PF Profiles and Four-Point Codes Seen in a Private Practice." *Multivariate Experimental Clinical Research, 7,* 123–147.

Rey, A. (1964). *L'examen Clinique en Psychologie* [The Clinical Examination in Psychology] (pp. 121–123). Paris: Presses Universitaires de France.

Rickers-Ovsiankina, M., Ed. (1960). *Rorschach Psychology.* New York: Wiley.

Riedlinger, T., and Riedlinger, J. (1994). "Psychedelic and Entactogenic Drugs in the Treatment of Depression." *Journal of Psychoactive Drugs, 26,* 41–55.

Rifkin, A., Doddi, S., Karajgi, B., Borenstein, M., and Wachspress, M. (1991). "Dosage of Haloperidol for Schizophrenics." *Archives of General Psychiatry, 48,* 166–170.

Robe, H. (1987). Personal communication.

Roberts, C., and Golding, S. (1991). "The Social Construction of Criminal Responsibility and Insanity." *Law and Human Behavior, 15,* 349–376.

Robinette, R. (1991). "The Relationship Between the Marlowe-Crowne Form C and the Validity Scales of the MMPI." *Journal of Clinical Psychology, 47,* 396–400.

Roffman, R., and Stephens, R. (1993). "Cannabis Dependence." In David L. Dunner, Ed., *Current Psychiatric Therapy.* Philadelphia: Saunders.

Rogers, C. (1951). *Client-Centered Therapy.* Boston: Houghton Mifflin.

Rogers, R. (1986). *Conducting Insanity Evaluations.* New York: Van Nostrand Reinhold.

_____ , Ed. (1988). *Clinical Assessment of Malingering and Deception.* New York: Guilford.

Rogers, R., Bagby, M., and Gillis, R. (1992). "Improvements in the M Test as a Screening Measure for Malingering." *Bulletin of the Americas Academy of Psychiatry and the Law, 20,* 101–104.

Rogers, R., Dolmetsch, R., and Cavanaugh, J. (1981). "An Empirical Approach to Insanity Evaluations." *Journal of Clinical Psychology, 37,* 683–687.

Rorschach, H. (1953). *Psychodiagnostics,* 5th ed. New York: Grune & Stratton.

Rossini, E., and Kaspar, J. (1987). "The Validity of the Bender-Gestalt Emotional Indicators." *Journal of Personality Assessment, 51,* 254–261.

Russell, M. T., and Karol, D. L. (1994). *The 16 PF Fifth Edition Administrator's Manual.* Champaign, IL: IPAT.

Sabine, D., and Meyer, R. (1992). "The Utility of the MMPI-2 Taped Version in a Low Socioeconomic Group." Unpublished paper.

_____ (1994). Unpublished paper.

Satz, P. (1987). Personal communication.

Satz, P., and Mogel, S. (1962). "An Abbreviation of the WAIS for Clinical Use." *Journal of Clinical Psychology, 18,* 77–79.

Schmidt, C. (1995). "Sexual Psychopathology and DSM-IV." In J. Oldham and M. Riba, Eds., *Review of Psychiatry.* Washington, DC: American Psychiatric Press.

Schnarch, D. (1992). *Constructing the Sexual Crucible.* New York: Norton.

Schneidman, E. (1985). *Definition of Suicide.* New York: Wiley.

Schretlen, D., Wilkins, S., Van Gorp, W., and Bobholz, J. (1992). "Cross-Validation of a Psychological Test Battery to Detect Faked Insanity." *Psychological Assessment, 4,* 77–83.

Schuyler, D. (1991). *A Practical Guide to Cognitive Therapy.* New York: Norton.

Schwartz, M. (1987). *Biofeedback.* New York: Guilford.

Scott, R., Prue, D., Denier, C., and King, A. (1986). "Worksite Smoking Intervention with Nursing Professionals." *Journal of Consulting and Clinical Psychology, 54,* 809–813.

Scott, R., and Stone, D. (1986). "MMPI Measures of Psychological Disturbance in Adolescent and Adult Victims of Father–Daughter Incest." *Journal of Clinical Psychology, 42,* 251–259.

Seamons, D., Howell, R., Carlisle, A., and Roe, A. (1981). "Rorschach Simulation of Mental Illness and Normality by Psychotic and Nonpsychotic Legal Offenders." *Journal of Personality Assessment, 45,* 130–135.

Seidman, S., and Rieder, R. (1994). "A Review of Sexual Behavior in the United States." *The American Journal of Psychatry, 151,* 330–341.

Segal, S., Watson, M. and Nelson, L. (1986). "Indexing Civil Commitment in Psychiatric Emergency Rooms." *Annals of the American Academy of Political and Social Science, 484,* 56–69.

Seltzer, L. (1986). *Paradoxical Strategies in Psychotherapy.* New York: Wiley.

Selye, H. (1956). *The Stress of Life.* New York: McGraw-Hill.

Serin, R., Peters, R., and Barbaree, H. (1990). "Predictors of Psychopathy and Release Outcome in a Criminal Population." *Psychological Assessment, 2,* 419–423.

Shafer, R. (1948). *Clinical Application of Psychological Tests.* New York: International Universities Press.

_____ (1954). *Psychoanalytic Interpretation in Rorschach Testing.* New York: Grune & Stratton.

Shapiro, D. (1984). *Psychological Evaluation and Expert Testimony.* New York: Van Nostrand Reinhold.

_____ (1991). *Forensic Psychological Assessment.* Needham Heights, MA: Allyn and Bacon.

Shatin, L. (1979). "Brief Form of the Competency Screening Test for Mental Competence to Stand Trial." *Journal of Clinical Psychology, 35,* 464–467.

Siegel, M. (1987). *Psychological Testing from Early Childhood Through Adolescence.* Madison, CT: International Universities Press.

Silver, L. (1992). *Attention-Deficit Hyperactivity Disorder: A Clinical Guide to Diagnosis and Treatment.* Washington, DC: American Psychiatric Press.

Silver, R., Isaacs, K., and Mansky, P. (1981). "MMPI Correlates of Affective Disorders." *Journal of Clinical Psychology, 37,* 836–839.

Silverman, L. (1976). "Psychoanalytic Theory: The Reports of My Death Are Greatly Exaggerated." *American Psychologist, 31,* 621–637.

Simon, R., Ed. (1995). *Posttraumatic Stress Disorder in Litigation.* Washington, DC: American Psychiatric Press.

Slobogin, C., Melton, G., and Showalter, C. (1984). "The Feasibility of a Brief Evaluation of Mental State at the Time of the Offense." *Law and Human Behavior, 8,* 305–320.

Slovenko, R. (1995). *Psychiatry and Criminal Culpability.* New York: Wiley.

Small, A., Madero, J., Gross, H., Teagno, L., et al. (1981). "A Comparative Analysis of Primary Anorexics and Schizophrenics on the MMPI." *Journal of Clinical Psychology, 37,* 773–736.

Smith, M., and Glass, G. (1977). "Meta-analysis of Psychotherapy Outcome Studies." *American Psychologist, 32,* 955–1008.

Smith, M., and Thelen, M. (1984). "Development and Validation of a Test for Bulimia." *Journal of Consulting and Clinical Psychology, 52,* 863–872.

Smith, S., and Meyer, R. (1980). "Working Between the Legal System and the Therapist." In D. Cox and R. Daitzman, Eds., *Exhibitionism.* New York: Garland.

_____ (1987). *Law, Behavior and Mental Health: Policy and Practice.* New York: New York University Press.

Snyder, S. (1986). "Pseudologia Fantastica in the Borderline Patient." *American Journal of Psychiatry, 143,* 1287–1290.

Solovay, M., Shenton, M., and Holzman, P. (1987). "Comparative Studies of Thought Disorders: 1. Mania: 2. Schizoaffective Disorder." *Archives of General Psychiatry, 44,* 13–30.

Spitzer, R. (1992). Personal communication.

Spitzer, R., Cohen, J., Fliess, J., and Endicott, J. (1967). "Quantification of Agreement in Psychiatric Diagnosis: A New Approach." *Archives of General Psychiatry, 17,* 83–87.

Spitzer, R., and Endicott, J. (1978). *Schedule of Affective Disorders and Schizophrenia.* New York: Biometrics Research.

Spitzer, R., Forman, J., and Nee, J. (1979). "DSM-III Field Trials: Initial Interrater Diagnostic Reliability." *American Journal of Psychiatry, 136,* 815–817.

Spivak, H., Rodin, G., and Sutherland, A. (1994). "The Psychology of Factitious Disorders." *Psychosomatics, 35,* 25–34.

Spotts, J., and Schontz, F. (1984). "Drug-Induced Ego States." *International Journal of the Addictions, 19,* 119–151.

State of New Jersey v. *Stasio,* 78 N.J. 467 (1979).

Steketee, G. (1993). *Treatment of Obsessive Compulsive Disorder.* New York: Guilford.

Stevenson, J., and Meares, R. (1992). "An Outcome Study of Psychotherapy for Patients with Borderline Personality Disorder." *American Journal of Psychiatry, 149,* 358–362.

Stone, M. (1990). *The Fate of Borderlines.* New York: Guilford.

Storr, A. (1990). *The Art of Psychotherapy,* 2d ed. New York: Routledge.

Stout, A., and Steege, J. (1985). "Psychological Assessment of Women Seeking Treatment for Premenstrual Syndrome." *Journal of Psychosomatic Research, 92,* 621–629.

Swann, A., Secunda, S., Koslow, S., Katz, M., et al. (1991). "Mania: Sympathoadrenal Function and Clinical State." *Psychiatry Research, 37,* 195–205.

Swiercinsky, D., Ed. (1985). *Testing Adults*. Kansas City: Test Corporation of America.

Sylvester, C., and Kruesi, M. (1994). "Child and Adolescent Psychopharmacotherapy: Progress and Pitfalls." *Psychiatric Annals, 24*, 83–90.

Taylor, C. (1995). "Treatment of Anxiety Disorders." In A. Schatzberg and C. Nemeroff, Eds., *Textbook of Psychiatry*. Washington, DC: American Psychiatric Press.

Teplin, L., Abram, K., and McClelland, G. (1994). "Does Psychiatric Disorder Predict Violent Crime among Released Jail Detainees?" *American Psychologist, 49*, 335–342.

Thelen, M., Farmer, J., Wonderlich, S., and Smith, M. (1991). "A Revision of the Bulimia Test: The BULIT-R." *Psychological Assessment, 3*, 119–124.

Tollefson, G. (1993). "Major Depression." In D. Dunner, Ed. *Current Psychiatric Therapy*. Philadelphia: Saunders.

Trethvithick, L., and Hosch, H. (1978). "MMPI Correlates of Drug Addiction Based on Drug of Choice." *Journal of Consulting and Clinical Psychology, 46*, 180.

Trull, T. (1991). "Discriminant Validity of the MMPI-Borderline Personality Disorder Scale." *Psychological Assessment, 3*, 232–238.

Tsushima, W., and Wedding, D. (1979). "MMPI Results of Male Candidates for Transsexual Surgery." *Journal of Personality Assessment, 43*, 385–387.

Turkat, D. (1990). *The Personality Disorders*. New York: Pergamon Press.

United States v. *Freeman*, 357 F.2d 606 (1966).

United States v. *Lions*, 731 F.2d 243 (1984).

United States v. *Tonero*, 735 F.2d 725 (1984).

Valenstein, E. (1986). *Great and Desperate Cures: The Rise and Decline of Psychosurgery and Other Radical Treatments for Mental Illness*. New York: Basic Books.

Van Gorp, W., and Meyer, R. (1986). "The Detection of Faking on the Millon Clinical Multiaxial Inventory (MCMI)." *Journal of Clinical Psychology, 42*, 742–748.

Van Gorp, W., Satz, P., Kiersch, M., and Henry, R. (1986). "Normative Data on the Boston Naming Test for a Group of Normal Older Adults." *Journal of Clinical and Experimental Neuropsychology, 8*, 702–705.

Van Oppen, P., Hoekstra, R., and Emmelkamp, P. (1995). The Structure of Obsessive-Compulsive Symptoms. *Behavior Research and Therapy, 33*, 15–23.

Virkkunen, M., and Linnoila, M. (1991). "How to Predict Impulsive Violence: The Biochemical Findings Among Habitually Violent Offenders." Abstracts of Ninth Biennial World Meeting of the International Society for Research on Aggression. Banff, Alberta, Canada. *Aggressive Behavior, 17*, 101.

Vitousek, K., and Manke, F. (1994). "Personality Variables and Disorders in Anorexia Nervosa and Bulimia Nervosa." *Journal of Abnormal Psychology, 103*, 137–147.

Vogel, G., Vogel, F., McAbee, R., and Thurmond, A. (1980). "Improvement of Depression by REM Sleep Deprivation." *Archives of General Psychiatry, 37*, 247–253.

Volavka, J. (1995). *Neurobiology of Violence*. Washington, DC: American Psychiatric Press.

Wagner, E., and Heise, M. (1981). "Rorschach and Hand Test Data Comparing Bipolar Patients in Manic and Depressive States." *Journal of Personality Assessment, 45*, 240–249.

Wagner, E., and Wagner, C. (1981). *The Interpretation of Psychological Test Data*. Springfield, IL: Thomas.

_____ (1978). "Similar Rorschach Patterning in Three Cases of Anorexia nervosa." *Journal of Personality Assessment, 42,* 426–429.

Walker, G. (1985). "The Brief Therapy of a Compulsive Gambler." *Journal of Family Therapy, 7,* 1–8.

Walker, J., Norton, G., and Ross, C., Eds. (1991). *Panic Disorder and Agoraphobia.* Pacific Grove, CA: Brooks/Cole.

Ward, C. (1991). "A Comparison of T Scores from the MMPI and the MMPI–2." *Psychological Assessment, 3,* 688–690.

Washton, A. (1991). *Cocaine Addiction: Treatment, Recovery, and Relapse Prevention.* New York: Norton.

Washton, A., and Gold, M. (1987). *Cocaine: A Clinician's Handbook.* New York: Guilford.

Watson, C. (1990). "Psychometric Posttraumatic Stress Disorder Measurement Techniques: A Review." *Psychological Assessment, 2,* 460–469.

Watson, C., Plemel, D., and Jacobs, L. (1978). "An MMPI Sign to Separate Organic from Functional Psychiatric Patients." *Journal of Clinical Psychology, 34,* 398–432.

Webb, J., McNamara, K., and Rodgers, D. (1981). *Configural Interpretations of the MMPI and CPI.* Columbus, OH: Ohio Psychology Publishing.

Wechsler, D. (1981). *WAIS-R Manual.* Cleveland, OH: The Psychological Corporation.

Weissberg, M. (1993). "Multiple Personality Disorder and Iatrogenesis: The Cautionary Tale of Anna O." *International Journal of Clinical and Experimental Hypnosis, 41(1),* 15–34.

Welsh, G. (1948). "An Extension of Hathaway's MMPI Profile Coding System." *Journal of Consulting Psychology, 12,* 343–344.

Wetter, M., Baer, R., Berry, D., Smith, G., and Larson, L. (1992). "Sensitivity of MMPI-2 Validity Scales to Random Responding and Malingering." *Psychological Assessment, 4,* 369–374.

Wetter, M., and Deitsch, S. (1996). "Faking Specific Disorders and Temporal Response Consistency on the MMPI-2." *Psychological Assessment.* In press.

Wettstein, R. (1989). "Psychiatric Malpractice." In A. Tasman, R. Hales, and A. Frances, Eds. *Review of Psychiatry,* vol. 8. Washington, DC: American Psychiatric Press.

Wettstein, R., Mulvey, E., and Rogers, R. (1991). "A Prospective Comparison of Four Insanity Defense Standards." *American Journal of Psychiatry, 148,* 21–27.

Wicksramasekera, I. (1976). "Aversive Behavior Rehearsal for Sexual Exhibitionism." In I. Wicksramasekera, Ed., *Biofeedback, Behavior Therapy, and Hypnosis.* Chicago: Nelson-Hall.

_____ (1988). *Clinical Behavioral Medicine.* New York: Plenum.

Widiger, T., Frances, A., Pincus, H., Davis, W., and First, M. (1991). "Toward an Empirical Classification for the DSM–IV." *Journal of Abnormal Psychology, 100,* 280–288.

Widiger, T., and Sanderson, C. (1987). "The Convergent and Discriminant Validity of the MCMI as a Measure of the DSM-III Personality Disorders." *Journal of Personality Assessment, 51,* 228–242.

Widiger, T., and Costa, P. (1994). "Personality and Personality Disorders." *Journal of Abnormal Psychology, 103,* 78–91.

Wiener, D., and Harmon, L. (1946). "Subtle and Obvious Keys for the MMPI." (Advisement Bulletin 16.) Minneapolis, MN: Regional Veteran's Administration Office.

Wiesel, F. (1994). "Neuroleptic Treatment of Schizophrenia." *British Journal of Psychiatry, 164* (Suppl. 23), 65–70.

Wiggins, E., and Brandt, J. (1988). "The Detection of Simulated Amnesia." *Law and Human Behavior, 12,* 57–79.

Wilson, T., and Walsh, B. (1991). "Eating Disorders in the DSM-IV." *Journal of Abnormal Psychology, 100,* 362–365.

Winder, P., O'Dell, J., and Karson, S. (1975). "New Motivational Distortion Scales for the 16 PF." *Journal of Personality Assessment, 39,* 532–537.

Winer, D. (1978). "Anger and Dissociation: A Case Study of Multiple Personality." *Journal of Abnormal Psychology, 87,* 368–372.

Winston, A., Laikin, M., Pollack, J., Samstag, L., et al. (1994). "Short–term Psychotherapy of Personality Disorders." *American Journal of Psychiatry, 151,* 190–194.

Winters, K., Weintraub, S., and Neale, V. (1981). "Validity of MMPI Codetypes in Identifying DSM-III Schizophrenics, Unipolars, and Bipolars." *Journal of Consulting and Clinical Psychology, 49,* 486–487.

Wolfe, B., and Maser, J. (Eds.) (1994). *Treatment of Panic Disorder.* Washington, DC: American Psychiatric Press.

Wolpe, J. (1987). "Carbon Dioxide Inhalation Treatments of Neurotic Anxiety." *Journal of Nervous and Mental Disease, 175,* 129–133.

Woody, J. (1992). *Treating Sexual Distress.* Newbury Park, CA: Sage.

World Health Organization (1979). *Schizophrenia: An International Follow-up Study.* New York: Wiley-Interscience.

Woychyshyn, C., McElheran, W., and Romney, D. (1992). "MMPI Validity Measures." *Journal of Personality Assessment, 58,* 138–148.

Yablonsky, L. (1976). *Psychodrama: Resolving Emotional Problems Through Role Playing.* New York: Basic Books.

Yager, J., Gwirtsman, H., and Edelstein, C. (1991). *Special Problems in Managing Eating Disorders.* Washington, DC: American Psychiatric Press.

Young, J., and Hillbrand, M. (1994). "Carbamazepine Lowers Aggression: A Review." *Bulletin of the American Academy of Psychiatry and the Law, 22,* 53–61.

Yudofsky, S., Williams, D., and Gorman, V. (1981). "Propranolol in the Treatment of Rage and Violent Behavior in Patients with Chronic Brain Syndrome." *American Journal of Psychiatry, 138,* 218–220.

Zeig, J., Ed. (1987). *The Evolution of Psychotherapy.* New York: Brunner/Mazel.

Zigler, E., and Glick, M. (1988). "Is Paranoid Schizophrenia Really Camouflaged Depression?" *American Psychologist, 43,* 284–290.

Zimmerman, I., and Woo-Sam, J. (1973). *Clinical Interpretation of the Wechsler Adult Intelligence Scale.* New York: Grune & Stratton.

Zimmerman, M. (1994). "Diagnosing Personality Disorders." *Archives of General Psychiatry, 51,* 225–245.

Ziskin, J., and Faust, D. (1988). *Coping with Psychiatric and Psychological Testimony,* 4th ed. Marina del Rey, CA: Law and Psychology Press.

Zook, A., and Sipps, G. (1985). "Cross-Validation of a Short Form of the Marlowe-Crowne Social Desirability Scale." *Journal of Clinical Psychology, 41,* 236–238.

Zuckerman, M., Buchsbaum, M., and Murphy, D. (1980). "Sensation Seeking and Its Biological Correlates." *Psychological Bulletin, 88,* 187–214.

Zuercher, E. (1996). *An End to Panic.* Oakland, CA: New Harbinger.

INDEX

(The many individual references in the text to various tests, e.g., WAIS-R, Rorschach, TAT, etc., and types of interventions, e.g., systematic desensitization, assertiveness training, etc., are not included here.)